TEACHER'S EDITION

L. Carey Bolster

H. Douglas Woodburn

Joella H. Gipson

Scott, Foresman and Company
Editorial Offices: Glenview, Illinois

Regional Sales Offices: Sunnyvale, California • Tucker, Georgia • Glenview, Illinois • Oakland, New Jersey • Dallas, Texas

Two-Year Program

Consumer and Career Mathematics, Second Edition, preceded by *Mathematics in Life, Second Edition*, provides a two-year general mathematics program. However, either book may be used independently at any grade level.

Mathematics in Life

Recommended for a first course in general mathematics. Emphasis in each chapter on basic mathematical skills and problem solving in consumer and career applications.

Unit 1 Whole Numbers

Unit 2 Decimals and the Metric System

Unit 3 Fractions, Mixed Numbers, and Probability

Unit 4 Ratio, Percent, and Statistics

Unit 5 Algebra

Unit 6 Geometry and Right-Triangle Relations

Consumer and Career Mathematics

Recommended for a final course in general mathematics, or for a course in consumer mathematics. Emphasis on mathematics needed in consumer and career situations with review of basic computational skills in Unit 1.

Unit 1 Mathematics Skills

Unit 2 Income, Banking, and Credit

Unit 3 Transportation

Unit 4 Housing

Unit 5 Taxes, Insurance, and Investments

Unit 6 Purchasing and Budgeting

ISBN: 0-673-23437-1

12345678910-KPH-9291908988887868584

Contents Table of Contents

Teacher's Edition

Student's Text

Unit and chapter titles are listed below. For a complete table of contents including lesson titles, tests, and features, see pages iii–viii in the student's text which follows after page T80.

Problem Solving: Consumer and Career Applications	Units 2–6 Consumer lessons feature examples in a problem-solution format that identify problem-solving strategies• and allow students to use mathematical skills in consumer situations. Related problems provide additional practice in solving similar problems. (See pages 346–347.) Career lessons allow students to gain experience in using mathematical skills in career situations and also feature the problem-solution examples. Related problems provide additional practice in using problem-solving strategies. (See pages 98–99.) Unit 1 Skill lessons provide related problems that contain applications of skills being taught on the page. Problem-solution examples contain practical settings that give a reason for learning mathematical skills. (See pages 34–37.) **Consumer and career applications provide exposure to problem-solving skills needed for survival in consumer situations.**	*pages T10–T13*
Skills	In Unit 1, problem-solution examples keyed by letter to exercise sets indicate different types of exercises within the same lesson. Estimation skills are emphasized throughout. (See pages 6–7.) **Skills lessons teach and reinforce basic skills.**	*page T13*

Enrichment Maintenance	Calculator Applications and Break Time in each chapter; Break Time/Mental Math• at the end of each unit; Skills Tune-Up at the end of each chapter in Units 2–6; Computer Applications• at the end of each unit in Units 2–6; Computer Literacy• in the back of the student's text; and Skills File in the back of the student's text **Enrichment and maintenance features allow ample flexibility in meeting individual differences.**	*pages T14–T15*
Built-in Testing	Chapter Reviews, Chapter Tests, and Unit Tests in the student's text; Unit Tests, End-of-Book Test, and Suggested Competency Test in the teacher's edition; and blackline masters packaged with the teacher's edition **Built-in testing helps teachers assess students' needs on a regular basis.**	*pages T16–T17*
Complete Teacher's Edition	Overprinted notes, answers, and warm-up exercises on lesson pages, a guide to management•, a suggested time schedule, and a special section of teacher notes keyed to each lesson **Complete teacher's edition makes the book extremely easy to manage.**	*pages T18–T43*
Supplementary Materials	*Consumer Forms and Problems Masters*, *Test Masters*, and *Solution Key* **Supplementary materials provide even more flexibility in using the program.**	*page T7*

•Indicates a new feature in *Consumer and Career Mathematics*, *Second Edition*

Authors and Readers/Consultants

Authors

L. Carey Bolster

Mr. Bolster is a Supervisor of Mathematics for the Baltimore County Public Schools. He works with elementary and secondary school teachers in curriculum development and instruction, and often conducts in-service workshops. He is coauthor of mathematics programs for the elementary and secondary levels.

H. Douglas Woodburn

Mr. Woodburn is Chairman of the Mathematics Department of Perry Hall Middle School in Baltimore County, Maryland. He has taught at the junior high, senior high, and college levels. He has reviewed articles submitted for publication in *The Mathematics Teacher* and *Arithmetic Teacher*.

Joella H. Gipson

Dr. Gipson is a Professor of Mathematics Education at Wayne State University in Detroit, Michigan. She has conducted pre-service and in-service workshops for teachers. She has written articles published in professional journals and is a member of many professional organizations.

Author of Test Masters

Dora A. Serna Cantu

Ms. Cantu is an Instructor of Mathematics at Laredo Junior College in Laredo, Texas. She has also taught mathematics at the secondary level. She has conducted workshops for elementary and secondary school teachers.

Readers/Consultants

Marita H. Eng

Ms. Eng is Chairman of the Mathematics Department of Sandalwood Junior-Senior High School in Jacksonville, Florida. She is coauthor of a series of computational skills workbooks.

Robert Y. Hamada

Mr. Hamada is an Instructional Specialist, Mathematics, in the Office of Instruction of the Los Angeles Unified School District. He is coauthor of a mathematics program for the elementary level.

Linda Borry Hausmann

Ms. Hausmann is Manager of Instructional Systems for EduSystems, Inc., in Minneapolis, Minnesota. She is author of a computerized music theory package.

William C. Messersmith, Jr.

Mr. Messersmith is a teacher of mathematics and computer programming at Rich Township High School in Richton Park, Illinois. He is also Coordinator of Data Processing Services.

Sidney Sharron

Mr. Sharron is a Supervisor in the Instructional Media and Resources Branch of the Los Angeles Unified School District. He has taught mathematics at the high school and college levels.

Program Materials

Student's Text

464 pages including answers to odd-numbered exercises.

Teacher's Edition

544 pages including reproduced student's pages with answers and notes overprinted plus 80 teacher pages at the front of the book.

Supplementary Materials

Consumer Forms and Problems Masters

64 duplicating masters. Provides consumer forms, such as checks and deposit slips, that can be used with lessons in the student's text. Also includes applications that reinforce and extend lessons in the student's text.

Test Masters

60 duplicating masters. Provides an alternate form for each chapter, unit, end-of-book, and competency test.

Solution Key

Contains answers for all exercises in the student's text. Steps needed to obtain answers are shown for selected exercises.

Units

The text is organized into six units.

Unit 1 focuses on mathematical skills. The unit may be used as a quick review or for reteaching.

Units 2–6 are organized according to consumer topics. The skills from Unit 1 are applied as needed in these units. The chapters or units may be taught independently of each other.

Chapters

Each unit contains three chapters. There are 18 chapters in all.

Unit 1 Mathematics Skills
- Chapter 1 Whole Numbers, Decimals, and Fractions
- Chapter 2 Equations, Proportions, and Percent
- Chapter 3 Measurement and Statistics

Unit 2 Income, Banking, and Credit
- Chapter 4 Income
- Chapter 5 Personal Banking
- Chapter 6 Consumer Credit

Unit 3 Transportation
- Chapter 7 Buying a Car
- Chapter 8 Automobile Operating Expenses
- Chapter 9 Travel

Unit 4 Housing
- Chapter 10 Renting and Decorating a Home
- Chapter 11 Buying a Home
- Chapter 12 Building a Home

Unit 5 Taxes, Insurance, and Investments
- Chapter 13 Income Tax
- Chapter 14 Health, Life, and Retirement Insurance
- Chapter 15 Investments

Unit 6 Purchasing and Budgeting
- Chapter 16 Buying Food
- Chapter 17 Buying, Making, and Renting Goods
- Chapter 18 Budgeting

Within chapters

Each chapter contains 4 to 9 lessons. A lesson can be from one to four pages long. See pages T10–T17 for samples of lessons, tests, and special features. A sample table of contents for a chapter is given below.

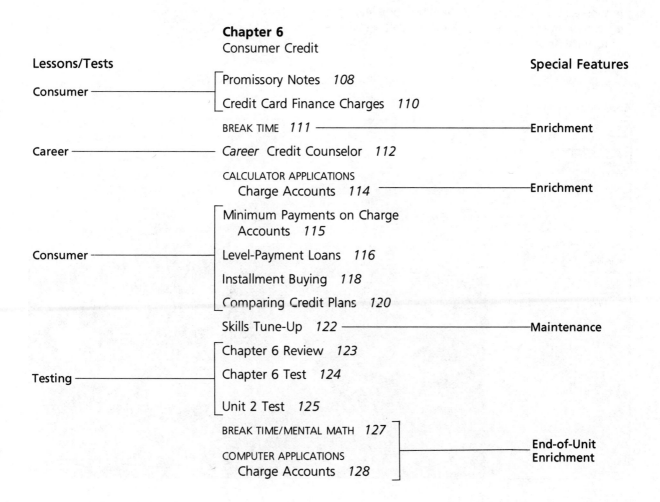

Chapter 6
Consumer Credit

Lessons/Tests		Special Features
Consumer	Promissory Notes *108*	
Consumer	Credit Card Finance Charges *110*	
	BREAK TIME *111*	Enrichment
Career	*Career* Credit Counselor *112*	
	CALCULATOR APPLICATIONS Charge Accounts *114*	Enrichment
Consumer	Minimum Payments on Charge Accounts *115*	
Consumer	Level-Payment Loans *116*	
Consumer	Installment Buying *118*	
Consumer	Comparing Credit Plans *120*	
	Skills Tune-Up *122*	Maintenance
Testing	Chapter 6 Review *123*	
Testing	Chapter 6 Test *124*	
Testing	Unit 2 Test *125*	
	BREAK TIME/MENTAL MATH *127*	End-of-Unit Enrichment
	COMPUTER APPLICATIONS Charge Accounts *128*	End-of-Unit Enrichment

Features Consumer Lessons

The major focus of the lessons in Units 2 through 6 is solving consumer-type problems.

Each consumer lesson includes
- a lesson title that indicates the content of the lesson.
- examples that feature consumer problems.
- worked-out solutions that identify a problem-solving strategy.
- related problems that provide practice in solving problems similar to those in the examples.

Consumer lesson, pages 78–81

Net Pay

Each pay period, employers subtract a specified amount from employees' gross pay for federal income tax.

The amount deducted is determined by an employee's gross pay, marital status, and number of **exemptions.** An exemption is a member of the family or a person who lived in the employee's home as a member of the family for the whole year.

The Internal Revenue Service of the United States Treasury Department provides tables which employers use to determine the amount to withhold for federal income tax. The tables are on pages 402–405.

SINGLE Persons—**WEEKLY** Payroll Period

And the wages are—		Exemptions claimed			
At least	But less than	0	1	2	3
		The amount of income tax to be withheld shall be—			
$135	$140	$19.00	$15.30	$11.80	$8.40
140	145	20.00	16.20	12.70	9.30
145	150	21.10	17.10	13.60	10.20
150	160	22.60	18.60	15.00	11.50
160	170	24.70	20.70	16.80	13.30
370	380	83.60	77.10	70.50	64.50
380	390	87.00	80.50	73.90	67.50
390	400	90.40	83.90	77.30	70.80
400	410	93.80	87.30	80.70	74.20
410	420	97.20	90.70	84.10	77.60

Problem

Marge Schaffer is single and earns $375.55 a week. She claims exemptions for herself and her father. How much is withheld from her paycheck each week for federal income tax?

Solution

Strategy
- Use the table for single persons and find the amounts that the salary is between.
  $375.55 is "at least $370 but less than $380."
- Follow the table across for the amount listed under 2 exemptions.
  $70.50

Conclusion
$70.50 is withheld from Marge's paycheck for federal income tax.

78

Related Problems

Use the appropriate table from pages 402–405 to find the amount withheld each week for federal income tax.

	Gross pay	Marital status	Exemptions claimed
1.	$125	Single	1
2.	$98	Single	1
3.	$175	Single	2
4.	$437	Single	1
5.	$437	Single	3
6.	$437	Married	2
7.	$437	Married	3
8.	$323	Married	2
9.	$418	Married	6
10.	$287	Married	5
11.	$247	Single	1
12.	$415	Married	4
13.	$170	Married	3
14.	$343	Single	1
15.	$542	Married	5

79

Other important aspects of a consumer lesson include

- minimal reading so that students can more readily focus on the mathematics involved in solving a problem.
- realistic photographs used for visual appeal and motivation.
- true-to-life forms, advertisements, and charts that bring the real world into the classroom.
- important terms that are marked in boldface type so that students can easily identify key ideas. A brief glossary is provided on pages 414–417.

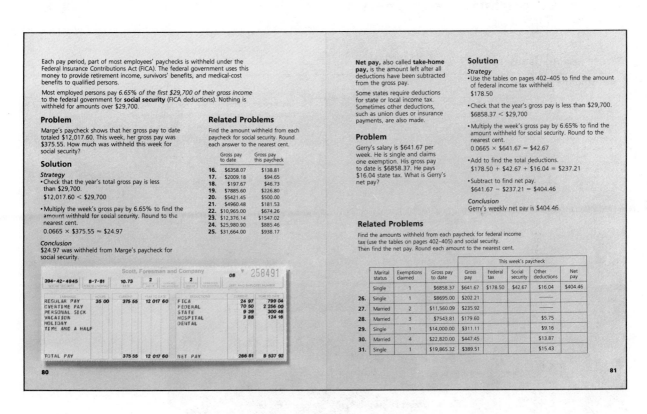

Each pay period, part of most employees' paychecks is withheld under the Federal Insurance Contributions Act (FICA). The federal government uses this money to provide retirement income, survivors' benefits, and medical-cost benefits to qualified persons.

Most employed persons pay *6.65% of the first $29,700 of their gross income* to the federal government for **social security** (FICA deductions). Nothing is withheld for amounts over $29,700.

Problem

Marge's paycheck shows that her gross pay to date totaled $12,017.60. This week, her gross pay was $375.55. How much was withheld this week for social security?

Solution

Strategy

- Check that the year's total gross pay is less than $29,700.
  $12,017.60 < $29,700
- Multiply the week's gross pay by 6.65% to find the amount withheld for social security. Round to the nearest cent.
  $0.0665 \times \$375.55 \approx \$24.97$

Conclusion
$24.97 was withheld from Marge's paycheck for social security.

Related Problems

Find the amount withheld from each paycheck for social security. Round each answer to the nearest cent.

	Gross pay to date	Gross pay this paycheck
16.	$6358.07	$138.81
17.	$2009.18	$94.65
18.	$197.67	$46.73
19.	$7885.60	$226.80
20.	$5421.45	$500.00
21.	$4960.48	$181.53
22.	$10,965.00	$674.26
23.	$12,376.14	$1547.02
24.	$25,980.90	$885.46
25.	$31,664.00	$938.17

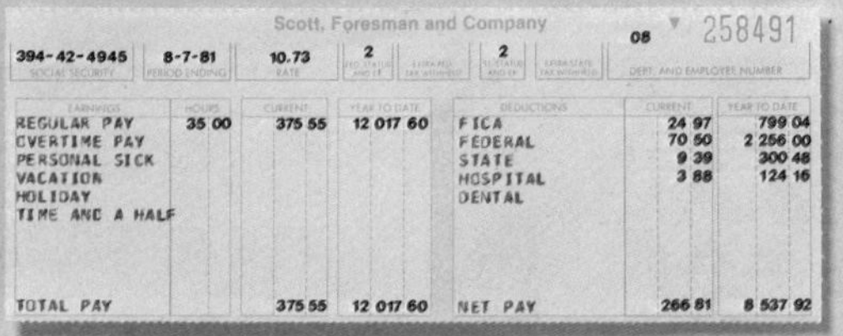

Scott, Foresman and Company
08 258491
394-42-4945 SOCIAL SECURITY
8-7-81 PERIOD ENDING
10.73 RATE
2
2
DEPT. AND EMPLOYEE NUMBER
EARNINGS HOURS CURRENT YEAR TO DATE
REGULAR PAY 35 00 375 55 12 017 60
OVERTIME PAY
PERSONAL SICK
VACATION
HOLIDAY
TIME AND A HALF
TOTAL PAY 375 55 12 017 60
DEDUCTIONS CURRENT YEAR TO DATE
FICA 24 97 799 04
FEDERAL 70 50 2 256 00
STATE 9 39 300 48
HOSPITAL 3 88 124 16
DENTAL
NET PAY 266 81 8 537 92

80

Net pay, also called **take-home pay,** is the amount left after all deductions have been subtracted from the gross pay.

Some states require deductions for state or local income tax. Sometimes other deductions, such as union dues or insurance payments, are also made.

Problem

Gerry's salary is $641.67 per week. He is single and claims one exemption. His gross pay to date is $6858.37. He pays $16.04 state tax. What is Gerry's net pay?

Solution

Strategy

- Use the tables on pages 402–405 to find the amount of federal income tax withheld.
  $178.50
- Check that the year's gross pay is less than $29,700.
  $6858.37 < $29,700
- Multiply the week's gross pay by 6.65% to find the amount withheld for social security. Round to the nearest cent.
  $0.0665 \times \$641.67 \approx \$42.67$
- Add to find the total deductions.
  $\$178.50 + \$42.67 + \$16.04 = \$237.21$
- Subtract to find net pay.
  $\$641.67 - \$237.21 = \$404.46$

Conclusion
Gerry's weekly net pay is $404.46.

Related Problems

Find the amounts withheld from each paycheck for federal income tax (use the tables on pages 402–405) and social security. Then find the net pay. Round each amount to the nearest cent.

				This week's paycheck				
	Marital status	Exemptions claimed	Gross pay to date	Gross pay	Federal tax	Social security	Other deductions	Net pay
	Single	1	$6858.37	$641.67	$178.50	$42.67	$16.04	$404.46
26.	Single	1	$8695.00	$202.21			——	
27.	Married	2	$11,560.09	$235.92			——	
28.	Married	3	$7543.81	$179.60			$5.75	
29.	Single	1	$14,000.00	$311.11			$9.16	
30.	Married	4	$22,820.00	$447.45			$13.87	
31.	Single	1	$19,865.32	$389.51			$15.43	

81

At least one lesson in every chapter of Units 2 through 6 is a career lesson. These lessons show how mathematical skills can be used in a career related to the chapter topic.

Each career lesson includes

- a lesson title that states the name of the career.
- a career cluster identified in the first line of the lesson. (The Careers Chart on pages 410–413 provides more information about jobs in various career clusters.)
- problem-solution examples that include a strategy for solving the stated problem.
- related problems that provide practice in solving problems related to the career.

Career lesson, pages 144–145

Automobile Salesperson

Career Cluster: Business Contact Beth Hall sells cars. For each car she sells, her commission is 25% of the dealer's profit. The profit is the difference between the selling price of the car and the amount the dealer paid for the car.

The dealer also has a bonus earnings plan. Each car is assigned from 1 to 5 points, depending on the model and how long it has been in stock. The amount of bonus earnings is determined by the number of points earned by the salesperson during the month. The dealer Beth works for uses this schedule.

Number of points per month	Bonus earnings
0–14	$0
15–20	$75
21–25	$350
26–29	$650
30–33	$800
34	$1200
35–39	$1400
40	$1500

Problem

During January, Beth earned 24 points for the sale of thirteen cars. The dealer's profit on the cars was $6500. What was Beth's gross pay for January?

Solution

Strategy

- Multiply by 25% to find the commission earnings.
  $0.25 \times \$6500 = \$1625$
- Read the table to find the amount of bonus earnings for 24 points.
  $350
- Add to find gross pay.

$1625	Commission earnings
+ 350	Bonus earnings
$1975	

Conclusion
Beth's gross pay for January was $1975.

144

Related Problems

Complete the table below to show Beth's total gross pay for the year.

	Month	Number of bonus points	Dealer's profit	Commission earnings	Bonus earnings	Gross pay
	January	24	$6500	$1625	$350	$1975
1.	February	33	$7254			
2.	March	30	$6820			
3.	April	33	$7010			
4.	May	37	$7416			
5.	June	39	$7936			
6.	July	28	$6413			
7.	August	20	$5400			
8.	September	32	$7212			
9.	October	22	$6135			
10.	November	19	$3700			
11.	December	13	$3610			
12.	Total	——	——			

13. Beth accumulated 33 bonus points in February. If she had received 1 more point, how much more gross pay would she have earned in February?
14. If Beth had received 1 less bonus point in March, how much less gross pay would she have earned that month?

For problems 15–17, assume that Beth sold one more car in August for a $375 dealer's profit and 3 bonus points.

15. What would Beth's commission earnings have been for August?
16. What would her bonus earnings have been for August?
17. What would her gross pay for August have been?

145

Features Skills Lessons

Skills lessons are featured in Unit 1.
These lessons teach the students essential computational and measurement skills.

Each skills lesson includes
- a lesson title that indicates the content of the lesson.
- a consumer-type setting that shows a need for the mathematical skills introduced.
- problem-solution examples that are keyed by letter to exercise sets.
- exercise sets keyed to examples.
- related problems that give students an opportunity to use skills taught in the lesson in consumer situations.
- whenever necessary, rules and generalizations that are set off in a box for easy reference.

Skills lesson, pages 8–9

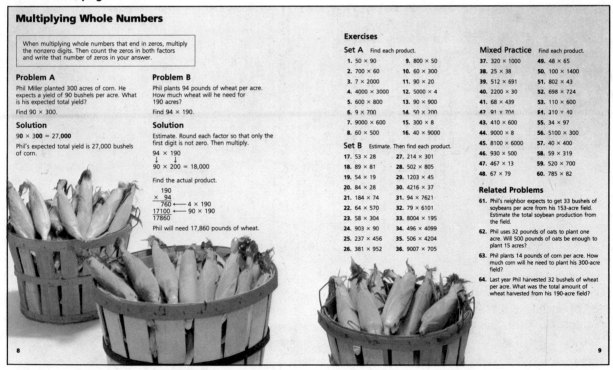

Multiplying Whole Numbers

> When multiplying whole numbers that end in zeros, multiply the nonzero digits. Then count the zeros in both factors and write that number of zeros in your answer.

Problem A

Phil Miller planted 300 acres of corn. He expects a yield of 90 bushels per acre. What is his expected total yield?

Find 90 × 300.

Solution

90 × 300 = 27,**000**

Phil's expected total yield is 27,000 bushels of corn.

Problem B

Phil plants 94 pounds of wheat per acre. How much wheat will he need for 190 acres?

Find 94 × 190.

Solution

Estimate. Round each factor so that only the first digit is not zero. Then multiply.

94 × 190
↓ ↓
90 × 200 = 18,000

Find the actual product.

$$\begin{array}{r} 190 \\ \times\ 94 \\ \hline 760 \\ 17100 \\ \hline 17860 \end{array} \quad \begin{array}{l} \\ \\ \leftarrow 4 \times 190 \\ \leftarrow 90 \times 190 \\ \\ \end{array}$$

Phil will need 17,860 pounds of wheat.

8

Exercises

Set A Find each product.

1. 50 × 90
2. 700 × 60
3. 7 × 2000
4. 4000 × 3000
5. 600 × 800
6. 9 × 700
7. 9000 × 600
8. 60 × 500
9. 800 × 50
10. 60 × 300
11. 90 × 20
12. 5000 × 4
13. 90 × 900
14. 50 × 200
15. 300 × 8
16. 40 × 9000

Set B Estimate. Then find each product.

17. 53 × 28
18. 89 × 81
19. 54 × 19
20. 84 × 28
21. 184 × 74
22. 64 × 570
23. 58 × 304
24. 903 × 90
25. 237 × 456
26. 381 × 952
27. 214 × 301
28. 502 × 805
29. 1203 × 45
30. 4216 × 37
31. 94 × 7621
32. 79 × 6101
33. 8004 × 195
34. 496 × 4099
35. 506 × 4204
36. 9007 × 705

Mixed Practice Find each product.

37. 320 × 1000
38. 25 × 38
39. 512 × 691
40. 2200 × 30
41. 68 × 439
42. 91 × 704
43. 410 × 600
44. 9000 × 8
45. 8100 × 6000
46. 930 × 500
47. 467 × 13
48. 67 × 79
49. 48 × 65
50. 100 × 1400
51. 802 × 43
52. 698 × 724
53. 110 × 600
54. 210 × 40
55. 34 × 97
56. 5100 × 300
57. 40 × 400
58. 59 × 319
59. 520 × 700
60. 785 × 82

Related Problems

61. Phil's neighbor expects to get 33 bushels of soybeans per acre from his 153-acre field. Estimate the total soybean production from the field.
62. Phil uses 32 pounds of oats to plant one acre. Will 500 pounds of oats be enough to plant 15 acres?
63. Phil plants 14 pounds of corn per acre. How much corn will he need to plant his 300-acre field?
64. Last year Phil harvested 32 bushels of wheat per acre. What was the total amount of wheat harvested from his 190-acre field?

9

Features **Maintenance and Enrichment**

Skills Tune-Up
At the end of each chapter in Units 2–6, there is a page containing sets of exercises that maintain important skills taught in Unit 1. References at the beginning of each set indicate the pages where the skill is taught.

page 104

Skills Tune-Up

Multiplying decimals, pages 10-11

1. 0.5 × 0.7
2. 0.8 × 0.3
3. 0.04 × 0.4
4. 0.01 × 0.6
5. 0.02 × 0.09
6. 0.4 × 0.08
7. 0.004 × 0.02
8. 0.03 × 0.011
9. 200 × 0.7
10. 0.9 × 600
11. 400 × 0.08
12. 0.05 × 110

Ratio and proportion, pages 30-31

Find the cross-products. Tell whether the ratios are equal.

1. $\frac{6}{30}$ $\frac{4}{20}$
2. $\frac{3}{13}$ $\frac{5}{15}$
3. $\frac{10}{12}$ $\frac{12}{14}$
4. $\frac{2.1}{0.7}$ $\frac{6}{2}$
5. $\frac{0.16}{0.06}$ $\frac{0.55}{0.40}$
6. $\frac{25.5}{15.3}$ $\frac{0.5}{0.3}$

Writing percents, decimals, and fractions, pages 32-33

Write as a decimal.

1. 17%	**13.** 6.75%
2. 8%	**14.** $1\frac{1}{2}$%
3. 1%	**15.** 32.8%
4. 25%	**16.** 8.5%
5. 96%	**17.** $5\frac{3}{4}$%
6. 3%	**18.** $16\frac{1}{8}$%
7. 99%	**19.** 103%
8. $6\frac{1}{4}$%	**20.** 924%
9. 7.75%	**21.** 856%
10. 15.6%	**22.** 160%
11. $12\frac{1}{2}$%	**23.** $\frac{1}{4}$%

Skills File
On pages 379–393, there are 15 sets of exercises involving skills from Unit 1. These may be used for more practice while teaching Unit 1, or as maintenance at any time. A reference on each Skills File set indicates where the skill is taught.

page 385

Skills File

Dividing decimals, pages 12-13

Find each quotient to the nearest hundredth.

1. 2)7.67	**21.** 95)98.9	**41.** 3.2)7.7	**61.** 0.19)0.82	**81.** 4.05)27
2. 7)35.63	**22.** 64)73.8	**42.** 7.4)1.3	**62.** 0.25)0.145	**82.** 8.33)42
3. 4)928.7	**23.** 39)80.4	**43.** 2.8)4.6	**63.** 0.64)0.309	**83.** 6.19)47
4. 3)640.9	**24.** 41)51.2	**44.** 6.1)9.2	**64.** 0.38)0.918	**84.** 1.72)35
5. 6)322.6	**25.** 53)65.23	**45.** 9.5)4.1	**65.** 0.51)0.836	**85.** 29.8)538
6. 5)472.3	**26.** 81)31.06	**46.** 8.3)7.2	**66.** 0.98)0.505	**86.** 70.2)746
7. 8)8901	**27.** 98)83.54	**47.** 5.9)2.8	**67.** 0.73)0.641	**87.** 40.1)864
8. 9)7132	**28.** 23)709.41	**48.** 4.1)98.2	**68.** 0.62)0.103	**88.** 93.2)601
	29. 77)471.29	**49.** 7.4)30.6	**69.** 3.24)41.72	**89.** 69.7)408

Break Time
This feature occurs at least once in each chapter. Included are recreational puzzles and/or problems.
The Break Time/Mental Math feature at the end of each unit teaches shortcuts to help students compute mentally. (See page 189.)

page 359

TOTAL

Break Time

Except for one counterfeit stone, all of these diamonds have the same weight. The counterfeit is slightly heavier than each of the other stones.

Describe how to use no more than two weighings of the diamonds on a balance scale to decide which stone is counterfeit.

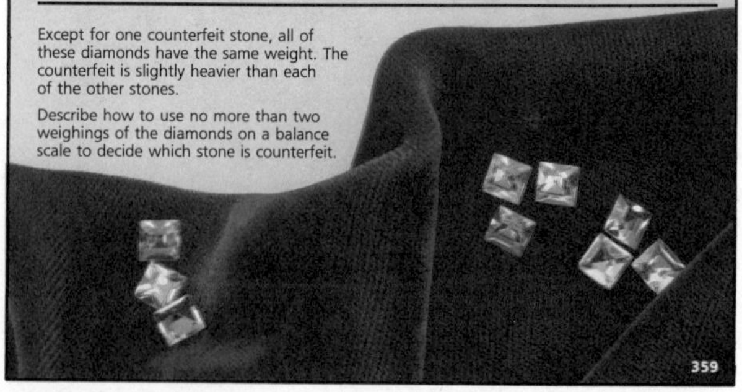

359

page 223

CALCULATOR APPLICATIONS

Amortization Tables

Many lending agencies provide their customers with an amortization table that shows how each monthly payment is divided between interest and principal. Scott Lynch is borrowing $40,000 at 13.5% annual interest for 25 years. His monthly payment will be $466.40. Use your calculator and the strategy on page 222 to complete these sections of Scott's amortization table.

	Payment number	Principal	Amount of interest	Amount paid on principal	New principal
	1	$40,000.00	$450.00	$16.40	$39,983.60
1.	2	$39,983.60			
2.	3				
3.	4				
4.	5				
5.	6				
6.	7				
7.	8				
8.	9				
	10				

Calculator Applications

In each chapter, there is a one-page feature containing consumer problems to be solved by using a four-function calculator. It reinforces and extends content of previous lessons.

page 128

COMPUTER APPLICATIONS

Charge Accounts

Sylvia Bishop has a charge account at Meyer's Department Store. She received this bill.

```
        MEYER'S DEPARTMENT STORE
        CHARGE-ACCOUNT STATEMENT

BEGINNING OF JULY
  BALANCE                         87.5
PAYMENTS DURING JULY              20
FINANCE CHARGE ON
  BALANCE OF $ 67.5                1.01
CHARGES DURING JULY               23.18
NEW BALANCE                       91.69
```

The bill was prepared using the program shown on the next page.

Lines 30, 50, 70, and 90 Only these values ... to prepare the ...

A semicolon at the end of the PRINT statement causes the computer to print the question mark for the INPUT statement on the same line.

All the calculations for preparing the bill are in the program.

Line 100 The unpaid balance (U) is calculated after the payment is made.

Line 110 The finance charge (F) is calculated using the unpaid balance and a rate of 1.5%.

Line 120 Many times the finance charge calculation will result in a part of a cent, so F ... Change F to a number of cents ... tenths of a cent

Computer Applications

At the end of each of Units 2–6, there is a two-page feature dealing with the use of the computer in consumer situations. The applications are related to the content of the unit.

page 399

COMPUTER LITERACY

The INT and TAB Functions

INT(X) is the greatest integer function. The computer will determine the greatest integer that is less than or equal to the number specified in parentheses following INT. Some examples are:

INT(8) = 8 INT(0.07) = 0
INT(3.87) = 3 INT(9/2) = 4

An important use for INT is to determine whether one number is divisible by another number. If so, the quotient will be the same as the INT of the quotient. Program A uses the INT function to determine the even integers between 1 and 10.

Give the output for each program.

1.
```
10 FOR X=1 TO 60
20 IF INT(X/5)=X/5 THEN 50
30 NEXT X
40 GO TO 70
50 PRINT X
60 GO TO 30
70 END
```

2.
```
10 READ N
20 PRINT "DIVISORS OF";N;"ARE:"
30 FOR D=1 TO N
40 IF INT(N/D)<>N/D THEN 60
50 PRINT D
60 NEXT D
70 GO TO 10
80 DATA 24,36,56,59
90 END
```

"PRICE 5% TAX TO...

Computer Literacy

Pages 394–399 focus on BASIC programming. The programs and exercises have been written so that they can either be run on a computer or be used as paper-and-pencil activities.

Testing

Testing Options Available with *Consumer and Career Mathematics, Second Edition*

Test	Student's Text	Teacher's Edition•	*Test Masters*
Chapter Review	–at the end of each chapter –reviews skills and applications taught in the chapter –items keyed to lesson pages –parallels, item-by-item, the chapter test		
Chapter Test	–at the end of each chapter –tests skills and applications taught in the chapter		–alternate form, item-by-item, of the chapter test in the student's text
Unit Test	–at the end of each unit –multiple-choice format –tests selected skills and applications taught in the unit –items keyed to lesson pages in overprinted teacher notes	–on pages T56–T68 –multiple-choice format –alternate form, item-by-item, of the test in the student's text	–multiple-choice format –alternate form, item-by-item, of the unit test in the student's text
End-of-Book Test		–on pages T69–T72 –multiple-choice format –tests selected skills and applications taught in the book –items keyed to chapters	–multiple-choice format –alternate form, item-by-item, of the end-of-book test in the teacher's edition
Suggested Competency Test		–on pages T73–T80 –multiple-choice format –tests selected applications –items keyed to consumer topics and to lesson pages	–multiple-choice format –alternate form, item-by-item, of the suggested competency test in the teacher's edition

•Also available as blackline masters packaged with the teacher's edition

Selected test pages

From the student's text:

Chapter Review
page 85

Chapter 4 Review

Hourly rate and overtime rate, pages 68–69

1. Don Marcy makes $4.86 per hour. Find his gross pay for 40 hours.
2. Kay Soto earns $4.50 per hour for a 40-hour work week and time and a half for overtime. One week she worked 56 hours. Find her gross pay for the week.

Hourly rate plus tips, pages 70–71

3. Mary Harvey makes $3.50 per hour plus tips. One week she worked 35 hours and earned $39.20 in tips. She kept 85% of her tips. Find her gross pay for the week.

Straight commission, pages 72–73

Net pay, pages 78–81

7. Max Steiner is married and claims 3 exemptions. He makes $289.46 per week. Use the table below to find the amount withheld from his weekly paycheck for federal income tax.

And the wages are—		Exemptions claimed			
At least	But less than	0	1	2	3
		The amount of income tax to be withheld shall be—			
250	260	36.50	32.50	28.50	24.80
260	270	38.60	34.60	30.60	26.60
270	280	40.70	36.70	32.70	28.60
280	290	42.80	38.80	34.80	30.70
290	300	45.10	40.90	36.90	32.80

8. Donna Adamson's gross pay for last week ... 6.65% was withheld ...

Chapter Test
page 86

Chapter 4 Test

1. Sheila makes $4.95 per hour. Find her gross pay for 40 hours.
2. Eric earns $6.50 per hour for a 40-hour work week and time and a half for overtime. One week he worked 54 hours. Find his gross pay for the week.
3. Rick makes $3.85 per hour plus tips. One week he worked 30 hours and earned $86.40 in tips. He kept 85% of the tips. Find his gross pay for the week.
4. Elaine makes 25% straight commission. One week she had sales of $1840. Find her gross pay for the week.

7. Julio is single and claims 1 exemption. He makes $198.53 per week. Use the table below to find the amount withheld from his weekly paycheck for federal income tax.

And the wages are—		Exemptions claimed			
At least	But less than	0	1	2	3
		The amount of income tax to be withheld shall be—			
170	180	26.80	22.80	18.80	15.10
180	190	28.90	24.90	20.90	16.90
190	200	31.00	27.00	23.00	18.90
200	210	33.60	29.10	25.10	21.00
210	220	36.20	31.20	27.20	23.10

8. Jim's gross pay for last week was $219.87. 6.65% was withheld for social security. Find the amount withheld. Round to the nearest cent.

Unit Test
page 125

Unit 2 Test

Choose the best answer.

1. Carol earns $5.25 per hour. What is her gross pay for a 38-hour week?
   A $43.25 C $57.75
   B $563 D $199.50
2. Nan kept 80% of her $195 in tips. How much did Nan keep?
   A $39 C $245.50
   B $156 D $175
3. Mr. Morrow sells cleaning supplies for a straight commission of 40%. How much did he earn on a sale of $982?
   C $245.50
7. Mert's Market has an opening for a job that pays $12,000 a year. At Gary's Grocery, the same job pays $948 a month. How much more does Mert's Market pay per year?
   A $624 C $11,376
   B $52 D $1000
8. Su Lin has checks for $135.48, $9.34, and $97.20 to deposit. If she wants $80 in cash, how much will she deposit in her account?
   A $162.02 C $242.02
   B $322.02 D $106.54
9. The balance forwarded on a check stub was ... A deposit of $100 was made ...

From the teacher's edition:

End-of-Book Test
page T69

End-of-Book Test Part A, Chapters 1-9

Choose the correct answer.

Chapter 1

1. 3.64 + 28.7 + 6.18
   A 12.69 (C) 38.52
   B 37.44 D 126.9
2. $5\frac{1}{4} \times \frac{2}{3}$
   A $7\frac{7}{8}$ C $5\frac{1}{6}$
   (B) $3\frac{1}{2}$ D $5\frac{2}{7}$

Chapter 2

3. Solve. $\frac{5}{7} = \frac{35}{w}$
   A $w = 35$ C $w = 42$
   B $w = 25$ (D) $w = 49$

... what number?

8. David's gross pay is $287 per week. Each week, $34.80 is withheld for federal income tax and $19.09 is withheld for social security. Find his net pay.
   (A) $233.11 C $340.89
   B $252.20 D $53.89

Chapter 5

9. Find the balance to be carried forward from this check stub.

	DOLLARS	CENTS
BAL. FOR'D	120	20
DEPOSITS	35	00

Suggested Competency Test
page T73

Test Suggested Competency Test

This test is designed to measure how well students can use mathematics in everyday life. The topics covered in this test are similar to topics found in competency tests that many schools require for graduation.

The test consists of 66 problems which are keyed to consumer topics. The chart below shows these consumer topics and the test problems that are keyed to each topic. More information about these consumer topics can be found in the index. The chart also shows the answers to the test problems and lists the page numbers of the lessons in the student's text where situations similar to those in the test problems can be found. Answers are also circled on the test pages in the Teacher's Edition.

Interpretation of test scores is left to the individual teacher. However, to demonstrate overall competency, a student should correctly answer at least one problem keyed to each consumer topic.

Consumer topic	Test problems	Answers	Page(s)
Gross pay	1	B	68–69
	2	C	
	3		

Consumer topic	Test problems	Answers	Page(s)
	34	A	194–195
	35	C	216–217
		B	228–229

page T74

Competency Test

Choose the correct answer.

1. Laura earns $6.50 per hour. What is her gross pay for a 30-hour work week?
   A $95 C $36.50
   (B) $195 D $200
2. Duane earns $3.50 per hour plus tips. Last week, he worked 40 hours and made $125 in tips. What was his gross pay for the week?
   A $140 (C) $265
   B $168.50 D $500
3. Linda earns 12% straight commission ...
6. Diana's gross pay is $245.62 a week. Each week, $21 is withheld for federal income tax and $16.33 is withheld for social security. Find Diana's net pay.
   A $37.33 C $218.31
   B $224.62 (D) $208.29
7. Last year, Randy received $8045 in wages, $135 in interest, and $75 in dividends. Find his adjusted gross income.
   A $8180 (C) $8255
   $8455

Teaching Aids

Management

The management guide suggests ways of planning, testing, and individualizing while using *Consumer and Career Mathematics, Second Edition*. See page T20.

Time Schedule

The suggested time schedule is a general guide to help you allocate periods of time to chapters within a unit. See page T21.

Teaching Notes

Notes and activities for each chapter include additional information and teaching suggestions. See pages T26–T43. Also included are general suggestions for the use of calculators and computers with the text. See pages T22–T25.

Reproducible Tests

Six unit tests, an end-of-book test, and a suggested competency test are provided. See pages T56–T80.

Answers and Lesson Notes

(1) **Objective** A brief statement of the objective for the lesson.

(2) **Notes** Helpful information and teaching suggestions.

(3) **Answers** Answers printed on a full-sized replica of the student's page.

(4) **Skills File Reference** Keys skills lessons in Unit 1 to additional practice exercises at the end of the student's text. (See page 13.)

Skills lesson, page 32

(1) Objectives: Write decimals and fractions as percents; write percents as decimals and fractions.

Writing Percents, Decimals, and Fractions

> Percent means hundredths.
> $1\% = 0.01 = \frac{1}{100}$

Problem A

From the real estate section of his newspaper, Sonny Gillespie learned that the cost of new homes in his city has increased by a factor of 0.575 over the past 5 years.

Write 0.575 as a percent.

Solution

$0.575 = 57.5\%$ Move the decimal point two places to the right and write a percent sign.

As a percent, 0.575 is 57.5%.

Problem B

The Gillespies have saved enough money to pay about $\frac{3}{8}$ of the cost of a house.

Write $\frac{3}{8}$ as a percent.

Solution

First write $\frac{3}{8}$ as a decimal.

$$\begin{array}{r} 0.375 \\ 8\overline{)3.000} \\ \underline{2\,4} \\ 60 \\ \underline{56} \\ 40 \\ \underline{40} \\ 0 \end{array}$$

Divide the numerator by the denominator.

$\frac{3}{8} = 0.375$

Then write the decimal as a percent.

$0.375 = 37.5\%$

As a percent, $\frac{3}{8}$ is 37.5%.

(2) Remind students that 37.5% could also be expressed as $37\frac{1}{2}\%$.

Problem C

Sonny read that mortgage interest rates are $5\frac{1}{4}\%$ higher than they were five years ago.

Write $5\frac{1}{4}\%$ as a decimal.

Solution

$5\frac{1}{4}\% = 5.25\%$ Write $5\frac{1}{4}$ as a decimal.

$5.25\% = 0.0525$ Drop the percent sign and move the decimal point 2 places to the left.

As a decimal, $5\frac{1}{4}\%$ is 0.0525.

Problem D

Often, 20% of the cost of a home is required as a down payment.

Write 20% as a fraction.

Solution

$20\% = \frac{20}{100}$ Drop the percent sign and write the number over 100.

$\frac{20}{100} = \frac{1}{5}$ Rename the fraction in lowest terms.

As a fraction, 20% is $\frac{1}{5}$.

Exercises

Set A Write as a percent.

(3)

1. 0.43 (43%)	**6.** 0.314 (31.4%)	**11.** 0.0745 (7.45%)
2. 0.71 (71%)	**7.** 0.225 (22.5%)	**12.** 0.0375 (3.75%)
3. 0.09 (9%)	**8.** 0.468 (46.8%)	**13.** 1.25 (125%)
4. 0.1 (10%)	**9.** 0.1975 (19.75%)	**14.** 3.74 (374%)
5. 0.027 (2.7%)	**10.** 0.2325 (23.25%)	**15.** 2.465 (246.5%)

32

(5) **Warm-up Exercises** Exercises that provide a quick review of the mathematical skills needed in a consumer or career lesson.

(6) **Extension Problems** Problems that extend the topic in the lesson. They are designated by a red circle.

(7) **Materials** A list of materials other than paper and pencil that are needed by the student to do the lesson.

(8) **Scoring Table** A table to convert raw test scores to percentage scores on each chapter and unit test.

(9) **References to Duplicating Masters** References to *Consumer Forms and Problems Masters* or to *Test Masters* where appropriate.

Consumer lesson, page 180

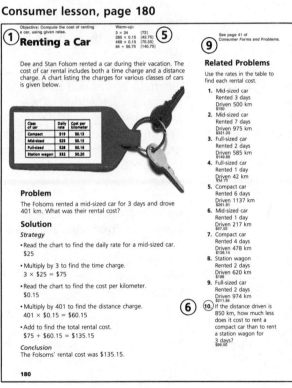

Objective: Compute the cost of renting a car, using given rates.

(1) **Renting a Car**

Warm-up: (5)
3 × 24 [72]
285 × 0.15 [42.75]
469 × 0.15 [70.35]
84 + 56.75 [140.75]

Dee and Stan Folsom rented a car during their vacation. The cost of car rental includes both a time charge and a distance charge. A chart listing the charges for various classes of cars is given below.

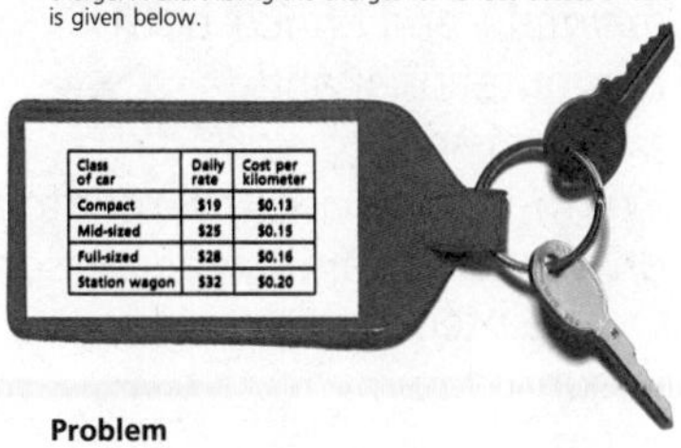

Class of car	Daily rate	Cost per kilometer
Compact	$19	$0.13
Mid-sized	$25	$0.15
Full-sized	$28	$0.16
Station wagon	$32	$0.20

Problem

The Folsoms rented a mid-sized car for 3 days and drove 401 km. What was their rental cost?

Solution

Strategy

- Read the chart to find the daily rate for a mid-sized car. $25
- Multiply by 3 to find the time charge. 3 × $25 = $75
- Read the chart to find the cost per kilometer. $0.15
- Multiply by 401 to find the distance charge. 401 × $0.15 = $60.15
- Add to find the total rental cost. $75 + $60.15 = $135.15

Conclusion
The Folsoms' rental cost was $135.15.

(9) See page 41 of *Consumer Forms and Problems.*

Related Problems

Use the rates in the table to find each rental cost.

1. Mid-sized car, Rented 3 days, Driven 500 km — $150
2. Mid-sized car, Rented 7 days, Driven 975 km — $321.25
3. Full-sized car, Rented 2 days, Driven 585 km — $149.60
4. Full-sized car, Rented 1 day, Driven 42 km — $34.72
5. Compact car, Rented 6 days, Driven 1137 km — $261.81
6. Mid-sized car, Rented 1 day, Driven 217 km — $57.55
7. Compact car, Rented 4 days, Driven 478 km — $138.14
8. Station wagon, Rented 2 days, Driven 620 km — $188
9. Full-sized car, Rented 2 days, Driven 974 km — $211.84

(6) (10.) If the distance driven is 850 km, how much less does it cost to rent a compact car than to rent a station wagon for 3 days? $98.50

180

Chapter test, page 250

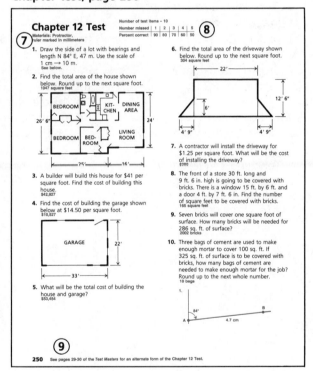

Chapter 12 Test

(7) Materials: Protractor, ruler marked in millimeters

Number of test items - 10

Number missed	1	2	3	4	5
Percent correct	90	80	70	60	50

(8)

1. Draw the side of a lot with bearings and length N 84° E, 47 m. Use the scale of 1 cm → 10 m. See below.
2. Find the total area of the house shown below. Round up to the next square foot. 1047 square feet

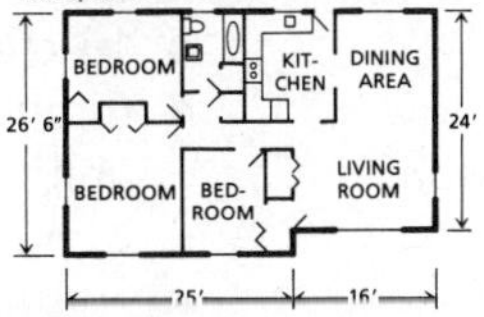

3. A builder will build this house for $41 per square foot. Find the cost of building this house. $42,927
4. Find the cost of building the garage shown below at $14.50 per square foot. $10,527

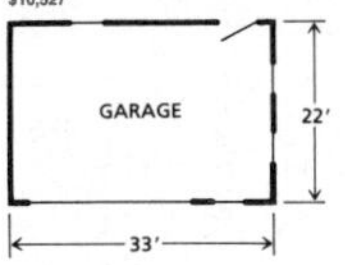

5. What will be the total cost of building the house and garage? $53,454
6. Find the total area of the driveway shown below. Round up to the next square foot. 304 square feet

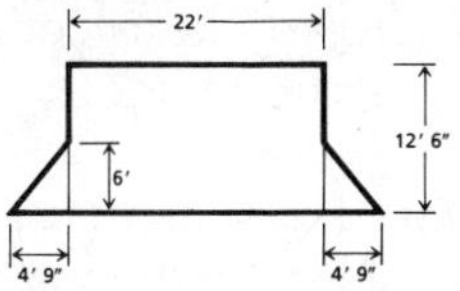

7. A contractor will install the driveway for $1.25 per square foot. What will be the cost of installing the driveway? $380
8. The front of a store 30 ft. long and 9 ft. 6 in. high is going to be covered with bricks. There is a window 15 ft. by 6 ft. and a door 4 ft. by 7 ft. 6 in. Find the number of square feet to be covered with bricks. 165 square feet
9. Seven bricks will cover one square foot of surface. How many bricks will be needed for 286 sq. ft. of surface? 2002 bricks
10. Three bags of cement are used to make enough mortar to cover 100 sq. ft. If 325 sq. ft. of surface is to be covered with bricks, how many bags of cement are needed to make enough mortar for the job? Round up to the next whole number. 10 bags

1.
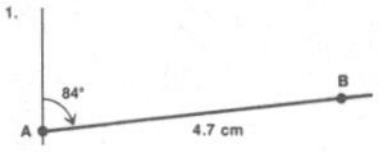

(9)

250 See pages 29-30 of the *Test Masters* for an alternate form of the Chapter 12 Test.

Management

Plan/Teach

Long range
- Table of contents
- Suggested time schedule on page T21
- Calculator notes on pages T22–T23
- Computer notes on pages T24–T25
- Suggested competency test keyed to consumer topics

Intermediate
- Overview of each chapter in teacher notes on pages T26–T43
- Activities and projects described in teacher notes

Short term
- Objectives for each lesson overprinted on page
- Teaching suggestions overprinted on page
- Additional notes found on pages T26–T43

Test

In the student's text
- 18 chapter reviews
- 18 chapter tests
- 6 multiple-choice unit tests

In the teacher's edition•
- 6 multiple-choice unit tests
- 1 multiple-choice end-of-book test
- 1 multiple-choice competency test

In the Test Masters
(alternate forms of tests in the student's text and the teacher's edition)
- 18 chapter tests
- 6 multiple-choice unit tests
- 1 multiple-choice end-of-book test
- 1 multiple-choice competency test

Maintain/Enrich

In the student's text

Maintain
- Skills Tune-Up
- Skills File

Enrich
- Break Time
- Break Time/Mental Math
- Calculator Applications
- Computer Applications
- Computer Literacy

In the teacher's edition
- Activities and projects described in teacher notes on pages T26–T43 that *maintain* and *enrich* both computational and problem-solving skills
- Warm-up exercises overprinted on consumer and career lessons
- Overprinted notes on the lesson page

In supplementary items
- *Consumer Forms and Problems Masters* that *maintain* and *enrich* problem-solving skills taught in the student's text

•Also available as blackline masters packaged with the teacher's edition

Schedule **Suggested Time Schedule**

The suggested schedule given below is a general guide to allocating periods of time to chapters within each unit. The schedule, which is based on a school year of 170 days, includes extra time for testing at the end of each chapter and unit.

	Chapter	Pages	Title	Days
Unit 1	1	4–22	Whole Numbers, Decimals, and Fractions	10
	2	24–40	Equations, Proportions, and Percent	9
	3	42–64	Measurement and Statistics	12
Unit 2	4	68–86	Income	10
	5	88–106	Personal Banking	10
	6	108–126	Consumer Credit	10
Unit 3	7	132–148	Buying a Car	8
	8	150–170	Automobile Operating Expenses	11
	9	172–188	Travel	9
Unit 4	10	194–214	Renting and Decorating a Home	10
	11	216–236	Buying a Home	11
	12	238–252	Building a Home	7
Unit 5	13	258–276	Income Tax	9
	14	278–298	Health, Life, and Retirement Insurance	10
	15	300–316	Investments	8
Unit 6	16	322–336	Buying Food	7
	17	338–354	Buying, Making, and Renting Goods	9
	18	356–374	Budgeting	10

Ways to Use the Calculator with *Consumer and Career Mathematics*, *Second Edition*

1. **With Calculator Applications**
   You may choose to use calculators with only the special feature called "Calculator Applications" in each chapter. This feature follows the theme of the chapter and focuses on ways of using a calculator with selected consumer topics. It reinforces and extends ideas taught in previous lessons.

2. **With consumer and career lessons in Units 2–6**
   Since the focus of these lessons is on solving problems, the use of calculators for computation would free the students to concentrate solely on problem solving.

3. **With exercises and related problems in selected lessons in Unit 1**
   Some lessons in this unit present mathematical concepts that *use* but do not *teach* computation. Using calculators with these lessons will help students learn the mathematical concepts without being slowed down by paper-and-pencil computation.

4. **Any combination of items 1–3**
   You may choose any combination that you prefer.

5. **Not at all**
   You may choose to omit the optional feature called "Calculator Applications" in each chapter and not use calculators at all during the year.

The use of the calculator with *Consumer and Career Mathematics*, *Second Edition*, is strictly optional. If you do plan to use the calculator in your classroom, a simple four-function calculator that adds, subtracts, multiplies, and divides is sufficient. Encourage students to use their estimation skills to determine if the answer in the display is reasonable. You might want to be aware of the following variations in calculators and **have students consult the manual for their specific calculator to determine the correct operating procedure**.

Variations

Calculator Displays
Most simple calculators show a maximum of 8 digits in the display. Some show only 6 digits, and some show more than 8 digits.

Many calculators show a zero before the decimal point when the number in the display is between 0 and 1. Some calculators do not show this zero.

Some calculators cut off, or truncate, a decimal when the display is filled. For example, a calculator answer for 2 ÷ 3 might be 0.6666666. Some calculators round instead of truncate and give the answer to 2 ÷ 3 as 0.6666667.

Calculator Key Sequences
Most four-function calculators have "algebraic logic." This means that to find 2 + 3, you press 2 [+] 3 [=]. Some calculators have "reverse logic." On these, you would press 2 [ENTER] 3 [+].

Most calculators will do operations in the order that they are entered. For example, if you press 2 [+] 3 [×] 4 [=], the calculator first adds 2 and 3 to get 5 and then multiplies by 4 to get 20. Some calculators (not many) are internally programmed to do multiplication before addition and would give 14 as the answer.

Many simple calculators have a feature that is referred to as "automatic constant." When you press 2 [×] 3 [=] the calculator automatically "remembers" the operation (multiplication) and the first number pressed (2). If you continue pressing the [=] key, the calculator will continue multiplying the number in the display by 2. Similar key sequences are possible for addition, subtraction, and division. Some calculators remember the second (instead of the first) number that is pressed. Some calculators have the automatic constant feature for only multiplication and division. Some do not have the automatic constant feature at all. Some calculators require the operation key to be pressed twice to engage the automatic constant. Some calculators have a [K] key or switch that must be used to engage the automatic constant.

Special Keys

Some calculators have two clear keys marked [C] ("clear") and [CE] ("clear entry"). On these calculators, pressing [CE] will clear or erase only the number in the display. Pressing [C] will clear the number in the display as well as all previous operations and numbers entered. Some calculators have just one key marked [C] or [C/CE]. On these calculators, pressing the key once clears the display and pressing it twice clears everything (except the memory). The [C] key is sometimes marked [AC] ("all clear") instead. Note that the clear key does not have to be pressed before each computation. For example, if you press 2 [+] 3 [=], the display will show 5. Then you can immediately press 4 [×] 7 [=] without first pressing any clear keys.

Many simple calculators have memory keys. Typically, memory keys are marked [M+] ("memory plus"), [M−] ("memory minus"), [MR] ("memory recall"), and [MC] ("memory clear"). When the calculator is first turned on, the number in memory is zero. Pressing the [M+] key will add whatever number is in the display at the time to whatever number is in the memory at the time to get a new number in memory. Pressing the [M−] key will subtract the number in the display from the number in memory to get a new number in memory. Pressing [MR] recalls the number in memory and shows it in the display. Pressing [MC] clears the memory (makes it zero). On some calculators the [M+] key will complete an operation and add the result to memory. Therefore, it is not necessary to press [=] before putting a number in memory. This is also true for the [M−] key. On some calculators the recall key is marked [RM] or [RCL] instead of [MR]. On some calculators the memory clear key is marked [CM] instead of [MC]. Some calculators have an [MS] or [STO] key instead of an [M+] key. The [MS] and [STO] keys put the display into the memory while erasing the previous number in memory.

Many simple calculators have a percent key. The use of the percent key varies a great deal from calculator to calculator. On some calculators, the [%] key can be used only with the operations multiplication and division. Other calculators have the capacity to compute add-on percent or discount percent in one step. On some calculators, the computation is performed when the [%] key is pressed. On these, pressing the [=] immediately after the [%] key may produce unwanted results.

Ways to Use the Computer with *Consumer and Career Mathematics*, *Second Edition*

1. **With a computer**

   Computer Literacy, pages 394–399
   These pages focus on BASIC programming statements and commands. You may wish to have students verify their answers to the computer literacy exercises by running them on the computer.

   Computer Applications, end of Units 2–6
   The exercises on these pages have been written for students to run on a computer. They provide students with experience keying in more complex programs. These lessons were written to give students exposure to real-world situations that use computer programs.

   Because there are variations in computers, it is recommended that you run these programs before assigning them to your students.

2. **As paper-and-pencil activities**

   Computer Literacy
   All of the exercises in this section have been written so that students can complete them as paper-and-pencil activities without running them on a computer. Using this plan, all students can gain exposure to BASIC programming language.

   Computer Applications
   Not all of the problems in this section can be completed as paper-and-pencil activities. Those problems that cannot be done in this manner are indicated on pages 191 and 255.

3. **Not at all**
   You may choose to omit the optional features called "Computer Literacy" and "Computer Applications."

The use of the computer with *Consumer and Career Mathematics*, *Second Edition,* is strictly optional. Two features have been included in the student text. One is called "Computer Literacy" and appears in the back of the student text. The other is called "Computer Applications" and appears at the end of each of Units 2–6.

The statements and commands presented in the computer literacy section are used on the computer applications pages without further explanation. Therefore, it is recommended that the computer literacy section be completed before using the applications pages. It is also recommended that the computer applications pages be done in the order in which they appear, as new programming techniques are included in each lesson.

Liberties have been taken in explaining some concepts to make them easier for students to understand; e.g., the computer does not return to the FOR statement as explained. This explanation has been given to make the concept of the loop easier to understand.

Computer Literacy

These pages in the back of the student's text provide exposure to the programming language BASIC and are not intended to represent a complete course in BASIC programming. Two or three statements or commands are explained in each one-page lesson. Examples of simple programs are shown using these statements.

All of the exercises on these pages have been written so that students can complete them as paper-and-pencil activities. One type of exercise is to give the output for specific input using programs that are given on the page. There are also exercises writing simple programs that are similar to the programs shown in the examples. These programs are short and should be easy for most students to write. Do not expect all of the students' programs to look the same. The programs should be checked to see if they give the desired output.

Computer Applications

Each of these lessons focuses on the use of the computer in consumer situations related to one or more of the topics taught in the unit. The objective for these pages is for students to be able to use an existing program. Students should understand what to enter when running each program, and they should be able to interpret the output. Students should not be expected to write programs as complex as these.

The modifications suggested for programs are intended as extensions and may not be appropriate for all students. You may wish to show students the modifications to the programs rather than to assign them. You could discuss how each line of the modification will change the output.

The programs were designed for use with a printer. However, the statements in the programs do not actually send output to the printer. Consult your manual to determine what modification is needed. If you do not have access to a printer, PRINT statements can be changed so that the output will appear on the screen in a more readable form. When using a screen for the output, you may want to add line 5 CLS to each program to clear the screen after the program is listed.

The DEF statement, which is used in the programs on pages 255 and 319, cannot be done without a disc in the computer. If your computer is not equipped with a disc drive system, the programs can be modified according to the directions in the overprinted note on page 254. Rounding, as explained using the DEF statement and the INT function, will work only for positive numbers.

PRINT statements appear before each INPUT statement so that what needs to be entered will appear on the screen. It is possible with some computers to include this information in the INPUT statement, i.e., 20 INPUT ''MONTH?'';M$. Check to see if this can be done on your computer. You may wish to have students modify the programs to fit this format.

The problems in the mortgage amortization lesson on page 255 use small numbers for the mortgage and the number of years to cut down on the use of computer time and paper. You might want to show an example using more realistic numbers. The problems in this lesson and the lesson on monthly car payments on page 191 cannot be done with paper and pencil due to the exponents in the formulas. All of the other lessons can be done with paper and pencil. You may wish to have students do some of the problems in each of the other lessons this way so that they understand what the computer does at each step of the program.

The teacher-edition answers for these lessons are often in an abbreviated form. For example, the complete amortization tables are not given since it should be necessary to check only the first several lines to determine if the student has made the correct entries.

For more complete forms of program outputs of odd-numbered problems, see Selected Answers in the back of the student's text. More complete forms of all answers may be found in the *Solution Key*.

Variations

With most computers, a statement does not have to fit on one line. The computer will automatically continue the same statement on the next line.

When a comma is used to separate items in a PRINT statement, it causes each item to be printed in a different zone. The number of characters in a zone and the number of zones on a line vary among computers.

Some computers round the answer to $\frac{2}{3}$ (.66666667), while others truncate (.66666666). Also, the number of significant digits may vary.

Features vary from computer to computer. You should be aware of the above variations and have students consult the manual for your particular system to determine the correct operating procedure for the computer system they use.

Notes Chapter 1

Whole Numbers, Decimals, and Fractions, pages 4–22

Overview

In Chapter 1, students will review computational skills involving whole numbers, decimals, and fractions. Most lessons also make use of estimation, a skill used frequently in real life. Estimation serves as a tool for checking answers both in the classroom and in everyday situations.

■ Materials relating to specific topics will be identified in the chapter overview by a square. You may want to check ahead to allow sufficient time to obtain the materials.

In preparation for teaching the consumer topics in this book, you might consider obtaining a list of federal publications dealing with consumer topics. Such a list is available through Consumer Information, Public Documents Distribution Center, Pueblo, Colorado 81009. You might also want a copy of *Sylvia Porter's Money Book for the 80's* (Softbound version © 1980, by Avon Books, 959 Eighth Avenue, New York, New York 10019).

Lesson Notes and Activities

pages 4–5 Rounding, as presented in this lesson, is important because it is used to estimate answers involving computation. To give students more practice, have them round sets of numbers found in an atlas or an almanac.

pages 6–7 Often numbers are rounded so that the estimated sum or difference can be found mentally. Encourage students to round when making purchases, estimate the total cost, and then estimate the amount of change they should receive when paying for the items.

pages 8–9 You might want to demonstrate some additional examples involving zeros, such as 205×83 and 307×309.

Have students experiment to find if there is a "best" method for rounding two-digit factors that end in 5. They will discover that rounding the smaller factor up and the larger factor down will produce the closest estimate of the product. An example follows.

$45 \times 75 = 3375$	Actual product
$50 \times 80 = 4000$	Normal rounding
$40 \times 80 = 3200$	Rounding smaller down, larger up
$50 \times 70 = 3500$	Rounding smaller up, larger down

pages 10–11 You might want to provide additional examples that involve writing extra zeros when placing the decimal point in the answer. Use exercises such as 0.006×5 and 0.004×0.02.

pages 12–13 You might want to discuss additional examples that involve zeros in the quotient. Exercises you could use are $13{,}065 \div 65$, $6900 \div 23$, and $4.575 \div 1.5$.

pages 14–15 The following skills involving fractions are reviewed: writing fractions with a common denominator, writing fractions in lowest terms, comparing fractions and mixed numbers, writing mixed numbers as fractions, and writing fractions as mixed numbers.

pages 16–17 In preparation for this lesson, you might want to review reciprocals. You might also explain why the "shortcut" works.

pages 18–19 Since the problems on page 18 deal with mixed numbers, you may want to review adding and subtracting fractions before using the lesson. Also review the renaming required for simplifying an answer, such as $8\frac{7}{5} = 9\frac{2}{5}$, and the renaming required for subtracting, such as $10\frac{1}{4} = 9\frac{5}{4}$.

page 20 Most of the answers to the calculator exercises are repeating decimals. You may wish to discuss the rounding of calculator answers.

Notes Chapter 2

Equations, Proportions, and Percent, pages 24–40

Overview

In Chapter 2, students will solve one-step and two-step equations and will use cross-products to solve proportions. They will also solve the three types of percent problems using equations. Encourage students to use estimation to check their answers whenever possible.

Lesson Notes and Activities

pages 24–25 Be sure students understand that the same number can be added to or subtracted from both sides of an equation without changing the solution. To solve an equation, students are taught to isolate the variable on one side of the equal sign. This can be accomplished by *undoing* the operation being performed on the variable. Addition *undoes* subtraction and subtraction *undoes* addition.

pages 26–27 You might remind students that they should rewrite the equation so that the variable is alone on one side of the equal sign. For this lesson they use the idea that multiplication *undoes* division and vice versa.

pages 28–29 Emphasize that in two-step equations one must *undo* the indicated operations in reverse order. Some students may find the following procedure helpful.

$3x + 2 = 11$	
x is multiplied by 3.	M3
2 is added to $3x$.	A2
To solve, do the opposite.	
Subtract 2.	S2
Then divide by 3.	D3

pages 30–31 Explain that ratios are used to express rates or comparisons. The ratio 7 to 4 can express a rate, such as 7 items for $4, or a comparison, such as 7 girls to 4 boys.

After discussing problem A, give students two ratios that are not equal and have them show that the cross-products are not equal.

- Activities that can be used to supplement a lesson or group of lessons are identified in the lesson notes by a dot. Often these activities require materials and/or information not found in the student's text.

  For an activity related to this lesson, have students bring in scale models or scale drawings. Have them measure parts of the model or drawing, and then use the scale to find the actual size.

pages 32–33 Mention that 100% of something is all of it and 0% of something is none of it. Discuss situations in which percents greater than 100% can occur and situations in which percents greater than 100% are not appropriate.

- Have students find baseball batting averages, which are usually expressed as decimals, and write them as percents. Also have them find basketball shooting percentages and express them as fractions or decimals.

pages 34–37 You may wish to show the proportion method for solving percent problems. The following proportions could be used for problems A, B, and C.

Problem A:	45% of $6.75 is what number?	$\frac{45}{100} = \frac{m}{6.75}$
Problem B:	What percent of $1.90 is $0.76?	$\frac{r}{100} = \frac{0.76}{1.90}$
Problem C:	20% of what number is $39?	$\frac{20}{100} = \frac{39}{p}$

- Have students find the percent of discount for sales advertisements in which only the regular price and sale price are given.

page 38 After students have completed this lesson, problems 1–9, have them determine for each problem, what single percent gives the same net cost. For problem 1 the net cost, to the nearest dollar, is $710. Since $710 is about 75% of $945, a single discount of 25% would give the same net cost.

Measurement and Statistics, pages 42–62

Overview

In the first part of Chapter 3, students will learn different units of measurement in the metric system. The topics covered are length, area, volume, capacity, mass, temperature, and time. In the second part of the chapter, students will read and construct bar, line, and circle graphs. They will also compute the mean, median, and mode for sets of data

- A source of information on the metric system is:
American National Metric Council
1625 Massachusetts Avenue, N.W.
Washington, D.C. 20036.

Lesson Notes and Activities

pages 42–43 Show the relative size of metric units of length on a meter stick.

- Choose items in the classroom for students to measure. You might suggest that they estimate before actually measuring. As they do more measuring in the metric system, their estimates should become more accurate.

pages 44–45 Note that in the metric system, cm^2 is the accepted symbol for square centimeter and cm^3 is the accepted symbol for cubic centimeter.

pages 46–47 Explain to students that a container with a volume of one cubic decimeter holds one liter of water. The mass of this water is one kilogram. If the volume of a container is one cubic centimeter, it will hold one milliliter of water, and the mass of the water will be one gram.

pages 48–49 You might review "moving" the decimal point to multiply or divide by a power of ten.

- Have students pick a topic, such as driving a car, cooking, or sports, and report on how it would be affected by a switch to the metric system.

pages 50–51 You might mention other temperatures when discussing the thermometer. For example, contrast a hot summer day (30°C) and a cold winter day ($^-$15°C), or a hot drink (75°C) and an iced drink (5°C).

It might also be interesting to note that a record low temperature of $^-$88°C was recorded in Antarctica on August 24, 1960, and a record high temperature of 58°C was recorded in North Africa on September 13, 1922.

pages 52–53 Have more able students find airplane arrival times, if they are given departure times, flight times, and time-zone changes.

pages 54–55 Discuss how choices of different values for the scales on a bar graph or line graph can affect the appearance of the graph.

pages 56–57 Point out that a circle graph is used to highlight a division of the whole rather than to show trends.

If a section of a circle graph contains an angle greater than 180°, this angle could be drawn first. Show students that to draw a 216° angle they can draw a 144° angle, since $360° - 216° = 144°$. An angle that is more than 180° and less than 360° is called a *reflex* angle.

- Have students survey classmates on something like favorite TV show, music group, football team, or candidate. Then have each student use the information to construct a graph.

pages 58–59 Help students see that the mean is never less than the least number nor greater than the greatest number in the set of data. Also, the mean need not be a number in the set.

- Have students collect data that interests them and find the mean, median, and mode for each set of data.

page 60 As an additional exercise, give students a set of data with one number missing, together with the average of the set. Have students find the missing number.

Notes Chapter 4

Income, pages 68–86

Overview

In Chapter 4, students will study two fundamental consumer concepts—gross pay and net pay. They will be shown several common wage systems and will learn how to compute gross pay for each. Deductions will be explained so that students can determine net pay.

- If you have not already done so, you might want to obtain the materials suggested in the Overview for Chapter 1. For Chapter 4, you might also want to get current salary schedules for various jobs. Such schedules often appear in the business sections of newspapers, or can be obtained through employment agencies. Current payroll withholding information and FICA schedules can be obtained from a payroll department or the district office of the Internal Revenue Service in your area.

Lesson Notes and Activities

pages 68–69 For less able students, give several examples of how regular pay is determined before having them compute overtime pay and gross pay.

pages 70–71 You might want to mention that when eating in a restaurant, most people give the waiter or waitress a tip for service. The tip is usually about 15% of the bill before tax is added. Determining the amount of a tip in a restaurant will be considered in Chapter 16.

pages 72–73 You might ask more able students how many dollars in sales Wendy needs in order to earn $500. They should solve "43% of what number is $500?" Wendy would need about $1163 in sales.

pages 74–75 When a person is paid a salary plus commission, the commission rate is usually less than the rate for straight commission.

page 76 You might ask more able students to find the straight commission rate that would give Scott the same gross pay on $17,000 in sales. They should solve "$1280 is what percent of $17,000?" The straight commission rate would be about 7.5%.

- Have each student select a career and research the training required, the number of openings annually, the opportunities for advancement, and the salary a new employee could expect to earn.

page 77 Selling-cost percent is one way of determining the effectiveness of a salesperson. The most effective person would have the lowest percent.

pages 78–81 The Internal Revenue Service is able to determine rather accurately the amount of income tax that an individual will be required to pay. This determination is based on income, marital status, and number of exemptions. The total amount withheld during the year should be sufficient to pay the person's federal income tax. Computing federal income tax will be discussed in Chapter 13.

The withholding tables and the percent withheld for FICA can change annually. The information given in the lesson uses data for 1981. If you have obtained more current rates, you might have students work the problems with them.

- Have a representative from an employment agency talk to the class about occupations, pay, and fringe benefits. Then conduct mock job interviews with students.

pages 82–83 You might summarize the different wage systems discussed in the chapter before the students use this lesson.

- Have students use employment ads from local newspapers to make a list of jobs that use the wage systems discussed in the chapter.

Notes Chapter 5

Personal Banking, pages 88–106

Overview

In Chapter 5, students will study the basic elements of personal banking—checking and savings accounts. They will learn how to keep records of their transactions and how to reconcile bank statements. They will also learn to compute simple and compound interest.

- You may want to obtain sample deposit slips, checks, check registers, and bank statements from local banks.

Lesson Notes and Activities

pages 88–89 If you have an actual deposit slip, point out that checks can also be entered on the reverse side.

pages 90–91 Mention that all of the checks in a checkbook should be numbered consecutively. Also point out that the numbers that appear just under the check number identify the city, the bank, and the Federal Reserve Bank. They are used to route the check back to the originating bank. The numbers at the bottom of the check identify the bank, the customer account, and the check. These numbers are machine readable.

pages 92–93 Explain that usually a checkbook will have either a register or stubs, but not both.

- Ask a local bank representative to speak to the class on the following topics:
  1. Checking systems: routing checks through the Federal Reserve System, dealing with checks written for more than is in the account, and stopping payment on a check
  2. Other banking services: safe-deposit boxes, traveler's checks, and so on
  3. Various kinds of savings accounts: regular accounts, passbook accounts, time accounts, and so on
  4. Career opportunities in banking

pages 94–96 Point out that some banks do not have a service charge for checking accounts; however, many of these banks require a minimum balance.

- Have students investigate the service charges and cost of checking at several local banks.
- As an ongoing activity, give each student a supply of checks that you have duplicated, along with a check register and an opening balance. Then, periodically give the students a list of bills to pay by check and deposits to make. After a given period of time, give the students a bank statement to reconcile.

page 97 If you have copies of bank statements from local banks, discuss the directions given for reconciling the statements. Discuss what to do if a bank error is found.

pages 98–99 Point out that the computation of simple interest can also be done with fractions. For example, the problem on page 98 can be solved with this equation:

$$I = \$300 \times \frac{55}{1000} \times \frac{1}{4}$$

pages 100–101 Compound interest can be computed in various ways. The student's text illustrates a method using the simple interest formula. Another method involves multiplying the principal by (1 + rate). Consider the problem on page 100 in which (1 + rate) is (1 + 0.08), or 1.08.

$1000 × 1.08 = $1080	First year
$1080 × 1.08 = $1166.40	Second year
$1166.40 − $1000 = $166.40	Total interest earned

pages 102–103 You may want to discuss the formula for compound interest with your more able students. This formula, $A = P(1 + r)^n$, was used to generate the compound interest table on page 102. Daily compounding will be discussed in Chapter 15.

Consumer Credit, pages 108–124

Overview

In Chapter 6, students will compute interest charges for borrowing money, and finance charges for buying on credit. Different methods of calculating finance charges on credit card purchases are shown. Students will also compare credit plans.

- You may want to assemble examples of the credit terms for major credit card companies and for local stores that have their own charge plans.

Lesson Notes and Activities

pages 108–109 In Chapter 5, the word *interest* means money received from a bank for use of funds put into a savings account. Now the term will be used to mean money paid to a lender for the use of borrowed money. Be sure students realize that interest can mean income *or* expense.

pages 110–111 You may wish to discuss some of the laws pertaining to consumer credit.

1. Consumers may withhold payment of a bill they believe to be incorrect, and the creditor must explain the billing within 90 days.
2. If a credit card is lost or stolen, the holder of the credit card is liable for only $50 in purchases that someone else charges.
3. Merchants or lenders who turn down an application for credit must explain why.
4. Any lending institution that buys an installment contract from a merchant may not demand payment for defective goods that the merchant refuses to repair or replace.
5. On accounts used by both husband and wife, all reports given to credit bureaus by lenders must include both spouses' names if both use the account or if either one of them requests dual reporting.

- Have students contact the credit departments of local stores to obtain information about the charge accounts they offer. After students report their findings to the class, discuss the similarities and differences in the credit plans.

pages 112–113 Finance charges cannot be figured on unpaid finance charges. Therefore, when the average daily balance is computed, outstanding finance charges are deducted from the unpaid balance. All payments received are applied to outstanding finance charges first, and then to previous purchases. The new balance is the sum of any outstanding finance charges, the balance after payments, the current finance charge, and the new purchases charged.

- Invite a guest speaker from a bank, a finance company, or a credit counseling service to talk to the class about such things as requirements needed to obtain a loan or charge account, prepayment clauses, credit traps, and the determination of interest rates.

page 114 This calculator application extends the previous lesson by having students determine the average daily balance and the current finance charges when new purchases have been made.

page 115 You might have several minimum-payment schedules available for comparison.

pages 116–117 Have students compare the amounts of the monthly payments for borrowing $300 at an annual rate of 16% for 12 months, 18 months, and 24 months.

- Have students research how credit ratings are determined, how a person can review his or her credit file, and how a person can correct a mistake in a credit rating.

pages 118–119 Problems 11–18 can be used as a basis for discussion of how finance charges vary with increased rates or increased time.

pages 120–121 Stress the importance of shopping for the best credit plan. Discuss the fact that it is easy to buy on credit, but it is not always easy to make the required payments.

Buying a Car, pages 132–148

Overview

Many students are interested in buying a car. In Chapter 7, they will learn how to compute the cost of a new car or used car, how to make an offer for a new car, and how to determine the cost of financing a car.

- Publications like *Buyer's Guide Reports New Car Prices* (DMR Publications Inc., 1410 East Capitol Drive, Milwaukee, Wisconsin 53211) list current sticker prices and available options. Such publications are available at magazine counters and book stores.

Lesson Notes and Activities

pages 132–133 Options can add greatly to the cost of a car. However, some options, such as radios, power steering, and air conditioning, can increase the resale value of a car.

You might want to extend this lesson by discussing the reasons that some people pick certain options. The discussion could include such things as protective equipment and different kinds of tires.

page 134 According to the 1981 *Buyer's Guide*, the estimated dealer cost factors range from 0.82 for a full-sized car to 0.87 for a subcompact car. Multiplying the sticker price by the cost factor gives a rough estimate of the dealer's cost.

page 135 Suggest that the students list the 24 possible winning arrangements, assume that each arrangement is correct, and then check the statements made by the frogs. For each frog exactly two statements must be true and exactly two statements must be false. If this is not the case, the arrangement being checked is incorrect.

pages 136–137 Before buying a used car, the buyer should take the car to a trusted mechanic who will inspect the entire car and make a list of any necessary repairs. When people buy a used car from a dealer, there is often a guarantee. It is important that the buyer understand what is covered by that guarantee.

- Have students find the total cost of a used car after investigating local fees and taxes.

pages 138–139 Students should understand that the lowest net price is what they pay for the car. Thus, the lowest selling price or the highest trade-in allowance will not necessarily determine the best deal.

- Have students do some comparison shopping for a new car. They should obtain the costs for local fees and taxes, and find the total cost of the new car.

pages 140–142 Explain to the students that if they know the interest rate, the principal (amount financed), and the time, they can find the approximate monthly payment by using the strategy on page 116 and the table on page 401. This is also the topic for the computer application for this unit.

- If the students selected a used car or new car to buy in previous activities, have them now determine how they would finance the car. Then have them compute the monthly payments.

page 143 Explain that truth-in-lending laws were passed to protect the consumer. If you have an installment contract available, discuss it with the class.

pages 144–145 Find out how various automobile salespeople are paid. Have students compare the different salary plans.

Automobile Operating Expenses, pages 150–170

Overview

In Chapter 8, students determine the cost of owning and operating a car. The cost of gasoline, depreciation, repairs, maintenance, and insurance are considered. Some attention is also given to using public transportation as an alternative to driving a car.

- You may wish to obtain current automobile insurance rates for your area.

Lesson Notes and Activities

pages 150–151 Point out that driving habits, road conditions, and the locale (whether highway or city) greatly influence fuel economy rates and thus affect gasoline costs. To determine the car's fuel economy rate, a driver usually keeps a record of gasoline purchases over a long period of time.

pages 152–153 As the rate of depreciation decreases, repair costs increase. When a car is between 6 and 7 years old, its market value is about the same as the annual repair and maintenance costs.

page 154 Discuss why rental cars depreciate at a faster rate than do privately owned cars.

page 155 When determining the percent of decrease (or increase), the change is compared to the original amount. Thus, in the example shown above problem 9, the change in the fuel economy rate is 0.41, which is about 4.81% of 8.53.

pages 156–159 Customers who feel that the labor costs on a bill are too high should ask to see the garage's trade manual. This manual allots specific times (in tenths of an hour) for performing certain repair work. This period of time, multiplied by the hourly charge for labor, should be close to the total charge for labor on the bill.

pages 160–161 Some companies give discounts to students who satisfactorily complete a course in driver education. In some states, young drivers are required to take this course.

Because of rising court settlements, encourage students to carry as much liability coverage as possible. Note that a 50/100 personal injury policy provides twice as much coverage as a 25/50 policy, but costs only 9% more. Students should understand that insurance companies are competitive; different companies will offer different premium quotations for the same coverage.

pages 162–163 As a car gets older and the market value decreases, many drivers decrease their premium by changing to a collision policy with a higher deductible amount, or by dropping their collision coverage.

- Have an insurance agent talk to your class about good-student driving discounts, the savings gained by adding the insurance for a student to a family policy, and so on. Also, inquire about high-risk drivers and their increased premium rates.

pages 164–165 Note that certain fixed costs exist whether or not a car is driven. Discuss costs that increase and costs that decrease as a car gets older.

- As an ongoing project, have students who own a car or who have access to a family car keep track of the costs of operating the car for a month. Have them summarize the fixed costs, variable costs, and depreciation. Suggest that they divide annual expenses such as depreciation, license fees, and insurance by 12 to find the monthly cost. Have them use this information to determine the cost per kilometer of operating the car during the month.

pages 166–167 If public transportation is available in your area, compare its cost with the cost of operating a car.

Travel, pages 172–186

Overview

The first part of Chapter 9 deals with interpreting distance charts, reading a road map, and estimating the cost of taking a trip by car. Students then learn about air fares and car rentals, and they compare the costs of different modes of travel.

- You can obtain road maps from the highway department, or local service stations. Updated air, bus, and train fares are available through the respective companies or from a travel agency. For additional information about travel agencies, contact the American Society of Travel Agents, 711 Fifth Avenue, New York, New York 10022.

Lesson Notes and Activities

pages 172–173 You could supplement the distance chart with distances, in kilometers, from your town or the nearest large city to the cities shown on the map.

pages 174–175 You might wish to use a map and discuss how such things as mountains and rivers influence where roads are built.

To extend the idea of the time a trip takes, show that for a given distance, if the rate is cut in half, the time is doubled. Similarly, if the rate is doubled, the time is cut in half.

- Have road maps available. Let students select a place to visit by car and then compute the distance and driving time based on a speed of 80 kilometers per hour.

pages 176–177 This lesson can be extended by having the students find the cost per day per person for the trip.

pages 178–179 Air fares change frequently. You might want to update the figures given on page 178.

- Have students contact representatives of different airlines to find the types of jobs available, the approximate number of employees, and the wages and benefits for various jobs.

page 180 Before a person can rent a car, certain requirements must be met. Generally, the person must be over 21 years of age (25 in some areas), have a valid driver's license, have the agency's credit card or another major credit card, and provide proof of insurance. If the person intends to pay cash, a deposit is required.

page 181 You might provide rate information from various car rental agencies. Have students calculate the cost of renting the same kind of car at each rate and then compare the results. Also discuss the fact that some rental companies have drop-off charges if the car is not returned to the agency from which it was rented.

pages 182–183 When choosing a method of travel, people must consider that buses are scheduled very frequently and go to many locations, trains offer sleeping rooms and space for moving around, and airplanes provide very fast service.

- Invite a travel agent to the class to speak about the services offered by a travel agent, the way the agent is paid, and the training necessary to become a travel agent.
- Have students decide on a trip they would like to take and research the cost of getting to the location using different methods of travel. Have them include meals and lodging, if these are required.

Renting and Decorating a Home, pages 194–214

Overview

In Chapter 10, students will encounter many aspects of renting and living in an apartment. Such things as determining the amount to spend for rent, selecting a place to rent, decorating an apartment, and personal property insurance will be covered.

- You might want to contact the gas company and the electric company in your area for current utility rates. You might also want to obtain personal property insurance rates for your area.

Lesson Notes and Activities

pages 194–195 The guideline given on page 194 is widely used. People tend to spend the maximum amount they can afford for housing.

pages 196–197 You might discuss why the cost of utilities varies in different parts of the country. If possible, compare the rates in different areas.

- Have students check local want ads for the least and the most expensive two-bedroom apartments in the area. Discuss the reasons for the differences in cost.
- Have the students use all of the ads they can find to determine the average cost of a two-bedroom apartment in the area.

pages 198–199 Billing for utilities varies, so you might want to discuss the procedures used in your area. Mention that a meter reader may leave a card to be completed by a consumer; therefore, it is important that the consumer be able to read the meter accurately.

- Have students obtain information concerning energy conservation. Discuss this idea with the class.
- Have students locate utility meters in their homes and take readings daily, weekly, or monthly. Have them use local rates to compute utility costs.

page 200 You might obtain the rate per kilowatt-hour in your area and have the students use this number when working the problems.

page 201 The number of squares in a rectangle is known as its "order." In this case, the order of the squared rectangle is 10. If some of the squares are the same size, the rectangle is an *imperfect-squared rectangle*.

pages 202–203 Mention that often an interior decorator will save a customer money by helping avoid costly mistakes.

- Have students measure a room and its furniture at home. Then have them use graph paper to make a new arrangement for the room.

pages 204–205 The number of tiles needed could also be estimated by dividing the total area by the area of each tile. However, this method does not account for partial tiles that may be needed to match patterns.

pages 206–207 This lesson assumes that the paint covers in one coat. To extend the lesson, discuss the amount of paint needed for two coats. You might also assume that the ceilings are to be painted a color different from that used for the walls.

pages 208–209 Explain that in most apartments tenants are required to use strippable wallpaper. In discussing the cost of wallpaper, point out that some wallpaper comes only in double or triple rolls.

- Have students measure a room at home and use their figures to determine the amount of paint and/or wallpaper needed to decorate it. Have them use costs from local merchants to figure the cost of the decorating.

pages 210–211 You might want to use current personal property insurance rates for your area.

Buying a Home, pages 216–236

Overview

Chapter 11 deals with the financial aspects of buying a home. It is not intended as a comprehensive study of the fine points of home ownership costs, but rather as a basic treatment of topics that consumers face when buying a home.

- You might want to obtain current information for your area relating to mortgage rates, real estate taxes, closing costs on buying a home, and homeowner's insurance.

Lesson Notes and Activities

pages 216–217 This lesson is similar to the first lesson in Chapter 10, but it deals with the purchase of a home rather than with renting. The guideline given on page 216 is flexible, but it can give an idea of the range a person should consider when buying a home.

- Have students use a local newspaper to find the costs of various kinds of housing in your area. Have them assume a 20% down payment and then use the guideline to determine the annual gross income needed to buy each home.

pages 218–219 A mortgage is a legal right to a piece of property, given as security to a lending institution that has loaned money.

Point out some of the advantages of mortgage loans, such as income tax deductions and the fact that during times of inflation repayment is made in ''cheaper'' dollars.

- Have students research the various types of loans available for buying a home.

pages 220–221 This lesson points out a fact that is often overlooked by people borrowing money—the interest on a long-term loan is often greater than the amount borrowed. However, the interest paid on a mortgage loan is tax deductible.

page 222 The concept of amortization will be pursued further in the next lesson where the students use calculators to do the computation.

page 223 You might show the students Scott's amortization table for the beginning of each of years 21 through 25.

Payment	Principal	Interest	Paid on principal	New principal
241	$20090.97	$226.02	$240.38	$19850.59
253	$17021.11	$191.49	$274.91	$16746.19
265	$13510.18	$151.99	$314.41	$13195.77
277	$ 9494.83	$106.82	$359.58	$ 9135.24
289	$ 4902.57	$ 55.15	$411.25	$ 4491.32

pages 224–225 If available, use current rate information for your area.

pages 226–227 Discuss why the assessed valuation of a home can change. Reasons include increased or decreased property value in the area and improvements made on the home.

pages 228–229 Discuss the role of the lawyer in the closing and what is meant by title search and title insurance.

pages 230–233 You might also discuss the idea of multiple listing by real estate agencies. The agency that lists the house might not sell it. In this case, the commission is divided between the listing and selling agencies.

Building a Home, pages 238–250

Overview

Some people buy a piece of property and plan to have a home constructed on it. In Chapter 12, students will learn how to draw a scale drawing of a piece of property, given bearings and lengths of sides. They will find the cost of building a house and garage and of installing a driveway. Attention is also given to determining the amount of materials needed when building with bricks.

- Charts are available that can be used to calculate building costs in a particular part of the country. You might want to obtain such a chart from an insurance broker.

Lesson Notes and Activities

pages 238–239 A surveyor usually expresses angle measures and distances more accurately than shown in this lesson.

As an extension of the lesson, you might have the students calculate the area of each figure in problems 9–12. Have them divide the figure into triangles, measure the bases and heights to scale, and compute the area.

- Have a local surveyor visit your class. The surveyor could bring a transit to class and explain its operation.

pages 240–242 Costs per square foot vary in different areas and with different builders. You might contact local builders for costs in your area.

page 243 If you have cost figures available for your area, you might want to compare them with the figures given.

pages 244–245 You may want to review finding the area of a triangle. Also mention that a concrete driveway would be more expensive than the asphalt driveway suggested in the lesson.

pages 246–247 You could extend this lesson by having the students calculate the cost of the bricks required for the house and the garage. The price of bricks varies according to the kind used. You might want to discuss the types of bricks that are available for construction.

Income Tax, pages 258–276

Overview

This chapter will cover some of the basic terminology and computation involved in preparing a federal income tax return. The lessons provide a background for students who will encounter a variety of tax forms throughout their lives. Attention is also given to various state income tax procedures.

- In order to teach the most up-to-date tax information using current forms, you may want to obtain classroom teaching units from the government. Contact the district office of the Internal Revenue Service in your area and ask for *Understanding Taxes* (Publication 21).

Lesson Notes and Activities

pages 258–259 This lesson introduces the W-2 form and the general instructions about who must file a tax return.

Point out that most people have to file a tax return. The related problems cover people in situations where income levels might be low—students working part time or older individuals who are no longer working full time.

pages 260–262 This lesson, along with the next two lessons, shows the students how to fill out tax return Form 1040A. You might want to discuss the differences in the requirements for filing Forms 1040 and 1040A. Also discuss what is meant by exemption, interest income, and dividend income.

page 263 Note that only parts of Tax Tables A, B, and C are shown on pages 406–408. If possible, have the entire set of tables available.

pages 264–265 Mention that if additional taxes are owed, a check must be sent to the IRS. Refunds are made automatically after the return is filed. Taxpayers are advised to keep all information regarding the preparation of their tax returns for several years.

pages 266–267 In this lesson, students use strategies learned in the previous three lessons to fill in Form 1040A. You might suggest that they refer to the form on page 266 when completing the related problems. For each problem they are to give the information for lines 11, 13, 15, and 16 or 17.

pages 268–270 Many people have their tax returns completed by a tax consultant. The fee paid to the consultant is deductible on the following year's tax return.

Most students will not itemize when they first file a return. However, itemizing can result in lower taxes for many adults. Tax forms list specific itemized deductions that are allowed.

- Have an income tax consultant speak to your class concerning the problems of students who are filing their first return. You can arrange for a speaker by contacting the district office of the IRS in your vicinity.
- Some students may be interested in Form 1040 and the directions for completing this form. The instruction book and the forms can be obtained from a post office, some banks, or an IRS office.

page 271 For additional information about tax withholding, estimated tax, and the penalty for underpayment, see IRS Publication 505, *Tax Withholding and Estimated Tax*.

pages 272–273 Each state may regulate its own income tax. The rules illustrated in this lesson are representative of some of the procedures used throughout the country. If your own state has an income tax, discuss the current filing procedures with the class.

- Obtain current state income tax forms for your state. Have students complete a form using initial data you have provided.

Health, Life, and Retirement Insurance, pages 278–298

Overview

Insurance can be a broad and difficult topic. The explanations of health insurance and different types of life insurance presented in Chapter 14 are simplified as much as possible.

- You might want to obtain current insurance rates for both males and females from an insurance broker. Updated social security retirement information can be obtained from your local social security office.

Lesson Notes and Activities

pages 278–279 Discuss the major types of health insurance coverage available:

1. Hospital expense insurance—provides benefits for hospital room and board, nursing care, and medical supplies.
2. Surgical expense coverage—pays most, if not all, of the expenses incurred for surgery.
3. Physician's expense coverage—is often included with items 1 and 2 above to form "basic" coverage.
4. Major medical insurance—protects the insured against prolonged hospital expenses.
5. Disability insurance—provides income in case of loss of work due to disabling injuries.

- Have students report on national health insurance, what it is, how it would affect the individual consumer, and how it would be financed.

pages 280–281 Explain that the rates for females are less than those for males because females have a greater life expectancy. You might want to obtain a mortality table and explain how it is compiled and how it affects insurance rates.

pages 282–285 Be sure students understand the difference between *face value* and *cash value*. Face value is the amount of money that the beneficiaries would receive if the insured were to die. Cash value is the cash amount available to the insured if the policy is surrendered or borrowed against. A person can borrow against cash value without relinquishing the policy, but the protection is then reduced by the amount of the loan until the loan is repaid. The amount one can borrow depends upon how long the policy has been in effect. Endowment insurance has a cash value, but it is specifically designed so that at the time it matures the insured is paid the policy's face value.

Most insurance companies have separate rates for males and females. The premium table shown on page 282 and the cash value table on page 284 are for males. With the exception of cash value at age 65, they can be used for a female by subtracting three years from her age. Using the resulting age in the table gives a close approximation of the rate for a female. However, since only part of the table on page 284 can be adapted for females, the problems on page 285 involve only males.

- Have students use the starting salaries for careers in which they are interested and the guideline of "four times annual gross pay" to determine an amount of life insurance to purchase. Have them find the annual premium for each type of life insurance using the age at which they would start working.

pages 286–287 Explain that one of an insurance agent's responsibilities is to advise a customer about the best type of health and/or life insurance to buy. Such things as age, marital status, and responsibilities are considered.

page 289 The solution to this puzzle is easy once the students realize they should work backward.

pages 290–291 For related problems 1 and 3–10, students could find the answers for females by subtracting 3 from the given age. (Problem 2 is excluded, as the rates for age 14 are not given in the table on page 282.)

Investments, pages 300–314

Overview

In Chapter 15, students will be introduced to several kinds of investments and will learn how each type earns money for the investor. The students will also compute annual yields in order to compare investments.

Lesson Notes and Activities

pages 300–301 Periodically the interest rate, as well as the maturity, on Series EE Bonds changes. The interest rate will probably be increased in the future, and the bonds will earn more than 9% compounded semiannually. However, the 9% rate is guaranteed.

- Have students investigate other kinds of bonds that are available and report their findings to the class.

pages 302–304 The table for interest compounded daily that is given on page 302 was derived from this formula:

$$A = P\left(1 + \frac{r}{365}\right)^d$$

In the formula, r is the nominal interest rate and d is the number of days the principal, P, has been on deposit. Ninety days is used for each quarter, and 365 days is used for one year. The entries in the table may vary slightly from figures quoted by local banks because of variations in the formula.

page 305 You might tell the students that the interest on \$2500 invested for 10 years at 7.75% simple interest is \$1937.50. The interest on \$2500 invested for 10 years at 7.75% compounded monthly is \$2912.95. Point out that interest compounded monthly differs only slightly from interest compounded daily.

pages 306–309 You might explain that some companies do not pay dividends to their stockholders. These companies invest their profits in new programs or facilities to provide for growth of the company.

- Let students start with a hypothetical amount of money and "buy and sell" stocks for a given period of time. Have them use newspaper stock quotations to keep track of the daily closings. You might require that they keep a specific stock for a given period of time before selling it. Discuss the results at the end of the designated time period.

pages 310–311 The buyer's price of a share of a mutual fund is called the *public offering price*. The seller's price is the *net asset value* (NAV). The net asset value is the net value of the fund's investments divided by the number of shares outstanding.

Mutual funds are managed by professional investment managers. This feature appeals to people without the time or experience to study stock markets. The management fee is deducted before the net asset value of the fund is computed.

You might mention that there are many types of mutual funds with different investment objectives. Some invest only in highly speculative issues, others in tax-exempt issues, and so on.

- Ask an investment counselor to discuss with the class the element of risk that is present in all types of investing.
- To emphasize that there really is no way to get rich quick, ask a law enforcement officer to discuss illegal get-rich schemes and confidence games.

Buying Food, pages 322–336

Overview

In Chapter 16, students study several topics related to buying food. They consider nutrition, calorie intake and expenditure, comparison shopping, and alternatives to preparing meals at home.

Lesson Notes and Activities

pages 322–323 To lose 1 kilogram of body weight per week, a person must consume 7000 fewer calories than the body expends (or about 1000 fewer calories per day). To approximate daily calorie expenditure, multiply a man's weight, in kilograms, by 40, and multiply a woman's weight by 35.

- Have students keep track of the food they eat for one week and then calculate their calorie intake each day. They will need to use a more comprehensive calorie chart than the one given on page 322.

pages 324–325 You might want to obtain a more complete chart giving the number of calories used in various activities. Such charts can be found in some exercise and physical fitness books.

- Have students keep a record of their activities for one week and calculate their calorie expenditure for each day. They should then compare each day's calorie expenditure with the day's calorie intake.

pages 326–328 Point out that in some stores, particularly those with electronic price scanners, the price of 2 items at 3 for \$1.00 would be \$0.67, not \$0.68 as shown in the problem. To find the price calculated by a scanner, multiply \$1.00 by $\frac{2}{3}$ and round up.

- Have each student take the same shopping list to a grocery store and record the prices of the items. Encourage them to find the best buys. Compare the students' results.
- Have students plan their own meals for one week, make a grocery list based on these plans, and then determine the cost by checking food ads. (Students should assume that they do not need to purchase staple items.) In preparation for Chapter 18 on budgeting, have the students revise their meal plans and try to save between 10% and 25% on food costs.
- Have students sample different brands of food, including store brands and generic items. Have them compare the taste, quality, and prices.

page 329 After students finish the problems, you might have them find the unit price for each item. Note that the prices in problems 2 and 9 are given as unit prices.

pages 330–331 Discuss the advantages and disadvantages of buying a side of beef. Consider the cost of freezing the beef and the fluctuating prices of beef at the grocery store during the time period in which the side of beef is being used.

pages 332–333 In comparing the costs of meals, you might want to discuss the value of a person's time spent preparing a meal at home.

- As preparation for Chapter 18, have students estimate their weekly (or monthly) expenditures on food, transportation, and recreation. Then have them start keeping track of their actual expenses. By the time you start Chapter 18, each student should have helpful data for planning a budget.

Buying, Making, and Renting Goods, pages 338–354

Overview

In Chapter 17, students consider three ways of obtaining goods: buying, making, and renting. They learn about buying merchandise through catalogs and about buying when items are on sale. There are several lessons that focus on the cost of making items. The last lesson deals with renting, rather than buying, equipment.

- You might want to have several catalogs and order forms available.

Lesson Notes and Activities

pages 338–340 Buying through catalogs is a major part of retail sales. The basic elements presented in this lesson are representative of most catalog sales.

- Have students bring catalogs from home. Compare order forms and the procedures used to determine the total cost. Discuss when state sales tax must be included.
- If catalogs are available for classroom use, prepare a series of cards, each with a description of items to be ordered. Have each student select a card and complete an order form.

page 341 Before using this lesson, you may wish to give the students more practice finding the total weight of several items when each weight is given in pounds and ounces.

pages 342–343 Discuss the advantages and disadvantages of making clothing.

pages 344–345 The information on page 344 is not intended to be all-inclusive. Seasonal reductions can vary from store to store and from city to city. A salesperson might be willing to explain to a customer when a particular item will be on sale and how much discount can be expected. Students might need help with such terms as *linens*, *white sales*, *major appliances*, and *small appliances*.

- Have each student select an item and find its cost at a particular store. Have the student reprice the item every two weeks and keep a record of price changes. Discuss why prices might change.

pages 346–347 Although two specific crafts are considered, the mathematics presented in this lesson can be applied to any craft projects.

All of the stained-glass and needlepoint designs considered are original, and the needlepoint designs have been hand painted on the canvas mesh. This accounts for the high prices. Mechanically produced designs, as well as self-designed patterns, would be far less expensive.

- Have students bring in examples of their own crafts. Discuss the cost of materials and the time involved. Then have students figure the percent of profit if they were to sell the items they made.

pages 348–349 Point out that the price of lumber varies greatly, depending on the quality. Lower-grade lumber can often be used satisfactorily for many parts of a building project.

pages 350–351 The idea of renting versus buying should be thoroughly discussed. Include such things as initial cost of the equipment, its upkeep, and its storage. You might suggest that money used to purchase an item could be used for other expenditures or for earning interest.

- Have students contact a local rental store and find out what items are available to rent. Have them compare prices and the billing procedures of the store with those presented in the lesson.
- Set up a hypothetical project for the class, such as furnishing a recreation room for a youth center. Items needed might include furniture, lighting, stereo equipment, games, and kitchen supplies. Have students investigate the cost of obtaining these goods by buying, making, or renting. They might also consider garage sales and resale stores.

Budgeting, pages 356–372

Overview

In Chapter 18, students will study the steps necessary for making a budget. They will examine the budgets of persons in two different economic situations. The students will then make decisions about changing these persons' lifestyles, depending on whether their budgets can be adjusted.

Lesson Notes and Activities

pages 356–359 Emphasize the importance of record keeping to find out exactly how money is spent. Note that many people have difficulty managing their money if they are faced with many variable expenses, or if they do not watch for the accumulation of small expenses that seem insignificant.

- Have each student make a guess about the amount of money he or she spends each week and then record every expenditure for the next 7 days. If students have already recorded expenses in anticipation of this chapter, they can use that data now.

pages 360–361 Mention that many people keep track of expenses for more than 3 months before finding an average. You might also discuss situations in which one of the numbers to be averaged is excessive. For example, suppose that in the problem on page 360 the monthly food expenditures were $15, $75, and $18. In this case, the average ($36) would not be representative of Julie's true monthly expenses.

pages 362–364 For people who are paid weekly, it is generally recommended that their monthly budget be based on 4 weeks' pay. The extra paycheck that they will receive every three months can be used for budget-breaking emergencies or for savings.

You might discuss the fact that savings are included in both budgets as fixed expenses. Experts recommend regular savings, preferably at least 5% of take-home pay. Note, too, that there are few installment payments in these budgets, although for some people such payments form a major part of their expenditures.

You might compare these budgets with local costs to help your students appreciate the reality of the large amounts listed for some budgeted items.

- Have students use the information they have collected regarding their spending habits and try to make a budget.
- Ask those students who plan to continue their education to try to develop a budget for this expense. Sources of income could include loans, scholarships, part-time work, and help from parents.

page 365 Note that to find the percent of increase, the change is compared to the original (previous year's) expenses.

pages 366–367 As an additional problem, you might have the students suggest how the Wrights' budget could be adjusted if, for example, Mrs. Wright stops working and the monthly take-home pay is decreased to $1200.

- Ask a representative of a financial counseling service to discuss the services that are available to consumers with budget problems. The representative might also give the class some general advice about budgeting.

pages 368–369 Be sure the students realize that bars of the same height in the graph do not necessarily represent the same amount of money. At levels D and F, families spend about the same percent of income for food. However, 23% of $21,000 is not the same as 23% of $35,000.

Page 55

1.

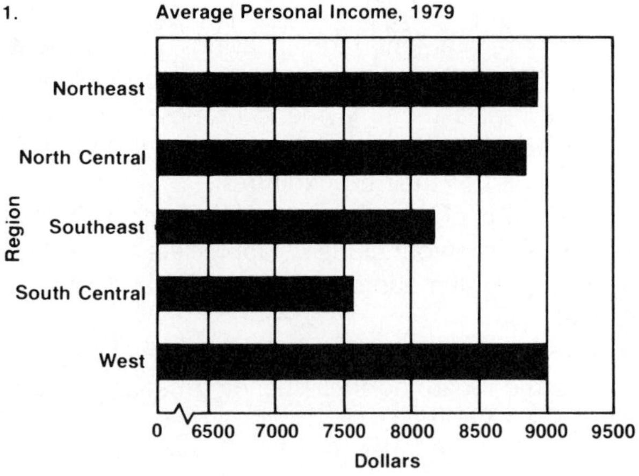
Average Personal Income, 1979
Northeast
North Central
Southeast
South Central
West
Region
0
6500
7000
7500
8000
8500
9000
9500
Dollars

2.

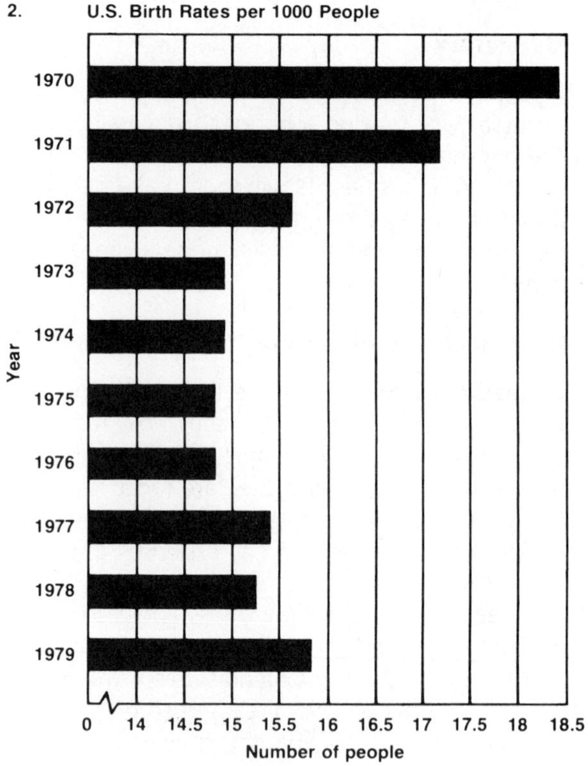
U.S. Birth Rates per 1000 People
1970
1971
1972
1973
1974
1975
1976
1977
1978
1979
Year
0
14
14.5
15
15.5
16
16.5
17
17.5
18
18.5
Number of people

3.

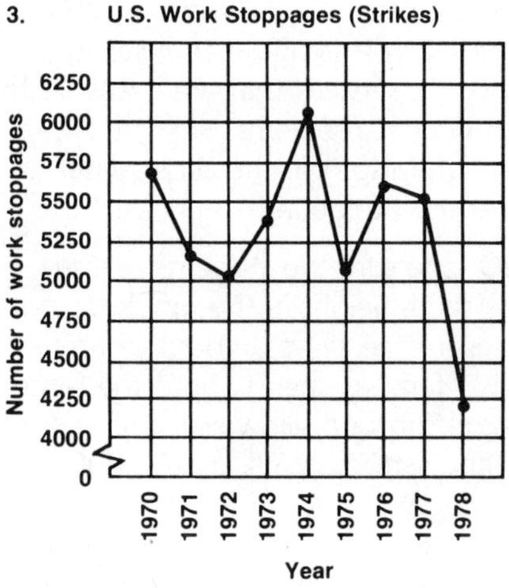
U.S. Work Stoppages (Strikes)
6250
6000
5750
5500
5250
5000
4750
4500
4250
4000
0
Number of work stoppages
1970
1971
1972
1973
1974
1975
1976
1977
1978
Year

4.

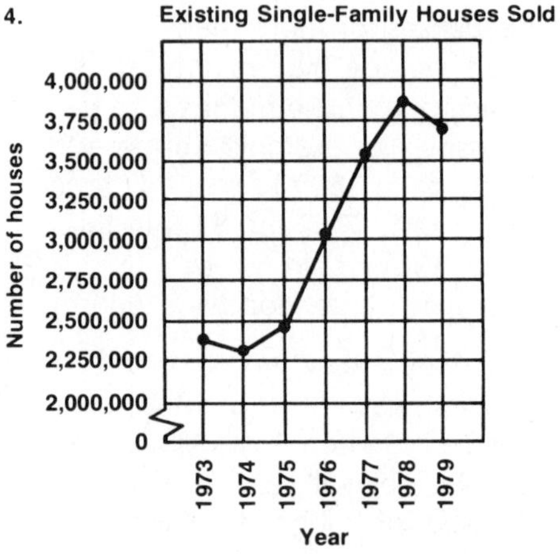
Existing Single-Family Houses Sold
4,000,000
3,750,000
3,500,000
3,250,000
3,000,000
2,750,000
2,500,000
2,250,000
2,000,000
0
Number of houses
1973
1974
1975
1976
1977
1978
1979
Year

Page 55

8. U.S. Travelers

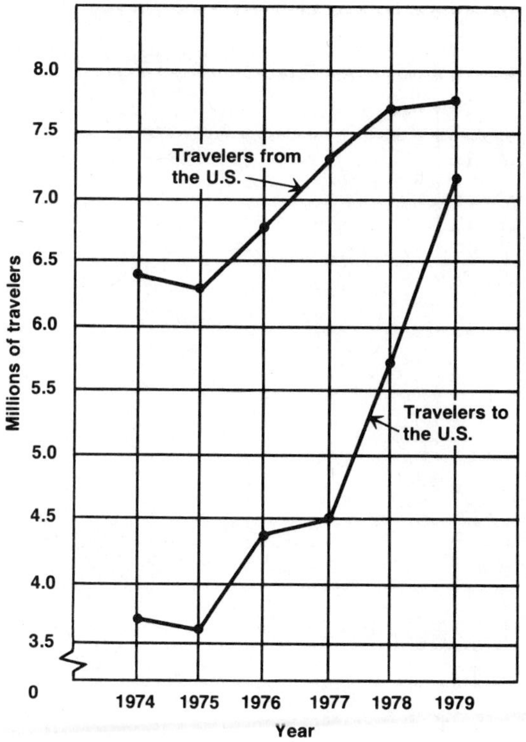

Page 57

13. Land Owned by the Federal Government, 1979

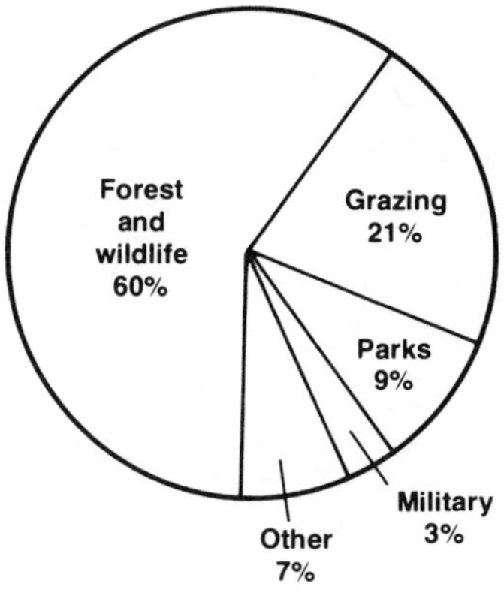

14. Major Issues Causing Work Stoppages, 1978

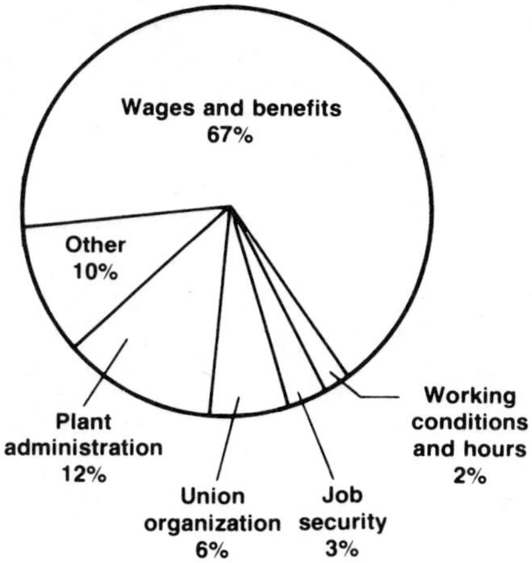

15. Estimated Voting Population by Age, 1980

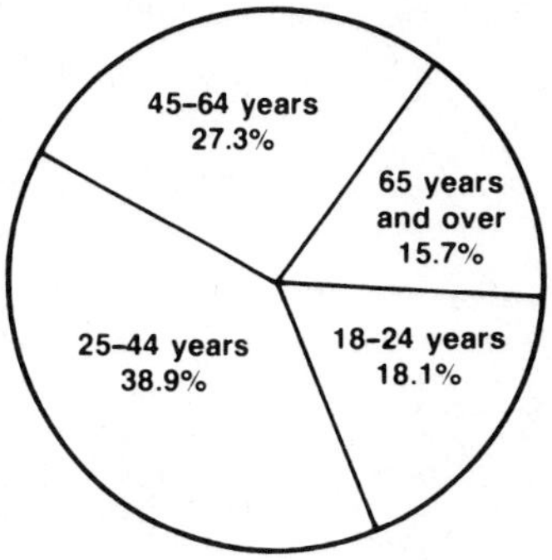

Additional Answers

Page 61

14. New Housing Units Started, 1976-1979

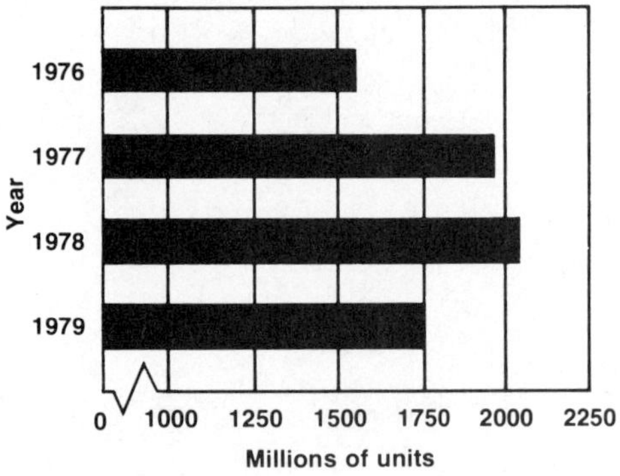

15. New Housing Units Started, 1976-1979

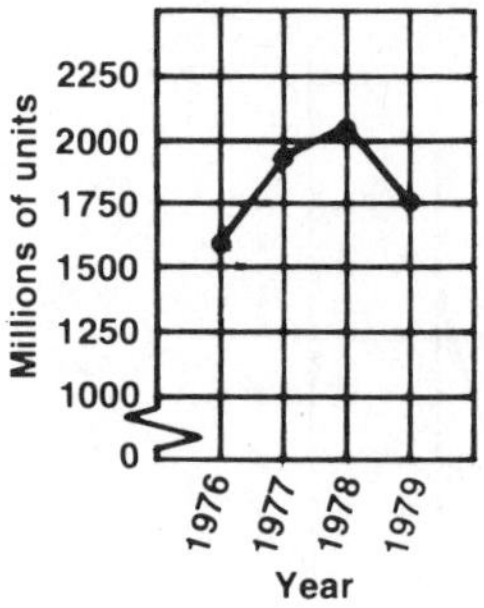

17. Distribution of Families by Number of Children Under 18 Years, 1979

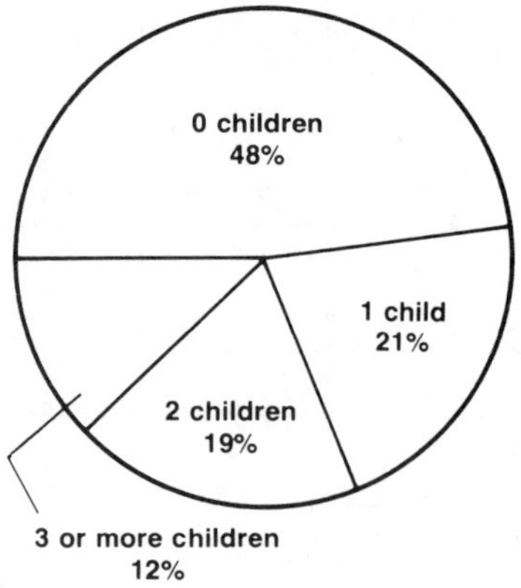

Page 62

14. Value of Farm Real Estate, 1977-1980

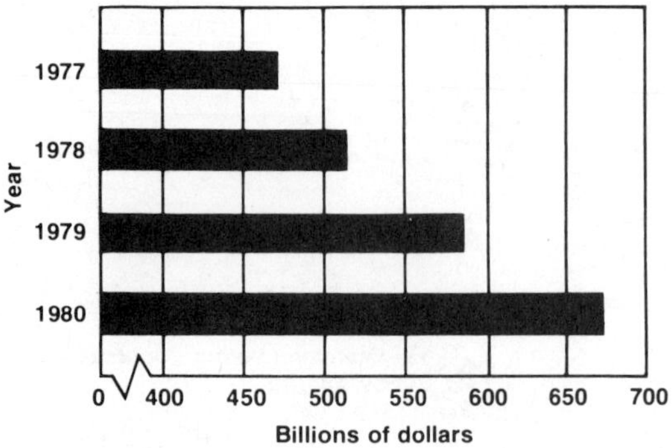

15. Value of Farm Real Estate, 1977-1980

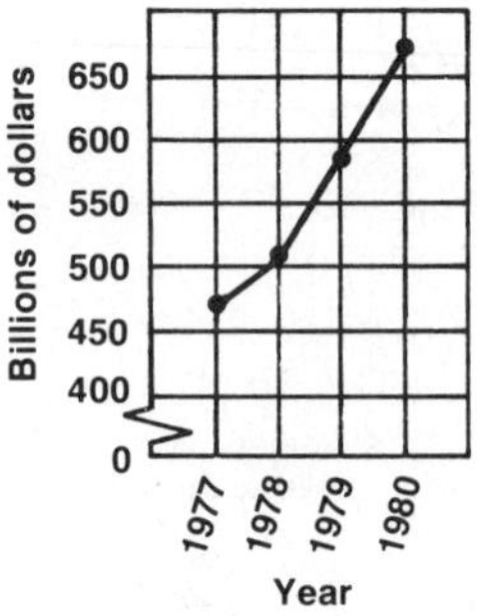

17. Persons Employed in Health Occupations, 1979

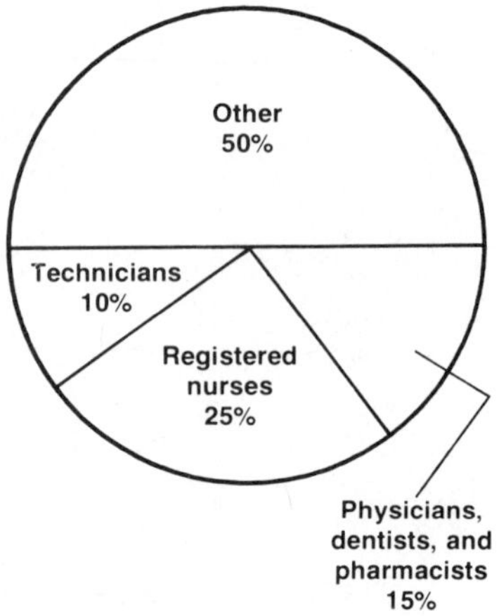

Page 71 Break Time

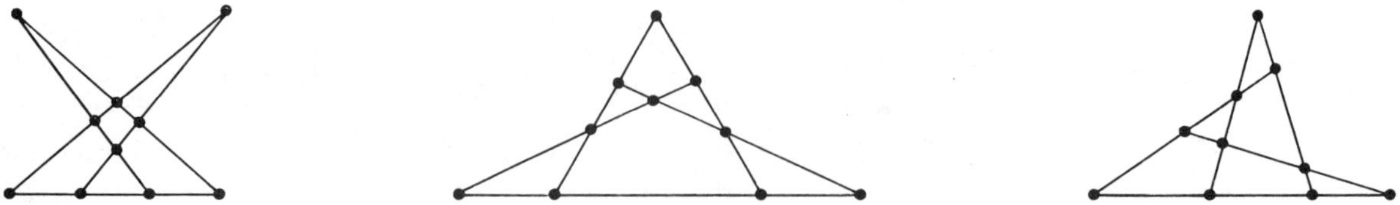

Page 142

11. SALE SUMMARY

Suggested Retail Price		$6845.00
Optional equipment	$ 739.00	
Destination charge	$ 260.00	
Sticker Price		$7844.00
Price reduction	$ 500.00	
Selling Price		$7344.00
Sales tax (4%)	$ 293.76	
License-plate fee	$ 18.00	
Title fee	$ 5.00	
Other charges	$ ----	
Total Cost		$7660.76
Trade-in allowance	$ ----	
Cash deposit	$3060.76	
Amount Financed		$4600.00
Finance charge	$ 965.36	
ANNUAL PERCENTAGE RATE		
Number of payments	24	
Monthly payment	$ 231.89	
Total of payments	$5565.36	
Total Sale Price (deferred-payment price)		$8626.12

12. SALE SUMMARY

Suggested Retail Price		$ ----
Optional equipment	$ ----	
Destination charge	$ ----	
Sticker Price		$ 9120.00
Price reduction	$ 547.20	
Selling Price		$ 8572.80
Sales tax (5%)	$ 428.64	
License-plate fee	$ 25.00	
Title fee	$ 6.00	
Other charges	$ ----	
Total Cost		$ 9032.44
Trade-in allowance	$2500.00	
Cash deposit	$1032.44	
Amount Financed		$ 5500.00
Finance charge	$1657.88	
ANNUAL PERCENTAGE RATE		
Number of payments	36	
Monthly payment	$ 198.83	
Total of payments	$7157.88	
Total Sale Price (deferred-payment price)		$10,690.32

Page 205

9.

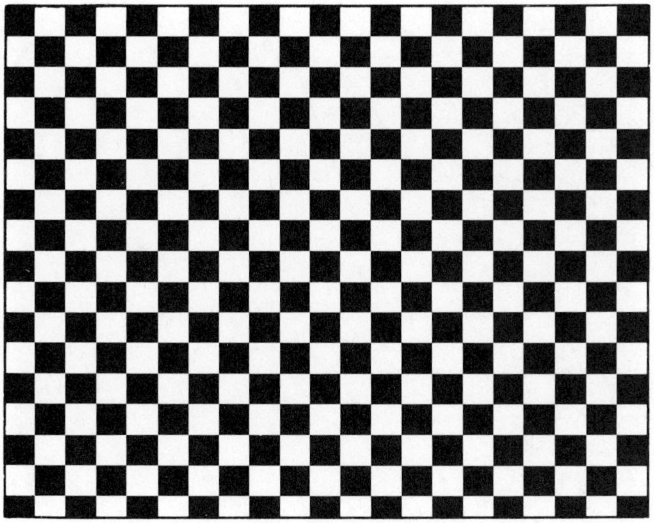

Answers Additional Answers

Page 239

1.

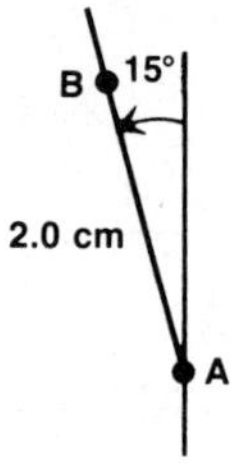

1 cm → 10 m

2.

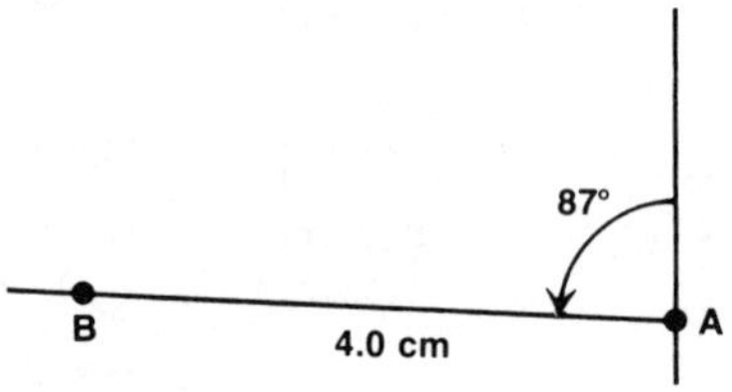

3.

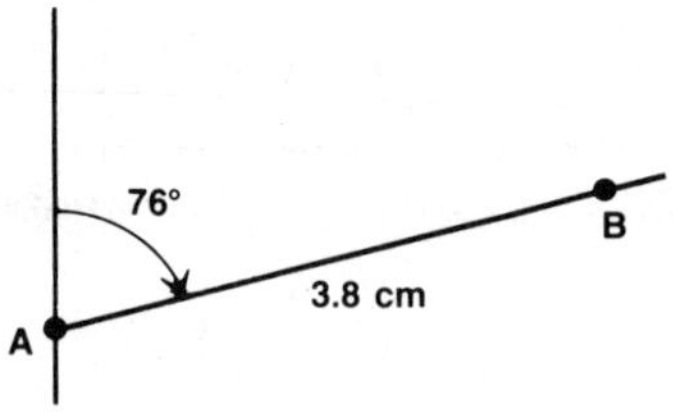

4.

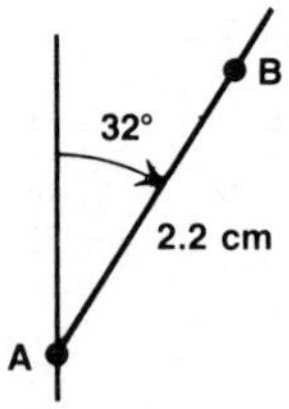

5.

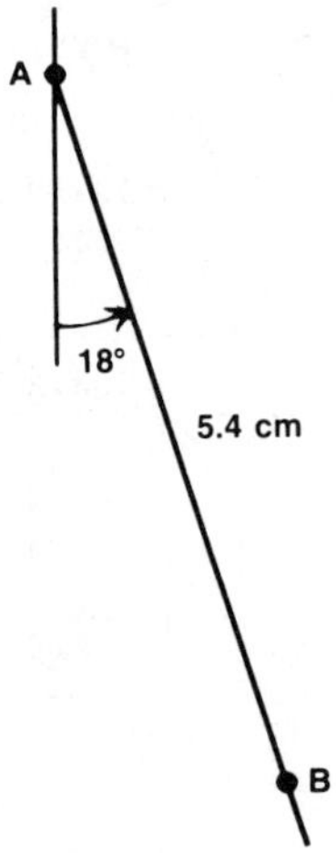

6.

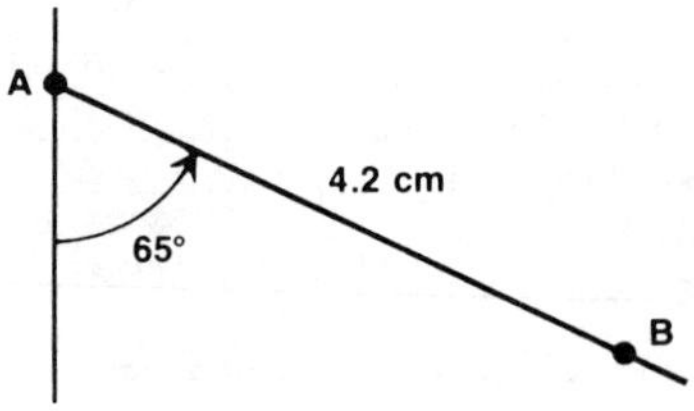

7.

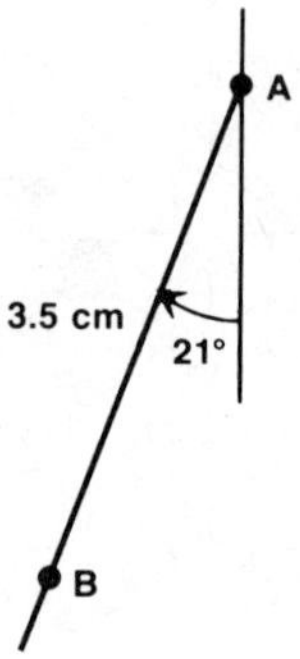

8.

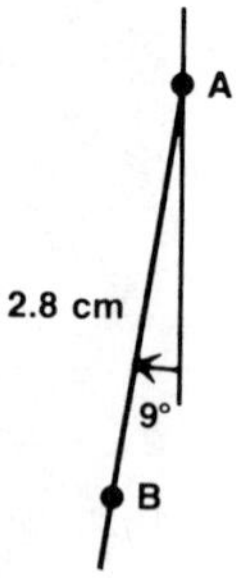

Page 239

9.

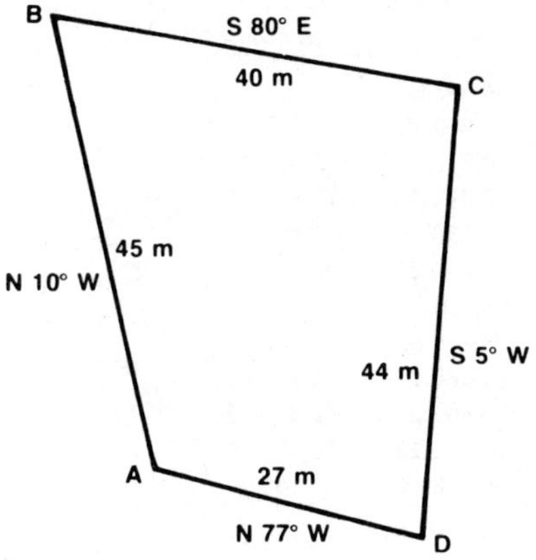

10.

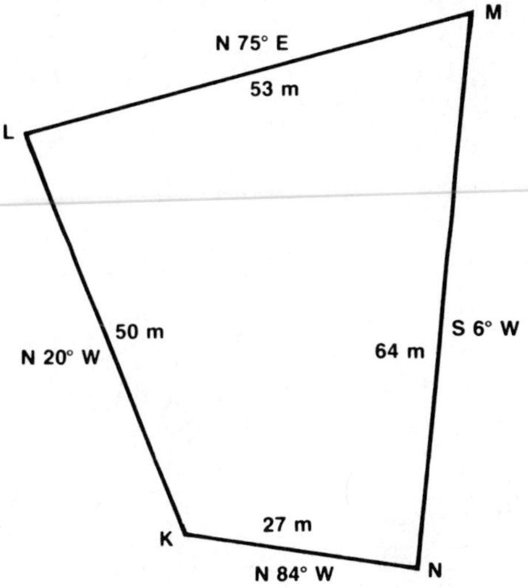

11.

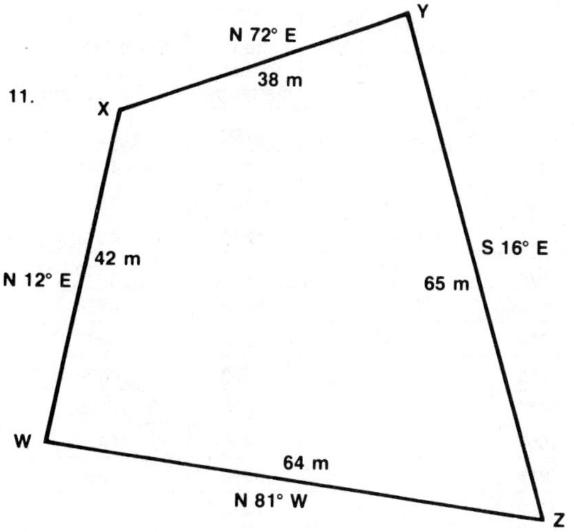

12.

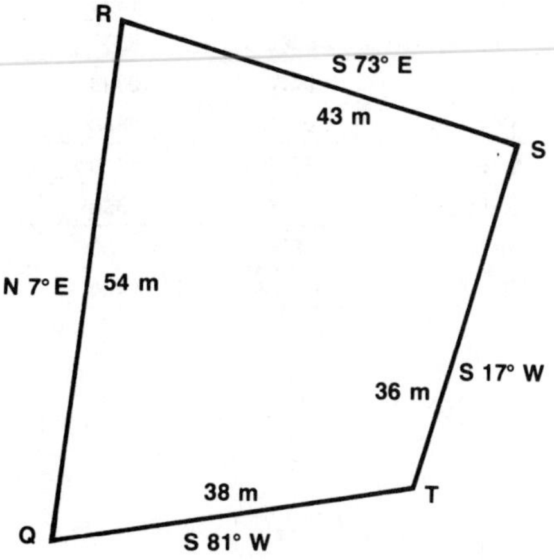

Page 294

1.

Work Sheet			
Year	Maximum annual income on which social security is paid	Actual annual earnings	Earnings subject to social security
1958	$ 4,200	$ 3290	$ 3290
1959	4,800	3760	3760
1960	4,800	3800	3800
1961	4,800	4270	4270
1962	4,800	4500	4500
1963	4,800	4960	4800
1964	4,800	4990	4800
1965	4,800	5300	4800
1966	6,600	5800	5800
1967	6,600	6430	6430
1968	7,800	6890	6890
1969	7,800	7430	7430
1970	7,800	7900	7800
1971	7,800	8100	7800
1972	9,000	7460	7460
1973	10,800	8000	8000
1974	13,200	8750	8750
1975	14,100	9060	9060
1976	15,300	9300	9300
1977	16,500	9470	9470
1978	17,700	9650	9650
1979	22,900	9970	9970
1980	25,900	10,350	10,350
1981	29,700	10,850	10,850
		Total	$169,030

Page 295

14.

Year	Retirement	
	at 63	at 65
1981	$ 4,843.20	
1982	9,686.40	
1983	14,529.60	$ 5,914.80
1984	19,372.80	11,829.60
1985	24,216.00	17,744.40
1986	29,059.20	23,659.20
1987	33,902.40	29,574.00
1988	38,745.60	35,488.80
1989	43,588.80	41,403.60
1990	48,432.00	47,318.40
1991	53,275.20	53,233.20
1992	58,118.40	59,148.00

Page 129

12. MEYER'S DEPARTMENT STORE
CHARGE-ACCOUNT STATEMENT

BEGINNING OF DECEMBER	
BALANCE	237.45
NO PAYMENT RECEIVED	
IF PAYMENT IS IN MAIL, THANK YOU	
PAYMENTS DURING DECEMBER	0
FINANCE CHARGE ON	
BALANCE OF $ 237.45	3.56
CHARGES DURING DECEMBER	24.86
NEW BALANCE	265.87

15.
```
75 PRINT "RETURNS";
76 INPUT R
101 IF R>U THEN 104
102 LET U=U−R
103 GO TO 110
104 LET A=0
105 LET A=R−U
106 LET F=0
107 GO TO 130
191 IF R=0 THEN 200
192 PRINT "$";R;"HAS BEEN CREDITED TO YOUR ACCOUNT"
225 IF A=0 THEN 230
226 PRINT "NEW BALANCE";TAB(30);"$";A;"CREDIT"
227 GO TO 240
```

16. MEYER'S DEPARTMENT STORE
CHARGE-ACCOUNT STATEMENT

BEGINNING OF APRIL	
BALANCE	20.72
PAYMENTS DURING APRIL	20.72
$ 20.72 HAS BEEN CREDITED TO YOUR ACCOUNT	
FINANCE CHARGE ON	
BALANCE OF $ 0	0
CHARGES DURING APRIL	0
NEW BALANCE	$ 20.72 CREDIT

17.
```
91 IF C1=0 THEN 97
97 PRINT "FINANCE CHARGE RATE";
98 INPUT Y
110 LET F=Y*U/100
```

Page 255

	PAYMENT NUMBER	PRINCIPAL	AMOUNT OF INTEREST	AMOUNT PAID ON PRINCIPAL	'NEW' PRINCIPAL
1.	1	2000	26.67	43.65	1956.35
	2	1956.35	26.08	44.24	1912.11
	36	69.12	.92	69.12	0
2.	1	6500	78.54	181.06	6318.94
	2	6318.94	76.35	183.25	6135.69
	30	256.4	3.1	256.4	0
3.	1	4475	56.87	110.01	4364.99
	2	4364.99	55.47	111.41	4253.58
	33	164.4	2.09	164.4	0
4.	1	8000	113.33	245.31	7754.69
	2	7754.69	109.86	248.78	7505.91
	27	353.47	5.01	353.47	0
5.	1	5000	62.5	179.94	4820.06
	2	4820.06	60.25	182.19	4637.87
	24	239.25	2.99	239.25	0
6.	1	7865	108.14	189.95	7675.05
	2	7675.05	105.53	192.56	7482.49
	33	293.92	4.04	293.92	0

Page 255

	PAYMENT NUMBER	PRINCIPAL	AMOUNT OF INTEREST	AMOUNT PAID ON PRINCIPAL	'NEW' PRINCIPAL
7.	1	3600	44.25	99.96	3500.04
	2	3500.04	43.02	101.19	3398.85
	30	142.43	1.75	142.43	0
8.	1	2200	32.08	107.77	2092.23
	2	2092.23	30.51	109.34	1982.89
	18	137.82	2.01	137.82	0
9.	1	4000	55.83	123.01	3876.99
	2	3876.99	54.12	124.72	3752.27
	27	176.18	2.46	176.18	0
10.	1	1600	24	167.38	1432.62
	2	1432.62	21.49	169.89	1262.73
	9	188.5	2.83	188.5	0
11.	1	9500	110.83	213.86	9286.14
	2	9286.14	108.34	216.35	9069.79
	36	320.83	3.74	320.83	0
12.	1	6195	85.18	168.23	6026.77
	2	6026.77	82.87	170.54	5856.23
	30	249.88	3.44	249.88	0

14. MORTGAGE AMORTIZATION TABLE

PRINCIPAL AMOUNT	$ 3000
ANNUAL INTEREST RATE	14.75%
TERM	24 MONTHS
MONTHLY PAYMENT	$ 145.11

PAYMENT NUMBER	PRINCIPAL	AMOUNT OF INTEREST	AMOUNT PAID ON PRINCIPAL	'NEW' PRINCIPAL
1	3000	36.88	108.23	2891.77
2	2891.77	35.54	109.57	2782.2
24	143.19	1.76	143.19	0

Page 255

16. MORTGAGE AMORTIZATION TABLE

PRINCIPAL AMOUNT	$ 3785
ANNUAL INTEREST RATE	15.5 %
TERM	30 MONTHS
MONTHLY PAYMENT	$ 152.99

PAYMENT NUMBER	PRINCIPAL	AMOUNT OF INTEREST	AMOUNT PAID ON PRINCIPAL	'NEW' PRINCIPAL
1	3785	48.89	104.1	3680.9
2	3680.9	47.54	105.45	3575.45
30	151.02	1.95	151.02	0

TOTAL PAID TO INTEREST	$ 804.68
TOTAL PAID TO PRINCIPAL	$ 3785

	$ 4589.68

17. MORTGAGE AMORTIZATION TABLE

PRINCIPAL AMOUNT	$ 2755
ANNUAL INTEREST RATE	17.5 %
TERM	6 MONTHS
MONTHLY PAYMENT	$ 482.89

PAYMENT NUMBER	PRINCIPAL	AMOUNT OF INTEREST	AMOUNT PAID ON PRINCIPAL	'NEW' PRINCIPAL
1	2755	40.18	442.71	2312.29
2	2312.29	33.72	449.17	1863.12
6	475.92	6.94	475.92	0

TOTAL PAID TO INTEREST	$ 142.31
TOTAL PAID TO PRINCIPAL	$ 2755

	$ 2897.31

Page 377

12.

TENS	1
FIVES	1
ONES	3
NICKELS	1
PENNIES	1
CHANGE	$ 18.06

13.

FIVES	1
ONES	3
NICKELS	1
PENNIES	1
CHANGE	$ 8.06

14.

NICKELS	1
PENNIES	1
CHANGE	$ .06

15.

```
85 IF S>=0 THEN 90
86 PRINT "NOT ENOUGH MONEY"
87 GO TO 50
```

16. NOT ENOUGH MONEY

ONES	2
DIMES	2
PENNIES	2
CHANGE	$ 2.22

17.

```
30 PRINT "AMOUNT OF MERCHANDISE";
40 INPUT M
45 LET X=M*.05
46 LET X=INT(X*100+.5) / 100
47 LET T=M+X
182 PRINT
183 PRINT "COST OF MERCHANDISE      $";M
184 PRINT "SALES TAX";TAB(22);"$";X
185 PRINT "TOTAL";TAB(22);"$";T
186 PRINT "AMOUNT GIVEN";TAB(22);"$";A
190 PRINT "CHANGE";TAB(22);"$";C
```

Page 377

18. QUARTERS 3
DIMES 1
PENNIES 3

COST OF MERCHANDISE	$	37.26
SALES TAX	$	1.86
TOTAL	$	39.12
AMOUNT GIVEN	$	40
CHANGE	$	.88

19.
```
27 LET M=0
28 PRINT "NO. OF ITEMS      COST/ITEM      COST"
30 PRINT "NUMBER OF ITEMS";
31 INPUT Q
32 IF Q=0 THEN 45
33 PRINT "COST PER ITEM";
34 INPUT P
35 LET E=Q*P
36 LET E=INT(E*100+.5) / 100
37 PRINT TAB(6);Q;TAB(17);P;TAB(25);E
38 LET M=M+E
39 GO TO 30
65 PRINT
```

Line 40 was deleted.

20.

NO. OF ITEMS	COST/ITEM	COST
3	.78	2.34
2	1.99	3.98
5	.87	4.35
2	1.44	2.88
1	5.79	5.79

FIVES 1
ONES 4
QUARTERS 2
DIMES 1
NICKELS 1
PENNIES 4

COST OF MERCHANDISE	$	19.34
SALES TAX	$	.97
TOTAL	$	20.31
AMOUNT GIVEN	$	30
CHANGE	$	9.69

Page 394

3.
```
2+4=  6
9-7=  2
 32  =8*4
 1.8  =9 / 5
```

The last two lines are indented because all numbers are treated as integers. One space is left in case a negative sign is needed.

4.
```
HELLO
MY NAME
IS
NOT
HAL.
```

5. Programs will vary.

```
10 PRINT "MARY FRASER"
20 PRINT "AGE 16 YEARS"
30 PRINT "AUBURNDALE HIGH SCHOOL"
40 END
```

6. Programs may vary.

```
10 PRINT 12+5
20 PRINT 9-4
30 PRINT 6*18
40 PRINT 15/3
50 END
```

Page 397

3. R = 5 C = 31.4
   R = 10 C = 62.8
   R = 17 C = 106.76
   OUT OF DATA AT LINE 10

4. REGULAR PRICE IS 15
   SALE PRICE IS 12
   REGULAR PRICE IS 22
   SALE PRICE IS 17.6
   REGULAR PRICE IS 27.5
   SALE PRICE IS 22
   REGULAR PRICE IS 30
   SALE PRICE IS 24
   REGULAR PRICE IS 42.75
   SALE PRICE IS 34.2
   OUT OF DATA AT LINE 10

5. ANDERSON PAY = 367.5
   JENSEN PAY = 505.25
   RIEDELL PAY = 570
   BRETZLAUF PAY = 408.5
   OUT OF DATA AT LINE 20

6. Programs may vary.

```
10 READ R,S
20 PRINT "AMOUNT OF DISCOUNT:  $";R-S
30 PRINT "RATE OF DISCOUNT:";(R-S) / R*100;"%"
40 DATA 20,18,35,28
50 END
```

Page 398

3. NUMBER: 1 COST: 19.95
   NUMBER: 2 COST: 39.9
   NUMBER: 3 COST: 59.85
   NUMBER: 4 COST: 79.8
   NUMBER: 5 COST: 99.75
   NUMBER: 6 COST: 119.7

4. YEAR: 1 INTEREST: $ 8
   YEAR: 2 INTEREST: $ 8.64
   YEAR: 3 INTEREST: $ 9.3312
   YEAR: 4 INTEREST: $ 10.077696
   YEAR: 5 INTEREST: $ 10.88391168

5. Programs may vary.

```
10 FOR H=1 TO 8
20 LET P=4.5*H
30 PRINT "HOURS:";H;"PAY:  $";P
40 NEXT H
50 END
```

Page 399

2. DIVISORS OF 24 ARE:
   1
   2
   3
   4
   6
   8
   12
   24
   DIVISORS OF 36 ARE:
   1
   2
   3
   4
   6
   9
   12
   18
   36

2. *continued*
   DIVISORS OF 56 ARE:
   1
   2
   4
   7
   8
   14
   28
   56
   DIVISORS OF 59 ARE:
   1
   59
   OUT OF DATA AT LINE 10

3.

PRICE	5% TAX	TOTAL
1.2	.06	1.26
6.8	.34	7.14
12.6	.63	13.23

OUT OF DATA AT LINE 20

4.

ACCOUNT	SERVICE CHARGE
# 1519	$ 1.6
# 1520	$ 1.5
# 1521	NO CHARGE
# 1522	$ 1.9

OUT OF DATA AT LINE 30

Tests Information and Answers

Information about the tests

On the following pages, you will find a test for each unit, an end-of-book test, and a suggested competency test. These tests may be copied and reproduced for classroom use and are provided as blackline masters with the Teacher's Edition.

Each unit test consists of 16 to 23 problems. There is one problem on a unit test related to each lesson in the unit. Each of these unit tests is an alternate form of the unit test that appears at the end of each unit in the student's text.

The end-of-book test consists of two parts, each with 18 problems. Part A covers chapters 1–9, and Part B covers chapters 10–18. There are two problems on the end-of-book test related to each chapter in the text.

Answers for the unit and end-of-book tests are listed below and are circled on the test pages in the Teacher's Edition.

Information about the suggested competency test, as well as answers for the test, appears on page T73.

An alternate form of each test is included in the *Test Masters*.

Answers for the tests

	Unit 1	Unit 2	Unit 3	Unit 4	Unit 5	Unit 6	End-of-Book Part A	End-of-Book Part B
1.	D	C	D	B	C	C	C	D
2.	B	B	B	D	A	A	B	B
3.	D	D	C	C	C	D	D	C
4.	A	B	A	B	B	B	C	B
5.	C	D	C	A	C	A	A	D
6.	D	C	D	A	D	C	A	B
7.	B	A	B	D	B	B	B	B
8.	A	D	D	C	C	D	A	A
9.	D	C	A	A	A	C	C	B
10.	C	B	C	C	D	A	A	B
11.	B	C	B	C	A	B	D	C
12.	A	A	D	D	C	D	B	A
13.	C	D	A	C	A	C	C	B
14.	D	B	C	D	C	D	D	B
15.	B	B	B	A	B	B	A	D
16.	C	A	C	B	D	A	D	A
17.	A	C	C	C	C		B	B
18.	B	D	D	D			C	D
19.	C	B	D	B				
20.	B	A	C	A				
21.	D	D						
22.	B							
23.	A							

Unit 1 Test **Mathematics Skills, pages 3-62**

Choose the best answer.

Pages 4-5

1. Round 3648 to the nearest hundred.

A 4000 **C** 3650

B 3700 **(D)** 3600

Pages 6-7

2. 86.45 − 32.81

A 54.44 **C** 54.64

(B) 53.64 **D** 119.26

Pages 8-9

3. 473 × 28

A 12,144 **C** 13,144

B 12,244 **(D)** 13,244

Pages 10-11

4. 7.42 × 3.6

(A) 26.712 **C** 25.702

B 26.612 **D** 25.512

Pages 12-13

5. 26.628 ÷ 4.2

A 5.12 **(C)** 6.34

B 6.28 **D** 6.41

Pages 14-15

6. Rename $\frac{16}{20}$ in lowest terms.

A $\frac{8}{10}$ **C** $\frac{3}{5}$

B $\frac{2}{5}$ **(D)** $\frac{4}{5}$

Pages 16-17

7. $4\frac{3}{4} \div 2\frac{1}{2}$

A $2\frac{1}{2}$ **C** $8\frac{3}{8}$

(B) $1\frac{9}{10}$ **D** $\frac{10}{19}$

Pages 18-19

8. $2\frac{5}{6} + 5\frac{3}{4}$

(A) $8\frac{7}{12}$ **C** $7\frac{7}{12}$

B $7\frac{4}{5}$ **D** $10\frac{5}{8}$

Pages 24-25

9. Solve. $h - 25.3 = 42.8$

A $h = 23.5$ **C** $h = 17.5$

B $h = 67.1$ **(D)** $h = 68.1$

Pages 26-27

10. Solve. $420 = 12y$

A $y = 5040$ **(C)** $y = 35$

B $y = 408$ **D** $y = 432$

Pages 28-29

11. Solve. $4a + 36 = 148$

A $a = 112$ **C** $a = 24$

(B) $a = 28$ **D** $a = 46$

Pages 30-31

12. Solve. $\frac{6}{x} = \frac{28}{42}$

(A) $x = 9$ **C** $x = 252$

B $x = 4$ **D** $x = 96$

Pages 32-33

13. Write 16% as a decimal.

A 16 **(C)** 0.16

B 1.6 **D** 0.016

Pages 34-37

14. 40% of what number is 80?

A 16 **C** 32

B 20 **(D)** 200

Pages 42-43
15. Choose the most sensible measure for the length of a nail.

A 5 mm **C** 5 m
(B) 5 cm **D** 5 km

Pages 44-45
16. Find the area of a rectangle that measures 4.0 meters by 6.2 meters.

A 2.48 m^2 **(C)** 24.8 m^2
B 20.4 m^2 **D** 49.6 m^2

Pages 46-47
17. Choose the most sensible measure for a container of liquid detergent.

(A) 2 L **C** 120 L
B 0.006 L **D** 40 L

Pages 48-49
18. 2675 g = ☐ kg

A 0.2675 **C** 26.75
(B) 2.675 **D** 267.5

Pages 50-51
19. Choose the most sensible temperature for hot soup.

A 22°C **(C)** 58°C
B 0°C **D** 118°C

Pages 52-53
20. Add 2 hours 15 minutes to 3:25 P.M.

A 6:40 P.M. **C** 5:30 P.M.
(B) 5:40 P.M. **D** 1:10 P.M.

Pages 54-55
21. Read the bar graph below and find how many more students watch comedy shows than drama shows.

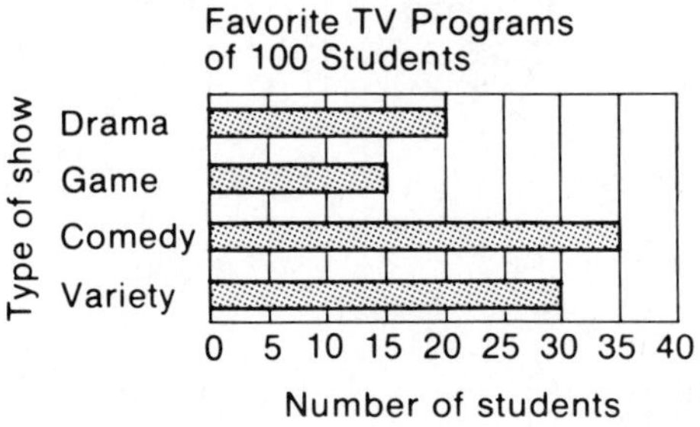

A 20 students **C** 35 students
B 5 students **(D)** 15 students

Pages 56-57
22. Read the circle graph below and find the amount spent for food by a family with an income of $16,000.

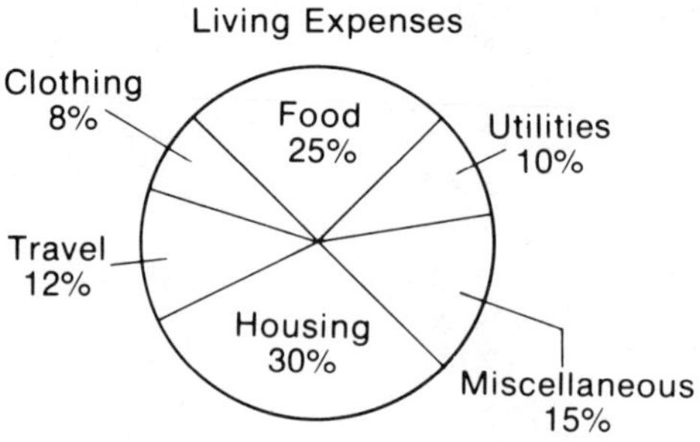

A $4800 **C** $1920
(B) $4000 **D** $2400

Pages 58-59
23. Find the mean for this set of numbers.

12, 14, 2, 10, 16, 10, 13

(A) 11 **C** 12
B 10 **D** 77

Unit 2 Test **Income, Banking, and Credit, pages 67–124**

Choose the best answer.

Pages 68-69

1. Andy earns $3.60 per hour. What is his gross pay for a 35-hour week?

   A $38.60 C $126

   B $76.50 D $161.60

Pages 70-71

2. Brad kept 75% of his $180 in tips. How much did Brad keep?

   A $45 C $175

   B $135 D $180

Pages 72-73

3. Anna sells cosmetics for a straight commission of 40%. How much did she earn on a sale of $26?

   A $15.60 C $36.40

   B $26 D $10.40

Pages 74-75

4. Ms. Ramirez is paid $250 a week plus 4% of all sales delivered. Last week, her total sales were $5200. Orders totaling $850 were canceled. Find Ms. Ramirez's gross pay for the week.

   A $174 C $558

   B $424 D $4350

Page 76

5. Michelle earns $200 a month plus 6% of her first $1000 in sales and 15% of her sales over $1000. Michelle's sales for the month were $3000. Find her gross pay.

   A $60 C $300

   B $360 D $560

Pages 78-81

6. Ron Carey's gross pay is $350 a week. His deductions are $77.40 for federal income tax and $20.47 for social security. What is his net pay?

   A $97.87 C $252.13

   B $447.87 D $272.60

Pages 82-83

7. Sam's Sales has a job opening paying $13,000 a year. At Dora's Discounts, the same job pays $950 a month. How much more does Sam's Sales pay per year?

   A $1600 C $11,400

   B $1400 D $133.33

Pages 88-89

8. Jan has checks for $14.53, $134.50, and $86.42 to deposit. If she wants $90 in cash, how much should she deposit in her account?

   A $59.03 C $149.03

   B $235.45 D $145.45

Pages 90-91

9. The balance forwarded on a check stub was $342.65. A deposit of $80 was made and a check for $30 was written. What was the balance carried forward?

   A $452.65 C $392.65

   B $110 D $422.65

Pages 92-93

10. Find the new balance in this account.

PAYMENT/DEBIT (−)	DEPOSIT/CREDIT (+)	BALANCE
		$510 62
$276 12	$	
	62 00	

   A $786.74 C $724.74

   B $296.50 D $234.50

Pages 94-96

11. The ending balance on a bank statement is $614.72. There is one outstanding deposit of $70.58 and one outstanding check of $42.25. What is the actual amount in the account?

   A $544.14 C $643.05

   B $586.39 D $685.30

Pages 98-99

12. A savings account of $1400 earns 6% simple interest per year. Find the interest earned in 6 months.

(A) $42 C $504

B $84 D $700

Pages 100-101

13. A savings account of $400 earns 7% interest compounded annually. Find the interest earned in 2 years.

A $28 C $457.96

B $29.96 (D) $57.96

Pages 102-103

14. Use the table below and find the interest on $500 at 8% compounded semiannually for 2 years.

Compound Interest Table			
No. of periods	4%	6%	8%
1	1.0400	1.0600	1.0800
2	1.0816	1.1236	1.1664
3	1.1248	1.1910	1.2597
4	1.1699	1.2625	1.3605

A $180.25 C $680.25

(B) $84.95 D $584.95

Pages 108-109

15. A promissory note for $2400 at an interest rate of 16% per year is due in 60 days. Find the amount of interest due. Use 360 days for 1 year.

A $384 C $400

(B) $64 D $40

Pages 110-111

16. The unpaid balance in an account was $120.50. A payment of $40 was made during the month. The finance charge is 1.5% per month of the balance after payments. Find the finance charge to the nearest cent.

(A) $1.21 C $0.40

B $2.41 D $0.60

Pages 112-113

17. In a charge account, the average daily balance for the month is $140.10. The finance charge is 1.8% per month of the average daily balance. Find the finance charge to the nearest cent.

A $252.18 (C) $2.52

B $27.60 D $142.62

Page 115

18. A store requires a minimum payment of 15% of the balance in an account if the balance is over $150. Find the minimum payment on a balance of $260.

A $16.50 C $26

B $22.50 (D) $39

Pages 116-117

19. Use the table below and find the amount of the monthly payment on a level-payment loan of $700 at 16% for 12 months. Round to the nearest cent.

Monthly Payment per $1 Borrowed			
Annual rate	Number of equal monthly payments		
	6	12	18
16%	0.17453	0.09073	0.06286

A $122.17 C $44

(B) $63.51 D $762.12

Pages 118-119

20. A loan of $730 will be repaid in 24 installments of $37.15 each. Find the finance charge.

(A) $161.60 C $568.40

B $148.60 D $891.60

Pages 120-121

21. Laurie financed a $1500 purchase with no down payment and 12 installments of $138.24 each. Find the total amount repaid.

A $158.88 C $1638.24

B $125 (D) $1658.88

Unit 3 Test **Transportation, pages 131-186**

Choose the best answer.

Pages 132-133

1. The suggested retail price of a car is $6244. Find the sticker price with automatic transmission ($370) and power steering ($180).

   A $6614 C $5694
   B $6424 (D) $6794

Page 134

2. Miguel offered a car dealer 10% less than the $7640 sticker price for a new car. What was Miguel's offer? Round to the nearest hundred dollars.

   A $6800 C $800
   (B) $6900 D $8400

Pages 136-137

3. A new car costs $9250 plus 4% sales tax. Find the sales tax.

   A $9620 (C) $370
   B $8880 D $3700

Pages 138-139

4. The selling price of a car is $7850. Find the net price with a trade-in allowance of $1320.

   (A) $6530 C $7850
   B $1320 D $9170

Pages 140-142

5. Mr. Wuttunee made a down payment of $1500 on a $8765 car. He financed the balance for 36 months with monthly payments of $270. Find the finance charge.

   A $9720 (C) $2455
   B $955 D $7265

Pages 144-145

6. For all cars she sells, Mary receives 25% of the dealer's profit. What does Mary receive on a dealer's profit of $5600?

   A $9800 C $4200
   B $140 (D) $1400

Pages 150-151

7. Erica drove 487 km and used 75 L of gasoline. Find her car's fuel economy rate to the nearest tenth.

   A 6.4 km/L C 36,525 km/L
   (B) 6.5 km/L D 6.6 km/L

Pages 152-153

8. Karen bought a new car for $8200 two years ago. The trade-in value now is 55% of the original selling price. Find the trade-in value now.

   A $451 C $11,890
   B $3690 (D) $4510

Page 154

9. To find the total depreciation of a car, multiply the monthly depreciation rate times the number of months times the original price. The original price of a car was $6700. Find the total depreciation after 12 months at 2.6% per month. Round to the nearest dollar.

   (A) $2090 C $4610
   B $209 D $8790

Pages 156-159

10. A mechanic is paid 40% of the labor charge on each job. What is the mechanic paid for a job in which the total charge for parts is $32.75 and the total labor charge is $82?

    A $13.10 (C) $32.80
    B $49.20 D $45.90

Pages 160-161

11. Curt pays a base premium of $335.75 for liability insurance. He also pays 20% of the base for increased bodily injury coverage and 8% of the base for increased property damage coverage. Find his annual premium.

    A $940.10 C $94.01
    (B) $429.76 D $241.74

Pages 162-163

12. Ron, age 18, is buying collision insurance with $100 deductible and comprehensive insurance with $50 deductible. Use this table and find his combined premium.

Teen driver	Collision premium for $100 deductible	Comprehensive premium for $50 deductible
Female	$318.16	$55.60
Male	$613.04	$55.60

A $931.20 C $373.76

B $557.44 D $668.64

Pages 164-165

13. Randy drove 16,000 km last year. His total car expenses were $4310. To the nearest tenth of a cent, what was the cost per kilometer to operate his car?

A 26.9¢ C 37.1¢

B 27.0¢ D 37.2¢

Pages 166-167

14. Sue takes the train and bus to and from work each day. The train ticket is $45 a month and the bus fare is $0.70 each way. Find Sue's monthly travel cost based on 20 working days per month.

A $28 C $73

B $59 D $77.50

Pages 172-173

15. Use the chart below to find the distance from Washington to San Francisco to Portland. Distances between cities are given in kilometers.

	Portland	St. Louis	San Francisco
St. Louis	3375		
San Francisco	1050	3424	
Washington	4504	1290	4620

A 5454 km C 9124 km

B 5670 km D 8929 km

Pages 174-175

16. To the nearest hour, what is the travel time for 310 km at a rate of 80 km/h?

A 6 hours C 4 hours

B 5 hours D 3 hours

Pages 176-177

17. Joyce plans to drive 1280 km in a car with a fuel economy rate of 8 km/L. She estimates that she will spend $0.40 per liter for gasoline, $28 for lodging, and $40 for meals. Estimate the total cost.

A $64 C $132

B $92 D $580

Pages 178-179

18. Find the total round-trip fare for one adult and one 7-year-old child from Jacksonville to Miami. The one-way adult fare is $96. Children (ages 2–11) pay $\frac{3}{4}$ of the adult fare.

A $72 C $144

B $168 D $336

Page 180

19. A car rents for $22 per day plus $0.15 per kilometer. Find the cost of renting the car for 3 days and driving 1200 kilometers.

A $66 C $180

B $84 D $246

Pages 182-183

20. For an adult, the one-way train fare from Denver to San Francisco is $142. Children (ages 2–11) pay $\frac{1}{2}$ of the adult fare. Find the total train fare for one adult and two children, ages 6 and 8, for a one-way train trip from Denver to San Francisco.

A $71 C $284

B $213 D $355

Unit 4 Test **Housing, pages 193–250**

Choose the best answer.

Pages 194-195

1. Lisa earns $5.60 per hour in a 40-hour work week. What is the most she should spend for rent each month? (Use the guideline of not spending more than one week's gross pay for shelter each month.)

A $56 **C** $45.60
B $224 **D** $896

Pages 196-197

2. Takashi rented an apartment for $325 per month plus utilities. Electricity costs will average $45 per month and heating costs will average $30 per month. How much will Takashi pay for rent and utilities each month?

A $75 **C** $370
B $355 **D** $400

Pages 198-199

3. Give the reading for this electric meter.

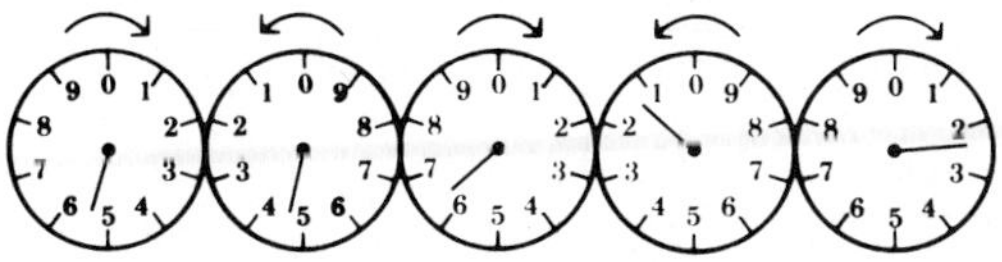

A 64612 **C** 54612
B 65723 **D** 21645

Pages 202-203

4. To the nearest tenth, what is the scale length of a room that is 3.6 m long? Use the scale of 1 cm→0.2 m.

A 7.2 cm **C** 72 cm
B 18 cm **D** 180 cm

Pages 204-205

5. How many tiles are needed to cover a floor 4.2 m by 5.6 m? Each tile is a square 20 cm by 20 cm.

A 588 tiles **C** 98 tiles
B 400 tiles **D** 49 tiles

Pages 206-207

6. A gallon of paint covers 400 sq. ft. About how much paint will be needed to paint the walls of a room 10 ft. by 11 ft.? The walls are 8 ft. high.

A 1 gallon **C** 3 gallons
B 2 gallons **D** 14 gallons

Pages 208-209

7. A roll of wallpaper covers 30 sq. ft. How many rolls are needed for a room 13 ft. by 17 ft. with walls 8 ft. high? Subtract $\frac{1}{2}$ roll for each of the 4 windows and 2 doors.

A 16 rolls **C** 10 rolls
B 12 rolls **D** 13 rolls

Pages 210-211

8. Sean has a $50-deductible insurance policy. His 2-year-old stereo was stolen and will cost $400 to replace. If the annual rate of depreciation is 8%, how much will the insurance company pay?

A $32 **C** $286
B $64 **D** $336

Pages 216-217

9. Carolyn earns $16,800 per year. What is the greatest amount she should borrow to buy a home? (Use the general guideline of 2 times annual income.)

A $33,600 **C** $16,800
B $67,200 **D** $8400

Pages 218-219

10. An amortization table shows that the monthly payment for a $1000 loan for 25 years at 15% interest is $12.81. Find the monthly payment on a 25-year home loan of $70,000 at 15% per year.

A $8967 **C** $896.70
B $700 **D** $1050

Pages 220-221

11. How much interest will Ms. Whitewolf pay on a loan of $40,000 for 30 years if the monthly payments are $475?

A $183,200 (C) $131,000

B $171,000 D $124,880

Page 222

12. Linda borrowed $66,000 at an annual interest rate of 14%. How much interest will she pay the first month?

A $9240 C $600

B $7700 (D) $770

Pages 224-225

13. Peter's basic premium for homeowner's insurance is $150. He has a $400 camera and a $700 coin collection he wants to insure separately. Use the table below and find the total premium for his insurance.

Personal property	One-year rate per $100 of value
Cameras, projectors	$1.65
Coin collections	$1.95

A $13.65 (C) $170.25

B $20.25 D $260

Pages 226-227

14. Find the assessed valuation of a home with a market value of $72,000. The rate of assessment is 60% of market value.

A $100,800 C $115,200

B $28,800 (D) $43,200

Pages 228-229

15. The lawyer's fee is 0.3% of the purchase price of a home. What is the lawyer's fee on a $78,000 home?

(A) $234 C $2340

B $30 D $23.40

Pages 230-233

16. A real estate salesperson's commission is 7% of the selling price of a home. For what amount should a house be listed if the seller wants at least $74,000? Round up to the next hundred dollars.

A $5180 C $79,200

(B) $79,600 D $796,000

Pages 238-239

17. Give the bearings of side AB.

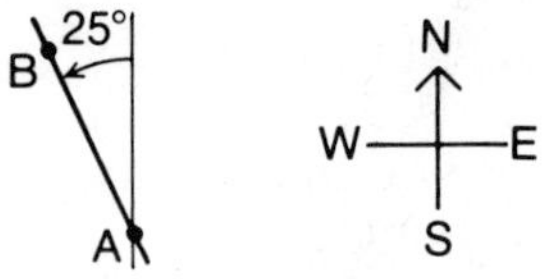

A N 25° E (C) N 25° W

B S 25° E D S 25° W

Pages 240-242

18. A builder charges $45 per square foot to build a one-story house. Find the cost of building a house 60 ft. long and 35 ft. wide.

A $156,500 C $42,750

B $21,000 (D) $94,500

Pages 244-245

19. A contractor will install a driveway for $1.30 per square foot. What is the cost of a driveway 10 ft. wide and 15 ft. long?

A $150 C $165

(B) $195 D $1500

Pages 246-247

20. The front of a garage is 10 ft. long and 9 ft. high. It contains one door 8 ft. by 7 ft. If a bricklayer uses 7 bricks per square foot of surface covered, about how many bricks will be needed for the garage front?

(A) 238 bricks C 486 bricks

B 50 bricks D 630 bricks

Unit 5 Test **Taxes, Insurance, and Investments, pages 257–314**

Choose the best answer.

Pages 258-259

1. Last year, Marie earned $1840.25, $630, $1582.65, and $86.62. Find her gross income.

   A $2470.25 (**C**) $4139.52
   B $4052.90 **D** $5392.46

Pages 260-262

2. Last year, Gary received $15,000 in salary, $240 in interest, and $420 in dividends. Find his adjusted gross income. Gary can claim a $100 exclusion for dividend income.

   (**A**) $15,560 **C** $15,660
   B $15,240 **D** $15,320

Page 263

3. A married couple files a joint tax return and claims 3 exemptions. Their adjusted gross income (line 11, Form 1040A) is $21,760. Use the tax table below to find their tax liability.

If line 11, Form 1040A is—		And the number of exemptions is—		
		2	3	4
Over	But not over	Your tax is—		
21,600	21,650	3,135	2,895	2,655
21,650	21,700	3,147	2,907	2,667
21,700	21,750	3,159	2,919	2,679
21,750	21,800	3,171	2,931	2,691

   A $2691 (**C**) $2931
   B $2919 **D** $3171

Pages 264-265

4. Scott has a tax liability of $2547 and a tax credit of $2694. Find his refund or balance due.

   A $5241 refund **C** $5241 balance due
   (**B**) $147 refund **D** $147 balance due

Pages 266-267

5. The Bentons claim 4 exemptions. Their adjusted gross income is $21,680 and their tax credit is $2534. Find their refund or balance due. (Use the tax table in problem 3.)

   A $133 refund (**C**) $133 balance due
   B $2667 refund **D** $2667 balance due

Pages 268-270

6. Use the information below and the tax table in problem 3 to find the Herreras' tax liability.

   Number of exemptions: 2
   Adjusted gross income: $22,150
   Zero bracket amount: $3400
   Itemized deductions
     State and local taxes: $1850
     Interest expenses: $1975

   A $2919 **C** $3147
   B $3171 (**D**) $3159

Pages 272-273

7. The state income tax for Illinois is 2.5% of taxable income. Find the tax on $14,000.

   A $35 **C** $2500
   (**B**) $350 **D** $3500

Pages 278-279

8. A health insurance company pays 80% of all medical expenses over the $50-deductible amount. What will the company pay on medical expenses of $1275?

   A $295 (**C**) $980
   B $500 **D** $1020

Pages 280-281

9. The annual premium for a 5-year term life insurance policy for an 18-year-old female is $2.05 per $1000. Find the annual premium on a $40,000 policy.

   (**A**) $82 **C** $2050
   B $410 **D** $4100

Pages 282-285

10. Mike bought $60,000 worth of straight life insurance at age 22. Use the table below and find the total cash value at age 65.

Straight Life—Cash Value per $1000			
Age at time of issue	Cash value at end of year		Cash value at age 65
	10	20	
20	$89	$241	$710
21	$91	$247	$703
22	$94	$254	$696

A $60,000 C $42,180

B $42,600 (D) $41,760

Pages 286-287

11. Tina's annual insurance premium is $462.50. How much more will she pay per year if she pays quarterly rather than annually? The factor for quarterly payment is 0.26.

(A) $18.50 C $120.25

B $15 D $481

Pages 290-291

12. Ben is buying straight life insurance at age 24. He wants to pay monthly premiums. How much of this insurance can he buy for a maximum of $70 a month? The factor for monthly premiums is 0.0875.

Annual Premiums per $1000 for Males			
Age	Straight life	20-payment life	20-year endowment
23	$13.79	$21.04	$42.20
24	$14.21	$21.54	$42.24
25	$14.64	$22.07	$42.27

A $58,000 (C) $56,000

B $57,000 D $55,000

Pages 292-295

13. The Holts receive monthly social security retirement benefits of $520.40 plus $262.30 for one dependent. Find their annual retirement benefit.

(A) $9392.40 C $3147.60

B $6244.80 D $782.70

Pages 300-301

14. The cost of a Series EE Savings Bond is $\frac{1}{2}$ of the face value. Find the cost of a $500 bond.

A $1000 (C) $250

B $150 D $500

Pages 302-304

15. Jean bought a $2000 CD that earns 8% interest compounded daily. She receives an interest check at the end of each year. How much interest does she receive at the end of each year?

Interest Factors per $1 Invested			
Annual rate	Interest period		
	6 mo.	9 mo.	1 yr.
7.5%	0.03767	0.05704	0.07788
8%	0.04024	0.06096	0.08328

A $155.76 C $121.92

(B) $166.56 D $2166.56

Pages 306-309

16. Mr. Chavez sold 60 shares of stock at $35.25 per share. He paid a commission of $40. How much did he receive?

A $2155 C $2115

B $2400 (D) $2075

Pages 310-311

17. SUN Mutual Fund is a no-load fund. The current selling price is $13.05 per share. Find the cost of 50 shares.

A $130.50 (C) $652.50

B $513.05 D $6525.50

Unit 6 Test **Purchasing and Budgeting, pages 321–372**

Choose the best answer.

Pages 322-323

1. Find the number of calories in 2 slices of whole-wheat bread if one slice contains 55 calories.

   A 57 calories (C) 110 calories

   B 100 calories D 27 calories

Pages 324-325

2. Jess weighs 68 kilograms. He played tennis for 1.5 hours. At 6.4 calories per kilogram per hour, how many calories did he use? Round to the nearest whole number.

   (A) 653 calories C 10 calories

   B 435 calories D 102 calories

Pages 326-328

3. Find the cost of 1.4 kg of bananas at \$0.85 per kilogram.

   A \$2.25 C \$1.40

   B \$1.85 (D) \$1.19

Pages 330-331

4. Before butchering, a side of beef weighed 140 kilograms. After butchering, the usable meat weighed 105 kilograms. What was the percent of loss?

   A 20% C 33%

   (B) 25% D 54%

Pages 332-333

5. Find the total cost of this meal for two people. The prices given are per person. Include a 15% tip.

Chicken	\$5.25
Beverage	\$0.75
Salad	\$1.50

   (A) \$17.25 C \$14.30

   B \$15 D \$8.63

Pages 338-340

6. Use the table below. Find the shipping and handling charges for an order weighing 2 lb. 10 oz. and going to zone 2.

Shipping and Handling Charges		
Shipping weight	Zones 1 & 2	Zone 3
1 lb. to 2 lb.	\$2.11	\$2.14
2 lb. 1 oz. to 3 lb.	\$2.39	\$2.43
3 lb. 1 oz. to 5 lb.	\$2.57	\$2.63
5 lb. 1 oz. to 10 lb.	\$2.84	\$2.91

   A \$2.57 (C) \$2.39

   B \$2.11 D \$2.43

Pages 342-343

7. If $1\frac{3}{4}$ yards of fabric is needed to make one jacket, how much fabric is needed to make 3 jackets?

   A $4\frac{3}{4}$ yards C $3\frac{3}{4}$ yards

   (B) $5\frac{1}{4}$ yards D 3 yards

Pages 344-346

8. The regular price of a stereo is \$500. The stereo is on sale. What is the sale price of the stereo if the discount is 20%?

   A \$100 C \$450

   B \$480 (D) \$400

Pages 346-347

9. A stained-glass lampshade takes 6 sq. ft. of blue glass at $3 a square foot. It also takes 2 pounds of solder at $7.75 a pound and 1 roll of foil at $3 a roll. Find the total cost of the materials for the lampshade.

A $13.75 (**C**) $36.50

B $15.50 **D** $33.50

Pages 348-349

10. Find the total cost of 5 boards, each 2 in. by 4 in. by 6 feet, at $0.18 per linear foot. Remember, when lumber is priced by the linear foot, the cost of each board depends only on its length.

(**A**) $5.40 **C** $10.80

B $9 **D** $1.08

Pages 350-351

11. A lawn aerator rents for $2.25 per hour. Find the cost of renting the aerator for 5 hours.

A $7.25 **C** $0.45

(**B**) $11.25 **D** $36.50

Pages 356-359

12. Find the total expense for entertainment for August. Round to the nearest dollar.

Entertainment expenses—August

Concert	$7.00
Soccer game	$8.50
Movie	$4.75

A $13 **C** $16

B $21 (**D**) $20

Pages 360-361

13. A 3-month spending record for gasoline, oil, and tolls is given below. Find the amount that should be budgeted per month for this variable expense.

Month 1	$64
Month 2	$63
Month 3	$59

A $186 (**C**) $62

B $64 **D** $63

Pages 362-364

14. Jackie's annual expenses total $874. To the nearest dollar, how much should she reserve each month to pay her annual expenses?

A $87 **C** $886

B $800 (**D**) $73

Pages 366-367

15. The Sakamotos usually budget $1800 for their summer vacation. This year they hope to save $540 by driving instead of flying to their destination. How much should they budget this year for the vacation?

A $540 **C** $150

(**B**) $1260 **D** $2340

Pages 368-369

16. One survey indicates that an average family spends 23% of its income on food. If the family income is $22,600, what is the amount spent for food?

(**A**) $5198 **C** $17,402

B $433 **D** $1883

End-of-Book Test **Part A, Chapters 1–9**

Choose the correct answer.

Chapter 1

1. $3.64 + 28.7 + 6.18$

A 12.69 — C 38.52
B 37.44 — D 126.9

2. $5\frac{1}{4} \times \frac{2}{3}$

A $7\frac{7}{8}$ — C $5\frac{1}{6}$
B $3\frac{1}{2}$ — D $5\frac{2}{7}$

Chapter 2

3. Solve. $\frac{5}{7} = \frac{35}{w}$

A $w = 35$ — C $w = 42$
B $w = 25$ — D $w = 49$

4. 12% of 200 is what number?

A $1666\frac{2}{3}$ — C 24
B $16\frac{2}{3}$ — D 2400

Chapter 3

5. Choose the most sensible measure for the length of a spoon.

A 15 cm — C 15 m
B 15 km — D 15 mm

6. Find the mean for this set of numbers.

16, 22, 22, 9, 6, 27

A 17 — C 102
B 22 — D 6

Chapter 4

7. Manuela earns $6.50 per hour as a tutor. What is her gross pay for 25 hours?

A $31.50 — C $130.25
B $162.50 — D $262.60

8. David's gross pay is $287 per week. Each week, $34.80 is withheld for federal income tax and $19.09 is withheld for social security. Find his net pay.

A $233.11 — C $340.89
B $252.20 — D $53.89

Chapter 5

9. Find the balance to be carried forward from this check stub.

	DOLLARS	CENTS
BAL. FOR'D	120	20
DEPOSITS	35	00
"		
TOTAL		
THIS PAYMENT	10	29
OTHER DEDUCTIONS		
BAL. FOR'D		

A $155.20 — C $144.91
B $85.20 — D $95.49

10. A savings account paid 7% simple interest per year. Find the amount of interest that $450 earned in 6 months.

A $15.75 — C $31.50
B $465.75 — D $189

Chapter 6

11. The average daily balance in a charge account for the month of May is $150. The finance charge is 1.8% per month of the average daily balance. Find the finance charge for May.

A $270 — C $27
B $83.33 — D $2.70

12. The cash price for a television set is $750. Mr. Halm plans to pay for the television set in 12 monthly installments of $71 each. What is the finance charge?

A $821 **C** $852

(B) $102 **D** $864

Chapter 7

13. The price of a used car is $2875. The state sales tax is 4% of the price of the car. Find the state sales tax.

A $2990 **(C)** $115

B $150 **D** $1150

14. The selling price of a new car is $8600. The trade-in allowance on a used car is $1930. Find the net price of the new car.

A $10,530 **C** $6530

B $5760 **(D)** $6670

Chapter 8

15. Takeo drove 850 km during April. He used 125 liters of gasoline. Find his car's fuel economy rate.

(A) 6.8 km/L **C** 6.4 km/L

B 6.6 km/L **D** 106,250 km/L

16. Sandy drove 15,000 km last year. Her total car expenses were $6150. Find the cost per kilometer to operate her car.

A 35.3¢ **C** 41.6¢

B 31¢ **(D)** 41¢

Chapter 9

17. Use the chart below to find the distance from Phoenix to San Francisco to Portland. Distances between cities are given in kilometers.

	Phoenix	Portland	St. Louis
Portland	2200		
St. Louis	2380	3375	
San Francisco	1288	1050	3424

A 2200 km **C** 1288 km

(B) 2338 km **D** 3250 km

18. Gail Parker is planning a trip. She estimates that she will spend $80 for gasoline and tolls, $40 for food, and $30 for lodging. Estimate the total cost of the trip.

A $130 **(C)** $150

B $120 **D** $110

End-of-Book Test Part B, Chapters 10–18

Choose the correct answer.

Chapter 10

1. Ken earns $8.75 per hour in a 40-hour work week. What is the most he should spend for rent per month? (Use the guideline of not spending more than one week's gross pay for shelter each month.)

   A $87.50 C $48.75

   B $300 (D) $350

2. Dara is planning to paint the walls of a room that measures 10 ft. by 12 ft. The walls are 8 ft. high. Find the total area to be painted.

   A 176 sq. ft. C 472 sq. ft.

   (B) 352 sq. ft. D 960 sq. ft.

Chapter 11

3. Bill Adams is buying a home that costs $72,000. He will make a 20% down payment and borrow the rest of the money. Find the amount of the loan.

   A $14,400 (C) $57,600

   B $56,400 D $86,400

4. The Simpsons paid a lawyer's fee of 0.4% of the purchase price of their home. What was the fee on their $78,500 home?

   A $31.40 C $31,400

   (B) $314 D $3140

Chapter 12

5. A garage costs $13 per square foot to build. Find the cost of building a garage that is 22 ft. long and 10 ft. wide.

   A $416 C $4670

   B $286 (D) $2860

6. A bricklayer needs 7 bricks to cover one square foot of surface. How many bricks are needed to cover 560 sq. ft.?

   A 5600 bricks C 80 bricks

   (B) 3920 bricks D 567 bricks

Chapter 13

7. Use the tax table below to find the tax liability for a person with one exemption and an adjusted gross income (line 11, Form 1040A) of $19,825.

If line 11, Form 1040A is—		And the number of exemptions is—		
		1	2	3
Over	But not over	Your tax is—		
19,750	19,800	3,761	3,438	3,138
19,800	19,850	3,778	3,453	3,153
19,850	19,900	3,795	3,468	3,168

   A $3453 C $3795

   (B) $3778 D $3761

8. Steve Momaday has a tax liability of $2467 and a tax credit of $2547. What is his refund or balance due?

   (A) $80 refund C $180 balance due

   B $180 refund D $80 balance due

Chapter 14

9. Pam Holt has a $50-deductible health insurance policy which pays 80% of the amount over the deductible. How much will the company pay on medical expenses of $1260?

   A $1210 C $1008

   (B) $968 D $242

10. Inez deposits $25 a month in a savings account that pays 7% interest compounded monthly. Use the table below to find the balance in the account at the end of 15 years.

Savings Balance (For $1 deposited each month with interest compounded monthly)		
Years	6%	7%
10	$163.88	$173.08
15	$290.82	$316.96
20	$462.04	$520.93

A $316.96 **C** $4815

(**B**) $7924 **D** $13,023.25

Chapter 15

11. The cost of any Series EE Savings Bond is $\frac{1}{2}$ of the face value. Find the cost of a $1000 bond.

A $50 (**C**) $500

B $2000 **D** $1000

12. Ms. Santos bought 50 shares of stock for $42.50 per share. What was the total amount invested?

(**A**) $2125 **C** $4375

B $2080 **D** $2170

Chapter 16

13. Find the cost of 1 can of orange juice at 6 cans for $1.19.

A $0.19 **C** $0.25

(**B**) $0.20 **D** $7.14

14. Sheila and Ed spent $12.80 for dinner in a restaurant. They left a 15% tip. Find the total cost of the dinner and tip.

A $12.95 **C** $1.92

(**B**) $14.72 **D** $19.20

Chapter 17

15. If $2\frac{3}{4}$ yards of fabric is needed to make one shirt, how much fabric is needed to make 6 shirts?

A $8\frac{3}{4}$ yards **C** $12\frac{3}{4}$ yards

B 12 yards (**D**) $16\frac{1}{2}$ yards

16. The regular price of a refrigerator is $549. What is the sale price with a 15% discount?

(**A**) $466.65 **C** $82.35

B $549 **D** $631.35

Chapter 18

17. A 3-month spending record for food is given below. Find the amount that should be budgeted per month for this variable expense.

Month 1 $125
Month 2 $113
Month 3 $122

A $110 **C** $1080

(**B**) $120 **D** $360

18. Glenn's annual expenses total $978. To the nearest dollar, how much should he reserve each month to pay his annual expenses?

A $19 **C** $80

B $11,736 (**D**) $82

Test Suggested Competency Test

This test is designed to measure how well students can use mathematics in everyday life. The topics covered in this test are similar to topics found in competency tests that many schools require for graduation.

The test consists of 66 problems which are keyed to consumer topics. The chart below shows these consumer topics and the test problems that are keyed to each topic. More information about these consumer topics can be found in the index. The chart also shows the answers to the test problems and lists the page numbers of the lessons in the student's text where situations similar to those in the test problems can be found. Answers are also circled on the test pages in the Teacher's Edition.

Interpretation of test scores is left to the individual teacher. However, to demonstrate overall competency, a student should correctly answer at least one problem keyed to each consumer topic.

Consumer topic	Test problems	Answers	Page(s)
Gross pay	1	B	68–69
	2	C	70–71
	3	C	72–73
Net pay	4	A	78–81
	5	D	78–81
	6	D	78–81
Income tax	7	C	260–262
	8	A	263
	9	B	264–265
Bank deposits	10	B	88–89
	11	C	88–89
	12	D	88–89
Checking accounts	13	A	90–91
	14	C	92–93
	15	D	94–96
Finance charges	16	B	112–113
	17	B	118–119
	18	A	118–119
Credit/ charge accounts	19	C	110–111
	20	D	115
	21	B	115
Savings plans	22	D	98–99
	23	C	300–301
	24	A	306–309
Buying a car	25	C	132–133
	26	B	136–137
	27	A	138–139
Automobile operating expenses	28	B	150–151
	29	A	152–153
	30	C	156–159
Travel	31	A	172–173
	32	B	174–175
	33	D	180

Consumer topic	Test problems	Answers	Page(s)
Buying or renting a home	34	A	194–195
	35	C	216–217
	36	B	228–229
Borrowing money	37	C	108–109
	38	C	218–219
	39	B	220–221
Home expenses	40	D	350–351
	41	A	224–225
	42	A	226–227
Insurance	43	C	162–163
	44	D	278–279
	45	B	282–285
Building costs and plans	46	A	202–203
	47	C	240–242
	48	D	244–245
Purchasing supplies	49	B	206–207
	50	C	246–247
	51	D	342–343
Sales tax and additional charges	52	A	136–137
	53	B	338–340
	54	A	332–333
Discounts	55	A	344–345
	56	A	344–345
	57	D	134
Unit pricing	58	C	326–328
	59	B	326–328
	60	D	326–328
Food	61	A	330–331
	62	C	322–323
	63	B	332–333
Budgeting	64	C	360–361
	65	A	366–367
	66	D	368–369

Competency Test

Choose the correct answer.

1. Laura earns $6.50 per hour. What is her gross pay for a 30-hour work week?

   A $95 (B) $195 C $36.50 D $200

2. Duane earns $3.50 per hour plus tips. Last week, he worked 40 hours and made $125 in tips. What was his gross pay for the week?

   A $140 B $168.50 (C) $265 D $500

3. Linda earns 12% straight commission selling books. One week, she had sales of $1650. What was her gross pay for the week?

   A $137.50 B $495 (C) $198 D $165

4. Maria's gross pay for last week was $400. The amount withheld for social security was 6.65% of her gross pay. How much was withheld for social security?

   (A) $26.60 B $6.65 C $373.40 D $134

5. Each week, the following amounts are withheld from Steve's gross pay: $70.50 for federal income tax and $24.61 for social security. How much is withheld each week for these items?

   A $45.89 B $274.89 C $465.11 (D) $95.11

6. Diana's gross pay is $245.62 a week. Each week, $21 is withheld for federal income tax and $16.33 is withheld for social security. Find Diana's net pay.

   A $37.33 B $224.62 C $218.31 (D) $208.29

7. Last year, Randy received $8045 in wages, $135 in interest, and $75 in dividends. Find his adjusted gross income.

   A $8180 B $8120 (C) $8255 D $8455

8. Virginia Whitehorse claims one exemption on her tax return. Her adjusted gross income (line 11, Form 1040A) is $16,980. Use the tax table below to find the amount of tax she must pay.

If line 11, Form 1040A is—		And the number of exemptions is—		
Over	But not over	1	2	3
		Your tax is—		
16,900	16,950	2,883	2,586	2,326
16,950	17,000	2,898	2,599	2,339

   (A) $2898 B $2599 C $2883 D $2339

9. Fred owes $3050 for income taxes. He has a tax credit of $3100. What is his refund or balance due?

   A $150 refund (B) $50 refund C $50 balance due D $150 balance due

Go on to the next page.

10. Tracy deposited checks for the following amounts: $25.40, $110.25, and $7.65. What was her total deposit?

A $117.90 **C** $77.20

B $143.30 **D** $135.65

11. Find the net deposit for this deposit slip.

CASH	CURRENCY		
	COIN		
LIST CHECKS SINGLY		125	00
		15	00
TOTAL FROM OTHER SIDE			
TOTAL			
LESS CASH RECEIVED		50	00
NET DEPOSIT			

A $140 **C** $90

B $190 **D** $50

12. Chris had checks to deposit for the following amounts: $25.50, $80, and $100. He wanted $75 in cash. What was his net deposit?

A $280.50 **C** $75

B $205.50 **D** $130.50

13. Find the balance to be carried forward from this check stub.

	DOLLARS	CENTS
BAL. FOR'D	96	40
DEPOSITS	25	00
TOTAL		
THIS PAYMENT	10	00
OTHER DEDUCTIONS		
BAL. FOR'D		

A $111.40 **C** $61.40

B $121.40 **D** $71.40

14. Chang had a balance of $575.49 in his checking account. He wrote a check for $220.32. What was the balance after Chang wrote this check?

A $795.81 **C** $355.17

B $220.32 **D** $255.17

15. Sue's bank statement showed a balance of $330.50 in her checking account. She had an outstanding deposit of $50 and an outstanding check for $62.50. Find the actual balance in Sue's checking account.

A $443 **C** $343

B $218 **D** $318

16. The balance in an account for the month of June was $185. The finance charge was 1.8% per month of the balance. What is the finance charge for June?

A $188.33 **C** $186.80

B $3.33 **D** $2.78

17. Frank is buying a stereo for $650. He plans to pay for the stereo in 12 monthly installments of $61 each. What is the finance charge?

A $732 **C** $54.17

B $82 **D** $568

18. The cost of a sofa is $550. Albert made a down payment of $130. He will pay the remainder in 18 monthly installments of $27 each. Find the finance charge.

A $66 **C** $486

B $344 **D** $64

Go on to the next page.

19. Dawn's unpaid balance in a charge account was $96. The finance charge is 1.5% per month of the unpaid balance. What is the new balance?

A $97.50 (**C**) $97.44

B $94.56 **D** $1.44

20. The unpaid balance in Juan's charge account was $78.50. A $20 payment and purchases of $25.25 were made during the month. The finance charge was $1.51. What is the new balance?

A $125.26 **C** $83.75

B $74.76 (**D**) $85.26

21. Sandy's charge-account statement showed a new balance of $150. Use the schedule below to find the minimum payment required.

New balance	Minimum payment
$0–$10	100% of balance
$10.01–$100	$10
$100.01–$200	$20
$200.01–$400	15% of balance
Over $400	20% of balance

A $10 **C** $22.50

(**B**) $20 **D** $170

22. A savings account paid 6% simple interest per year. Find the amount of interest that $400 earned in 6 months ($\frac{1}{2}$ year).

A $144 **C** $412

B $24 (**D**) $12

23. After 10 years, the redemption value of a $50 Series EE Savings Bond is $60.29. What is the redemption value of a $100 Series EE Bond after 10 years?

A $100 (**C**) $120.58

B $110.29 **D** $160.29

24. Charles bought 50 shares of stock at $42 per share. What was the total amount that Charles invested?

(**A**) $2100 **C** $119

B $92 **D** $2000

25. The suggested retail price of a new car is $7800. Find the sticker price with these options.

Automatic transmission	$350
Power steering	$180
Air conditioning	$600

A $1130 (**C**) $8930

B $6670 **D** $8150

26. The price of a used car is $1900. The state sales tax is $76. The license-plate fee is $30. The title fee is $6. Find the total cost.

A $1986 **C** $112

(**B**) $2012 **D** $1788

27. The selling price of a new car is $9600. The trade-in allowance on a used car is $2530. Find the net price of the new car.

(**A**) $7070 **C** $12,130

B $7030 **D** $7130

Go on to the next page.

28. Tamiko drove 2040 km during July. She used 300 liters of gasoline. Find her car's fuel economy rate.

A 5.7 km/L **C** 6 km/L

B 6.8 km/L **D** 7 km/L

29. Three years ago, John bought a new car for $7400. Because of depreciation, the trade-in value of a three-year-old car is 40% of the price of the car when it was new. What is the trade-in value?

A $2960 **C** $4500

B $7104 **D** $4400

30. The repair bill for June's car showed $38 for labor, $26.52 for parts, and $7.20 for oil and grease. What was the total amount of the bill?

A $64.52 **C** $71.72

B $33.72 **D** $45.20

31. Use the chart below to find the distance from Memphis to Denver. Distances between cities are given in kilometers.

	Dallas	Denver	Houston
Denver	1262		
Houston	395	1652	
Los Angeles	2259	1826	2501
Memphis	747	1667	903

A 1667 km **C** 903 km

B 1826 km **D** 747 km

32. Shelly drove 570 km at an average speed of 80 km/h. To the nearest hour, what was the travel time?

A 8 hours **C** 6 hours

B 7 hours **D** 5 hours

33. Len rented a car for 2 days and drove 600 kilometers. He was charged $25 per day plus $0.15 per kilometer driven. Find the rental cost.

A $50 **C** $115

B $90 **D** $140

34. Don earns $7 per hour for a 40-hour work week. What is the most he should spend for rent each month? (Use the guideline of not spending more than one week's gross pay for shelter each month.)

A $280 **C** $28

B $470 **D** $140

35. Kathy earns $1750 per month. What is the greatest amount she should consider borrowing for a home? (Use the general guideline of 2 times annual income.)

A $21,000 **C** $42,000

B $35,000 **D** $3500

36. The Willoyas paid a lawyer's fee of 0.5% of the purchase price of their home. What was the fee on their $91,000 home?

A $910 **C** $4550

B $455 **D** $45,500

37. A promissory note for $200 at an interest rate of 15% per year is due in 1 year. What is the amount of interest due?

A $170 **C** $30

B $230 **D** $15

Go on to the next page.

38. What is the monthly payment on a loan of $42,000 for 25 years at an annual interest rate of 12.5%? Use the amortization table below.

Amortization of a $1000 Loan			
	Monthly payment		
Interest rate	20-year loan	25-year loan	30-year loan
12.0%	$11.01	$10.53	$10.29
12.5%	$11.36	$10.90	$10.67
13.0%	$11.72	$11.28	$11.06

A $477.12 　 **(C)** $457.80

B $473.76 　 **D** $442.26

39. Find the total amount of interest that will be paid on a loan of $34,000 for 20 years if the amount paid in monthly payments totals $5064 each year.

A $101,280 　 **C** $422

(B) $67,280 　 **D** $135,280

40. Find the cost of renting a floor sander for 2 days at $22.50 per day.

A $44 　 **C** $50

B $22.50 　 **(D)** $45

41. Kelly's basic premium for homeowner's insurance is $120. She also wants to insure a $100 camera separately. Use the table below and find the total premium for her insurance.

Personal property	One-year rate per $100 of value
Jewelry	$1.40
Cameras, projectors	$1.65
Musical instruments	$0.69

(A) $121.65 　 **C** $220

B $1.65 　 **D** $121.40

42. The assessed valuation of the Garcias' home is $40,000. The real estate tax is $3.50 per $100 of assessed valuation. Find their real estate tax.

(A) $1400 　 **C** $350

B $400 　 **D** $140,000

43. The premium for Mary's collision insurance is $170.72. The premium for her comprehensive insurance is $55.60. What is Mary's combined premium for collision and comprehensive insurance?

A $115.12 　 **(C)** $226.32

B $94.92 　 **D** $307.05

44. Bill has a $50-deductible health insurance policy which pays 80% of the amount over the deductible. His medical expenses are $550. How much will be paid by the insurance company?

A $440 　 **C** $150

B $500 　 **(D)** $400

45. Dan bought $60,000 worth of straight life insurance at age 26. Use the table below and find the cash value of the insurance after 15 years.

Straight Life—Cash Value per $1000				
Age at time of issue	Cash value at end of year			
	5	10	15	20
25	$31	$102	$176	$278
26	$32	$105	$181	$286
27	$33	$109	$186	$295

A $11,160 　 **C** $17,160

(B) $10,860 　 **D** $6300

Go on to the next page.

46. What is the scale length of a dining room that is 4 m long? Use the scale of 1 cm ⟶ 0.25 m.

(A) 16 cm C 2.8 cm
B 8 cm D 1 cm

47. A house costs $42 per square foot to build. Find the cost of building a house that covers 1500 square feet.

A $6300 (C) $63,000
B $42,000 D $1542

48. A contractor will install a driveway for $1.25 per square foot. What is the cost of installing a driveway 10 feet wide and 20 feet long?

A $125.25 C $225
B $200 (D) $250

49. The total wall area to be painted is 1200 sq. ft. If one gallon of paint covers about 400 sq. ft., how many gallons of paint must be purchased?

A 2 gallons C 4 gallons
(B) 3 gallons D 5 gallons

50. Seven bricks will cover one square foot of surface. How many bricks will be needed to cover 119 sq. ft.?

A 126 bricks (C) 833 bricks
B 17 bricks D 710 bricks

51. Gail is making skirts for the cheerleaders. She needs $1\frac{1}{4}$ yards for one skirt. How much fabric does she need for six skirts?

A $7\frac{1}{4}$ yards C $4\frac{4}{5}$ yards
B $6\frac{1}{4}$ yards (D) $7\frac{1}{2}$ yards

52. The price of a car is $8300. The state sales tax is 4% of the price of the car. Find the state sales tax.

(A) $332 C $33.20
B $322 D $3320

53. Kim ordered a 10-ounce item from a catalog. The item with sales tax cost $8.19. She lives in zone 2. Use the table below and find the total amount she must enclose with the order.

Shipping and Handling Charges			
Shipping weight	Local zone	Zones 1 & 2	Zone 3
1 oz. to 8 oz.	$1.27	$1.34	$1.36
9 oz. to 15 oz.	$1.49	$1.60	$1.64

A $9.68 C $9.83
(B) $9.79 D $9.53

54. Mark's dinner cost $7. He left a 15% tip. Find the amount of the tip.

(A) $1.05 C $8.05
B $1.50 D $10.50

55. A $10 wallet is on sale at a 20% discount. What is the amount of the discount?

(A) $2 C $5
B $0.20 D $8

56. The regular price of a sweater is $30. With a 20% discount, what is the sale price of the sweater?

(A) $24 C $15
B $28 D $6

Go on to the next page.

57. A new car has a sticker price of $6700. The dealer agreed to Jan's offer to pay 10% less than the sticker price. What was Jan's offer?

A $7370 **C** $670
B $6623 **(D)** $6030

58. Find the unit price of a 4-kg bag of potatoes priced at $1.96 a bag.

A $7.84 per kg **(C)** $0.49 per kg
B $5.99 per kg **D** $0.50 per kg

59. Which is the best buy for apple juice?

1-liter bottle for $0.79
2-liter bottle for $1.48
3-liter bottle for $2.26
4-liter bottle for $3.09

A 1-L bottle **C** 3-L bottle
(B) 2-L bottle **D** 4-L bottle

60. Find the cost of 3 loaves of bread at 2 loaves for $1.28.

A $0.64 **C** $2.56
B $3.84 **(D)** $1.92

61. If ground beef costs $3.99 per kilogram, find the value of 12 kg of ground beef.

(A) $47.88 **C** $8.01
B $15.99 **D** $48

62. Find the total number of calories for the following breakfast.

$\frac{1}{2}$ grapefruit	55 calories
2 slices bacon	90 calories
1 poached egg	80 calories
1 glass milk	160 calories

A 225 calories **(C)** 385 calories
B 395 calories **D** 285 calories

63. The Smyth family had dinner in a restaurant. The bill was $32.80. They left a 15% tip. Find the cost of the dinner and the tip.

A $4.92 **C** $27.88
(B) $37.72 **D** $33.29

64. A 3-week spending record for food is shown below. Find the amount that should be budgeted per week for this variable expense.

Week 1	$42
Week 2	$32
Week 3	$34

A $32 **(C)** $36
B $34 **D** $108

65. Thelma budgets $58 per month for lunch. If she takes her lunch to work part of the time, she can cut this expense in half. Find the new amount she should budget for lunch.

(A) $29 **C** $87
B $116 **D** $58

66. An average family spends 22% of its income for food. If the family income is $26,000 per year, what is the amount spent for food?

A $31,720 **C** $2600
B $20,280 **(D)** $5720

Stop. End of test.

L. Carey Bolster

H. Douglas Woodburn

Joella H. Gipson

Scott, Foresman and Company
Editorial Offices: Glenview, Illinois

Regional Sales Offices: Sunnyvale, California • Tucker, Georgia • Glenview, Illinois • Oakland, New Jersey • Dallas, Texas

Authors

L. Carey Bolster
Supervisor of Mathematics
Baltimore County Public Schools
Towson, Maryland

H. Douglas Woodburn
Chairman of the Mathematics Department
Perry Hall Middle School
Baltimore County, Maryland

Joella H. Gipson
Professor, College of Education
Wayne State University
Detroit, Michigan

Readers/Consultants

Marita H. Eng
Mathematics Department Chairman
Sandalwood Junior-Senior High School
Jacksonville, Florida

Robert Y. Hamada
Instructional Specialist, Mathematics
Los Angeles Unified School District
Los Angeles, California

Linda Borry Hausmann
Manager of Instructional Systems
EduSystems, Inc.
Minneapolis, Minnesota

William C. Messersmith, Jr.
Teacher/Coordinator of Data Processing Services
Rich Township High School
Richton Park, Illinois

Sidney Sharron
Supervisor, Instructional Media and Resources Branch
Los Angeles Unified School District
Los Angeles, California

ISBN: 0–673–23436–3

12345678910-KPK-9392919089888786

Acknowledgements

For permission to reproduce indicated information on the following pages, acknowledgment is made to:

4–5, 1980 Census Forms, Courtesy Bureau of the Census.

66, 88, 90, 92, 94–95, 97, and *108,* Deposit slip, check, check register, bank statements, and promissory note, Reprinted by permission of Glenview State Bank, Glenview, Illinois.

120, Piano, Courtesy Andrews-Edwards Music Service, Wilmette, Illinois

135, Puzzle, from MATHEMATICS: PROBLEM SOLVING THROUGH RECREATIONAL MATHEMATICS by Bonnie Averbach and Orin Chein. W.M. Freeman and Company. Copyright © 1980. Reprinted by permission.

224–225, Violin and accessories, Courtesy Fritz Reuter and Sons, Chicago.

232, Table, adapted from "Averages for Selected Metropolitan Areas for All Major Lenders," from Federal Home Loan Bank Board *News.* Courtesy Federal Home Loan Bank Board.

258, 260, 264, and *266,* Form W-2, "Who Must File" instructions, and Form 1040A, Courtesy Internal Revenue Service.

293, Table, Courtesy Social Security Administration.

300–301, United States Savings Bonds, Courtesy United States Department of the Treasury.

302, Certificate of deposit, Reprinted by permission of Glenview State Bank, Glenview, Illinois.

309, Puzzle, from MATHEMATICAL PUZZLES AND PASTIMES by Aaron Bakst. Copyright © 1965 by Van Nostrand Reinhold Company. Reprinted by permission of the publisher.

346–347, Stained glass, Courtesy Stained Glass & More, Northfield, Illinois.

347, Needlepoint, Courtesy Needlepoint & More, Northfield, Illinois. Designs, Courtesy Dede Needleworks, San Francisco.

402–405, Tables for wage-bracket method of withholding, Courtesy Internal Revenue Service.

406–409, 1980 Tax Tables and Schedules, Courtesy Internal Revenue Service.

Photographs

Unless otherwise credited, all photographs are the property of Scott, Foresman and Company.

19, Stacy Pick/Lensman; *42,* Focus on Sports; *52,* Jon Brenneis/FPG; *138–139,* Used with permission; *178–179,* E. Simonsen/H. Armstrong Roberts; *192–193, 215,* and *237,* Cameramann International; *247,* Michael Philip Manheim/ Photo Researchers.

Original Art

15, Susan Atlas Kelley; *26–27,* Garrett Reese; *33* and *253,* John Youssi; *42, 44, 49, 111,* and *173,* Jack Wallen; *50–51, 65, 127, 189,* and *375,* Sandy Rabinowitz; *135,* Pat Dypold; *233,* Dick Martin; *332,* Johanna Yount Baldwin; *344,* Bobbye Cochran.

Unit 1 Mathematics Skills

Chapter 1
Whole Numbers, Decimals, and Fractions

Chapter 2
Equations, Proportions, and Percent

Chapter 3
Measurement and Statistics

End-of-Unit Materials

Unit 2 Income, Banking, and Credit

Unit 3 Transportation

Chapter 7
Buying a Car

Chapter 8
Automobile Operating Expenses

Chapter 9
Travel

End-of-Unit Materials

Unit 4 Housing

Chapter 10
Renting and Decorating a Home

Chapter 11
Buying a Home

Chapter 12
Building a Home

End-of-Unit Materials

Unit 5 Taxes, Insurance, and Investments

Chapter 13
Income Tax

Chapter 14
Health, Life, and Retirement Insurance

Chapter 15
Investments

End-of-Unit Materials

Unit 6 Purchasing and Budgeting

Chapter 16 Buying Food

Chapter 17 Buying, Making, and Renting Goods

Chapter 18 Budgeting

End-of-Unit Materials

End-of-Book Materials

CONSUMER
AND
CAREER
MATHEMATICS
SECOND
EDITION

Unit 1 Mathematics Skills

Chapter 1 Whole Numbers, Decimals, and Fractions

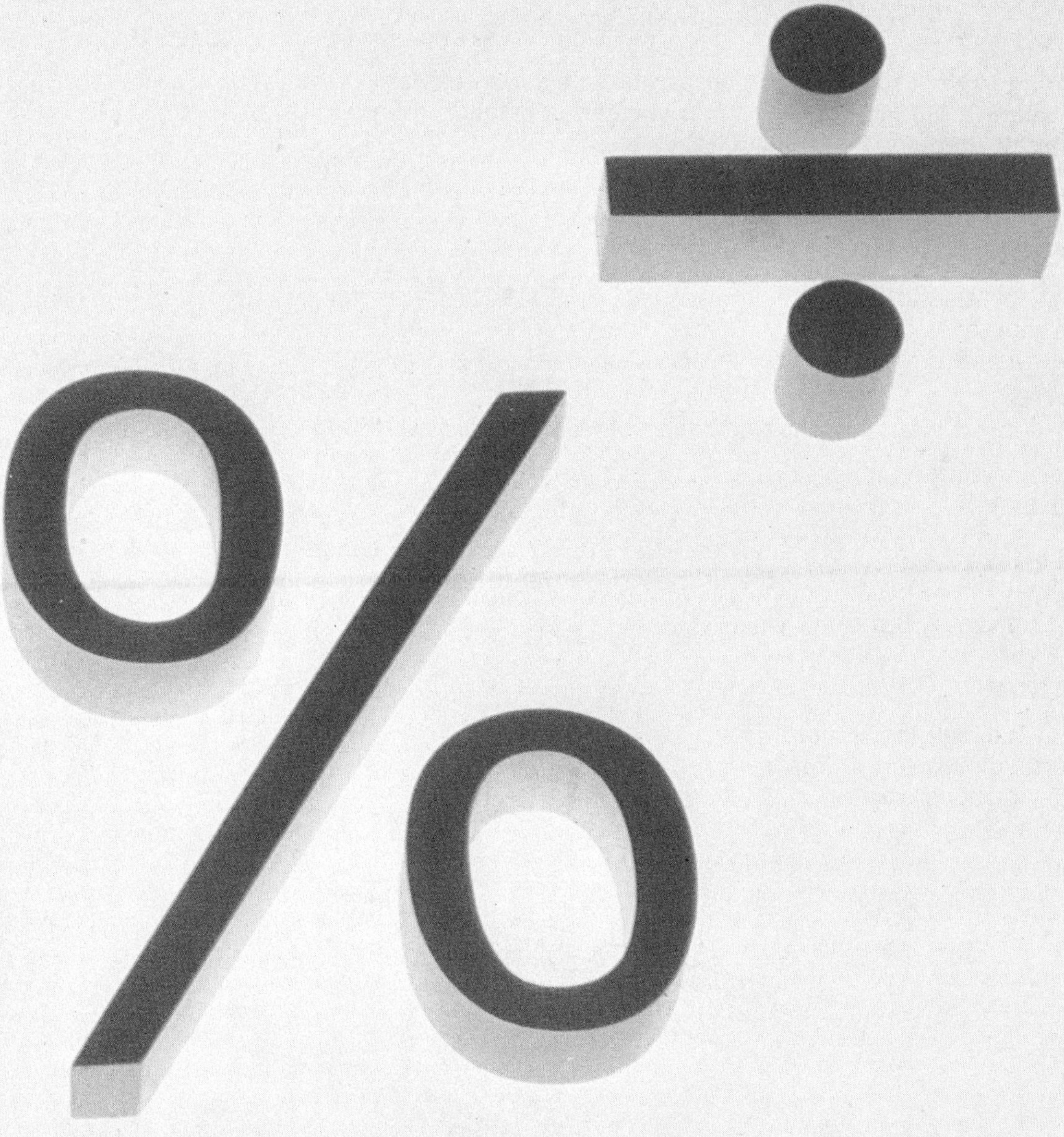

Objectives: Round whole numbers to the nearest thousand, nearest hundred, and nearest ten; round decimals to the nearest whole number, nearest tenth, and nearest hundredth.

Rounding Whole Numbers and Decimals

See page T26 for additional notes and activities for Chapter 1.

> When rounding a number, look at the digit to the right of the place to which you are rounding. If the digit is 5 or greater, round up. If the digit is less than 5, round down.

Generalizations and rules needed for the lesson are given at the beginning of most skills lessons.

Problem A

Examples in a Problem/Solution format provide students with models for completing the exercises and the related problems.

According to the United States Census, the population of Hampstead, Maryland, in 1980 was 24,862. What was the population rounded to the nearest thousand?

Round 24,862 to the nearest thousand.

Solution

Look at the digit to the right of the thousands place. It is greater than 5, so round up.

2**4**,**8**62

Thousands place (4) — 8 is greater than 5. Round up to 25,000.

To the nearest thousand, the population of Hampstead was 25,000.

Problem B

Remind students that population density is a measure of the average number of people in a given area.

The population density of Hampstead was 70.342 people per square kilometer. What was the density to the nearest tenth?

Round 70.342 to the nearest tenth.

Solution

Look at the digit to the right of the tenths place. It is less than 5, so round down.

70.**34**2

Tenths place (3) — 4 is less than 5. Round down to 70.3.

To the nearest tenth, the density of Hampstead was 70.3 people per square kilometer.

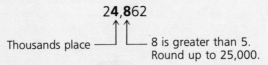

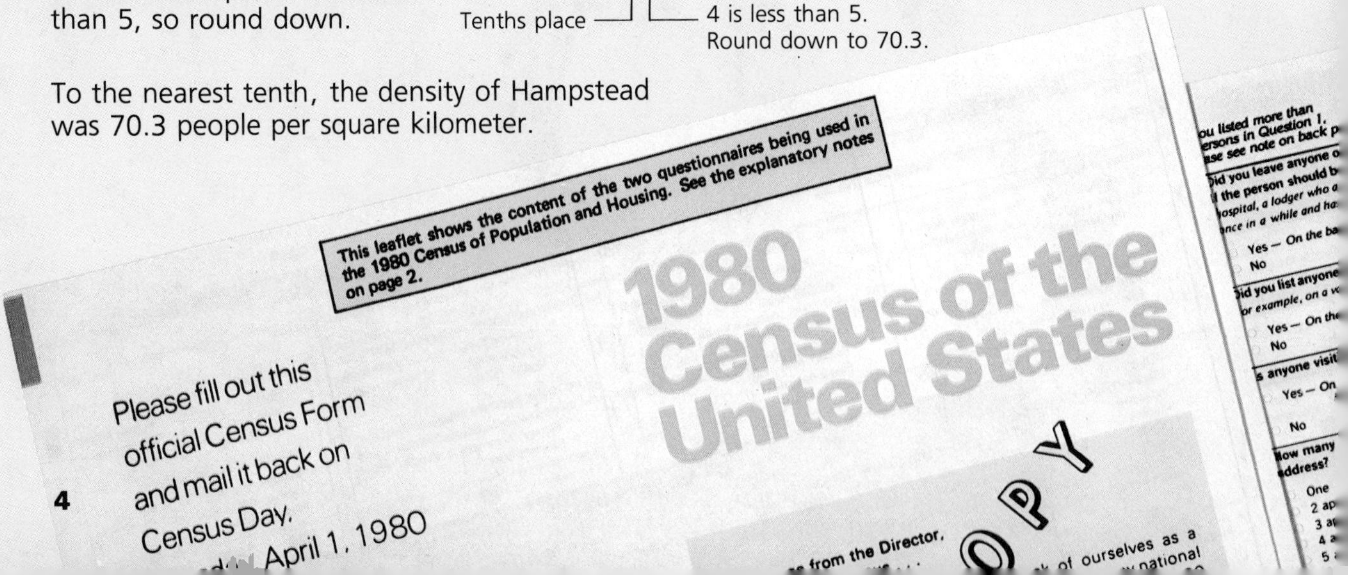
This leaflet shows the content of the two questionnaires being used in the 1980 Census of Population and Housing. See the explanatory notes on page 2.
1980 Census of the United States
Please fill out this official Census Form and mail it back on Census Day.
April 1, 1980
COPY

Each exercise set contains exercises that are the same type as the Problem/Solution example with the same letter. The set of related problems contains applications of the skills taught.

Answers to odd-numbered exercises are given at the end of the student's text on pages 418-451.

Exercises

Set A Round each number to the nearest thousand, nearest hundred, and nearest ten.

1. 1536
2000; 1500; 1540
2. 2321
2000; 2300; 2320
3. 4872
5000; 4900; 4870
4. 855
1000; 900; 860
5. 927
1000; 900; 930
6. 5013
5000; 5000; 5010
7. 6005
6000; 6000; 6010
8. 80,089
80,000; 80,100; 80,090
9. 7002
7000; 7000; 7000
10. 16,010
16,000; 16,000; 16,010

Set B Round each number to the nearest whole number, nearest tenth, and nearest hundredth.

11. 12.684
13; 12.7; 12.68
12. 5.27
5; 5.3; 5.27
13. 13.882
14; 13.9; 13.88
14. 17.5039
18; 17.5; 17.50
15. 47.973
48; 48.0; 47.97
16. 126.1293
126; 126.1; 126.13
17. 320.709
321; 320.7; 320.71
18. 97.005
97; 97.0; 97.01
19. 100.084
100; 100.1; 100.08
20. 10.002
10; 10.0; 10.00

Related Problems

21. In 1980, Maryland had a population of about 4,216,446. What was the population to the nearest million?
4,000,000
22. In 1980, the population density of Maryland was 151.378 people per square kilometer. What was the density to the nearest tenth of a square kilometer?
151.4 people per square kilometer

Typical monthly electric bills (for 1980, 500 kilowatt-hours) for homes in four Maryland cities are listed below. Round each amount to the nearest ten cents and to the nearest dollar.

	City	Typical bill	Nearest ten cents	Nearest dollar
23.	Elkton	$28.06	$28.10	$28
24.	Greenbelt	$29.62	$29.60	$30
25.	Rockville	$30.15	$30.20	$30
26.	Frederick	$27.12	$27.10	$27

See Skills File, page 379, for more practice.

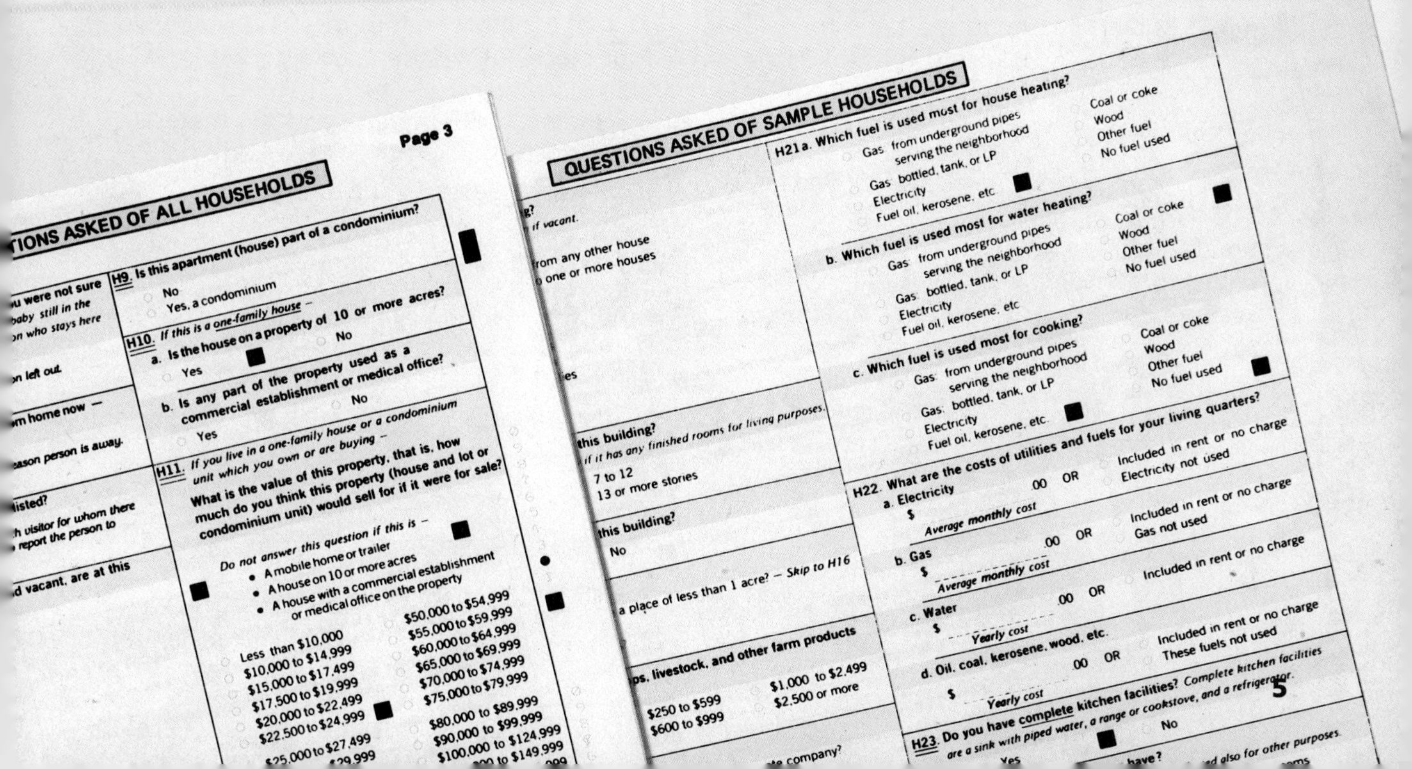

Objectives: Estimate sums and differences of whole numbers and decimals; add and subtract whole numbers and decimals.

Adding and Subtracting Whole Numbers and Decimals

> When adding or subtracting decimals, write the numbers so that the decimal points align.

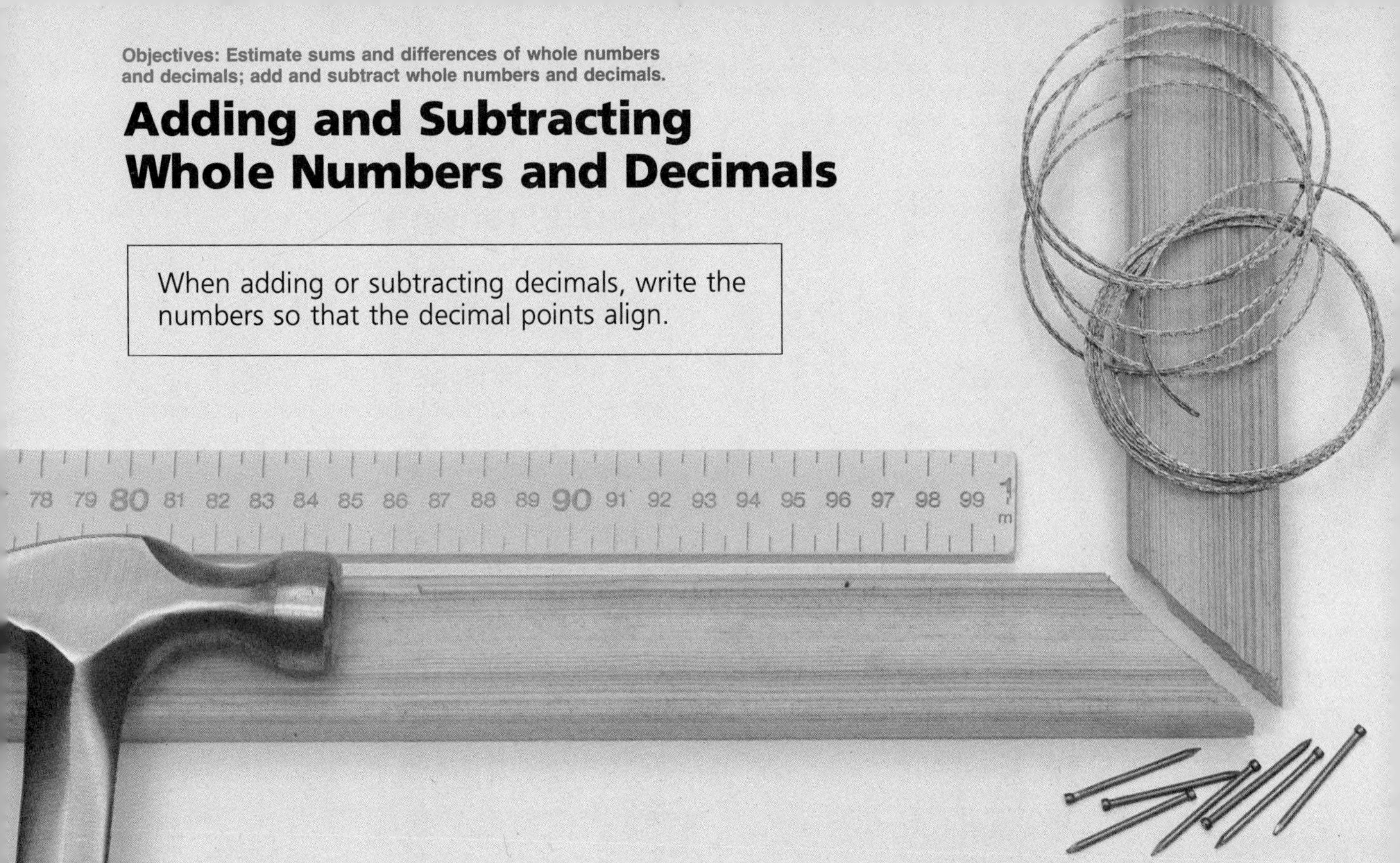

Problem A

Jim and Robin Rada bought a table for \$88, a chair for \$185, and a lamp for \$43. How much money did they spend?

Find \$88 + \$185 + \$43.

Solution

Stress estimation skills, as they are of prime importance with the use of calculators.

Estimate. Round each number to the same place and add.

88 ⟶	90
185 ⟶	190
43 ⟶	+ 40
	320

Find the actual sum.

$$\begin{array}{r} 88 \\ 185 \\ +\ 43 \\ \hline 316 \end{array}$$

Jim and Robin spent \$316.

The estimate is close to the actual sum, so the answer is reasonable.

You might point out that extra zeros may be annexed when adding or subtracting ragged decimals.

7.349 + 0.8 ⟶ $\begin{array}{r} 7.349 \\ +\ 0.800 \\ \hline \end{array}$

Problem B

To make picture frames, the Radas needed four pieces of wooden molding with the following measures: 2.36 meters, 4.8 meters, 1.52 meters, and 1.4 meters. How much molding did they need in all?

Find 2.36 + 4.8 + 1.52 + 1.4.

Solution

Estimate. Round each number to the same place and add.

2.36 ⟶	2
4.8 ⟶	5
1.52 ⟶	2
1.4 ⟶	+ 1
	10

Find the actual sum.

$$\begin{array}{r} 2.36 \\ 4.8 \\ 1.52 \\ +\ 1.4 \\ \hline 10.08 \end{array}$$

Align the decimal points.

The Radas needed 10.08 meters of molding.

Problem C

A frostless refrigerator costs $949, and a regular refrigerator costs $425. How much less does the regular refrigerator cost?

Find $949 − $425.

Solution

Estimate the difference.		Find the actual difference.
949 ⟶	900	949
425 ⟶	− 400	− 425
	500	524

The regular refrigerator costs $524 less.

Problem D

A bolt of fabric contained 8 meters of fabric. Robin bought 6.8 meters. How much fabric was left on the bolt?

Find 8 − 6.8.

Solution

Estimate the difference.		Find the actual difference.
8 ⟶	8	8.**0**
6.8 ⟶	− 7	− 6.8
	1	1.2

Sometimes you need to write extra zeros.

There was 1.2 meters of fabric left.

Exercises

Estimate each sum or difference. Then find each actual sum or difference.

Estimates may vary. Sample answers are given.

Set A

1. 42 + 28 + 39
110; 109

2. 23 + 46 + 267
340; 336

3. 74 + 12 + 18
100; 104

4. 86 + 58 + 17
170; 161

5. 62 + 129 + 243
430; 434

6. 81 + 56 + 25 + 34
200; 196

7. 93 + 8 + 17 + 18
140; 136

8. 267 + 194 + 301
800; 762

9. 356 + 217 + 592
1200; 1165

10. 101 + 463 + 786
1400; 1350

Set B

11. 4.7 + 40.25
45; 44.95

12. 63.91 + 12.28
76; 76.19

13. 1.82 + 3.47 + 1.9
7; 7.19

14. 1.31 + 0.35 + 2.5
4; 4.16

15. 2.34 + 6.79 + 5.28 + 4.05
18; 18.46

16. 1.04 + 3.71 + 8.65 + 7.249
21; 20.649

17. 0.57 + 0.93 + 0.15 + 1.08
3; 2.73

Set C

18. 31 − 19
10; 12

19. 82 − 38
40; 44

20. 67 − 42
30; 25

21. 91 − 7
80; 84

22. 806 − 489
300; 317

23. 983 − 779
200; 204

Set D

24. 47.3 − 21.2
26; 26.1

25. 95.85 − 8.16
88; 87.69

26. 73.51 − 41.6
32; 31.91

27. 40.933 − 36.2
5; 4.733

28. 53.9 − 8
46; 45.9

29. 27.31 − 18
9; 9.31

30. 18 − 5.6
12; 12.4

31. 27 − 12.45
15; 14.55

32. 83.73 − 17.008
67; 66.722

33. 45.6 − 14.986
31; 30.614

Related Problems

Extension problems are indicated with red circles.

34. Estimate the total cost of these items: tacks—$0.89; hammer—$2.95; varnish—$3.49; wire—$0.59.
$8

(35.) How much change would Jim receive if he paid for the items in problem 34 with a $20 bill?
$12.08

See Skills File, pages 380 and 381, for more practice.

Objectives: Estimate products of whole numbers; multiply whole numbers.

Multiplying Whole Numbers

You may wish to review the terms *factor* and *product.*

> When multiplying whole numbers that end in zeros, multiply the nonzero digits. Then count the zeros in both factors and write that number of zeros in your answer.

Problem A

Phil Miller planted 300 acres of corn. He expects a yield of 90 bushels per acre. What is his expected total yield?

Find 90 × 300.

Solution

9**0** × 3**00** = 27,**000**

Phil's expected total yield is 27,000 bushels of corn.

Problem B

Phil plants 94 pounds of wheat per acre. How much wheat will he need for 190 acres?

Find 94 × 190.

Solution

Point out that rounding each factor facilitates mental estimation.

Estimate. Round each factor so that only the first digit is not zero. Then multiply.

$$\begin{array}{ccccc} 94 & \times & 190 & & \\ \downarrow & & \downarrow & & \\ 90 & \times & 200 & = & 18{,}000 \end{array}$$

Find the actual product.

$$\begin{array}{r l} 190 & \\ \times\ \ 94 & \\ \hline 760 & \longleftarrow 4 \times 190 \\ 17100 & \longleftarrow 90 \times 190 \\ \hline 17860 & \end{array}$$

Phil will need 17,860 pounds of wheat.

Exercises

Set A Find each product.

1. 50 × 90
   4500
2. 700 × 60
   42,000
3. 7 × 2000
   14,000
4. 4000 × 3000
   12,000,000
5. 600 × 800
   480,000
6. 9 × 700
   6300
7. 9000 × 600
   5,400,000
8. 60 × 500
   30,000
9. 800 × 50
   40,000
10. 60 × 300
    18,000
11. 90 × 20
    1800
12. 5000 × 4
    20,000
13. 90 × 900
    81,000
14. 50 × 200
    10,000
15. 300 × 8
    2400
16. 40 × 9000
    360,000

Set B Estimate. Then find each product.

Encourage students to estimate mentally.

17. 53 × 28
    1500; 1484
18. 89 × 81
    7200; 7209
19. 54 × 19
    1000; 1026
20. 84 × 28
    2400; 2352
21. 184 × 74
    14,000; 13,616
22. 64 × 570
    36,000; 36,480
23. 58 × 304
    18,000; 17,632
24. 903 × 90
    81,000; 81,270
25. 237 × 456
    100,000; 108,072
26. 381 × 952
    400,000; 362,712
27. 214 × 301
    60,000; 64,414
28. 502 × 805
    400,000; 404,110
29. 1203 × 45
    50,000; 54,135
30. 4216 × 37
    160,000; 155,992
31. 94 × 7621
    720,000; 716,374
32. 79 × 6101
    480,000; 481,979
33. 8004 × 195
    1,600,000; 1,560,780
34. 496 × 4099
    2,000,000; 2,033,104
35. 506 × 4204
    2,000,000; 2,127, 224
36. 9007 × 705
    6,300,000; 6,349,935

Each exercise in mixed practice is the same type of exercise as in one of the other sets in the lesson.

Mixed Practice Find each product.

37. 3200 × 100
    320,000
38. 50 × 19
    950
39. 256 × 1382
    353,792
40. 1100 × 60
    66,000
41. 34 × 878
    29,852
42. 182 × 352
    64,064
43. 205 × 1200
    246,000
44. 8000 × 9
    72,000
45. 9000 × 5400
    48,600,000
46. 775 × 600
    465,000
47. 467 × 13
    6071
48. 67 × 79
    5293
49. 78 × 40
    3120
50. 200 × 700
    140,000
51. 802 × 43
    34,486
52. 1396 × 362
    505,352
53. 120 × 550
    66,000
54. 280 × 30
    8400
55. 17 × 194
    3298
56. 3060 × 500
    1,530,000
57. 80 × 200
    16,000
58. 29 × 649
    18,821
59. 260 × 1400
    364,000
60. 205 × 314
    64,370

Related Problems

61. Phil's neighbor expects to get 33 bushels of soybeans per acre from his 153-acre field. Estimate the total soybean production from the field.
    6000 bushels
62. Phil uses 32 pounds of oats to plant one acre. Will 500 pounds of oats be enough to plant 15 acres?
    Yes
63. Phil plants 14 pounds of corn per acre. How much corn will he need to plant his 300-acre field?
    4200 pounds
64. Last year Phil harvested 32 bushels of wheat per acre. What was the total amount of wheat harvested from his 190-acre field?
    6080 bushels

See Skills File, page 382, for more practice.

Objectives: Estimate products of decimals; multiply decimals.

Multiplying Decimals

When multiplying decimals, multiply as with whole numbers. Then add the number of decimal places in the factors to find the number of decimal places in the product. You might have to write extra zeros.

Problem A

A kilowatt-hour (kW•h) is the amount of electricity used to light a 100-watt light bulb for 10 hours.

Patsy Bowen's dishwasher uses about 0.9 kilowatt-hour of electricity per load. At $0.05 per kilowatt-hour, what is the cost of the electricity for one dishwasher load?

Find $0.05 × 0.9.

Solution

$$\begin{array}{r l} 0.9 & \longleftarrow \text{1 decimal place} \\ \times\ 0.05 & \longleftarrow \text{2 decimal places} \\ \hline 0.\mathbf{045} & \longleftarrow \text{3 decimal places} \end{array}$$

The electric cost for one dishwasher load is about $0.045.

Problem B

At $0.048 per kilowatt-hour, what is the cost per week to operate a refrigerator that uses about 42.5 kilowatt-hours of electricity a week?

Find $0.048 × 42.5.

Solution

Estimate. Round each factor to get a number with one nonzero digit. Then multiply.

$$\begin{array}{c c c c c} 0.048 & \times & 42.5 & & \\ \downarrow & & \downarrow & & \\ 0.05 & \times & 40 & = & 2 \end{array}$$

Find the actual product.

$$\begin{array}{r l} 42.5 & \longleftarrow \text{1 decimal place} \\ \times\ 0.048 & \longleftarrow \text{3 decimal places} \\ \hline 3400 & \\ 17000 & \\ \hline 2.0400 & \longleftarrow \text{4 decimal places} \end{array}$$

The cost per week to operate the refrigerator is about $2.04.

Exercises

Set A Find each product.

1. 0.4 × 0.2
   0.08
2. 0.3 × 0.1
   0.03
3. 0.08 × 0.8
   0.064
4. 0.7 × 0.03
   0.021
5. 0.09 × 0.04
   0.0036
6. 0.6 × 0.06
   0.036
7. 0.008 × 0.7
   0.0056
8. 0.005 × 5
   0.025
9. 0.005 × 500
   2.5
10. 6 × 0.03
    0.18
11. 9 × 0.009
    0.081
12. 0.005 × 2
    0.01
13. 5000 × 0.8
    4000
14. 0.09 × 0.08
    0.0072
15. 0.4 × 0.05
    0.02
16. 0.001 × 0.01
    0.00001
17. 0.03 × 5000
    150
18. 600 × 0.05
    30
19. 900 × 0.006
    5.4
20. 0.09 × 700
    63

Set B Estimate. Then find each product.

21. 0.56 × 320
    180; 179.2
22. 2.7 × 0.043
    0.12; 0.1161
23. 0.79 × 0.052
    0.04; 0.04108
24. 86 × 0.42
    36; 36.12
25. 38.7 × 0.62
    24; 23.994
26. 4.5 × 11.6
    50; 52.2
27. 9.58 × 0.014
    0.1; 0.13412
28. 9.4 × 47.8
    450; 449.32
29. 8.808 × 2.1
    18; 18.4968
30. 0.3204 × 75
    24; 24.03
31. 0.45 × 1121
    500; 504.45
32. 2.9 × 1.989
    6; 5.7681
33. 0.946 × 0.187
    0.18; 0.176902
34. 0.609 × 1.97
    1.2; 1.19973
35. 83.1 × 0.288
    24; 23.9328
36. 587 × 4.62
    3000; 2711.94
37. 4.001 × 89.9
    360; 359.6899
38. 55.04 × 0.0436
    2.4; 2.399744
39. 5.603 × 3.21
    18; 17.98563
40. 61.91 × 0.873
    54; 54.04743

Mixed Practice Find each product.

41. 0.04 × 0.8
    0.032
42. 2.59 × 35
    90.65
43. 17 × 0.83
    14.11
44. 12.34 × 5.7
    70.338
45. 0.12 × 0.02
    0.0024
46. 4.8 × 6.3
    30.24
47. 120 × 0.03
    3.6
48. 0.158 × 44.2
    6.9836
49. 0.413 × 5.5
    2.2715
50. 1500 × 0.4
    600
51. 0.88 × 1409
    1239.92
52. 0.5 × 0.007
    0.0035
53. 0.601 × 80.7
    48.5007
54. 11 × 0.003
    0.033
55. 0.014 × 50
    0.7
56. 13 × 0.03
    0.39

Related Problems

57. At $0.049 per kilowatt-hour, what is the electric cost per year to operate a frostless refrigerator that uses about 1690 kilowatt-hours a year?
    $82.81
58. At $0.049 per kilowatt-hour, what is the electric cost per year to operate a standard electric water heater that uses about 6340 kilowatt-hours a year?
    $310.66
59. At $0.049 per kilowatt-hour, what is the electric cost per year to operate a "miser" electric water heater that uses about 5890 kilowatt-hours a year?
    $288.61
60. For one year, how much less is the electric cost for a miser water heater than for a standard water heater?
    $22.05

See Skills File, page 383, for more practice.

Objective: Divide whole numbers and decimals.

Dividing Whole Numbers and Decimals

You may wish to review the terms *dividend, divisor, quotient,* and *remainder.*

> When rounding a quotient, divide until there is one more decimal place than required. Write extra zeros in the dividend if necessary.
>
> When dividing by a decimal, make the divisor a whole number by "moving" the decimal point. Then "move" the decimal point in the dividend the same direction and the same number of places.

Problem A

The Masemore Construction Company owns property with 1375 feet of frontage along Willow View Road. How many lots 65 feet wide will fit along the road? How many feet of frontage will be left over?

Find 1375 ÷ 65.

Solution

```
      21 R10
65)1375
   130 <--- 2 × 65
    75
    65 <--- 1 × 65
    10
```

Use estimation to decide if the answer is reasonable. Round the quotient and the divisor and multiply.

21 × 65
↓ ↓
20 × 70 = 1400

Since 1400 is close to 1375, the estimate indicates that the answer, 21 R10, is reasonable.

Twenty-one 65-foot lots will fit along the road. There will be 10 feet of frontage left over.

Problem B

Marlin Masemore plans to divide a 22.8-acre plot of land into 18 lots. To the nearest hundredth of an acre, how large will each lot be?

Find 22.8 ÷ 18.

Solution

Remind students that zeros may be annexed without changing the value of a number.

```
     1.266 ≈ 1.27
18)22.800
   18
    4 8
    3 6
    1 20
    1 08
     120
     108
      12
```

Remember that ≈ means "is approximately equal to."

Continue dividing to the thousandths place. Then round to the nearest hundredth.

Use estimation to decide if the answer is reasonable. Round the quotient and the divisor and multiply.

1.27 × 18
↓ ↓
1 × 20 = 20

The answer is reasonable.

To the nearest hundredth of an acre, each lot will be 1.27 acres.

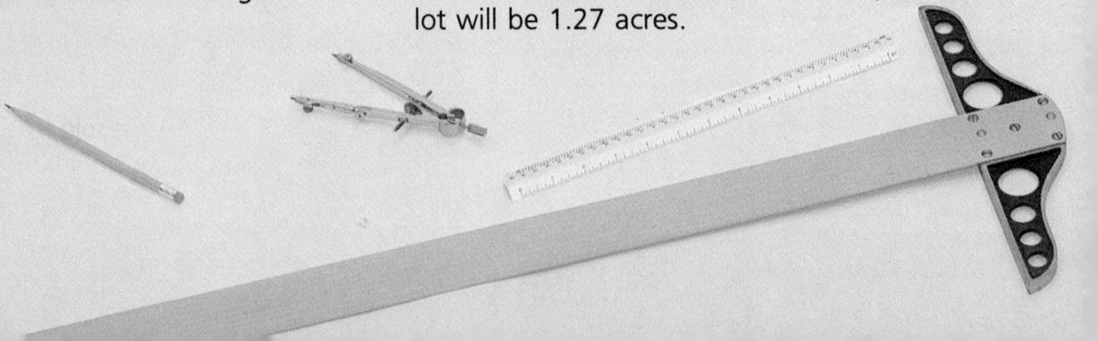

Problem C

Marlin bought a 2.1-acre plot of land for $975. To the nearest dollar, what was the price per acre?

Find $975 ÷ 2.1.

Solution

```
         46 4.2  ≈ 464
2.1)975.0 0
    84
    135
    126
      9 0
      8 4
        6 0
        4 2
        1 8
```

Continue dividing to the tenths place. Then round to the nearest whole number.

Use estimation to decide if the answer is reasonable.

$$464 \times 2.1$$
$$\downarrow \quad\quad \downarrow$$
$$500 \times 2 = 1000$$

The answer is reasonable.

To the nearest dollar, the price per acre was $464.

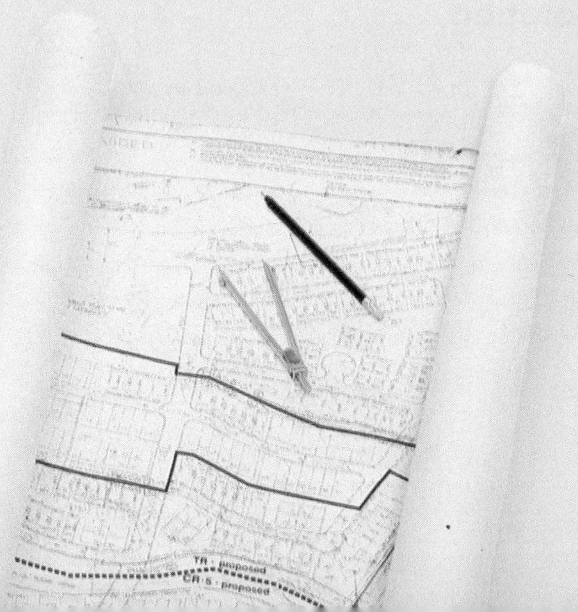

Exercises

Stress that students can use estimation to determine if their answers are reasonable.

Set A

Find each quotient. Estimate to decide if the answer is reasonable.

1. 3152 ÷ 8
394
2. 2128 ÷ 7
304
3. 830 ÷ 23
36 R2
4. 963 ÷ 49
19 R32
5. 3875 ÷ 78
49 R53
6. 2359 ÷ 61
38 R41
7. 39,565 ÷ 84
471 R1
8. 209,915 ÷ 32
6559 R27
9. 95,140 ÷ 543
175 R115
10. 182,216 ÷ 902
202 R12

Set B

Find each quotient to the nearest hundredth. Estimate to decide if the answer is reasonable.

11. 268.7 ÷ 9
29.86
12. 1834 ÷ 6
305.67
13. 41.52 ÷ 19
2.19
14. 5.42 ÷ 12
0.45
15. 15.6 ÷ 79
0.20
16. 79.9 ÷ 39
2.05
17. 118.62 ÷ 56
2.12
18. 21.6 ÷ 14
1.54
19. 1168 ÷ 242
4.83
20. 42.89 ÷ 381
0.11

Set C

Find each quotient to the nearest whole number. Estimate to decide if the answer is reasonable.

21. 71.52 ÷ 9.32
8
22. 58.9 ÷ 8.4
7
23. 11.53 ÷ 2.66
4
24. 4.4 ÷ 1.83
2
25. 19 ÷ 3.56
5
26. 0.08 ÷ 0.04
2
27. 9.3 ÷ 3.1
3
28. 604 ÷ 97.1
6
29. 0.635 ÷ 0.07
9
30. 8.3 ÷ 0.23
36

Related Problems

31. Marlin wants to put 14 lots along a plot of land with 1250 feet of road frontage. To the nearest tenth of a foot, how wide will each lot be?
89.3 feet
32. A 77.5-acre farm sold for $65,000. Find the price per acre, to the nearest dollar.
$839

See Skills File, pages 384 and 385, for more practice.

Objective: Compare and rename fractions and mixed numbers.

Comparing and Renaming Fractions and Mixed Numbers

You may wish to review the terms *multiple, common multiple, least common multiple, common factor,* and *greatest common factor.*

Multiplying or dividing both the numerator and the denominator of a fraction by the same number does not change the value of the fraction.

A fraction is in lowest terms if the only number that will divide both the numerator and the denominator is 1.

Problem A

Mrs. Gourley's Home Ec class plans to make rye bread. The recipe for *Grandma's Rye Bread* calls for $5\frac{2}{3}$ cups of flour. The recipe for *Old-Fashioned Rye Bread* calls for $5\frac{3}{4}$ cups of flour. Which recipe uses less flour?

Compare $5\frac{2}{3}$ and $5\frac{3}{4}$.

Solution

Since $5\frac{2}{3}$ and $5\frac{3}{4}$ have the same whole number, consider only the fractions, $\frac{2}{3}$ and $\frac{3}{4}$.

List the multiples of 4 until you have a multiple of 3.

4 8 **12** 12 is a common multiple of 4 and 3.

Write each fraction with a denominator of 12.

$\frac{2}{3} = \frac{2 \times 4}{3 \times 4} = \frac{8}{12}$

$\frac{3}{4} = \frac{3 \times 3}{4 \times 3} = \frac{9}{12}$

Compare $\frac{8}{12}$ and $\frac{9}{12}$.

$\frac{8}{12} < \frac{9}{12}$

$\downarrow \quad \downarrow$

$\frac{2}{3} < \frac{3}{4}$

Remember, $>$ means "is greater than," and $<$ means "is less than." $8 < 9$, so $\frac{8}{12} < \frac{9}{12}$.

$5\frac{2}{3} < 5\frac{3}{4}$

The recipe for *Grandma's Rye Bread* uses less flour.

Problem B

Sheila bought $\frac{24}{36}$ of a yard (24 inches) of elastic for a skirt.

Rename $\frac{24}{36}$ in lowest terms.

Solution

Point out that reducing some fractions to lowest terms may be done in one step or in several.

$\frac{24}{36} = \frac{24 \div 6}{36 \div 6} = \frac{4}{6}$

$\frac{4}{6} = \frac{4 \div 2}{6 \div 2} = \frac{2}{3}$

$\frac{2}{3}$ is in lowest terms because the only number that divides both 2 and 3 is 1.

$\frac{24}{36} = \frac{2}{3}$

In lowest terms, $\frac{24}{36}$ is $\frac{2}{3}$.

Problem C

Rick bought $2\frac{3}{4}$ yards of fabric for pillows.

Rename $2\frac{3}{4}$ as a fraction.

Solution

$2\frac{3}{4} = \frac{4 \times 2 + 3}{4} = \frac{11}{4}$

Multiply 2 by 4 to find the number of fourths in 2. Then add 3.

$2\frac{3}{4} = \frac{11}{4}$

As a fraction, $2\frac{3}{4}$ is $\frac{11}{4}$.

Problem D

Jamie measured $\frac{5}{4}$ cups of milk for biscuits. Rename $\frac{5}{4}$ as a mixed number.

Solution

$\frac{5}{4}$ means $5 \div 4$.

$$\begin{array}{r} 1\frac{1}{4} \\ 4\overline{)5} \\ \underline{4} \\ 1 \end{array}$$

Divide the numerator by the denominator. Then express the remainder as a fraction.

As a mixed number, $\frac{5}{4}$ is $1\frac{1}{4}$.

Exercises

Set A Compare these fractions or mixed numbers. Replace ● with <, >, or =.

1. $\frac{3}{4}$ ● $\frac{9}{16}$ >
2. $\frac{4}{7}$ ● $\frac{1}{2}$ >
3. $\frac{1}{3}$ ● $\frac{2}{5}$ <
4. $\frac{5}{6}$ ● $\frac{8}{9}$ <
5. $\frac{3}{4}$ ● $\frac{3}{5}$ >
6. $\frac{1}{2}$ ● $\frac{8}{16}$ =
7. $2\frac{4}{9}$ ● $2\frac{5}{12}$ >
8. $8\frac{1}{3}$ ● $9\frac{1}{6}$ <
9. $1\frac{5}{6}$ ● $1\frac{5}{8}$ >

Set B Rename in lowest terms.

10. $\frac{8}{10}$ $\frac{4}{5}$
11. $\frac{18}{24}$ $\frac{3}{4}$
12. $\frac{24}{40}$ $\frac{3}{5}$
13. $\frac{10}{25}$ $\frac{2}{5}$
14. $\frac{75}{100}$ $\frac{3}{4}$
15. $\frac{42}{56}$ $\frac{3}{4}$
16. $\frac{22}{66}$ $\frac{1}{3}$
17. $\frac{24}{72}$ $\frac{1}{3}$

Set C Rename as a fraction.

18. $2\frac{4}{5}$ $\frac{14}{5}$
19. $9\frac{2}{3}$ $\frac{29}{3}$
20. 4 $\frac{4}{1}$
21. $4\frac{5}{12}$ $\frac{53}{12}$
22. $2\frac{5}{16}$ $\frac{37}{16}$
23. $6\frac{7}{8}$ $\frac{55}{8}$
24. $3\frac{5}{6}$ $\frac{23}{6}$
25. $7\frac{1}{10}$ $\frac{71}{10}$

Set D Rename as a mixed number.

26. $\frac{28}{5}$ $5\frac{3}{5}$
27. $\frac{14}{3}$ $4\frac{2}{3}$
28. $\frac{24}{7}$ $3\frac{3}{7}$
29. $\frac{72}{8}$ 9
30. $\frac{42}{12}$ $3\frac{1}{2}$
31. $\frac{24}{10}$ $2\frac{2}{5}$
32. $\frac{34}{6}$ $5\frac{2}{3}$
33. $\frac{48}{16}$ 3

Related Problems

34. A recipe for salad dressing calls for $\frac{5}{8}$ cup of oil and $\frac{3}{4}$ cup of vinegar. Does the recipe use more oil or more vinegar?
Vinegar

35. Dan has $\frac{2}{3}$ cup of oil. His recipe calls for $\frac{7}{8}$ cup. Does he have enough oil?
No

See Skills File, page 386, for more practice.

Break Time

In the division below, replace each symbol with a different digit. Identical symbols represent the same digit.

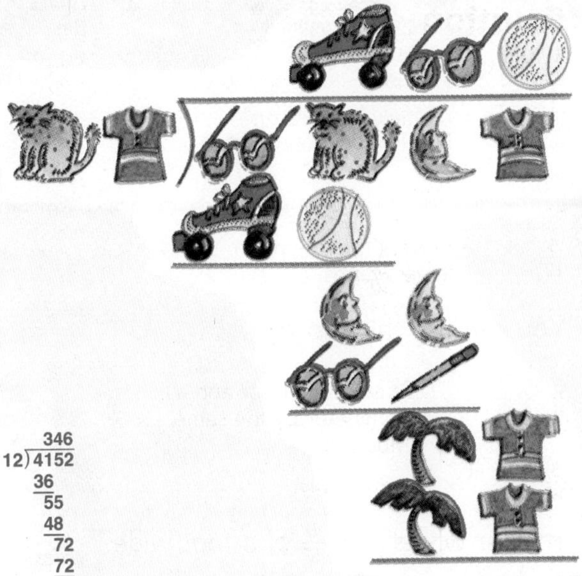

$$\begin{array}{r} 346 \\ 12\overline{)4152} \\ \underline{36} \\ 55 \\ \underline{48} \\ 72 \\ \underline{72} \end{array}$$

The Break Time feature occurs in each chapter. It is an interesting problem or puzzle that usually does not involve computational skills. Encourage students of all ability levels to try the Break Times.

Objectives: Estimate products and quotients of mixed numbers; multiply and divide fractions and mixed numbers.

Multiplying and Dividing Fractions and Mixed Numbers

> When multiplying fractions, first multiply the numerators. Then multiply the denominators.
>
> To divide fractions and mixed numbers, multiply the dividend by the reciprocal of the divisor.

Problem A

The wheels on John Sauble's car are $\frac{5}{8}$ as wide as the wheels on his pickup truck. The truck wheels are $\frac{2}{3}$ of a foot wide. How wide are the car wheels?

Find $\frac{5}{8} \times \frac{2}{3}$.

Solution

Encourage students to simplify fractions before multiplying.

$\frac{5}{8} \times \frac{2}{3}$

$\frac{5 \times 2}{8 \times 3}$ Multiply numerators. Multiply denominators.

$\frac{10}{24}$

$\frac{5}{12}$ Express the answer in lowest terms.

You can use this shortcut.

$\frac{5}{\cancel{8}_{4}} \times \frac{\cancel{2}^{1}}{3}$ Divide a numerator and a denominator by the same number, 2.

$\frac{5}{12}$ Then multiply.

The car wheels are $\frac{5}{12}$ of a foot wide.

Problem B

The fuel tank of John's semitrailer truck holds $3\frac{1}{3}$ times as much as the fuel tank of his car. The car fuel tank holds $14\frac{1}{2}$ gallons. How much does the truck fuel tank hold?

Find $3\frac{1}{3} \times 14\frac{1}{2}$.

Solution

Students are directed to estimate only with mixed numbers to eliminate the possibility of rounding to zero.

Estimate. Round each factor to the nearest whole number. If the fraction is $\frac{1}{2}$ or greater, round up. If the fraction is less than $\frac{1}{2}$, round down.

$3\frac{1}{3} \times 14\frac{1}{2}$

$\downarrow \quad \downarrow$

$3 \times 15 = 45$

Find the actual product.

$3\frac{1}{3} \times 14\frac{1}{2}$

$\frac{10}{3} \times \frac{29}{2}$ Rename the mixed numbers as fractions.

$\frac{\cancel{10}^{5}}{3} \times \frac{29}{\cancel{2}_{1}}$ Divide a numerator and a denominator by the same number, 2. Then multiply.

$\frac{145}{3}$

$48\frac{1}{3}$ Rename the answer as a mixed number.

The truck fuel tank holds $48\frac{1}{3}$ gallons.

See page 14 of
Consumer Forms and Problems.

Problem C

John drove his pickup truck 170 miles in $3\frac{3}{4}$ hours. What was his average speed?

Find $170 \div 3\frac{3}{4}$.

Solution

$170 \div 3\frac{3}{4}$

$\frac{170}{1} \div \frac{15}{4}$ — Rename the whole or mixed numbers as fractions.

$\frac{170}{1} \times \frac{4}{15}$ — Multiply the dividend by the reciprocal of the divisor. Remember, $\frac{15}{4}$ and $\frac{4}{15}$ are reciprocals because $\frac{15}{4} \times \frac{4}{15} = 1$.

$\frac{\overset{34}{\cancel{170}}}{1} \times \frac{4}{\underset{3}{\cancel{15}}}$ — Simplify.

$\frac{136}{3}$ — Multiply.

$45\frac{1}{3}$ — Express the answer as a mixed number.

Use estimation to decide if the answer is reasonable. Round the quotient and the divisor and multiply.

$45\frac{1}{3} \times 3\frac{3}{4}$

$\downarrow \qquad \downarrow$

$45 \times 4 = 180$

Since 180 is close to 170, the estimate indicates that the answer, $45\frac{1}{3}$ is reasonable.

John's average speed was $45\frac{1}{3}$ miles per hour.

You may wish to have students experiment to find out when the quotient is less than one and when it is greater than one. They will discover that when the dividend is greater than the divisor, the quotient is greater than one. When the dividend is less than the divisor, the quotient is less than one.

Exercises

Set A Find each product.

1. $\frac{1}{2} \times \frac{5}{6}$ $\frac{5}{12}$ **3.** $\frac{3}{5} \times \frac{5}{6}$ $\frac{1}{2}$ **5.** $\frac{1}{5} \times 4$ $\frac{4}{5}$

2. $\frac{1}{4} \times \frac{2}{3}$ $\frac{1}{6}$ **4.** $\frac{7}{10} \times \frac{15}{28}$ $\frac{3}{8}$ **6.** $\frac{7}{8} \times 6$ $5\frac{1}{4}$

Set B Estimate. Then find each product.

7. $3\frac{1}{2} \times 1\frac{1}{5}$ 4; $4\frac{1}{5}$ **10.** $2\frac{11}{12} \times 6$ 18; $17\frac{1}{2}$

8. $2\frac{3}{16} \times 1\frac{3}{5}$ 4; $3\frac{1}{2}$ **11.** $4 \times 8\frac{7}{8}$ 36; $35\frac{1}{2}$

9. $4\frac{1}{3} \times 3\frac{3}{5}$ 16; $15\frac{3}{5}$ **12.** $1\frac{5}{6} \times 5\frac{1}{3}$ 10; $9\frac{7}{9}$

Set C Find each quotient. Estimate to decide if the answer is reasonable.

13. $2\frac{2}{3} \div 3\frac{1}{5}$ $\frac{5}{6}$ **16.** $6\frac{3}{8} \div 2\frac{1}{8}$ 3

14. $3\frac{1}{8} \div 1\frac{1}{4}$ $2\frac{1}{2}$ **17.** $4\frac{1}{3} \div 1\frac{1}{6}$ $3\frac{5}{7}$

15. $4\frac{1}{5} \div 2\frac{1}{3}$ $1\frac{4}{5}$ **18.** $8\frac{5}{6} \div 2\frac{2}{3}$ $3\frac{5}{16}$

Mixed Practice Multiply or divide.

19. $1\frac{2}{3} \div \frac{7}{9}$ $2\frac{1}{7}$ **24.** $\frac{1}{2} \times 4\frac{1}{2} \times 3\frac{1}{3}$ $7\frac{1}{2}$

20. $5\frac{1}{3} \times \frac{1}{2}$ $2\frac{2}{3}$ **25.** $3\frac{1}{3} \div \frac{5}{6}$ 4

21. $12\frac{3}{8} \div 8\frac{1}{4}$ $1\frac{1}{2}$ **26.** $\frac{5}{6} \div 2\frac{1}{2}$ $\frac{1}{3}$

22. $3 \div 1\frac{1}{3}$ $2\frac{1}{4}$ **27.** $\frac{1}{2} \times \frac{2}{3} \times \frac{5}{8}$ $\frac{5}{24}$

23. $2\frac{5}{8} \times \frac{5}{6}$ $2\frac{3}{16}$ **28.** $2\frac{1}{2} \div 3\frac{1}{8}$ $\frac{4}{5}$

Related Problems

29. At 50 miles per hour, how far can John drive in $7\frac{1}{2}$ hours?
375 miles

30. John's semitrailer truck travels $8\frac{1}{3}$ miles per gallon of fuel. How much fuel will be used during a 3200-mile trip?
384 gallons

See Skills File, pages 387 and 388, for more practice.

Objectives: Estimate sums and differences of fractions and mixed numbers; add and subtract fractions and mixed numbers.

Adding and Subtracting Fractions and Mixed Numbers

> When adding or subtracting fractions and mixed numbers, write the fractions with a common denominator.

Problem A

Melinda Tanaka bought stock when the selling price was $8\frac{3}{4}$ ($8\frac{3}{4}$ dollars) per share. During the next quarter (three months), the value of a share rose $3\frac{7}{8}$ ($3\frac{7}{8}$ dollars). What was the new selling price of the stock?

Find $8\frac{3}{4} + 3\frac{7}{8}$.

Solution

Be sure that students can rename mixed numbers when simplifying answers $\left(12\frac{11}{8} = 13\frac{3}{8}\right)$ and when subtracting $\left(15\frac{1}{4} = 14\frac{5}{4}\right)$.

Estimate. Round to the nearest whole number.

$$\begin{array}{lr} 8\frac{3}{4} \longrightarrow & 9 \\ 3\frac{7}{8} \longrightarrow & +\ 4 \\ \hline & 13 \end{array}$$

Find the actual sum.

$$\begin{array}{r} 8\frac{3}{4} = 8\ \frac{6}{8} \\ +\ 3\frac{7}{8} = 3\ \frac{7}{8} \\ \hline 11\frac{13}{8} \end{array}$$

Write the fractions with a common denominator. Then add the numerators and use the common denominator. Add the whole numbers.

$11\frac{13}{8} = 11 + 1\frac{5}{8} = 12\frac{5}{8}$ Simplify the answer.

The new selling price of the stock was $12\frac{5}{8}$ ($12\frac{5}{8}$ dollars).

Problem B

The high and low prices for a given quarter were $15\frac{1}{4}$ ($15\frac{1}{4}$ dollars) and $12\frac{3}{8}$ ($12\frac{3}{8}$ dollars). Find the difference between the high and the low prices.

Find $15\frac{1}{4} - 12\frac{3}{8}$.

Solution

Estimate. Round to the nearest whole number.

$$\begin{array}{lr} 15\frac{1}{4} \longrightarrow & 15 \\ 12\frac{3}{8} \longrightarrow & -\ 12 \\ \hline & 3 \end{array}$$

Find the actual difference.

$$\begin{array}{r} 15\frac{1}{4} = 15\frac{2}{8} = 14\frac{10}{8} \\ -\ 12\frac{3}{8} = 12\frac{3}{8} = 12\ \frac{3}{8} \\ \hline 2\ \frac{7}{8} \end{array}$$

Write the fractions with a common denominator. Since $\frac{3}{8}$ cannot be subtracted from $\frac{2}{8}$, rename $15\frac{2}{8}$ as $14\frac{10}{8}$. Then subtract.

The difference between the high and the low prices was $2\frac{7}{8}$ ($2\frac{7}{8}$ dollars).

Exercises

Set A Find each sum.

1. $\frac{1}{8} + \frac{1}{3}$ $\frac{11}{24}$
2. $\frac{5}{6} + \frac{1}{4}$ $1\frac{1}{12}$
3. $\frac{3}{7} + \frac{1}{2}$ $\frac{13}{14}$
4. $\frac{3}{4} + \frac{4}{5}$ $1\frac{11}{20}$
5. $\frac{9}{16} + \frac{5}{8}$ $1\frac{3}{16}$
6. $\frac{1}{12} + \frac{2}{3}$ $\frac{3}{4}$
7. $\frac{1}{4} + \frac{5}{9}$ $\frac{29}{36}$
8. $\frac{3}{7} + \frac{1}{3}$ $\frac{16}{21}$
9. $\frac{1}{2} + \frac{5}{8} + \frac{5}{6}$ $1\frac{23}{24}$
10. $\frac{2}{3} + \frac{1}{2} + \frac{3}{5}$ $1\frac{23}{30}$

Estimate. Then find each sum.

11. $2\frac{1}{3} + 4\frac{5}{6}$ 7; $7\frac{1}{6}$
12. $7\frac{3}{5} + 9\frac{1}{10}$ 17; $16\frac{7}{10}$
13. $1\frac{3}{4} + 1\frac{1}{10}$ 3; $2\frac{17}{20}$
14. $2\frac{6}{7} + 3\frac{1}{3}$ 6; $6\frac{4}{21}$
15. $6\frac{2}{3} + 4\frac{1}{4}$ 11; $10\frac{11}{12}$
16. $4\frac{7}{8} + 1\frac{4}{5}$ 7; $6\frac{27}{40}$
17. $12\frac{3}{8} + \frac{2}{3}$ 13; $13\frac{1}{24}$
18. $3\frac{5}{7} + \frac{1}{2}$ 5; $4\frac{3}{14}$
19. $8\frac{1}{16} + 2\frac{7}{8}$ 11; $10\frac{15}{16}$
20. $4\frac{4}{5} + 5\frac{2}{3}$ 11; $10\frac{7}{15}$
21. $2\frac{1}{4} + 1\frac{1}{5} + 4\frac{1}{2}$ 8; $7\frac{19}{20}$
22. $10\frac{2}{3} + 3\frac{7}{8} + 4\frac{1}{6}$ 19; $18\frac{17}{24}$

Set B Find each difference.

23. $\frac{5}{8} - \frac{1}{2}$ $\frac{1}{8}$
24. $\frac{3}{5} - \frac{1}{2}$ $\frac{1}{10}$
25. $\frac{11}{12} - \frac{2}{3}$ $\frac{1}{4}$
26. $\frac{3}{4} - \frac{2}{5}$ $\frac{7}{20}$
27. $\frac{7}{8} - \frac{5}{6}$ $\frac{1}{24}$
28. $\frac{1}{3} - \frac{1}{4}$ $\frac{1}{12}$
29. $\frac{3}{8} - \frac{1}{3}$ $\frac{1}{24}$
30. $\frac{1}{2} - \frac{2}{7}$ $\frac{3}{14}$
31. $4 - \frac{3}{5}$ $3\frac{2}{5}$
32. $10 - \frac{5}{16}$ $9\frac{11}{16}$

Estimate. Then find each difference.

33. $6\frac{1}{8} - 2\frac{7}{8}$ 3; $3\frac{1}{4}$
34. $27\frac{1}{3} - 18$ 9; $9\frac{1}{3}$
35. $16 - 4\frac{3}{8}$ 12; $11\frac{5}{8}$
36. $11 - 2\frac{5}{12}$ 9; $8\frac{7}{12}$
37. $12\frac{1}{3} - 7\frac{1}{9}$ 5; $5\frac{2}{9}$
38. $14\frac{5}{8} - 5\frac{3}{4}$ 9; $8\frac{7}{8}$
39. $15\frac{1}{2} - 1\frac{11}{16}$ 14; $13\frac{13}{16}$
40. $17\frac{5}{6} - 9\frac{2}{3}$ 8; $8\frac{1}{6}$
41. $12\frac{3}{5} - 4\frac{3}{4}$ 8; $7\frac{17}{20}$
42. $16\frac{2}{9} - 2\frac{5}{6}$ 13; $13\frac{7}{18}$
43. $10\frac{1}{3} - 4\frac{7}{8}$ 5; $5\frac{11}{24}$
44. $11\frac{1}{4} - 3\frac{5}{6}$ 7; $7\frac{5}{12}$

Related Problems

45. Melinda bought another stock for $7\frac{1}{8}$. During the next quarter, it rose $4\frac{1}{2}$. Then, during the following quarter, it rose $4\frac{3}{4}$. What was the price of the stock at the end of the two quarters? $16\frac{3}{8}$

46. At the beginning of the fourth quarter, the price of a stock was $16\frac{3}{8}$. During the quarter, the price fell $2\frac{7}{8}$. What was the price at the end of the quarter? $13\frac{1}{2}$

See Skills File, pages 389 and 390, for more practice.

CALCULATOR APPLICATIONS

Fractions as Decimals

Each chapter contains an optional set of problems to be done with a four-function calculator. These problems use or extend concepts taught previously in the chapter.

Stock quotations in newspapers list figures for stocks in fractional form. For instance, a price of $43\frac{3}{8}$ means $43\frac{3}{8}$ dollars. When used in computation, the figures are often written as decimals.

Write $43\frac{3}{8}$ as a decimal to the nearest thousandth.

First, use your calculator to find the decimal for $\frac{3}{8}$ to the nearest thousandth.

$\frac{3}{8} = 3 \div 8 = 0.375$

Then, use 0.375 for $\frac{3}{8}$ to rewrite $43\frac{3}{8}$.

$$\begin{aligned} 43\tfrac{3}{8} &= 43 + \tfrac{3}{8} \\ &= 43 + 0.375 \\ &= 43.375 \end{aligned}$$

Students could use this key sequence with mixed numbers:
Numerator [÷] Denominator [+] Whole number [=]

As a decimal to the nearest thousandth, $43\frac{3}{8}$ is 43.375.

Write each fraction or mixed number as a decimal to the nearest thousandth.

1. $\frac{5}{6}$ 0.833	**9.** $\frac{15}{52}$ 0.288	**17.** $2\frac{4}{5}$ 2.800	**25.** $17\frac{3}{11}$ 17.273
2. $\frac{7}{9}$ 0.778	**10.** $\frac{13}{16}$ 0.813	**18.** $10\frac{7}{8}$ 10.875	**26.** $20\frac{33}{111}$ 20.297
3. $\frac{11}{13}$ 0.846	**11.** $\frac{75}{70}$ 1.071	**19.** $14\frac{5}{12}$ 14.417	**27.** $53\frac{4}{9}$ 53.444
4. $\frac{20}{21}$ 0.952	**12.** $\frac{36}{17}$ 2.118	**20.** $27\frac{11}{16}$ 27.688	**28.** $12\frac{4}{99}$ 12.040
5. $\frac{5}{8}$ 0.625	**13.** $\frac{97}{37}$ 2.622	**21.** $31\frac{1}{15}$ 31.067	**29.** $15\frac{33}{99}$ 15.333
6. $\frac{23}{40}$ 0.575	**14.** $\frac{111}{24}$ 4.625	**22.** $40\frac{1}{18}$ 40.056	**30.** $8\frac{17}{99}$ 8.172
7. $\frac{7}{18}$ 0.389	**15.** $\frac{114}{15}$ 7.600	**23.** $2\frac{2}{11}$ 2.182	**31.** $6\frac{35}{99}$ 6.354
8. $\frac{37}{60}$ 0.617	**16.** $\frac{250}{100}$ 2.500	**24.** $3\frac{5}{9}$ 3.556	**32.** $4\frac{98}{99}$ 4.990

Chapter 1 Review

Items in the review cover each problem type in the chapter, lesson by lesson. The lesson titles and text pages are included so that students may refer back to these pages if necessary. Answers to all review problems are given at the end of the student's text.

Rounding whole numbers and decimals, pages 4–5

1. Round 7481 to the nearest thousand, nearest hundred, and nearest ten.
7000; 7500; 7480
2. Round 23.716 to the nearest whole number, nearest tenth, and nearest hundredth.
24; 23.7; 23.72

Adding and subtracting whole numbers and decimals, pages 6–7

3. $26 + 52 + 63$
141
4. $2.1 + 0.36 + 5.82$
8.28
5. $91 - 57$
34
6. $65.2 - 23.74$
41.46

Multiplying whole numbers, pages 8–9

7. 30×700
21,000
8. 576×42
24,192

Multiplying decimals, pages 10–11

9. 50×0.07
3.5
10. 5.23×6.7
35.041

Dividing whole numbers and decimals, pages 12–13

11. $9312 \div 16$
582
12. Find the quotient to the nearest hundredth for $43.6 \div 7$.
6.23
13. Find the quotient to the nearest whole number for $84.1 \div 0.24$.
350

Comparing and renaming fractions and mixed numbers, pages 14–15

14. Compare. Replace ● with $<$, $>$, or $=$.
$4\frac{2}{3}$ ● $4\frac{3}{5}$
$>$
15. Rename $\frac{12}{18}$ in lowest terms. $\frac{2}{3}$
16. Rename $4\frac{7}{8}$ as a fraction. $\frac{39}{8}$
17. Rename $\frac{28}{3}$ as a mixed number. $9\frac{1}{3}$

Multiplying and dividing fractions and mixed numbers, pages 16–17

18. $\frac{1}{3} \times \frac{5}{7}$ $\frac{5}{21}$
19. $1\frac{1}{6} \times 2\frac{2}{3}$ $3\frac{1}{9}$
20. $\frac{3}{4} \div \frac{1}{6}$ $4\frac{1}{2}$
21. $3\frac{1}{2} \div 1\frac{1}{4}$ $2\frac{4}{5}$

Adding and subtracting fractions and mixed numbers, pages 18–19

22. $\frac{3}{4} + \frac{1}{5}$ $\frac{19}{20}$
23. $2\frac{1}{3} + 3\frac{7}{8}$ $6\frac{5}{24}$
24. $\frac{7}{8} - \frac{2}{5}$ $\frac{19}{40}$
25. $5\frac{2}{3} - 2\frac{1}{9}$ $3\frac{5}{9}$

Chapter 1 Test

For each test, a table is given to help score the test.

Number of test items–25

Number missed	1	2	3	4	5	6	7	8	9	10	11	12
Percent correct	96	92	88	84	80	76	72	68	64	60	56	52

1. Round 3172 to the nearest thousand, nearest hundred, and nearest ten.
3000; 3200; 3170

2. Round 58.236 to the nearest whole number, nearest tenth, and nearest hundredth.
58; 58.2; 58.24

3. $32 + 74 + 25$
131

4. $8.12 + 3.27 + 5.64$
17.03

5. $83 - 26$
57

6. $57.36 - 24.71$
32.65

7. 20×800
16,000

8. 324×67
21,708

9. 0.7×0.04
0.028

10. 4.62×32
147.84

11. $3728 \div 6$
621 R2

12. Find the quotient to the nearest hundredth for $56.2 \div 9$.
6.24

13. Find the quotient to the nearest whole number for $15.55 \div 0.32$.
49

14. Compare. Replace ● with <, >, or =.
$2\frac{11}{12}$ ● $2\frac{3}{4}$
>

15. Rename $\frac{18}{27}$ in lowest terms. **$\frac{2}{3}$**

16. Rename $6\frac{2}{3}$ as a fraction. **$\frac{20}{3}$**

17. Rename $\frac{35}{4}$ as a mixed number. **$8\frac{3}{4}$**

18. $\frac{1}{2} \times \frac{3}{8}$ **$\frac{3}{16}$**

19. $1\frac{3}{4} \times 3\frac{1}{3}$ **$5\frac{5}{6}$**

20. $\frac{5}{6} \div \frac{4}{5}$ **$1\frac{1}{24}$**

21. $4\frac{2}{3} \div 3\frac{1}{2}$ **$1\frac{1}{3}$**

22. $\frac{2}{3} + \frac{1}{4}$ **$\frac{11}{12}$**

23. $2\frac{2}{5} + 1\frac{1}{3}$ **$3\frac{11}{15}$**

24. $\frac{5}{6} - \frac{2}{3}$ **$\frac{1}{6}$**

25. $4\frac{7}{8} - 1\frac{1}{2}$ **$3\frac{3}{8}$**

The Chapter Test parallels the Chapter Review, item for item.
The student's text does not contain any answers for test problems.

 See pages 1-2 of the *Test Masters* for an alternate form of the Chapter 1 Test.

Chapter 2 Equations, Proportions, and Percent

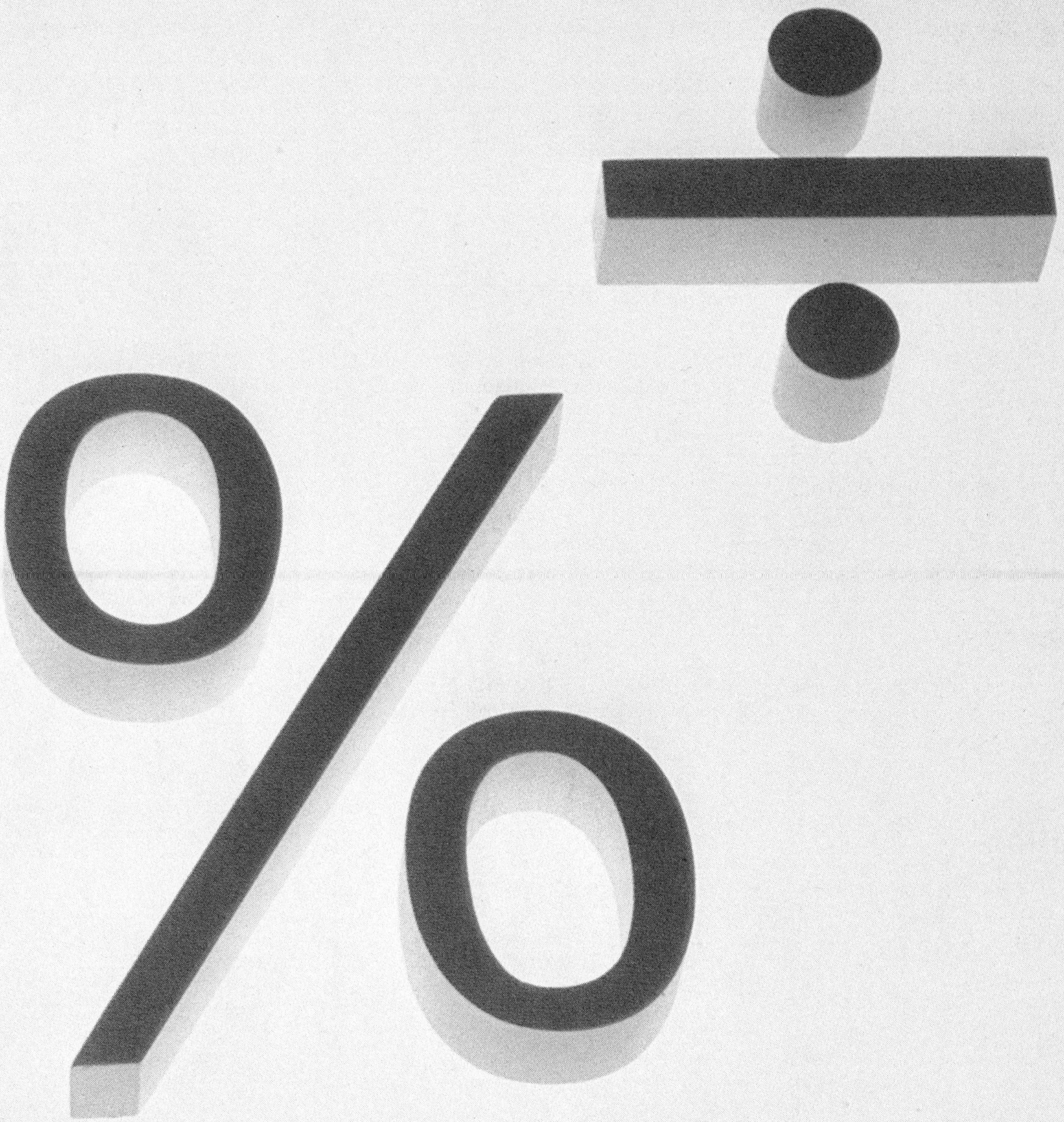

Objective: Solve addition and subtraction equations.

Addition and Subtraction Equations

See page T27 for additional notes and activities for Chapter 2.

> To solve an addition equation, subtract the same number from both sides. To solve a subtraction equation, add the same number to both sides.

Problem A

Bud ordered some prints of a photograph. The total bill was \$5.25, including postage. If the prints cost \$4.65, how much was postage?

Solve. $p + 4.65 = 5.25$

You might have students write a "skeleton" of the problem to lead them into the equation. For example:

postage + cost of prints = total cost

$p \quad + \quad 4.65 \quad = \quad 5.25$

Solution

$p + 4.65 = 5.25$	4.65 is added to p.
$p + 4.65 - 4.65 = 5.25 - 4.65$	To undo the addition, subtract 4.65 from both sides of the equation.
$p = 0.60$	

Check:

$p + 4.65 = 5.25$	Substitute 0.60 for p in the original equation.
$0.60 + 4.65 \stackrel{?}{=} 5.25$	
$5.25 = 5.25$	

The postage was \$0.60.

The equation for problem A might also be written as: $4.65 + p = 5.25$.

Problem B

Bud ordered film from a mail-order company and paid \$0.37 a roll less than the retail price. If he paid \$1.76 per roll, what was the retail price?

Solve. $r - 0.37 = 1.76$

Solution

$r - 0.37 = 1.76$	0.37 is subtracted from r.
$r - 0.37 + 0.37 = 1.76 + 0.37$	To undo the subtraction, add 0.37 to both sides of the equation.
$r = 2.13$	

Check:

$r - 0.37 = 1.76$	Substitute 2.13 for r in the original equation.
$2.13 - 0.37 \stackrel{?}{=} 1.76$	
$1.76 = 1.76$	

The retail price was \$2.13.

Problem B could also be solved with this equation: $r - 1.76 = 0.37$.

You might go through selected exercises orally and ask students what they would do to solve each equation.

Exercises

Point out that the variable can be on either side of the equation.

Set A Solve and check.

1. $a + 6 = 21$
$a = 15$

2. $d + 28 = 37$
$d = 9$

3. $f + 1.87 = 3.4$
$f = 1.53$

4. $x + 3.3 = 4$
$x = 0.7$

5. $9.2 = c + 2.9$
$c = 6.3$

6. $4 = b + 3.01$
$b = 0.99$

7. $8 = 3.9 + y$
$y = 4.1$

8. $4.7 = 2.7 + w$
$w = 2$

9. $m + 83 = 104$
$m = 21$

10. $r + 21 = 76.5$
$r = 55.5$

11. $t + 8.4 = 17.3$
$t = 8.9$

12. $x + 0.4 = 1.8$
$x = 1.4$

13. $2.7 + m = 8.7$
$m = 6$

14. $4.32 = r + 1.9$
$r = 2.42$

Set B Solve and check.

15. $g - 13 = 10$
$g = 23$

16. $m - 2 = 4$
$m = 6$

17. $h - 0.25 = 1.13$
$h = 1.38$

18. $a - 0.03 = 1.8$
$a = 1.83$

19. $7 = n - 17$
$n = 24$

20. $17 = r - 8$
$r = 25$

21. $0.09 = k - 0.7$
$k = 0.79$

22. $x - 0.8 = 1.3$
$x = 2.1$

23. $100 = m - 47$
$m = 147$

24. $3.4 = y - 8.1$
$y = 11.5$

25. $t - 31 = 4.8$
$t = 35.8$

26. $a - 8 = 7.4$
$a = 15.4$

27. $0.92 = x - 7.1$
$x = 8.02$

28. $0.4 = m - 3$
$m = 3.4$

Mixed Practice Solve and check.

29. $52 = 25 + t$
$t = 27$

30. $d - 47 = 77$
$d = 124$

31. $21 + m = 33$
$m = 12$

32. $32 = a + 6.3$
$a = 25.7$

33. $t - 0.26 = 0.67$
$t = 0.93$

34. $r + 4.08 = 5$
$r = 0.92$

35. $3.6 = s - 2$
$s = 5.6$

36. $26 = v + 22$
$v = 4$

37. $w - 43.19 = 8$
$w = 51.19$

38. $9.6 = 6.21 + x$
$x = 3.39$

39. $8 = y - 45$
$y = 53$

40. $z + 200 = 599$
$z = 399$

41. $p - 78 = 13$
$p = 91$

42. $7.9 = a - 30.7$
$a = 38.6$

43. $3.6 + b = 6.36$
$b = 2.76$

44. $s + 12.6 = 32$
$s = 19.4$

45. $3.5 = z - 5.55$
$z = 9.05$

46. $d - 3.8 = 6.3$
$d = 10.1$

47. $87.6 + g = 121$
$g = 33.4$

48. $17.6 = 3.1 + x$
$x = 14.5$

Related Problems

Write an equation for each problem. Then solve and check.
Equations may vary.

49. By using a coupon, Peg saved \$1.25 when she ordered prints. If she paid \$11.85, what was the regular price?
$r - 1.25 = 11.85$; \$13.10

50. Yana bought a camera case for \$14.75 plus tax. If his total bill was \$15.49, how much was the tax?
$t + 14.75 = 15.49$; \$0.74

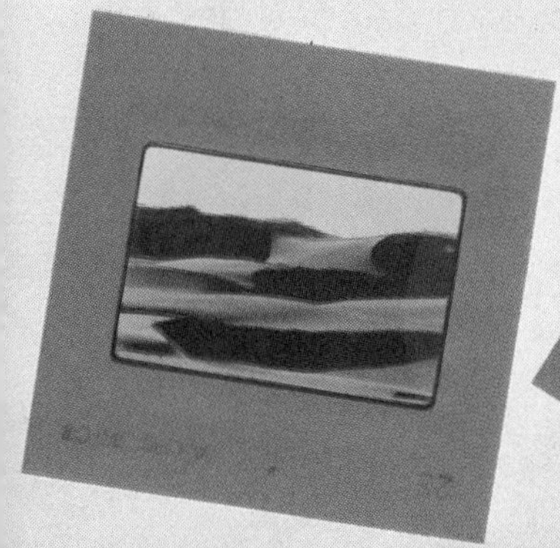

Objectives: Solve multiplication and division equations; combine like terms to solve equations.

Multiplication and Division Equations

> To solve a multiplication equation, divide both sides by the same number.
> To solve a division equation, multiply both sides by the same number.

Problem A

How many games were bowled if $82.45 was paid at a special rate of $0.85 per game?

Solve. $0.85g = 82.45$

Solution

$0.85g = 82.45$ — $0.85g$ means $0.85 \times g$.

$\frac{0.85g}{0.85} = \frac{82.45}{0.85}$ — To undo the multiplication, divide both sides of the equation by 0.85.

$g = 97$

Check:

$$0.85g = 82.45$$
$$0.85(97) \stackrel{?}{=} 82.45$$
$$82.45 = 82.45$$

Be sure students understand the use of parentheses to show multiplication.

97 games were bowled.

Problem B

A team's average was 86.2 pins per game in 15 games. What was the total number of pins?

Solve. $\frac{p}{15} = 86.2$

Solution

$\frac{p}{15} = 86.2$ — $\frac{p}{15}$ means $p \div 15$.

$\frac{p}{15}(15) = 86.2(15)$ — To undo the division, multiply both sides of the equation by 15.

$p = 1293$

Check:

$$\frac{p}{15} = 86.2$$
$$\frac{1293}{15} \stackrel{?}{=} 86.2$$
$$86.2 = 86.2$$

The total number of pins was 1293.

Before solving this problem, you may want to have students practice combining like terms, such as $9x + 5x$, $12n - 7n$, and $16r - r$.

Problem C

There are 8 students in the beginning bowling class and 9 students in the advanced class. Each student rented shoes, and the total charge for shoe rental was $12.75. What was the rental charge for each pair of shoes?

Solve. $8c + 9c = 12.75$

Solution

$8c + 9c = 12.75$ — Combine like terms. $8c$ and $9c$ are like terms because 8 and 9 are both multiplied by c. $8c + 9c = (8 + 9)c = 17c$

$17c = 12.75$

$\frac{17c}{17} = \frac{12.75}{17}$ — To undo the multiplication, divide both sides by 17.

$c = 0.75$

Check:

$$8c + 9c = 12.75$$
$$8(0.75) + 9(0.75) \stackrel{?}{=} 12.75$$
$$6 + 6.75 \stackrel{?}{=} 12.75$$
$$12.75 = 12.75$$

The rental charge for each pair of shoes was $0.75.

Exercises

Set A Solve and check.

1. $3a = 141$
$a = 47$

2. $1.2b = 8.4$
$b = 7$

3. $153 = 9c$
$c = 17$

4. $0.8x = 72$
$x = 90$

5. $3.15 = 3.5x$
$x = 0.9$

Set B Solve and check.

6. $\frac{d}{5} = 0.08$
$d = 0.4$

7. $\frac{f}{0.2} = 3$
$f = 0.6$

8. $0.45 = \frac{g}{0.7}$
$g = 0.315$

9. $\frac{r}{0.8} = 19$
$r = 15.2$

10. $0.04 = \frac{h}{25}$
$h = 1$

Set C Solve and check.

11. $7a + 8a = 45$
$a = 3$

12. $10c - 2c = 32$
$c = 4$

13. $99 = 5t + 6t$
$t = 9$

14. $0.2d + 2.2d = 48$
$d = 20$

15. $84 = 15x - 8x$
$x = 12$

Mixed Practice

Solve and check.

16. $0.5r = 17.5$
$r = 35$

17. $\frac{f}{0.16} = 0.6$
$f = 0.096$

18. $17c + 28c = 45$
$c = 1$

19. $47y = 0$
$y = 0$

20. $2b + 2b + 3b = 56$
$b = 8$

21. $0.09z = 8.1$
$z = 90$

22. $\frac{x}{5.07} = 1.1$
$x = 5.577$

23. $1.08 = 0.27s$
$s = 4$

24. $12a + a = 26$
$a = 2$

25. $318x - 167x = 0$
$x = 0$

26. $\frac{d}{0.5} = 0.8$
$d = 0.4$

27. $3.5 = 0.07x$
$x = 50$

28. $105 = 16q - q$
$q = 7$

29. $\frac{k}{4.018} = 0$
$k = 0$

30. $0.22 = \frac{m}{1.7}$
$m = 0.374$

Related Problems

Write an equation for each problem. Then solve and check.

Equations may vary.

31. The cost of bowling one game is $0.85. How many games could Tim bowl for $7.65?
$0.85g = 7.65$; 9 games

32. The women's league had 2 sessions. In the first session, 108 games were bowled. In the second, 159 games were bowled. If a total of $253.65 was collected, what was the cost of each game?
$108c + 159c = 253.65$; $0.95

33. In Sandy's league, there are 5 people on every team. Each team bowls 3 games a week. The league bowls a total of 135 games per week. How many teams are in the league?
$15t = 135$; 9 teams

Objective: Solve two-step equations.

Two-Step Equations

Problem A

Before he retired, Bill Oberle purchased a 4-unit apartment building as an investment. From the rent he collects each month, Bill pays out \$600 for expenses. How much rent must he charge for each of the 4 apartments if he wants to make \$500 profit each month? The amount of rent is the same for each of the apartments.

Solve. $4r - 600 = 500$

Solution

$$4r - 600 = 500$$

r is multiplied by 4 and 600 is subtracted from 4*r*.

$$4r - 600 + 600 = 500 + 600$$

To undo the subtraction, add 600 to both sides.

$$4r = 1100$$

$$\frac{4r}{4} = \frac{1100}{4}$$

To undo the multiplication, divide both sides by 4.

$$r = 275$$

Check:

$$4r - 600 = 500$$
$$4(275) - 600 \stackrel{?}{=} 500$$
$$1100 - 600 \stackrel{?}{=} 500$$
$$500 = 500$$

Bill must charge \$275 rent for each apartment.

You might use the following steps to help students understand the equation.

Let r = rent from 1 apartment
$4r$ = total rent

total rent − expenses = profit
Then: $4r - 600 = 500$

Let x = total rental income

$\frac{x}{2}$ = Ruth's share of rental income

rental income + salary = total income

Then: $\frac{x}{2} + 450 = 980$

Problem B

Ruth Santos and her son own an apartment building together. They split the rental income equally. Ruth's monthly income is \$980. She earns \$450 per month at a part-time job. The rest of her monthly income is her share of the rental income. What is the total rental income?

Solve. $\frac{x}{2} + 450 = 980$

Solution

$$\frac{x}{2} + 450 = 980$$

x is divided by 2 and 450 is added to $\frac{x}{2}$.

$$\frac{x}{2} + 450 - 450 = 980 - 450$$

$$\frac{x}{2} = 530$$

To undo the addition, subtract 450 from both sides.

$$\frac{x}{2}(2) = 530(2)$$

$$x = 1060$$

To undo the division, multiply both sides by 2.

Check: $\frac{x}{2} + 450 = 980$

$$\frac{1060}{2} + 450 \stackrel{?}{=} 980$$

$$530 + 450 \stackrel{?}{=} 980$$

$$980 = 980$$

The total rental income is \$1060.

Exercises

Set A Solve and check.

1. $5a + 3 = 8$
   $a = 1$
2. $3s - 14 = 16$
   $s = 10$
3. $7n + 2 = 65$
   $n = 9$
4. $11 = 6 + 2r$
   $r = 2.5$
5. $0 = 2b - 7$
   $b = 3.5$
6. $12x + 32 = 89$
   $x = 4.75$
7. $45 = 13m - 20$
   $m = 5$
8. $29 = 4a + 16$
   $a = 3.25$
9. $105n - 6 = 99$
   $n = 1$
10. $79x + 45 = 282$
    $x = 3$

Set B Solve and check.

11. $\frac{m}{2} + 3 = 6$
    $m = 6$
12. $\frac{a}{3} - 7 = 5$
    $a = 36$
13. $\frac{t}{7} + 9 = 10$
    $t = 7$
14. $24 = 11 + \frac{c}{4}$
    $c = 52$
15. $0 = \frac{n}{4} - 9$
    $n = 36$
16. $\frac{a}{10} + 12 = 18$
    $a = 60$
17. $\frac{b}{6} - 21 = 3$
    $b = 144$
18. $4 = \frac{x}{6} - 4$
    $x = 48$
19. $\frac{x}{9} + 49 = 58$
    $x = 81$
20. $38 = \frac{a}{2} - 6$
    $a = 88$

Mixed Practice Solve and check.

21. $20 = 5z - 20$
    $z = 8$
22. $12 + 2c = 12$
    $c = 0$
23. $\frac{x}{2} + 6 = 15$
    $x = 18$
24. $2.9 + \frac{d}{5} = 3.5$
    $d = 3$
25. $1.2 + 6m = 2.4$
    $m = 0.2$
26. $0.9n - 4.7 = 1.6$
    $n = 7$
27. $0.1x - 0.1 = 0.1$
    $x = 2$
28. $40 = 32 + \frac{y}{9}$
    $y = 72$
29. $1 = \frac{b}{0.1} - 39$
    $b = 4$
30. $43 = 7 + 3w$
    $w = 12$

Related Problems

Write an equation for each problem. Then solve and check.

31. Larry Houser owns a building with 3 apartments. He pays out \$450 in monthly expenses. How much rent does Larry charge for each apartment if his monthly profit is \$315? He charges the same amount of rent for each apartment.
    $3r - 450 = 315$; \$255
32. Kay and her sister share an apartment. They each pay half of the rent, but Kay pays \$25 extra per month for the use of a garage. Kay pays \$175 per month. What is the monthly rent for the apartment?
    $\frac{r}{2} + 25 = 175$; \$300

Objectives: Find cross-products to tell if two ratios are equal; solve a proportion by using cross-products.

Ratio and Proportion

> Equal ratios form a proportion. Two ratios are equal if their cross-products are equal. If the cross-products are not equal, the ratios are not equal.

Problem A

For less able students, you may want to discuss problem A and assign set A before discussing problem B.

To create a new billboard, a designer first made a sketch on which the picture was 11.5 centimeters wide. Using a scale of 0.5 to 12, the designer computed the actual width of the picture on the billboard to be 276 centimeters. Did the designer compute the actual width correctly?

Tell whether these ratios are equal. $\frac{0.5}{12} \stackrel{?}{=} \frac{11.5}{276}$ ← Width of sketch / ← Actual width

Solution

$$\frac{0.5}{12} \times \frac{11.5}{276}$$

$0.5 \times 276 \quad 12 \times 11.5$

Multiply 0.5 × 276 and 12 × 11.5 to find cross-products.

$138 = 138$

$\frac{0.5}{12} = \frac{11.5}{276}$

The cross-products are equal, so the ratios are equal.

The designer computed the actual width correctly.

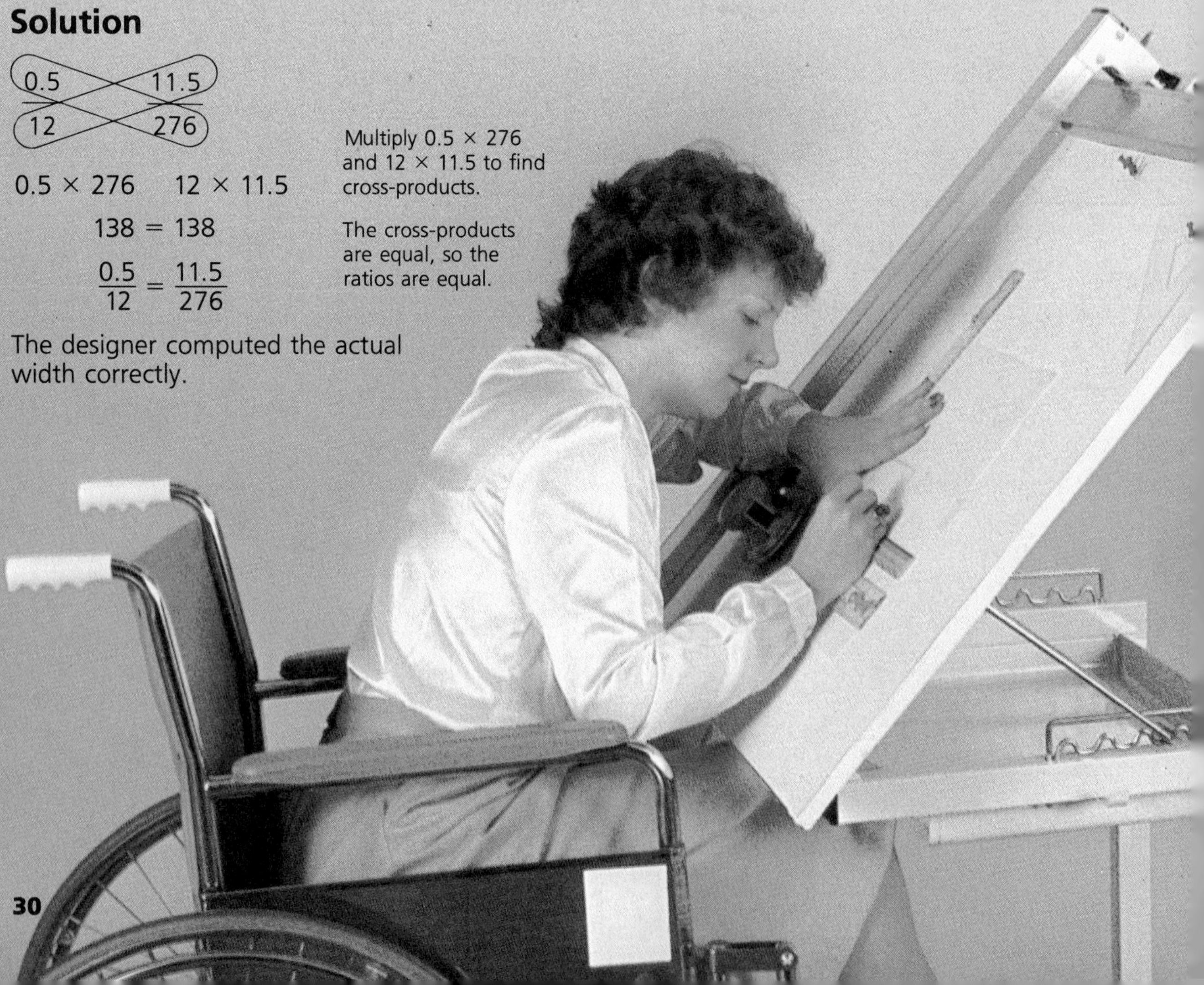

See page 15 of
Consumer Forms and Problems.

Problem B

A painted billboard is built so that the ratio of height to width is 0.5 to 2. If the board is 4 meters high, how wide is it?

Solve. $\frac{0.5}{2} = \frac{4}{w}$ ⟵ Height, ⟵ Width

Solution

$$\frac{0.5}{2} = \frac{4}{w}$$

$0.5 \times w = 2 \times 4$ Find the cross-products.

$0.5w = 8$

$\frac{0.5w}{0.5} = \frac{8}{0.5}$ To undo the multiplication, divide both sides by 0.5.

$w = 16$

Check: $\frac{0.5}{2} = \frac{4}{w}$ Substitute 16 for w in the original proportion.

$\frac{0.5}{2} \overset{?}{=} \frac{4}{16}$

$0.5 \times 16 \overset{?}{=} 2 \times 4$ Find the cross-products.

$8 = 8$ The cross-products are equal, so the ratios are equal, and $w = 16$.

The billboard is 16 meters wide.

Exercises

Set A Find the cross-products. Tell whether the ratios are equal.

1. $\frac{7}{28}$ $\frac{3}{12}$ 84 = 84
2. $\frac{20}{100}$ $\frac{7}{35}$ 700 = 700
3. $\frac{5}{6}$ $\frac{37}{42}$ 210 ≠ 222
4. $\frac{30}{8}$ $\frac{70}{21}$ 630 ≠ 560
5. $\frac{24}{64}$ $\frac{3}{8}$ 192 = 192
6. $\frac{20}{35}$ $\frac{12}{21}$ 420 = 420
7. $\frac{11}{12}$ $\frac{44}{48}$ 528 = 528
8. $\frac{32}{63}$ $\frac{4}{9}$ 288 ≠ 252
9. $\frac{8}{1.2}$ $\frac{2}{0.3}$ 2.4 = 2.4
10. $\frac{3.5}{4.2}$ $\frac{10}{14}$ 49 ≠ 42
11. $\frac{10.8}{6}$ $\frac{3.6}{2}$ 21.6 = 21.6
12. $\frac{0.6}{9}$ $\frac{0.4}{6}$ 3.6 = 3.6
13. $\frac{0.5}{0.25}$ $\frac{0.4}{0.2}$ 0.1 = 0.1
14. $\frac{0.3}{0.5}$ $\frac{3}{4.5}$ 1.35 ≠ 1.5
15. $\frac{50.4}{100}$ $\frac{4.2}{9}$ 453.6 ≠ 420
16. $\frac{75}{81}$ $\frac{2.5}{2.7}$ 202.5 = 202.5

Set B Solve and check.

17. $\frac{a}{20} = \frac{6}{8}$ $a = 15$
18. $\frac{11}{33} = \frac{c}{15}$ $c = 5$
19. $\frac{12}{d} = \frac{4}{3}$ $d = 9$
20. $\frac{24}{9} = \frac{8}{f}$ $f = 3$
21. $\frac{x}{5} = \frac{3}{4}$ $x = 3.75$
22. $\frac{16}{g} = \frac{10}{2}$ $g = 3.2$
23. $\frac{3}{5} = \frac{h}{7}$ $h = 4.2$
24. $\frac{24}{25} = \frac{6}{w}$ $w = 6.25$
25. $\frac{0.75}{1} = \frac{30}{x}$ $x = 40$
26. $\frac{r}{14} = \frac{0.7}{10}$ $r = 0.98$
27. $\frac{5}{0.9} = \frac{s}{36}$ $s = 200$
28. $\frac{x}{1.4} = \frac{2.4}{2.8}$ $x = 1.2$
29. $\frac{0.03}{0.5} = \frac{t}{0.1}$ $t = 0.006$
30. $\frac{0.06}{v} = \frac{0.3}{4}$ $v = 0.8$
31. $\frac{y}{1.6} = \frac{1.5}{4.8}$ $y = 0.5$
32. $\frac{0.25}{0.3} = \frac{100}{x}$ $x = 120$

Related Problems

The ratio of height to width on a standard printed billboard is 1 to 2.25.

33. If the height is 8 meters, find the width.
    18 meters
34. Could a standard printed billboard be 4 meters high and 9 meters wide?
    Yes

See Skills File, page 391, for more practice.

Objectives: Write decimals and fractions as percents; write percents as decimals and fractions.

Writing Percents, Decimals, and Fractions

> Percent means hundredths.
> $1\% = 0.01 = \frac{1}{100}$

Problem A

From the real estate section of his newspaper, Sonny Gillespie learned that the cost of new homes in his city has increased by a factor of 0.575 over the past 5 years.

Write 0.575 as a percent.

Solution

$0.575 = 57.5\%$ — Move the decimal point two places to the right and write a percent sign.

As a percent, 0.575 is 57.5%.

Problem B

The Gillespies have saved enough money to pay about $\frac{3}{8}$ of the cost of a house.

Write $\frac{3}{8}$ as a percent.

Solution

First write $\frac{3}{8}$ as a decimal.

$$\begin{array}{r} 0.375 \\ 8\overline{)3.000} \\ \underline{2\,4} \\ 60 \\ \underline{56} \\ 40 \\ \underline{40} \\ 0 \end{array}$$

Divide the numerator by the denominator.

$\frac{3}{8} = 0.375$

Then write the decimal as a percent.

$0.375 = 37.5\%$

As a percent, $\frac{3}{8}$ is 37.5%.

Remind students that 37.5% could also be expressed as $37\frac{1}{2}\%$.

Problem C

Sonny read that mortgage interest rates are $5\frac{1}{4}\%$ higher than they were five years ago.

Write $5\frac{1}{4}\%$ as a decimal.

Solution

$5\frac{1}{4}\% = 5.25\%$ — Write $5\frac{1}{4}$ as a decimal.

$5.25\% = 0.0525$ — Drop the percent sign and move the decimal point 2 places to the left.

As a decimal, $5\frac{1}{4}\%$ is 0.0525.

Problem D

Often, 20% of the cost of a home is required as a down payment.

Write 20% as a fraction.

Solution

$20\% = \frac{20}{100}$ — Drop the percent sign and write the number over 100.

$\frac{20}{100} = \frac{1}{5}$ — Rename the fraction in lowest terms.

As a fraction, 20% is $\frac{1}{5}$.

Exercises

Set A Write as a percent.

1. 0.43 **43%**
2. 0.71 **71%**
3. 0.09 **9%**
4. 0.1 **10%**
5. 0.027 **2.7%**
6. 0.314 **31.4%**
7. 0.225 **22.5%**
8. 0.468 **46.8%**
9. 0.1975 **19.75%**
10. 0.2325 **23.25%**
11. 0.0745 **7.45%**
12. 0.0375 **3.75%**
13. 1.25 **125%**
14. 3.74 **374%**
15. 2.465 **246.5%**

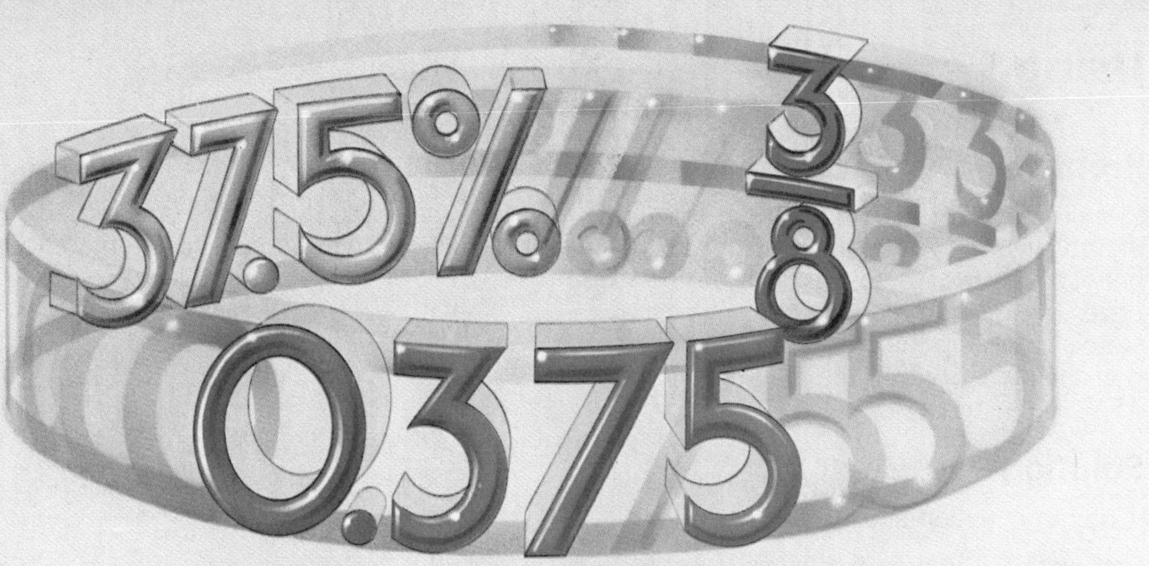

Set B Write as a percent.

16. $\frac{3}{4}$ 75%	**21.** $\frac{17}{25}$ 68%	**26.** $\frac{9}{16}$ 56.25%
17. $\frac{1}{2}$ 50%	**22.** $\frac{27}{50}$ 54%	**27.** $\frac{12}{32}$ 37.5%
18. $\frac{1}{4}$ 25%	**23.** $\frac{1}{20}$ 5%	**28.** $\frac{1}{8}$ 12.5%
19. $\frac{4}{5}$ 80%	**24.** $\frac{2}{25}$ 8%	**29.** $\frac{11}{5}$ 220%
20. $\frac{8}{20}$ 40%	**25.** $\frac{5}{8}$ 62.5%	**30.** $\frac{27}{4}$ 675%

Set C Write as a decimal.

31. 23% 0.23	**36.** 9.25% 0.0925	**41.** $32\frac{1}{4}$% 0.3225
32. 7% 0.07	**37.** 8.75% 0.0875	**42.** $12\frac{1}{10}$% 0.121
33. 2% 0.02	**38.** 24.8% 0.248	**43.** 135% 1.35
34. 14% 0.14	**39.** $3\frac{1}{2}$% 0.035	**44.** 216% 2.16
35. 13.5% 0.135	**40.** $4\frac{3}{4}$% 0.0475	**45.** 107% 1.07

Set D Write as a fraction in lowest terms.

46. 10% $\frac{1}{10}$	**51.** 75% $\frac{3}{4}$	**56.** 18% $\frac{9}{50}$
47. 70% $\frac{7}{10}$	**52.** 60% $\frac{3}{5}$	**57.** 61% $\frac{61}{100}$
48. 25% $\frac{1}{4}$	**53.** 35% $\frac{7}{20}$	**58.** 93% $\frac{93}{100}$
49. 50% $\frac{1}{2}$	**54.** 21% $\frac{21}{100}$	**59.** 109% $1\frac{9}{100}$
50. 40% $\frac{2}{5}$	**55.** 47% $\frac{47}{100}$	**60.** 107% $1\frac{7}{100}$

Related Problems

Use this information for problems 61–64.

Mortgage payments now take $0.35 of each income dollar.

Real estate taxes rose 22% in 6 years.

In 6 years, repair and maintenance costs have increased by $\frac{3}{4}$.

61. Write the increase in real estate taxes as a decimal. 0.22

62. Write the increase in real estate taxes as a fraction in lowest terms. $\frac{11}{50}$

63. Write the increase in repair and maintenance costs as a percent. 75%

64. Mortgage payments take what percent of the income? 35%

See Skills File, page 392, for more practice.

Objectives: Find a percent of a number; find what percent one number is of another; find a number when a percent of it is known.

Using Percent

Problem A

Be sure students understand that "cost" as used here means the amount the store pays for the item.

Nita Singh determines the markup for items in a retail store. The markup is the difference between the store's cost and the selling price. The markup rate is a percent of the store's cost. Find the markup on a shirt that cost the store $6.75 if the markup rate is 45%.

Solution

Write an equation and solve it.

First write the information in this form:

___% *of* ___ *is* ______.

45% *of* cost *is* markup.

$0.45 \times 6.75 = m$

$3.0375 = m$

$3.04 \approx m$ Round to the next higher cent.

The markup is $3.04.

Discuss the advantages of buying certain items wholesale rather than retail.

Problem B

Find the markup rate for plant food if the store's cost was $1.90 and the markup is $0.76.

Solution

___% *of* ___ *is* ______.

___% *of* cost *is* markup.

$r \times 1.90 = 0.76$ Write an equation and solve it.

$$\frac{r \times 1.90}{1.90} = \frac{0.76}{1.90}$$

$r = 0.4$

$0.4 = 40\%$ Write 0.4 as a percent.

The markup rate is 40%.

Problem C

An ad says, "20% off our regular price. Save $39!" What is the regular price?

Solution

___% *of* ___________ *is* ___________.

<u>20%</u> *of* <u>regular price</u> *is* <u>amount saved</u>.

$0.20 \times p = 39$ Write an equation and solve it.

$$\frac{0.20p}{0.20} = \frac{39}{0.20}$$

$$p = 195$$

The regular price is $195.

Exercises

Encourage students to use estimation as a check.

Set A

1. 25% of 56 is ___.
   14
2. 1% of 225 is ___.
   2.25
3. 5% of 50 is ___.
   2.5
4. 12.6% of 18.5 is ___.
   2.331
5. Find 7% of 462.
   32.34
6. Find 5% of 150.
   7.5
7. Find 42.5% of 50.
   21.25
8. Find 250% of 22.
   55
9. 60% of 70 is what number?
   42
10. 32% of 14 is what number?
    4.48
11. What number is 9.5% of 7.5?
    0.7125
12. What number is $10\frac{1}{2}$% of 40?
    4.2

Set B

13. ___% of 35 is 21.
    60%
14. ___% of 36 is 5.4.
    15%
15. ___% of 44 is 38.72.
    88%
16. ___% of 80 is 2.8.
    3.5%
17. What percent of 40 is 30?
    75%
18. What percent of 128 is 80?
    62.5%
19. What percent of 75 is 6?
    8%
20. What percent of 100 is 190?
    190%
21. 9 is what percent of 60?
    15%
22. 27 is what percent of 450?
    6%
23. 1350 is what percent of 2000?
    67.5%
24. 56 is what percent of 64?
    87.5%

Set C

25. 95% of ____ is 38.
40

26. 11% of ____ is 22.
200

27. 86% of ____ is 77.4.
90

28. $6\frac{1}{4}$% of ____ is 7.5.
120

29. 8% of what number is 36?
450

30. 40% of what number is 22?
55

31. 52% of what number is 5.72?
11

32. 20.2% of what number is 13.13?
65

33. 21 is 70% of what number?
30

34. 110 is 125% of what number?
88

35. 36 is 25% of what number?
144

36. 2.5 is 40% of what number?
6.25

Mixed Practice

37. 25% of 68 is ____.
17

38. ____% of 55 is 33.
60%

39. 5% of ____ is 8.
160

40. $12\frac{1}{2}$% of 24 is ____.
3

41. 4% of ____ is 14.
350

42. 37.5% of 40 is ____.
15

43. ____% of 24 is 18.
75%

44. 14% of ____ is 10.5.
75

45. ____% of 500 is 235.
47%

46. $62\frac{1}{2}$% of 64 is ____.
40

47. 180% of ____ is 26.1.
14.5

48. ____% of 7.95 is 1.59.
20%

See page 16 of
Consumer Forms and Problems.

Related Problems

Find the markup for each item. Round to the next higher cent.

	Item	Store's cost	Markup rate	
49.	Red begonias	$0.89	40%	$0.36
50.	Wood stain	$7.86	27%	$2.13
51.	Shampoo	$1.16	14%	$0.17
52.	Slacks	$7.99	46%	$3.68

53. A store's cost for batteries was $0.48 and the markup was $0.10. Find the markup rate to the nearest percent.
21%

54. A sale is advertised as follows: "25% off our regular price. Save $8." What is the regular price?
$32

55. Janice bought shoes on sale at 10% off the regular price of $29. How much did she save?
$2.90

56. A store's cost for jeans was $7.50 and the markup was $3.75. What was the markup rate?
50%

57. As an employee, Nita is given a 15% discount on all items in the store. She bought a table and saved $21. What was the regular price of the table?
$140

58. Nita used her 15% discount when she bought a lamp. If the regular price of the lamp was $36, how much did she save?
$5.40

(59.) There is a 75% markup rate for curtains. If the store's cost is $8.50, find the markup and the selling price.
$6.38; $14.88

(60.) A camera that regularly sells for $45 is on sale for 25% off. Find the sale price.
$33.75

See Skills File, page 393, for more practice.

Break Time

There are 3 boxes of flowers. One box has 1 dozen roses, one has 1 dozen carnations, and one has 6 roses and 6 carnations. Each cover is labeled, but someone has switched all the covers.

Select a box. With your eyes closed, open the box, take out a flower, and close the lid. When you open your eyes and see the flower you took, how can you tell which flowers are in which box?

Select the box labeled 6 roses, 6 carnations.

If you pick a rose, this box has 1 dozen roses. Then the box marked 1 dozen roses must have 1 dozen carnations and the box marked 1 dozen carnations has 6 roses and 6 carnations. (Remember, ALL the covers were switched.)

The argument is similar if a carnation is picked from the box.

CALCULATOR APPLICATIONS

Percent and Discounts

Retail stores are often given discounts when they order large quantities of goods. One wholesale firm offers a $20\frac{3}{4}\%$ discount to retail stores on orders up to \$400. If the total amount of the order is more than \$400, an additional discount is given. This discount is $5\frac{1}{4}\%$ of the cost after the first discount. Find the net cost of a \$765 order.

Total amount of order: \$765

Amount of 1st discount: $\$765 \times 0.2075 = \$158.7375 \approx \$158.74$
Cost after 1st discount: $\$765 - \$158.74 = \$606.26$

Amount of 2nd discount: $\$606.26 \times 0.0525 = \$31.82865 \approx \$31.83$
Cost after 2nd discount: $\$606.26 - \$31.83 = \$574.43$

The net cost is \$574.43.

Possible key sequence:
765 [M+] [×] .2075 [=] [M−] [MR] [×] .0525 [=] [M−] [MR]

For each problem, use the discounts described above to find the net cost of the order. The total amount of the order is given.

Because of rounding, answers may vary if students use a key sequence similar to the one shown above.

1. \$945 **\$709.59**
2. \$475.30 **\$356.90**
3. \$847.29 **\$636.23**
4. \$328 **\$259.94**
5. \$627.90 **\$471.49**
6. \$1023 **\$768.17**
7. \$1847.24 **\$1387.08**
8. \$1329.67 **\$998.44**
9. \$3216.42 **\$2415.19**

An alternate method is to use the complements of the percents given. For example:

$100\% - 20\frac{3}{4}\% = 79\frac{1}{4}\%$

$100\% - 5\frac{1}{4}\% = 94\frac{3}{4}\%$

$765 \times 0.7925 \times 0.9475 \approx 574.43$

Another firm offers a single 25% discount on orders over \$200. Buyers pay an additional $\frac{1}{2}\%$ of the net cost for insurance. For each problem, find the total amount of the order, the net cost, and the final cost including insurance.

10. \$179.48
\$565.55
\$739.15

11. \$429.37
\$65.42
\$517.16

12. \$821.18
\$651.33
\$47.24

	Total amount of order	Net cost	Final cost
10.	\$1484.18	\$1113.13	\$1118.70
11.	\$1011.95	\$758.96	\$762.75
12.	\$1519.75	\$1139.81	\$1145.51

Chapter 2 Review

Addition and subtraction equations, pages 24–25

Solve and check.

1. $d + 3.5 = 8$
   $d = 4.5$
2. $15.8 = m + 7.3$
   $m = 8.5$
3. $f - 0.74 = 7.25$
   $f = 7.99$
4. $5.8 = g - 2.15$
   $g = 7.95$

Multiplication and division equations, pages 26–27

Solve and check.

5. $8x = 424$
   $x = 53$
6. $17.5 = 2.5t$
   $t = 7$
7. $\frac{b}{9} = 0.24$
   $b = 2.16$
8. $3a + 9a = 48$
   $a = 4$

Two-step equations, pages 28–29

Solve and check.

9. $7c + 2 = 37$
   $c = 5$
10. $23 = 5y - 17$
    $y = 8$
11. $\frac{a}{4} - 9 = 8$
    $a = 68$
12. $\frac{x}{2} + 2 = 5$
    $x = 6$

Ratio and proportion, pages 30–31

Find the cross-products. Tell whether the ratios are equal.

13. $\frac{50}{65}$ $\frac{4}{5}$
    $250 \neq 260$
14. $\frac{9}{24}$ $\frac{1.2}{3.2}$
    $28.8 = 28.8$

Solve and check.

15. $\frac{c}{56} = \frac{3}{7}$
    $c = 24$
16. $\frac{0.25}{2} = \frac{11}{t}$
    $t = 88$

Writing percents, decimals, and fractions, pages 32–33

Write as a percent.

17. 0.06 6%
18. 0.465 46.5%
19. $\frac{19}{25}$ 76%
20. $\frac{5}{16}$ 31.25%

Write as a decimal.

21. 57% 0.57
22. $5\frac{3}{4}\%$ 0.0575

Write as a fraction in lowest terms.

23. 41% $\frac{41}{100}$
24. 38% $\frac{19}{50}$

Using percent, pages 34–37

25. Find 6% of 527.
    31.62
26. $37\frac{1}{2}\%$ of 64 is what number?
    24
27. 9 is what percent of 60?
    15%
28. What percent of 56 is 49?
    87.5%
29. 24% of what number is 10.8?
    45
30. 18 is 12% of what number?
    150

Chapter 2 Test

Number of test items – 30

Number missed	1	2	3	4	5	6	7	8	9	10	11	12	13	14	15
Percent correct	97	93	90	87	83	80	77	73	70	67	63	60	57	53	50

Solve and check.

1. $a + 7 = 11$
$a = 4$

2. $14.7 = x + 4$
$x = 10.7$

3. $p - 6 = 5.2$
$p = 11.2$

4. $9 = h - 12$
$h = 21$

5. $6t = 162$
$t = 27$

6. $4.2 = 3a$
$a = 1.4$

7. $\frac{d}{7} = 0.14$
$d = 0.98$

8. $4t + 5t = 36$
$t = 4$

9. $6x + 4 = 22$
$x = 3$

10. $31 = 9b - 14$
$b = 5$

11. $\frac{r}{6} - 8 = 3$
$r = 66$

12. $\frac{s}{3} + 2 = 6$
$s = 12$

Find the cross-products. Tell whether the ratios are equal.

13. $\frac{3}{8} \quad \frac{12}{32}$
$96 = 96$

14. $\frac{5.6}{8.1} \quad \frac{8}{9}$
$50.4 \neq 64.8$

Solve and check.

15. $\frac{2}{3} = \frac{n}{39}$
$n = 26$

16. $\frac{3.2}{d} = \frac{16}{7}$
$d = 1.4$

Write as a percent.

17. 0.24 24%

18. 0.327 32.7%

19. $\frac{3}{20}$ 15%

20. $\frac{7}{8}$ 87.5%

Write as a decimal.

21. 49% 0.49

22. $21\frac{1}{2}\%$ 0.215

Write as a fraction in lowest terms.

23. 39% $\frac{39}{100}$

24. 24% $\frac{6}{25}$

Compute.

25. Find 8% of 43.
3.44

26. $12\frac{1}{2}\%$ of 88 is what number?
11

27. 7 is what percent of 25?
28%

28. What percent of 125 is 15?
12%

29. 18% of what number is 4.5?
25

30. 36 is 30% of what number?
120

 See pages 3-4 of the *Test Masters* for an alternate form of the Chapter 2 Test.

Chapter 3 Measurement and Statistics

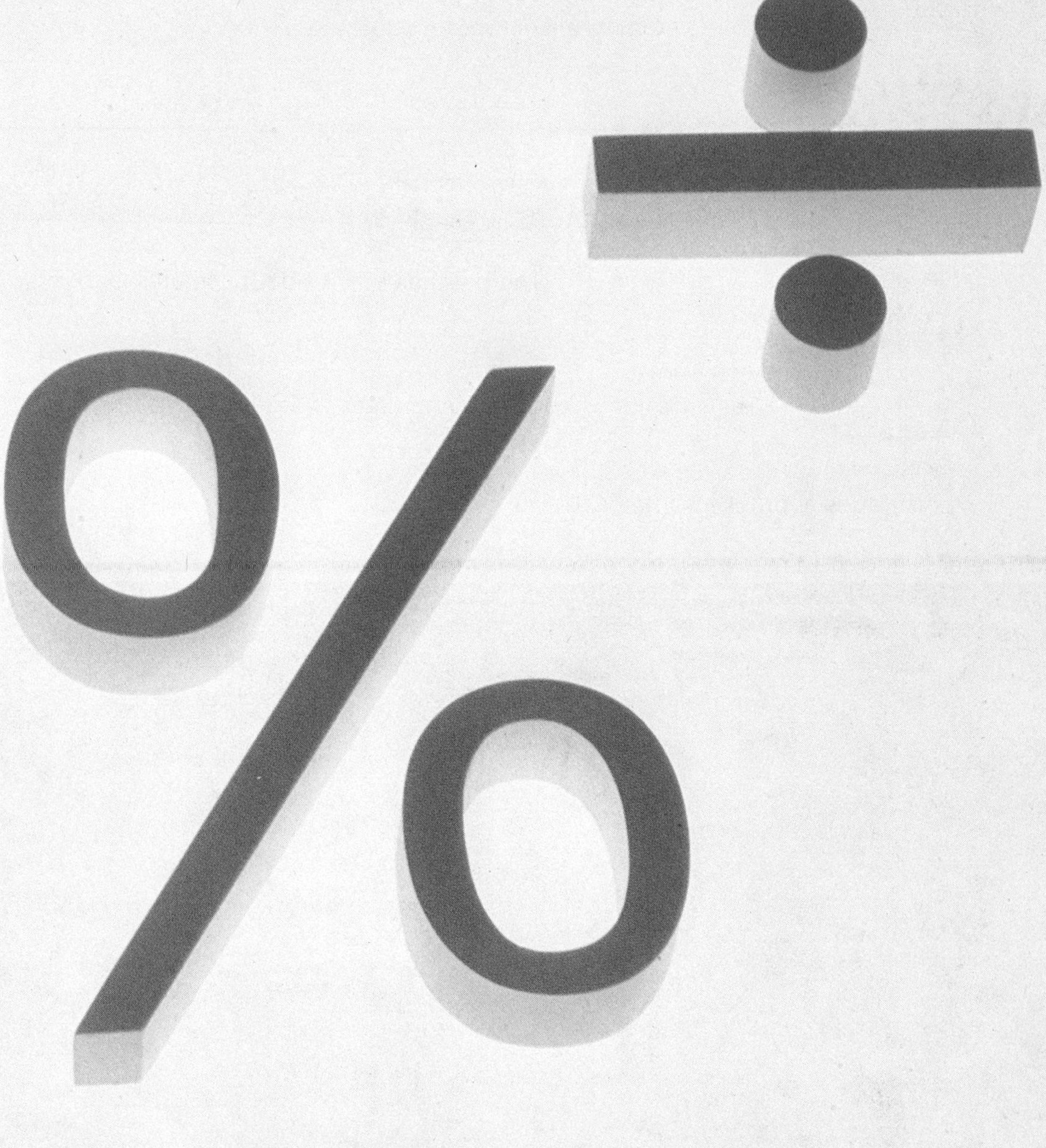

Objective: Choose sensible measures involving metric units of length.

Metric Units of Length

See page 400 for a table of metric measures.

See page T28 for additional notes and activities for Chapter 3.

Commonly used metric units of length are the **millimeter** (mm), the **centimeter** (cm), the **meter** (m), and the **kilometer** (km).

Important terms appear in boldface type.

Point out that the metric symbols do not require a period.

Objects are not shown actual size.

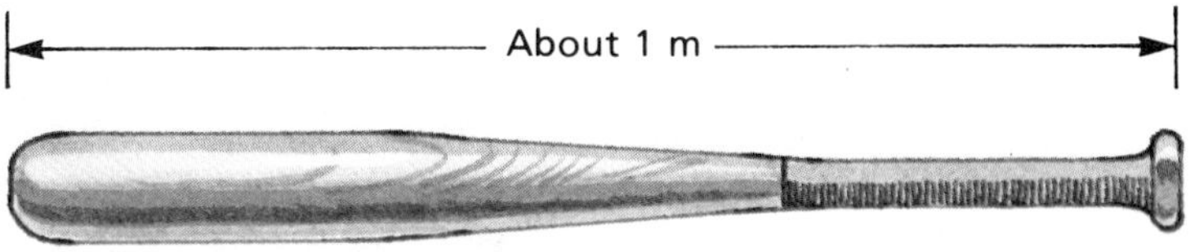

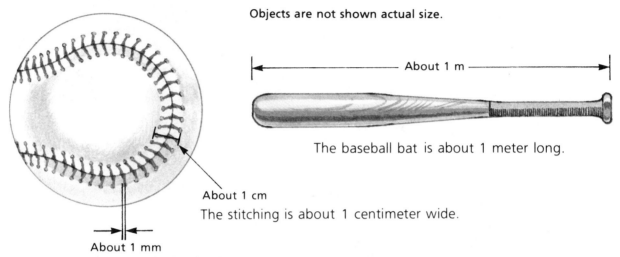

The baseball bat is about 1 meter long.

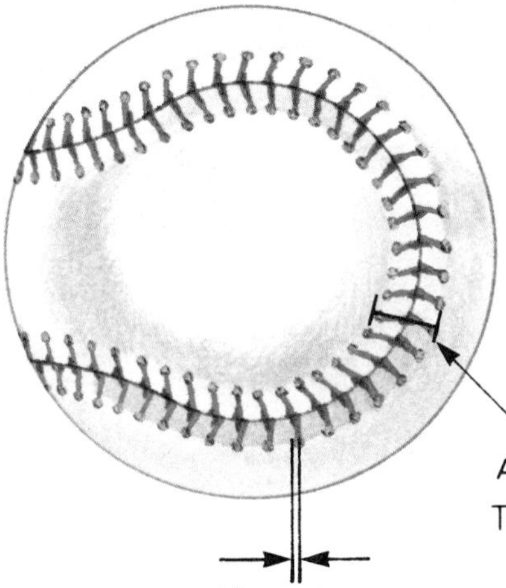

The stitching is about 1 centimeter wide.

The string is about 1 millimeter thick.

One kilometer is about 9 times around a baseball diamond.

See page 17 of
Consumer Forms and Problems.

There are 1000 millimeters in 1 meter.
There are 100 centimeters in 1 meter.
There are 1000 meters in 1 kilometer.

Problem A

Gina plans to make a suit. She estimated the length of the material needed.

Choose the most sensible measure for the length of the material needed.

4 mm   4 cm   4 m

Solution

Use the information on page 42 to make a sensible selection.

The length of the material needed is about 4 m.

Problem B

The Walkers are planning a trip from New York to Chicago. They estimated the distance one way.

Choose the most sensible measure for the distance from New York to Chicago.

1353 km   26 km   2 km

Solution

Use the information on page 42 to make a sensible selection.

The distance from New York to Chicago is about 1353 km.

Exercises

Set A   Choose the most sensible measure.

1. Average depth of the Atlantic Ocean
   3.87 cm   3.87 m   3.87 km
2. Height of a giant redwood tree
   110 cm   110 m   110 km
3. Length of a peanut
   14 mm   14 cm   14 m
4. Height of a toaster
   18 mm   18 cm   18 m
5. Distance from Denver to New Orleans
   2130 cm   2130 m   2130 km

Set B   Choose the most sensible measure.

6. Diameter of a long-playing record
   0.8 cm   12 cm   30 cm
7. Length of a hockey rink
   60 m   300 m   1000 m
8. Width of a lane on an expressway
   0.5 m   3.0 m   30.0 m
9. Distance from New York to Los Angeles
   6 km   250 km   4590 km
10. Thickness of this book
    25 mm   100 mm   500 mm

Related Problems   Answers will vary.

11. Estimate the length of your classroom in meters.
12. Estimate the width of your classroom in meters.
13. Estimate the height of the blackboard in centimeters.
14. Estimate the length of a paper clip.
15. Estimate the height of your teacher.

Objective: Compute area and volume using metric measures.

Area and Volume

Some metric units of area are the square millimeter (mm^2), the square centimeter (cm^2), the square meter (m^2), and the square kilometer (km^2).

Some metric units of volume are the cubic millimeter (mm^3), the cubic centimeter (cm^3), and the cubic meter (m^3).

Problem A

What is the area of the front face of this concrete block?

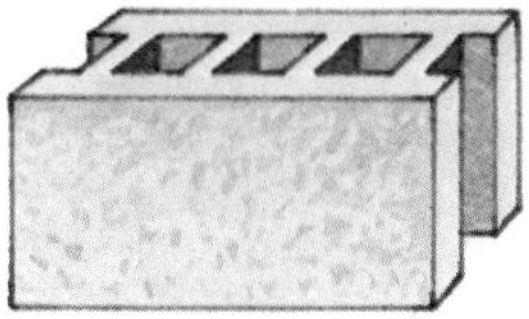

Problem B

What is the area of one triangular face of this roof?

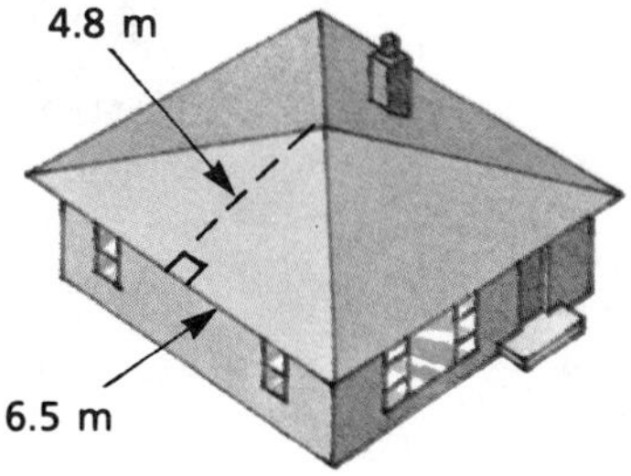

Problem C

What is the volume of this brick? Round the answer to the nearest tenth of a cubic centimeter.

Solution

The **area** of a rectangle is the length times the width.

$A = l \times w$

$A = 400 \times 200$

$A = 80{,}000$

The area is 80,000 mm^2.

Be sure students read the measures correctly: cm^2 is read "square centimeter," not "centimeter squared."

Solution

The area of a triangle is $\frac{1}{2}$ times the base times the height.

$A = \frac{1}{2} \times b \times h$

$A = \frac{1}{2} \times 6.5 \times 4.8$

$A = 15.6$

The area is 15.6 m^2.

Solution

The **volume** of a rectangular prism is the length times the width times the height.

$V = l \times w \times h$

$V = 19.5 \times 9.0 \times 5.5$

$V \approx 965.3$

The volume is about 965.3 cm^3.

Point out that height *h* can also mean depth, as in related problem 17.

Exercises

Set A Use the given dimensions to find the area of each rectangle to the nearest tenth.

	Length	Width	
1.	28 mm	14 mm	**392.0 mm^2**
2.	6.2 m	3.5 m	**21.7 m^2**
3.	4.1 km	2.3 km	**9.4 km^2**
4.	17.3 cm	25.9 cm	**448.1 cm^2**
5.	11.6 m	27.8 m	**322.5 m^2**

Set B Use the given dimensions to find the area of each triangle to the nearest tenth.

	Base	Height	
6.	23 m	16 m	**184.0 m^2**
7.	35 mm	12 mm	**210.0 mm^2**
8.	1.5 cm	1.0 cm	**0.8 cm^2**
9.	11.2 m	6.5 m	**36.4 m^2**
10.	34.5 cm	11.5 cm	**198.4 cm^2**

Set C Use the given dimensions to find the volume of each rectangular prism to the nearest tenth.

	Length	Width	Height	
11.	37 mm	13 mm	17 mm	**8177.0 mm^3**
12.	8.0 m	4.0 m	2.3 m	**73.6 m^3**
13.	9.0 cm	2.7 cm	4.3 cm	**104.5 cm^3**
14.	8.1 m	6.2 m	3.7 m	**185.8 m^3**
15.	27.7 cm	21.5 cm	1.9 cm	**1131.5 cm^3**

Related Problems

16. Find the area of a rectangular driveway that measures 15.2 m by 5.5 m.
83.6 m^2

17. How many cubic meters of sand are needed to fill a sandbox 1.7 m long, 1.5 m wide, and 0.3 m deep? Round the answer to the nearest tenth.
0.8 m^3

18. Hoffmans' patio is shaped like a triangle. The base of the triangle is 6.1 m, and the height is 6.1 m. What is the area of the patio to the nearest tenth?
18.6 m^2

Break Time

Copy this picture. Try to place eight dots on the diagram so that two dots are on each circle and two dots are on each straight line.

Answers will vary.
One answer is shown.

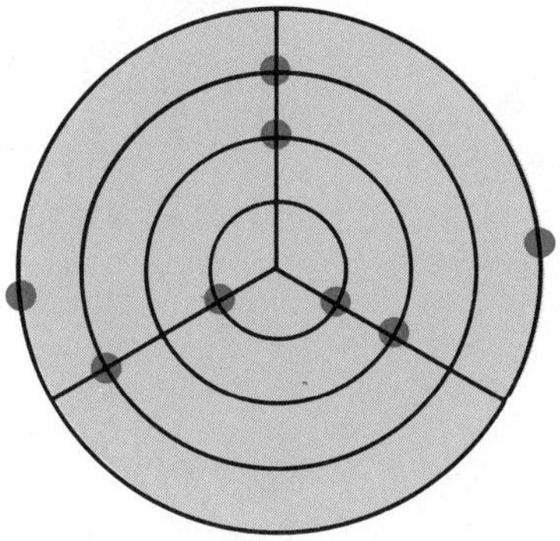

Objective: Choose sensible measures involving metric units of capacity and mass.

Metric Units of Capacity and Mass

The lowercase "l" is the international symbol for liter. Since this can be confused with the numeral "1," the symbol "L" is recommended for use in the United States.

> Commonly used metric units of capacity are the **liter** (L) and the **milliliter** (mL).
>
> Commonly used metric units of mass are the **kilogram** (kg), the **gram** (g), and the **milligram** (mg).

The mass of your math book is about 1 kilogram.

The amount of orange juice in this jar is 1 liter.

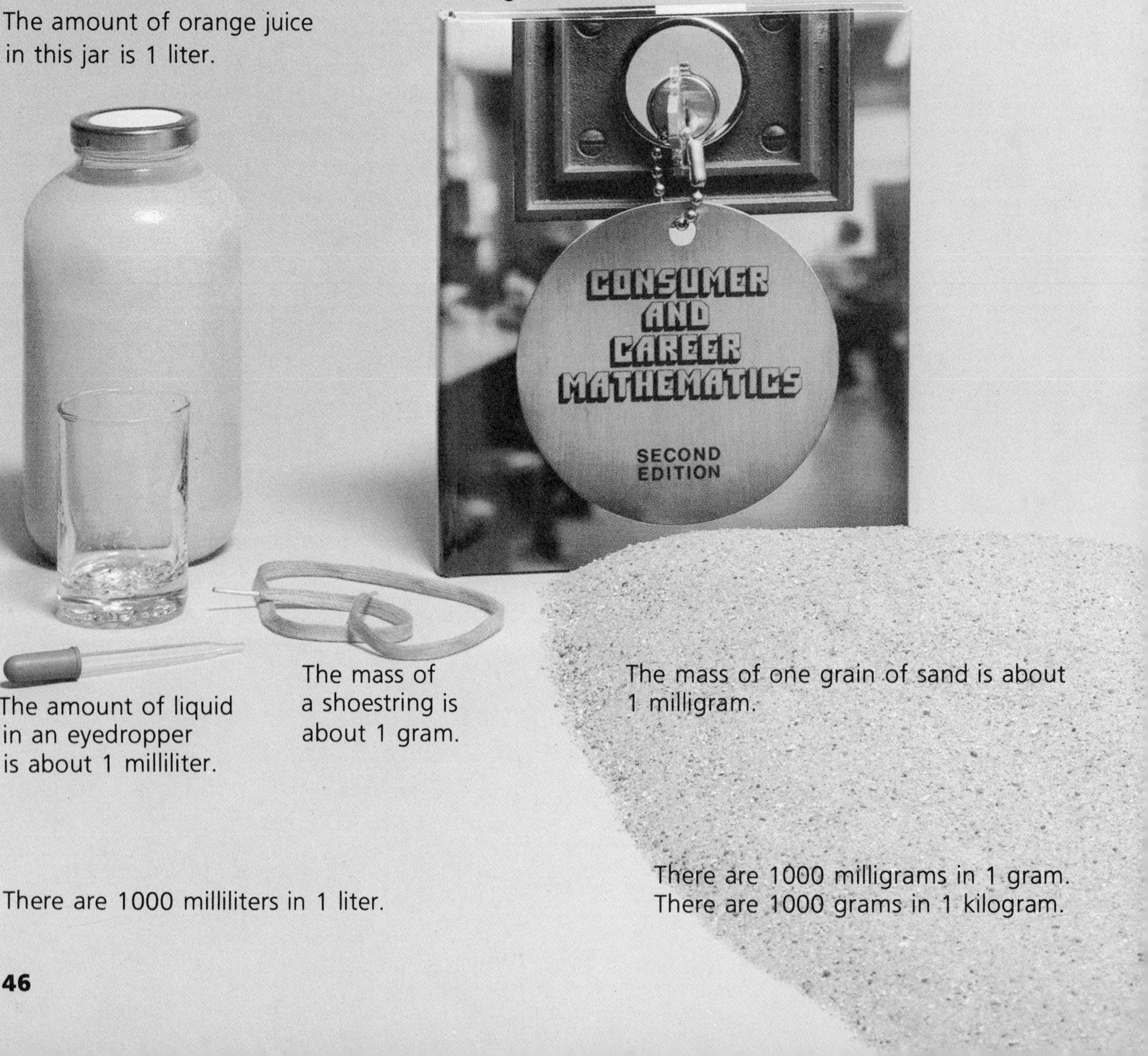

The amount of liquid in an eyedropper is about 1 milliliter.

The mass of a shoestring is about 1 gram.

The mass of one grain of sand is about 1 milligram.

There are 1000 milliliters in 1 liter.

There are 1000 milligrams in 1 gram.
There are 1000 grams in 1 kilogram.

Problem A

Tina's car is almost out of gas. She estimated the amount of gas the tank will hold.

Choose the more sensible measure for the capacity of a gas tank in a car.

60 mL   60 L

Solution

Use the information on page 46 to make a sensible selection.

The capacity of a gas tank is about 60 L.

Problem B

Chris plans to ship a lawn mower to a relative. He estimated the mass of the lawn mower.

Choose the most sensible measure for the mass of a lawn mower.

5 kg   35 kg   1000 kg

Solution

Use the information on page 46 to make a sensible selection.

The mass of a lawn mower is about 35 kg.

Exercises

Set A Choose the more sensible measure of capacity.

1. Glass of milk
   250 mL   250 L
2. Bottle of antifreeze
   2 mL   2 L
3. Washing machine
   40 mL   40 L
4. Can of paint
   4 L   25 L
5. Tube of toothpaste
   15 mL   150 mL

Set B Choose the most sensible measure for the mass of each object.

6. Brick
   2 kg   150 kg   900 kg
7. Car key
   0.8 g   85 g   8500 g
8. Paper clip
   0.5 mg   5 mg   500 mg
9. Hockey puck
   165 mg   165 g   165 kg
10. TV set
    50 mg   50 g   50 kg

Related Problems

Give the most sensible unit of measure for each of these items.

11. Capacity of an aquarium **Liter**
12. Mass of a tennis ball **Gram**
13. Capacity of a spoon **Milliliter**
14. Mass of a portable typewriter **Kilogram**
15. Mass of a letter **Gram**

Objective: Convert from one metric unit of measure to another.

Renaming Metric Units of Measure

> To rename a larger metric unit of measure as a smaller unit, *multiply* by a number such as 10, 100, or 1000.
>
> To rename a smaller metric unit of measure as a larger unit, *divide* by a number such as 10, 100, or 1000.

The chart below lists the metric prefixes and their values.
It can help you to find equal metric measures.

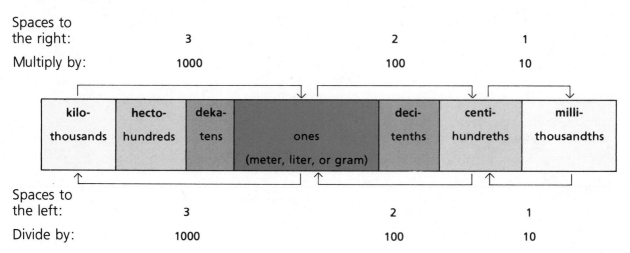

Spaces to the right:	3	2	1
Multiply by:	1000	100	10

kilo-	hecto-	deka-		deci-	centi-	milli-
thousands	hundreds	tens	ones (meter, liter, or gram)	tenths	hundredths	thousandths

Spaces to the left:	3	2	1
Divide by:	1000	100	10

Problem A

Dick completed a 20-kilometer running race. How many meters did he run?

20 km = ▒ m

Solution

Changing from kilometers to meters is like moving 3 places to the right on the chart. So multiply by 1000.

$1000 \times 20 = 20{,}000$

20 km = 20,000 m

Dick ran 20,000 meters.

Problem B

Lynn needs 150 centimeters of ribbon, but the ribbon is sold only by the meter. How many meters of ribbon should she buy?

150 cm = ▒ m

Solution

Changing from centimeters to meters is like moving 2 places to the left on the chart. So divide by 100.

$150 \div 100 = 1.5$

150 cm = 1.5 m

Lynn should buy 1.5 meters of ribbon.

Instead of using multiplication and division, you may wish to have students simply move the decimal point a certain number of places as shown in the chart.

Exercises

Set A

1. 5 m = ▒ cm — 500 cm

2. 0.8 km = ▒ m — 800 m

3. 9.3 cm = ▒ mm — 93 mm

4. 2.1 m = ▒ mm — 2100 mm

5. 12.75 m = ▒ cm — 1275 cm

6. 3 L = ▒ mL — 3000 mL

7. 0.5 L = ▒ mL — 500 mL

8. 45 kg = ▒ g — 45,000 g

9. 2.1 g = ▒ mg — 2100 mg

10. 0.84 kg = ▒ g — 840 g

Set B

11. 935 m = ▒ km — 0.935 km

12. 160.4 cm = ▒ m — 1.604 m

13. 429 mm = ▒ m — 0.429 m

14. 1250 m = ▒ km — 1.25 km

15. 67 mm = ▒ cm — 6.7 cm

16. 1578 mL = ▒ L — 1.578 L

17. 84 mL = ▒ L — 0.084 L

18. 716 g = ▒ kg — 0.716 kg

19. 1375 mg = ▒ g — 1.375 g

20. 42.6 g = ▒ kg — 0.0426 kg

Mixed Practice

21. 23 km = ▒ m — 23,000 m

22. 971 m = ▒ km — 0.971 km

23. 18 cm = ▒ mm — 180 mm

24. 3.5 m = ▒ mm — 3500 mm

25. 6 cm = ▒ m — 0.06 m

26. 14 L = ▒ mL — 14,000 mL

27. 250 mL = ▒ L — 0.25 L

28. 837 g = ▒ kg — 0.837 kg

29. 1296 mg = ▒ g — 1.296 g

30. 8.3 kg = ▒ g — 8300 g

Related Problems

Use this recipe to answer problems 31–34.

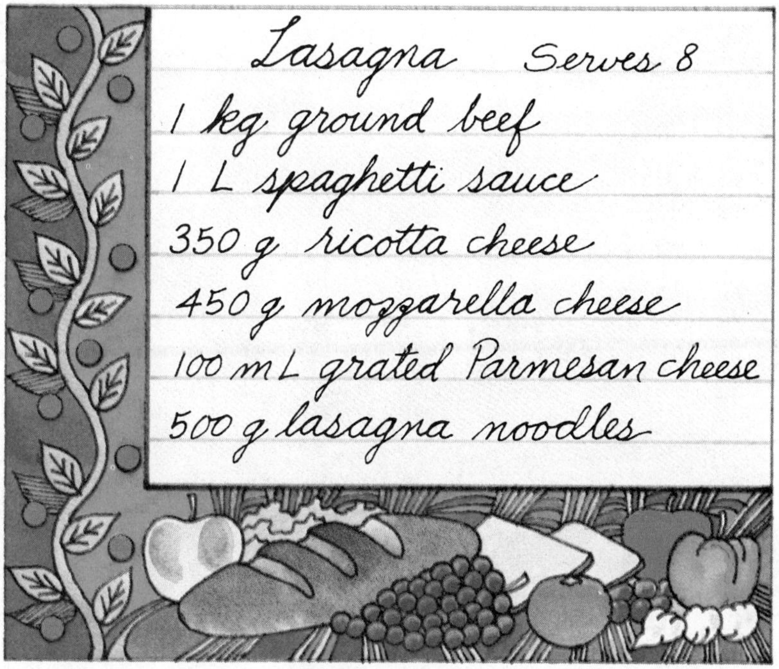

Lasagna Serves 8
1 kg ground beef
1 L spaghetti sauce
350 g ricotta cheese
450 g mozzarella cheese
100 mL grated Parmesan cheese
500 g lasagna noodles

31. How many grams of ground beef are needed?
1000 grams

32. How many liters of Parmesan cheese are needed?
0.1 liters

33. Perry plans to make lasagna for 4 people. How many milliliters of spaghetti sauce does he need?
500 milliliters

34. Anne plans to make a double recipe. How many kilograms of noodles does she need?
1 kilogram

Objective: Choose sensible temperatures involving degrees Celsius.

Temperature

Temperature can be measured with several different scales. The Celsius scale is commonly used in countries that use the metric system.

Problem

Ben plans to make an ice-skating rink in his backyard. To decide whether the conditions are suitable, he first estimates the outdoor temperature.

Choose the more sensible temperature in degrees Celsius (°C) for a winter day in Gary, Indiana.

$^-5$°C   25°C

Solution

Consult the Celsius thermometer shown at the right.

The more sensible temperature is $^-5$°C.

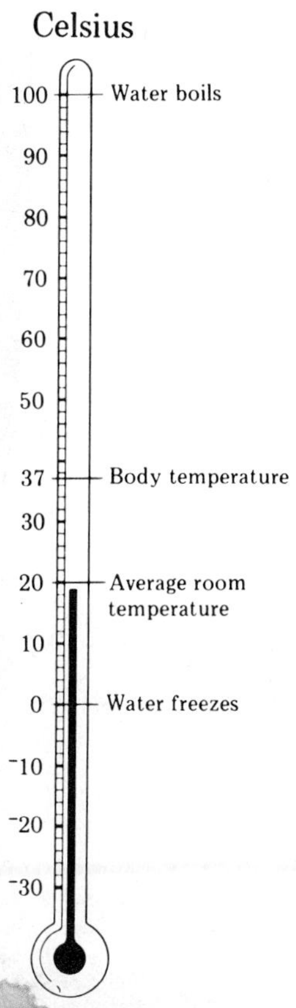

Exercises

Choose the more sensible temperature.

1. Frozen orange juice
0°C 20°C

2. Hot summer day
32°C 15°C

3. Snowball
18°C 3°C

4. Sauna
22°C 60°C

5. Warm dinner rolls
50°C 125°C

6. Ocean water
118°C 18°C

7. Sick person
39.8°C 100.4°C

8. Setting on a home thermostat
50°C 20°C

9. Cold milk
10°C 50°C

10. Melted cheese
-5°C 40°C

Heat loss from the body is caused by temperature and wind. A person can feel colder than the actual temperature because of the effect of the wind in combination with cold temperatures. Wind speeds over 60 kilometers per hour have little additional effect.

Related Problems

Use the wind-chill index for problems 11–15.

Wind-Chill Index

Wind speed (km/h)	Thermometer reading (°C)								
	0	-5	-10	-15	-20	-25	-30	-35	-40
	Wind chill (°C) (equivalent temperature)								
Calm	0	-5	-10	-15	-20	-25	-30	-35	-40
10	-4	-10	-15	-21	-27	-32	-38	-43	-49
15	-8	-14	-20	-26	-32	-38	-45	-51	-57
20	-10	-17	-23	-30	-37	-43	-50	-56	-63
25	-12	-19	-26	-33	-40	-47	-54	-61	-68
30	-14	-21	-28	-36	-43	-50	-57	-64	-71
35	-16	-23	-30	-38	-45	-52	-60	-67	-74
40	-17	-24	-32	-39	-47	-54	-62	-69	-77
45	-18	-25	-33	-41	-48	-56	-64	-71	-79
50	-19	-26	-34	-42	-50	-57	-65	-73	-81
55	-19	-27	-35	-43	-51	-59	-67	-74	-82
60	-20	-28	-36	-44	-52	-60	-68	-76	-83

Little danger Increasing danger Great danger

11. The thermometer reading is -10°C and the wind speed is 30 km/h. Find the wind chill.
-28°C

12. The thermometer reading is -5°C and the wind speed is 45 km/h. Find the wind chill.
-25°C

13. If the wind chill is -34°C and the wind speed is 50 km/h, what is the thermometer reading?
-10°C

14. If the thermometer reading is -30°C and the wind chill is -50°C, what is the wind speed?
20 km/h

15. At one time the wind chill was -20°C. An hour later the wind chill was -16°C. If the thermometer reading was 0°C at both times, what was the difference in wind speeds?
25 km/h

Objectives: Add two amounts of time; add an amount of time to a starting time to find the ending time; find an amount of elapsed time.

Time

The abbreviation "A.M." represents the time from midnight to noon; "P.M." represents the time from noon to midnight.

All times are given in multiples of 5 minutes.

Problem A

A trip to Crystal Lake took 4 hours 45 minutes by train plus 2 hours 30 minutes by bus. How long did the trip take?

Add 4 hours 45 minutes and 2 hours 30 minutes.

Solution

First add the minutes. Then add the hours.

$$\begin{array}{r} 4 \text{ hours } 45 \text{ minutes} \\ +\ 2 \text{ hours } 30 \text{ minutes} \\ \hline 6 \text{ hours } 75 \text{ minutes} \end{array}$$

There are 60 minutes in 1 hour.
Since 75 minutes = 1 hour 15 minutes, 6 hours 75 minutes is the same as 7 hours 15 minutes.

The trip took 7 hours 15 minutes.

See page 18 of
Consumer Forms and Problems.

Problem B

The departure time on a flight from New York to Miami was 11:20 A.M. If the flight took 2 hours 25 minutes, what was the arrival time in Miami?

Add 2 hours 25 minutes to 11:20 A.M.

Solution

First add the hours to the departure time. Remember that the first hour after 12:00 noon is 1:00 P.M.

11:20 A.M. + 2 hours ⟶ 1:20 P.M.

Then add the minutes.

1:20 + 25 minutes ⟶ 1:45 P.M.

The arrival time was 1:45 P.M.

Problem C

Mr. Bedoni left St. Louis at 10:30 A.M. and drove to Chicago. He arrived in Chicago at 5:15 P.M. How long did Mr. Bedoni drive?

Find how much time there is from 10:30 A.M. to 5:15 P.M.

Solution

First find the number of hours. Remember that the first hour after 12:00 noon is 1:00 P.M.

10:30 A.M. to 4:30 P.M. ⟶ 6 hours

Then find the number of minutes remaining.

4:30 P.M. to 5:15 P.M. ⟶ 45 minutes

Mr. Bedoni drove 6 hours 45 minutes.

Exercises

Set A Add.

1. 3 hours 15 minutes + 5 hours 20 minutes
   8 hours 35 minutes
2. 2 hours 35 minutes + 7 hours 50 minutes
   10 hours 25 minutes
3. 4 hours 25 minutes + 3 hours 55 minutes
   8 hours 20 minutes
4. 5 hours 45 minutes + 5 hours 15 minutes
   11 hours 0 minutes

Set B

5. Add 3 hours 20 minutes to 8:15 A.M.
   11:35 A.M.
6. Add 6 hours 5 minutes to 9:25 A.M.
   3:30 P.M.
7. Add 8 hours 15 minutes to 10:10 P.M.
   6:25 A.M.
8. Add 12 hours 35 minutes to 12:05 P.M.
   12:40 A.M.

Set C

9. How much time is there from 4:30 P.M. to 7:40 P.M.?
   3 hours 10 minutes
10. How much time is there from 7:15 A.M. to 3:35 P.M.?
    8 hours 20 minutes
11. How much time is there from 11:45 A.M. to 6:20 P.M.?
    6 hours 35 minutes
12. How much time is there from 1:30 A.M. to 12:45 P.M.?
    11 hours 15 minutes

Related Problems

13. Pete and Liz drove to Yosemite National Park. Pete drove 3 hours 20 minutes. Liz drove 4 hours 45 minutes. What was the total driving time?
    8 hours 5 minutes
14. A car was parked in a parking lot from 8:50 A.M. until 9:20 P.M. the same day. How long was the car parked?
    12 hours 30 minutes
15. Joe went sailing with some friends. They left at 10:30 A.M. and returned 5 hours 45 minutes later. What time did they return?
    4:15 P.M.

Objective: Make bar graphs and line graphs.

Bar Graphs and Line Graphs

Materials: Graph paper

Problem A

Paul Marcello is planning a national advertising campaign. He needs to make a **bar graph** that shows the estimated advertising expenditures for 1979.

Make a bar graph for this set of data.

1979 estimated advertising expenditures

Newspapers	$14 billion
Magazines	$3 billion
Television	$10 billion
Radio	$4 billion
Direct mail	$7 billion
Other	$10 billion

Solution

List the six types of advertising on the vertical scale.

Units on the horizontal scale can be billions of dollars. Since the largest number is 14, the scale can stop at 15.

Draw bars to show the billions of dollars spent for each type of advertising.

Write a title for the graph.

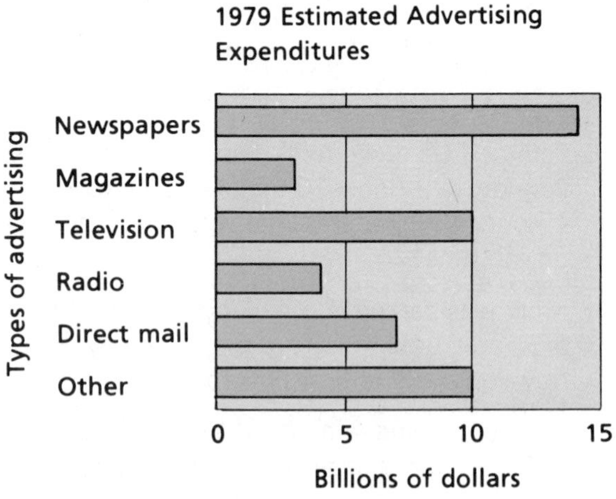

Bar graphs can also be done vertically.

Problem B

Kathy Odina is doing research on school enrollment trends. She needs to make a **line graph** that shows the number of students enrolled in high schools for the years 1973 to 1979.

Make a line graph for this set of data.

High school enrollment, 1973–1979

1973	15.3 million
1974	15.4 million
1975	15.7 million
1976	15.7 million
1977	15.8 million
1978	15.5 million
1979	15.1 million

Solution

Draw and label the vertical and horizontal scales. The broken vertical scale means that numbers are missing.

Find the line for 1973. Mark a point on that line for 15.3.

Locate the points for the other years. Connect the points with a line.

Write a title for the graph.

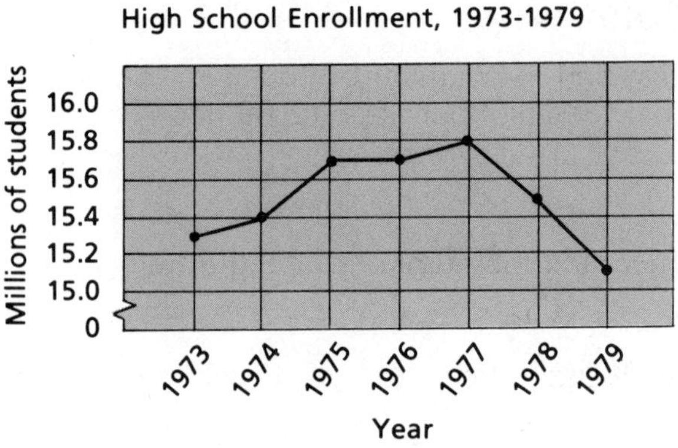

See pages 11 and 12 of
Consumer Forms and Problems.

Exercises

Set A Make a bar graph for each set of data.
See Additional Answers beginning on page T44.

1. Average personal income in 1979 by region

Northeast	$8900
North Central	$8800
Southeast	$8200
South Central	$7600
West	$9000

2. U.S. birth rates per 1000 people

1970	18.4	1975	14.8
1971	17.2	1976	14.8
1972	15.6	1977	15.4
1973	14.9	1978	15.3
1974	14.9	1979	15.8

Set B Make a line graph for each set of data.
See Additional Answers beginning on page T44.

3. Number of work stoppages (strikes) in the U.S.

1970	5716	1975	5031
1971	5138	1976	5648
1972	5010	1977	5506
1973	5353	1978	4230
1974	6074		

4. Existing single-family houses sold

1973	2,334,000
1974	2,272,000
1975	2,452,000
1976	3,002,000
1977	3,547,000
1978	3,863,000
1979	3,701,000

Discuss with students how the choice of scale can make the differences in the data appear more or less extreme.

Related Problems

Use the bar graph below for problems 5–7.

Advertising Expenditures by Selected Media in 1975 and 1979

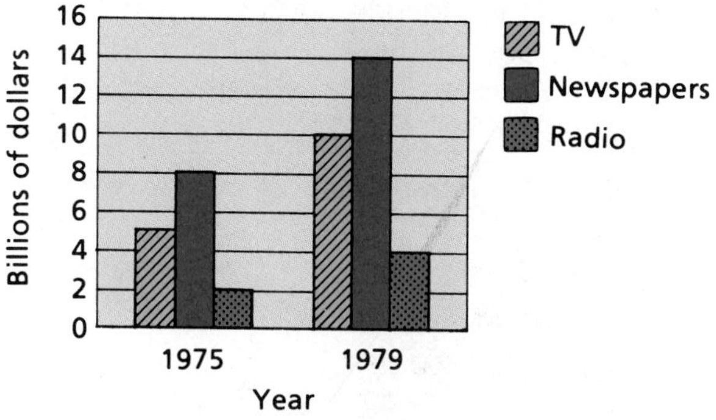

5. How much more was spent on television advertising in 1979 than in 1975?
$5 billion

6. How many times as much was spent on newspaper advertising as on radio advertising in 1975? in 1979?
4 times; 3.5 times

7. What was the total amount spent on advertising for these selected media in 1975? in 1979?
$15 billion; $28 billion

8. Erica Schmidt works for an international airline. She wants to make a graph that shows the number of travelers to and from the U.S. for each year from 1974 to 1979. Make two line graphs on the same grid for this set of data. Use one line graph to show the travelers to the U.S. and the other to show the travelers from the U.S. Label each line graph.
See Additional Answers beginning on page T44.

	To the U.S.	From the U.S.
1974	3.7 million	6.4 million
1975	3.6 million	6.3 million
1976	4.4 million	6.8 million
1977	4.5 million	7.3 million
1978	5.7 million	7.7 million
1979	7.2 million	7.8 million

Objective: Read and make circle graphs.

Circle Graphs

Materials: Protractor

Problem A

Ann Winters read a report in a news magazine that included the **circle graph** below. It shows the countries with the greatest energy usage. The total amount of energy used worldwide was estimated at 8,020,000,000 metric tons. About how many metric tons of energy were used by the United States?

Countries with Greatest Energy Usage

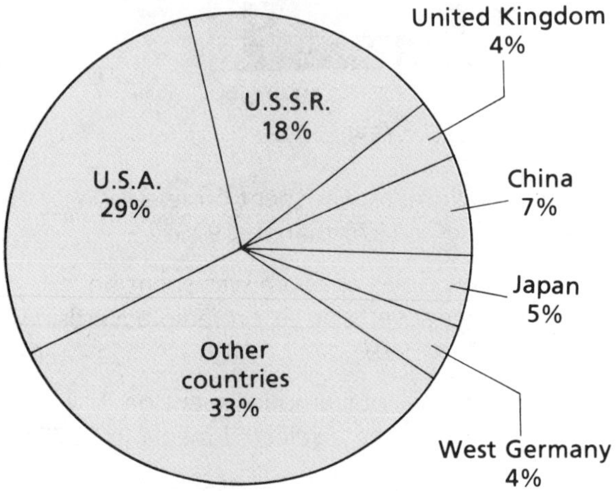

Solution

Read the circle graph to find what percent of the energy was used by the United States.

29%

Then find 29% of 8,020,000,000.

$0.29 \times 8{,}020{,}000{,}000 = 2{,}325{,}800{,}000$

The United States used about 2,325,800,000 metric tons of energy.

Problem B

You might review angle measurement and construction.

Jorge Alvaro is preparing a report on the cost of living. He wants to make a circle graph that shows how a typical family's income is spent.

Make a circle graph for this set of data.

Living expenses

Category	Percent of income
Food	25%
Housing	30%
Utilities	10%
Travel	12%
Clothing	8%
Miscellaneous	15%

Solution

Remind students that there are 360° in a circle.

Multiply 360° by each percent to find the size of each **central angle.** Round each answer to the nearest degree.

Food	$0.25 \times 360° = 90°$
Housing	$0.30 \times 360° = 108°$
Utilities	$0.10 \times 360° = 36°$
Travel	$0.12 \times 360° \approx 43°$
Clothing	$0.08 \times 360° \approx 29°$
Miscellaneous	$0.15 \times 360° = 54°$

Draw a circle. Then use a protractor to draw each central angle. Label each section. Write a title for the graph.

Living Expenses

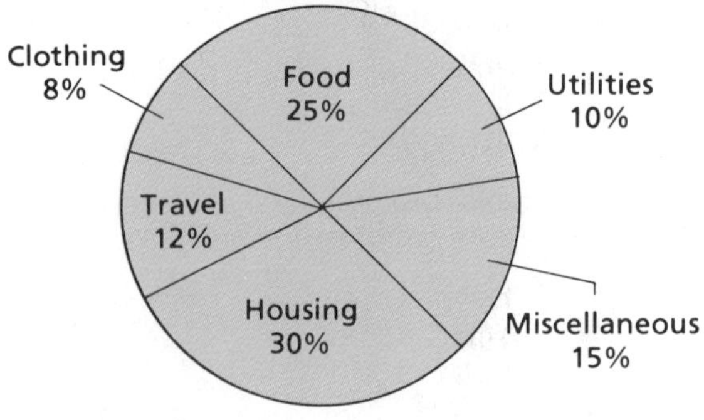

Exercises

In set B, the measure of each central angle is given to the nearest degree. For graphs, see Additional Answers beginning on page T44.

Set A

Use the circle graph in problem A for exercises 1–6. About how many metric tons were used by each of the following?

1. U.S.S.R. 1,443,600,000 t
2. United Kingdom 320,800,000 t
3. China 561,400,000 t
4. Japan 401,000,000 t
5. West Germany 320,800,000 t
6. Other countries 2,646,600,000 t

Use the circle graph in problem B for exercises 7–12. If the Wilsons' income was $17,500, about how much was spent in each category?

7. Housing $5250
8. Travel $2100
9. Clothing $1400
10. Food $4375
11. Utilities $1750
12. Miscellaneous $2625

Set B

Make a circle graph for each set of data.

13. Land owned by the federal government in 1979

Type (use)	Percent of total	
Forest and wildlife	60%	216°
Grazing	21%	76°
Parks	9%	32°
Military	3%	11°
Other	7%	25°

14. Major issues causing work stoppages in 1978

Issue	Percent of work stoppages	
Wages and benefits	67%	241°
Working conditions and hours	2%	7°
Job security	3%	11°
Union organization	6%	22°
Plant administration	12%	43°
Other	10%	36°

Have students draw smaller angles first; discuss *reflex* angles.

15. Estimated voting population by age in 1980

Age	Percent of population	
18–24 years	18.1%	65°
25–44 years	38.9%	140°
45–64 years	27.3%	98°
65 years and over	15.7%	57°

Related Problems

Lisa Sadler made the circle graph below to show the distribution of workers by occupation throughout the country. The total number of employed persons in 1979 was about 97,000,000.

Distribution of Workers by Occupation in 1979

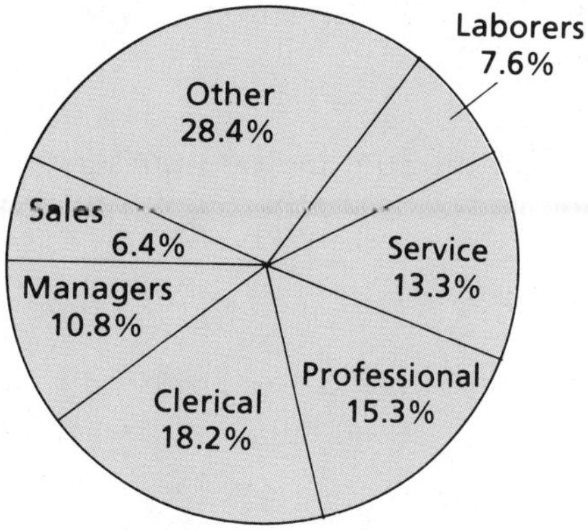

16. About how many more clerical workers were there than professional workers? 2,813,000 clerical workers
17. About how many more managers were there than laborers? 3,104,000 managers
18. About what was the total number of workers in sales occupations or in service occupations? 19,109,000 workers
19. About what percent of the total number of employed persons were clerical workers or laborers? 25.8%

Objective: Compute the mean, median, and mode for a set of numbers.

Mean, Median, and Mode

The sum of a set of numbers divided by the number of addends is the average, or the **mean.** When a set of numbers is arranged in order, the middle number is the **median.** In a set of numbers, the number that appears most often is the **mode.**

Problem A

Ricky Doran bowled 132, 146, 121, 118, and 138. What was his mean score?

Find the mean for these numbers.

Solution

Add the bowling scores.

$$\begin{array}{r} 132 \\ 146 \\ 121 \\ 118 \\ +\ 138 \\ \hline 655 \end{array}$$

Then divide the sum by the number of addends. In this case, there are 5 addends.

$$5\overline{)655} = 131$$

Ricky's mean bowling score was 131.

Problem B

A girls' basketball team played seven games this season. Their scores were 56, 59, 61, 56, 64, 43, and 81. A boys' basketball team played eight games this season. Their scores were 95, 41, 78, 81, 69, 102, 59, and 75. What was the median score for each team?

Find the median for each set of numbers.

Solution

The numbers can be written in ascending or descending order when the median or the mode is to be found.

Arrange the girls' scores in order.

43, 56, 56, **59,** 61, 64, 81

The middle number is 59.

Arrange the boys' scores in order.

41, 59, 69, **75, 78,** 81, 95, 102

In this set of numbers there are two middle numbers, 75 and 78. The median is the average of 75 and 78.

$75 + 78 = 153 \qquad 153 \div 2 = 76.5$

The median score for the girls' team was 59. The median score for the boys' team was 76.5.

Set B 11. 7
12. 8
13. 21
14. 73
15. 25
16. 305
17. 121
18. 16.5
19. 10.3
20. 2.4

Problem C

During the golf season, Norma shot 85, 86, 97, 102, 86, 93, 91, 97, and 86. What was the mode of her golf scores?

Find the mode for these numbers.

Solution

Arrange the numbers in order.

85, **86, 86, 86,** 91, 93, 97, 97, 102

86 appears most often.

The mode of her golf scores was 86.

Some sets of numbers, such as 16, 19, 20, 21, 25, and 27, have no mode. Some sets of numbers, such as 6, 6, 8, 9, 11, 11, and 14, have more than one mode.

Set C 21. 7
22. No mode
23. 21
24. 73
25. 29
26. 301 and 309
27. 116 and 132
28. 15
29. 10.3
30. 2.4

Exercises

Set A Find the mean for each set of numbers.

1. 8, 9, 7, 2, 3, 7, 6
   6
2. 9, 7, 13, 5, 3, 11
   8
3. 47, 21, 89, 12, 21
   38
4. 73, 87, 78, 69, 73, 58
   73
5. 29, 23, 21, 25, 24, 31, 29
   26
6. 309, 305, 309, 301, 301
   305
7. 116, 132, 116, 104, 132, 126
   121
8. 21, 18, 14, 15, 15, 18, 20, 15
   17
9. 10.3, 10.1, 10.2, 10.6, 10.3
   10.3
10. 2.2, 2.3, 2.5, 2.4, 2.6, 2.4
    2.4

Set B Exercises 11–20. Find the median for each set of numbers in Set A.

See above.

Set C Exercises 21–30. Find the mode for each set of numbers in Set A.

See above.

Related Problems

In bowling, a handicap is the number of points given to the player with the lower mean score to equalize the chances of winning. The amount of the handicap is the difference in the mean scores of the players.

For each problem, find the mean score for each player. Then tell which player should get the handicap. Indicate the amount of the handicap.

31. Bob's scores: 119, 131, 127, 147
    Matt's scores: 172, 136, 165, 151
    Bob 131, Matt 156; handicap: Bob, 25
32. Jill's scores: 127, 131, 146, 136
    Sue's scores: 96, 107, 85, 120
    Jill 135, Sue 102; handicap: Sue, 33
33. Bev's scores: 113, 117, 121, 117, 127
    John's scores: 114, 105, 136, 99, 121
    Bev 119, John 115; handicap: John, 4

CALCULATOR APPLICATIONS

Finding the Mean

Find the mean for each set of numbers. Round each answer to the nearest tenth.

1. 282, 919, 464, 737
600.5

2. 1537, 2491, 1764, 3248, 2073
2222.6

3. 1234, 5678, 6789
4567

4. 1122, 3344, 5566, 7788, 9900
5544

5. 27,634   47,092
90,185   53,264
36,243
50,883.6

6. 364,257   423,765
170,843   857,091
963,251
555,841.4

7. 84,076.3   65,308.7
58,732.1   42,435.4
93,457.8
68,802.1

8. 525.371   976.32
624.57   425.09
139.84   840.16
588.6

9. 532.96   4.308
647.91   17.852
3.54
241.3

10. 17.562   3.354
23.98   22.731
104.16   0.634
28.7

Find the mean for each set of data. Round each answer to the nearest whole number.

11. Number of students attending school during a one-week period
1757 students

Monday	1842
Tuesday	1730
Wednesday	1753
Thursday	1813
Friday	1647

12. Salaries in one department
$12,290

Baker	$6,790
Carson	$13,500
Mason	$8,470
Omachi	$20,620
Pena	$18,575
Roberts	$7,250
Thomas	$10,825

13. Attendance at football games
56,501 people

Sept. 22	62,153
Sept. 29	48,139
Oct. 6	57,204
Oct. 13	64,379
Oct. 20	35,702
Oct. 27	71,428

14. U.S. motor vehicle factory sales
12,112,250 sales

1976	11,480,000
1977	12,642,000
1978	12,871,000
1979	11,456,000

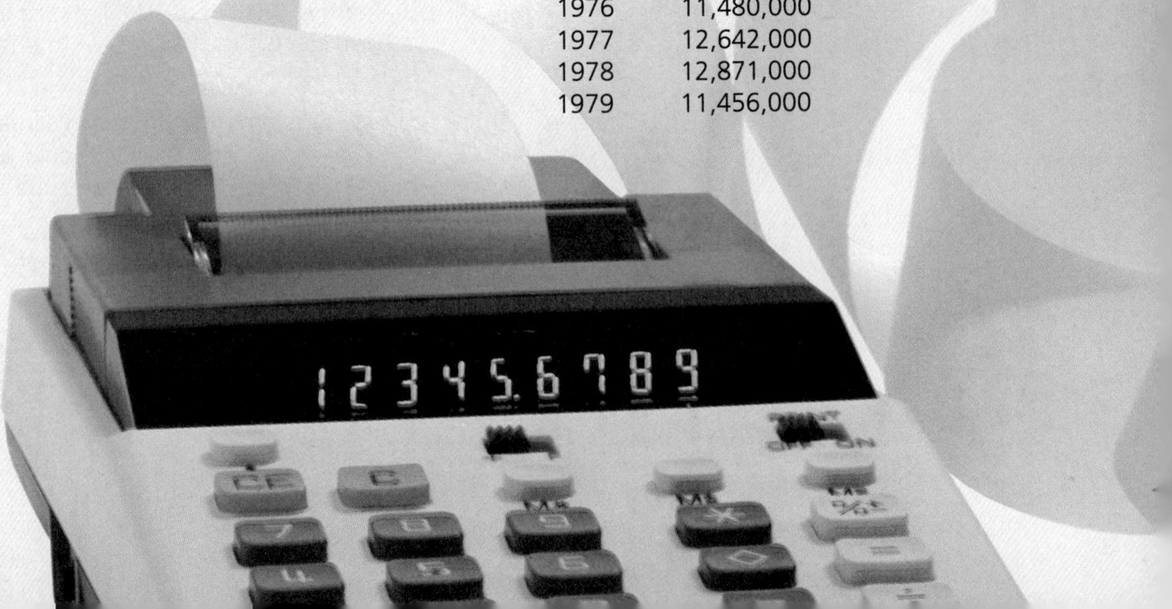

Chapter 3 Review

Materials: Graph paper, protractor

Metric units of length, pages 42–43

Choose the most sensible measure.

1. Length of a paper clip
   3 mm   3 cm   3 m
2. Width of a desk
   1 m   4 m   10 m

Area and volume, pages 44–45

3. Find the area of a rectangle 7.0 m by 4.8 m.
   33.6 m²
4. Find the area of a triangle with a base of 9.4 cm and a height of 11.0 cm.
   51.7 cm²
5. Find the volume of a rectangular prism 14.3 cm by 7.2 cm by 5.6 cm to the nearest tenth.
   576.6 cm³

Metric units of capacity and mass, pages 46–47

Choose the more sensible measure.

6. Gas tank of a motorcycle
   13 mL   13 L
7. Can of peaches
   25 g   600 g

Renaming metric units of measure, pages 48–49

8. 7.63 kg = ▦ g
   7630 g
9. 34 cm = ▦ m
   0.34 m

Temperature, pages 50–51

10. Choose the more sensible temperature for melted wax.
    20°C   80°C

Time, pages 52–53

11. Add. 6 hours 20 minutes + 3 hours 45 minutes.
    10 hours 5 minutes
12. Add 4 hours 10 minutes to 3:55 P.M.
    8:05 P.M.
13. How much time is there from 10:35 A.M. to 2:20 P.M.?
    3 hours 45 minutes

Bar graphs and line graphs, pages 54–55

14. Make a bar graph for this set of data.
    See Additional Answers beginning on page T44.

    New housing units started, 1976–1979

1976	1550 million	1978	2020 million
1977	1990 million	1979	1750 million

15. Make a line graph for the data in problem 14.
    See Additional Answers beginning on page T44.

Circle graphs, pages 56–57

Use the circle graph for problem 16.

Households Using Fuel Oil in 1979

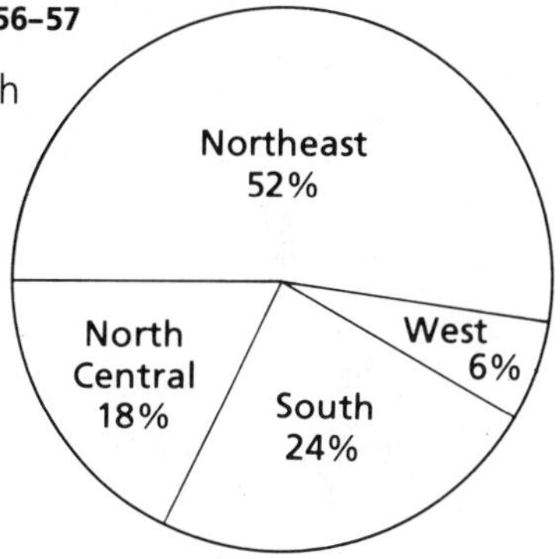

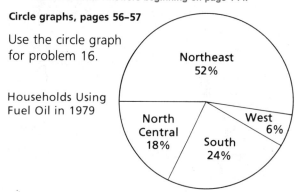

16. In 1979, the total number of households using fuel oil to heat their homes was about 17,000,000. How many of these were in the Northeast?
    8,840,000 households
17. Make a circle graph for this set of data.
    See Additional Answers beginning on page T44.

    Distribution of families by number of children under 18 years (1979)

Number of children	Percent of total
0	48% 173°
1	21% 76°
2	19% 68°
3 or more	12% 43°

Mean, median, and mode, pages 58–59

For problems 18–20, use this set of numbers.

21, 15, 23, 10, 14, 28, 21, 12

Find the

18. mean.
    18
19. median.
    18
20. mode.
    21

Chapter 3 Test

Materials: Graph paper, protractor

Number of test items - 20

Number missed	1	2	3	4	5	6	7	8	9	10
Percent correct	95	90	85	80	75	70	65	60	55	50

Choose the most sensible measure.

1. Length of a canoe
4 mm   4 cm   4 m

2. Length of a wrench
1 cm   26 cm   315 cm

3. Find the area of a rectangle 3.0 m by 7.2 m.
21.6 m²

4. Find the area of a triangle with a base of 8.6 cm and a height of 13.0 cm.
55.9 cm²

5. Find the volume of a rectangular prism 11.4 cm by 5.7 cm by 7.1 cm to the nearest tenth.
461.4 cm³

Choose the more sensible measure.

6. Carton of grapefruit juice
900 mL   900 L

7. Whole chicken
1.2 kg   24.5 kg

8. 3.7 m = ▒ cm
370 cm

9. 482 g = ▒ kg
0.482 kg

10. Choose the more sensible temperature for a warm shower.
30°C   80°C

11. Add. 8 hours 15 minutes + 4 hours 55 minutes.
13 hours 10 minutes

12. Add 3 hours 45 minutes to 9:45 A.M.
1:30 P.M.

13. How much time is there from 1:10 P.M. to 5:45 P.M.?
4 hours 35 minutes

14. Make a bar graph for this set of data.
See Additional Answers beginning on page T44.
Value of farm real estate, 1977–1980

1977	$470 billion	1979	$580 billion
1978	$510 billion	1980	$670 billion

15. Make a line graph for the data in problem 14.
See Additional Answers beginning on page T44.

Use the circle graph below for problem 16.

Households Using Electricity in 1979

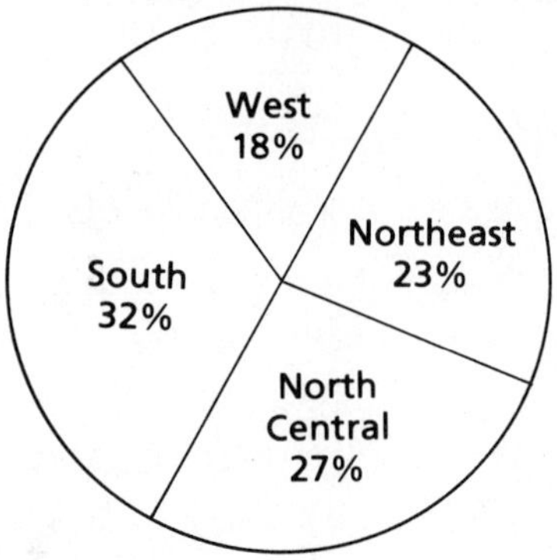

16. In 1979, the total number of households using electricity to heat their homes was about 80,000,000. How many of these were in the South?
25,600,000 households

17. Make a circle graph for this set of data.
See Additional Answers beginning on page T44.
Persons employed in health occupations in 1979

Type	Percent of total
Physicians, dentists, and pharmacists	15% **54°**
Registered nurses	25% **90°**
Technicians	10% **36°**
Other	50% **180°**

For problems 18–20, use this set of numbers.

15, 22, 23, 16, 22, 12, 16

Find the

18. mean.
18

19. median.
16

20. mode.
22 and 16

See pages 5-6 of the *Test Masters* for an alternate form of the Chapter 3 Test.

Unit 1 Test

Number of test items - 23

Number missed	1	2	3	4	5	6	7	8	9	10	11
Percent correct	96	91	87	83	78	74	70	65	61	57	52

Choose the best answer.

Pages 4–5

1. Round 4753 to the nearest hundred.

A 5000 **C** 4700

(**B**) 4800 **D** 4750

Pages 6–7

2. 96.27 − 64.83

A 161.10 (**C**) 31.44

B 32.64 **D** 32.34

Pages 8–9

3. 783 × 94

(**A**) 73,602 **C** 66,502

B 68,592 **D** 72,602

Pages 10–11

4. 8.32 × 4.7

A 3.8104 (**C**) 39.104

B 381.04 **D** 38.104

Pages 12–13

5. 28.236 ÷ 3.9

A 0.724 **C** 7.31

B 0.731 (**D**) 7.24

Pages 14–15

6. Rename $\frac{12}{20}$ in lowest terms.

A $\frac{6}{10}$ **C** $\frac{4}{5}$

B $\frac{3}{4}$ (**D**) $\frac{3}{5}$

Pages 16–17

7. $5\frac{3}{5} \div 2\frac{1}{3}$

A $10\frac{3}{15}$ **C** $13\frac{1}{15}$

(**B**) $2\frac{2}{5}$ **D** $\frac{5}{12}$

Pages 18–19

8. $3\frac{3}{4} + 1\frac{1}{6}$

(**A**) $4\frac{11}{12}$ **C** $4\frac{4}{10}$

B $3\frac{4}{10}$ **D** $3\frac{1}{8}$

Pages 24–25

9. Solve. $d - 25.1 = 34.7$

(**A**) $d = 59.8$ **C** $d = 11.6$

B $d = 9.6$ **D** $d = 10.4$

Pages 26–27

10. Solve. $384 = 16y$

A $y = 6144$ (**C**) $y = 24$

B $y = 368$ **D** $y = 400$

Pages 28–29

11. Solve. $8b + 42 = 138$

(**A**) $b = 12$ **C** $b = 14.5$

B $b = 22.5$ **D** $b = 16$

Pages 30–31

12. Solve. $\frac{6}{c} = \frac{21}{28}$

A $c = 4.5$ **C** $c = 9$

(**B**) $c = 8$ **D** $c = 98$

Pages 32–33

13. Write 8% as a decimal.

A 0.8 **C** 8

B 0.008 (**D**) 0.08

Pages 34–37

14. Find 15% of 90.

A 1350 **C** 600

(**B**) 13.5 **D** 135

A unit test occurs at the end of each three chapters. The test covers selected skills or applications taught in each lesson of the unit. The multiple-choice style was chosen to help prepare students for taking standardized tests.

Each page reference shown in red indicates where a skill or application is taught. You might give students these references if you assign these two pages as an open-book test.

Pages 42–43

15. Choose the most sensible measure for the length of an adult's hand.

A 19 mm **C** 19 m

B 19 cm **D** 19 km

Pages 44–45

16. Find the area of a rectangle that measures 6.0 meters by 9.7 meters.

A 582 m^2 **C** 474 m^2

B 47.4 m^2 **D** 58.2 m^2

Pages 46–47

17. Choose the most sensible measure for a container of liquid bleach.

A 0.003 L **C** 4 L

B 125 L **D** 68 L

Pages 48–49

18. 3476 g = ▒ kg

A 0.3476 **C** 3.476

B 347.6 **D** 34.76

Pages 50–51

19. Choose the most sensible water temperature for outdoor swimming.

A 23°C **C** 79°C

B 4°C **D** 101°C

Pages 52–53

20. Add 3 hours 25 minutes to 4:15 P.M.

A 7:30 P.M. **C** 7:40 P.M.

B 1:10 P.M. **D** 8:40 P.M.

Pages 54–55

21. How many more TV sets per 1000 population are there in Australia than in France?

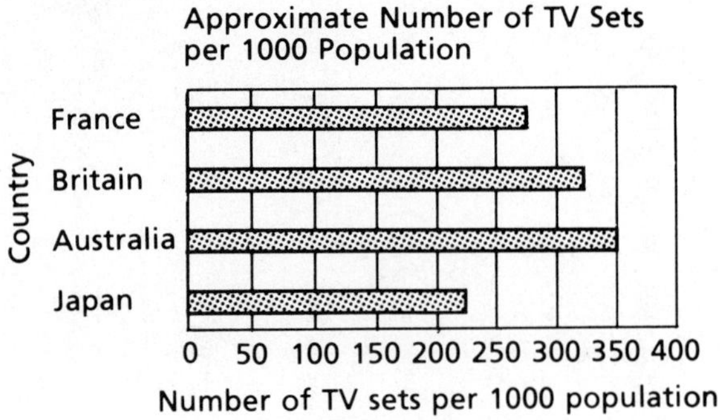

A 50 sets **C** 100 sets

B 75 sets **D** 275 sets

Pages 56–57

22. Read the circle graph below and find the cost of labor on a home that costs $78,000 to build.

Major Cost Items in Building a House

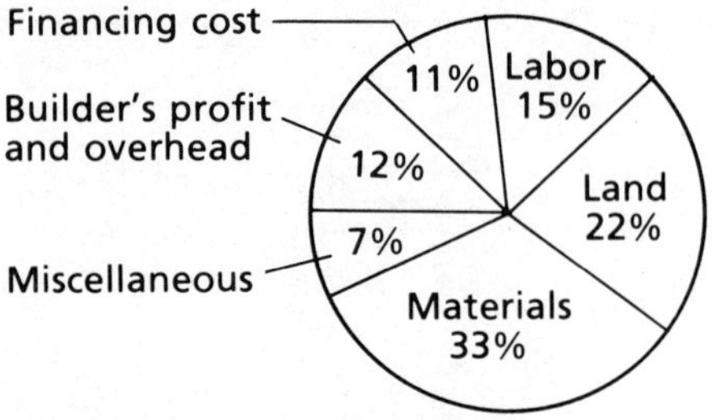

A $17,160 **C** $5200

B $11,700 **D** $9300

Pages 58–59

23. Find the mean for this set of numbers.

13, 18, 4, 15, 9, 18, 21

A 15 **C** 18

B 98 **D** 14

 For an alternate form of the Unit 1 Test, see pages T57–T58 of this book and pages 7–8 of the *Test Masters*.

Here is a method of adding a long column of one-digit numbers in which you use your fingers to show the tens. First look at the usual way of adding these numbers.

The Break Time/Mental Math feature occurs at the end of each unit. It shows shortcuts to help students compute mentally. Encourage all students to try these shortcuts.

Usual Method

	THINK
9	
8	9 + 8 = 17
7	17 + 7 = 24
5	24 + 5 = 29
6	29 + 6 = 35
+ 8	35 + 8 = 43
43	

Another Method

	THINK	Show using your fingers
9		
8	9 + 8 = 17	 Show one ten.
7	7 + 7 = 14	 Show another ten.
5	4 + 5 = 9	 No additional tens.
6	9 + 6 = 15	 Show another ten.
+ 8	5 + 8 = 13	 Show another ten.
43	Your fingers show 4 tens. There are 3 ones.	

Add, using your fingers to show the tens. Write only the answer.

1. 5 + 8 + 8 + 7 + 3 + 9 + 4
   44
2. 7 + 4 + 9 + 5 + 3 + 9 + 4 + 6
   47
3. 6 + 8 + 9 + 4 + 6 + 2 + 9 + 7 + 4
   55
4. 5 + 7 + 9 + 3 + 6 + 9 + 7 + 8 + 2
   56
5. 3 + 9 + 9 + 5 + 8 + 6 + 8 + 7 + 5 + 1 + 7
   68
6. 9 + 7 + 8 + 2 + 7 + 5 + 1 + 4 + 9 + 8 + 7 + 5
   72
7. 3 + 3 + 8 + 2 + 9 + 7 + 5 + 6 + 9 + 1 + 7 + 9
   69
8. 5 + 5 + 5 + 6 + 6 + 6 + 7 + 7 + 7 + 8 + 8 + 8
   78
9. 3 + 7 + 9 + 1 + 7 + 8 + 4 + 9 + 7 + 8 + 2 + 9 + 4 + 4 + 8
   90
10. 6 + 9 + 1 + 3 + 6 + 8 + 2 + 5 + 8 + 7 + 4 + 8 + 3 + 9 + 2
    81

The Computer Literacy feature on pages 394–399 provides exposure to the programming language BASIC. It could be used at this time.

Unit 2 Income, Banking, and Credit

Chapter 4 Income

Objective: Compute gross pay by using hourly and overtime rates.

Hourly Rate and Overtime Rate

See page T29 for additional notes and activities for Chapter 4.

Important terms appear in boldface type.

Ruben Betances is a mailer for a stereo manufacturer. He usually works 8 hours a day, 5 days a week.

When he works more than 8 hours in one day, Ruben is paid at an **overtime rate** for the extra hours. The overtime rate is 1.5 times the regular hourly rate. This is called **time and a half.**

Ruben's **gross pay** is the sum of his regular pay and his overtime pay.

Problem

The Problem/Solution format provides students with a strategy for completing the related problems.

One week Ruben worked his regular 40 hours and 4.75 hours of overtime. If his regular hourly rate is \$5.50 per hour, what was his gross pay for the week?

Solution

Point out that partial hours are given as decimals instead of minutes.

Strategy

- Multiply hourly rate by 40 to find regular pay.
  $40 \times \$5.50 = \$220.00$
- Multiply hourly rate by 1.5 to find overtime rate.
  $1.5 \times \$5.50 = \$8.25$
- Multiply by 4.75 to find overtime pay. Round to the nearest cent.
  $4.75 \times \$8.25 \approx \$39.19$
- Add to find gross pay.
  $\$220.00 + \$39.19 = \$259.19$

You might show the actual product before rounding.
$4.75 \times \$8.25 = \$39.1875$ which rounds to \$39.19.

Conclusion

Ruben's gross pay was \$259.19.

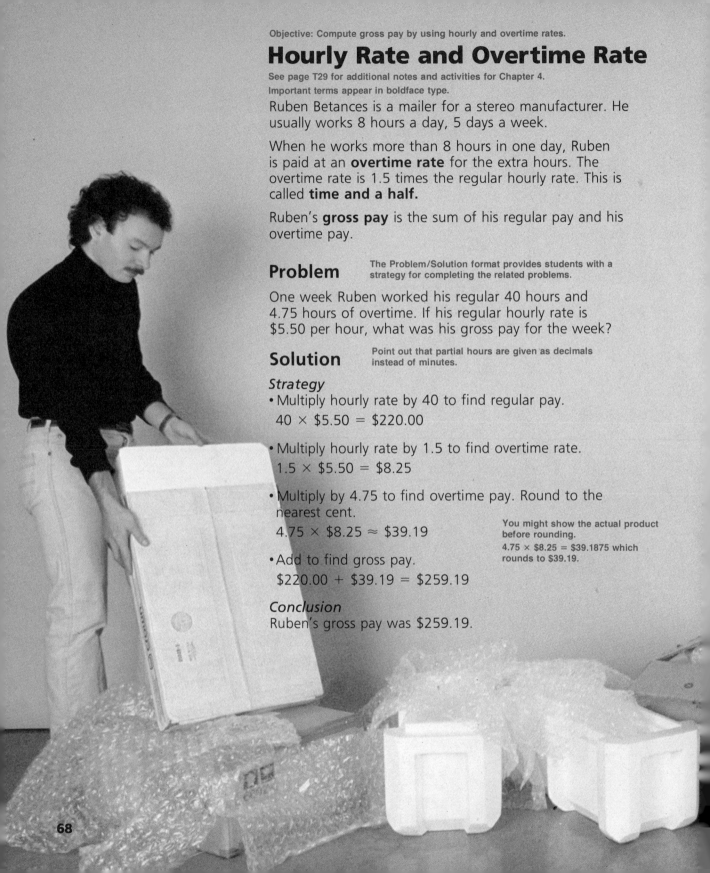

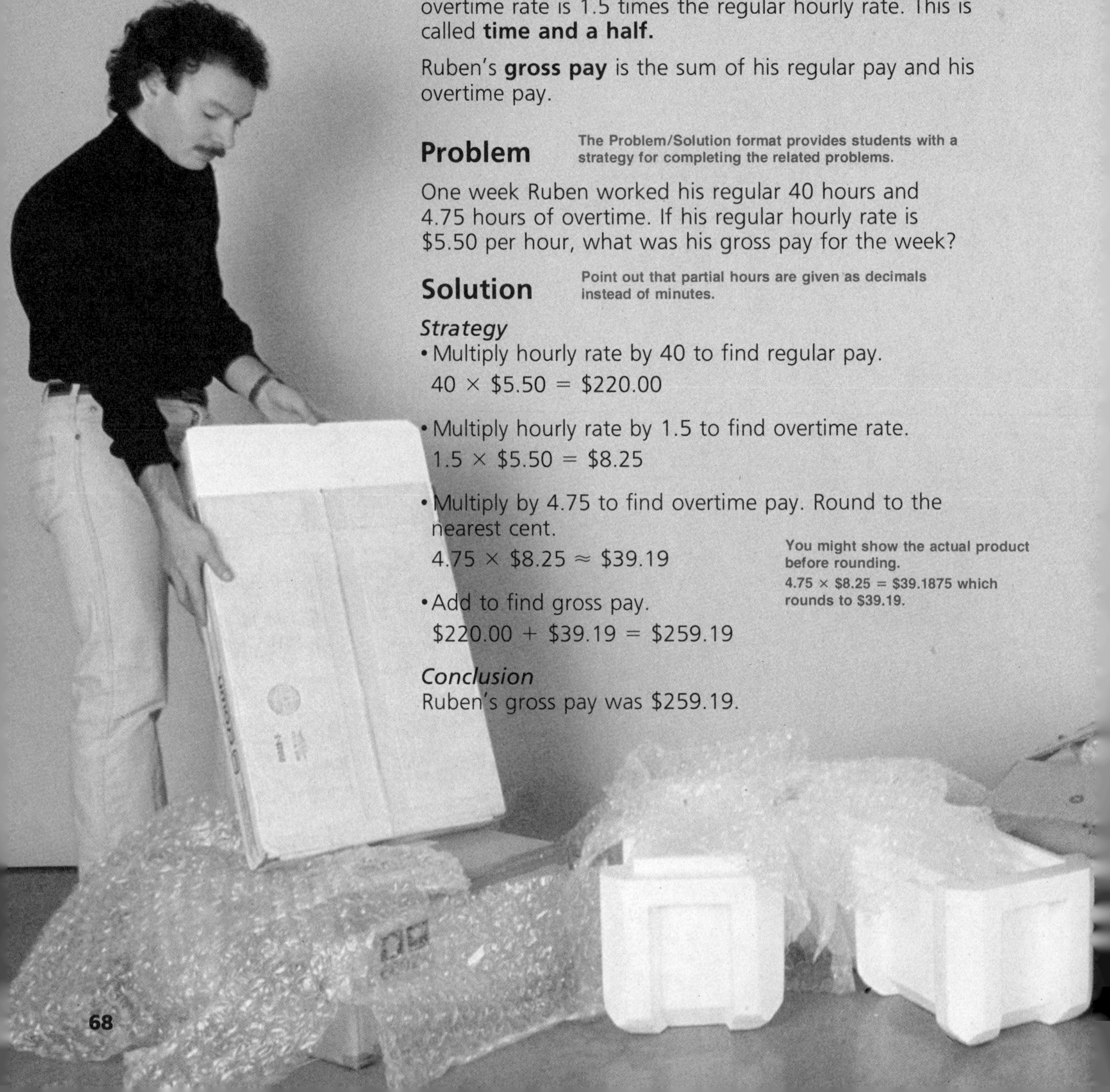

Warm-up: 40 × 4.10 [164]
36 × 5.45 [196.20]
1.5 × 6.58 [9.87]
193.56 + 7.53 [201.09]

Warm-up exercises in each lesson of Units 2-6 provide a quick skills review of the mathematical skills used in the lesson.

See pages 19-20 of *Consumer Forms and Problems.*

Related Problems

Answers to the odd-numbered problems are given at the end of the student's text on pages 418–451.

Complete the table to find the gross pay for each employee. Round each amount to the nearest cent.

	Job	Regular hours	Regular hourly rate	Regular pay	Overtime hours	Overtime rate (time and a half)	Overtime pay	Gross pay
	Mailer	40	$5.50	$220.00	4.75	$8.25	$39.19	$259.19
1.	Steamfitter	40	$10.10	$404.00	0	——	——	$404.00
2.	Sheet-metal worker	38	$10.39	$394.82	0	——	——	$394.82
3.	Power truck operator	40	$6.50	$260.00	5	$9.75	$48.75	$308.75
4.	Operating engineer	40	$9.50	$380.00	6	$14.25	$85.50	$465.50
5.	Floor molder	40	$6.20	$248.00	8	$9.30	$74.40	$322.40
6.	Millwright	40	$8.72	$348.80	12	$13.08	$156.96	$505.76
7.	Machinist	40	$8.02	$320.80	2.25	$12.03	$27.07	$347.87
8.	Ironworker	40	$10.85	$434.00	15	$16.28	$244.20	$678.20
9.	Tool and die maker	40	$8.53	$341.20	3.5	$12.80	$44.80	$386.00
10.	Electroplater	40	$6.75	$270.00	6.75	$10.13	$68.38	$338.38
11.	Instrument maker	40	$8.03	$321.20	5.25	$12.05	$63.26	$384.46

(12.) Ann Altaha is a stationary engineer. Her regular hourly rate is $7.93 for a 40-hour week. She is paid double time (two times the hourly rate) for each hour she works on holidays. She is paid time and a half for all other overtime. One week Ann worked 53.5 hours, including 8 hours on a holiday. Find her gross pay for that week. Round each amount to the nearest cent.
$509.53

Extension problems are indicated with red circles.

Objective: Compute gross pay for employees paid hourly wages plus tips.

Hourly Rate Plus Tips

Earl Johnson is a waiter in a large restaurant in Chicago. His weekly pay is determined by both his hourly rate and the tips he earns. Earl gives part of his tips to other employees who help him serve his customers.

Solutions to percent problems like the one below will appear throughout the text without a variable.

Problem

Earl is paid \$4.15 an hour for a 40-hour week. One week he worked 40 hours and earned \$215 in tips. Earl kept 75% of his tips and gave the other 25% of his tips to the other employees. What was Earl's gross pay for the week?

Solution

Strategy

- Multiply to find regular pay.
  $40 \times \$4.15 = \$166.00$
- Multiply his tips by 75% to find his share of the tips.
  $0.75 \times \$215 = \$161.25$
- Add to find gross pay.
  $\$166.00 + \$161.25 = \$327.25$

Conclusion

Earl's gross pay was \$327.25.

Warm-up: 3.42 × 19.4 [66.348]
100% − 35% [65%]
75% of 150 [112.5]
80% of 219 [175.2]

See page 21 of *Consumer Forms and Problems.*

Related Problems

Problem 9 can be extended if you add the condition that Sue must give $0.50 per haircut to the owner of the shop.

Find each person's gross pay for the week.

	Name	Hourly rate	Hours worked	Tips		Gross pay
				Amount	Percent kept	
1.	Linda Taylor	$4.00	40	$250	100%	$410.00
2.	Phillip Witt	$4.35	25	$115	100%	$223.75
3.	David Glenn	$4.18	40	$164	80%	$298.40
4.	Vicki Farnsworth	$4.75	35	$183	75%	$303.50
5.	Dick Grove	$6.20	40	$212	85%	$428.20
6.	Irene Luciano	$4.90	36.4	$148	85%	$304.16
7.	Clyde Beagle	$7.10	34.7	$143	90%	$375.07

8. Roger Marks is a porter. He earns $4.75 an hour plus tips. He worked 35 hours and earned $175 in tips. What was his gross pay?
$341.25

9. Sue Bowersox is a barber. She charges $7.50 for each haircut. She gave 65 haircuts and earned $62.50 in tips. What was her gross pay?
$550

10. Ray Inada is a musician earning $6.75 an hour for a 40-hour week. He makes time and a half for overtime. One week Ray worked 45 hours and made $185 in tips. Find his gross pay. Round each amount to the nearest cent.
$505.65

Break Time

The Break Time feature occurs in each chapter. It is an interesting problem or puzzle that usually does not involve computational skills. Encourage students of all ability levels to try the Break Times.

A farmer planted 10 trees in 5 rows of 4 each. Two ways are shown. Draw three other ways.
See Additional Answers beginning on page T44.

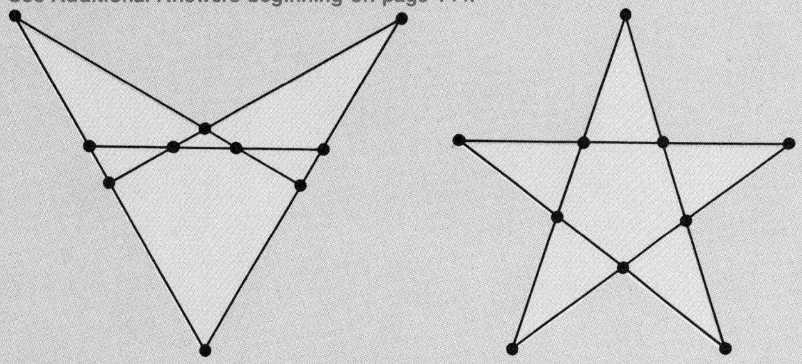

Objective: Compute earnings for employees paid straight commission.

Straight Commission

Wendy McClure works part time selling products for Home Cosmetics, Inc. She is paid a **commission,** or a certain portion of the money from the sales, as her pay.

Since this commission is the only pay that Wendy earns, it is called **straight commission.**

Problem

One customer ordered two bottles of cologne that cost $5.49 each. Wendy's commission on the cologne was 43%. How much did Wendy earn on this sale?

Solution

Strategy

- Multiply to find the total amount of the sale.

  $2 \times \$5.49 = \$10.98$

- Multiply by 43% to find the earnings. Round to the nearest cent.

  $0.43 \times \$10.98 \approx \$4.72$

Conclusion

Wendy earned $4.72 on this sale.

Warm-up:
5 × 2.98 [14.9]
4 × 3.17 [12.68]
35% of 19.50 [6.825]
20% of 105 [21]

Related Problems

Find the amount of commission for each item. Round each answer to the nearest cent.

	Item	Price	Commission	
1.	Night cream	$3.50	45%	$1.58
2.	Cleansing cream	$2.69	45%	$1.21
3.	Eyeshadow	$2.99	43%	$1.29
4.	Mascara	$2.49	43%	$1.07
5.	Blush	$4.49	37%	$1.66

	Item	Price	Commission	
6.	Moisturizer	$3.29	35%	$1.15
7.	Lipstick	$1.99	41%	$0.82
8.	After-shave lotion	$6.99	33%	$2.31
9.	Air freshener	$1.49	25%	$0.37
10.	Jewelry case	$16.99	45%	$7.65

Complete the table. The commission for each item is 40%. Round each answer to the nearest cent.

	Item	Quantity	Price each	Total price	Commission earned
11.	Bath crystals	2	$5.99	$11.98	$4.79
12.	Suntan lotion	3	$2.99	$8.97	$3.59
13.	Eyeliner	1	$2.29	$2.29	$0.92
14.	Hand lotion	2	$2.99	$5.98	$2.39
15.	Perfumed soap	3	$1.50	$4.50	$1.80
16.	Hair spray	2	$2.49	$4.98	$1.99
17.	Bath talc	4	$2.99	$11.96	$4.78

18. Find the total amount of the sale and the total commission earned for problems 11–17.
$50.66; $20.26

This lesson could be extended by finding the amount Pat must send to the company with the customer's order. The total price minus the commission is the amount sent.

Objective: Compute earnings for employees paid salary plus commission.

Bookkeeper

See the Careers Chart beginning on page 410 for more information about the careers in this cluster.

The career lesson in each chapter features an occupation in which mathematical skills are needed. The lesson is an integral part of the development of the chapter topic.

Career Cluster: Business Detail Carolyn Tarahata owns Business Services, Inc. Her firm prepares payroll information for Becker's Home Center. Carolyn computes the gross pay for each employee.

Problem

Greg Ritter is paid $125 a week plus a commission of 1.5% on all sales delivered. Last week, he sold $7400 worth of furniture. Orders totaling $475 were canceled. What was Carolyn's computation of Greg's gross pay for the week?

Solution

Commissions are paid when orders are delivered. Thus, cancellations must be subtracted from total sales.

Strategy

- Subtract the canceled sales from the total sales to find the sales delivered.
  $\$7400 - \$475 = \$6925$
- Multiply by 1.5% to find the commission earnings. Round to the nearest cent.
  $0.015 \times \$6925 \approx \$103.88$
- Add to find gross pay.
  $\$125.00 + \$103.88 = \$228.88$

Conclusion

Carolyn's computation of Greg's gross pay was $228.88.

Warm-up: 3125 − 473 [2652]
2.5% of 5326 [133.15]
496.35 + 87.50 [583.85]
576.38 + 237.50 [813.88]

Related Problems

In problems 9-12, students must subtract the minimum sales from the total sales to determine the amount on which commission is paid.

Find the gross pay for each of the Becker employees.
Round each amount to the nearest cent.

	Name	Total sales	Cancellations	Commission	Weekly salary	Gross pay
1.	Mary Andrulewicz	$8,500	——	1.5%	$115	$242.50
2.	Gloria Wren	$7,860	——	1.5%	$120	$237.90
3.	Bill Bowen	$10,432	$357	2%	$135	$336.50
4.	Jay Baldwin	$9,136	$425	2%	$100	$274.22
5.	Lorraine Hill	$11,089	$718	1.5%	$110	$265.57
6.	Tom Gill	$9,976	$387	1.5%	$110	$253.84
7.	Carol Reynolds	$7,659	$195	3%	$95	$318.92
8.	Mike Merrill	$8,564	$87	2%	$100	$269.54

9. Jerry Cohen sells mattresses and springs. He receives a salary of $255 a week plus a commission of 2% on all sales over $800. Last week he sold $1500 worth of bedding. Find his gross pay.
$269

10. Neil McCall receives a salary of $330 a week plus a commission of 1.5% on all sales over $1800. Last week he sold $3700 worth of carpeting. Find his gross pay.
$358.50

11. Shannon Michaels sells major appliances. Her salary is $680 per month plus a commission of 3.5% on all sales over $8000. Find her gross pay for the month if her sales were $12,400.
$834

12. Dick Nair sells tires for a monthly salary of $840 plus a 2% commission on all sales over $4800. If he sold $4650 worth of tires last month, what was his gross pay?
$840

Objective: Compute gross pay for employees paid salary and graduated commission.

Warm-up: 4% of 7000 [280]
3.5% of 5400 [189]
16,000 − 7800 [8200]
378 + 493 [871]

Graduated Commission

See page 22 of *Consumer Forms and Problems*.

Scott Palmer sells pipe and steel products for large construction projects. He is paid a monthly salary plus a **graduated commission.** His commission rate depends upon his total sales.

Problem

Scott's monthly salary is $350. In addition, he receives 5% commission on the first $9000 of his sales and 6% commission on all sales over $9000.

Last month Scott sold $17,000 worth of products. What was his gross pay?

Solution

Strategy

- Multiply $9000 by 5% to find the earnings on the first $9000 of his sales.
  0.05 × $9000 = $450
- Subtract $9000 from the total sales to find the amount that earns commission at 6%.
  $17,000 − $9000 = $8000
- Multiply $8000 by 6% to find the earnings on sales over $9000.
  0.06 × $8000 = $480
- Add to find the gross pay.
  $350 + $450 + $480 = $1280

Conclusion

Scott's gross pay was $1280.

Related Problems

For each problem, find the gross pay from the total sales and the commission given.

	Salary	Commission	Total sales
1.	$500 $1020.00	5% of first $5000; 6% of sales over $5000	$9,500
2.	$535 $1011.00	4% of first $2000; 5.5% of sales over $2000	$9,200
3.	$475 $1225.00	8% of first $5000; 10% of sales over $5000	$8,500
4.	$525 $1059.00	5.5% of first $8500; 7% of sales over $8500	$9,450
5.	$0 $1264.75	10% of all sales plus 5% of sales over $4300	$9,865
6.	$0 $1311.00	4% of first $1500; 5% of next $1500; 7% of sales over $3000	$19,800

CALCULATOR APPLICATIONS

Selling-Cost Percent

Employers may use selling-cost percent to compare the work of their salespeople. The lower the selling-cost percent, the more efficient the salesperson.

Selling-cost percent can be found by dividing the total earnings by the total sales and then expressing that quotient as a percent.

Emily Fiene sold $87,000 worth of goods last year. Her salary was $12,300 plus a commission of 2% of her sales.

$0.02 \times \$87,000 = \$1740$ Commission earnings

$\$12,300 + \$1740 = \$14,040$ Total earnings

$\$14,040 \div \$87,000 \approx 0.161$ Rounded to 3 decimal places

Emily's selling-cost percent is 16.1%.

Find each selling-cost percent to the nearest tenth.

	Salesperson	Salary	Commission	Sales	Total earnings	Selling-cost percent
	Emily Fiene	$12,300	2% of all sales	$87,000	$14,040	16.1%
1.	Tom Auer	$5,823	5% of all sales	$65,000	**$9073.00**	**14.0%**
2.	Carole Nitz	$7,123	7.25% of all sales	$88,500	**$13,539.25**	**15.3%**
3.	Pete Vaughn	$6,100	6.135% of all sales	$74,865	**$10,692.97**	**14.3%**
4.	Andy Ricco	$5,036	3.35% of first $1800; 4.7% of sales over $1800	$89,547	**$9220.41**	**10.3%**
5.	Dan Statz	$4,538	5.5% of first $20,000; 8.5% of sales over $20,000	$133,457	**$15,281.85**	**11.5%**
6.	Vicky Sayo	$5,200	6.7% of first $25,000; 9.2% of sales over $25,000	$189,419	**$22,001.55**	**11.6%**
7.	Ben Griffin	$0	10.23% straight commission	$158,889	**$16,254.34**	**10.2%**
8.	Mike Ryan	$0	11.85% straight commission	$126,453	**$14,984.68**	**11.8%**
9.	Jenny Fox	$3,500	11.21% straight commission	$117,582	**$16,680.94**	**14.2%**
10.	Liz Wille	$7,400	3.47% of first $25,000; 6.23% of next $25,000; 7.35% of sales over $50,000	$298,468	**$28,087.40**	**9.4%**
11.	Dave Bock	$6,000	3.73% of first $45,000; 6.85% of next $45,000; 7.35% of sales over $90,000	$215,386	**$19,976.87**	**9.3%**

12. Which three people had the best selling-cost percents?
Dave Bock, Liz Wille, Ben Griffin

Each chapter contains an optional set of problems to be done with a four-function calculator. These problems use or extend concepts taught previously in the chapter.

Objectives: Find the amount withheld from gross pay for federal income tax and social security; find the total amount of deductions and compute the net pay.

Net Pay

Each pay period, employers subtract a specified amount from employees' gross pay for federal income tax.

The amount deducted is determined by an employee's gross pay, marital status, and number of **exemptions.** An exemption is a member of the family or a person who lived in the employee's home as a member of the family for the whole year.

The Internal Revenue Service of the United States Treasury Department provides tables which employers use to determine the amount to withhold for federal income tax. The tables are on pages 402–405.

SINGLE Persons—**WEEKLY** Payroll Period

And the wages are—		Exemptions claimed			
At least	But less than	0	1	2	3
		The amount of income tax to be withheld shall be—			
$135	$140	$19.00	$15.30	$11.80	$8.40
140	145	20.00	16.20	12.70	9.30
145	150	21.10	17.10	13.60	10.20
150	160	22.60	18.60	15.00	11.50
160	170	24.70	20.70	16.80	13.30
370	380	83.60	77.10	70.50	64.50
380	390	87.00	80.50	73.90	67.50
390	400	90.40	83.90	77.30	70.80
400	410	93.80	87.30	80.70	74.20
410	420	97.20	90.70	84.10	77.60

Problem

Marge Schaffer is single and earns $375.55 a week. She claims exemptions for herself and her father. How much is withheld from her paycheck each week for federal income tax?

Solution

Strategy

- Use the table for single persons and find the amounts that the salary is between.

  $375.55 is "at least $370 but less than $380."

- Follow the table across for the amount listed under 2 exemptions.

  $70.50

Conclusion

$70.50 is withheld from Marge's paycheck for federal income tax.

Warm-up:
6.65% of 458 [30.457]
6.65% of 250 [16.625]
89.35 + 14.67 + 5.28 [109.30]
576.28 − 137.49 [438.79]

See pages 318-319 for a computer application related to this lesson.

Related Problems

Problems 4-7 can be used for a class discussion on the effect that marital status and number of exemptions have on the amount withheld for federal income tax.

Use the appropriate table from pages 402–405 to find the amount withheld each week for federal income tax.

	Gross pay	Marital status	Exemptions claimed	
1.	$125	Single	1	$13.50
2.	$98	Single	1	$8.40
3.	$175	Single	2	$18.80
4.	$437	Single	1	$97.50
5.	$437	Single	3	$84.40
6.	$437	Married	2	$70.60
7.	$437	Married	3	$65.20
8.	$323	Married	2	$43.20
9.	$418	Married	6	$46.20
10.	$287	Married	5	$23.30
11.	$247	Single	1	$39.00
12.	$415	Married	4	$55.50
13.	$170	Married	3	$10.70
14.	$343	Single	1	$67.10
15.	$542	Married	5	$85.20

Point out that both the amount withheld for federal income tax and the amount withheld for FICA are based on gross pay.

You may wish to allow students to use calculators for these problems.

Each pay period, part of most employees' paychecks is withheld under the Federal Insurance Contributions Act (FICA). The federal government uses this money to provide retirement income, survivors' benefits, and medical-cost benefits to qualified persons.

Most employed persons pay *6.65% of the first $29,700 of their gross income* to the federal government for **social security** (FICA deductions). Nothing is withheld for amounts over $29,700.

Problem

Marge's paycheck shows that her gross pay to date totaled $12,017.60. This week, her gross pay was $375.55. How much was withheld this week for social security?

Solution

Strategy

- Check that the year's total gross pay is less than $29,700.

  $12,017.60 < $29,700

- Multiply the week's gross pay by 6.65% to find the amount withheld for social security. Round to the nearest cent.

  0.0665 × $375.55 ≈ $24.97

Conclusion

$24.97 was withheld from Marge's paycheck for social security.

Related Problems

Find the amount withheld from each paycheck for social security. Round each answer to the nearest cent.

	Gross pay to date	Gross pay this paycheck	
16.	$6358.07	$138.81	$9.23
17.	$2009.18	$94.65	$6.29
18.	$197.67	$46.73	$3.11
19.	$7885.60	$226.80	$15.08
20.	$5421.45	$500.00	$33.25
21.	$4960.48	$181.53	$12.07
22.	$10,965.00	$674.26	$44.84
23.	$12,376.14	$1547.02	$102.88
24.	$25,980.90	$885.46	$58.88
25.	$31,664.00	$938.17	None

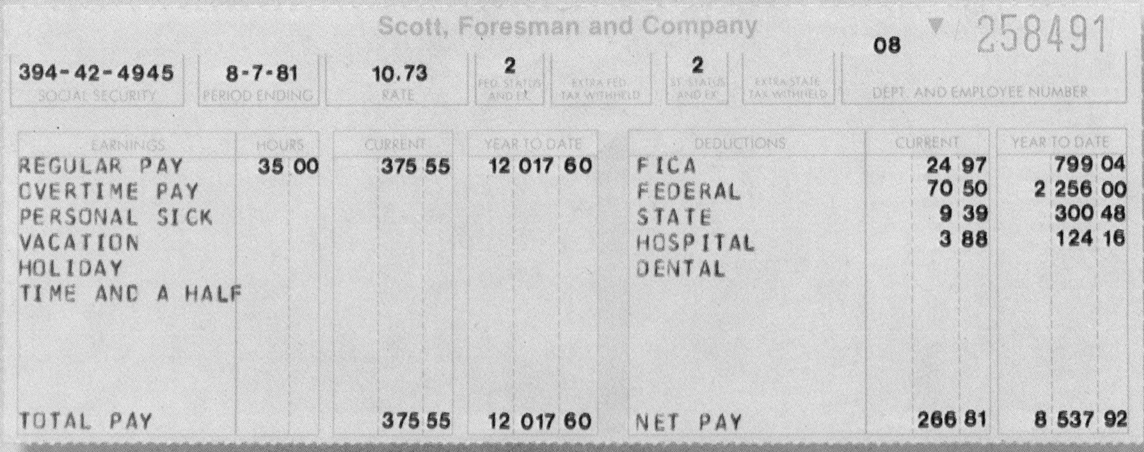

Scott, Foresman and Company

SOCIAL SECURITY	PERIOD ENDING	RATE	FED. STATUS AND EX.	EXTRA FED. TAX WITHHELD	ST. STATUS AND EX.	EXTRA STATE TAX WITHHELD	DEPT. AND EMPLOYEE NUMBER
394-42-4945	8-7-81	10.73	2		2		08 258491

EARNINGS	HOURS	CURRENT	YEAR TO DATE	DEDUCTIONS	CURRENT	YEAR TO DATE
REGULAR PAY	35 00	375 55	12 017 60	FICA	24 97	799 04
OVERTIME PAY				FEDERAL	70 50	2 256 00
PERSONAL SICK				STATE	9 39	300 48
VACATION				HOSPITAL	3 88	124 16
HOLIDAY				DENTAL		
TIME AND A HALF						
TOTAL PAY		375 55	12 017 60	NET PAY	266 81	8 537 92

See page 23 of
Consumer Forms and Problems.

Net pay, also called **take-home pay,** is the amount left after all deductions have been subtracted from the gross pay.

Some states require deductions for state or local income tax. Sometimes other deductions, such as union dues or insurance payments, are also made.

Problem

Gerry's salary is $641.67 per week. He is single and claims one exemption. His gross pay to date is $6858.37. He pays $16.04 state tax. What is Gerry's net pay?

Solution

Strategy

- Use the tables on pages 402–405 to find the amount of federal income tax withheld.
  $178.50
- Check that the year's gross pay is less than $29,700.
  $6858.37 < $29,700
- Multiply the week's gross pay by 6.65% to find the amount withheld for social security. Round to the nearest cent.
  $0.0665 \times \$641.67 \approx \$42.67$
- Add to find the total deductions.
  $\$178.50 + \$42.67 + \$16.04 = \$237.21$
- Subtract to find net pay.
  $\$641.67 - \$237.21 = \$404.46$

Conclusion

Gerry's weekly net pay is $404.46.

Related Problems

You may wish to allow students to use calculators for these problems.

Find the amounts withheld from each paycheck for federal income tax (use the tables on pages 402–405) and social security. Then find the net pay. Round each amount to the nearest cent.

				This week's paycheck				
	Marital status	Exemptions claimed	Gross pay to date	Gross pay	Federal tax	Social security	Other deductions	Net pay
	Single	1	$6858.37	$641.67	$178.50	$42.67	$16.04	$404.46
26.	Single	1	$8695.00	$202.21	**$29.10**	**$13.45**	———	**$159.66**
27.	Married	2	$11,560.09	$235.92	**$24.60**	**$15.69**	———	**$195.63**
28.	Married	3	$7543.81	$179.60	**$10.70**	**$11.94**	$5.75	**$151.21**
29.	Single	1	$14,000.00	$311.11	**$58.10**	**$20.69**	$9.16	**$223.16**
30.	Married	4	$22,820.00	$447.45	**$62.70**	**$29.76**	$13.87	**$341.12**
31.	Single	1	$19,865.32	$389.51	**$80.50**	**$25.90**	$15.43	**$267.68**

This lesson could be extended by having the students determine what percent of gross pay is actually received by each employee in the problems. The results could be the basis of a class discussion.

Objective: Use information from ads to compute and compare wages for various jobs.

Jobs in Classified Ads

Bobbi Gill is looking for a job as a secretary. She uses the "help wanted" section of the classified ads in her daily paper.

Problem

The problems require students to apply skills learned in all of the previous lessons in this chapter.

Bobbi found these two ads that interest her. Which job pays more? How much more per year does it pay?

A

MEDICAL SECRETARY
NO STENO!
$1,250-$1,500 MONTH
No medical experience necessary. You'll deal with patients for our client, get information for charts, histories. Talk with hospital personnel to set up surgeries, therapy. Good typing desired. No Saturdays! Exceptional benefits.

B

Secretary
PRIVATE OFFICE-$15,500
Assist partner in all functions of running client office. Project work. Min. 2 yrs. office exp., type 55 wpm, & top image req. No fee.
Gains Employment.

A true comparison of the amounts that different jobs "pay" should include a comparison of the fringe benefits.

Solution

Strategy

- Multiply the monthly salary of Job A by 12 to find the yearly salary.
  $12 \times \$1250 = \$15{,}000$
- The yearly salary for Job B is given in the ad.
  $15,500
- Compare the yearly salaries.
  $\$15{,}000 < \$15{,}500$
- Subtract to find the difference in salaries.
  $\$15{,}500 - \$15{,}000 = \$500$

Conclusion

Job B pays $500 more per year than Job A.

Related Problems

Have students read through the ads in class before they begin work on the problems. Explain the abbreviations used in classifieds.

Use these ads and the strategies from the previous lessons in this chapter to solve problems 1–10.

C

DRAFTERS!!!
CAREER POSITION WITH THE
"BEST"
$15-$17,000 TO START
Here's your opportunity to join a leader in the instrumentation field. Work independently on design drafting assignments, including tolerances and math calculations. All talented drafters will be considered for this promotable position. Outstanding hours, benefits and location. Call:
977-4800
BEST AGENCY
150 S. Peach, Suite 700,

D

PIZZA DELIVERY
$4.50-$5.50 per hour. Full or part time. Must have car. No. side loc. Will train.

E

Medical Opportunity
ASCP LAB TECHNICIAN
For surgi-center on northwest side. 6 hours. 4 days/week. 8 a.m. to 2 p.m. $250/week. Call Monday through Friday, 10 a.m. to 2 p.m.

F

MOLD MAKERS
Days and Nights. We offer a stable 50 hour work week and many generous benefits
1. Free hospitalization ins.
2. Free life insurance
3. Free disability benefits
4. 9 paid holidays
5. 2 weeks paid vacation
6. Attendance bonus plan
7. 20% night premium

We will pay top rates for qualified individuals.
CONNER CORP.

G

RETAIL STORE MANAGER
$350 Weekly
+ Profit Shar. +
Ins. Benefits
Must have experience in managing women's lingerie, sportswear, or dress shop. Send resume with salary history to: MSL 538 Journal 535

H

RETAIL STORE MANAGER
Management experience necessary. Prefer soft goods or back country sports equipment background. Evanston location. Near public transportation. Minimum $18,000 with full benefit package. Call Mr. Fraser

I

Help Wanted
SALES/TEACHING AIDS
MANAGER TRAINEE
$1200 PER MONTH TO START
GUARANTEED COMMISSION
AUTOMATIC INCREASE TO $1700 AFTER 3 MONTHS IF YOU MEET OUR REQUIREMENTS
These positions are offered by a new division of one of the largest companies of its kind in our industry. All company benefits. Those accepted will be offered positions with $40,000 per year potential after 6 month manager training program.
Call Mr. Sheridan 282-4314

Warm-up: 215 × 52 [11,180]
4.15 × 40 [166]
9150 − 8900 [250]
125.60 + 38.40 [164]

See pages 1-2 and 24 of *Consumer Forms and Problems*.

J

SALES
TERRITORY MGR.
FOOD SERVICE
$23,000 + COMM.
Well known institutional food service co. needs person with 2 or more yrs. exp. in food service mgmt. & vending. Your bkgd. in institutional trade can help you get this top position. Contact Ms. Anderson, Pvt. Emp. Agy., 180 N. Lakewood, Rm. 1500.

K

SALES
FINANCIAL PLANNING
Earn $300-$500 in comm. per week Part Time, prefer college degree and background in Teaching, Sales or Management. Call Mon. and Tues. betwn. 9 & 5 Ms. Haas

L

WAITRESSES
TOP TIPS
••••
Coffee Shops & Dining Rms
Full Time or Lunch Only
In the Loop's Finest Buildings
Great Income & Benefits
Insurance, Free Meals & Uniforms
55 E Apple, Rm 3533,

M

Secretary LEARN
WORD PROCESSING
$1,333-$1,416 MONTH
Train to use the latest in our client's word processing equipment. Just good office skills, some secretarial background and desire to get into interesting, higher paying field. Any familiarity with word processing is a plus

N

WORD-PROCESSOR: $14,560
Expanding Corp. Hdqr's. client seeking exp. word-proc. to join progressive dept. Definite promotion opp'ts. Min 6 mo's. exp. & typing 60 wpm req. No fee. 943-6676. Gains Employment.

1. Charles is looking for a job as a word processor. Which of the jobs advertised pays more per year? How much more does it pay?
M; $2432

2. Danny is looking for a delivery job. How much more would he make in a 40-hour week if he is offered the highest pay rather than the lowest pay in the ad?
$40

3. Mona is looking for a job as a retail store manager. Which of the jobs advertised pays more per year? How much more does it pay? (Use 52 weeks for 1 year.)
G; $200

4. Barbara was hired as a manager trainee in sales of teacher aids. She met the requirements to receive the automatic increase. What was her salary for the first six months?
$8700

5. Cheryl was hired as a drafter at the lowest salary in the ad. After 6 months she received a 15% raise. What was her gross pay for the year?
$16,125

6. Bob was hired as a mold maker on the night shift. The position of mold maker pays $10.50 per hour for the first 40 hours and time and a half for the additional hours. What is Bob's weekly gross pay?
$693

7. Bernard accepted the position as a lab technician. He is single and claims 1 exemption. Along with federal income tax and social security, $6.25 is deducted from each check for state tax. What is his net pay per week?
$185.52

8. Jack was hired for the sales/financial planning position for a straight commission of 16%. His first week's sales were $585, $1128, $456, and $298. How much did he earn from these sales? Did he receive the advertised commission?
$394.72; yes

9. Kelly received the position as territory manager of a food service. She received 4% commission on the first $20,000 in sales, and 6.5% commission on all sales over $20,000. What was her gross pay for the year if the sales were $32,500?
$24,612.50

10. Carla interviewed for the job as a waitress. She would earn $5.50 an hour and work 7 hours a day, 5 days a week, in the coffee shop. She was told that tips averaged $18 per day. A position in the dining room paid $200 for a 5-day week. Tips averaged $35 a day. At which place could Carla earn more money? How much more could she earn?
Dining room; $92.50 per week

Skills Tune-Up

After Unit 1, a Skills Tune-Up page occurs at the end of each chapter. It contains sets of maintenance exercises that can be used at any time. The exercise sets are referenced to pages where the particular skills are taught. Answers to odd-numbered exercises are given at the end of the student's text.

Rounding whole numbers and decimals, pages 4–5

Round each number to the nearest thousand, nearest hundred, and nearest ten.

1. 668
   1000; 700; 670
2. 923
   1000; 900; 920
3. 1246
   1000; 1200; 1250
4. 7958
   8000; 8000; 7960
5. 5042
   5000; 5000; 5040
6. 2003
   2000; 2000; 2000
7. 65,191
   65,000; 65,200; 65,190
8. 71,544
   72,000; 71,500; 71,540
9. 87,897
   88,000; 87,900; 87,900
10. 28,028
   28,000; 28,000; 28,030

Round each number to the nearest whole number, nearest tenth, and nearest hundredth.

11. 3.283
   3; 3.3; 3.28
12. 11.754
   12; 11.8; 11.75
13. 74.521
   75; 74.5; 74.52
14. 20.196
   20; 20.2; 20.20
15. 152.802
   153; 152.8; 152.80
16. 647.033
   647; 647.0; 647.03
17. 391.475
   391; 391.5; 391.48
18. 18.912
   19; 18.9; 18.91
19. 84.666
   85; 84.7; 84.67
20. 100.349
   100; 100.3; 100.35
21. 478.977
   479; 479.0; 478.98

Subtracting whole numbers and decimals, pages 6–7

1. 47 − 16
   31
2. 84 − 27
   57
3. 74 − 8
   66
4. 83 − 6
   77
5. 26 − 17
   9
6. 59 − 55
   4
7. 44.2 − 31.7
   12.5
8. 63.4 − 4.8
   58.6
9. 45.34 − 32.63
   12.71
10. 64.43 − 37.83
   26.6
11. 80.41 − 64.6
   15.81
12. 52.83 − 43.5
   9.33
13. 6.092 − 2.61
   3.482
14. 63.944 − 16.35
   47.594
15. 83.364 − 66.019
   17.345
16. 97.087 − 34.521
   62.566
17. 0.45 − 0.097
   0.353
18. 48.04 − 12.07
   35.97
19. 18.5 − 17.9
   0.6
20. 8.07 − 7.44
   0.63
21. 8.103 − 3
   5.103
22. 79.002 − 63
   16.002
23. 93 − 21.6
   71.4
24. 24 − 0.8
   23.2
25. 5 − 0.61
   4.39
26. 65 − 32.05
   32.95
27. 61.5 − 48.984
   12.516

Multiplying whole numbers, pages 8–9

1. 30 × 50
   1500
2. 90 × 40
   3600
3. 70 × 600
   42,000
4. 200 × 800
   160,000
5. 900 × 600
   540,000
6. 8000 × 60
   480,000
7. 90 × 2000
   180,000
8. 500 × 6000
   3,000,000
9. 43 × 7
   301
10. 17 × 26
   442
11. 1700 × 2000
   3,400,000
12. 50 × 91
   4550
13. 9 × 873
   7857
14. 430 × 800
   344,000
15. 425 × 5
   2125
16. 855 × 37
   31,635
17. 5100 × 700
   3,570,000
18. 49 × 63
   3087
19. 84 × 48
   4032
20. 490 × 99
   48,510
21. 68 × 506
   34,408
22. 240 × 600
   144,000
23. 9478 × 23
   217,994
24. 892 × 7172
   6,397,424
25. 9075 × 894
   8,113,050
26. 100 × 460
   46,000
27. 594 × 3652
   2,169,288

Chapter 4 Review

Items in the review cover each problem type in the chapter, lesson by lesson. The lesson titles and text pages are included so that students may refer back to these pages if necessary. Answers to all review problems are given at the end of the student's text.

Hourly rate and overtime rate, pages 68–69

1. Don Marcy makes $4.86 per hour. Find his gross pay for 40 hours.
$194.40

2. Kay Soto earns $4.50 per hour for a 40-hour work week and time and a half for overtime. One week she worked 56 hours. Find her gross pay for the week.
$288

Hourly rate plus tips, pages 70–71

3. Mary Harvey makes $3.50 per hour plus tips. One week she worked 35 hours and earned $39.20 in tips. She kept 85% of her tips. Find her gross pay for the week.
$155.82

Straight commission, pages 72–73

4. Dwayne Johnson makes 15% straight commission. One week he had sales of $1560. Find his gross pay for the week.
$234

Bookkeeper, pages 74–75

5. Dottie Koontz receives a salary of $150 per week plus a commission of 5% on all sales delivered. Last week she had sales of $3000 and cancellations of $1200. Find her gross pay for the week.
$240

Graduated commission, page 76

6. Dale Keller is paid $350 per month plus a commission of 3% of the first $2000 of his sales, and 4.5% of all his sales over $2000. He sold $4500 worth of lumber last month. Find his gross pay for the month.
$522.50

Net pay, pages 78–81

7. Max Steiner is married and claims 3 exemptions. He makes $289.46 per week. Use the table below to find the amount withheld from his weekly paycheck for federal income tax.
$30.70

And the wages are—		Exemptions claimed			
At least	But less than	0	1	2	3
		The amount of income tax to be withheld shall be—			
250	260	36.50	32.50	28.50	24.80
260	270	38.60	34.60	30.60	26.60
270	280	40.70	36.70	32.70	28.60
280	290	42.80	38.80	34.80	30.70
290	300	45.10	40.90	36.90	32.80

8. Donna Adamson's gross pay for last week was $365.48. 6.65% was withheld for social security. Find the amount withheld. Round to the nearest cent.
$24.30

9. Dick Laba's gross pay is $256.72 a week. $28.50 is withheld for federal income tax, $17.07 for social security, and $3.15 for insurance. Find his net pay.
$208.00

Jobs in classified ads, pages 82–83

10. Use the ads shown. Which job pays more? How much more does it pay per year?
B; $420

A

Receptionist
FRONT DESK
PEOPLE MEETER
$11,400 TO START
Plush offices! Lots of variety! A chance to polish your office basics! Our client anxious to hire!
JAROSZ PERSONNEL
985 Nash, Suite 315
Oak Brook
Des Plaines

B

Help Wanted

RECEPTIONIST
TELEPHONE
Growing food company near Loop needs a telephone receptionist with light typing. Must have good phone voice. $985/mo.

Chapter 4 Test

For each test, a table is given to help score the test.

Number of test items–10

Number missed	1	2	3	4	5
Percent correct	90	80	70	60	50

1. Sheila makes $4.95 per hour. Find her gross pay for 40 hours.
$198

2. Eric earns $6.50 per hour for a 40-hour work week and time and a half for overtime. One week he worked 54 hours. Find his gross pay for the week.
$396.50

3. Rick makes $3.85 per hour plus tips. One week he worked 30 hours and earned $86.40 in tips. He kept 85% of the tips. Find his gross pay for the week.
$188.94

4. Elaine makes 25% straight commission. One week she had sales of $1840. Find her gross pay for the week.
$460

5. Kristen receives a salary of $110 per week plus a commission of 8% of all sales delivered. Last week she had sales of $4000 and cancellations of $1700. Find her gross pay for the week.
$294

6. Marjorie is paid $125 per week plus a commission of 3% on the first $3000 of sales, and 5.5% of all sales over $3000. She sold $4000 worth of appliances. Find her gross pay for the week.
$270

7. Julio is single and claims 1 exemption. He makes $198.53 per week. Use the table below to find the amount withheld from his weekly paycheck for federal income tax.
$27.00

And the wages are—		Exemptions claimed			
At least	But less than	0	1	2	3
		The amount of income tax to be withheld shall be—			
170	180	26.80	22.80	18.80	15.10
180	190	28.90	24.90	20.90	16.90
190	200	31.00	27.00	23.00	18.90
200	210	33.60	29.10	25.10	21.00
210	220	36.20	31.20	27.20	23.10

8. Jim's gross pay for last week was $219.87. 6.65% was withheld for social security. Find the amount withheld. Round to the nearest cent.
$14.62

9. Julie's gross pay is $369.24 a week. $57.30 is withheld for federal income tax, $24.55 for social security, and $5.85 for insurance. Find her net pay.
$281.54

10. Use the ads shown. Which job pays more? How much more does it pay per year?
A; $220

A

Management Trainee
SHARP LADIES
SHARP GUYS
Fun job calling on Lawyers, Doctors and Executive type personnel. Representing new corporation in Chicago. Positions available in person. Positions available in Management and Marketing. Car necessary - earn while you learn.
$1060/MO
Mr. Huffman

B

MANAGEMENT
TRAINEES
Our multi million dollar corp. is looking for 8 ambitious people to start training for management positions in our consumer oriented field. No exp necessary. Will train the right people. $12,500
Call Julie Graves

The Chapter Test parallels the Chapter Review, item for item.
The student's text does not contain any answers for test problems.

 See pages 9-10 of the *Test Masters* for an alternate form of the Chapter 4 Test.

Chapter 5 Personal Banking

Objective: Complete a deposit slip for a checking account.

Deposit Slips

See page T30 for additional notes and activities for Chapter 5.

James Morrison has a checking account. The money that he puts into his account is called a **deposit**. Often when making a deposit, he keeps some cash for spending money. The **net deposit** is the actual amount that is put into the account.

Problem

James is making a deposit. He has checks for \$237.31 and \$176.25. He wants to keep \$50 in cash. Find his net deposit.

You may wish to discuss endorsing a check and explain making a check payable only to depositor's account when banking by mail.

Solution

Strategy

- List each check separately on the deposit slip.
- Add to find the total.
- Subtract the cash received from the total to find the net deposit.

When receiving cash while making a deposit, the signature of the depositor is required on the line below the date.

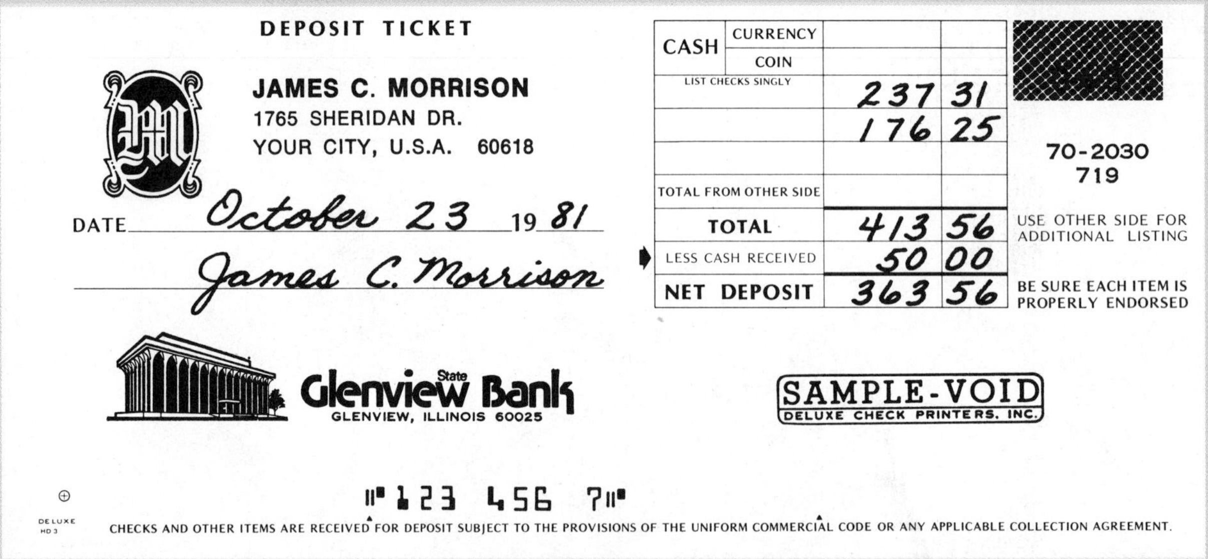
DEPOSIT TICKET

JAMES C. MORRISON
1765 SHERIDAN DR.
YOUR CITY, U.S.A. 60618

DATE October 23 19 81

James C. Morrison

CASH	CURRENCY		
	COIN		
LIST CHECKS SINGLY		237	31
		176	25
TOTAL FROM OTHER SIDE			
TOTAL		413	56
LESS CASH RECEIVED		50	00
NET DEPOSIT		363	56

70-2030
719

USE OTHER SIDE FOR ADDITIONAL LISTING

BE SURE EACH ITEM IS PROPERLY ENDORSED

State Glenview Bank
GLENVIEW, ILLINOIS 60025

SAMPLE-VOID
DELUXE CHECK PRINTERS, INC.

⑈123 456 7⑈

DELUXE HD 3

CHECKS AND OTHER ITEMS ARE RECEIVED FOR DEPOSIT SUBJECT TO THE PROVISIONS OF THE UNIFORM COMMERCIAL CODE OR ANY APPLICABLE COLLECTION AGREEMENT.

Conclusion

James's net deposit was \$363.56.

Emphasize that the net deposit is the amount added to the checking account.

Warm-up: 57.46 + 186.60 + 13.74 [257.80]
48.70 + 29.63 + 127.30 [205.63]
267.51 − 80 [187.51]
342.89 − 175 [167.89]

See pages 3 and 25 of *Consumer Forms and Problems.*

Related Problems

Complete each deposit slip.

1.

CASH	CURRENCY		
	COIN		
LIST CHECKS SINGLY		478	23
		36	42
TOTAL FROM OTHER SIDE			
TOTAL		514	65
LESS CASH RECEIVED		60	00
NET DEPOSIT		454	65

2.

CASH	CURRENCY		
	COIN		
LIST CHECKS SINGLY		715	95
		139	24
		78	78
TOTAL FROM OTHER SIDE			
TOTAL		933	97
LESS CASH RECEIVED		80	00
NET DEPOSIT		853	97

3.

CASH	CURRENCY		
	COIN	7	86
LIST CHECKS SINGLY		18	84
		27	36
		16	25
TOTAL FROM OTHER SIDE			
TOTAL		70	31
LESS CASH RECEIVED			
NET DEPOSIT		70	31

4.

CASH	CURRENCY		
	COIN	18	56
LIST CHECKS SINGLY		205	16
		19	43
		8	62
TOTAL FROM OTHER SIDE			
TOTAL		251	77
LESS CASH RECEIVED		32	00
NET DEPOSIT		219	77

5.

CASH	CURRENCY		
	COIN	54	75
LIST CHECKS SINGLY		218	97
		108	29
		37	17
TOTAL FROM OTHER SIDE			
TOTAL		419	18
LESS CASH RECEIVED		75	00
NET DEPOSIT		344	18

6.

CASH	CURRENCY		
	COIN	37	17
LIST CHECKS SINGLY		49	26
		123	47
		35	91
TOTAL FROM OTHER SIDE			
TOTAL		245	81
LESS CASH RECEIVED		65	00
NET DEPOSIT		180	81

7. Roy had checks to deposit for the following amounts: $23.78, $116.29, $108.25, and $8.75. He wanted $75 in cash. What was his net deposit?
$182.07

8. Linda had checks to deposit for the following amounts: $97.18, $208.36, $29.16, and $8.64. She wanted $35 in cash. What was her net deposit?
$308.34

9. Rosa had checks to deposit for the following amounts: $327.67, $53.77, $184.23, and $3.85. She wanted $100 in cash. What was her net deposit?
$469.52

10. Marc had checks to deposit for the following amounts: $1025.76, $879.24, $548.92, and $353.88. He wanted $75 in cash. What was his net deposit?
$2732.80

Objectives: Write the amount of a check in words; complete a check stub.

Checks and Check Stubs

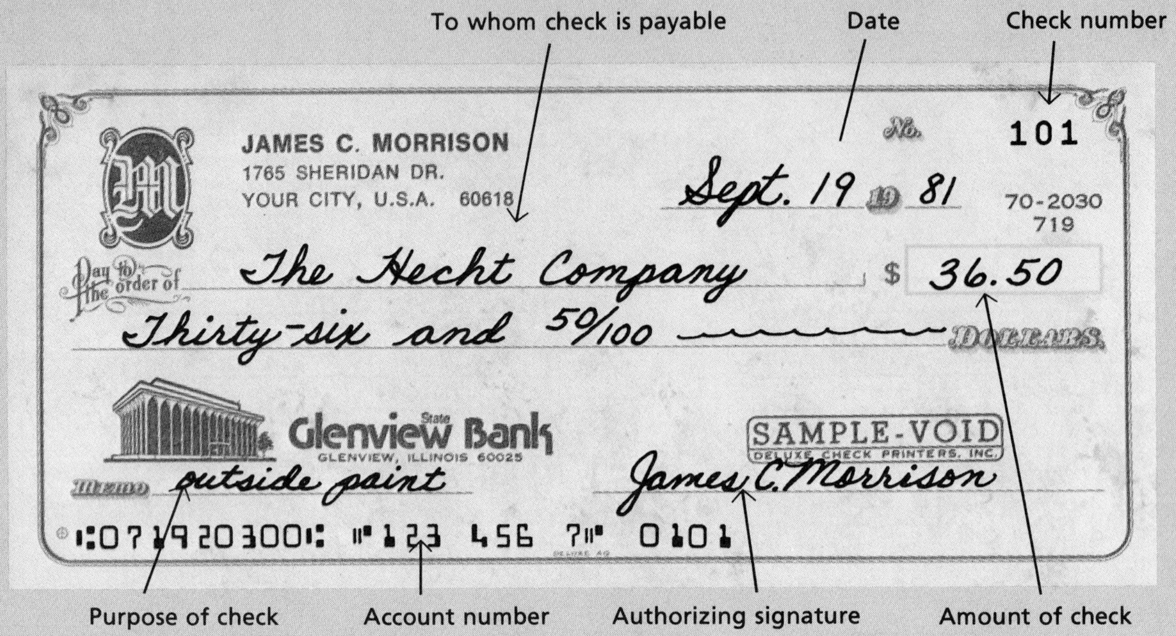

The amount of a check is written in both words and numbers. If there is a difference in these amounts, the bank would honor the amount written in words.

Problem

How should $457.17 be written in words on a check?

Remind students that writing "and" between "hundred" and "fifty" is incorrect.

Solution

Always use ink and fill the entire space so that no one can change the amount that is written.

Explain that if the amount of the check does not include any cents, the students should write "and $^{00}/_{100}$."

Four hundred fifty-seven and 17/100 —— DOLLARS

Related Problems

Write each amount in words as it would appear on a check.

1. $27.81
   Twenty-seven and $\frac{81}{100}$
2. $45.63
   Forty-five and $\frac{63}{100}$
3. $60.00
   Sixty and $\frac{00}{100}$
4. $72.54
   Seventy-two and $\frac{54}{100}$
5. $15.00
   Fifteen and $\frac{00}{100}$
6. $18.08
   Eighteen and $\frac{08}{100}$
7. $395.13
   Three hundred ninety-five and $\frac{13}{100}$
8. $639.00
   Six hundred thirty-nine and $\frac{00}{100}$
9. $1002.30
   One thousand two and $\frac{30}{100}$

Warm-up: Write in words.
30 [thirty]
40 [forty]
59 [fifty-nine]
87 [eighty-seven]

See pages 4 and 26 of *Consumer Forms and Problems.*

When James wrote the check to the Hecht Company, he filled in the attached **check stub**. The stub is a record of the check. When completed, the stub shows how much money is left in the account.

Problem

If the balance brought forward was $347.59 and a deposit of $63.20 was made, what was the new balance after James wrote the check shown on page 90?

Solution

Strategy
- List the balance brought forward from the last stub.
- List all deposits.
- Add the balance brought forward and all deposits made since the last stub was completed to find the total.
- Subtract the amount of this check from the total to find the new balance to be carried forward to the next stub.

Conclusion
The new balance was $374.29.

Explain that the stub is the only record of the check that a person has until the canceled check is returned by the bank. Stubs should be filled in carefully before the check is written.

101 $ 36.50

Sept. 19 19 81
TO The Hecht Co.
(paint)

	DOLLARS	CENTS
BAL. FOR'D	347	59
DEPOSITS	63	20
"		
TOTAL	410	79
THIS PAYMENT	36	50
OTHER DEDUCTIONS		
BAL. FOR'D	374	29

Related Problems

Complete each check stub.

10.

	DOLLARS	CENTS
BAL. FOR'D	65	29
DEPOSITS		
"		
TOTAL	65	29
THIS PAYMENT	18	40
OTHER DEDUCTIONS		
BAL. FOR'D	46	89

11.

	DOLLARS	CENTS
BAL. FOR'D	86	20
DEPOSITS	37	50
"	23	16
TOTAL	146	86
THIS PAYMENT	48	95
OTHER DEDUCTIONS		
BAL. FOR'D	97	91

12.

	DOLLARS	CENTS
BAL. FOR'D	17	86
DEPOSITS	39	42
"	8	63
TOTAL	65	91
THIS PAYMENT	15	29
OTHER DEDUCTIONS		
BAL. FOR'D	50	62

13. On a check stub the balance brought forward was $475.80. Deposits of $163.20 and $87.25 were made. The amount of this check is $287.45. Find the balance carried forward to the next stub.
$438.80

Objective: Make entries of checks and deposits in a check register and find the new balance in the checking account.

Check Registers

Many people use a **check register** rather than check stubs to record their checks. The same information is written on both.

Problem

David Halstead had a balance of $431.18 in his account. On September 29, he wrote check number 342 for $289.00. This check was made out to Realty Associates to pay his rent. What was the balance after David wrote this check?

Solution

Strategy

- Write the check number, date, description of check, and amount of check in the check register.
- Subtract the amount of the check from the old balance to find the new balance.

You may wish to explain that the column in the register headed by the checkmark can be used to mark off checks returned by the bank. This helps in reconciling the bank statement.

NUMBER	DATE	DESCRIPTION OF TRANSACTION	PAYMENT/DEBIT (-)	√ T	FEE (IF ANY) (-)	DEPOSIT/CREDIT (+)	BALANCE
							$ 431 18
342	9/29	Realty Associates (rent)	$ 289 00		$	$	289 00
							142 18

Conclusion
The balance was $142.18.

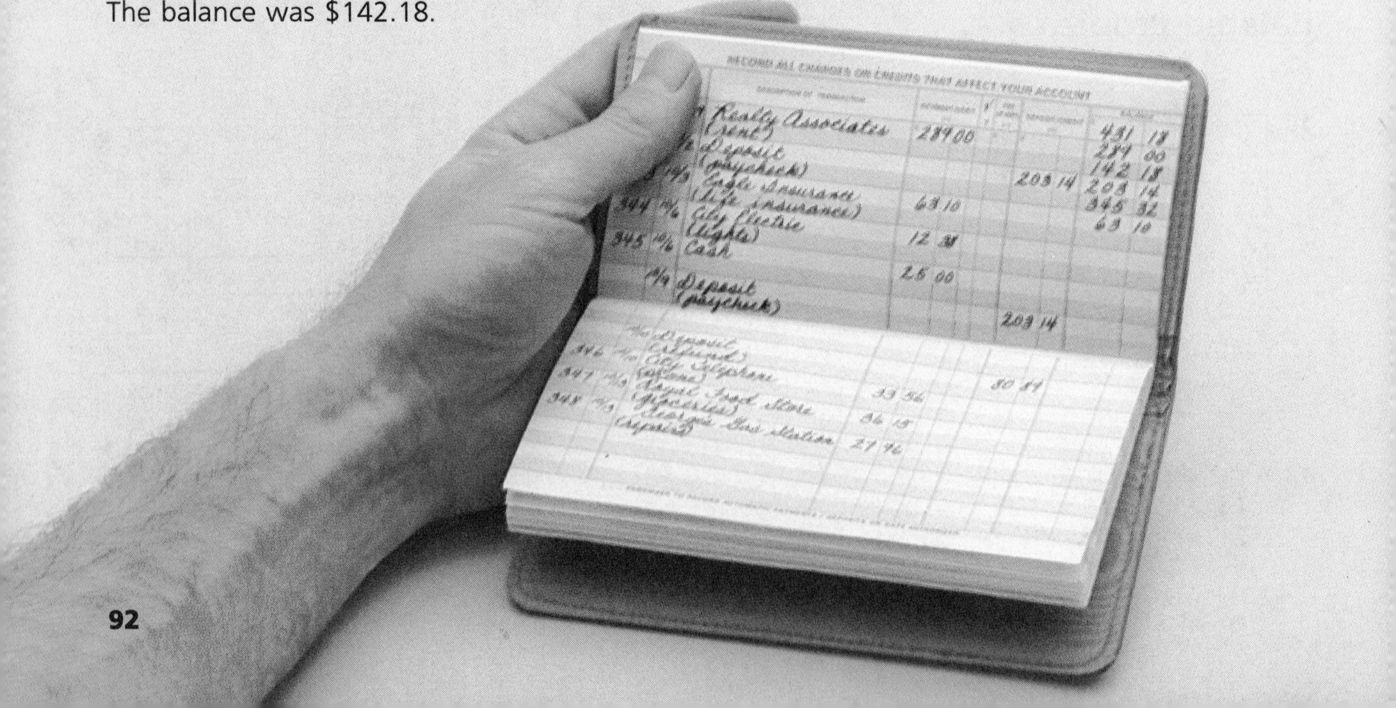

Warm-up: 146.89 − 23.80 [123.09]
73.25 − 19.47 [53.78]
347.28 + 84.29 [431.57]
18.37 + 259.86 [278.23]

See pages 5 and 27 of *Consumer Forms and Problems.*

Problem

David made a deposit of $203.14 on October 2. Find the new balance.

Solution

Strategy
- Write the date and the amount of deposit in the check register.
- Add the old balance and the deposit to find the new balance.

NUMBER	DATE	DESCRIPTION OF TRANSACTION	PAYMENT/DEBIT (−)	√ T	FEE (IF ANY) (−)	DEPOSIT/CREDIT (+)	BALANCE
							$ 431 18
342	9/29	Realty Associates	$ 289 00		$	$	289 00
		(rent)					142 18
	10/2	Deposit				203 14	203 14
		(paycheck)					345 32

Conclusion
The new balance is $345.32.

Related Problems

Find each new balance. The last balance on each page of the partial check register becomes the beginning balance for the next page of the check register.

	NUMBER	DATE	PAYMENT/DEBIT (−)	√ T	FEE (IF ANY) (−)	DEPOSIT/CREDIT (+)	BALANCE
							$ 345 32
1.	343	10/3	$ 63 10		$	$	63 10
							282 22
2.	344	10/6	12 38				12 38
							269 84
3.	345	10/6	25 00				25 00
							244 84
4.		10/9				203 14	203 14
							447 98
5.		10/10				80 89	80 89
							528 87
6.	346	10/10	33 56				33 56
							495 31
7.	347	10/13	36 15				36 15
							459 16
8.	348	10/13	27 96				27 96
							431 20

	NUMBER	DATE	PAYMENT/DEBIT (−)	√ T	FEE (IF ANY) (−)	DEPOSIT/CREDIT (+)	BALANCE
							$ 431 20
9.	349	10/15	$ 57 66		$	$	57 66
							373 54
10.		10/16				203 14	203 14
							576 68
11.	350	10/19	144 34				144 34
							432 34
12.	351	10/19	109 20				109 20
							323 14
13.	352	10/19	18 48				18 48
							304 66
14.	353	10/22	50 00				50 00
							254 66
15.		10/23				203 14	203 14
							457 80
16.	354	10/27	73 56				73 56
							384 24

You may wish to explain "void" checks and how to record them in a check register.
Also, stop-payment orders and overdrafts could be discussed at this time.

Objective: Reconcile a bank statement with a check register.

Reconciling a Bank Statement

Each month David Halstead receives a **bank statement** for his checking account. He also receives the checks that the bank has paid from his account during the month. These are called **canceled checks**.

David **reconciles** the bank statement with his check register. This means that he determines if the check register agrees with the bank statement.

Sometimes David has recorded deposits and checks in his check register that are not listed on the bank statement. These are called **outstanding deposits** and **outstanding checks**.

The service charge is the amount the bank charges for handling the account.

Point out that canceled checks are receipts for payments made. They should always be saved.

Explain that outstanding deposits are deposits made too late to be recorded on the bank statement. Outstanding checks are checks that have been written but have not cleared the bank by the statement date.

BALANCE LAST STATEMENT	DEPOSITS AND CREDITS		CHECKS AND DEBITS		SERVICE CHARGE	BALANCE THIS STATEMENT
	NO.	TOTAL AMOUNT	NO.	TOTAL AMOUNT		
142.18	4	690.31	9	418.63	4.75	409.11

CHECKING ACCOUNT TRANSACTIONS

DATE	DEBITS	CREDITS	DESCRIPTION
10/02		203.14	DEPOSIT
10/09		203.14	DEPOSIT
10/10		80.89	DEPOSIT
10/16		203.14	DEPOSIT
10/30	4.75		SERVICE CHARGE

CHECKS

DATE	CHECK NO	AMOUNT	DATE	CHECK NO	AMOUNT
10/08	343	63.10	10/13	344	12.38
10/14	345	25.00	10/19	346	33.56
10/20	347	36.15	10/23	348	27.96
10/26	349	57.66	10/28	350	144.34
10/29	352	18.48			

Problem

The same check register is used for this lesson as for the lesson on pages 92–93. You might have students look at the register to see which deposits and checks are outstanding.

The balance in David's check register is \$384.24. He determined that he has an outstanding deposit of \$203.14 and that check #351 for \$109.20, check #353 for \$50.00, and check #354 for \$73.56 are outstanding. Does his check register agree with his bank statement? Find the actual amount in his checking account.

Explain that the dates shown on the bank statement are the dates that the bank recorded the transactions. These dates will not necessarily agree with the dates recorded in the check register.

Warm-up: 34.78 + 295.47 + 28.60 [358.85]
23.56 + 197.68 + 53 [274.24]
378.47 − 358.85 [19.62]
264.92 − 15 [249.92]

Solution

The directions given are similar to those that appear on the back of most bank statements.

Strategy

- Complete the form on the back of the bank statement to reconcile the bank statement with the check register.

BALANCE YOUR CHECK BOOK
by doing these things

Fill in Below Amounts from Your BANK STATEMENT and CHECK BOOK

Balance shown on BANK STATEMENT . . .	$ 409.11	Balance shown in Your CHECK Book . . .	$ 384.24
Add Deposits Not on Statement	$ 203.14	Add any Deposits Not Already Entered in Check Book	$
Sub-Total	$ 612.25	Sub-Total	$ 384.24
Subtract Checks Issued But Not on Statement:	$ 109.20 50.00 73.56	Subtract Service Charges and other Bank Charges Not in Check Book	$ 4.75
Total	$ 232.76	Total	$ 4.75
BALANCE	$ 379.49	BALANCE	$ 379.49

- Since the adjusted statement balance and the adjusted check register are the same, the statement is reconciled.
- Subtract the service charge from the previous balance in the check register to find the actual amount. $384.24 − $4.75 = $379.49

Conclusion

The check register and the bank statement agree. The actual amount in David's account was $379.49.

Explain how to find errors if the statement and the check register don't reconcile.

See pages 6 and 28 of
Consumer Forms and Problems.

Related Problems

Reconcile the bank-statement information with the check-register balance. Find the actual amount in each checking account.

1. Statement ending balance: $41.27
   Outstanding deposits: $27.70, $12.30
   Outstanding check: $9.98
   Service charge: $4.21
   Check-register balance: $75.50
   $71.29
2. Statement ending balance: $151.93
   Outstanding deposit: $100.00
   Outstanding checks: $10.00, $24.13, $200.00
   Service charge: $6.60
   Check-register balance: $24.40
   $17.80
3. Statement ending balance: $67.38
   Outstanding deposits: $15.45, $12.55
   Outstanding checks: $18.45, $17.12, $20.20
   Service charge: $5.50
   Check-register balance: $45.11
   $39.61
4. Statement ending balance: $235.00
   Outstanding deposits: $12.00, $13.00
   Outstanding checks: $9.75, $11.25, $10.00
   Service charge: $6.00
   Check-register balance: $235.00
   $229
5. Statement ending balance: $392.41
   Outstanding deposits: $32.41, $50.12, $49.46
   Outstanding checks: $42.75, $73.12, $63.30, $88.71, $81.80
   Service charge: $7.15
   Check-register balance: $181.87
   $174.72

6. A portion of Joe Sanchez's check register is shown. Find the actual amount in Joe's checking account on August 30. You may find arithmetic errors in Joe's check register. The bank statement showed an ending balance of $73.47; a deposit of $45.00; check #981, check #982, and check #983; and a service charge of $5.50.

NUMBER	DATE	DESCRIPTION OF TRANSACTION	PAYMENT/DEBIT (-)	√ T	FEE (IF ANY) (-)	DEPOSIT/CREDIT (+)	BALANCE	
							$ 120 00	
981	8/5	Sadkin Hardware (tools)	$ 10 25	✓	$	$	10 25 109 75	
	8/8	Deposit		✓		45 00	45 00 154 75	
982	8/10	Granger's Store (for groceries)	25 35	✓			25 35 129 40	
983	8/15	Tony Navarro (for car repair)	50 43	✓			50 43 ~~79 97~~	78.97
	8/27	Deposit				52 60	52 60 ~~132 57~~	131.57
984	8/30	Northwest Telephone	32 52				32 52 ~~100 05~~	99.05
	8/30	Service Charge			5.50		5 50 93 55	

CALCULATOR APPLICATIONS

Checking Accounts

Point out that the dates on the bank statement for the deposits do not agree with the dates in the check register. This often occurs when deposits are made by mail.

Many people use the single-line method of recording entries in their check registers. Each new balance is written on the same line as the entry to which it corresponds.

Find each new balance. The last balance on each page of the check register becomes the beginning balance for the next page of the check register.

	NUMBER	DATE	PAYMENT/DEBIT (−)	√ T	FEE (IF ANY) (−)	DEPOSIT/CREDIT (+)	BALANCE
							$1005.07
	719	8/26	$103.82	√	$	$	901.25
1.	720	8/28	111.26	√			789.99
2.	721	8/28	273.69	√			516.30
3.		8/31		√		887.51	1403.81
4.	722	9/1	386.89	√			1016.92
5.	723	9/3	270.93	√			745.99
6.	724	9/9	521.57	√			224.42
7.	725	9/11	211.40	√			13.02

	NUMBER	DATE	PAYMENT/DEBIT (−)	√ T	FEE (IF ANY) (−)	DEPOSIT/CREDIT (+)	BALANCE
							$13.02
8.		9/15	$	√	$	$428.60	441.62
9.	726	9/21	219.74				221.88
10.	727	9/24	202.55	√			19.33
11.		9/30				628.35	647.68
12.	728	9/30	77.78				569.90
13.	729	10/2	35.40				534.50
14.	730	10/2	187.65				346.85
15.		9/30			6.80		340.05

15. Reconcile the check register above with this bank statement. Find the actual amount in the checking account. See above.

BALANCE LAST STATEMENT	DEPOSITS AND CREDITS NO.	DEPOSITS AND CREDITS TOTAL AMOUNT	CHECKS AND DEBITS NO.	CHECKS AND DEBITS TOTAL AMOUNT	SERVICE CHARGE	BALANCE THIS STATEMENT
1005.07	2	1316.11	8	2082.11	6.80	232.27

CHECKING ACCOUNT TRANSACTIONS

DATE	DEBITS	CREDITS	DESCRIPTION
09/01		887.51	DEPOSIT
09/16		428.60	DEPOSIT
09/30	6.80		SERVICE CHARGE

CHECKS

DATE	CHECK NO	AMOUNT	DATE	CHECK NO	AMOUNT
09/01	719	103.82	09/02	720	111.26
09/04	721	273.69	09/08	722	386.89
09/11	723	270.93	09/15	724	521.57
09/21	725	211.40	09/28	727	202.55

Objective: Compute simple interest for a savings account by using the formula $i = p \times r \times t$.

Personal Banking Representative

See the Careers Chart beginning on page 410 for more information about the careers in this cluster.

Career Cluster: Business Contact Debbie Haverl is a personal banking representative for the Edgar State Bank. She advises customers on the various services offered by the bank. John and Andrea Warren want to open a savings account. The amount the Warrens deposit is called the **principal**. The amount that the bank will pay the Warrens for leaving their money in a savings account is called the **interest**.

Debbie uses the simple interest formula to find the amount of interest that will be paid.

$$\underset{\text{Interest}}{\underset{\uparrow}{\boldsymbol{I}}} = \underset{\text{Principal}}{\underset{\uparrow}{\boldsymbol{P}}} \times \underset{\text{Rate}}{\underset{\uparrow}{\boldsymbol{R}}} \times \underset{\text{Time}}{\underset{\uparrow}{\boldsymbol{T}}}$$

Problem

The Warrens opened a savings account by depositing \$300. After 3 months, what was the amount of interest at $5\frac{1}{2}\%$ per year?

Solution

Strategy

- Write the percent as a decimal.

  $5\frac{1}{2}\% = 0.055$

- Write the time as part of a year.

  3 months is $\frac{3}{12}$, or $\frac{1}{4}$, year. $\frac{1}{4} = 0.25$

- Use the formula. Round to the nearest cent.

  $I = P \times R \times T$
  $I = \$300 \times 0.055 \times 0.25$
  $I \approx \$4.13$

Conclusion

The interest earned was \$4.13.

Related Problems

Compute the simple interest for each savings account. Round each amount to the nearest cent.

	Principal	Interest rate	Time	
1.	$50	5%	6 mo.	$1.25
2.	$200	$5\frac{3}{4}$%	1 yr.	$11.50
3.	$350	6.5%	18 mo.	$34.13
4.	$175	6.25%	9 mo.	$8.20
5.	$348	$5\frac{1}{2}$%	15 mo.	$23.93
6.	$225	4.75%	30 mo.	$26.72
7.	$285	5.35%	27 mo.	$34.31
8.	$615	$6\frac{1}{2}$%	2 yr.	$79.95
9.	$425	5.25%	39 mo.	$72.52
10.	$3210	6%	1 yr. 9 mo.	$337.05
11.	$3750	$6\frac{1}{4}$%	3 mo.	$58.59
12.	$2940	4.8%	2 yr. 3 mo.	$317.52
13.	$5000	5.65%	3 yr. 3 mo.	$918.13
14.	$1290	$6\frac{3}{4}$%	2 yr. 6 mo.	$217.69
15.	$720	6.2%	3 yr. 9 mo.	$167.40

Break Time

Use each number and operation symbol to form an equation.
Answers may vary.

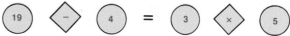

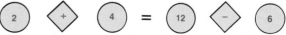

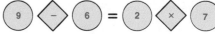

2 4 6 12 + −

2 + 4 = 12 − 6

3 4 5 19 − ×

19 − 4 = 3 × 5

2 6 7 9 11 + − ×

11 + 9 − 6 = 2 × 7

2 3 4 4 96 × × ÷

3 × 4 × 4 = 96 ÷ 2

Warm-up: Write 5% as a decimal. [0.05]
Write $6\frac{1}{2}$% as a decimal. [0.065]
300 × 0.07 × 1.5 [31.5]
545 × 0.06 × 0.25 [8.175]

Objective: Compute the total interest for a savings account when the interest is compounded annually, semiannually, or quarterly.

Compound Interest

Huang Ching put his money into a savings account that paid **compound interest**. This means that the interest is computed on the sum of the principal *and* the previously earned interest.

Problem

Huang put $1000 in a savings account that paid 8% interest compounded annually. How much interest was earned in 2 years?

Solution

Stress that each year's interest is added to the principal before the next year's interest is computed. This is the difference between simple interest and compound interest.

Strategy

- Huang made the table below by using the simple interest formula.
- Find the interest for the first year.

Year	Principal plus previous interest	Interest for the year $P \times R \times T = I$
1	$1000	$1000 × 0.08 × 1 = $80.00
2	$1000 + $80 = $1080	$1080 × 0.08 × 1 = $86.40

- Add the principal and the interest. Then find the interest for the second year.
- Add the interest earned each year to find the total interest.
  $80.00 + $86.40 = $166.40

Conclusion

The interest earned in 2 years was $166.40.

Related Problems

You may wish to allow students to use calculators for this lesson.

Compute the interest earned by the amount in each of these savings accounts. The interest is compounded annually. Round each answer to the nearest cent.

1. $100 at 7% for 4 years
   $31.08
2. $500 at 8% for 3 years
   $129.86
3. $300 at 6% for 5 years
   $101.46
4. $250 at 6.5% for 2 years
   $33.56
5. $1000 at 7.5% for 3 years
   $242.30
6. $3000 at 7.75% for 3 years
   $752.95

Warm-up: Write 7.5% as a decimal. [0.075]
Write 8.25% as a decimal. [0.0825]
$2000 \times 0.05 \times 0.25$ [25]
$3600 \times 0.065 \times 0.5$ [117]

Interest compounded semiannually is computed every 6 months.
Interest compounded quarterly is computed every 3 months.

Problem

Alicia Melendez put $1500 in a savings account that paid 8% interest compounded quarterly. How much interest was earned in 1 year?

Solution

Emphasize that time must be expressed in years. Thus 3 months is one-fourth or 0.25 of a year.

Strategy
- Alicia made the table below using the simple interest formula.
- Find the interest for the first quarter.

Qtr.	Principal plus previous interest	Interest for the year $P \times R \times T = I$
1	$1500	$1500 × 0.08 × 0.25 = $30
2	$1500.00 + $30.00 = $1530.00	$1530.00 × 0.08 × 0.25 = $30.60
3	$1530.00 + $30.60 = $1560.60	$1560.60 × 0.08 × 0.25 ≈ $31.21
4	$1560.60 + $31.20 = $1591.80	$1591.80 × 0.08 × 0.25 ≈ $31.84

- Add the principal and the interest. Then find the interest for the next 3 quarters. Round to the nearest cent.
- Add the interest earned each quarter to find the total interest.
  $30.00 + $30.60 + $31.21 + $31.84 = $123.65

Conclusion
The interest earned in one year was $123.65.

Related Problems

Problems 12–14 could be the basis of a class discussion on the effect of different compounding periods.

Find the interest earned by each amount for the given time. Round each answer to the nearest cent.

7. $400 at 7% compounded quarterly for 1 year
   $28.74
8. $300 at 6% compounded semiannually for 2 years
   $37.65
9. $560 at 8% compounded semiannually for 3 years
   $148.59
10. $220 at 7% compounded quarterly for 1 year
   $15.82
11. $1000 at 6.5% compounded semiannually for 2 years
   $136.48
12. $500 at 6% compounded quarterly for 1 year
   $30.68
13. $500 at 6% compounded semiannually for 1 year
   $30.45
14. $500 at 6% compounded annually for 1 year
   $30

Compound Interest Tables

Compound interest tables are designed to allow people to compute compound interest without extensive calculating.

COMPOUND INTEREST TABLE

No. of Periods	1.5%	2%	2.5%	3%	3.5%	4%	5%	6%	7%	8%
1	1.0150	1.0200	1.0250	1.0300	1.0350	1.0400	1.0500	1.0600	1.0700	1.0800
2	1.0302	1.0404	1.0506	1.0609	1.0712	1.0816	1.1025	1.1236	1.1449	1.1664
3	1.0457	1.0612	1.0769	1.0927	1.1087	1.1248	1.1576	1.1910	1.2250	1.2597
4	1.0614	1.0824	1.1038	1.1255	1.1475	1.1699	1.2155	1.2625	1.3108	1.3605
5	1.0773	1.1041	1.1314	1.1593	1.1877	1.2167	1.2763	1.3382	1.4026	1.4693
6	1.0934	1.1262	1.1597	1.1941	1.2293	1.2653	1.3401	1.4186	1.5007	1.5869
7	1.1098	1.1487	1.1887	1.2299	1.2723	1.3159	1.4071	1.5036	1.6058	1.7138
8	1.1265	1.1717	1.2184	1.2668	1.3168	1.3686	1.4775	1.5938	1.7182	1.8059
9	1.1434	1.1951	1.2489	1.3048	1.3629	1.4233	1.5513	1.6895	1.8385	1.9990
10	1.1605	1.2190	1.2801	1.3439	1.4106	1.4802	1.6289	1.7908	1.9672	2.1589
11	1.1779	1.2434	1.3121	1.3842	1.4600	1.5395	1.7103	1.8983	2.1049	2.3316
12	1.1956	1.2682	1.3449	1.4258	1.5111	1.6010	1.7959	2.0122	2.2522	2.5182
13	1.2136	1.2936	1.3785	1.4685	1.5640	1.6651	1.8856	2.1329	2.4098	2.7196
14	1.2318	1.3195	1.4130	1.5126	1.6187	1.7317	1.9799	2.2609	2.5785	2.9372
15	1.2502	1.3459	1.4483	1.5580	1.6753	1.8009	2.0789	2.3966	2.7590	3.1722
16	1.2690	1.3728	1.4845	1.6047	1.7340	1.8730	2.1829	2.5404	2.9522	3.4259
17	1.2880	1.4002	1.5216	1.6528	1.7947	1.9479	2.2920	2.6928	3.1588	3.7000
18	1.3073	1.4282	1.5597	1.7024	1.8575	2.0258	2.4066	2.8543	3.3799	3.9960
19	1.3270	1.4568	1.5987	1.7535	1.9225	2.1068	2.5270	3.0256	3.6165	4.3157
20	1.3469	1.4859	1.6386	1.8061	1.9898	2.1911	2.6533	3.2071	3.8697	4.6610
21	1.3671	1.5157	1.6796	1.8603	2.0594	2.2788	2.7860	3.3996	4.1406	5.0338
22	1.3876	1.5460	1.7216	1.9161	2.1315	2.3699	2.9253	3.6035	4.4304	5.4365
23	1.4084	1.5769	1.7646	1.9736	2.2061	2.4647	3.0715	3.8198	4.7405	5.8715
24	1.4295	1.6084	1.8087	2.0328	2.2833	2.5633	3.2251	4.0489	5.0724	6.3412
25	1.4509	1.6407	1.8539	2.0938	2.3673	2.6658	3.3864	4.2919	5.4274	6.8485

Warm-up: 8% ÷ 2 = ■% [4]
9% ÷ 2 = ■% [4.5]
2600 × 1.0600 [2756]
4000 × 3.1722 [12,688.8]

Problem

Ginny Leatherman had $550 in a savings account that paid 7% interest compounded semiannually. How much interest was earned in 3 years?

Solution

Strategy

- Divide 7% by the number of times the interest is compounded each year.
  $7 \div 2 = 3.5$
- Multiply the number of years by the number of times the interest is compounded each year to find the total number of periods.
  $2 \times 3 = 6$
- Read the entry from the table.
  1.2293
- Multiply by the principal to find the total amount in the account. Round to the nearest cent.
  $\$550 \times 1.2293 \approx \$676.12$
- Subtract the principal from the total amount to find the interest.
  $\$676.12 - \$550.00 = \$126.12$

Conclusion

The interest earned was $126.12.

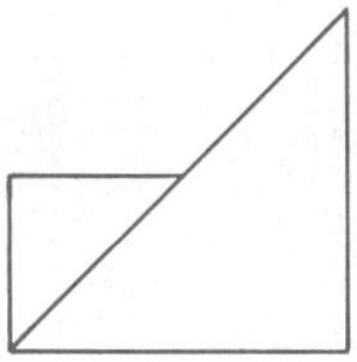

Side view

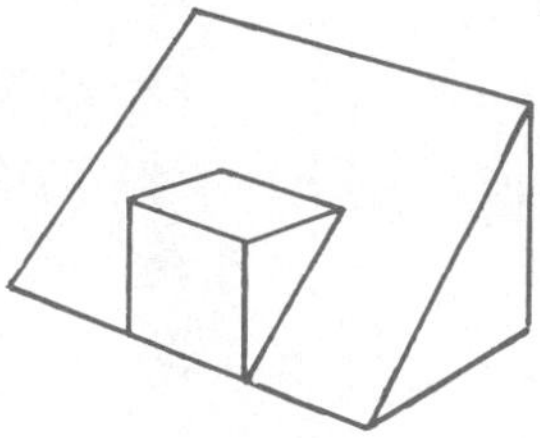

Three-dimensional view

Give several examples to insure that the students can use the table before assigning the problems.

Related Problems

You may wish to allow students to use calculators.

Use the compound interest table to find the interest earned by each amount for the given time. Round each answer to the nearest cent.

1. $100 at 6% compounded annually for 4 years
   $26.25
2. $370 at 7% compounded annually for 5 years
   $148.96
3. $750 at 8% compounded annually for 15 years
   $1629.15
4. $435 at 5% compounded annually for 8 years
   $207.71
5. $400 at 10% compounded semiannually for 3 years
   $136.04
6. $850 at 7% compounded semiannually for 8 years
   $623.90
7. $575 at 8% compounded semiannually for 11 years
   $787.69
8. $1000 at 6% compounded semiannually for 12 years
   $1032.80
9. $2000 at 8% compounded quarterly for 5 years
   $971.80
10. $1500 at 6% compounded quarterly for 6 years
    $644.25
11. $1800 at 10% compounded quarterly for 4 years
    $872.10
12. $2500 at 12% compounded quarterly for 3 years
    $1064.50

Break Time

The picture below shows both the top view and the front view of a three-dimensional figure. Draw the side view.

See left.

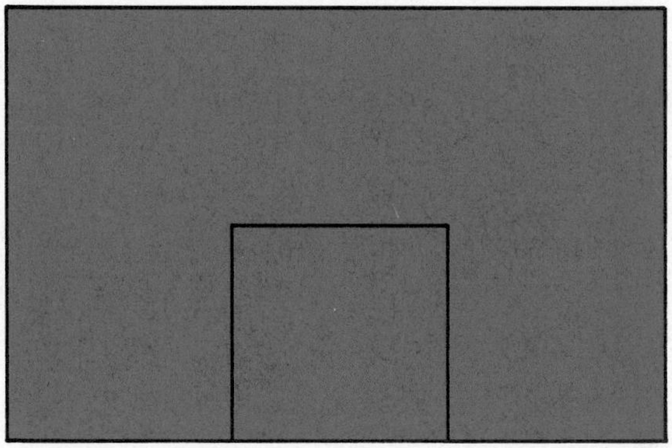

Skills Tune-Up

Multiplying decimals, pages 10-11

1. 0.5×0.7 0.35
2. 0.6×0.4 0.24
3. 0.08×0.2 0.016
4. 0.06×0.1 0.006
5. 0.03×0.06 0.0018
6. 0.8×0.04 0.032
7. 0.002×0.04 0.00008
8. 0.11×0.003 0.00033
9. 700×0.2 140
10. 0.6×900 540
11. 800×0.04 32
12. 0.05×110 5.5
13. 0.003×700 2.1
14. 600×0.008 4.8
15. 0.005×0.004 0.00002
16. 0.002×0.007 0.000014
17. 4000×0.0011 4.4
18. 8.3×1.7 14.11
19. 8.32×4.2 34.944
20. 9.1×3.46 31.486
21. 13.5×0.018 0.243
22. 5.661×6.46 36.57006
23. 80.33×1.911 153.51063
24. 7.49×0.6008 4.499992
25. 49.217×0.032 1.574944
26. 4.627×0.0037 0.0171199
27. 0.054×31.5 1.701
28. 0.014×782.3 10.9522

Ratio and proportion, pages 30-31

Find the cross-products. Tell whether the ratios are equal.

1. $\frac{2}{40}$ $\frac{3}{60}$ $120 = 120$
2. $\frac{3}{13}$ $\frac{5}{15}$ $45 \neq 65$
3. $\frac{4}{12}$ $\frac{12}{35}$ $140 \neq 144$
4. $\frac{1.4}{0.6}$ $\frac{7}{3}$ $4.2 = 4.2$
5. $\frac{0.32}{0.05}$ $\frac{0.66}{0.20}$ $0.064 \neq 0.033$
6. $\frac{15.3}{25.5}$ $\frac{0.3}{0.5}$ $7.65 = 7.65$

Solve and check.

7. $\frac{4}{5} = \frac{n}{45}$ $n = 36$
8. $\frac{15}{a} = \frac{3}{20}$ $a = 100$
9. $\frac{x}{54} = \frac{5}{18}$ $x = 15$
10. $\frac{14}{3} = \frac{7}{c}$ $c = 1.5$
11. $\frac{16}{d} = \frac{3.2}{4.2}$ $d = 21$
12. $\frac{1.4}{0.7} = \frac{a}{0.45}$ $a = 0.9$
13. $\frac{0.04}{0.36} = \frac{9}{y}$ $y = 81$
14. $\frac{42}{x} = \frac{26}{0.13}$ $x = 0.21$

Writing percents, decimals, and fractions, pages 32-33

Write as a decimal.

1. 17% 0.17
2. 8% 0.08
3. 1% 0.01
4. 25% 0.25
5. 96% 0.96
6. 3% 0.03
7. 99% 0.99
8. $6\frac{1}{4}\%$ 0.0625
9. 7.75% 0.0775
10. 15.6% 0.156
11. $12\frac{1}{2}\%$ 0.125
12. 1.5% 0.015
13. 6.75% 0.0675
14. $1\frac{1}{2}\%$ 0.015
15. 32.8% 0.328
16. 8.5% 0.085
17. $5\frac{3}{4}\%$ 0.0575
18. $16\frac{1}{8}\%$ 0.16125
19. 103% 1.03
20. 924% 9.24
21. 856% 8.56
22. 160% 1.6
23. $\frac{1}{4}\%$ 0.0025
24. $\frac{2}{5}\%$ 0.004

Write as a fraction in lowest terms.

25. 50% $\frac{1}{2}$
26. 90% $\frac{9}{10}$
27. 35% $\frac{7}{20}$
28. 75% $\frac{3}{4}$
29. 60% $\frac{3}{5}$
30. 37% $\frac{37}{100}$
31. 24% $\frac{6}{25}$
32. 83% $\frac{83}{100}$
33. 20% $\frac{1}{5}$
34. 15% $\frac{3}{20}$
35. 9% $\frac{9}{100}$
36. 56% $\frac{14}{25}$
37. 33% $\frac{33}{100}$
38. 5% $\frac{1}{20}$
39. 45% $\frac{9}{20}$
40. 87% $\frac{87}{100}$
41. 95% $\frac{19}{20}$
42. 67% $\frac{67}{100}$
43. $37\frac{1}{2}\%$ $\frac{3}{8}$
44. $16\frac{1}{2}\%$ $\frac{33}{200}$
45. 110% $1\frac{1}{10}$
46. 675% $6\frac{3}{4}$
47. 350% $3\frac{1}{2}$
48. 140% $1\frac{2}{5}$

Chapter 5 Review

Deposit slips, pages 88-89

1. Find the total and the net deposit for this deposit slip.

CASH	CURRENCY		
	COIN	8	75
LIST CHECKS SINGLY		29	80
		37	40
		5	23
TOTAL FROM OTHER SIDE			
TOTAL		81	18
LESS CASH RECEIVED		25	00
NET DEPOSIT		56	18

Checks and check stubs, pages 90-91

2. Write $38.72 in words as it would appear on a check.
Thirty-eight and $\frac{72}{100}$

3. Find the balance carried forward for this check stub.

	DOLLARS	CENTS
BAL. FOR'D	93	57
DEPOSITS	95	76
"	11	29
TOTAL	206	62
THIS PAYMENT	75	20
OTHER DEDUCTIONS		
BAL. FOR'D	131	42

Check registers, pages 92-93

For problems 4 and 5, find each new balance.

	NUMBER	DATE	PAYMENT/DEBIT (−)		√ T	FEE (IF ANY) (−)	DEPOSIT/CREDIT (+)		BALANCE	
									$ 283	26
		10/8	$			$	$ 136	18	136	18
4.									419	44
	127	10/9	34	70					34	70
5.									384	74

Reconciling a bank statement, pages 94-96

6. Reconcile the bank-statement information with the check-register balance. Find the actual amount in the checking account.
$109.11
Statement ending balance: $196.50
Outstanding deposit: $57.56
Outstanding checks: $19.70, $125.25
Service charge: $4.75
Check-register balance: $113.86

Personal banking representative, pages 98-99

7. A savings account paid 6.5% simple interest. Find the amount of interest that $1200 earned in 9 months.
$58.50

Compound interest, pages 100-101

8. Sylvia put $800 in a savings account that paid 6% interest compounded annually. Find the interest earned in 2 years.
$98.88

9. Carl put $1000 in a savings account that paid 8% interest compounded quarterly. Find the interest earned in 1 year. Round to the nearest cent.
$82.43

Compound interest tables, pages 102-103

10. Use the table below to find the amount of interest earned on $400 at 6% interest compounded semiannually for 5 years.
$137.56

No. of Periods	1.5%	2%	2.5%	3%
1	1.0150	1.0200	1.0250	1.0300
2	1.0302	1.0404	1.0506	1.0609
7	1.1098	1.1487	1.1887	1.2299
8	1.1265	1.1717	1.2184	1.2668
9	1.1434	1.1951	1.2489	1.3048
10	1.1605	1.2190	1.2801	1.3439

Chapter 5 Test

Number of test items - 10

Number missed	1	2	3	4	5
Percent correct	90	80	70	60	50

1. Find the total and the net deposit for this deposit slip.

CASH	CURRENCY		
	COIN		
LIST CHECKS SINGLY		18	50
		43	82
		459	27
TOTAL FROM OTHER SIDE			
TOTAL		521	59
LESS CASH RECEIVED		35	00
NET DEPOSIT		486	59

2. Write $52.43 in words as it would appear on a check.
Fifty-two and $\frac{43}{100}$

3. Find the balance carried forward for this check stub.

	DOLLARS	CENTS
BAL. FOR'D	100	69
DEPOSITS	47	29
"	126	35
TOTAL	274	33
THIS PAYMENT	225	80
OTHER DEDUCTIONS		
BAL. FOR'D	48	53

For problems 4 and 5, find each new balance.

	NUMBER	DATE	PAYMENT/DEBIT (-)		√ T	FEE (IF ANY) (-)	DEPOSIT/CREDIT (+)		BALANCE	
									$ 114	53
		11/20	$			$	$ 126	74	126	74
4.									241	27
	311	11/24	78	16					78	16
5.									163	11

6. Reconcile the bank-statement information with the check-register balance. Find the actual amount in the checking account.
$61.96
Statement ending balance: $147.80
Outstanding deposit: $57.26
Outstanding checks: $37.86, $105.24
Service charge: $6.25
Check-register balance: $68.21

7. A savings account paid 7.5% simple interest. Find the amount of interest that $700 earned in 6 months.
$26.25

8. Joan put $500 in a savings account that paid 7% interest compounded annually. Find the interest earned in 2 years.
$72.45

9. Ray put $2000 in a savings account that paid 8% interest compounded semiannually. Find the interest earned in 1 year.
$163.20

10. Use the table below to find the amount of interest earned on $5000 at 8% interest compounded quarterly for 4 years.
$1864

No. of Periods	1.5%	2%	2.5%	3%
1	1.0150	1.0200	1.0250	1.0300
2	1.0302	1.0404	1.0506	1.0609
16	1.2690	1.3728	1.4845	1.6047
17	1.2880	1.4002	1.5216	1.6528
18	1.3073	1.4282	1.5597	1.7024
19	1.3270	1.4568	1.5987	1.7535
20	1.3469	1.4859	1.6386	1.8061

 See pages 11-12 of the *Test Masters* for an alternate form of the Chapter 5 Test.

Chapter 6 Consumer Credit

Objective: Compute the interest and the total amount due on a promissory note.

Promissory Notes

See page T31 for additional notes and activities for Chapter 6.

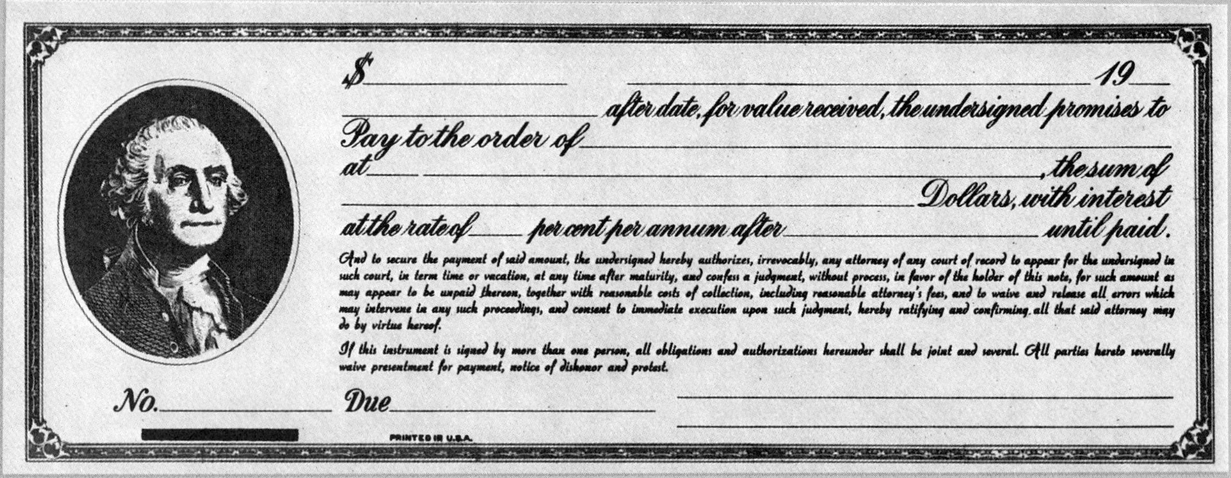

$ ______________ ______________ 19____

______________ after date, for value received, the undersigned promises to

Pay to the order of ______________

at ______________, the sum of

______________ Dollars, with interest

at the rate of ____ per cent per annum after ______________ until paid.

And to secure the payment of said amount, the undersigned hereby authorizes, irrevocably, any attorney of any court of record to appear for the undersigned in such court, in term time or vacation, at any time after maturity, and confess a judgment, without process, in favor of the holder of this note, for such amount as may appear to be unpaid thereon, together with reasonable costs of collection, including reasonable attorney's fees, and to waive and release all errors which may intervene in any such proceedings, and consent to immediate execution upon such judgment, hereby ratifying and confirming all that said attorney may do by virtue hereof.

If this instrument is signed by more than one person, all obligations and authorizations hereunder shall be joint and several. All parties hereto severally waive presentment for payment, notice of dishonor and protest.

No. ______________ Due ______________

PRINTED IN U.S.A.

When Dennis Nelson borrowed money from his bank, the bank required that he sign a **promissory note.** In the note, he agreed to repay the **principal,** or the amount borrowed, along with the **interest,** by a certain date. The interest is the amount the bank charges for the use of the money.

The bank used the simple interest formula to compute the amount of interest due.

$$I = P \times R \times T$$

I — Interest, P — Principal, R — Rate, T — Time

Problem

Dennis signed a promissory note for $2500 at an interest rate of 17.5% per year. The note is due in 120 days. Find the amount of interest and the total amount due. Use 360 days for 1 year.

Solution

Strategy

- Express the interest rate and time as fractions.

  $17.5\% = 0.175 = \frac{175}{1000}$

  120 days is $\frac{120}{360}$, or $\frac{1}{3}$, year.

- Use the simple interest formula to compute the interest due. Round to the nearest cent.

  $I = P \times R \times T$

  $I = \$2500 \times \frac{175}{1000} \times \frac{1}{3}$

  $I \approx \$145.83$

- Add the principal and the interest to find the total amount due.

  $\$2500 + \$145.83 = \$2645.83$

Conclusion

Dennis will pay $145.83 in interest. The total amount due will be $2645.83.

Warm-up: 8 months = ■ year [$\frac{2}{3}$] 1 yr. 3 mo. = ■ year [$\frac{5}{4}$]

120 days = ■ year [$\frac{1}{3}$] $1600 \times \frac{185}{1000} \times \frac{1}{4}$ [74]

Related Problems

Note that problems 7-10 are in terms of months.

Find the amount of interest due. Round to the nearest cent.

1. $850 at 18% for 90 days
   $38.25
2. $1100 at 15% for 30 days
   $13.75
3. $730 at 14.5% for 60 days
   $17.64
4. $1500 at 13.5% for 120 days
   $67.50
5. $2000 at 20% for 1 day
   $1.11
6. $600 at 17.5% for 15 days
   $4.38
7. $2300 at 15% for 4 months
   $115
8. $1350 at 18.5% for 8 months
   $166.50
9. $500 at 17% for 15 months
   $106.25
10. $4850 at 18% for 18 months
    $1309.50

For each promissory note, find the amount of interest due. Round to the nearest cent. Then find the total amount due.

11. *120 days* AFTER DATE I, WE, OR EITHER OF US, PROMISE TO PAY TO THE ORDER OF *First National Bank*
One thousand eight hundred and 00/100 DOLLARS
WITH INTEREST FOR VALUE RECEIVED AT *18* % PER YEAR.

$108 interest
$1908 total due

12. *1 yr. 3 mo.* AFTER DATE I, WE, OR EITHER OF US, PROMISE TO PAY TO THE ORDER OF *Prairie State Bank*
Nine hundred twenty-five and 00/100 DOLLARS
WITH INTEREST FOR VALUE RECEIVED AT *18.5* % PER YEAR.

$213.91 interest
$1138.91 total due

13. *2 yr. 6 mo.* AFTER DATE, I, WE, OR EITHER OF US, PROMISE TO PAY TO THE ORDER OF *Lincoln Bank*
Two thousand four hundred and 00/100 DOLLARS
WITH INTEREST FOR VALUE RECEIVED AT *14* % PER YEAR.

$840 interest
$3240 total due

14. *50 days* AFTER DATE I, WE, OR EITHER OF US, PROMISE TO PAY TO THE ORDER OF *Northeast National Bank*
Nine hundred seventy-five and 00/100 DOLLARS
WITH INTEREST FOR VALUE RECEIVED AT *17.5* % PER YEAR.

$23.70 interest
$998.70 total due

Objectives: Compute the finance charge for a charge account, using the balance after payments; find the new balance.

Credit Card Finance Charges

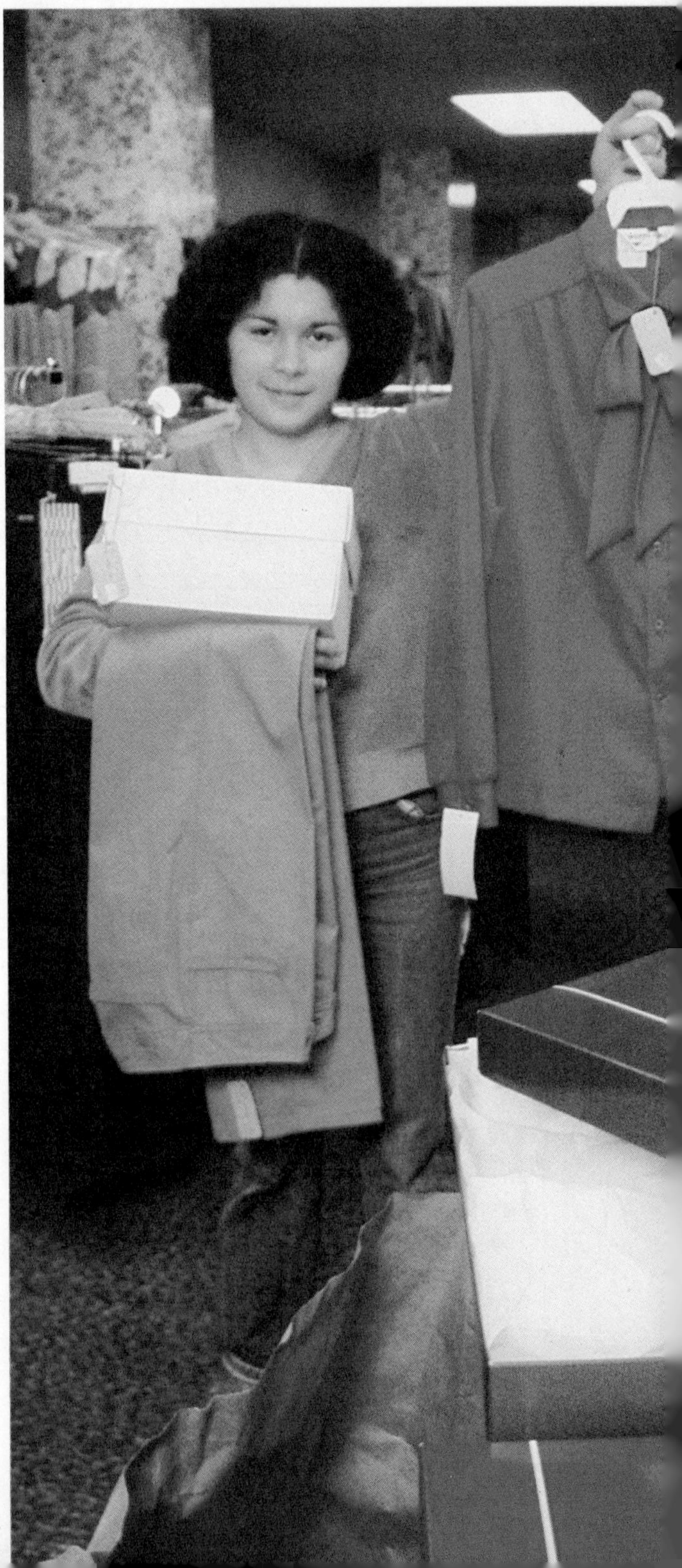

Marilyn Running Deer has a credit card that allows her to charge all of her purchases at Engel's, a local department store. Once a month, she receives a statement of the balance due on her account.

When Marilyn pays less than the full amount owed, she has to pay a **finance charge** the next month. The finance charge is the amount that the store charges for the privilege of delaying payment.

Engel's computes the finance charge on the balance that remains after payments have been subtracted from the unpaid balance. Engel's does not charge its customers a finance charge on new purchases.

Problem

Marilyn's unpaid balance from last month is \$87.50. This month she has made a payment of \$20 and charged purchases totaling \$23.18. The finance charge is 1.5% per month. What is the new balance?

Point out that 1.5% per month is 18% per year.

Solution

Strategy

- Subtract to find the balance after payment.

  $\$87.50 - \$20.00 = \$67.50$

- Multiply by 1.5% to find the finance charge on the balance after payment. Round to the nearest cent.

  $0.015 \times \$67.50 \approx \$1.01$

- Add to find the new balance.

Balance after payment		Finance charge		Purchases		New balance
\$67.50	+	\$1.01	+	\$23.18	=	\$91.69

Conclusion

The new balance is \$91.69.

Warm-up: Round to the nearest hundredth.
1.5% of 38.50 [0.58]
1.5% of 75.20 [1.13]
1.5% of 326.81 [4.90]
1.5% of 1200 [18]

See page 29 of *Consumer Forms and Problems.*

Related Problems

Complete the table. The finance charge is 1.5% per month of the balance after payments. Round the finance charge to the nearest cent.

	Unpaid balance	Payments	Balance after payments	Finance charge	Purchases	New balance
1.	$47.16	$0	$47.16	$0.71	$0	$47.87
2.	$79.62	$0	$79.62	$1.19	$46.13	$126.94
3.	$126.38	$20.00	$106.38	$1.60	$0	$107.98
4.	$148.18	$25.00	$123.18	$1.85	$30.57	$155.60
5.	$72.33	$50.00	$22.33	$0.33	$9.98 $14.68	$47.32
6.	$342.75	$10.00	$332.75	$4.99	$6.23 $10.39	$354.36
7.	$183.77	$10.00	$173.77	$2.61	$17.43 $12.21	$206.02
8.	$234.90	$36.00	$198.90	$2.98	$18.95 $19.34	$240.17
9.	$83.21	$83.21	$0	$0	$20.94	$20.94
10.	$223.14	$10.00 $13.14	$200.00	$3.00	$0	$203.00
11.	$158.19	$8.19	$150.00	$2.25	$35.60	$187.85
12.	$0	$0	$0	$0	$12.00 $16.49 $49.40	$77.89

See pages 128–129 for a computer application related to this lesson.

Break Time

A farmer counted the number of cows and chickens by counting heads and legs. If he counted 35 heads and 78 legs, how many cows and chickens did he have?

4 cows and 31 chickens

Objectives: Compute the finance charge for a charge account, using average daily balance; find the new balance.

Credit Counselor

See the Careers Chart beginning on page 410 for more information about the careers in this cluster.

Warm-up:
189.60 × 20 [3792]
137.91 + 0.86 + 82.13 [220.90]
Round to the nearest hundredth.
0.018 × 135.62 [2.44]
8612 ÷ 31 [277.81]

Career Cluster: Social Service Lee Jones is a counselor for a consumer protection agency. She helps people understand the cost of buying on credit.

Jim Nawrocki has a credit card from a company that uses the **average daily balance** to compute finance charges. The company computes the unpaid balance in the account each day of the month. The finance charge is based on the average of these daily unpaid amounts. Ms. Jones showed Jim how a weighted balance was used to find the average daily balance in his account.

Problem

See Calculator Applications on page 114 for a situation in which new purchases are included when determining the average daily balance and current finance charges.

Jim's unpaid balance on April 1 was $132.40. He charged $23.14 on April 15 and made a payment of $20 on April 21. The finance charge was 1.8% per month of the average daily balance. There was no finance charge on new purchases. What were the finance charge and the new balance as of April 30?

Solution

Explain how to count days: April 1-20 is 20 days, not 19; April 22-30 is 9 days, not 8. Total number of days should equal the number of days in the month.

Strategy

- Multiply to find each weighted balance. Add to find the total.

Dates	Payment	Unpaid balance	Days	Weighted balance (unpaid balance × days)
April 1–20	——	$132.40	20	$2648.00
April 21	$20	$112.40	1	$112.40
April 22–30	——	$112.40	9	$1011.60
		Total	30	$3772.00

- Divide to find the average daily balance to the nearest cent.

Total weighted balance ÷ Total days ≈ Average daily balance

$3772 ÷ 30 ≈ $125.73

- Multiply to find the finance charge to the nearest cent.

Monthly rate × Average daily balance ≈ Finance charge

0.018 × $125.73 ≈ $2.26

- Subtract to find the balance after payment.

$132.40	Unpaid balance
− 20.00	Payment
$112.40	Balance after payment

- Add to find the new balance.

$112.40	Balance after payment
2.26	Finance charge
+ 23.14	Purchases
$137.80	New balance

Conclusion

The finance charge was $2.26. The new balance was $137.80.

You may want to have students compare the finance charges and new balances for a given unpaid balance using the procedure on pages 110-111 and the average daily balance method shown here.

Related Problems

On June 1, the unpaid balance in Jim's account was $147.19. On June 11, he made a $25 payment. A purchase of $19.82 was made on June 17.

Complete this table to find the total weighted balance.

	Dates	Payment	Unpaid balance	Days	Weighted balance (unpaid balance × days)
1.	June 1–10	——	$147.19	10	$1471.90
2.	June 11	$25	$122.19	1	$122.19
3.	June 12–30	——	$122.19	19	$2321.61
4.			Total	30	$3915.70

5. Use the information in the table to find Jim's average daily balance to the nearest cent.
$130.52

6. The finance charge is 1.8% of the average daily balance. There is no finance charge on new purchases. Find Jim's finance charge to the nearest cent.
$2.35

7. What is the balance after payment?
$122.19

8. Find the new balance in Jim's account on June 30.
$144.36

Find the finance charge to the nearest cent and the new balance at the end of the month. The finance charge is 1.8% per month of the average daily balance. There is no finance charge on new purchases.

9. Jan. 1: Unpaid balance of $34
Jan. 7: Payment of $10
New purchase of $18
$0.47; $42.47

10. Sept. 1: Unpaid balance of $88.14
Sept. 22: Payment of $25
No new purchases
$1.45; $64.59

11. Aug. 1: Unpaid balance of $108.75
Aug. 21: Payment of $60
New purchase of $32.98
$1.57; $83.30

12. May 1: Unpaid balance of $235.89
No payment during the month
New purchases of $76.54 and $33.65
$4.25; $350.33

Point out that when no payment is made during the month, the average daily balance is the same as the unpaid balance.

CALCULATOR APPLICATIONS

Charge Accounts

Some companies *include* new purchases when they determine a customer's average daily balance. They do this only when the customer has an unpaid balance from the previous month.

Alice Chen has a credit card from a company that uses this method. The finance charge is 1.8% per month. Complete the chart below to find the amount of the finance charge and the new balance in Alice's account on December 31.

	Dates	Payments	Purchases	Unpaid balance	Days	Weighted balance (unpaid balance × days)
	Dec. 1–8	——	——	$435.78	8	$3486.24
1.	Dec. 9	——	$23.97	$459.75	1	$459.75
2.	Dec. 10	$50.00	——	$409.75	1	$409.75
3.	Dec. 11–14	——	——	$409.75	4	$1639.00
4.	Dec. 15	——	$12.31	$422.06	1	$422.06
5.	Dec. 16–23	——	——	$422.06	8	$3376.48
6.	Dec. 24	——	$18.99	$441.05	1	$441.05
7.	Dec. 25–28	——	——	$441.05	4	$1764.20
8.	Dec. 29	——	$15.79	$456.84	1	$456.84
9.	Dec. 30–31	——	——	$456.84	2	$913.68
10.	Total	$50.00	$71.06	——	31	$13,369.05

11. Find the average daily balance to the nearest cent.

Total weighted balance		Total days		Average daily balance
$13,369.05	÷	31	≈	$431.26

12. Find the amount of the finance charge to the nearest cent.

Monthly rate		Average daily balance		Finance charge
0.018	×	$431.26	≈	$7.76

13. Find the new balance in the account.

	$435.78	Unpaid balance	
−		Total of payments	$50.00
		Balance after payments	$385.78
		Balance after payments	$385.78
		Total of purchases	$71.06
+		Finance charge	$7.76
		New balance	$464.60

Objectives: Compute the new balance in a charge account; use a table to find the minimum monthly payment.

See page 30 of *Consumer Forms and Problems.*

Minimum Payments on Charge Accounts

Most credit companies require that the customer make a **minimum payment** on the account each month. The amount of this payment depends upon the balance in the account.

A minimum-payment schedule may look like this.

New balance	Minimum payment
$0–$10	100% of balance
$10.01–$100	$10
$100.01–$200	$20
$200.01–$400	15% of balance
Over $400	20% of balance

Warm-up:
375.58 − 250 [125.58]
143.56 + 2.15 + 29.56 [175.27]
Round to the nearest hundredth.
15% of 262.73 [39.41]
20% of 582.12 [116.42]

Problem

Claire Thompson's charge-account statement showed an unpaid balance of $198.42. During the month, she made a payment of $150 and charged purchases of $227.65. The finance charge on the statement was $0.73. What was her new balance at the end of the month? What was the minimum payment required?

Solution

Strategy

- Subtract to find the balance after payment.

	$198.42	Unpaid balance
−	150.00	Payment
	$ 48.42	Balance after payment

- Add to find the new balance.

	$ 48.42	Balance after payment
	0.73	Finance charge
+	227.65	Purchases
	$276.80	New balance

- Read the schedule for minimum-payment terms. 15% of balance
- Multiply to find the minimum payment. $0.15 \times \$276.80 = \$41.52$

Conclusion

The new balance was $276.80. The minimum payment required was $41.52.

Related Problems

Complete the table. Use the minimum-payment schedule above. Round to the nearest cent.

	Unpaid balance	Payment	Balance after payment	Finance charge	Purchases	New balance	Minimum payment
1.	$52.16	$10.00	$42.16	$0.78	$11.76	$54.70	$10.00
2.	$85.49	$10.00	$75.49	$1.13	$76.35	$152.97	$20.00
3.	$127.36	$20.00	$107.36	$1.61	$85.50	$194.47	$20.00
4.	$178.28	$20.00	$158.28	$2.37	$107.00	$267.65	$40.15
5.	$225.93	$35.00	$190.93	$2.86	$0	$193.79	$20.00
6.	$418.73	$125.00	$293.73	$4.41	$0	$298.14	$44.72
7.	$129.68	$120.00	$9.68	$0.15	$0	$9.83	$9.83
8.	$629.58	$629.58	$0	$0	$9.55	$9.55	$9.55

Remind students that a customer is not limited to paying only the minimum payment. The customer can pay any amount more than the minimum or pay the entire new balance and thus avoid a finance charge.

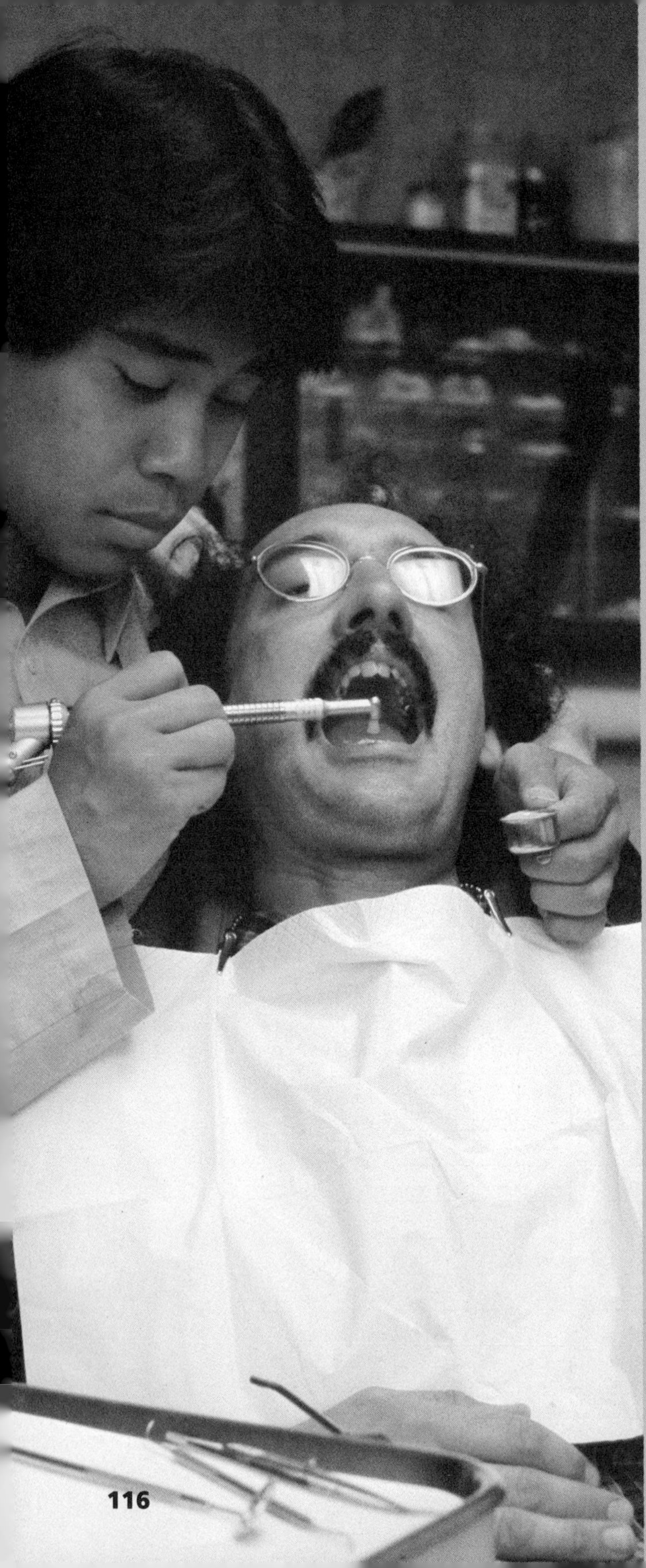

Objective: Find the amount of the monthly payment for a level-payment loan.

Level-Payment Loans

For many people, the best credit arrangement is a **level-payment loan.** This type of loan is repaid in equal monthly payments.

The calculations needed to determine the amount of each payment are very complicated, so lenders use a table like the one on page 401. Part of the table is shown below.

Monthly Payment per $1 Borrowed				
Annual rate	Number of equal monthly payments			
	6	12	18	24
16%	0.17453	0.09073	0.06286	0.04896
16.5%	0.17478	0.09097	0.06309	0.04920
17%	0.17503	0.09120	0.06333	0.04944

Problem

Don Delfonso wants to borrow $300 for 6 months to pay dental bills. The annual interest on the level-payment loan will be 16% of the unpaid balance. How much will each monthly payment be?

Solution

Strategy

- Read the table for 16% with 6 payments.
  0.17453
- Multiply to find the monthly payment on $300. Round to the nearest cent.
  $0.17453 \times \$300 \approx \$52.36$

Conclusion

Each monthly payment will be $52.36.

Most lending institutions set up a level-payment method for their customers to pay off a loan because it is easier for the customer. A mortgage loan is a common type of level-payment loan.

Warm-up: Round to the nearest hundredth.

0.06381×250 [15.95]

0.05041×400 [20.16]

0.17403×500 [87.02]

$900 \times \frac{18}{100} \times \frac{1}{12}$ [13.5]

Related Problems

Use the table on page 401 to find the amount of the monthly payment for each level-payment loan. Round to the nearest cent.

1. $500 at 18.5% for 6 months
   $87.89
2. $350 at 16% for 12 months
   $31.76
3. $700 at 15.5% for 6 months
   $122
4. $875 at 12% for 36 months
   $29.06
5. $300 at 22% for 30 months
   $13.09
6. $1100 at 14% for 24 months
   $52.81
7. $950 at 16% for 24 months
   $46.51
8. $950 at 16% for 36 months
   $33.40
9. $2500 at 18% for 18 months
   $159.53
10. $2500 at 16.5% for 18 months
   $157.73

Problem

Each month, part of Don's payment is used to repay one month's interest. The rest of the payment reduces the amount owed on the loan. How much will Don still owe on his $300 loan after the first payment of $52.36?

Solution

Strategy

- Use the simple interest formula to find the amount of interest at 16% per year for 1 month ($\frac{1}{12}$ year).

$I = P \times R \times T$

$I = \$300 \times \frac{16}{100} \times \frac{1}{12}$

$I = \$4$

- Add the amount of the loan and the interest to find the total amount owed.

$\$300 + \$4 = \$304$

Point out that the interest is added to the amount owed before the payment is subtracted.

- Subtract $52.36 to find the amount owed after the first payment.

$\$304.00 - \$52.36 = \$251.64$

Conclusion

Don will still owe $251.64 after the first payment.

Related Problems

Complete the table to find Don's schedule for repaying his loan. Round to the nearest cent.

	End of month	Amount owed	Interest for the month	Total owed	Payment	Amount still owed
	1	$300.00	$4.00	$304.00	$52.36	$251.64
11.	2	$251.64	$3.36	$255.00	$52.36	$202.64
12.	3	$202.64	$2.70	$205.34	$52.36	$152.98
13.	4	$152.98	$2.04	$155.02	$52.36	$102.66
14.	5	$102.66	$1.37	$104.03	$52.36	$51.67
15.	6	$51.67	$0.69	$52.36	$52.36	$0
16.	Total	——	$14.16	——	$314.16	——

Objective: Compute the finance charge on an installment purchase.

Installment Buying

Instead of paying full price for an item at the time of purchase, people often pay only part of the price, or the **down payment.** The remainder is **financed** and paid in monthly **installments.** Buying on an installment plan is similar to borrowing money with a level-payment loan.

Like all credit arrangements, buying an item on installment costs more than paying in full at the time of purchase. The additional cost is the finance charge.

Problem

The Jamisons bought a color television set. The price, including tax, was $736.70. They signed an installment contract agreeing to pay 15% of the price as a down payment. The remainder, plus a finance charge, will be paid in 18 monthly installments of $41.16 each. What is the amount of the finance charge on the Jamisons' account?

Solution

Strategy

- Multiply the price by 15% to find the down payment. Round to the nearest cent.
  $0.15 \times \$736.70 \approx \$110.51$
- Subtract to find the amount financed.
  $\$736.70 - \$110.51 = \$626.19$
- Multiply the monthly installment by 18 to find the total amount paid in installments.
  $18 \times \$41.16 = \$740.88$
- Subtract to find the amount of the finance charge.
  $\$740.88 - \$626.19 = \$114.69$

Conclusion

The amount of the finance charge is $114.69.

In this problem, the annual rate is 22%.
The maximum legal interest rate varies from state to state.

Warm-up: 18 × 25.16 [452.88]
24 × 15.77 [378.48]
459.18 − 116.24 [342.94]
381.50 − 103.79 [277.71]

Related Problems

Complete the table. Round to the nearest cent.

	Item	Cash price	Down payment	Amount financed	Installments: Number of months	Installments: Monthly payment	Installments: Total paid in installments	Finance charge
	TV set	$736.70	$110.51	$626.19	18	$41.16	$740.88	$114.69
1.	Tool set	$249.50	——	$249.50	12	$23.11	$277.32	$27.82
2.	Lawn mower	$269.15	——	$269.15	18	$17.43	$313.74	$44.59
3.	Refrigerator	$829.95	$100.00	$729.95	24	$37.15	$891.60	$161.65
4.	Rug	$151.25	$25.00	$126.25	12	$11.69	$140.28	$14.03
5.	Water heater	$199.20	$25.00	$174.20	30	$7.43	$222.90	$48.70
6.	Typewriter	$289.16	$30.00	$259.16	24	$13.19	$316.56	$57.40
7.	Furniture	$615.23	10%	$553.71	36	$20.58	$740.88	$187.17
8.	Air conditioner	$499.85	20%	$399.88	24	$20.35	$488.40	$88.52
9.	Oven	$289.67	30%	$202.77	36	$7.53	$271.08	$68.31
10.	Sewing machine	$385.35	10%	$346.81	30	$14.78	$443.40	$96.59

Complete the table. Round to the nearest cent. To find the monthly payment for these installment plans, use the strategy from the previous lesson and the table on page 401.

	Amount financed	Annual rate	Installments: Number of months	Installments: Monthly payment	Installments: Total paid in installments	Finance charge
11.	$500	18%	12	$45.84	$550.08	$50.08
12.	$500	18%	24	$24.96	$599.04	$99.04
13.	$500	18%	36	$18.08	$650.88	$150.88
14.	$500	21%	12	$46.56	$558.72	$58.72
15.	$500	21%	24	$25.70	$616.80	$116.80
16.	$500	21%	36	$18.84	$678.24	$178.24
17.	$500	21.5%	24	$25.82	$619.68	$119.68
18.	$500	21.5%	36	$18.97	$682.92	$182.92

Objective: Compare various credit plans to determine which plan costs less.

Comparing Credit Plans

Students need to realize that they not only need to shop for the best price on an item, but they should also "shop for a loan" if they plan to finance the item.

People can often choose from a variety of credit plans to finance a major purchase. They should compare the plans before deciding which one to use.

Problem

Victor Lopez wants to buy a piano for $1289. He can borrow $1289 from his credit union at an annual rate of 15%. He would repay the credit union $44.69 per month for 36 months.

Victor can also finance the $1289 through the piano dealer at an annual rate of 21%. He would repay the dealer $84.09 per month for 18 months.

What is the cost of credit for each plan? Which plan costs less?

Solution

Strategy

- Multiply to find the total amount to be repaid to the credit union.
  36 × $44.69 = $1608.84
- Subtract to find the cost of borrowing the money from the credit union.
  $1608.84 − $1289.00 = $319.84
- Multiply to find the total amount to be repaid to the dealer.
  18 × $84.09 = $1513.62
- Subtract to find the cost of financing through the dealer.
  $1513.62 − $1289.00 = $224.62

Conclusion

The cost of credit for borrowing the money from the credit union is $319.84. The cost of credit for financing through the dealer is $224.62. Financing the piano through the dealer costs less.

Warm-up: 36 × 239.25 [8613]
24 × 187.48 [4499.52]
498.84 − 436.92 [61.92]
1213.85 − 1087.26 [126.59]

See page 31 of
Consumer Forms and Problems.

Related Problems

Use strategies from previous lessons to solve these problems.

Two stores are offering the same model home freezer for $469.95.

1. Ace Appliance Store will finance the purchase over 18 months with monthly payments of $31.12. What is the cost of credit for this plan?
   $90.21
2. Lakeview Department Store offers a 24-month payment plan with monthly payments of $23.92. What is the cost of credit for this plan?
   $104.13
3. Which store's plan costs less?
   Ace Appliance Store

Al Marvin wants to borrow $800 to buy carpentry tools.

4. He can borrow $800 on a level-payment loan and repay it in 6 monthly installments of $141.22. What is the cost of credit for this plan?
   $47.32
5. He can borrow $800 on a promissory note at 18% interest for 6 months. What is the cost of credit for this plan?
   $72
6. Which plan costs less?
   The level-payment loan in problem 4

Gladys Smith needs to borrow $2800 for medical expenses. Use the table on page 401.

7. She can borrow $2800 at 18% for 30 months on a level-payment loan. What is the monthly payment? Round to the nearest cent.
   $116.59
8. She can borrow $2800 at 17% for 36 months on a level-payment loan. What is the monthly payment?
   $99.82
9. Gladys knows that the most she can repay is $100 per month. Which credit plan will fit into her budget?
   The 17% loan for 36 months in problem 8

George Menendez is buying a canoe for $357.88.

10. He can use his credit card to make the purchase. Use the schedule on page 115 to find the amount of his minimum monthly payment for the first month. Round to the nearest cent.
    $53.68
11. He can buy the canoe on an installment plan. The contract calls for no down payment and 18 monthly payments at an annual rate of 22%. Use the table on page 401 to find the monthly payment.
    $23.52
12. Which first-month payment is less?
    The installment plan in problem 11

Emily Franconi owes $400 on a credit card account.

13. She could borrow $400 from a savings and loan association and repay the loan in 4 equal payments of $104.11 each. What is the cost of credit for this plan?
    $16.44
14. She could pay $100 per month on her account and pay finance charges of 2% per month on the balance after payment. Complete the table to find the cost of credit for this plan. Round to the nearest cent.
    $12.57

Unpaid balance	Payment	Balance after payment	Finance charge (2%)	New balance
$400	$100	$300	$6	$306
$306	$100	$206.00	$4.12	$210.12
$210.12	$100	$110.12	$2.20	$112.32
$112.32	$100	$12.32	$0.25	$12.57
$12.57	$12.57	$0	$0	$0
Total	———	———	$12.57	———

15. Which plan costs less?
    The $100 a month at 2% per month in problem 14

Skills Tune-Up

Dividing whole numbers, pages 12–13

1. 7812 ÷ 3
   2604
2. 3124 ÷ 9
   347 R1
3. 1098 ÷ 6
   183
4. 5642 ÷ 7
   806
5. 6614 ÷ 4
   1653 R2
6. 1997 ÷ 4
   499 R1
7. 3885 ÷ 87
   44 R57
8. 2059 ÷ 19
   108 R7
9. 5971 ÷ 57
   104 R43
10. 8274 ÷ 42
    197
11. 2716 ÷ 66
    41 R10
12. 2488 ÷ 28
    88 R24
13. 6412 ÷ 14
    458
14. 4880 ÷ 86
    56 R64
15. 8176 ÷ 39
    209 R25
16. 8449 ÷ 71
    119
17. 3266 ÷ 72
    45 R26
18. 77,765 ÷ 24
    3240 R5
19. 45,493 ÷ 67
    679
20. 45,049 ÷ 58
    776 R41
21. 65,971 ÷ 29
    2274 R25
22. 468,635 ÷ 81
    5785 R50
23. 299,641 ÷ 82
    3654 R13
24. 513,122 ÷ 62
    8276 R10
25. 971,169 ÷ 86
    11,292 R57
26. 563,806 ÷ 802
    703
27. 64,737 ÷ 743
    87 R96
28. 829,740 ÷ 283
    2931 R267

Dividing decimals, pages 12–13

Find the quotient to the nearest hundredth.

1. 14.69 ÷ 8
   1.84
2. 47.13 ÷ 7
   6.73
3. 20.34 ÷ 31
   0.66
4. 34.02 ÷ 41
   0.83
5. 4.154 ÷ 46
   0.09
6. 1.741 ÷ 67
   0.03
7. 6.5 ÷ 1.2
   5.42
8. 87.2 ÷ 0.6
   145.33
9. 0.7 ÷ 6.5
   0.11
10. 1.6 ÷ 4.4
    0.36
11. 48.58 ÷ 7.6
    6.39
12. 10.23 ÷ 4.8
    2.13
13. 0.731 ÷ 0.16
    4.57
14. 3.261 ÷ 0.57
    5.72
15. 56 ÷ 0.2
    280
16. 35 ÷ 0.7
    50
17. 8.7 ÷ 1.54
    5.65
18. 2.56 ÷ 8.75
    0.29
19. 6.41 ÷ 8.17
    0.78
20. 7.32 ÷ 4.75
    1.54
21. 0.1531 ÷ 2.87
    0.05
22. 0.614 ÷ 0.314
    1.96
23. 0.851 ÷ 0.613
    1.39
24. 0.3498 ÷ 0.071
    4.93
25. 0.6649 ÷ 0.092
    7.23
26. 0.9368 ÷ 0.045
    20.82

Multiplying fractions and mixed numbers, pages 16–17

1. $\frac{2}{3} \times \frac{1}{5}$ $\frac{2}{15}$
2. $\frac{3}{8} \times \frac{1}{2}$ $\frac{3}{16}$
3. $\frac{4}{5} \times \frac{1}{4}$ $\frac{1}{5}$
4. $\frac{1}{3} \times \frac{1}{2}$ $\frac{1}{6}$
5. $\frac{5}{8} \times \frac{4}{5}$ $\frac{1}{2}$
6. $\frac{7}{12} \times \frac{3}{7}$ $\frac{1}{4}$
7. $\frac{4}{9} \times 15$ $6\frac{2}{3}$
8. $30 \times \frac{3}{10}$ 9
9. $\frac{4}{5} \times 2\frac{1}{4}$ $1\frac{4}{5}$
10. $1\frac{7}{8} \times \frac{4}{5}$ $1\frac{1}{2}$
11. $5\frac{5}{7} \times \frac{7}{8}$ 5
12. $2\frac{1}{2} \times 2\frac{1}{4}$ $5\frac{5}{8}$
13. $\frac{1}{2} \times 6\frac{1}{4}$ $3\frac{1}{8}$
14. $2 \times 3\frac{5}{7}$ $7\frac{3}{7}$
15. $5\frac{1}{3} \times 1\frac{1}{8}$ 6
16. $1\frac{1}{2} \times 8\frac{1}{2}$ $12\frac{3}{4}$
17. $14 \times 1\frac{1}{8}$ $15\frac{3}{4}$
18. $9\frac{2}{7} \times 2\frac{4}{5}$ 26
19. $\frac{5}{8} \times \frac{16}{21} \times \frac{3}{4}$ $\frac{5}{14}$
20. $7 \times 2\frac{4}{7} \times \frac{3}{5}$ $10\frac{4}{5}$
21. $\frac{2}{5} \times 10 \times 4\frac{1}{6}$ $16\frac{2}{3}$

Chapter 6 Review

Promissory notes, pages 108–109

1. A promissory note for $1500 at 18% interest per year is due in 3 months. What is the total amount due?
$1567.50

Credit card finance charges, pages 110–111

2. The unpaid balance in an account was $127.30. A payment of $20 was made. The finance charge is 1.5% per month of the balance after payment. What is the new balance? (Round the finance charge to the nearest cent.)
$108.91

Credit counselor, pages 112–113

3. On June 1, the unpaid balance in a charge account was $120. On June 15, a payment of $75 was made. There were no new purchases made. What was the average daily balance in the account during the month of June? (June has 30 days.)
$80

4. The average daily balance in an account for the month of February was $130.50. The finance charge was 1.8% per month of the average daily balance. What was the finance charge for February to the nearest cent?
$2.35

Minimum payments on charge accounts, page 115

5. The unpaid balance in an account was $75. A $20 payment and purchases of $155 were made during the month. The finance charge was $1.83. What was the new balance in the account?
$211.83

6. The new balance in an account is $255.68. Use the schedule below to find the minimum payment required. Round to the nearest cent.
$51.14

New balance	Minimum payment
$0–$20	100% of balance
$20.01–$100	$20
$100.01–$300	20% of balance

Level-payment loans, pages 116–117

7. Use the table below to find the amount of the monthly payment on a level-payment loan of $800 at 16% for 18 months. Round to the nearest cent.
$50.29

Monthly Payment per $1 Borrowed				
Annual rate	Number of equal monthly payments			
	6	12	18	24
16%	0.17453	0.09073	0.06286	0.04896

8. A level-payment loan of $500 is to be repaid in 12 monthly payments of $45.84 each. The annual interest is 18% of the unpaid balance. Part of each payment is used to repay one month's interest. The rest of each payment reduces the amount owed on the loan. How much will still be owed on the loan after the first payment?
$461.66

Installment buying, pages 118–119

9. The cash price of a sofa was $429.50. The customer agreed to pay 20% of the price as a down payment. The remainder will be paid in 24 monthly installments of $17.15 each. What is the amount of the finance charge?
$68

Comparing credit plans, pages 120–121

10. Jim Adolf needs to borrow $500. Plan A will allow him to repay the $500 in 18 monthly payments of $32.62 each. For Plan B, he can repay the loan in 12 monthly payments of $46.56 each. Which payment plan costs less?
Plan B

Chapter 6 Test

Number of test items - 10

Number missed	1	2	3	4	5
Percent correct	90	80	70	60	50

1. A promissory note for $300 at 19% interest per year is due in 6 months. What is the total amount due?
$328.50

2. The unpaid balance in an account was $175. A payment of $60 was made. The finance charge is 1.5% per month of the balance after payment. What is the new balance? (Round the finance charge to the nearest cent.)
$116.73

3. On April 1, the unpaid balance in a charge account was $75. On April 21, a payment of $15 was made. There were no new purchases. What was the average daily balance in the account during the month of April? (April has 30 days.)
$70

4. The average daily balance in an account for the month of September was $60.50. The finance charge was 1.8% per month of the average daily balance. What was the finance charge for September to the nearest cent?
$1.09

5. The unpaid balance in an account was $65. A $25 payment and purchases of $89 were made during the month. The finance charge was $1.60. What was the new balance in the account?
$130.60

6. The new balance in an account is $231.15. Use the schedule below to find the minimum payment required. Round to the nearest cent.
$57.79

New balance	Minimum payment
$0–$25	100% of balance
$25.01–$100	$25
$100.01–$300	25% of balance

7. Use the table below to find the amount of the monthly payment on a level-payment loan of $2000 at 18% for 12 months.
$183.36

Monthly Payment per $1 Borrowed				
Annual rate	Number of equal monthly payments			
	6	12	18	24
18%	0.17553	0.09168	0.06381	0.04992

8. A level-payment loan of $600 is to be repaid in 18 monthly payments of $37.72 each. The annual interest is 16% of the unpaid balance. Part of each payment is used to repay one month's interest. The rest of each payment reduces the amount owed on the loan. How much will still be owed on the loan after the first payment?
$570.28

9. The cash price of a refrigerator was $850. The customer agreed to pay $127.50 as a down payment. The remainder will be paid in 18 monthly installments of $46.79 each. What is the amount of the finance charge?
$119.72

10. Nancy James needs to borrow $1000. Plan A will allow her to repay the $1000 in 6 monthly payments of $176.02 each. In Plan B, she can repay the loan in 18 monthly payments of $64.28 each. Which payment plan costs less?
Plan A

 See pages 13-14 of the *Test Masters* for an alternate form of the Chapter 6 Test.

Unit 2 Test

Number of test items - 21

Number missed	1	2	3	4	5	6	7	8	9	10
Percent correct	95	90	86	81	76	71	67	62	57	52

Choose the best answer.

Pages 68–69

1. Carol earns $5.25 per hour. What is her gross pay for a 38-hour week?

A $43.25 **C** $57.75

B $563 **D** $199.50

Pages 70–71

2. Nan kept 80% of her $195 in tips. How much did Nan keep?

A $39 **C** $245.50

B $156 **D** $175

Pages 72–73

3. Mr. Morrow sells cleaning supplies for a straight commission of 40%. How much did he earn on a sale of $982?

A $392.80 **C** $245.50

B $589.20 **D** $3928

Pages 74–75

4. Vince is paid $175 a week plus 4% of all sales delivered. Last week his total sales were $4500. Orders totaling $750 were canceled. Find Vince's gross pay for the week.

A $355 **C** $150

B $325 **D** $180

Page 76

5. Maria earns $150 a month plus 8% of her first $1000 in sales and 15% of her sales over $1000. Maria's sales for the month were $5500. Find her gross pay.

A $590 **C** $905

B $825 **D** $1415

Pages 78–81

6. Dale Snowbird's gross pay is $375 a week. His deductions are $77.10 for federal tax and $24.94 for social security. What is his net pay?

A $102.04 **C** $272.96

B $297.90 **D** $477.04

Pages 82–83

7. Mert's Market has an opening for a job that pays $12,000 a year. At Gary's Grocery, the same job pays $948 a month. How much more does Mert's Market pay per year?

A $624 **C** $11,376

B $52 **D** $1000

Pages 88–89

8. Su Lin has checks for $135.48, $9.34, and $97.20 to deposit. If she wants $80 in cash, how much will she deposit in her account?

A $162.02 **C** $242.02

B $322.02 **D** $106.54

Pages 90–91

9. The balance forwarded on a check stub was $225.75. A deposit of $100 was made and a check for $50 was written. What was the balance carried forward?

A $325.75 **C** $150

B $275.75 **D** $175.75

Pages 92–93

10. Find the new balance in this account.

NUMBER	DATE	PAYMENT/DEBIT (−)	√ T	DEPOSIT/CREDIT (+)	BALANCE
					$ 1434 28
181	7/5	$ 389 09		$	
	7/19			45 00	

A $344.09 **C** $1045.19

B $1000.19 **D** $1090.19

Pages 94–96

11. The ending balance on a bank statement is $427.32. There is one outstanding deposit of $105.50 and one outstanding check of $39.84. What is the actual amount in the account?

A $361.66 **C** $281.98

B $572.66 **D** $492.98

A unit test occurs at the end of each three chapters. It tests selected applications taught in each lesson of the unit. The multiple-choice style was chosen to help prepare students for taking standardized tests.

Each page reference shown in red indicates where an application is taught. You might give students these references if you assign these two pages as an open-book test.

Pages 98–99

12. A savings account of $1600 earns 7% simple interest per year. Find the interest earned in 9 months.

(A) $84 C $112

B $1008 D $1200

Pages 100–101

13. A savings account of $500 earns 9% interest compounded annually. Find the interest earned in 2 years.

A $594.05 C $49.05

B $545 (D) $94.05

Pages 102–103

14. Find the interest on $300 at 8% compounded semiannually for 1 year.

COMPOUND INTEREST TABLE

No. of Periods	4%	5%	6%	7%	8%
1	1.0400	1.0500	1.0600	1.0700	1.0800
2	1.0816	1.1025	1.1236	1.1449	1.1664

A $324.48 (C) $24.48

B $49.92 D $349.92

Pages 108–109

15. A promissory note for $1500 at an interest rate of 18% per year is due in 30 days. Find the amount of interest due. Use 360 days for 1 year.

(A) $22.50 C $270

B $8100 D $225

Pages 110–111

16. The unpaid balance in an account was $95.50. A payment of $50 was made during the month. The finance charge is 1.5% per month of the balance after payments. Find the finance charge to the nearest cent.

A $1.43 C $0.75

(B) $0.68 D $0.71

Pages 112–113

17. In a charge account, the average daily balance for the month is $189.50. The finance charge is 1.8% per month of the average daily balance. Find the finance charge to the nearest cent.

A $341.11 C $34.72

(B) $3.41 D $192.91

Page 115

18. A store requires a minimum payment of 20% of the balance in the account if the balance is over $200. Find the minimum payment on a balance of $330.20.

A $40 C $26.04

B $106.04 (D) $66.04

Pages 116–117

19. Find the amount of the monthly payment on a level-payment loan of $500 at 17% for 18 months. Round to the nearest cent.

Monthly Payment per $1 Borrowed			
Annual rate	Number of equal monthly payments		
	6	12	18
17%	0.17503	0.09120	0.06333

A $45.60 (C) $31.67

B $31.43 D $85

Pages 118–119

20. A loan of $850 will be repaid in 12 installments of $79.55 each. Find the finance charge.

(A) $104.60 C $954.60

B $745.40 D $929.55

Pages 120–121

21. Elsa financed a $2400 purchase with no down payment and 12 installments of $220.03 each. Find the total amount repaid.

A $240.36 (C) $2640.36

B $200 D $2620.03

 For an alternate form of the Unit 2 Test, see pages T59–T60 of this book and pages 15–16 of the *Test Masters*.

Break Time

The Break Time/Mental Math feature occurs at the end of each unit. It shows shortcuts to help students compute mentally. Encourage all students to try these shortcuts.

Mental Math

A jogging suit costs $17, and jogging shoes cost $24. Find the total cost mentally.

If one addend is a multiple of 10 (10, 20, 30, and so on), the addition is easier.

Here is one way to find 17 + 24 mentally.

THINK

> Add 3 to 17 to get a multiple of 10.
> 17 + 3 = 20
>
> Add 20 and 24. 20 + 24 = 44
>
> Subtract the 3 you added. 44 − 3 = 41

Here is another way.

THINK

> Subtract 4 from 24 to get a multiple of 10. 24 − 4 = 20
>
> Add 20 and 17. 20 + 17 = 37
>
> Add the 4 you subtracted. 37 + 4 = 41

The total cost is $41.

Use a *multiple-of-10* method to find each sum mentally. Write only the answer. In problems 22–28, add two numbers at a time.

1. 49 + 25
74

2. 12 + 78
90

3. 57 + 25
82

4. 19 + 63
82

5. 28 + 37
65

6. 49 + 32
81

7. 61 + 28
89

8. 79 + 14
93

9. 27 + 39
66

10. 44 + 66
110

11. 66 + 95
161

12. 77 + 77
154

13. 23 + 98
121

14. 84 + 48
132

15. 56 + 48
104

16. 18 + 23
41

17. 135 + 39
174

18. 36 + 256
292

19. 17 + 465
482

20. 134 + 259
393

21. 338 + 174
512

22. 36 + 44 + 8
88

23. 27 + 19 + 12
58

24. 16 + 58 + 11
85

25. 57 + 18 + 51
126

26. 63 + 49 + 77
189

27. 38 + 89 + 12
139

28. 23 + 99 + 36
158

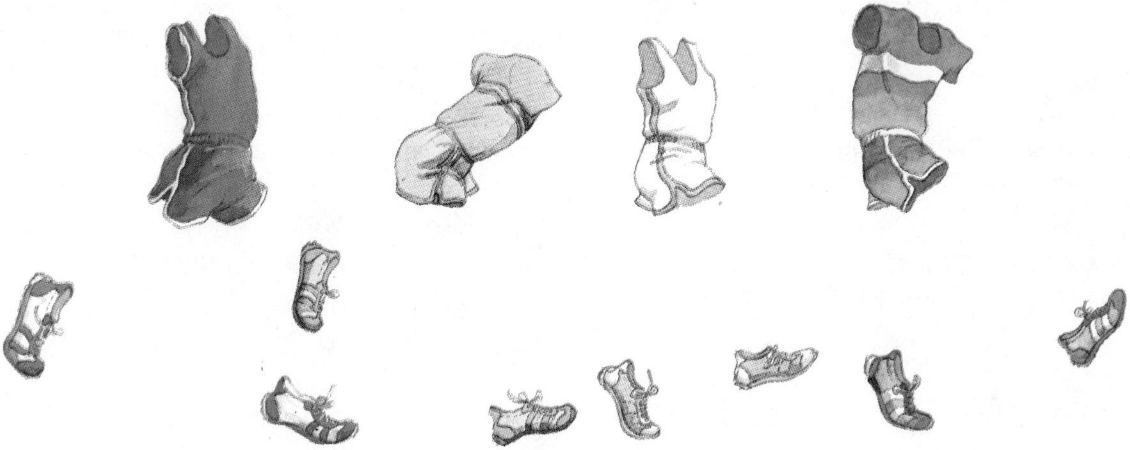

The Computer Applications feature occurs at the end of each unit. The applications are related to the content of the unit.

Students should review the programming techniques provided in the Computer Literacy feature on pages 394–399 before they begin Computer Applications.

Charge Accounts

Problems on page 111 can be done using the program shown.

Sylvia Bishop has a charge account at Meyer's Department Store. She received this bill.

```
        MEYER'S DEPARTMENT STORE
        CHARGE-ACCOUNT STATEMENT

BEGINNING OF JULY
  BALANCE                          87.5
PAYMENTS DURING JULY               20
FINANCE CHARGE ON
  BALANCE OF $ 67.5                 1.01
CHARGES DURING JULY                23.18
NEW BALANCE                        91.69
```

Remind students that 87.5 means $87.50.

The bill was prepared using the program shown on the next page.

Lines 30, 50, 70, and 90 Only these values need to be entered to prepare the bill.

Data required	*Name*
Name of month	M$
Balance at beginning of month	B
Total payments	P
Total charges	C

Lines 20, 40, 60, and 80 A PRINT statement before each INPUT statement shows what data to enter.

A semicolon at the end of the PRINT statement causes the computer to print the question mark for the INPUT statement on the same line.

All the calculations for preparing the bill are in the program.

Line 100 The unpaid balance (U) is calculated after the payment is made.

Line 110 The finance charge (F) is calculated using the unpaid balance and a rate of 1.5%.

Line 120 Many times the finance charge calculation will result in a part of a cent, so F must be rounded. Change F to a number of cents (∗100). Add .5, then drop any tenths of a cent (INT), and then change F back to dollars and cents (/100). Give students some numbers to round using this technique.

Line 130 The unpaid balance, finance charge, and total charges are added. The sum is the new balance (N) to be used for next month.

Lines 140–230 After the bill is calculated, PRINT statements are used to print the bill.

Line 160 A PRINT statement with nothing following the word "PRINT" causes a blank line in the printout.

For the programs in Computer Applications, any PRINT statement that directly precedes an INPUT statement is included to prompt students to input the correct data. Answers do not include output from this type of statement.

The semicolon at the end of lines 20, 40, 60, and 80 causes the question mark for the INPUT statements to print on the same line.

These problems can be used either with a computer or as a paper-and-pencil activity.

```
10 REM  MEYER'S CHARGE ACCOUNTS
20 PRINT "MONTH";
30 INPUT M$
40 PRINT "BEGINNING BALANCE";
50 INPUT B
60 PRINT "PAYMENT";
70 INPUT P
80 PRINT "CHARGES";
90 INPUT C
100 LET U=B-P
110 LET F=.015*U
120 LET F=INT(F*100+.5)/100
130 LET N=U+F+C
140 PRINT TAB(8);"MEYER'S DEPARTMENT STORE"
150 PRINT TAB(8);"CHARGE-ACCOUNT STATEMENT"
160 PRINT
170 PRINT "BEGINNING OF ";M$
180 PRINT "  BALANCE";TAB(30);B
190 PRINT "PAYMENTS DURING ";M$;TAB(30);P
200 PRINT "FINANCE CHARGE ON"
210 PRINT "  BALANCE OF $";U;TAB(31);F
220 PRINT "CHARGES DURING ";M$;TAB(30);C
230 PRINT "NEW BALANCE";TAB(30);N
240 END
```

Answers for computer applications are often in an abbreviated form. In all program modifications shown, the changes and/or additions incorporate previous modifications and will vary. Samples are given.

Give the output for the program above when

1. M$ is AUGUST, B is 211.85, P is 50.00, and C is 37.82.
See below.

2. M$ is SEPTEMBER, B is 748.53, P is 35.00, and C is 52.77.
NEW BALANCE $777.00

3. M$ is JANUARY, B is 37.42, P is 37.42, and C is 23.51.
NEW BALANCE $23.51

4. M$ is APRIL, B is 126.73, P is 25.00, and C is 0.
NEW BALANCE $103.26

5. M$ is JUNE, B is 83.92, P is 40.00, and C is 27.35.
NEW BALANCE $71.93

6. the balance at the beginning of May was $438.22, the payment was $62, and the charge was $16.87.
NEW BALANCE $398.73

7. the balance at the beginning of February was $287.93, the payment was $35, and the charge was $29.68.
NEW BALANCE $286.40

8. the balance at the beginning of November was $16.58, the payment was $16.58, and there were no new charges.
NEW BALANCE $0

9. the balance at the beginning of October was $87.21, the payment was $10, and the charge was $19.58.
NEW BALANCE $97.95

10. the balance at the beginning of March was $549.03, the payment was $20, and there were no new charges.
NEW BALANCE $536.97

13.
```
15 LET C=0
90 INPUT C1
91 IF C1=0 THEN 100
92 LET C=C+C1
93 GO TO 90
```
With this modification, zero must be entered for the last input for line 90 so the program can continue.

11.
```
182 IF P>0 THEN 190
183 IF B=0 THEN 190
184 PRINT "NO PAYMENT RECEIVED"
185 PRINT "IF PAYMENT IS IN MAIL, THANK YOU"
```

11. Modify the program so that it prints a statement about not receiving a payment.
See above.

12. Give the output when M$ is December, B is 237.45, P is 0, and C is 24.86.
See Additional Answers on page T51.

13. Modify the program so that more than one purchase can be entered. Have the computer total the purchases.
See below.

14. Give the output when M$ is June, B is 356.92, P is 60.00, and C is 12.98, 45.87, and 123.66.
NEW BALANCE $483.88

15. Modify the program so that credit for returned purchases can also be entered. Interest should not be charged on amounts to be credited.
See Additional Answers on page T51.

16. Give the output when M$ is April, B is 20.72, P is 20.72, C is 0, and the $20.72 purchase is returned for credit.
See Additional Answers on page T51.

17. Modify the program so that the rate of the finance charge is part of the input.
See Additional Answers on page T51.

18. Give the output when M$ is January, B is 386.92, P is 50.00, C is 8.95 and 17.47, and the finance charge rate is 1.8%.
NEW BALANCE $369.40

1.
```
        MEYER'S DEPARTMENT STORE
        CHARGE-ACCOUNT STATEMENT

BEGINNING OF AUGUST
  BALANCE                      211.85
PAYMENTS DURING AUGUST         50
FINANCE CHARGE ON
  BALANCE OF $ 161.85           2.43
CHARGES DURING AUGUST          37.82
NEW BALANCE                    202.1
```

Unit 3 Transportation

Chapter 7 Buying a Car

Objective: Compute the sticker price of a new car.

New Car Sticker Price

See page T32 for additional notes and activities for Chapter 7.

The sticker price of a new car is the suggested retail price plus the cost of optional equipment plus the destination charge. A portion of a new car sticker and a sample price list for some options are shown below.

MODEL: Compact (2-door)
SUGGESTED RETAIL PRICE: $6833.49
Vehicle Identification Number:
3W18J2B675498

The following items are included at NO EXTRA CHARGE unless replaced by optional equipment.

- 2.5-liter L4 engine
- 4-speed manual transmission
- Fiberglass-belted blackwall tires
- Rack and pinion steering

Optional Equipment — **Compact (2-door)**

Engines	
2.8-liter V6 w/4-speed manual transmission	$125
2.5-liter L4 w/automatic transmission	$370
2.8-liter V6 w/automatic transmission	$495
Tires	
Fiberglass-belted, whitewall	$75
Steel-belted, blackwall	
with 2.5-liter engine	$95
with 2.8-liter engine	$67
Steel-belted, whitewall	
with 2.5-liter engine	$110
with 2.8-liter engine	$78
Steel-belted, wide-oval, billboard-lettered	
with 2.5-liter engine	$135
with 2.8-liter engine	$119
Comfort and convenience	
Power steering	$179
Power front disc brakes	$86
Air conditioner	$625
Electric rear-window defogger	$115
Cruise control	$145
Entertainment	
AM radio	$51
AM-FM radio	$68
AM-FM stereo radio with front and rear dual speakers	$100
AM-FM stereo radio with tape player and front and rear dual speakers	$174
AM-FM stereo radio with 40 channel CB	$413
Appearance and protection	
Styled wheel covers	$59
Deluxe wire wheel covers	$129
Sunroof, tempered removable glass	$261
Landau top	$175
Vinyl top	$149
Protective body-side moldings	$44
Door-edge guards	$15
Bumper guards, front and rear	$38
Special-order paint	$181
Body-side accent stripe	$47
Sport-style mirrors, driver's remote	$53
Sport-style mirrors, both remote	$80

Problem

Jason Lee is buying a new 2-door compact car. The options on the car include automatic transmission (2.5-liter engine), AM-FM stereo radio with front and rear dual speakers, and steel-belted, whitewall tires. The destination charge is $285. Find the sticker price of Jason's new car.

You might discuss the various options available on cars today. For this car, tires cost less with a 2.8-liter engine because part of the cost is included in the price of the engine.

Solution

Strategy

- Read the price list. Then add to find the sticker price.

$6833.49	Suggested retail price
370.00	Automatic transmission
100.00	AM-FM stereo radio
110.00	Steel-belted, whitewall tires
+ 285.00	Destination charge
$7698.49	

Conclusion

The sticker price of the car is $7698.49.

Warm-up: 4927 + 862 + 57 [5846]
5620 + 78 + 498 [6196]
6295 + 89 + 142 [6526]
7432 + 658 + 265 [8355]

See page 32 of *Consumer Forms and Problems*.

Related Problems

You could recommend that students use estimation to check their answers.

Use the suggested retail price and list of options given on page 132 for problems 1–10.

For problems 1–3, find the sticker price of a new compact car with the options given. The destination charge is $305.

1. AM-FM stereo radio with front and rear dual speakers
Air conditioner
Body-side accent stripe
Fiberglass-belted, whitewall tires
Landau top
$8160.49

2. 2.8-liter, V6 engine with automatic transmission
Power steering
Power front disc brakes
AM-FM stereo radio and tape player with front and rear dual speakers
Electric rear-window defogger
Steel-belted, blackwall tires
Bumper guards, front and rear
$8292.49

3. AM radio
Sport-style mirrors, driver's remote
Automatic transmission (2.5-liter engine)
Air conditioner
Cruise control
Styled wheel covers
Vinyl top
Special-order paint
$8771.49

7. AM radio $51
Sport-style mirrors, driver's remote $53
Steel-belted, blackwall tires $67
with 2.8-liter engine

9. AM-FM stereo radio $413
with 40 channel CB
Sport-style mirrors, both remote $80
Steel-belted, wide oval, $119
billboard-lettered tires
with 2.8-liter engine

Nancy Parkins plans to buy a new compact car. She does not want to spend more than $8000. In problems 4 and 5, find the sticker price of a car with the options listed and a destination charge of $265. Then tell whether Nancy could buy either car.

4. AM-FM radio
Air conditioner
Electric rear-window defogger
Steel-belted, whitewall tires (2.5-liter engine)
Deluxe wire wheel covers
Protective body-side moldings
$8189.49; no

5. Power steering
AM-FM stereo radio with tape player and front and rear dual speakers
Sport-style mirrors, both remote
Steel-belted, wide-oval, billboard-lettered tires (2.5-liter engine)
Sunroof, tempered removable glass
Door-edge guards
Body-side accent stripe
$7989.49; yes

Jay Murphy wants to buy a new compact car. The options will include a 2.8-liter, V6 engine with 4-speed manual transmission, power steering, power front disc brakes, and styled wheel covers. The destination charge will be $285.

6. Find the sticker price of Jay's car.
$7567.49

7. Jay would also like a radio, sport-styled mirrors, and steel-belted tires. List the least expensive of each of these options.
See left.

8. What is the sticker price of the car Jay wants with the options in problem 7?
$7738.49

9. List the most expensive of each of the options in problem 7.
See left.

10. What is the sticker price of the car Jay wants with the options in problem 9?
$8179.49

Objective: Determine a reasonable price to offer for a new car, using a percentage guideline.

Warm-up:
10% of 7425 [742.5]
10% of 5693 [569.3]
10% of 6310 [631]
10% of 8700 [870]

Making an Offer for a Car

The price of most cars includes both dollars and cents. In the remaining lessons in this chapter the cents are omitted to simplify the computations.

Walter Choi bought a new car. He bargained on the price of the car since he knows that the sticker price includes a profit for the dealer.

Walter used this guideline: Offer the dealer 10% less than the sticker price. Round the offer to the nearest hundred dollars.

1. $8300
2. $6600
3. $8800
4. $11,600
5. $7100
6. $8500
7. $8400
8. $9200
9. $6700
10. $7600

Problem

Walter selected a new subcompact car. The sticker price was $6970. What was Walter's offer for the car?

Solution

A reasonable offer could also be found by multiplying the sticker price by 90%.

Strategy

- Multiply the sticker price by 10% to find the price reduction. $0.10 \times \$6970 = \$697$
- Subtract and round the answer to the nearest hundred to find the amount Walter offered. $\$6970 - \$697 \approx \$6300$

Conclusion

Walter's offer for the car was $6300.

Related Problems

Use the guideline to find an offer for each car.

See above.

	Model	Sticker price
1.	Mid-sized	$9,200
2.	Subcompact	$7,300
3.	Full-sized	$9,780
4.	Sports car	$12,856
5.	Compact	$7,895
6.	Station wagon	$9,467
7.	Mid-sized	$9,386
8.	Full-sized	$10,212
9.	Subcompact	$7,480
10.	Compact	$8,427

Break Time

The hop-off at the Toad County Frog Jump featured four participants—Croaker, Longjump, Hopalong, and Gribbit.

After the contest, the following statements were made.

I won. Hopalong came in second. Hopalong beat Gribbit by 5cm. Gribbit beat Longjump.
I took first place. Gribbit came in second. Longjump came in third. Croaker was a distant last.
I won. Croaker beat Gribbit. Gribbit did better than Hopalong. Hopalong beat Croaker.
I won. Croaker came in second. Hopalong beat Longjump. Longjump finished last.
CROAKER
HOPALONG
LONGJUMP
GRIBBIT

If each of the four participants made two true statements and told two lies, what was the order of finish in the race?

First: Gribbit; second: Hopalong; third: Longjump; fourth: Croaker

Objective: Compute the total cost of buying a car.

Finding Total Cost of a Car

Teri Bright plans to buy a used car. She must consider the total cost of the car. Besides price, the total cost includes sales tax, a title fee, a license-plate fee, and any repairs needed on the car.

Problem

The price of the used car Teri wants to buy is $1985. The state sales tax is 4% of the price of the car. There is a title fee of $5. The license-plate fee is $22. Teri took the car to a mechanic and found that the car needs a tune-up that would cost $92.45. What is the total cost of the car?

Solution

Strategy

- Multiply the price by 4% to find the sales tax.

  $0.04 \times \$1985 = \$79.40$

- Add to find the total cost of the car.

$1985.00	Price
79.40	Sales tax
5.00	Title fee
22.00	License-plate fee
+ 92.45	Repairs
$2183.85	

Conclusion

The total cost of the car is $2183.85.

Warm-up: 5% of 935 [46.75]
2.5% of 1560 [39]
4.5% of 2490 [112.05]
1895 + 47.50 + 3 + 28 [1973.50]

Related Problems

In some states, sales tax is not charged if a car is purchased from a private party.

Complete the table for each used car.

	Price	Sales tax	Amount of sales tax	Title fee	License-plate fee	Repairs	Total cost
	$1985	4%	$79.40	$5.00	$22	$92.45	$2183.85
1.	$825	5%	$41.25	$8.00	$20	$142.50	$1036.75
2.	$1495	4%	$59.80	$4.00	$30	$81.45	$1670.25
3.	$2295	3%	$68.85	$5.50	$24	——	$2393.35
4.	$1395	——	——	$10.00	$56	$163.79	$1624.79
5.	$1845	7%	$129.15	$6.00	$18	——	$1998.15
6.	$2995	6%	$179.70	$9.50	$75	$97.40	$3356.60
7.	$3575	——	——	$7.00	$100	$56.95	$3738.95
8.	$4350	4.5%	$195.75	$12.50	$48	——	$4606.25
9.	$2768	5.5%	$152.24	$4.50	$35	$264.18	$3223.92

Floyd Gates is comparing the total cost of different-sized used cars. His state has a 4% sales tax and a $6.50 title fee. Floyd can buy a 6-month license plate for $15. There is also a city sales tax of 1.5%.

The price of a used subcompact car is $1876.

10. Find the state sales tax.
$75.04

11. Find the city sales tax.
$28.14

12. The car needs new brakes that will cost $95.35. Find the total cost of the car.
$2096.03

The price of a used compact car is $2920.

13. Find the state sales tax.
$116.80

14. Find the city sales tax.
$43.80

15. This car needs new spark plugs. Floyd can do the work himself for a cost of $11.80. Find the total cost of the car.
$3113.90

16. Find the difference in the total cost of the subcompact car and the compact car.
$1017.87

Martha O'Brien wants to buy a new car. The state sales tax is 5%. The title fee is $6.

17. The sticker price of a new full-sized car is $8945. The license-plate fee is $34. What is the total cost of the car?
$9432.25

18. The sticker price of a new mid-sized car is $8250. The license-plate fee is $22. What is the total cost of the car?
$8690.50

19. Find the difference in the total cost of the full-sized car and the mid-sized car.
$741.75

Objective: Determine the best buy on a car by comparing the net price offered by various dealers.

Shopping for a Car

Amy and Dudley Davis want to buy a new compact station wagon. They will receive a trade-in allowance from the dealer for their present car. The total cost less the trade-in allowance is the net price.

Sometimes a discount can be shown as an overstated trade-in allowance.

Problem

Amy and Dudley have shopped at three car dealerships and have found these prices for the same car.

Dealer	Selling price	Trade-in allowance
Penn Sales, Inc.	\$8560	\$1845
Richard Motors	\$8500	\$1830
Walker Motors, Ltd.	\$8455	\$1775

What is the lowest net price, and which car dealer offers it?

Solution

Strategy

- Subtract to find the net price at Penn Sales, Inc.

  \$8560 − \$1845 = \$6715

- Subtract to find the net price at Richard Motors.

  \$8500 − \$1830 = \$6670

- Subtract to find the net price at Walker Motors, Ltd.

  \$8455 − \$1775 = \$6680

- Compare the net prices.

  \$6670 < \$6680 < \$6715

Conclusion

The lowest net price is \$6670, offered by Richard Motors.

Many dealers will not negotiate the sticker price of a new car if they know the customer is trading in an old car. The customer should first find out how much the new car will cost, then talk about the trade-in allowance.

Warm-up: 8570 − 1695 [6875]
9430 − 2580 [6850]
7295 − 1400 [5895]
11,367 − 2640 [8727]

See page 33 of *Consumer Forms and Problems.*

Related Problems

Point out that the lowest net price is not always the result of using the highest trade-in allowance or the lowest selling price.

Find the net price for each new car. Then indicate which dealer offers the lowest net price.

Subcompact model

Suburban, Ltd.

	Dealer	Selling price	Trade-in allowance	
1.	Suburban, Ltd.	$7385	$1260	$6125
2.	Oak St. Motors	$7435	$1200	$6235
3.	Field Sales	$7495	$1330	$6165

Compact model

Colonial Motors

	Dealer	Selling price	Trade-in allowance	
4.	Pollard Motors	$8330	$1500	$6830
5.	Central Sales	$8450	$1645	$6805
6.	Colonial Motors	$8090	$1485	$6605

Mid-sized model

Heritage, Ltd.

	Dealer	Selling price	Trade-in allowance	
7.	Lutz Motor Co.	$9143	$2435	$6708
8.	Oak Park Sales	$9328	$2470	$6858
9.	Heritage, Ltd.	$9208	$2510	$6698

Full-sized model

Cass St. Motors

	Dealer	Selling price	Trade-in allowance	
10.	Cass St. Motors	$9842	$2580	$7262
11.	Morris, Inc.	$9767	$2425	$7342
12.	Wagner Motors	$9985	$2610	$7375

Luxury sedan

Prospect Sales

	Dealer	Selling price	Trade-in allowance	
13.	Serota Motors	$11,204	$2665	$8539
14.	Prospect Sales	$11,284	$2850	$8434
15.	Viking Motors	$11,175	$2730	$8445

Sports car

Congress Motors

	Dealer	Selling price	Trade-in allowance	
16.	Village Imports	$13,529	$3135	$10,394
17.	Congress Motors	$13,589	$3375	$10,214
18.	Matulis Imports	$13,759	$3460	$10,299

John Lauer is buying a new mid-sized car. The sticker price of the car is $8775.

19. The dealer agreed to John's offer to pay 8% less than the sticker price. Find the selling price.
$8073

20. The state sales tax is 7% of the selling price of the car. Find the amount of state sales tax.
$565.11

21. The title fee is $6.50 and the license-plate fee is $28. Find the total cost of the car.
$8672.61

22. The trade-in allowance on the car he owns now is $2390. Find the net price.
$6282.61

Some states compute sales tax on the selling price. Some states compute sales tax on the net price. Have students find out how your state computes the tax.

Objectives: Compute the finance charge for a new car loan; compute the total sale price of a new car.

Financing a Car

Bud Elliot must finance the new compact car he plans to buy. Financing a car is similar to buying on the installment plan.

The total down payment could include a trade-in allowance and a cash deposit made at the time the car is purchased. The remainder is the amount to be financed.

The sum of the down payment and the total paid in monthly installments is the total sale price, or deferred-payment price.

Problem

The total cost of the car Bud plans to buy is \$8450. His total down payment is \$1400. Bud can finance the rest of the cost for 36 months. His monthly payments will be \$260.22. Find the finance charge on the loan. Then find the total sale price.

Solution

Strategy See page 118 for a similar strategy.

- Subtract the down payment from the total cost to find the amount to be financed. $\$8450 - \$1400 = \$7050$
- Multiply the monthly installments by 36 to find the total paid in monthly installments. $36 \times \$260.22 = \$9367.92$
- Subtract the amount to be financed from the total paid in monthly installments to find the amount of the finance charge. $\$9367.92 - \$7050 = \$2317.92$
- Add the total paid in monthly installments to the down payment to find the total sale price. $\$9367.92 + \$1400 = \$10{,}767.92$

The total sale price is also equal to total cost plus the finance charge.

Conclusion

The finance charge on Bud's loan will be \$2317.92. The total sale price will be \$10,767.92.

See pages 190–191 for a computer application related to this lesson.

Warm-up: 207.59 × 36 [7473.24]
268.03 × 24 [6432.72]
8230 − 1500 [6730]
9254.87 − 7350 [1904.87]

See page 34 of *Consumer Forms and Problems.*

Related Problems

Problems 3 and 7 have the same amount of money financed. The annual percentage rate is 18% in both cases. Point out how the finance charge increases with the length of the loan.

For each car financed, find the finance charge and the total sale price.

	Model	Total cost	Down payment	Installments					Total sale price
				Amount financed	Monthly payment	Number of months	Total paid in monthly installments	Finance charge	
	Compact	$8,450	$1400	$7050	$260.22	36	$9367.92	$2317.92	$10,767.92
1.	Compact	$7,740	$1740	$6000	$302.45	24	$7258.80	$1258.80	$8998.80
2.	Full-sized	$9,204	$3450	$5754	$209.47	36	$7540.92	$1786.92	$10,990.92
3.	Station wagon	$9,848	$2995	$6853	$437.26	18	$7870.68	$1017.68	$10,865.68
4.	Subcompact	$6,732	$1235	$5497	$231.60	30	$6948.00	$1451.00	$8183.00
5.	Mid-sized	$8,655	$2475	$6180	$572.48	12	$6869.76	$689.76	$9344.76
6.	Sports car	$13,147	$4350	$8797	$320.24	36	$11,528.64	$2731.64	$15,878.64
7.	Full-sized	$9,918	$3065	$6853	$201.31	48	$9662.88	$2809.88	$12,727.88
8.	Compact	$7,960	$1975	$5985	$380.45	18	$6848.10	$863.10	$8823.10
9.	Mid-sized	$8,539	$3650	$4889	$247.64	24	$5943.36	$1054.36	$9593.36
10.	Subcompact	$6,825	$1525	$5300	$490.96	12	$5891.52	$591.52	$7416.52

The annual percentage rates used vary from 17.5% to 20%.

Harry Bretzlauf purchased a new compact car.

A summary of his purchase is shown at the right.

Other charges might include insurance, etc.

S A L E   S U M M A R Y

Suggested Retail Price		$ 6775.40
Optional equipment	$ 959.00	
Destination charge	$ 280.00	
Sticker Price		$ 8014.40
Price reduction	$ 750.00	
Selling Price		$ 7264.40
Sales tax (5 %)	$ 363.22	
License-plate fee	$ 30.00	
Title fee	$ 4.50	
Other charges	$ N/A	
Total Cost		$ 7662.12
Trade-in allowance	$ 1645.00	
Cash deposit	$ 817.12	
Amount financed		$ 5200.00
Finance charge	$ 1029.92	
ANNUAL PERCENTAGE RATE	18%	
Number of payments	24	
Monthly payment	$ 259.58	
Total of payments	$ 6229.92	
Total Sale Price (deferred-payment price)		$ 8692.00

Use the strategies on pages 132–141 to fill in a sale summary for problems 11 and 12.

11. Bessie Papanos bought a new compact car with a suggested retail price of $6845. The optional equipment cost $739 and the destination charge was $260. She agreed to a price reduction of $500. The sales tax was 4% of the selling price. The title fee was $5 and the license-plate fee was $18. Bessie's cash deposit was $3060.76. The remaining cost was financed for 24 months. Her monthly payments are $231.89.
$965.36; $8626.12

12. Ed Verenski bought a new mid-sized car with a sticker price of $9120. The dealer agreed to Ed's offer to pay 6% less than the sticker price. The sales tax was 5% of the selling price. The license-plate fee was $25 and the title fee was $6. Ed received a $2500 trade-in allowance and paid a $1032.44 cash deposit. He financed the remaining cost for 36 months. His monthly payments are $198.83.
$1657.88; $10,690.32

The finance charge and total sale price are given here.
See Additional Answers beginning on page T44 for complete sale summary.

CALCULATOR APPLICATIONS

Annual Percentage Rates

Truth-in-Lending laws require the lender to show the finance charge and the annual percentage rate on an installment contract.

An approximation of the annual percentage rate can be found by using the following formula when the payments are made monthly.

$$\text{Approximate annual percentage rate} = \frac{24 \times \text{Finance charge}}{\text{Amount financed} \times (\text{Total number of payments} + 1)}$$

Mel Nelson is financing the cost of a car for 36 months. The finance charge is \$1815.40. Find the approximate annual percentage rate.

$$\text{Approximate annual percentage rate} = \frac{24 \times \$1815.40}{\$5600 \times (36 + 1)}$$

≈ 0.2103 Round to the nearest ten-thousandth.

$= 21.03\%$ Write as a percent.

The approximate annual percentage rate is 21.03%.

Possible key sequence: 5600 [×] 37 [=] [M+] 24 [×] 1815.40 [=] [÷] [MR] [=]

Find the approximate annual percentage rate. Round to the nearest hundredth of a percent.

	Amount financed	Finance charge	Number of payments	Approximate annual percentage rate
1.	\$4975	\$731.33	18	18.57%
2.	\$5590	\$1693.77	36	19.65%
3.	\$7250	\$1959.50	30	20.92%
4.	\$6435	\$1312.74	24	19.58%
5.	\$6435	\$656.37	12	18.83%
6.	\$6435	\$1969.11	36	19.85%
7.	\$8100	\$1348.65	18	21.03%
8.	\$4627	\$971.67	24	20.16%

Objective: Compute monthly gross pay for an automobile salesperson who is paid a commission and a bonus.

Automobile Salesperson

Career Cluster: Business Contact Beth Hall sells cars. For each car she sells, her commission is 25% of the dealer's profit. The profit is the difference between the selling price of the car and the amount the dealer paid for the car.

The dealer also has a bonus earnings plan. Each car is assigned from 1 to 5 points, depending on the model and how long it has been in stock. The amount of bonus earnings is determined by the number of points earned by the salesperson during the month. The dealer Beth works for uses this schedule.

Number of points per month	Bonus earnings
0–14	$0
15–20	$75
21–25	$350
26–29	$650
30–33	$800
34	$1200
35–39	$1400
40	$1500

Problem

During January, Beth earned 24 points for the sale of thirteen cars. The dealer's profit on the cars was $6500. What was Beth's gross pay for January?

Solution

Strategy

- Multiply by 25% to find the commission earnings.

  $0.25 \times \$6500 = \$1625$

- Read the table to find the amount of bonus earnings for 24 points.

  $350

- Add to find gross pay.

$1625	Commission earnings
+ 350	Bonus earnings
$1975	

Conclusion

Beth's gross pay for January was $1975.

Warm-up: 25% of 5900 [1475]
25% of 6348 [1587]
1645 + 450 [2095]
1273 + 1150 [2423]

Related Problems

Complete the table below to show Beth's total gross pay for the year.

	Month	Number of bonus points	Dealer's profit	Commission earnings	Bonus earnings	Gross pay
	January	24	$6500	$1625	$350	$1975
1.	February	33	$7254	$1813.50	$800	$2613.50
2.	March	30	$6820	$1705.00	$800	$2505.00
3.	April	33	$7010	$1752.50	$800	$2552.50
4.	May	37	$7416	$1854.00	$1400	$3254.00
5.	June	39	$7936	$1984.00	$1400	$3384.00
6.	July	28	$6413	$1603.25	$650	$2253.25
7.	August	20	$5400	$1350.00	$75	$1425.00
8.	September	32	$7212	$1803.00	$800	$2603.00
9.	October	22	$6135	$1533.75	$350	$1883.75
10.	November	19	$3700	$925.00	$75	$1000.00
11.	December	13	$3610	$902.50	$0	$902.50
12.	Total	——	——	$18,851.50	$7500	$26,351.50

13. Beth accumulated 33 bonus points in February. If she had received 1 more point, how much more gross pay would she have earned in February? $400

14. If Beth had received 1 less bonus point in March, how much less gross pay would she have earned that month? $150

For problems 15–17, assume that Beth sold one more car in August for a $375 dealer's profit and 3 bonus points.

15. What would Beth's commission earnings have been for August? $1443.75

16. What would her bonus earnings have been for August? $350

17. What would her gross pay for August have been? $1793.75

Skills Tune-Up

Subtracting whole numbers and decimals, pages 6–7

1. 98 − 64
34
2. 74 − 45
29
3. 32 − 8
24
4. 60 − 7
53
5. 83 − 16
67
6. 49 − 40
9
7. 85.6 − 64.5
21.1
8. 73.7 − 4.8
68.9
9. 43.36 − 25.16
18.2
10. 92.75 − 38.27
54.48
11. 53.47 − 32.5
20.97
12. 80.53 − 34.8
45.73
13. 6.041 − 2.26
3.781
14. 57.349 − 24.78
32.569
15. 87.103 − 65.831
21.272
16. 55.028 − 52.356
2.672
17. 0.37 − 0.007
0.363
18. 35.68 − 4.649
31.031
19. 73.6 − 72.7
0.9
20. 17.3 − 16.7
0.6
21. 23.789 − 18
5.789
22. 9.006 − 7
2.006
23. 58 − 31.4
26.6
24. 82 − 39.3
42.7
25. 5 − 3.04
1.96
26. 43 − 26.32
16.68
27. 95 − 47.496
47.504

Writing percents, decimals, and fractions, pages 32–33

Write as a decimal.

1. 29%
0.29
2. 5%
0.05
3. 9%
0.09
4. 16%
0.16
5. 82%
0.82
6. 2%
0.02
7. 73%
0.73
8. $3\frac{3}{4}\%$
0.0375
9. 18.42%
0.1842
10. 6.3%
0.063
11. $67\frac{1}{2}\%$
0.675
12. 4.5%
0.045
13. 8.25%
0.0825
14. $10\frac{1}{2}\%$
0.105
15. 18.4%
0.184
16. 7.5%
0.075
17. $8\frac{1}{4}\%$
0.0825
18. 525%
5.25
19. $20\frac{1}{2}\%$
0.205
20. 115%
1.15
21. 405%
4.05
22. $5\frac{3}{8}\%$
0.05375
23. 250%
2.5
24. 400%
4

Write as a percent.

25. 0.56
56%
26. 0.83
83%
27. 0.03
3%
28. 0.08
8%
29. 0.5
50%
30. 0.17
17%
31. 0.49
49%
32. 0.9
90%
33. 0.053
5.3%
34. 0.528
52.8%
35. 0.339
33.9%
36. 0.75
75%
37. 0.906
90.6%
38. 0.159
15.9%
39. 0.0125
1.25%
40. 0.8237
82.37%
41. 0.3225
32.25%
42. 0.0875
8.75%
43. 0.9054
90.54%
44. 3.87
387%
45. 5.06
506%
46. 2.48
248%
47. 1.121
112.1%
48. 8.675
867.5%

Percent problems, pages 34–37

1. 14% of 35 is ____.
4.9
2. 65% of 30 is ____.
19.5
3. Find $3\frac{1}{4}\%$ of 1200.
39
4. Find 75% of 493.
369.75
5. What number is 5% of 4140?
207
6. What number is 4% of 425?
17
7. 13.2% of 50 is what number?
6.6
8. 27% of 32 is what number?
8.64
9. ____% of 56 is 7.
12.5%
10. ____% of 80 is 12.
15%
11. ____% of 210 is 6.3.
3%
12. ____% of 78 is 62.4?
80%
13. What percent of 75 is 24?
32%
14. What percent of 150 is 144?
96%
15. 77 is what percent of 175?
44%
16. 336 is what percent of 1600?
21%
17. 12% of ____ is 3.
25
18. 95% of ____ is 756.2.
796
19. 44% of ____ is 149.6.
340
20. $4\frac{1}{2}\%$ of ____ is 54.
1200
21. 76% of what number is 2.28?
3
22. 85% of what number is 51?
60
23. 21 is 70% of what number?
30
24. 6.8 is 80% of what number?
8.5

Chapter 7 Review

New car sticker price, pages 132–133

1. The suggested retail price of a new mid-sized car is $7725. The destination charge is $265. Find the sticker price with these options.
   $9264
   Automatic transmission $370
   Power steering $179
   Air conditioner $625
   AM-FM stereo radio $100

Making an offer for a car, page 134

2. Marcie selected a new subcompact car. The sticker price was $6790. Marcie offered the dealer 10% less than the sticker price. What was Marcie's offer for the car? Round the offer to the nearest hundred dollars.
   $6100

Finding total cost of a car, pages 136–137

3. The price of a used subcompact car is $1975. The state sales tax is 5% of the price of the car. Find the amount of the state sales tax.
   $98.75
4. The price of a used compact car is $2895. The license-plate fee is $32 and the title fee is $6.50. The car needs repairs that will cost $47.35. The state sales tax is 4% of the price. Find the total cost of the car.
   $3096.65

Shopping for a car, pages 138–139

5. The selling price of a new car is $9360. The dealer offered a trade-in allowance of $2685. Find the net price.
   $6675
6. Which dealer offers the lowest net price?
   Sayo Imports

Dealer	Selling price	Trade-in allowance	
Sayo Imports	$9253	$1765	$7488
Crown Sales	$9408	$1810	$7598
Park Motors	$9317	$1795	$7522

Financing a car, pages 140–142

7. Greg is financing $7135 of the cost of his new sports car for 18 months. His monthly payment is $456.93. Find the finance charge.
   $1089.74
8. The total cost of Sam's new car is $9745. He made a total down payment of $3700. Sam is financing the remaining cost for 24 months. His monthly payment is $304.72. Find the total sale price.
   $11,013.28

Automobile salesperson, pages 144–145

9. During the month of November, Weber Motors made a profit of $5415 on the cars sold by Sue Willis. Find Sue's commission earnings if she is paid 20% of the profit.
   $1083
10. The dealer Joe works for follows the bonus earnings plan shown below.

Number of points per month	Bonus earnings
0–14	$0
15–20	$75
21–25	$350
26–29	$650
30–33	$800

Joe earned 27 bonus points for the sale of fifteen cars. The dealer's profit was $6220. Joe's commission earnings are 25% of the dealer's profit. Find Joe's gross pay.
$2205

Chapter 7 Test

Number of test items - 10					
Number missed	1	2	3	4	5
Percent correct	90	80	70	60	50

1. The suggested retail price of a new compact car is $6844. The destination charge is $285. Find the sticker price of the car with these options.
$7942
Automatic transmission $370
Power front disc brakes $86
Power steering $179
Steel-belted, whitewall tires $110
AM-FM radio $68

2. A new full-sized car has a sticker price of $9410. Mary offered the dealer 10% less than the sticker price. What was Mary's offer for the car? Round the offer to the nearest hundred dollars.
$8500

3. The price of a used mid-sized car is $4425. The state sales tax is 4% of the price of the car. Find the amount of the state sales tax.
$177

4. The price of a used subcompact car is $2385. The sales tax is 5% of the price. The license-plate fee is $28 and the title fee is $7.50. The car needs repairs that will cost $63.45. Find the total cost of the car.
$2603.20

5. The selling price of a new car is $8850. The dealer offered a trade-in allowance of $2975. Find the net price.
$5875

6. Which dealer offers the lowest net price?
Perrini Imports

Dealer	Selling price	Trade-in allowance	
Auer Auto	$8758	$2200	**$6558**
Ridge Motors	$8694	$2250	**$6444**
Perrini Imports	$8627	$2300	**$6327**

7. Justin is financing $8365 of the cost of his new luxury sedan for 24 months. His monthly payment is $417.58. Find the finance charge.
$1656.92

8. The total cost of Bill's new car is $7875. He made a total down payment of $1900. Bill is financing the remaining cost for 36 months. His monthly payment is $219.04. Find the total sale price.
$9785.44

9. During September, Fargo Motors made a profit of $4560 on the cars sold by Janice Whitecrow. Find Janice's commission earnings if she is paid 25% of the profit.
$1140

10. The dealer Lily works for follows the bonus earnings plan shown below.

Number of points per month	Bonus earnings
0–14	$0
15–20	$75
21–25	$350
26–29	$650
30–33	$800

Lily earned 31 bonus points for the sale of twelve cars. The dealer's profit was $5310. Lily's commission earnings are 20% of the dealer's profit. Find Lily's gross pay.
$1862

 See pages 17-18 of the *Test Masters* for an alternate form of the Chapter 7 Test.

Chapter 8 Automobile Operating Expenses

Objectives: Find a car's fuel economy rate in kilometers per liter; find the cost of gasoline in cents per kilometer.

Finding Gasoline Costs

See page T33 for additional notes and activities for Chapter 8.

The cost of gasoline for a car depends partly on the car's **fuel economy rate.** Fuel economy rates can be expressed as the number of kilometers traveled on one liter of gasoline.

Monica Shang and her brother Vincent kept records of their gasoline purchases during October. Each started with a full tank of gasoline and filled the tank every time more was needed.

Problem

Gasoline costs used in this lesson are based on a price of $0.38 per liter.

Monica drives a 6-cylinder mid-sized car. Her record for October is shown at the right. What was her car's fuel economy rate and her cost of gasoline per kilometer traveled during October?

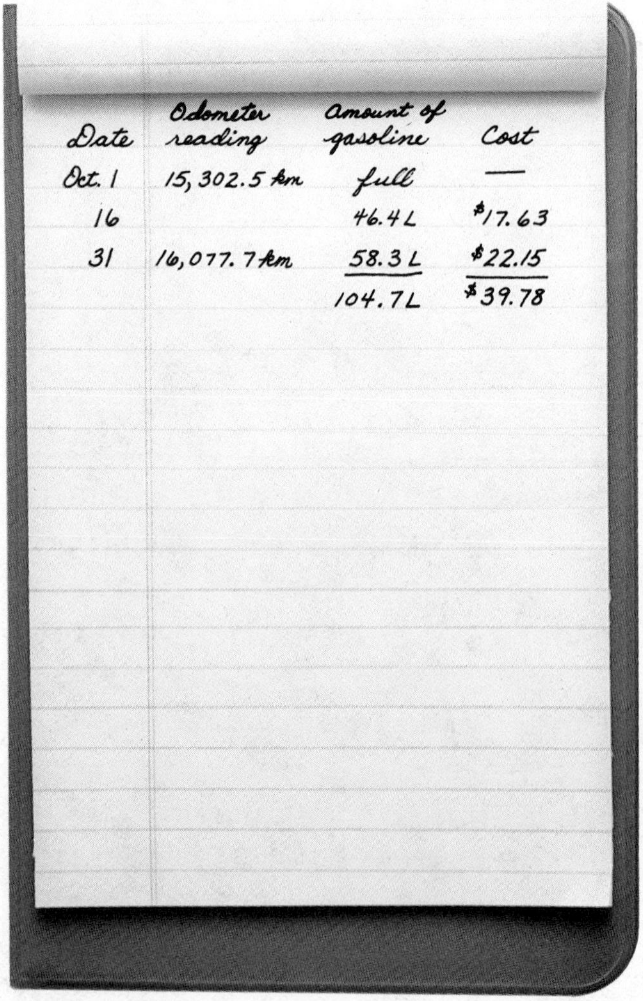
Date
Odometer reading
Amount of gasoline
Cost
Oct. 1
15,302.5 km
full
—
16
46.4 L
$17.63
31
16,077.7 km
58.3 L
$22.15
104.7 L
$39.78

Solution

Strategy

- Subtract to find the number of kilometers traveled in October.

Oct. 31 reading		Oct. 1 reading		Kilometers traveled
16,077.7	−	15,302.5	=	775.2

- Divide to find the car's fuel economy rate in kilometers per liter. Round to the nearest tenth.

Kilometers traveled		Liters of gas used		Kilometers per liter
775.2	÷	104.7	≈	7.4

- Divide to find the cost of gasoline for each kilometer traveled. Round to the nearest tenth of a cent.

Total cost		Kilometers traveled		Cost per kilometer
$39.78	÷	775.2	≈	$0.051 or 5.1¢

Conclusion

Monica's car had a fuel economy rate of about 7.4 kilometers per liter. The cost of gasoline was about 5.1 cents per kilometer traveled during October.

Warm-up: 12,956.7 − 12,428.9 [527.8]
38.5 + 42 + 56.8 [137.3]
435.6 ÷ 60.5 [7.2]
13.11 ÷ 524.4 [0.025]

See page 35 of *Consumer Forms and Problems.*

Related Problems

Vincent Shang has an 8-cylinder full-sized car. He kept this record of gasoline purchases.

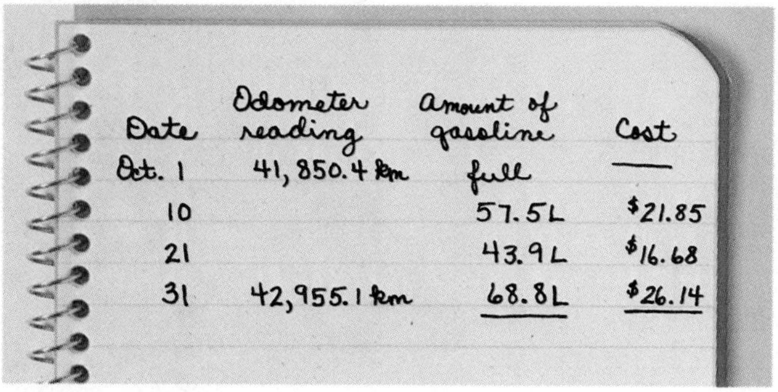

Date	Odometer reading	Amount of gasoline	Cost
Oct. 1	41,850.4 km	full	—
10		57.5 L	$21.85
21		43.9 L	$16.68
31	42,955.1 km	68.8 L	$26.14

1. How many kilometers did Vincent drive his car during the month?
   1104.7 kilometers
2. How many liters of gasoline did he buy?
   170.2 liters
3. Find his car's fuel economy rate. Round the answer to the nearest tenth.
   6.5 kilometers per liter
4. What was Vincent's total cost of gasoline for the month?
   $64.67
5. To the nearest tenth of a cent, find Vincent's cost of gasoline for each kilometer traveled.
   5.9¢ per kilometer
6. Vincent drives his car about 10,000 km in a year. How much might he spend on gasoline in a year?
   $590
   Ask for Monica's yearly cost of gasoline if she drives about 10,000 km each year. [$510]

For each car, find the distance traveled and its fuel economy rate to the nearest tenth. Then find the cost of gasoline per kilometer. Round to the nearest tenth of a cent.

	Odometer reading (km)		Distance traveled (km)	Amount of gasoline	Fuel economy rate (km/L)	Total cost of gasoline	Cost per kilometer
	Oct. 1	Oct. 31					
7.	45,800.2	46,149.7	349.5	57.0 L	6.1	$21.66	6.2¢
8.	62,521.3	63,343.3	822.0	68.5 L	12.0	$26.03	3.2¢
9.	18,462.5	18,704.5	242.0	60.5 L	4.0	$22.99	9.5¢
10.	13,520.9	13,976.9	456.0	48.0 L	9.5	$18.24	4.0¢
11.	8,743.1	9,085.6	342.5	76.0 L	4.5	$28.88	8.4¢
12.	38,465.0	38,883.0	418.0	41.8 L	10.0	$15.89	3.8¢

Objective: Compute the trade-in value and the amount of depreciation of a car, using information from a graph.

Depreciation

The graph below shows how the trade-in value of a car decreases yearly. This loss in value is called **depreciation.** The percents given in the graph are based on the price of the car when it was new.

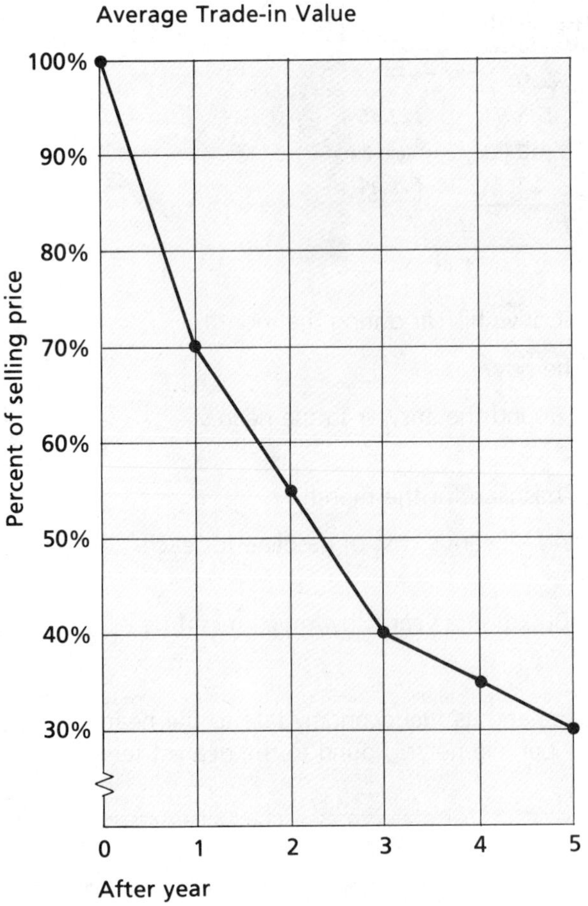

This graph represents an average decline in value for many different cars. Percents are rounded to the nearest 5%.

Problem

Keith and Evelyn McLane bought a new car for $6300 two years ago. What is the approximate trade-in value of the car, and how much has the car depreciated?

Solution

Strategy

- Read the graph to find the average trade-in value after two years.

  55% of selling price

- Multiply the selling price by 55% to find the trade-in value.

  $0.55 \times \$6300 = \$3465$

- Subtract to find the amount of depreciation.

$6300	Selling price
− 3465	Trade-in value
$2835	Depreciation

Conclusion

After two years the trade-in value of the McLanes' car is $3465. The car has depreciated $2835 in two years.

Related Problems

Warm-up: 55% of 5400 [2970]
30% of 8700 [2610]
70% of 6500 [4550]
6300 − 1895 [4405]

The selling prices of ten different cars are given. For each car, find its trade-in value each year for 5 years. Use the graph on page 152 to help you. Then subtract the trade-in value after 5 years from the selling price to find the car's depreciation after 5 years.

	Selling price	Trade-in value after					Depreciation after 5 years
		1 year	2 years	3 years	4 years	5 years	
1.	$5800	$4060	$3190	$2320	$2030	$1740	$4060
2.	$6000	$4200	$3300	$2400	$2100	$1800	$4200
3.	$6200	$4340	$3410	$2480	$2170	$1860	$4340
4.	$6600	$4620	$3630	$2640	$2310	$1980	$4620
5.	$7100	$4970	$3905	$2840	$2485	$2130	$4970
6.	$7700	$5390	$4235	$3080	$2695	$2310	$5390
7.	$8500	$5950	$4675	$3400	$2975	$2550	$5950
8.	$9000	$6300	$4950	$3600	$3150	$2700	$6300
9.	$9700	$6790	$5335	$3880	$3395	$2910	$6790
10.	$10,300	$7210	$5665	$4120	$3605	$3090	$7210

Most dealers consult a book to determine trade-in value for a car of a given model and year. However, it is to a customer's advantage to be able to estimate the trade-in value.

Objectives: Compute the total depreciation of a rental car; compute the selling price of a rental car, based on depreciation.

Selling Price Based on Depreciation

Warm-up: 7800 − 3249 [4551]
8000 − 2713 [5287]

Round to the nearest whole number.
0.027 × 8 × 5900 [1274]
0.025 × 27 × 7100 [4793]

A local rental agency is planning to sell some of its cars. The selling price of each car will depend partly upon how much the car has depreciated. The agency bases the amount of depreciation on the age of the car in months.

Age of car (months)	Monthly rate of depreciation
11 or less	2.7%
12 through 23	2.6%
24 through 35	2.5%

The percentages from the graph on page 152 are not used here because rental cars, police cars, and taxicabs usually have received harder use than privately owned cars.

This rule is used for computing the amount of depreciation.

Monthly rate × Number of months × Original price = Total depreciation

Problem

The agency has a car that was purchased 1 year 4 months (16 months) ago for $6800. Find the total depreciation and the selling price based on depreciation.

Solution

Strategy

- Read the table to find the monthly rate of depreciation for 16 months.

  2.6%

- Multiply to find the total depreciation. Round to the nearest dollar.

Monthly rate		Number of months		Original price		Total depreciation
0.026	×	16	×	$6800	≈	$2829

- Subtract from the original price to find the selling price based on depreciation.

  $6800 − $2829 = $3971

Conclusion

The car depreciated $2829 in 16 months. The selling price based on depreciation is $3971.

Related Problems

Find the total depreciation for each car. Round each answer to the nearest dollar.

	Original price	Age of car	
1.	$5720	21 months	$3123
2.	$5720	30 months	$4290
3.	$7500	9 months	$1823
4.	$6500	18 months	$3042
5.	$5200	24 months	$3120
6.	$6450	1 year 2 months	$2348
7.	$7325	1 year 7 months	$3619
8.	$6650	2 years 3 months	$4489
9.	$7000	1 year 11 months	$4186
10.	$7325	2 years 8 months	$5860
11.	$8500	1 year	$2652
12.	$9000	1 month	$243

13–24. Find the selling price based on depreciation for each car in problems 1–12.

13. $2597
14. $1430
15. $5677
16. $3458
17. $2080
18. $4102
19. $3706
20. $2161
21. $2814
22. $1465
23. $5848
24. $8757

CALCULATOR APPLICATIONS

Fuel Economy

A car's fuel economy rate usually decreases if the car is driven at high speeds or if air conditioning is used. This table gives the fuel economy rates of five different cars driven at various speeds without air conditioning and with air conditioning.

Fuel Economy Rates

	Without air conditioning				With air conditioning			
	Speed in km/h				Speed in km/h			
Car	48	64	80	96	48	64	80	96
	Kilometers per liter				Kilometers per liter			
A	9.16	8.53	8.12	7.58	7.89	7.78	7.56	7.37
B	10.06	10.45	8.70	6.30	7.83	7.75	6.67	5.88
C	8.64	8.50	7.44	6.87	8.94	7.40	7.32	7.37
D	7.28	7.31	6.85	6.34	6.87	7.15	6.93	5.98
E	7.79	8.20	6.64	6.04	7.15	7.13	6.82	6.19

Key sequence for problems 9–12:
a [−] *b* [÷] *a* [=]

At each speed, find the average of the fuel economy rates for the five cars without air conditioning.

1. 48 km/h
8.586 km/L

2. 64 km/h
8.598 km/L

3. 80 km/h
7.55 km/L

4. 96 km/h
6.626 km/L

At each speed, find the average of the fuel economy rates for the five cars with air conditioning.

5. 48 km/h
7.736 km/L

6. 64 km/h
7.442 km/L

7. 80 km/h
7.06 km/L

8. 96 km/h
6.558 km/L

The table below shows that the fuel economy rate of car A without air conditioning is 4.81% less at 80 km/h than at 64 km/h. Complete the table to find the percent of decrease for the other cars without air conditioning. Round to the nearest hundredth of a percent.

	Car	64 km/h rating (*a*)	80 km/h rating (*b*)	Change due to speed ($c = a - b$)	Percent decrease in fuel economy ($d = c \div a$)
	A	8.53	8.12	0.41	4.81%
9.	B	**10.45**	**8.70**	**1.75**	**16.75%**
10.	C	**8.50**	**7.44**	**1.06**	**12.47%**
11.	D	**7.31**	**6.85**	**0.46**	**6.29%**
12.	E	**8.20**	**6.64**	**1.56**	**19.02%**

Objective: Compute the total amount of a repair bill and the amount the mechanic will be paid.

Automobile Mechanic

See the Careers Chart beginning on page 410 for more information about the careers in this cluster.

Warm-up:	25.89 + 13 + 5.20	[44.09]
	37.90 + 43.18 + 63.47	[144.55]
	40% of 16.50	[6.60]
	40% of 139.50	[55.80]

Career Cluster: Trades Russell Brandau is a mechanic at a gas station. Most of his work involves tuning engines and replacing parts that are worn out. Russell is paid 40% of the total charge for labor on each bill.

I HEREBY AUTHORIZE ALL REPAIR WORK AS DESCRIBED AND ALL NECESSARY REPLACEMENT OF PARTS.
xLaura Red Eagle

CUSTOMER	PHONE	OFFICE USE ONLY
Laura Red Eagle	555-0770	

ADDRESS	CALL WHEN READY AM PM
8 Angeline Dr.	

MAKE	MODEL	ODOMETER
	6 cylinder	23,020

TIME RECEIVED	TIME PROMISED	WRITTEN BY
8 AM	5 PM	Russ

LICENSE NO.	SERIAL NO.	DATE
		11-27

PARTS	
1 oil filter	$5.95
1 fuel filter	4.00
1 air filter	6.25
8 spark plugs	13.20
1 set points	5.75
1 condenser	2.50
Total	$37.65

JOB DESCRIPTION	LABOR
20,000-km Inspection	
Engine tune-up	$55.00
Cln. battery, check PCV valve,	
new air filter, gap new plugs,	
check distributor cap and rotor,	
replace and gap points, adjust	
dwell, check timing & choke,	
new fuel filter	
Change oil, Lube chassis	4.50

GAS, OIL, GREASE	
5 L oil @ 1.30	$6.50
Grease	2.00
Total	$8.50

CANFIELD SERVICE
4th St. & Highway A
Canfield, Nebraska

TOTAL LABOR	$59.50
TOTAL PARTS	37.65
GAS, OIL, GREASE	8.50
OTHER	
TOTAL AMOUNT	$105.65

As shown here, a copy of the mechanic's work order is often used as the customer's bill. This work order should provide the customer with a detailed description of the work. Also, the customer should request to be called for approval or refusal of any additional repair work.

Problem

Laura Red Eagle brought in her car for a 20,000-kilometer inspection. What is the total amount of her bill? How much will Russell be paid for the work he did on the car?

Solution

Strategy

- Record the totals from the 3 sections of the bill.
- Add to find the total amount of the bill.
  $59.50 + $37.65 + $8.50 = $105.65
- Multiply the total charge for labor by 40% to find the amount Russell will be paid for the work.
  0.40 × $59.50 = $23.80

Conclusion

Laura's total bill is $105.65. Russell will be paid $23.80 for the work he did on the car.

You may want to include sales tax on the "Parts" portion of the bill. Enter this amount under "Other" on the final section of the bill.

Related Problems

Russell has completed the following work on Duane Beatty's car. Find the total for each section of the bill.

1.

JOB DESCRIPTION	LABOR
Tune - up	$55.00
Oil change, lube	4.50
Put on 2 snow tires	6.00

$65.50

2.

PARTS	
Oil Filter	$4.95
Hose bracket	1.05

$6.00

3.

GAS, OIL, GREASE	
4 L oil @ 1.30	$5.20
Grease	1.50

$6.70

4. What is the total amount of Duane's bill?
$78.20

5. How much will Russell be paid? (Find 40% of the total charge for labor.)
$26.20

Russell did the work listed on this bill.

JOB DESCRIPTION	LABOR
Aim headlights	$ 6.40
Adjust rear brakes	6.75
Check ignition timing	9.50

6. What is the total charge for labor?
$22.65
7. How much will Russell be paid for this job?
$9.06

Find the total amount of each bill.
Encourage students to check their answers by using estimation.

8. *Labor*

Replace muffler and tailpipe	$32.75
Parts	
Muffler	$45.15
Pipe	$14.90
Clamps	$2.60
Hanger	$11.53
Hanger	$3.36

$110.29

9. *Labor*

Replace front and rear shock absorbers	$36.00
Parts	
2 heavy-duty front shocks with fittings	$38.98
2 heavy-duty rear shocks with fittings	$38.98

$113.96

Break Time

Do your skills go from A to Z?

Trace the letter A and cut it into 4 pieces that can be put together to form the letter Z. Try to do this without turning any piece over.

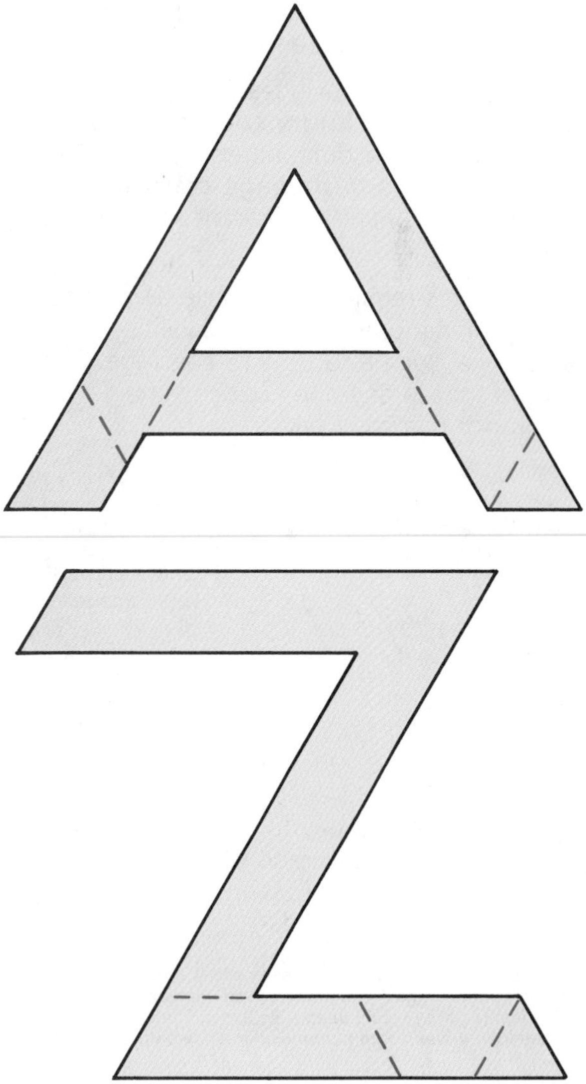

See page 36 of *Consumer Forms and Problems*.

10. Find the total amount charged for labor in the two bills in problems 8 and 9.
$68.75

11. How much will Russell be paid from these two bills?
$27.50

Many people keep records of all of their bills during the year. How much did each of these people spend last year on automobile maintenance and repair?

12. Laura Red Eagle

Jan.	$26.25	June	$34.50
Mar.	$17.80	Aug.	$61.42
Apr.	$28.40	Nov.	$107.15

$275.52

13. Duane Beatty

Feb.	$91.88	Aug.	$25.25
July	$45.20	Nov.	$74.15

$236.48

If some of your students do auto maintenance and repairs themselves, ask them to estimate how much money they save by doing this.

Objective: Compute the annual premium for automobile liability insurance, using information from a table.

Automobile Liability Insurance

Suppose you were a driver involved in an automobile accident in which someone was injured. If the court decided that you owed that person $35,000, could you pay? Most people could not, so they buy **liability insurance**. They pay **premiums** to an insurance company. The company then agrees to pay certain accident costs.

Liability insurance includes two types of coverage. **Bodily injury coverage** protects you financially if someone else is injured by your car. **Property damage coverage** protects you financially if someone's property is damaged by your car.

Some states require automobile owners to carry a minimum amount of liability insurance, such as 25/50/15 coverage. This means that in any one accident, the insurance company pays:

Bodily Injury
$25,000 maximum to each person you injure

Property Damage
$15,000 maximum to all persons whose property you damage

25/50/15

$50,000 maximum to all persons you injure

The premium you pay for liability insurance depends on the coverage you want, your age, where you live, how much you drive, and your driving record.

Premium rates quoted in this lesson and the next are for individual coverage. Premiums for teen-aged drivers covered on a family policy would usually be lower. The category "teen-aged driver" used here includes drivers up to age 25.

This table shows how annual premiums are figured by one company in a certain area. The base rates used here are for teen-aged drivers in the city. Rates vary greatly for different age groups and different localities.

BASE COVERAGE	BASE PREMIUMS
25/50/15	Teen male: $335.75 Teen female: $174.25

Premiums for Additional Coverage		
Type of coverage	Amount of coverage	Premium rate (Pay 100% of base plus:)
Bodily injury	50/100	9% of base
	100/300	20% of base
	250/500	33% of base
Property damage	25	2% of base
	50	5% of base
	100	8% of base

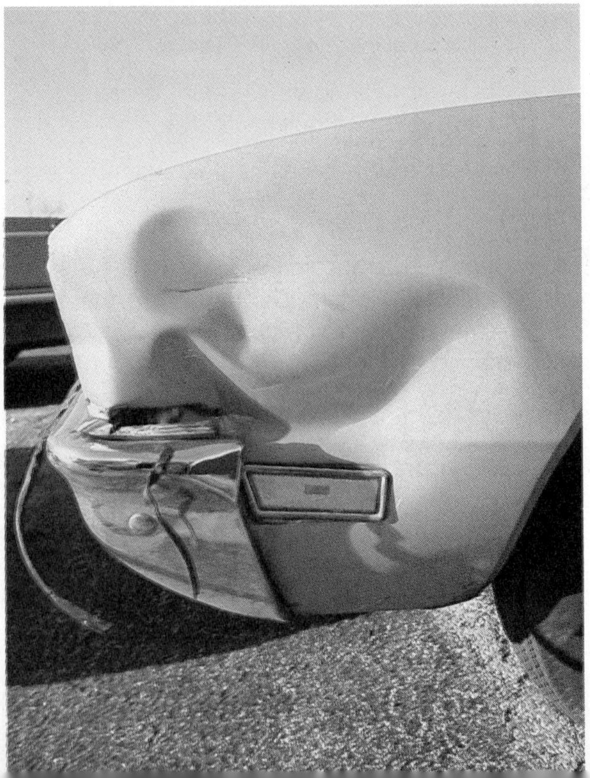

Warm-up: 100 + 33 + 8 [141]

Round to the nearest hundredth.
1.11 × 333.75 [370.46]
1.25 × 174.25 [217.81]
1.41 × 257.15 [362.58]

Problem

Gloria Stiller is 18. She bought liability insurance with 50/100/25 coverage. What is her annual premium? Remember, she must pay the base premium for a teen female, plus the premiums for additional coverage.

Solution

Strategy

- Use a percent to show the base premium rate.

  100% of base

- Read the table to find the premium rate for bodily injury coverage of 50/100.

  9% of base

- Read the table to find the premium rate for property damage coverage of 25.

  2% of base

- Add to find the total premium rate for 50/100/25 coverage.

	100%	of base
	9%	of base
+	2%	of base
	111%	of base

- Multiply the base premium by 111% to find the annual premium. Round to the nearest cent.

  $1.11 \times \$174.25 \approx \$193.42$

Conclusion

Gloria's annual premium for liability insurance is $193.42.

Drivers from 16 to 25 years old represent about 22% of all licensed drivers, but they are involved in about 39% of all highway accidents. For this reason, their insurance rates are higher than those for other age categories. Males in this age category pay more than females because statistics show that they drive more and have more accidents.

Related Problems

If your liability insurance coverage is 250/500/100, what is the maximum amount the insurance company will pay

1. to each person you injure?
$250,000

2. to all persons you injure?
$500,000

3. to all persons whose property you damage?
$100,000

Find the premium that Gloria Stiller would pay for each type of coverage.

4. 50/100/50
$198.65

5. 100/300/50
$217.81

6. 250/500/100
$245.69

7. 100/300/100
$223.04

8. 25/50/25
$177.74

Gloria's brother Ray is 19. Find the annual premium he would pay for each type of coverage.

9. 25/50/25
$342.47

10. 50/100/50
$382.76

11. 100/300/100
$429.76

12. 250/500/100
$473.41

13. 50/100/25
$372.68

14. Katy Olson is 17. Her liability insurance coverage is 50/100/25. She wants to change it to 100/300/25. How much will her annual premium increase?
$19.17

Objective: Compute the combined annual premium for automobile collision and comprehensive insurance, using information from a table.

Automobile Collision and Comprehensive Insurance

Liability insurance is only one part of a total automobile insurance program. Many automobile owners also buy insurance to protect themselves financially in case of damage to their own cars. This kind of coverage is usually required if you apply for an auto loan.

Collision insurance pays for the repair of damage on your car caused by an accident.

Comprehensive insurance pays for repair or replacement of your car in case of fire, theft, vandalism, or an act of nature, such as a flood.

To figure the premium for collision and comprehensive insurance, the insurance company classifies your car according to its age and the amount of extra equipment it has. Your premium will be less if your policy has a **deductible** feature. For example, with $100 deductible, you agree to pay the first $100 of any repair bill. Other deductibles are usually available.

This table shows one company's premium rates for Gloria Stiller's city.

Annual Premiums for Collision and Comprehensive Insurance

Car	Driver	Collision premium for		Comprehensive premium for	
		$50 ded.	$100 ded.	No ded.	$50 ded.
Class B	Teen female	$338.66	$318.16	$69.20	$55.60
	Teen male	$652.54	$613.04	$69.20	$55.60
	Female, 25 and over	$181.72	$170.72	$69.20	$55.60
	Single male, 25–30	$264.32	$248.32	$69.20	$55.60
Class C	Teen female	$383.76	$359.16	$81.60	$64.80
	Teen male	$739.44	$692.04	$81.60	$64.80
	Female, 25 and over	$205.92	$192.72	$81.60	$64.80
	Single male, 25–30	$299.52	$280.32	$81.60	$64.80
Class F	Teen female	$402.62	$377.20	$89.60	$76.20
	Teen male	$775.78	$726.80	$89.60	$76.20
	Female, 25 and over	$216.04	$202.40	$89.60	$76.20
	Single male, 25–30	$314.24	$294.40	$89.60	$76.20

This table quotes premiums for a new car in one geographical territory. Class B cars have 4 or 6 cylinders and few options. Class F cars are the high-powered cars with many options.

Problem

Gloria Stiller's car is rated as Class C. What would be her annual combined premium for collision insurance with $100 deductible and comprehensive insurance with no deductible?

Driver categories listed in the table are not all-inclusive. For example, there are separate categories for a married male under 25 and over 25, also for male or female over 65.

Warm-up: 195.85 + 36.20 [232.05]
218.50 + 46.75 [265.25]
187.32 + 54.60 [241.92]
752.08 + 37.50 [789.58]

Solution

Strategy

- Read the table to find Gloria's collision premium. Remember, she is 18, so find the heading "Teen female" in the Class C section.
  $359.16
- Read the table to find Gloria's comprehensive premium.
  $81.60
- Add to find the combined premium.
  $359.16 + $81.60 = $440.76

Conclusion

Gloria's combined premium for collision and comprehensive insurance is $440.76.

Related Problems

Problems 1-3, 4-7, and 8-9 indicate premiums for drivers in different categories who have the same coverage.

Use the rates shown in this lesson to complete the table.

	Driver	Class	Collision		Comprehensive		Combined premium
			Deductible	Premium	Deductible	Premium	
	Teen female	C	$100	$359.16	None	$81.60	$440.76
1.	Teen male	C	$100	**$692.04**	None	**$81.60**	**$773.64**
2.	Female, 25 and over	C	$100	**$192.72**	None	**$81.60**	**$274.32**
3.	Single male, 25-30	C	$100	**$280.32**	None	**$81.60**	**$361.92**
4.	Teen female	B	$50	**$338.66**	$50	**$55.60**	**$394.26**
5.	Teen male	B	$50	**$652.54**	$50	**$55.60**	**$708.14**
6.	Female, 25 and over	B	$50	**$181.72**	$50	**$55.60**	**$237.32**
7.	Single male, 25-30	B	$50	**$264.32**	$50	**$55.60**	**$319.92**
8.	Teen female	F	$100	**$377.20**	$50	**$76.20**	**$453.40**
9.	Teen male	F	$100	**$726.80**	$50	**$76.20**	**$803.00**

10. Find Gloria Stiller's total annual premium for automobile insurance. Include liability, collision, and comprehensive insurance.
$634.18
Refer to page 161 for Gloria's liability insurance premium.

Objective: Compute the annual cost of owning and operating a car.

Annual Expenses

Gregory Brent, age 32, bought a new 6-cylinder mid-sized car 3 years ago. He financed the car with a two-year loan. This record shows his annual expenses.

	First year	Second year	Third year
Distance traveled	16,700 km	16,000 km	15,000 km
Depreciation	$1950.00	$975.00	$845.00
Fixed Costs			
Loan payments	$3250.00	$3250.00	—
Insurance	$458.49	$460.81	$423.13
License and fees	$49.00	$49.00	$49.00
Garage, tolls, parking	$275.00	$314.00	$256.00
Variable Costs			
Gas	$918.20	$902.00	$855.00
Repair, maintenance	$208.50	$245.39	$275.80
Radial tires	—	—	$144.70

Note that the changes in gasoline costs reflect changes in price per liter as well as in distances traveled.

Problem

During the first year that Greg owned his car, what was the cost per kilometer traveled?

Solution

Strategy

- Add to find the total fixed costs for the first year.

$$\begin{array}{r} \$3250.00 \\ 458.49 \\ 49.00 \\ +\quad 275.00 \\ \hline \$4032.49 \end{array}$$

- Add to find the total variable costs.

$$\begin{array}{r} \$918.20 \\ +\quad 208.50 \\ \hline \$1126.70 \end{array}$$

- Add to find the total cost for the year, including depreciation.

$$\begin{array}{rl} \$1950.00 & \text{Depreciation} \\ 4032.49 & \text{Fixed costs} \\ +\quad 1126.70 & \text{Variable costs} \\ \hline \$7109.19 & \end{array}$$

- Divide by the number of kilometers traveled to find the cost per kilometer. Round to the nearest tenth of a cent.

$\$7109.19 \div 16{,}700 \approx \$0.426$ or 42.6¢

Conclusion

During the first year, Greg's car cost him about 42.6¢ per kilometer.

Warm-up:
1640 + 783.25 + 1852.56 [4275.81]
986 + 148.63 + 792.06 [1926.69]

Round to the nearest thousandth.
1460.54 ÷ 6960 [0.210]
5630.22 ÷ 14,700 [0.383]

See page 37 of *Consumer Forms and Problems.*

Related Problems

You might have students check their answers to problems 1-3 and 7-9 by estimating.

For problems 1-6, use Greg's records for the second year.

1. Find the total fixed costs.
   $4073.81
2. Find the total variable costs.
   $1147.39
3. Find the total cost for the year, including depreciation, fixed costs, and variable costs.
   $6196.20
4. Find the cost per kilometer. Round the answer to the nearest tenth of a cent.
   38.7¢ per kilometer
5. In the second year, which expenses decreased?
   Depreciation; gas
6. In the second year, which expenses increased?
   Insurance; garage, tolls, parking; repairs and maintenance

For problems 7-11, use Greg's records for the third year.

7. Find the total fixed costs.
   $728.13
8. Find the total variable costs.
   $1275.50
9. Find the total cost for the year, including depreciation, fixed costs, and variable costs.
   $2848.63
10. Find the cost per kilometer. Round the answer to the nearest tenth of a cent.
    19.0¢ per kilometer
11. What new expense did Greg have during the third year?
    Radial tires
12. Why is the cost during the third year so much less than during the first or second year?
    The loan has been paid off.

Objective: Find the monthly cost of transportation for people who do not own a car.

Alternatives to Owning a Car

Some people choose not to own a car because they can use **public transportation** such as buses, subways, trains, and taxicabs.

Problem

Ruth Steele lives 35 km from her place of work in the city. She takes a bus to and from the train station in her town for $0.60 each way. Ruth buys a monthly train ticket for $47.90. She walks to her office from the train station in the city. Find Ruth's monthly cost of traveling to and from work. Assume that each month has 20 working days.

Solution

Strategy

- Multiply to find the monthly cost of the bus.

Cost per trip		Trips per day		Days per month		Cost per month
$0.60	×	2	×	20	=	$24.00

- Add the cost of the train to the cost of the bus to find the total monthly cost.

$24.00	Bus
+ 47.90	Train
$71.90	

Conclusion

Ruth's monthly cost of traveling to and from work is $71.90.

Warm-up: 0.55 × 40 [22]
2.75 × 40 [110]
14 + 39.60 [53.60]
12 × 185 [2220]

Related Problems

For problems 1-6, find the monthly cost of traveling to and from work. Assume that each month has 20 working days.

1. $0.65 bus fare each way
   $45.60 monthly train ticket
   $71.60
2. $65.50 monthly train ticket
   $4.50 taxicab fare each way
   $245.50
3. $0.70 bus fare each way
   $0.20 bus transfer each way
   $36
4. $0.75 bus fare each way
   $0.45 subway transfer each way
   $48
5. $0.75 subway fare each way
   $0.30 subway transfer each way
   $42
6. $2.00 per week to neighbor for ride to and from bus stop
   $0.75 fare each way for express bus
   $38
7. Brett Bauman lives in one town and works in another. He takes two buses, one for $0.60 each way and the other for $0.75 each way. Find his monthly cost of traveling to and from work.
   $54
8. Find Brett's yearly cost of traveling to and from work.
   $648
9. Brett travels about 24,000 km to and from work each year. How much does he pay per kilometer?
   2.7¢ per kilometer
10. Last year Brett drove his car to and from work. His annual expenses were about $2700 to drive the 24,000 km. How much did he pay per kilometer? Round the answer to the nearest tenth of a cent.
    11.3¢ per kilometer

Another alternative to owning a car is **leasing** a car. A person pays a monthly fee to use a car. The car is returned at the end of the lease period. This table shows typical monthly leasing fees.

Monthly leasing fees				
Model	12 mo.	24 mo.	30 mo.	36 mo.
Compact	$195	$147	$138	$135
Mid-sized	$212	$158	$148	$145
Full-sized	$258	$189	$178	$175

Problem

Rick Velez leased a compact car for 24 months. What was his total cost for leasing the car?

Solution

Strategy

- Read the table to find the monthly fee. $147
- Multiply by 24 to find the total cost. 24 × $147 = $3528

Conclusion

Rick's total cost for leasing the car is $3528.

Related Problems

Find the total cost of leasing each car.

		Model	Number of months		Model	Number of months	
$3792	**11.**	Mid-sized	24	**16.**	Compact	30	$4140
$4536	**12.**	Full-sized	24	**17.**	Mid-sized	30	$4440
$2340	**13.**	Compact	12	**18.**	Compact	36	$4860
$2544	**14.**	Mid-sized	12	**19.**	Mid-sized	36	$5220
$3096	**15.**	Full-sized	12	**20.**	Full-sized	36	$6300

Skills Tune-Up

Adding whole numbers and decimals, pages 6-7

1. 12 + 26 + 14 52
2. 4 + 17 + 56 77
3. 94 + 37 + 26 157
4. 34 + 40 + 74 148
5. 74 + 52 + 63 189
6. 82 + 47 + 74 203
7. 48 + 34 + 57 + 93 232
8. 86 + 7 + 23 + 42 158
9. 74 + 62 + 86 + 98 320
10. 202 + 155 + 343 700
11. 357 + 444 + 931 1732
12. 378 + 950 + 509 1837
13. 336 + 687 + 543 1566
14. 8.1 + 2.56 10.66
15. 3.2 + 9.65 12.85
16. 27.36 + 14.51 41.87
17. 29.24 + 30.27 59.51
18. 0.4 + 0.9 + 0.5 1.8
19. 6.8 + 3.4 + 8.67 18.87
20. 0.09 + 1.06 + 0.18 1.33
21. 9.81 + 4.75 + 7.04 21.6
22. 7.89 + 6.7 + 4.47 19.06
23. 0.73 + 0.59 + 0.12 1.44
24. 7.92 + 3.89 + 3.25 15.06
25. 4.364 + 3.49 + 0.05 7.904
26. 2.01 + 4.6 + 6.7 + 8.2 21.51
27. 6.8 + 9.37 + 137.9 154.07
28. 195.3 + 89.2 + 0.7 285.2

Multiplying decimals, pages 10-11

1. 0.3 × 0.6 0.18
2. 0.4 × 0.5 0.2
3. 0.09 × 0.4 0.036
4. 0.07 × 0.3 0.021
5. 0.05 × 0.06 0.003
6. 0.11 × 0.04 0.0044
7. 0.003 × 0.08 0.00024
8. 0.06 × 0.011 0.00066
9. 800 × 0.4 320
10. 600 × 0.7 420
11. 180 × 0.02 3.6
12. 0.09 × 500 45
13. 0.008 × 700 5.6
14. 400 × 0.001 0.4
15. 0.006 × 0.005 0.00003
16. 0.003 × 0.009 0.000027
17. 7000 × 0.0012 8.4
18. 3.4 × 4.2 14.28
19. 5.22 × 6.6 34.452
20. 5.2 × 8.23 42.796
21. 15.6 × 0.023 0.3588
22. 8.367 × 9.72 81.32724
23. 17.2 × 2.044 35.1568
24. 4.17 × 0.3596 1.499532
25. 16.76 × 0.374 6.26824
26. 0.0027 × 5.46 0.014742
27. 2.77 × 1.98 5.4846
28. 38.09 × 0.006 0.22854

Renaming fractions and mixed numbers, pages 14-15

Rename as a fraction.

1. $1\frac{3}{8}$ $\frac{11}{8}$
2. $3\frac{2}{3}$ $\frac{11}{3}$
3. $2\frac{5}{6}$ $\frac{17}{6}$
4. $7\frac{3}{4}$ $\frac{31}{4}$
5. $5\frac{1}{5}$ $\frac{26}{5}$
6. $2\frac{7}{8}$ $\frac{23}{8}$
7. $9\frac{1}{2}$ $\frac{19}{2}$
8. $6\frac{4}{5}$ $\frac{34}{5}$
9. $3\frac{5}{9}$ $\frac{32}{9}$
10. $12\frac{2}{3}$ $\frac{38}{3}$
11. $6\frac{3}{10}$ $\frac{63}{10}$
12. 5 $\frac{5}{1}$
13. 12 $\frac{12}{1}$
14. $4\frac{7}{12}$ $\frac{55}{12}$
15. $2\frac{3}{16}$ $\frac{35}{16}$
16. $8\frac{6}{7}$ $\frac{62}{7}$
17. $5\frac{9}{10}$ $\frac{59}{10}$
18. $7\frac{1}{12}$ $\frac{85}{12}$
19. $4\frac{8}{11}$ $\frac{52}{11}$
20. $3\frac{5}{16}$ $\frac{53}{16}$

Rename as a mixed number.

21. $\frac{9}{4}$ $2\frac{1}{4}$
22. $\frac{17}{5}$ $3\frac{2}{5}$
23. $\frac{3}{2}$ $1\frac{1}{2}$
24. $\frac{23}{6}$ $3\frac{5}{6}$
25. $\frac{13}{6}$ $2\frac{1}{6}$
26. $\frac{10}{7}$ $1\frac{3}{7}$
27. $\frac{14}{3}$ $4\frac{2}{3}$
28. $\frac{11}{2}$ $5\frac{1}{2}$
29. $\frac{65}{15}$ $4\frac{1}{3}$
30. $\frac{45}{8}$ $5\frac{5}{8}$
31. $\frac{21}{16}$ $1\frac{5}{16}$
32. $\frac{36}{27}$ $1\frac{1}{3}$
33. $\frac{19}{8}$ $2\frac{3}{8}$
34. $\frac{48}{9}$ $5\frac{1}{3}$
35. $\frac{36}{20}$ $1\frac{4}{5}$
36. $\frac{37}{12}$ $3\frac{1}{12}$
37. $\frac{67}{9}$ $7\frac{4}{9}$
38. $\frac{48}{32}$ $1\frac{1}{2}$

Chapter 8 Review

Finding gasoline costs, pages 150-151

1. Daniel drove 1482.4 km during August. He bought 218 liters of gasoline. Find his car's fuel economy rate.
6.8 kilometers per liter

Depreciation, pages 152-153

2. Estela bought a new $5600 car 3 years ago. How much has her car depreciated? Use the guideline that after 3 years the trade-in value is 40% of the price of the car when it was new.
$3360

Selling price based on depreciation, page 154

3. A rental agency is selling a car that was purchased 15 months ago for $6200. Find the total depreciation by multiplying the monthly rate times the number of months times the original price. Use this table.
$2418

Age of car (months)	Monthly rate of depreciation
11 or less	2.7%
12 through 23	2.6%
24 through 35	2.5%

Automobile mechanic, pages 156-159

Use this repair bill for problems 4 and 5.

TOTAL LABOR	$ 48.00
TOTAL PARTS	17.25
GAS, OIL, GREASE	6.50
OTHER	
TOTAL AMOUNT	

4. What is the total amount of this bill?
$71.75
5. The mechanic is paid 40% of the labor charge for each job. How much will the mechanic be paid for this job?
$19.20

Automobile liability insurance, pages 160-161

6. Gordon is 18. How much is his annual premium for liability coverage of 50/100/25? Use the table on page 160. Round the answer to the nearest cent.
$372.68

Automobile collision and comprehensive insurance, pages 162-163

7. Marsha, age 17, has a Class C car. She is buying collision insurance with $50 deductible and comprehensive insurance with $50 deductible. How much is her annual combined premium? Use the table on page 162.
$448.56

Annual expenses, pages 164-165

8. Kim Foss drove 15,000 km last year. She recorded these expenses for her car during the year:

Depreciation	$1380.00
Fixed costs	$2267.15
Variable costs	$485.33

Find the cost per kilometer. Round the answer to the nearest tenth of a cent.
27.5¢ per kilometer

Alternatives to owning a car, pages 166-167

9. Harley takes the bus and the train to and from work. Bus fare is $0.60 each way. His monthly train ticket is $35.10. Find Harley's monthly cost of traveling to and from work. Assume that there are 20 working days in a month.
$59.10
10. Glen leased a compact car for 12 months. Find his total cost for leasing the car. Use this table. $2340

Monthly leasing fees				
Model	12 mo.	24 mo.	30 mo.	36 mo.
Compact	$195	$147	$138	$135
Mid-sized	$212	$158	$148	$145

Chapter 8 Test

Number of test items - 10

Number missed	1	2	3	4	5
Percent correct	90	80	70	60	50

1. Annette drove 1020.7 km during July. She bought 173 liters of gasoline. Find her car's fuel economy rate.
5.9 kilometers per liter

2. Howard Chinn bought a new $5900 car 5 years ago. How much has his car depreciated? Use the guideline that after 5 years the trade-in value is 30% of the price of the car when it was new.
$4130

3. A rental agency is selling a car that was purchased 30 months ago for $6500. Find the total depreciation by multiplying the monthly rate times the number of months times the original price. Use this table.
$4875

Age of car (months)	Monthly rate of depreciation
11 or less	2.7%
12 through 23	2.6%
24 through 35	2.5%

Use this repair bill for problems 4 and 5.

TOTAL LABOR	$ 68.40
TOTAL PARTS	15.50
GAS, OIL, GREASE	5.50
OTHER	
TOTAL AMOUNT	

4. What is the total amount of this bill?
$89.40

5. A mechanic is paid 40% of the labor charge for each job. How much will the mechanic be paid for this job?
$27.36

6. Elvina is 19. How much is her annual premium for liability coverage of 100/300/50? Use the table on page 160. Round the answer to the nearest cent.
$217.81

7. Nick, age 17, has a Class B car. He is buying collision insurance with $100 deductible and comprehensive insurance with $50 deductible. How much is his annual combined premium? Use the table on page 162.
$668.64

8. Hector Lopez drove 15,000 km last year. He recorded these expenses for his car during the year:

Depreciation	$975.00
Fixed costs	$1745.09
Variable costs	$792.73

Find the cost per kilometer. Round the answer to the nearest tenth of a cent.
23.4¢ per kilometer

9. Lynn takes the bus and the train to and from work. Bus fare is $0.65 each way. Her monthly train ticket is $47.95. Find Lynn's monthly cost of traveling to and from work. Assume that there are 20 working days in a month.
$73.95

10. Dick leased a full-sized car for 36 months. Find his total cost for leasing the car. Use this table.
$6300

Monthly leasing fees				
Model	12 mo.	24 mo.	30 mo.	36 mo.
Compact	$195	$147	$138	$135
Mid-sized	$212	$158	$148	$145
Full-sized	$258	$189	$178	$175

 See pages 19-20 of the *Test Masters* for an alternate form of the Chapter 8 Test.

Chapter 9 Travel

Objective: Find the distance of a route using a distance chart.

Reading a Distance Chart

See page T34 for additional notes and activities for Chapter 9.

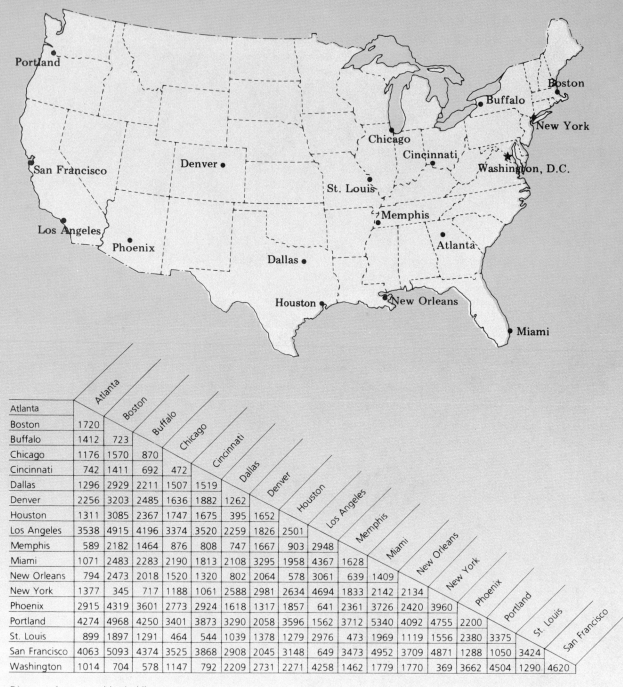

	Atlanta	Boston	Buffalo	Chicago	Cincinnati	Dallas	Denver	Houston	Los Angeles	Memphis	Miami	New Orleans	New York	Phoenix	Portland	St. Louis	San Francisco
Atlanta																	
Boston	1720																
Buffalo	1412	723															
Chicago	1176	1570	870														
Cincinnati	742	1411	692	472													
Dallas	1296	2929	2211	1507	1519												
Denver	2256	3203	2485	1636	1882	1262											
Houston	1311	3085	2367	1747	1675	395	1652										
Los Angeles	3538	4915	4196	3374	3520	2259	1826	2501									
Memphis	589	2182	1464	876	808	747	1667	903	2948								
Miami	1071	2483	2283	2190	1813	2108	3295	1958	4367	1628							
New Orleans	794	2473	2018	1520	1320	802	2064	578	3061	639	1409						
New York	1377	345	717	1188	1061	2588	2981	2634	4694	1833	2142	2134					
Phoenix	2915	4319	3601	2773	2924	1618	1317	1857	641	2361	3726	2420	3960				
Portland	4274	4968	4250	3401	3873	3290	2058	3596	1562	3712	5340	4092	4755	2200			
St. Louis	899	1897	1291	464	544	1039	1378	1279	2976	473	1969	1119	1556	2380	3375		
San Francisco	4063	5093	4374	3525	3868	2908	2045	3148	649	3473	4952	3709	4871	1288	1050	3424	
Washington	1014	704	578	1147	792	2209	2731	2271	4258	1462	1779	1770	369	3662	4504	1290	4620

Distances between cities in kilometers

Warm-up: 347 + 869 + 852 [2068]
329 + 37 + 824 [1190]
27 + 1280 + 427 [1734]
3401 − 2948 [453]

See page 38 of
Consumer Forms and Problems.

Students will need to change the order of the cities to read the chart for some problems.

Problem

Gene Papiri is driving from Boston to Dallas. He plans to stop in Memphis on his way to Dallas. How many kilometers will he travel?

Solution

Strategy

- Find Memphis on the chart and follow the chart across to the distance in kilometers listed under Boston.

  2182

- Find Memphis on the chart and follow the chart across to the distance in kilometers listed under Dallas.

  747

- Add to find the total distance.

  2182 + 747 = 2929

Conclusion

Gene will travel about 2929 kilometers.

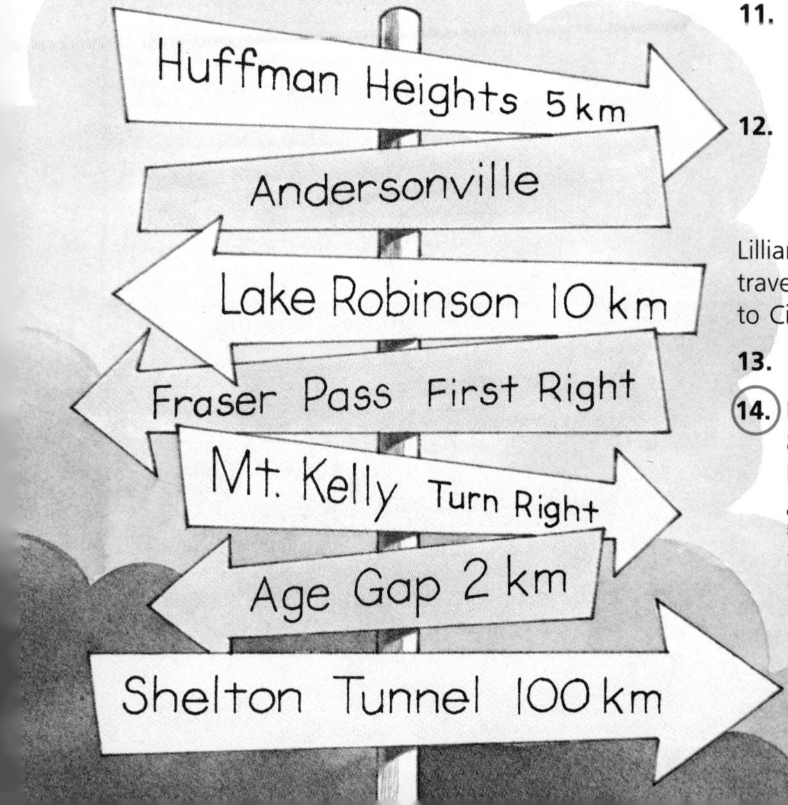

Related Problems

Find the distance along each route.

1. Washington to St. Louis to San Francisco
   4714 kilometers
2. Miami to New Orleans to Phoenix
   3829 kilometers
3. Cincinnati to Chicago to Denver
   2108 kilometers
4. New York to Memphis to Los Angeles
   4781 kilometers
5. Portland to St. Louis to Atlanta
   4274 kilometers
6. Dallas to St. Louis to Buffalo
   2330 kilometers
7. New Orleans to Los Angeles to Portland
   4623 kilometers
8. Buffalo to Atlanta to Miami
   2483 kilometers
9. Vancouver, British Columbia, is about 515 km north of Portland. Find the distance from New Orleans to Los Angeles to Portland to Vancouver.
   5138 kilometers
10. Toronto, Ontario, is about 165 km north of Buffalo. Find the distance from Toronto to Buffalo to Atlanta to Miami.
    2648 kilometers
11. How much farther is the distance from Houston to Washington by way of Cincinnati than by way of Atlanta?
    142 kilometers
12. How much farther is the distance from Phoenix to Chicago by way of Dallas than by way of Denver?
    172 kilometers

Lillian Barton is a regional sales manager. She is traveling from New York to Atlanta to Memphis to Cincinnati to Chicago to New York.

13. How far will Lillian travel?
    4434 kilometers
14. If Lillian drives at an average rate of 80 kilometers per hour, about how many hours will she spend driving? Round your answer to the nearest hour.
    55 hours

To extend the lesson, give students the rate of travel and ask for the resulting travel time.

Objective: Find the distance of a route and the travel time required, using a map.

Finding Distance and Travel Time

On this map of Wyoming, national interstate highways are shown in green, U.S. highways and state highways are in red, and other roads are in blue. Distances between dots are given in kilometers.

How to determine the scale

0 20 40 60 Kilometers

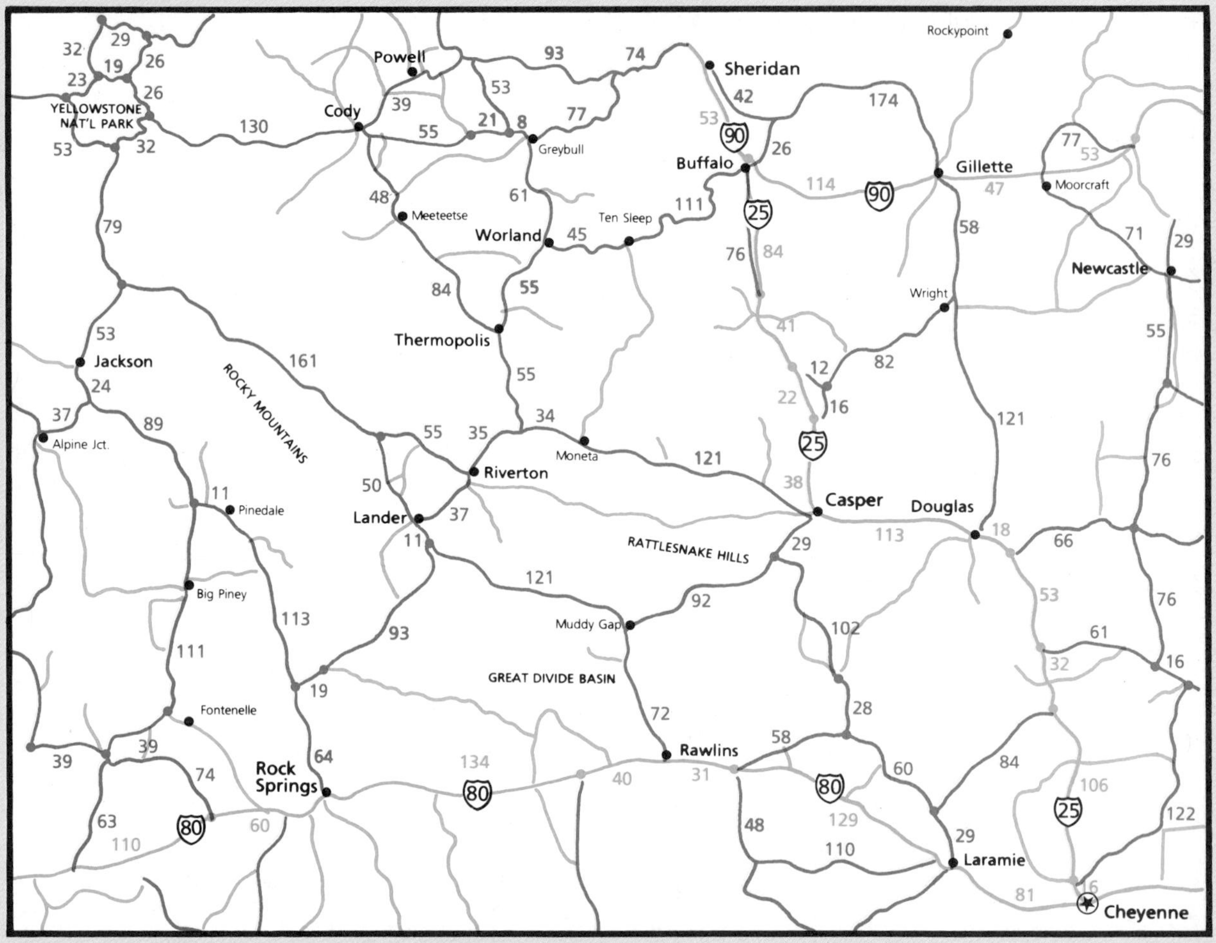

Problem

What is the distance from Sheridan to Casper? At a rate of 80 kilometers per hour (km/h), what is the travel time for this distance?

Solution

Strategy

- Add to find the total number of kilometers. $53 + 84 + 41 + 22 + 38 = 238$
- Divide to find the travel time. $238 \div 80 \approx 3$

Conclusion

The distance from Sheridan to Casper is about 238 km and the travel time is about 3 hours.

Warm-up: 234 + 467 [701]
685 + 372 + 549 [1606]
576 ÷ 80 [7.2]
380 ÷ 80 [4.75]

Related Problems

Find the distance along each route. Then find the travel time to the nearest hour. Use a rate of 80 km/h.

1. Sheridan to Powell
167 kilometers; 2 hours

2. Gillette to Douglas
179 kilometers; 2 hours

3. Rock Springs to Laramie
334 kilometers; 4 hours

4. Rawlins to Cheyenne
241 kilometers; 3 hours

5. Sheridan to Gillette by interstate
167 kilometers; 2 hours

6. Sheridan to Gillette by U.S. highway
216 kilometers; 3 hours

7. Casper to Douglas to Cheyenne
338 kilometers; 4 hours

8. Casper to Laramie to Cheyenne
329 kilometers; 4 hours

9. Jackson to Pinedale to Rock Springs
301 kilometers; 4 hours

Problem

Julie Burdic plans to drive from Riverton to Casper on a local road. What is the measured distance from Riverton to Casper?

Solution

Strategy

• Using the scale of the map, mark off and label segments on a card.

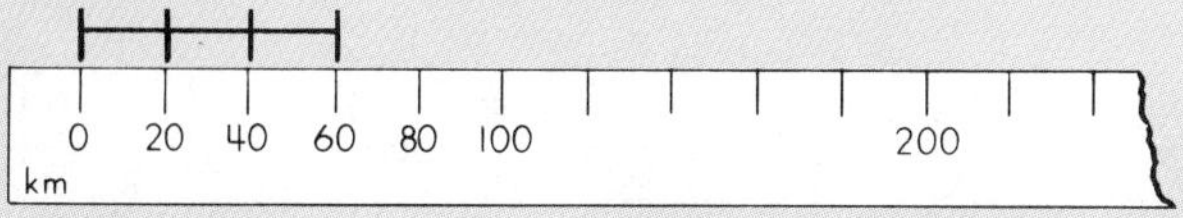

• Use the card to measure the most direct distance between Riverton and Casper.

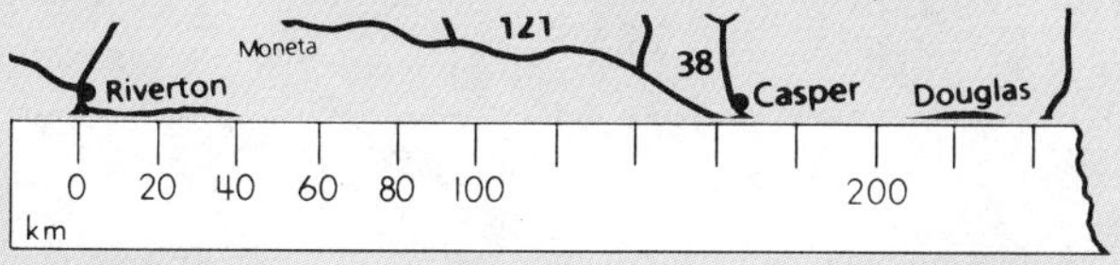

Conclusion

The measured distance from Riverton to Casper is about 170 km.

See page 39 of *Consumer Forms and Problems.*

Answers are given using the straight line distance between points. Answers close to these are acceptable. You might allow a difference of 15 km or have students round to the nearest 10 km.

Related Problems

Measure to find the distance along each of these routes.

10. Ten Sleep to Moneta
100 kilometers

11. Wright to Newcastle
110 kilometers

12. Rockypoint to Gillette
80 kilometers

13. Greybull to Meeteetse
80 kilometers

14. Alpine Jct. to Big Piney
100 kilometers

15. Fontenelle to Rock Springs
80 kilometers

For each route, use the numbers on the map to compute the distance. Then measure to find the distance.

	Route	Computed distance	Measured distance
16.	Rock Springs to Rawlins	174 km	170 km
17.	Lander to Muddy Gap	132 km	120 km
18.	Pinedale to Rock Springs	177 km	150 km
19.	Rawlins to Laramie	160 km	150 km
20.	Muddy Gap to Casper	121 km	110 km

For problems 21 and 22, use 40 km/h for the rate of travel on the roads shown in blue and 80 km/h for other roads.

21. To the nearest hour, what is the travel time from Riverton to Douglas?
6 hours

22. Which route takes more time, Wright to Newcastle or Wright to Gillette to Moorcraft to Newcastle?
Wright to Newcastle

Objective: Estimate the total expenses incurred while traveling.

Expenses on the Road

Many people estimate their total expenses for a trip. The expenses might include costs for gasoline, food, and lodging.

Problem

Amy and Alex Thorson plan to drive the 1562 km from Los Angeles to Portland. They estimate that gas will cost \$0.40 per liter and that their car's fuel economy rate will be about 7.8 km/L. They will spend 2 nights in motels for about \$45 per night. They estimate that 12 meals (6 each for 2 people) will cost about \$8 each. They are allowing \$50 for other expenses. Find the total estimate for the cost of the trip.

Solution

Strategy

- Divide total distance by fuel economy rate to find the number of liters of gas needed to the nearest liter.

  $1562 \div 7.8 \approx 200$

- Multiply by \$0.40 to find the cost of gas.

  $\$0.40 \times 200 = \$80$

- Multiply motel cost by 2 to find the cost of lodging.

  $2 \times \$45 = \$90$

- Multiply \$8 by 12 to find the cost of meals.

  $12 \times \$8 = \$96$

- Add to find the total estimate, including \$50 for other expenses.

  $\$80 + \$90 + \$96 + \$50 = \$316$

Conclusion

The total estimate for the cost of the trip is \$316.

It is often wise to add 10% or 15% to estimated expenses to ensure that you have enough money.

Warm-up: 1974 ÷ 8.4 [235]
864 ÷ 7.2 [120]
516 × 0.40 [206.4]
289 × 0.40 [115.6]

See page 40 of *Consumer Forms and Problems.*

Related Problems

You may wish to discuss the advantages and disadvantages of paying with cash, with traveler's checks, or with credit cards.

Find the total estimate for each trip. Round the amount of gasoline to the nearest liter. Assume gasoline costs $0.40 per liter.

1. Clifford White Feather plans to drive from Chicago to Minneapolis, a distance of 665 km. His car's fuel economy rate is about 8 km/L. He plans to have 2 meals for $6 each.
$45.20
2. Lucinda Beran plans to drive 500 km from Pittsburgh to Philadelphia. Her car's fuel economy rate is about 9 km/L. She is allowing $10 for tolls and $5 for food. She plans to stay overnight in a motel for about $37.50.
$74.90
3. Mr. and Mrs. Robb and their four sons are taking a 2300-km camping trip. They plan to spend $40 for campsites. The camper rental fee is $35 per day. While pulling a camper, their car has a fuel economy rate of 3 km/L. They estimate $30 per day for food for the 5-day trip.
$671.80
4. Kristen and Jamie Cooper plan to drive 157 km to Houston to shop. The car's fuel economy rate is about 8.2 km/L. They are each allowing $7 for lunch and $200 for shopping. They expect to pay $6 for parking. They will return home that evening.
$435.20
5. Ron Finkner is taking his two children to an amusement park. Tickets for the park cost $8 each. Ron expects to pay about $6 each for food. The park is 125 km from their home. The car's fuel economy rate is about 8.8 km/L. They will return home in the evening.
$53.20
6. Six people are taking a van on a 400-km round trip to a football game. The van's fuel economy rate is about 5 km/L. Tickets to the game cost $12 each. Each person plans to spend $25 for food. Motel rooms cost $50 per room. Three rooms will be needed for one night. To the nearest cent, what is the estimated cost of the trip per person?
$67.33

Break Time

Four jumbo jets and three super jets can carry as many passengers in five trips as three jumbo jets and five super jets can carry in four trips.

Which jet is bigger, jumbo or super?
Super

Objective: Compute air fares by using various plans from a fare summary.

Air Travel

For any given air trip, there are usually several different fares available. This summary lists types of service and the fares available for flights from Chicago to various other U.S. cities.

This summary of fares is based on information as of June 1, 1981.

FARE SUMMARY from Chicago to							
Fare code	Denver	Houston	Los Angeles	Miami	Minneapolis/ St. Paul	New Orleans	New York/ Newark
One way							
F	$294	$223	$470	$226	$142	$198	$258
Y	$210	$185	$336	$219	$109	$165	$184
FN	$210	$185	$336	$219	$109	$165	$184
YN	$168	$148	$269	$175	$87	$132	$147
Round trip							
Ex	$289	$240	$520	$373	$186	$259	$316

Fares include Federal Transportation Tax. All fares and service are subject to change.

Notice that the fare for coach (Y) is the same as the fare for night first class (FN).

Explanation of codes

F—First class FN—Night first class
Y—Coach YN—Night coach
Children's fare (ages 2–11) for above: $\frac{3}{4}$ of adult fare

Ex—Excursion (round trip only)
Children's fare (ages 2–11) for above: One-way adult coach fare

Warm-up: $\frac{3}{4} \times 60$ [45]
$\frac{3}{4} \times 256$ [192]
2×445 [890]
3×179 [537]

Problem

Kathi Bishop and her children, ages 8 and 14, plan to fly from Chicago to Houston. What is the total fare if they fly night coach?

Solution

Strategy

- Read the table to find the night coach (YN) fare.
  $148
- Multiply by $\frac{3}{4}$ to find the child's fare.
  $\frac{3}{4} \times \$148 = \$111$
- Add two adult fares and one child's fare to find the total.
  $148 + $148 + $111 = $407

Conclusion
The total fare for Kathi and her children is $407.

You might point out the difference in cost between the answers to problems 4 and 5.

Related Problems

Find the total one-way fare from Chicago.

1. One adult flying coach to New York
   $184
2. Four adults flying coach to New York
   $736
3. One adult and two children, ages 10 and 15, flying coach to Denver
   $577.50
4. Two adults and three children, ages 3, 5, and 8, flying first class to Los Angeles
   $1997.50
5. Two adults and three children, ages 4, 7, and 10, flying night coach to Los Angeles
   $1143.25

Find the total round-trip fare from Chicago.

6. One adult flying round trip night first class to Miami
   $438
7. One adult and one child, age 7, flying round trip first class to Minneapolis
   $497
8. Two adults and one child, age 3, flying excursion to New Orleans
   $683
9. One adult and three children, ages 4, 9, and 15, flying excursion to New York
   $1000
10. If Kathi Bishop and her children fly round trip from Chicago to Houston, how much money could they save by flying excursion rather than by flying night coach?
    $149

Objective: Compute the cost of renting a car, using given rates.

Renting a Car

Warm-up:

3 × 24 [72]
285 × 0.15 [42.75]
469 × 0.15 [70.35]
84 + 56.75 [140.75]

See page 41 of *Consumer Forms and Problems.*

Dee and Stan Folsom rented a car during their vacation. The cost of car rental includes both a time charge and a distance charge. A chart listing the charges for various classes of cars is given below.

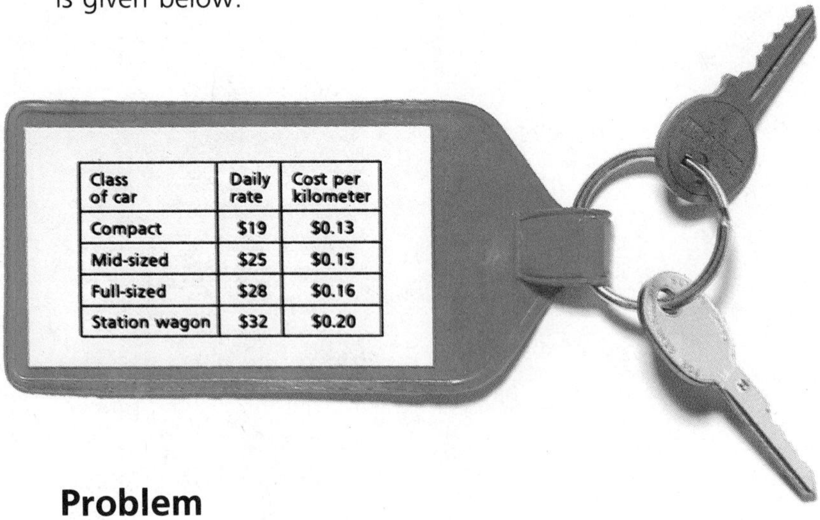

Class of car	Daily rate	Cost per kilometer
Compact	$19	$0.13
Mid-sized	$25	$0.15
Full-sized	$28	$0.16
Station wagon	$32	$0.20

Problem

The Folsoms rented a mid-sized car for 3 days and drove 401 km. What was their rental cost?

Solution

Strategy

- Read the chart to find the daily rate for a mid-sized car.
  $25
- Multiply by 3 to find the time charge.
  $3 \times \$25 = \$75$
- Read the chart to find the cost per kilometer.
  $0.15
- Multiply by 401 to find the distance charge.
  $401 \times \$0.15 = \$60.15$
- Add to find the total rental cost.
  $\$75 + \$60.15 = \$135.15$

Conclusion

The Folsoms' rental cost was $135.15.

Related Problems

Use the rates in the table to find each rental cost.

1. Mid-sized car
   Rented 3 days
   Driven 500 km
   $150
2. Mid-sized car
   Rented 7 days
   Driven 975 km
   $321.25
3. Full-sized car
   Rented 2 days
   Driven 585 km
   $149.60
4. Full-sized car
   Rented 1 day
   Driven 42 km
   $34.72
5. Compact car
   Rented 6 days
   Driven 1137 km
   $261.81
6. Mid-sized car
   Rented 1 day
   Driven 217 km
   $57.55
7. Compact car
   Rented 4 days
   Driven 478 km
   $138.14
8. Station wagon
   Rented 2 days
   Driven 620 km
   $188
9. Full-sized car
   Rented 2 days
   Driven 974 km
   $211.84
10. If the distance driven is 850 km, how much less does it cost to rent a compact car than to rent a station wagon for 3 days?
    $98.50

CALCULATOR APPLICATIONS

Car-Rental Costs

Complete the table. Find the number of kilometers driven by subtracting the "start" reading from the "end" reading. Use the rental rates given on page 180.

	Class	Odometer		Distance driven	Distance charge	Number of days	Time charge	Rental cost
		Start	End					
1.	Mid-sized	6,285	7,113	828 km	$124.20	7	$175	$299.20
2.	Mid-sized	11,247	11,697	450 km	$67.50	4	$100	$167.50
3.	Full-sized	9,505	10,049	544 km	$87.04	4	$112	$199.04
4.	Full-sized	8,377	8,424	47 km	$7.52	1	$28	$35.52
5.	Station wagon	30,621	31,000	379 km	$75.80	3	$96	$171.80
6.	Station wagon	27,926	28,555	629 km	$125.80	3	$96	$221.80

The rental agency has this special rate.

COMPACT GETAWAY SPECIAL

7 days w/1600 km	**$129**
Each day over 7	**$19**
Each km over 1600	**$0.20**

For $129 a customer can rent a compact car for as long as 7 days and drive it as far as 1600 km. However, if the car is kept longer and/or driven farther, there are extra charges. If a car is rented for 10 days and driven 2000 km, the extra charges are for 3 days (10 − 7) and for 400 km (2000 − 1600).

$129	Basic charge
57	Extra time (3 × $19)
+ 80	Extra distance (400 × $0.20)
$266	Rental cost

Find the rental cost using the *Compact Getaway Special* rate.

7. Rent for 10 days; drive 1700 km
$206

8. Rent for 9 days; drive 2054 km
$257.80

9. Rent for 10 days; drive 1200 km
$186

10. Rent for 5 days; drive 1961 km
$201.20

11. Rent for 3 days; drive 1400 km
$129

12. Rent for 8 days; drive 737 km
$148

13. Rent for 7 days; drive 2700 km
$349

14. Using the rental rates on page 180, find the cost of renting a compact car for 7 days and driving 2700 km.
$484

15. Use your answers to problems 13 and 14. Which rate costs less? How much less does the rate cost?
Compact Getaway Special; $135

Objective: Compute and compare the costs of traveling by various modes of transportation.

Travel Agent

Warm-up:
$\frac{1}{2} \times 168$ [84]
$\frac{3}{4} \times 176$ [132]
4×318 [1272]
$285 + 70 + 14$ [369]

Career Cluster: Business Contact Gordon Wickes is a travel agent at the Cross-Country Travel Agency. He points out to his customers the advantages of various methods of travel.

Gordon prepared this chart for a trip from Denver to San Francisco.

One-way costs, per person		Denver to San Francisco	
	Bus	Train	Plane
Adult fare	$115	Coach $142 Single slumber $202 Bedroom (2 people) $519	F $318 Y $204 FN $227 YN $182
Children's fare (ages 2–11)	$\frac{1}{2}$ adult fare	$\frac{1}{2}$ adult fare	$\frac{3}{4}$ adult fare
Meals	About $20	About $35	No charge
Transportation to center of city	None	None	$8–$20

Air fares in this chart are coded as explained on page 178.

Problem

Harriet Kaplan and her daughter, age 10, asked Gordon for an estimate of the cost of taking a bus from Denver to San Francisco. What was Gordon's estimate of their travel expenses?

Solution

Strategy

- Read the table to find the adult fare. $115
- Multiply by $\frac{1}{2}$ to find a child's fare. $\frac{1}{2} \times \$115 = \$57.50$
- Multiply the meal cost by 2 to find the cost of food for two people. $2 \times \$20 = \$40$
- Add to find the total. $\$115 + \$57.50 + \$40 = \$212.50$

Conclusion

Gordon's estimate was $212.50.

Related Problems

Find the travel expenses for one adult going from Denver to San Francisco.

1. By bus
   $135
2. By train, single slumber
   $237
3. By plane, coach (Y). Allow $8 for bus to hotel.
   $212
4. By plane, first class (F). Allow $18 for taxi to hotel.
   $336

Find the travel expenses for two adults and one child, age 8, going from Denver to San Francisco.

5. By bus
   $347.50
6. By train, coach
   $460
7. By plane, coach (Y). Allow $8 each for bus to hotel.
   $585
8. By plane, first class (F). Allow $18 for a taxi for all three people.
   $892.50
9. Find the round-trip cost from Denver to San Francisco for four adults using two bedrooms on the train.
   $2356
10. Which method costs less for four adults going round trip from Denver to San Francisco: by train, renting two bedrooms; or by plane, flying night coach (YN)? How much less?
    Flying night coach; $900

Skills Tune-Up

Dividing decimals, pages 12–13

Find the quotient to the nearest hundredth.

1. $43.17 \div 4$ 10.79
2. $53.56 \div 8$ 6.70
3. $5.857 \div 77$ 0.08
4. $0.0095 \div 0.14$ 0.07
5. $8.71 \div 0.62$ 14.05
6. $87.5 \div 6.2$ 14.11
7. $5.4 \div 6.7$ 0.81
8. $1.7 \div 3.24$ 0.52
9. $32.1 \div 5.12$ 6.27
10. $5.98 \div 5.06$ 1.18
11. $71.9 \div 6.02$ 11.94
12. $42.1 \div 6.92$ 6.08

Find the quotient to the nearest whole number.

13. $28.7 \div 5$ 6
14. $96.9 \div 8$ 12
15. $21.41 \div 3.7$ 6
16. $18.98 \div 9.3$ 2
17. $15.09 \div 5.2$ 3
18. $0.345 \div 0.06$ 6
19. $0.561 \div 0.07$ 8
20. $68 \div 0.4$ 170
21. $64 \div 0.8$ 80
22. $0.353 \div 0.174$ 2
23. $0.7456 \div 0.023$ 32
24. $0.3331 \div 0.042$ 8

Adding fractions and mixed numbers, pages 18–19

1. $\frac{1}{3} + \frac{3}{4}$ $1\frac{1}{12}$
2. $\frac{1}{14} + \frac{3}{7}$ $\frac{1}{2}$
3. $\frac{7}{12} + \frac{3}{4}$ $1\frac{1}{3}$
4. $\frac{4}{7} + \frac{2}{21}$ $\frac{2}{3}$
5. $\frac{1}{2} + \frac{4}{7}$ $1\frac{1}{14}$
6. $\frac{2}{15} + \frac{2}{3}$ $\frac{4}{5}$
7. $\frac{8}{9} + \frac{5}{12}$ $1\frac{11}{36}$
8. $5\frac{1}{8} + \frac{11}{12}$ $6\frac{1}{24}$
9. $\frac{1}{6} + 3\frac{9}{10}$ $4\frac{1}{15}$
10. $4\frac{3}{4} + \frac{2}{9}$ $4\frac{35}{36}$
11. $5\frac{3}{4} + 2\frac{7}{12}$ $8\frac{1}{3}$
12. $7\frac{4}{5} + 8\frac{9}{20}$ $16\frac{1}{4}$
13. $4\frac{7}{9} + 3\frac{1}{18}$ $7\frac{5}{6}$
14. $3\frac{1}{4} + 1\frac{7}{8}$ $5\frac{1}{8}$
15. $1\frac{1}{3} + 5\frac{3}{5}$ $6\frac{14}{15}$
16. $2\frac{7}{10} + 8\frac{1}{6}$ $10\frac{13}{15}$
17. $5\frac{9}{16} + 2\frac{5}{8}$ $8\frac{3}{16}$
18. $3\frac{3}{8} + 5\frac{1}{5}$ $8\frac{23}{40}$
19. $4\frac{9}{10} + 3\frac{1}{2} + 10\frac{3}{5}$ 19
20. $13\frac{1}{3} + 4\frac{4}{5} + 6\frac{1}{2}$ $24\frac{19}{30}$
21. $8\frac{1}{3} + 6\frac{3}{4} + 3\frac{5}{8}$ $18\frac{17}{24}$

Subtracting fractions and mixed numbers, pages 18–19

1. $\frac{5}{6} - \frac{1}{3}$ $\frac{1}{2}$
2. $\frac{3}{4} - \frac{1}{2}$ $\frac{1}{4}$
3. $\frac{7}{8} - \frac{1}{2}$ $\frac{3}{8}$
4. $\frac{2}{3} - \frac{1}{5}$ $\frac{7}{15}$
5. $\frac{7}{8} - \frac{1}{6}$ $\frac{17}{24}$
6. $\frac{2}{3} - \frac{1}{2}$ $\frac{1}{6}$
7. $\frac{4}{7} - \frac{1}{2}$ $\frac{1}{14}$
8. $\frac{7}{10} - \frac{1}{4}$ $\frac{9}{20}$
9. $3 - \frac{5}{8}$ $2\frac{3}{8}$
10. $12 - \frac{1}{5}$ $11\frac{4}{5}$
11. $6\frac{1}{8} - 3\frac{5}{8}$ $2\frac{1}{2}$
12. $9\frac{5}{8} - 3\frac{7}{8}$ $5\frac{3}{4}$
13. $11 - 6\frac{2}{3}$ $4\frac{1}{3}$
14. $6 - 5\frac{7}{10}$ $\frac{3}{10}$
15. $13\frac{7}{8} - 4\frac{5}{16}$ $9\frac{9}{16}$
16. $16\frac{4}{5} - 9\frac{3}{4}$ $7\frac{1}{20}$
17. $19\frac{3}{10} - 12\frac{5}{6}$ $6\frac{7}{15}$
18. $8\frac{1}{3} - 4\frac{8}{15}$ $3\frac{4}{5}$
19. $15\frac{5}{6} - 9\frac{1}{2}$ $6\frac{1}{3}$
20. $16\frac{3}{10} - 7\frac{7}{15}$ $8\frac{5}{6}$
21. $10\frac{1}{4} - 2\frac{5}{6}$ $7\frac{5}{12}$

Chapter 9 Review

Reading a distance chart, pages 172–173

1. Use the chart below to find the distance from Atlanta to Cincinnati to Chicago.
1214 kilometers

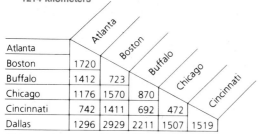

	Atlanta	Boston	Buffalo	Chicago	Cincinnati
Atlanta					
Boston	1720				
Buffalo	1412	723			
Chicago	1176	1570	870		
Cincinnati	742	1411	692	472	
Dallas	1296	2929	2211	1507	1519

Distances between cities in kilometers

Finding distance and travel time, pages 174–175

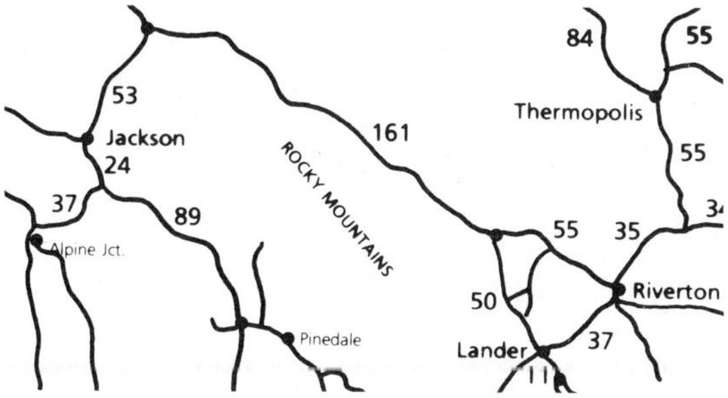

2. Distances on the map are given in kilometers. What is the distance from Jackson to Riverton?
269 kilometers

3. Copy the card below to measure the distance between Jackson and Pinedale. 100 kilometers

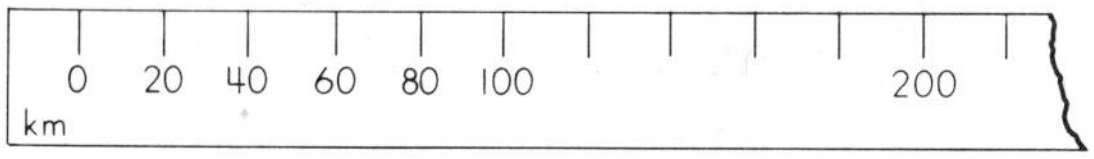

Expenses on the road, pages 176–177

4. Warren Crown has planned a 1260-km trip. His car's fuel economy rate is about 6.2 km/L. If gas costs $0.40 per liter, find the cost of gas for Warren's trip. (Round the amount of gas to the nearest liter.)
$81.20

5. Linda Nelson has planned a trip. She is allowing $50 for gasoline, $20 for meals, and $3 for tolls. Find her total travel expense.
$73

Air travel, pages 178–179

FARE SUMMARY from Chicago to			
Fare code	Denver	Houston	Los Angeles
One way			
F	$294	$223	$470
Y	$210	$185	$336

6. Find the total one-way fare for two adults and one child, age 6, flying coach (Y) from Chicago to Houston. A child's fare is $\frac{3}{4}$ of an adult fare.
$508.75

7. Find the round-trip fare for two adults flying first class (F) from Chicago to Los Angeles.
$1880

Renting a car, page 180

8. Molly Little Horse rented a car for 4 days, driving it 673 km. She was charged $25 per day and $0.15 per kilometer driven. Find her rental cost.
$200.95

Travel agent, pages 182–183

One-way costs Denver to San Francisco				
	Train		Plane	
Adult fare	Coach	$142	F	$318
	Single slumber	$202	Y	$204
	Bedroom (2 people)	$519	FN	$227
			YN	$182

9. Find the total travel expense for three adults going from Denver to San Francisco by train in 3 single slumbers.
$606

10. Find the travel expense for three adults flying first class (F) from Denver to San Francisco and sharing a taxi for $15.
$969

Chapter 9 Test

Number of test items - 10					
Number missed	1	2	3	4	5
Percent correct	90	80	70	60	50

1. Use the chart below to find the distance from Dallas to Chicago to Boston.
3077 kilometers

	Atlanta	Boston	Buffalo	Chicago	Cincinnati	Dallas
Atlanta						
Boston	1720					
Buffalo	1412	723				
Chicago	1176	1570	870			
Cincinnati	742	1411	692	472		
Dallas	1296	2929	2211	1507	1519	
Denver	2256	3203	2485	1636	1882	1262

Distances between cities in kilometers

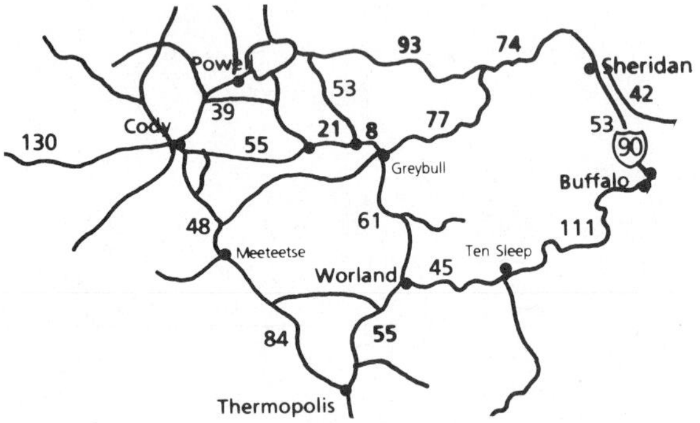

2. Distances on the map are given in kilometers. What is the distance from Cody to Greybull?
84 kilometers

3. Copy the card below to measure the distance between Cody and Thermopolis.
120 kilometers

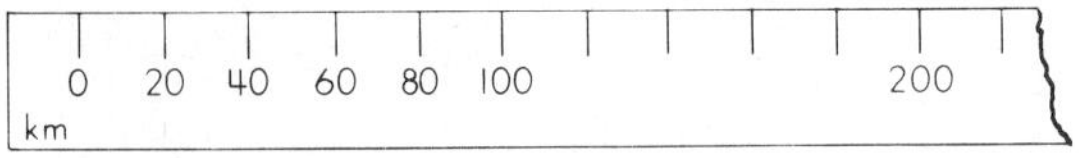

4. Bill Binkoff has planned a 926-km trip. His car's fuel economy rate is about 7.2 km/L. If gas costs $0.40 per liter, find the cost of gas for Bill's trip. (Round the amount of gas to the nearest liter.)
$51.60

5. Dave Olson has planned a trip. He is allowing $60 for gasoline, $35 for meals, and $90 for motels. Find Dave's total travel expense.
$185

FARE SUMMARY from Chicago to			
Fare code	Denver	Houston	Los Angeles
One way			
F	$294	$223	$470
Y	$210	$185	$336

6. Find the total one-way fare for two adults and one child, age 4, flying first class (F) from Chicago to Denver. A child's fare is $\frac{3}{4}$ of an adult fare.
$808.50

7. Find the round-trip fare for two adults flying coach (Y) from Chicago to Houston.
$740

8. Lee Parks rented a car for 5 days, driving it 523 km. She was charged $28 per day and $0.16 per kilometer driven. Find her rental cost.
$223.68

One-way costs Denver to San Francisco				
	Train		Plane	
Adult fare	Coach	$142	F	$318
	Single slumber	$202	Y	$204
	Bedroom (2 people)	$519	FN	$227
			YN	$182

9. Find the travel expense for two adults going from Denver to San Francisco by train in 2 single slumbers.
$404

10. Find the travel expense for two adults flying coach (Y) from Denver to San Francisco and sharing a taxi for $18.
$426

Unit 3 Test

Number of test items - 20

Number missed	1	2	3	4	5	6	7	8	9	10
Percent correct	95	90	85	80	75	70	65	60	55	50

Choose the best answer.

Pages 132–133

1. The suggested retail price of a car is $5950. Find the sticker price with power steering ($185) and a radio ($58).

   A $243 C $5707
   B $6193 D $8135

Page 134

2. Martha Long Bow offered a dealer 10% less than the $8929 sticker price for a new car. What was Martha's offer? Round to the nearest hundred dollars.

   A $900 C $8700
   B $9600 D $8000

Pages 136–137

3. A used car costs $2125 plus 5% sales tax. Find the sales tax.

   A $2231.25 C $106.25
   B $10.62 D $1062.50

Pages 138–139

4. The selling price of a car is $8930. Find the net price with a trade-in allowance of $1685.

   A $7300 C $7245
   B $10,615 D $7692

Pages 140–142

5. Ann made a down payment of $1200 on a $7695 car. She financed the balance for 36 months with monthly payments of $240.25. Find the finance charge.

   A $2154 C $7350
   B $6495 D $2450

Pages 144–145

6. For all cars he sells, Hal receives 25% of the dealer's profit. What does Hal receive on a dealer's profit of $9800?

   A $245 C $7350
   B $12,250 D $2450

Pages 150–151

7. Ben Valdez drove 528 km and used 85 L of gasoline. Find his car's fuel economy rate to the nearest tenth.

   A 6.3 km/L C 44,880 km/L
   B 6.0 km/L D 6.2 km/L

Pages 152–153

8. Chang bought a new car for $7500 five years ago. The trade-in value now is 30% of the original selling price. Find the trade-in value now.

   A $2250 C $5250
   B $9750 D $225

Page 154

9. To find the total depreciation of a car, multiply the monthly depreciation rate times the number of months times the original price. The original price of a car was $8295. Find the total depreciation after 30 months at 2.5% per month. Round to the nearest dollar.

   A $2089 C $6200
   B $2074 D $6221

Pages 156–159

10. A mechanic is paid 40% of the labor charge on each job. What is the mechanic paid for a job in which the total charge for parts is $21.75 and the total labor charge is $65?

    A $8.70 C $86.75
    B $26 D $34.70

Pages 160–161

11. Joan pays a base premium of $174.25 for liability insurance. She also pays 20% of the base for increased bodily injury coverage and 8% of the base for increased property damage coverage. Find her annual premium.

    A $48.79 C $125.46
    B $209.10 D $223.04

Pages 162–163

12. Lucy, age 19, is buying collision and comprehensive insurance, both with $50 deductible. Find her combined premium.

Driver	Collision premium for $50 deductible	Comprehensive premium for $50 deductible
Teen female	$338.66	$55.60
Teen male	$652.54	$55.60

A $283.06 **C** $394.26

B $708.14 **D** $237.32

Pages 164–165

13. Sonia drove 14,000 km last year. Her total car expenses were $4920. To the nearest tenth of a cent, what was the cost per kilometer to operate her car?

A 40¢ **C** 30¢

B 35.2¢ **D** 35.1¢

Pages 166–167

14. Joy takes the train and bus to and from work each day. The train ticket is $55.85 a month and the bus fare is $0.75 each way. Find Joy's monthly travel cost based on 20 working days per month.

A $57.35 **C** $70.85

B $56.60 **D** $85.85

Pages 172–173

15. Use the chart to find the distance from Chicago to Buffalo to Atlanta. Distances between cities are given in kilometers.

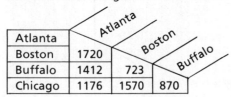

	Atlanta	Boston	Buffalo
Atlanta			
Boston	1720		
Buffalo	1412	723	
Chicago	1176	1570	870

A 2282 km **C** 2135 km

B 2746 km **D** 3616 km

Pages 174–175

16. To the nearest hour, what is the travel time for 385 km at a rate of 80 km/h?

A 4 hours **C** 5 hours

B 3 hours **D** 6 hours

Pages 176–177

17. Stuart plans to drive 1350 km in a car with a fuel economy rate of 9 km/L. He estimates he will spend $0.40 per liter for gasoline, $30 for lodging, and $55 for meals. Estimate the total cost.

A $60 **C** $540

B $145 **D** $625

Pages 178–179

18. Find the total round-trip air fare for one adult and one 10-year-old child from New Orleans to Chicago. The one-way adult fare is $165. Children (ages 2–11) pay $\frac{3}{4}$ of the adult fare.

A $288.75 **C** $123.75

B $577.50 **D** $330

Page 180

19. A car rents for $21 per day plus $0.14 per kilometer. Find the cost of renting the car for 2 days and driving 1000 km.

A $42 **C** $182

B $140 **D** $161

Pages 182–183

20. For an adult, the one-way bus fare from Denver to San Francisco is $115. Children (ages 2–11) pay $\frac{1}{2}$ of the adult fare. Find the total bus fare for one adult and two children, ages 5 and 9, for a one-way bus trip from Denver to San Francisco.

A $230 **C** $57.50

B $172.50 **D** $287.50

 For an alternate form of the Unit 3 Test, see pages T61–T62 of this book and pages 23–24 of the *Test Masters*.

Break Time

The scenic route through Great Mountain Park is 83 km long. The direct route is 59 km long. How much shorter is the direct route?

If the number that is subtracted is a multiple of 10, the subtraction is easier.

Find 83 − 59 mentally.

THINK

Add 1 to 59 to get a multiple of 10. 59 + 1 = 60

Add 1 to 83. 83 + 1 = 84

Subtract 60 from 84. 84 − 60 = 24

The direct route is 24 km shorter.

Find 61 − 23 mentally.

THINK

Subtract 3 from 23 to get a multiple of 10. 23 − 3 = 20

Subtract 3 from 61. 61 − 3 = 58

Subtract 20 from 58. 58 − 20 = 38

The answer is 38.

Use a *multiple-of-10* method to subtract mentally. Write only the answer.

1. 73 − 29
44
2. 41 − 18
23
3. 95 − 37
58
4. 86 − 59
27
5. 62 − 25
37
6. 47 − 19
28
7. 91 − 47
44
8. 75 − 42
33
9. 56 − 27
29
10. 95 − 38
57
11. 82 − 69
13
12. 42 − 16
26
13. 81 − 45
36
14. 76 − 17
59
15. 63 − 26
37
16. 69 − 48
21
17. 87 − 22
65
18. 51 − 14
37
19. 87 − 29
58
20. 99 − 52
47
21. 126 − 19
107
22. 153 − 28
125
23. 283 − 48
235
24. 394 − 87
307
25. 275 − 56
219
26. 118 − 59
59
27. 204 − 76
128
28. 263 − 89
174

Auto Financing

The problems on page 141 can be extended using the program for problem 20 by giving annual interest rates instead of monthly payments.

Steve Larson plans to buy a new car. He is comparing the cost of financing a loan at different lending institutions. Steve wrote the program shown to help him compare loans. He can try combinations of different interest rates and numbers of months to repay to calculate a monthly payment that will fit his budget.

Lines 30, 50, and 70 Only these values need to be entered to calculate the monthly payment.

Data required	*Name*
Amount to be financed	P
Annual rate of interest (%)	Y
Number of months to repay	N

Lines 20, 40, and 60 A PRINT statement before each INPUT statement shows what to enter.

Line 80 The annual interest rate is first divided by 100 so that it is in decimal form, and then it is divided by 12 fo find the rate per month.

Line 90 A formula is used to find the monthly payment (A). The symbol "^" is used to raise a number to a power.

These are some examples of the computation the computer would perform for the symbol ^.

Part of statement	*Computation*
5^2	5×5
3^4	$3 \times 3 \times 3 \times 3$
8^N (6 is entered for N)	$8 \times 8 \times 8 \times 8 \times 8 \times 8$

The number following ^ indicates the number of times the number preceding ^ is used as a factor. In this program, the number N following ^ is entered in line 70 and can vary each time the program is run. The number preceding ^ depends upon the data entered in line 50 and the result of the computation in line 80. Without a computer, the computation in line 90 would be very complicated and tedious.

Line 100 The amount of the monthly payment is rounded to the nearest cent.

Lines 110–140 The given values are printed along with the monthly payment so that different financing plans can be compared.

Steve can borrow \$5000 at 18% annual interest. By running the program, he found that the monthly payments for 24 months would be \$249.62, and the monthly payments for 36 months would be \$180.76.

These problems should be done using a computer. Modifications can be paper-and-pencil activities.

```
10 REM  MONTHLY PAYMENT PROGRAM
20 PRINT "AMOUNT TO FINANCE";
30 INPUT P
40 PRINT "INTEREST RATE";
50 INPUT Y
60 PRINT "NUMBER OF MONTHS";
70 INPUT N
80 LET I=(Y/100)/12
90 LET A=P*((I*(1+I)^N)/((1+I)^N-1))
100 LET A=INT(A*100+.5)/100
110 PRINT "AMOUNT TO FINANCE   $";P
120 PRINT "ANNUAL INTEREST RATE";Y;"%"
130 PRINT "NUMBER OF MONTHS";N
140 PRINT "MONTHLY PAYMENT   $";A
150 END
```

15.
```
20 PRINT "TOTAL COST";
30 INPUT T
32 PRINT "DOWN PAYMENT";
33 INPUT D
34 LET P=T-D
105 PRINT "TOTAL COST     $";T
106 PRINT "DOWN PAYMENT     $";D
```

Answers for computer applications are often in an abbreviated form. In all program modifications shown, the changes and/or additions incorporate previous modifications and will vary. Samples are given.

Give the output for the program above when

1. P is 2500, Y is 17, and N is 18.
   See below.
2. P is 4800, Y is 18, and N is 30.
   MONTHLY PAYMENT $199.87
3. P is 5250, Y is 19, and N is 24.
   MONTHLY PAYMENT $264.65
4. P is 6400, Y is 18.5, and N is 36.
   MONTHLY PAYMENT $232.98
5. P is 7185, Y is 17.75, and N is 36.
   MONTHLY PAYMENT $258.85
6. \$3850 is to be financed at 18% annually for 24 months.
   MONTHLY PAYMENT $192.21
7. \$7210 is to be financed at 16.75% annually for 36 months.
   MONTHLY PAYMENT $256.16
8. \$5500 is to be financed at 17% annually for 30 months.
   MONTHLY PAYMENT $226.32
9. \$6820 is to be financed at 17.5% annually for 18 months.
   MONTHLY PAYMENT $433.53
10. \$9000 is to be financed at 16.5% annually for 42 months.
    MONTHLY PAYMENT $283.51

For which finance plan is the monthly payment lower:

11. \$3000 at 17.5% annually for 24 months, or \$3500 at 18% annually for 30 months?
    $3500 at 18% annually for 30 months
12. \$6600 at 19% annually for 36 months, or \$6250 at 17.5% annually for 30 months?
    $6600 at 19% annually for 36 months
13. \$4785 at 18.5% annually for 18 months, or \$5000 at 17% annually for 24 months?
    $5000 at 17% annually for 24 months
14. \$7100 at 16.5% annually for 30 months, or \$6800 at 18% annually for 30 months?
    $6800 at 18% annually for 30 months
15. Modify the program so that the total cost of the car and the down payment are entered. Calculate the amount to be financed in the program.
    See above.
16. Give the output when the total cost of the car is \$7259, the down payment is \$2000, the annual interest rate is 17%, and the number of monthly payments is 30.
    MONTHLY PAYMENT $216.40
17. For which finance plan is the monthly payment lower: financing a car with a total cost of \$8745 and a \$4000 down payment at 16.5% annually for 28 months, or financing a car with a total cost of \$9282 and a \$5000 down payment at 16.8% annually for 24 months? $8745 with a $4000 down payment at 16.5% annually for 28 months
18. Modify the program to include the cost of financing as part of the output.
    See below.
19. Give the output when the total cost of the car is \$8378, the down payment is \$3500, the annual interest rate is 18.5%, and the number of monthly payments is 24.
    See below.
20. Modify the program to include the total sale price as part of the output. Remember that the total sale price is the sum of the monthly payments and the down payment.
    See below.
21. Give the output when the total cost of the car is \$10,583, the down payment is \$4000, the annual interest rate is 16.75%, and the number of monthly payments is 30.

    TOTAL SALE PRICE $ 12102.4
    MONTHLY PAYMENT $ 270.08

1. AMOUNT TO FINANCE $ 2500
   ANNUAL INTEREST RATE 17 %
   NUMBER OF MONTHS 18
   MONTHLY PAYMENT $ 158.33

18.
```
104 LET C=A*N-P
135 PRINT "COST OF FINANCING     $";C
```

19. COST OF FINANCING $ 995.04
    MONTHLY PAYMENT $ 244.71

20.
```
107 LET S=A*N+D
136 PRINT "TOTAL SALE PRICE     $";S
```

Unit 4 Housing

Chapter 10 Renting and Decorating a Home

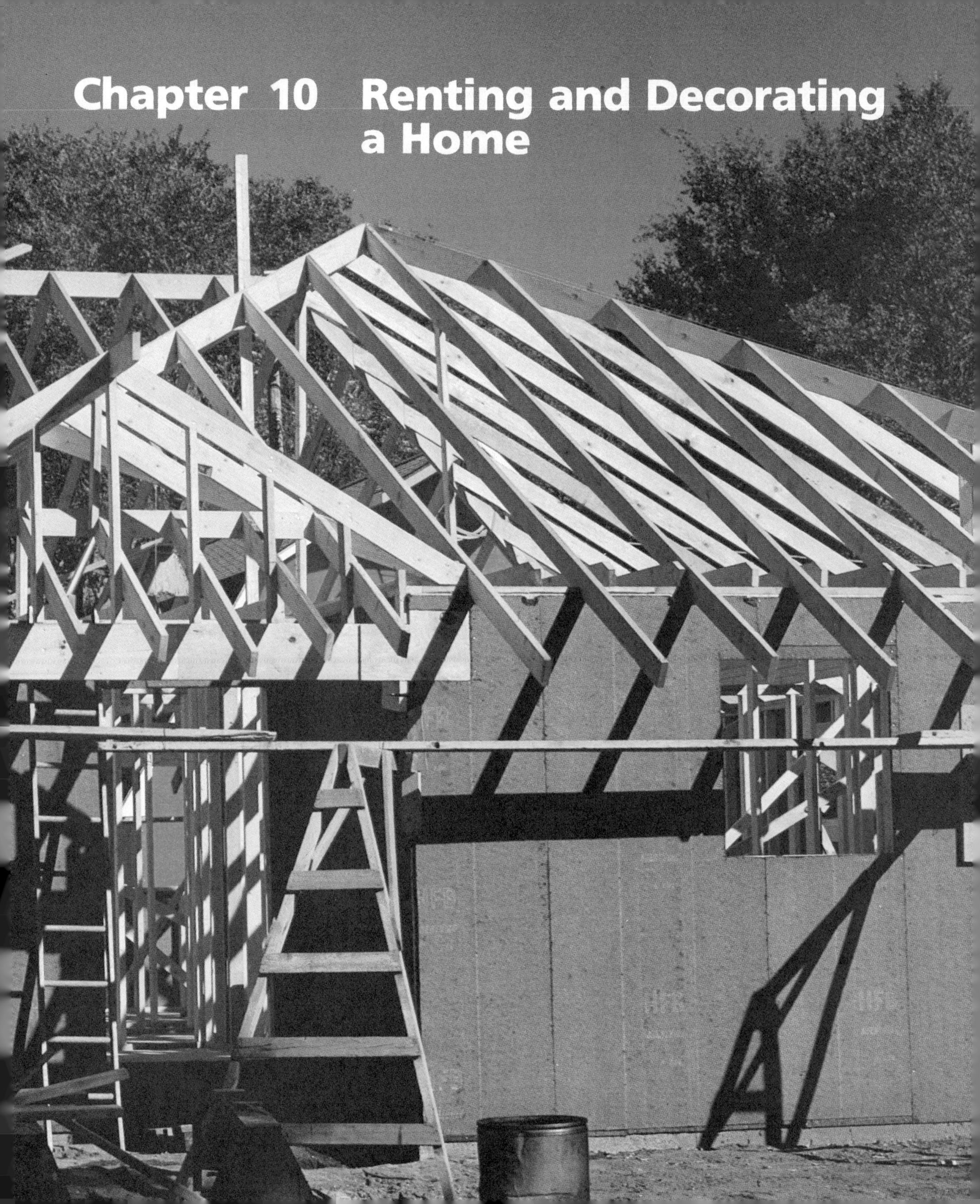

Objective: Compute a reasonable amount to spend for rent by using a common guideline.

Amount to Spend for Rent

See page T35 for additional notes and activities for Chapter 10.

Emily Coale and Paul Hines are trying to determine how much they can spend for rent when they get married. A common guideline is: *Do not spend more than one week's gross pay for shelter each month*.

Problem

Paul works 40 hours per week at $6.80 per hour. Emily is unemployed now. What is the most they can spend for rent?

Solution

Strategy

• Multiply hourly pay by 40 to find weekly pay. $40 \times \$6.80 = \$272$

Conclusion

Paul and Emily should not spend more than $272 per month for rent.

Related Problems

Remind students that they can use estimation to check their answers. Note that annual salaries are given in problems 9–12.

For each problem, use the given pay rate to find the maximum amount that should be spent for rent each month. Assume a 40-hour work week.

1. $6.30 per hour
$252

2. $5.75 per hour
$230

3. $8.60 per hour
$344

4. $7.80 per hour
$312

5. $7.25 per hour
$290

6. $9.50 per hour
$380

7. $12.50 per hour
$500

8. $10.95 per hour
$438

9. $10,816 per year
$208

10. $11,180 per year
$215

11. $15,600 per year
$300

12. $19,500 per year
$375

Warm-up: 40 × 6.25 [250]
10,260 ÷ 12 [855]
0.28 × 12,800 [3584]
2472 ÷ 12 [206]

Emily and Paul read in a survey that families who rent spend about 28% of their annual net income on shelter. This amount includes utilities.

Remind students of the difference between net and gross income.

Problem

Paul's annual net income is $10,750. According to the survey, about how much will Paul and Emily probably spend for shelter each month?

Solution

Strategy

- Multiply annual net income by 0.28 to find expected annual amount for shelter. $0.28 \times \$10,750 = \$3010$
- Divide by 12 to find monthly amount for shelter. Round to the nearest dollar. $\$3010 \div 12 \approx \$251$

Conclusion

Paul and Emily will probably spend about $251 for shelter each month.

Related Problems

Using the 28% from the survey, find the expected monthly payment for shelter for the net incomes given. Round each answer to the nearest dollar.

13. $9802
$229
14. $7633
$178
15. $11,468
$268
16. $10,575
$247
17. $15,650
$365
18. $18,000
$420
19. $21,000
$490
20. $12,042
$281

21. Emily is looking for a full-time job. If she can earn at least $5 per hour for a 40-hour week, how much could she and Paul spend for rent each month? (Use the guideline on page 194.)
$472

22. If Emily gets a job that gives her a net income of $7640 per year, about how much would she and Paul spend for shelter each month? Round your answer to the nearest dollar. (Use the survey.)
$429

Objective: Compare the costs of renting by finding the expected monthly expenses.

Selecting a Place to Rent

Unfurnished Apartments for Rent Cont'd 175

3 BEDROOM lower, $325 month; 2 bedroom upper, $275 month.

3 BEDROOM apartment, upper, westside, 1 mo. security deposit required. No pets. $250 plus utilities. 1-7.

3 ROOM LOWER. Close to medical center & town. Off-street parking. Adults only. plus electric.

5 ROOM UPPER. Off-street parking. Washer/dryer hookup. Separate utilities. Security deposit. Lease. Prefer older couple. No pets.

5 ROOM upper apartment, westside, carpeting & all utilities. $310 per mo. Available April 1.

OAK CREEK. Aurora. Sublease deluxe 1 bedroom apartment. Air-conditioning, carpeted, heat, pool. Available 3/1. $265/mo.

PLANO. Modern 2 bedroom apartment. Heat & appliances furnished. New carpeting, air-conditioned. $250/mo. Security deposit required. or Emerson

RENT WITH or without option to buy. Applying security toward option. Financing arranged. Bright sunny 3 bedroom, 1½ bath townhome, central air, full carpet & no wax, full basement. On Monomoy St. $340/mo. Call Paul at

S.W. EXCELLENT 2 bedroom duplex with garage, large yard, appliances, disposal, air-conditioning, utility room, 1½ baths. 1 yr. lease. 1 mos. security. preferably between 9 & 1.

MODERN apartment. Living room, kitchen, bath, partly furnished. West Aurora. $160. Utilities separate.

SPACIOUS 1 & 2 bedroom apartments. No pets.

SPACIOUS 2 bedroom townhouse. Appliances, air-conditioning, washer/dryer hookup. No pets.

SPECIAL
1 MONTH FREE RENT
bedroom deluxe apartment with gas included for heat, cooking & hot water. New carpeting, air, appliances, laundry, security system. Near E-W tollway. RTA at door.
MARYWOOD CIRCLE APARTMENTS

CONTEMPORARY tapestry ame for deluxe Crest Creek Condo, $220.

SUBLET 1 and 2 bedroom apartments available at reduced rates. Heritage Green Apartments.

SUGAR GROVE, new, 2 bedroom apartment, large rooms, $385 month, plus security deposit. Call days, evenings.

SUGAR GROVE: 2 bedroom apartment, $275 per month.

Meadow Green

No Security Deposit Needed
1 Month's Rent Will Move You In

- Tennis Courts
- Pool
- Playground
- Schools
- Shopping Centers
- All-elec. apts.

$290 plus elec.
1 BR
2 BR $325
OPEN DAILY 10 TO 6
Equal Housing Opportunity

Middletown
Country Club Living
1 & 2 Bedrm apts avail.
TENNIS
POOL
CLUBHOUSE
Your Own Washer/Dryer
Carpet thru-out
$265 plus utilities
2 BR $295
OPEN DAILY 10-6
Equal Housing Opportunity

CRANBROOK SQUARE
Next to Cranbrook Road Plaza
$320 Plus elec.
2 B.R., one bath
Available very soon
- Washer & Dryer
- Pool
- Tennis Courts
- Ind Controlled Heat & A/C
- All-electric Apts.

1 B.R. $275
OPEN DAILY 9-5 P.M.
SAT. & SUN. 12-6 P.M.
Equal Housing Opportunity

COPLEY AREA. 1 bedroom upper, full bath, carpeted, appliances, carport. All utilities included. $255/mo. No children or pets. Also, available furnished.

RIVER BEND APARTMENTS
We Have What You Need
Studios, 1 & 2 Bedrooms—From $210
- Spacious rooms
- Fully carpeted and newly decorated
- Air conditioning and appliances
- No heating bills

Colony Point Apts.
1, 2, & 3 Bedrooms
$260 1 Bedrm.
2 Bedroom $285
We Pay All Utilities
Directions: Route 37 north to Colony Point Drive
Mon.-Fri. 10-5
Sat. 12-4
Sun. 12-5
Equal Housing Opportunity

750 Nichols Rd.
Modern 1 & 2 bdrm. apts. Newly dec. Tile bath, hardwd floors. 1 bdrm. from $245—2 bdrm. from $270. Gas heat. All util. included except elec. Across from tennis, golf and park. Excl. trans.

SUMMIT—lg. 2 bdrm. twnhse. appl. crpt. bsmt. $285 + util.

2 Weeks free rent, 1 & 2 bedroom apartments. Call Peggy

West Aurora Plaza, deluxe 2 bedroom, garage, no children or pets. $265 month.

WEST SIDE--3 bedroom apartment, $350 month. Call Ed Kirch, charles b. doss & co.,

WEST. 1 bedroom. Open immediately. 517 Penn. Call after 4:30. $225 plus deposit.

WESTSIDE RESIDENTIAL area, 2 bedroom duplex, carpeted living & dining room, basement & garage, no pets. Security deposit. $250 per mo. 554

WESTSIDE. NEAT upper 2 bedroom apartment in quiet area. All appliances furnished.

YORKVILLE--Condos for rent including redecorated model. 2 bedroom, 1½ bath with 2 car attached garage. Situated on the Fox River.

The Villas
OPEN HOUSE
- Spacious rooms
- Dishwasher
- Large closets
- Convenient to shopping, schools
- Gas heat

2 BR
$240 plus elec.
Route 67 and I-21
Equal Housing Opportunity

SE, 1 room apartment, mature adult. Utilities furnished, deposit, $185.

SOUTHEAST, large sunny upper, heat included, off street parking, mature adult, no pets, lease/deposit.

UPPER 2 rooms & bath, utilities paid, off-street parking, 1-2 adults.

WEST ZENITH --Presidential Villas deluxe 1 & 2 bedrooms. Dishes, linens & TV available. NO LEASE. Call 10

Resorts, Cottages for Rent 220

BLUEBERRY HILL resort-/campground. Lake cottages. Hayward area.

Wanted to Rent 225

FAMILY WANTS to rent house with land to keep horse. Reasonable. Call after 6:30 p.m.

Antiques Continued 260

24th annual
ANTIQUE SHOW
55 Outstanding Dealers from 12 states, with over 25 FURNITURE DEALERS,
To Insure Authenticity EVERY ITEM SCREENED!
FRI., SAT., MAR. 13 & 14
11 a.m. - 9:30 p.m.
SUN., MARCH 15
11 a.m. - 5:00 p.m.
County Fairgrounds
Randall Rd., St. Charles,
Managed by:
Antique Dealers Association
Sponsored by:
ANTIQUE SHOW & SALE
Luncheon/Dinner Served

FOX VALLEY Flea Market, 410 Hill Ave., Aurora. Inside. Open every Sat. & Sun. all year, 8 a.m. to 4:30 p.m. Dealers & buyers wanted.

ANTIQUE SHOW and Flea Market, Sun. March 15. 8 a.m.-4 p.m. 4-H Fairgrounds, U.S. 30, Amboy, Ill. Meals. Admission $1. Robert Mitchell.

OPEN Sat. & Sun.--Regal Antiques, 640 E. New York St., Business Rte. 30.--Adv.

ANTIQUE BELL upright telephone-brass, $100. World War I bayonet & helmet, $35.

Garage Sales 265

GIGANTIC GARAGE SALE
Take a big 35% off on merchandise already reduced, 33% to 50% off. Savings on clothing for men, women, children.
FRIENDLY RESTAURANT
In the garage next to our store

MOVING SALE. Fri. Sa Sun. 8 am to 5 pm. Mens suit 50xl; executive desk; typ writer; easy chair; end bles; dinette; table sa tools; toys; clothes; ot household items. Al ter. Longwood Manor (Rt near E-W Tollway) ville.

For Sale Miscellaneous 275

(2)-20 in. Clark buff chines. 1 yr. $1100 for (1)-18 in. automatic scrubber machine, shape, $500. Toro lawnm 21 in. high speed, full der, 1 yr. $200.

1 MAN'S fine white VS mond. Best offer. carat.

1972 AMC GREMLIN.

Warm-up: 295 + 35 + 15 [345]
315 + 65 [380]
550 ÷ 2 [275]
480 ÷ 2 [240]

See page 42 of *Consumer Forms and Problems.*

Mike and Jake Amano plan to rent one of the two-bedroom units described in the ads on page 196. After investigating the cost of utilities, they came to the following conclusions.

— "Plus utilities" means that the tenants pay gas heat and electricity.

— The cost of gas heat averages about $60 per month.

— The cost of electricity, without electric heat, averages about $25 per month.

— The cost of electricity for an all-electric apartment averages about $90 per month.

Discuss with students local utility rates.

Problem

About how much will Mike and Jake pay for rent and utilities each month if they rent a two-bedroom unit at Middletown Apartments?

Solution

Strategy

• Read the ad and the guidelines above to determine the rent and the utility costs. Then add to find the total.

$295	Rent
60	Gas
+ 25	Electricity
$380	

Conclusion

Mike and Jake will probably pay about $380 each month for rent and utilities if they rent at Middletown Apartments.

Related Problems

Find the expected monthly total for rent and utilities for a two-bedroom unit at each location.

1. Summit
$370
2. 750 Nichols Road
$295
3. Cranbrook Square
$410
4. Meadow Green
$415
5. Colony Point
$285
6. The Villas
$265

7. List in order all the two-bedroom units and their monthly totals for rent and utilities. Begin with the least expensive.
See above.
8. Find the difference in monthly totals between the least expensive and the most expensive two-bedroom units.
$150
9. If Jake and Mike decide to split the rent and utility costs on a two-bedroom apartment at Cranbrook Square, about how much would each one pay every month?
$205

7.

The Villas	$265
Colony Point	$285
750 Nichols Road	$295
Summit	$370
Middletown Apartments	$380
Cranbrook Square	$410
Meadow Green	$415

You might also wish to discuss the "extras" offered at some locations, and that these extras often influence people's choices of apartments.

Objective: Read an electric meter and compute electric usage.

Meter Reader

Career Cluster: Business Detail Rhonda Davis works for the electric company as a meter reader. From the readings Rhonda takes, the company can determine the number of kilowatt-hours of electricity that a customer uses during a specific period of time.

Problem

Point out to students that the arrows indicate the direction in which to read each dial.

What is the reading on the dials of this electric meter?

Solution

Rhonda reads the dials from left to right. When the hand on any dial is between two numbers, she uses the smaller number. When the hand is between 9 and 0, as on the second dial, she thinks of the 0 as 10.

The reading is 29635.

Warm-up: 59,630 − 59,210 [420]
64,100 − 63,279 [821]
26,341 − 25,981 [360]
37,005 − 36,184 [821]

See pages 43–44 of *Consumer Forms and Problems.*

9.

Feb.-April	677
April-June	643
June-Aug.	1828
Aug.-Oct.	1134
Oct.-Dec.	547

Related Problems

Rhonda read the meter at the Radows' home every two months for a year. Give the reading for each date.

1. December 1, 1980 58915

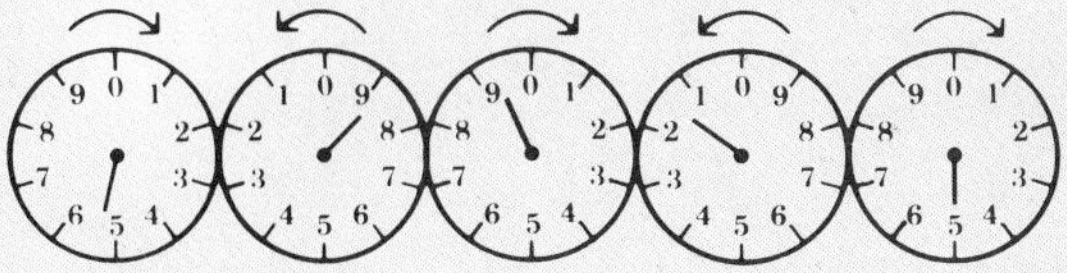

2. February 2, 1981 59602

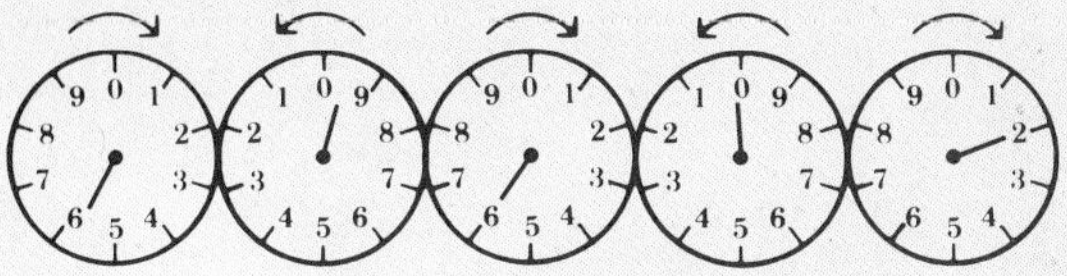

3. April 1, 1981 60279

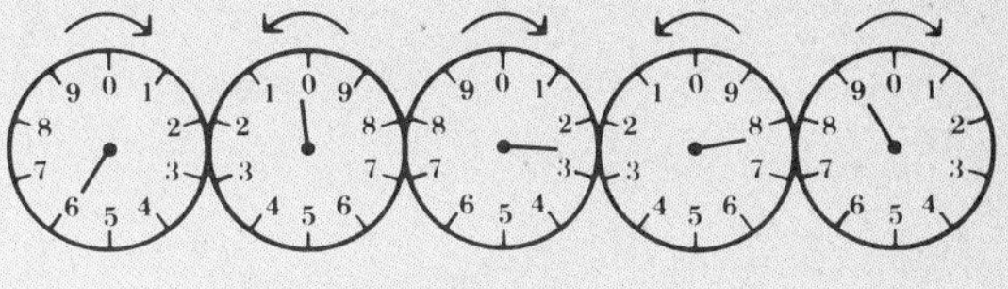

4. June 1, 1981 60922

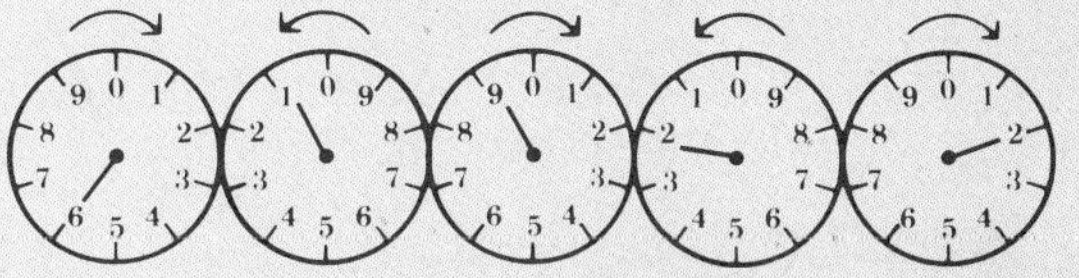

5. August 3, 1981 62750

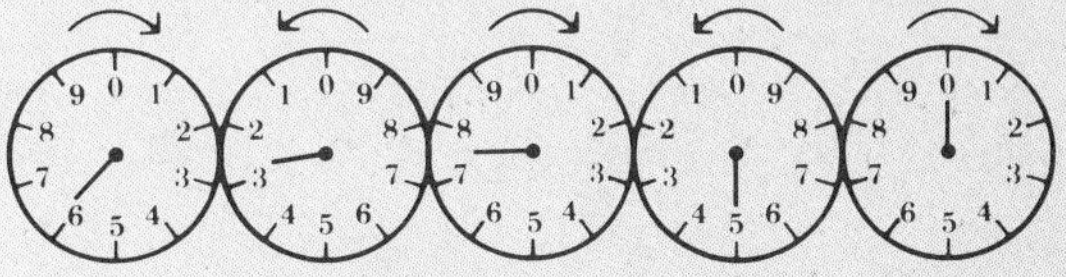

6. October 1, 1981 63884

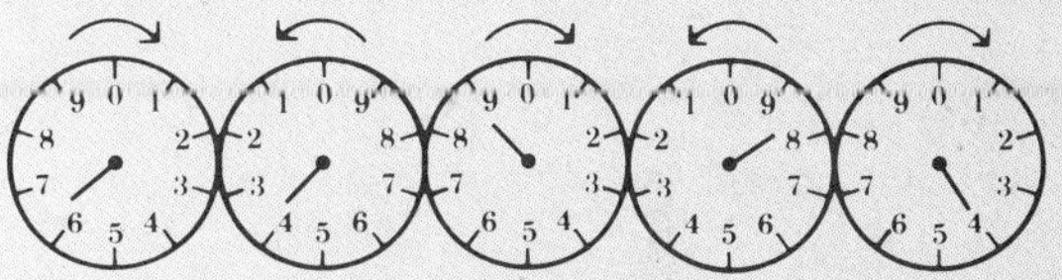

7. December 1, 1981 64431

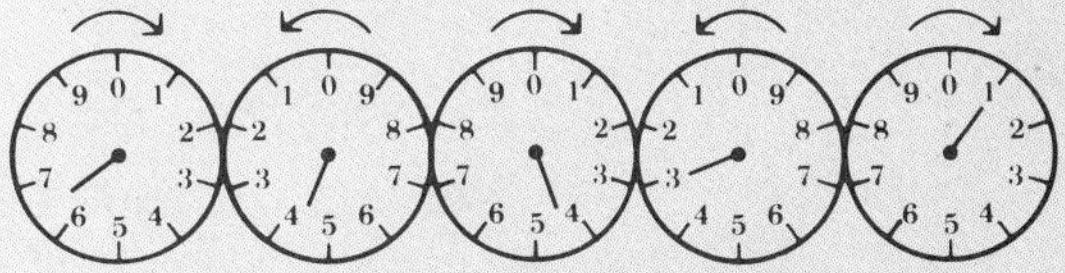

8. How many kilowatt-hours were used between December 1, 1980, and February 2, 1981? (Subtract the December reading from the February reading.)
687 kilowatt-hours

9. Find the number of kilowatt-hours used during each of the other 2-month periods.
See above.

10. During which 2-month period was electric usage greatest?
June 1 to August 3

Discuss with students that air conditioning is probably responsible for the great increase in electric usage for this time period.

CALCULATOR APPLICATIONS

Electricity Costs

The amount of electricity used to light a 100-watt light bulb for 10 hours is a **kilowatt-hour** (kW·h).

On the average, a freezer uses 1195 kW·h of electricity per year. Find the annual cost of electricity to operate the freezer when the rate is 4.973¢ per kilowatt-hour.

First, multiply the rate by 0.01 to change cents to dollars.

$4.973 \times 0.01 = 0.04973 \quad 4.973¢ = \$0.04973$

After changing the rate from cents to dollars, students could use the automatic constant feature with these repetitive calculations.

Then, multiply the annual usage by the rate to find the annual cost. Round the answer to the nearest cent.

$\$0.04973 \times 1195 \approx \$59.43$

The annual cost of electricity for the freezer is $59.43.

Students can use this key sequence: Rate [×] .01 [×] Usage [=]

Find the annual cost of electricity for each appliance listed below. Use a rate of 4.973¢ per kilowatt-hour.

	Appliance		Average annual usage (kW·h)	
1.	Hair dryer	**$0.90**	18	**17. $0.90**
2.	Microwave oven	**$9.45**	190	**$9.53**
3.	Iron	**$7.16**	144	**$7.22**
4.	Range with oven	**$58.43**	1175	**$58.95**
5.	Dishwasher	**$18.05**	363	**$18.21**
6.	Trash compactor	**$2.49**	50	**$2.51**
7.	Toaster	**$1.94**	39	**$1.96**
8.	Clothes dryer	**$49.38**	993	**$49.82**

	Appliance		Average annual usage (kW·h)	
9.	Clothes washer (automatic)	**$22.13**	445	**17. $22.33**
10.	Air conditioner (window)	**$60.92**	1225	**$61.46**
11.	Vacuum cleaner	**$2.29**	46	**$2.31**
12.	Television (black and white)	**$13.03**	262	**$13.14**
13.	Television (color)	**$22.78**	458	**$22.98**
14.	Radio	**$4.28**	86	**$4.31**
15.	Stereo	**$5.42**	109	**$5.47**
16.	Shaver	**$0.10**	2	**$0.10**

17. Find the annual cost of electricity for the appliances in the list. Use a rate of 5.017¢ per kilowatt-hour.
See above.

Square	A	B	C	D	G	H	I	J
Length of side (cm)	44	28	33	16	19	26	60	45

Break Time

The drawing below shows a perfect-squared rectangle. The rectangle is made up of squares A through J, all of different sizes. As shown, square E measures 7 cm on each side. Square F measures 12 cm on each side. Without measuring, find the dimensions of the other squares. What are the length and the width of the rectangle? **Length is 105 cm; width is 104 cm.**

The rectangle in this drawing is not actual size.

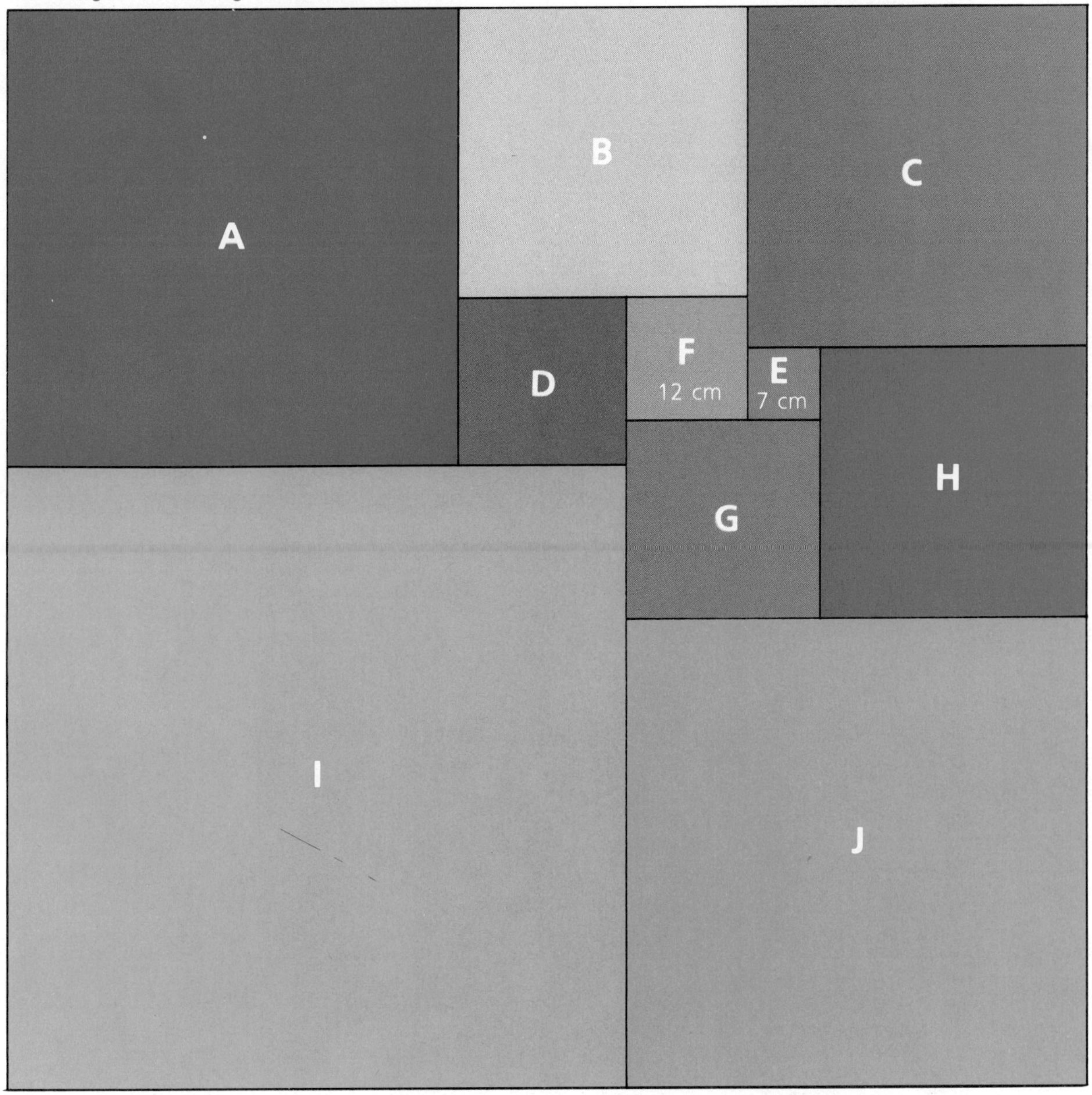

Objective: Find the scale dimensions for rooms and furniture.

Interior Designer

Materials: Graph paper

See the Careers Chart beginning on page 410 for more information about the careers in this cluster.

Career Cluster: Arts Raul Cruz is an interior designer for Bentley's Furniture Store. He made a **scale drawing** of Arlene Novak's living room floor. Raul showed her possible arrangements for the furniture she plans to buy.

Problem

On his drawing, Raul used 1 cm to represent 0.2 m. Arlene's living room is 4.73 m long. To the nearest tenth of a centimeter, what is the scale length of the living room?

Solution

Strategy

- Write a proportion to find the scale length.

$$\frac{1}{0.2} = \frac{n}{4.73} \begin{array}{l} \longleftarrow \text{Scale length (cm)} \\ \longleftarrow \text{Actual length (m)} \end{array}$$

- Write the cross-products and solve for n. Round your answer to the nearest tenth.

$$1 \times 4.73 = 0.2 \times n$$
$$4.73 = 0.2n$$
$$23.7 \approx n$$

Conclusion

To the nearest tenth of a centimeter, the scale length of the living room is 23.7 cm.

Warm-up: $\frac{1}{0.4} = \frac{n}{3.6}$ [$n = 9$] $\frac{1}{0.35} = \frac{n}{1.47}$ [$n = 4.2$]

$\frac{1}{0.25} = \frac{n}{1.9}$ [$n = 7.6$] $\frac{1}{0.5} = \frac{n}{3.5}$ [$n = 7$]

See pages 11–12 of *Consumer Forms and Problems.*

Related Problems

For problems 1–14, round your answers to the nearest tenth of a centimeter.

1. The living room is 3.40 m wide. What is the scale width of the room? Use a scale of 1 cm ⟶ 0.2 m.
17.0 cm

Find the scale dimensions of each piece of furniture. Use a scale of 1 cm ⟶ 0.2 m.

2. Sofa: 2.10 m by 0.86 m
10.5 cm by 4.3 cm

3. Love seat: 1.53 m by 0.86 m
7.7 cm by 4.3 cm

4. Chair: 0.80 m by 0.86 m
4.0 cm by 4.3 cm

5. Library table: 1.49 m by 0.58 m
7.5 cm by 2.9 cm

6. End table: 0.65 m by 0.55 m
3.3 cm by 2.8 cm

7. Antique desk: 1.28 m by 0.60 m
6.4 cm by 3.0 cm

Raul made a scale drawing for another customer, using a scale of 1 cm ⟶ 0.25 m. Find the scale dimensions of the room and of each piece of furniture.

8. Bedroom: 3.60 m by 3.45 m
14.4 cm by 13.8 cm

9. Bed: 1.95 m by 1.35 m
7.8 cm by 5.4 cm

10. Night table: 0.57 m by 0.40 m
2.3 cm by 1.6 cm

11. Chair: 0.65 m by 0.46 m
2.6 cm by 1.8 cm

12. Bench: 1.08 m by 0.43 m
4.3 cm by 1.7 cm

13. Triple dresser: 1.68 m by 0.48 m
6.7 cm by 1.9 cm

14. Five-drawer chest: 0.90 m by 0.48 m
3.6 cm by 1.9 cm

15. Use the scale dimensions in problem 8 to draw the outline of the bedroom on centimeter graph paper. Include a closet, a window, and a door.
Outline should be 14.4 cm by 13.8 cm.

16. Make scale drawings of the furniture for the bedroom (problems 9–14). Cut out the furniture and make an arrangement for the room.
Answers will vary.

Objective: Compute the number and the cost of tiles needed to cover a floor.

Installing Floor Tiles

Materials: Graph paper

Lin Hong rents a house and wants to put floor tiles in the den. His landlord will pay for the materials if Lin installs the tiles. Each tile is a square 30 cm by 30 cm.

Problem

Lin's den measures 4.6 m by 3.9 m. How many tiles are needed for the floor?

	Length	Width	Total
1.	8	5	40
2.	14	14	196
3.	15	13	195
4.	13	11	143
5.	21	17	357
6.	15	10	150

Solution

Strategy

- Change each dimension to centimeters. Length: 4.6 m = 460 cm; Width: 3.9 m = 390 cm
- Divide each dimension by 30 to find the number of tiles needed. Round up to the next whole number. Length: $460 \div 30 \approx 16$; Width: $390 \div 30 = 13$
- Multiply to find the total number of tiles needed.

Number of tiles needed for length		Number of tiles needed for width		Total number of tiles needed
16	×	13	=	208

Conclusion

Lin needs 208 tiles for the floor.

Explain to students that cut edges are generally not abutted with finished edges of tiles.

Related Problems

For each problem, find the number of tiles needed for the length and the width. Then find the total number of tiles needed for each room.

See above.

1. Bathroom: 2.4 m by 1.5 m
2. Bedroom: 4.2 m by 4.1 m
3. Dining room: 4.4 m by 3.9 m
4. Utility room: 3.8 m by 3.3 m
5. Recreation room: 6.3 m by 5.0 m
6. Kitchen: 4.4 m by 2.8 m

Warm-up: 3.7 m = ■ cm [370]
5.62 m = ■ cm [562]
420 ÷ 30 [14]
255 ÷ 30 [≈ 9]

See pages 11–12 of *Consumer Forms and Problems.*

Problem

Lin wants to make a design with the tiles. He used graph paper to make the design shown below.

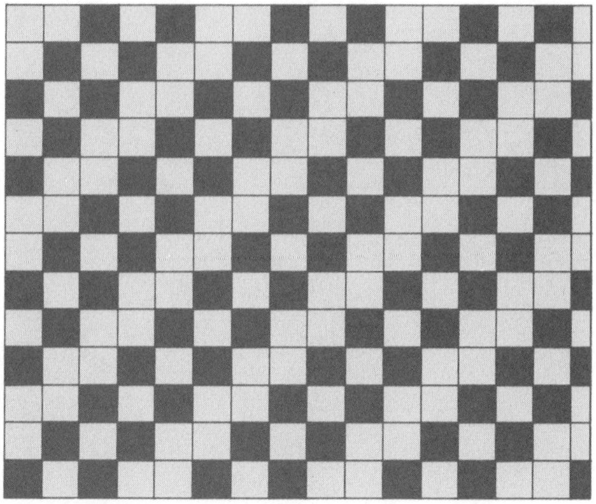

Find the cost of the brown tiles if a package of 5 tiles costs $6.50.

Solution

Strategy

- Count the number of brown tiles needed. Count each partial tile as a whole tile.

  83

- Divide by 5 to find the number of packages needed. Round up to the next whole number.

  $83 \div 5 \approx 17$

- Multiply $6.50 by 17 to find the total cost.

  17 × $6.50 = $110.50

Conclusion

The brown tiles will cost $110.50.

Related Problems

7. At $6.50 for a package of 5, find the cost of the beige tiles for Lin's den.
$162.50

8. What is the cost of all the tiles for Lin's den?
$273

9. Make a regular checkerboard pattern for Lin's recreation room on graph paper. (See problem 5.) He wants the design in green and blue, starting with a blue tile in the upper left-hand corner.
See Additional Answers beginning on page T44.

10. How many blue tiles are needed in the recreation room?
179 tiles

11. How many green tiles are needed in the recreation room?
178 tiles

12. At $6 for a package of 5 tiles, what is the cost of the blue tiles?
$216

13. At the same price, what is the cost of the green tiles?
$216

14. What is the total cost of the tiles for Lin's recreation room?
$432

Objective: Compute the amount of paint needed to paint a room.

Painting an Apartment

Russell and Marie Atkin are planning to paint their apartment. They know that one gallon of paint will cover about 400 sq. ft.

Problem

Discuss with your class that in many consumer settings, the answers are rounded up. This is especially true when determining quantities of materials needed for various projects.

The Atkins' bedroom is 16 ft. by 14 ft. The walls are 8 ft. high. How many gallons of paint will they need to paint the walls and the ceiling?

Solution

To help students visualize this concept, you might make a simple paper or cardboard model.

Strategy

- Draw a simple sketch of the room and a sketch showing the four walls placed end to end.

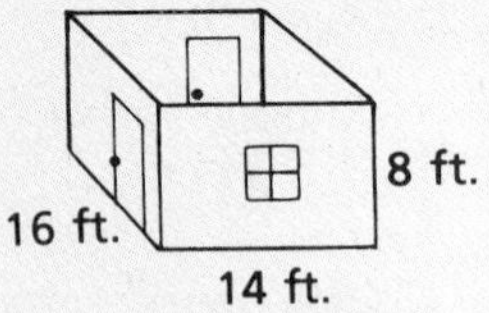

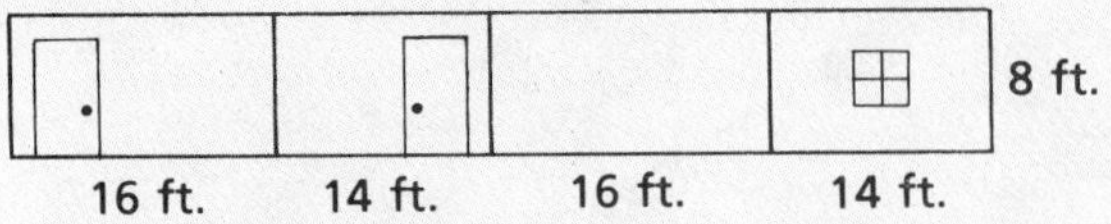

- Add to find the length of the long rectangle in feet. It is the same as the perimeter of the room. $16 + 14 + 16 + 14 = 60$
- Multiply total length by the wall height to find the area of the walls in square feet. $8 \times 60 = 480$
- Multiply length times width to find the area of the ceiling in square feet. $16 \times 14 = 224$
- Add to find the total area of walls and ceiling in square feet. $480 + 224 = 704$

The areas of the doors and the windows are included to allow for a safe margin of error.

- Divide by 400 to find the number of gallons needed. Round up to the next whole number. $704 \div 400 \approx 2$

Conclusion

Marie and Russell will need 2 gallons of paint.

Warm-up: 8 × 72 [576]
15 × 12 [180]
400 + 156 [556]
684 ÷ 400 [≈ 2]

Related Problems

Marie and Russell measured the other rooms to determine how much paint they would need. Then they made this chart.

Room	Room dimensions
Den	14 ft. by 11 ft.
Living room	18 ft. by 12 ft.
Entrance	6 ft. by 5 ft.
Dining room	12 ft. by 11 ft.
Hallway	25 ft. by 5 ft.

Complete the table below to find the number of gallons of paint needed for each room. Remember, the walls are 8 ft. high.

	Room	Wall area (square feet)	Ceiling area (square feet)	Total area to be painted (square feet)	Amount of paint needed (gallons)
	Bedroom	480	224	704	2
1.	Den	400	154	554	2
2.	Living room	480	216	696	2
3.	Entrance	176	30	206	1
4.	Dining room	368	132	500	2
5.	Hallway	480	125	605	2

6. Paint is $10.49 per gallon. What will be the total bill for all the paint?
$115.39

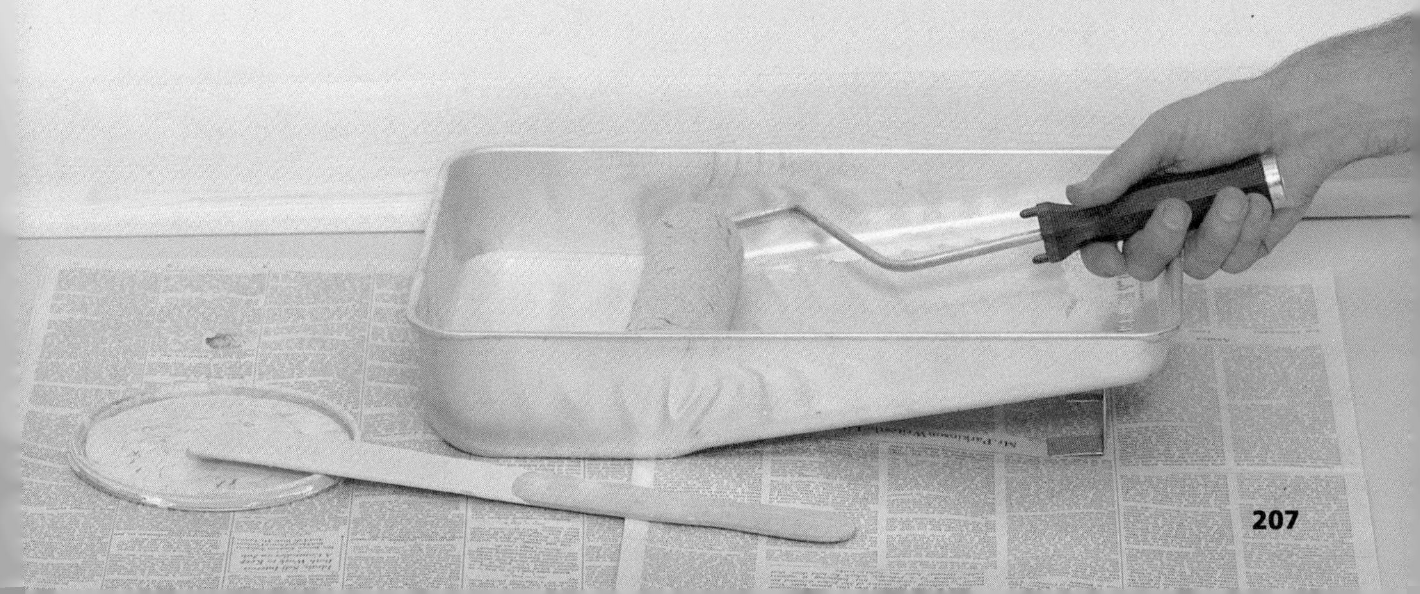

Objective: Determine the number of rolls of wallpaper needed to paper a room.

Ordering Wallpaper

There are actually 36 sq. ft. of paper in a roll of wallpaper. Because the patterns must be matched, some paper is always discarded. For this reason, it is recommended that the area be divided by 30, not 36.

Mary Grace Gettings plans to wallpaper her den. The clerk at the wallpaper store gave her these guidelines to help her decide how much paper to order.

— Find the total area of the walls, disregarding all openings.

— Divide the total area by 30. (Each roll of paper covers about 30 sq. ft.)

— Subtract $\frac{1}{2}$ roll for each window or single door and 1 roll for each picture window, double door, or other large opening.

Problem

A drawing of Mary Grace's den is shown below. How many rolls of wallpaper should she order?

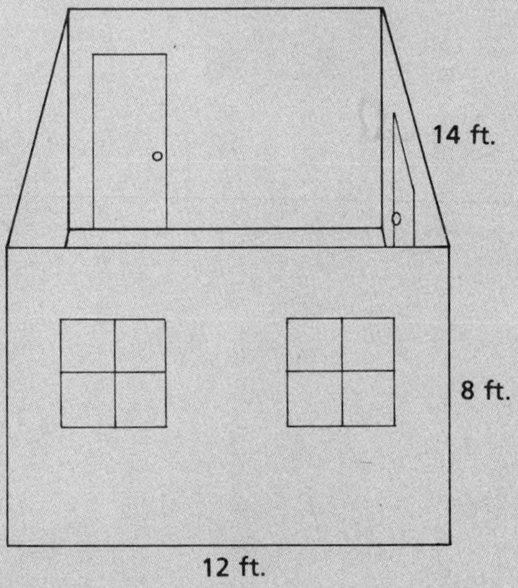

Solution

Have students use the same strategy for finding the area of the walls that was used on page 206.

Strategy

- Add the lengths of the walls to find the perimeter of the room in feet.

  $12 + 14 + 12 + 14 = 52$

- Multiply the total length by the wall height to find the total area of the walls in square feet.

  $8 \times 52 = 416$

- Divide by 30 to find the total number of rolls needed, disregarding openings. Round up to the next whole number.

  $416 \div 30 \approx 14$

- Subtract 2 rolls to allow for the 4 openings.

  $(4 \times \frac{1}{2} = 2)$

  $14 - 2 = 12$

Conclusion

Mary Grace should order 12 rolls of wallpaper.

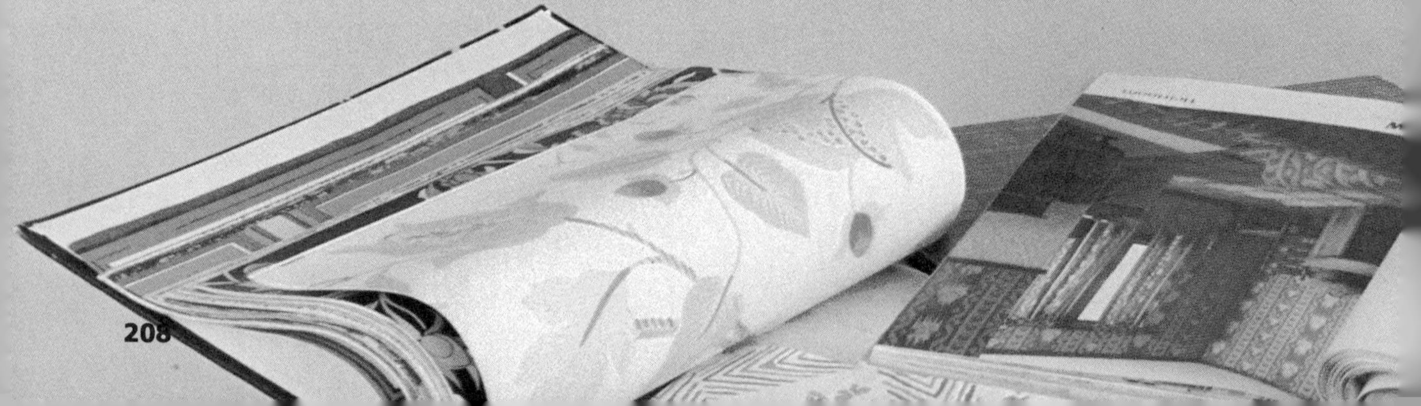

Warm-up: 9×64 [576]
8×48 [384]
$6 \times \frac{1}{2}$ [3]
$510 \div 30$ [17]

Related Problems

Mary Grace wants to paper both her dining room and her living room. The walls in both rooms are 8 ft. high.

The dining room is 16 ft. long and 14 ft. wide. There are three windows, one door, and a large archway in the room.

1. Find the area of the walls, disregarding all openings.
   480 sq. ft.
2. Find the number of rolls of paper needed. (Disregard openings.)
   16 rolls
3. Find the number of rolls that should be subtracted for the openings.
   3 rolls
4. How many rolls of wallpaper should Mary Grace order?
   13 rolls
5. Find the cost of the paper at $8.49 per roll.
   $110.37

Mary Grace's living room is 22 ft. long and 18 ft. wide. It has one window, one door, a large archway, and a picture window.

6. Find the area of the walls, disregarding all openings.
   640 sq. ft.
7. Find the number of rolls of paper needed. (Disregard openings.)
   22 rolls
8. Find the number of rolls that should be subtracted for the openings.
   3 rolls
9. How many rolls of wallpaper should Mary Grace order for the living room?
   19 rolls
10. Mary Grace wants to paper the living room for $140. What is the most she can spend per roll? Round your answer to the nearest cent.
    $7.37
11. Mary Grace plans to cover the bathroom walls with vinyl covering. The room is 9 ft. long and 6 ft. wide. The height of the wall area to be covered is 4 ft. The room has one window and one door. How many rolls of vinyl are needed?
    3 rolls
12. The vinyl covering is $14.75 per roll. Find the cost of covering the walls.
    $44.25

Objective: Compute the amount of money paid by an insurance company for stolen or destroyed property.

Personal Property Insurance

Jeff Scott carries renter's insurance. This type of insurance covers losses or damage to personal property caused by misfortunes such as fire or theft. Jeff's insurance agent gave him the information shown here. To determine the amount of depreciation, Jeff needs to know the age and the replacement cost of any article lost or destroyed.

Item	Average useful years	Annual rate of depreciation
Athletic equipment	5	20%
Barbecue	8	12%
Bicycle	5	20%
Clock—Electric	15	7%
—Grandfather	30	3%
Furniture—Card tables, chairs	10	10%
—Children's	5	20%
—Desks, tables	20	5%
—Lamps	20	5%
—Wood-frame (example: sofa)	10	10%
Golf clubs	8	12%
Stereo	12	8%
Television	8	12%
Tools	20	5%
Typewriter—Home	20	5%
—Office	5	20%

Warm-up: 7% of 42 [2.94]
12% of 250 [30]
16.25 × 7 [113.75]
138.25 − 50 [88.25]

See page 7 of
Consumer Forms and Problems.

You might discuss with your class that it is usually better to use replacement cost than original purchase price of an item.

Problem

Jeff's apartment was burglarized and his typewriter was taken. The typewriter is 3 years old and will cost $175 to replace. Jeff has a $50-deductible insurance policy. How much can Jeff expect to receive from the insurance company?

Solution

Strategy

- Read the list to find the annual rate of depreciation for the typewriter. 5% per year
- Multiply the replacement cost by the rate of depreciation. $0.05 \times \$175 = \$8.75$
- Multiply to find the depreciation for 3 years. $3 \times \$8.75 = \$26.25$
- Subtract to find the present value. $\$175 - \$26.25 = \$148.75$
- Subtract the deductible amount from the present value to find the insurance benefit. $\$148.75 - \$50 = \$98.75$

Conclusion

Jeff can expect to receive $98.75 from the insurance company.

Related Problems

You can extend the problem situations by having students determine the amount needed to replace the lost or destroyed items.

The storage area in Tom Smith's apartment building was damaged by water. The items he lost are listed below. Find the value for each item after depreciation.

	Item	Replacement cost		Age in years
1.	Bicycle	$150	$90.00	2
2.	Golf clubs	$175	$70.00	5
3.	Barbecue	$65	$57.20	1
4.	Electric clock	$75	$59.25	3
5.	Circular saw	$110	$88.00	4
6.	Camping equipment	$355	$213.00	2
7.	Desk	$175	$131.25	5

Use the athletic-equipment rate for the camping equipment.

8. Tom has a $50-deductible policy. How much will he receive from the insurance company?
$658.70

Donna Littlebird had a fire in her apartment. The following items were destroyed. Find the value for each item after depreciation.

	Item	Replacement cost		Age in years
9.	Sofa	$580	$406.00	3
10.	Chair	$225	$180.00	2
11.	Chair	$185	$129.50	3
12.	End table	$120	$108.00	2
13.	Stereo	$325	$273.00	2
14.	Television	$535	$470.80	1
15.	Lamp	$60	$51.00	3

16. Donna has a $100-deductible policy. How much will she receive from the insurance company?
$1518.30

Discuss with students the need for renter's insurance.

Skills Tune-Up

Dividing whole numbers, pages 12–13

1. 3577 ÷ 7 511
2. 2336 ÷ 8 292
3. 1948 ÷ 6 324 R4
4. 7448 ÷ 8 931
5. 18,968 ÷ 4 4742
6. 5812 ÷ 6 968 R4
7. 6832 ÷ 54 126 R28
8. 8189 ÷ 27 303 R8
9. 5745 ÷ 53 108 R21
10. 4275 ÷ 19 225
11. 8154 ÷ 67 121 R47
12. 2235 ÷ 65 34 R25
13. 2112 ÷ 48 44
14. 3366 ÷ 30 112 R6
15. 7038 ÷ 34 207
16. 2449 ÷ 71 34 R35
17. 3792 ÷ 47 80 R32
18. 69,184 ÷ 46 1504
19. 63,762 ÷ 53 1203 R3
20. 62,043 ÷ 82 756 R51
21. 140,668 ÷ 18 7814 R16
22. 110,653 ÷ 58 1907 R47
23. 377,166 ÷ 88 4285 R86
24. 595,038 ÷ 714 833 R276
25. 188,496 ÷ 924 204
26. 452,953 ÷ 806 561 R787
27. 648,713 ÷ 394 1646 R189

Multiplying fractions and mixed numbers, pages 14–15

1. $\frac{5}{6} \times \frac{1}{4}$ $\frac{5}{24}$
2. $\frac{3}{4} \times \frac{1}{6}$ $\frac{1}{8}$
3. $\frac{4}{5} \times \frac{5}{14}$ $\frac{2}{7}$
4. $\frac{4}{5} \times \frac{3}{8}$ $\frac{3}{10}$
5. $\frac{3}{8} \times \frac{2}{9}$ $\frac{1}{12}$
6. $\frac{9}{14} \times 7$ $4\frac{1}{2}$
7. $8 \times \frac{7}{16}$ $3\frac{1}{2}$
8. $8\frac{1}{3} \times \frac{3}{5}$ 5
9. $2\frac{3}{5} \times \frac{6}{13}$ $1\frac{1}{5}$
10. $\frac{4}{15} \times 3\frac{3}{4}$ 1
11. $5\frac{5}{6} \times \frac{3}{14}$ $1\frac{1}{4}$
12. $3\frac{5}{9} \times 1\frac{3}{8}$ $4\frac{8}{9}$
13. $5\frac{5}{8} \times 4\frac{4}{5}$ 27
14. $4\frac{1}{4} \times 2\frac{2}{3}$ $11\frac{1}{3}$
15. $1\frac{5}{7} \times 5\frac{1}{4}$ 9
16. $7 \times 2\frac{1}{4}$ $15\frac{3}{4}$
17. $12\frac{1}{5} \times 2$ $24\frac{2}{5}$
18. $\frac{7}{10} \times \frac{5}{8} \times \frac{1}{7}$ $\frac{1}{16}$
19. $5\frac{2}{5} \times 3\frac{1}{2} \times \frac{5}{9}$ $10\frac{1}{2}$
20. $7 \times 1\frac{3}{8} \times 2\frac{6}{7}$ $27\frac{1}{2}$

Ratio and proportion, pages 30–31

Find the cross-products. Tell whether the ratios are equal.

1. $\frac{4}{14}$ $\frac{2}{6}$ $24 \neq 28$
2. $\frac{14}{21}$ $\frac{6}{9}$ $126 = 126$
3. $\frac{15}{20}$ $\frac{64}{80}$ $1200 \neq 1280$
4. $\frac{225}{4.5}$ $\frac{100}{2}$ $450 = 450$
5. $\frac{12}{16}$ $\frac{9}{9.8}$ $117.6 \neq 144$
6. $\frac{99}{5}$ $\frac{2.97}{0.15}$ $14.85 = 14.85$

Solve and check.

7. $\frac{18}{21}$ $\frac{a}{35}$ $a = 30$
8. $\frac{n}{24} = \frac{20}{8}$ $n = 60$
9. $\frac{64}{8} = \frac{24}{c}$ $c = 3$
10. $\frac{16}{x} = \frac{32}{9}$ $x = 4.5$
11. $\frac{26.5}{36} = \frac{n}{7.2}$ $n = 5.3$
12. $\frac{2.7}{d} = \frac{1.2}{4.8}$ $d = 10.8$
13. $\frac{0.3}{2.4} = \frac{50}{n}$ $n = 400$
14. $\frac{x}{17} = \frac{5.2}{34}$ $x = 2.6$

Chapter 10 Review

Amount to spend for rent, pages 194–195

1. Linda earns $7.85 per hour in a 40-hour work week. If she uses the "week's gross pay" guideline (do not spend more than one week's gross pay for shelter each month), what is the most she can spend for rent each month?
   $314

2. A survey states that people who rent spend about 28% of their annual net income on shelter. If Fred's net income is $10,200 per year, about how much will he probably spend on shelter each month?
   $238

Selecting a place to rent, pages 196–197

3. Sam estimates that his electric bill will be about $40 per month and that his gas bill will be about $55 per month. If the rent for his apartment is $275, what will be the monthly total for rent and utilities?
   $370

Meter reader, pages 198–199

4. Give the reading for this electric meter.
   40593

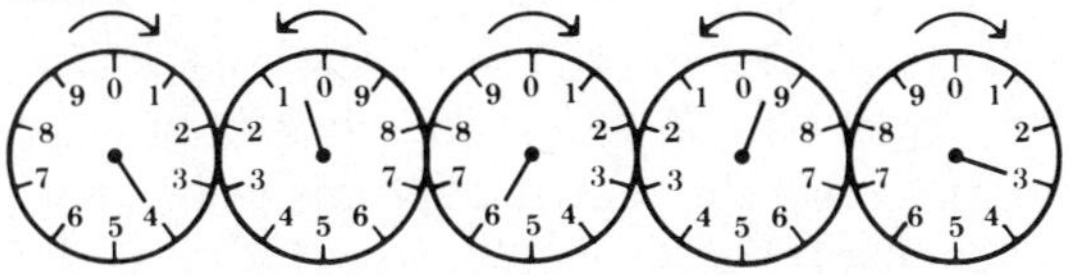

Interior designer, pages 202–203

5. Using a scale of 1 cm ⟶ 0.2 m, find the scale length of a room 4.40 m long.
   22 cm

Installing floor tiles, pages 204–205

6. How many floor tiles will be needed to cover a floor 5.6 m by 4.5 m? Each tile is a square 30 cm by 30 cm.
   285 tiles

7. The tiles Cathy wants for her bathroom floor cost $6.50 for a package of 5 tiles. Find the total cost if she needs 48 tiles.
   $65

Painting an apartment, pages 206–207

8. Eleanor plans to paint the walls and the ceiling of her den. The room measures 12 ft. by 12 ft., and the walls are 8 ft. high. If one gallon of paint covers about 400 sq. ft., how much paint will Eleanor need?
   2 gallons

Ordering wallpaper, pages 208–209

9. Jack wants to wallpaper his study. The room measures 15 ft. by 16 ft., and the walls are 8 ft. high. The room has 3 windows and 1 door. Find the number of rolls of wallpaper Jack should order. (Each roll of paper covers about 30 sq. ft. Subtract $\frac{1}{2}$ roll for each window or door.)
   15 rolls

Personal property insurance, pages 210–211

10. Juanita's renter's insurance is a $100-deductible policy. Her television set was stolen, and it will cost $365 to replace. The set was 2 years old. If the annual rate of depreciation is 12%, how much will she receive from the insurance company?
    $177.40

Chapter 10 Test

Number of test items - 10

Number missed	1	2	3	4	5
Percent correct	90	80	70	60	50

1. Duane earns $8.95 per hour in a 40-hour work week. If he uses the "week's gross pay" guideline (do not spend more than one week's gross pay for shelter each month), what is the most he can spend for rent each month?
$358

2. A survey states that people who rent spend about 28% of their annual net income on shelter. If Jane's net income is $11,400 per year, about how much will she probably spend on shelter each month?
$266

3. Margo is interested in renting an apartment for $325 per month. She estimates that her electric bill will be about $35 per month and that her gas bill will be about $50 per month. What will be the monthly total for rent and utilities?
$410

4. Give the reading for this electric meter.
24936

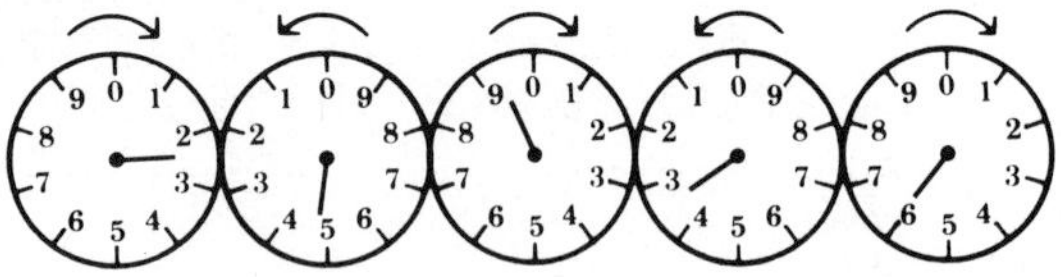

5. Using a scale of 1 cm ⟶ 0.25 m, find the scale length of a sofa that is 2.75 m long.
11 cm

6. How many tiles will be needed to cover a floor 5.2 m by 3.6 m? Each tile is a square 30 cm by 30 cm.
216 tiles

7. The tiles Ned wants for his den floor cost $6 for a package of 5 tiles. Find the total cost if he needs 72 tiles.
$90

8. Marty plans to paint the walls and the ceiling of his living room. The room measures 18 ft. by 12 ft., and the walls are 8 ft. high. If one gallon of paint covers about 400 sq. ft., how much paint will Marty need?
2 gallons

9. Anna is going to wallpaper her dining room. The room measures 16 ft. by 14 ft., and the walls are 8 ft. high. The room has 2 doors and 2 windows. Find the number of rolls of wallpaper Anna should order. (Each roll of paper covers about 30 sq. ft. Subtract $\frac{1}{2}$ roll for each window or door.)
14 rolls

10. Beverly's renter's insurance is a $50-deductible policy. Her stereo was destroyed in a fire, and it will cost $285 to replace. The stereo was 3 years old. If the annual rate of depreciation is 8%, how much will she receive from the insurance company?
$166.60

 See pages 25–26 of the *Test Masters* for an alternate form of the Chapter 10 Test.

Chapter 11 Buying a Home

Objective: Use a general guideline to compute the maximum amount to borrow for a home.

Amount to Borrow for a Home

See page T36 for additional notes and activities for Chapter 11.

Edward and Marta Rivera are thinking of buying their own home. They will need to borrow most of the money to pay for it. To help them decide how much they can afford to borrow, their banker gave this advice: *Do not consider borrowing more than 2 times your annual gross income.*

Problem

Edward earns $6.50 per hour working 40 hours a week. Marta earns $1150 per month. How much can they consider borrowing?

You might discuss various types of housing available for purchase—such as single-family homes and condominiums. Factors to consider are cost, location, and maintenance. Recall that condominium owners usually pay a monthly maintenance fee.

Solution

Strategy

• Multiply Edward's hourly income by 40 to find his weekly income.	40 × $6.50 = $260
• Multiply by 52 to find Edward's annual income.	52 × $260 = $13,520
• Multiply Marta's monthly income by 12 to find her annual income.	12 × $1150 = $13,800
• Add to find the Riveras' annual gross income.	$13,520 + $13,800 = $27,320
• Multiply by 2 to find the greatest amount they can consider borrowing.	2 × $27,320 = $54,640

Conclusion

The Riveras can consider borrowing $54,640.

Warm-up: 3.75 × 40 [150]
795 × 12 [9540]
235 × 52 [12,220]
34,600 × 2 [69,200]

Related Problems

Use the general guideline to determine the greatest amount a person earning each salary could consider borrowing for a home while earning the given income. Assume a 40-hour work week.

1. $18,000 per year
   $36,000
2. $31,400 per year
   $62,800
3. $780 per month
   $18,720
4. $1150 per month
   $27,600
5. $280 per week
   $29,120
6. $455 per week
   $47,320
7. $6.80 per hour
   $28,288
8. $13.50 per hour
   $56,160
9. $5.50 per hour
   $22,880
10. $12.50 per hour
    $52,000

For problems 11–13, assume a 40-hour work week.

11. Richard earns $9.50 per hour. Maria earns $625 per month. Can they consider a $58,000 loan?
    No
12. Lenny earns $6.50 per hour. Helene earns $375 per week. Can they consider a $60,500 loan?
    Yes
13. Ann earns $175 per week. Harvey earns $5.75 per hour. Can they consider a $40,000 loan?
    Yes
14. Barbara earns $4.25 per hour in a 20-hour work week. Frank earns $21,500 per year. Can they consider a $68,000 loan?
    No

Down Payment and Monthly Payment

Most people do not pay for a house with cash. At the time of purchase, they pay part of the price with a down payment. They borrow the rest of the money from a lending institution. This **mortgage loan** is paid back in equal monthly payments. An **amortization table** is used to find the amount of each monthly payment.

Problem

Paula Jeffers is interested in buying a condominium for $48,000. At the savings and loan company, she was told she needs 20% of $48,000 for the down payment. She can borrow the rest of the money at 12.5% annual interest, to be paid back over 25 years. How much does Paula need for the down payment? What will her monthly payment be?

Amortization of a $1000 Loan

Interest rate	Monthly payment		
	20-year loan	25-year loan	30-year loan
10.0%	$9.66	$9.09	$8.78
10.5%	$9.99	$9.45	$9.15
11.0%	$10.33	$9.81	$9.53
11.5%	$10.66	$10.16	$9.90
12.0%	$11.01	$10.53	$10.29
12.5%	$11.36	$10.90	$10.67
13.0%	$11.72	$11.28	$11.06
13.5%	$12.07	$11.66	$11.45
14.0%	$12.44	$12.04	$11.85
14.5%	$12.80	$12.42	$12.25
15.0%	$13.17	$12.81	$12.64
15.5%	$13.54	$13.20	$13.05
16.0%	$13.92	$13.59	$13.45
16.5%	$14.29	$13.99	$13.86
17.0%	$14.67	$14.38	$14.26
17.5%	$15.05	$14.78	$14.67
18.0%	$15.44	$15.18	$15.08

Solution

Strategy

- Multiply by 20% to find the amount of the down payment.

  $0.20 \times \$48{,}000 = \$9600$

- Subtract to find the amount of the loan.

  $\$48{,}000 - \$9600 = \$38{,}400$

- Read the table to find the monthly payment for $1000 for 25 years at 12.5% interest.

  $10.90

- Multiply to find the monthly payment. Think of 38,400 as 38.4 thousands.

  $38.4 \times \$10.90 = \$418.56$

Conclusion

Paula's down payment is $9600. Her monthly payment will be $418.56.

Class discussion for this lesson might include the different types of lending institutions that give mortgage loans. Also discuss the fact that the interest rate often depends on the availability of money, much of which comes from deposits in savings accounts.

Warm-up: 35,700 is ■ thousands. [37.5]
10% of 36,000 [3600]
36,000 − 3600 [32,400]
7.69 × 31.5 [242.235]

Related Problems

Problems 9–15 point out the importance of "shopping" for a mortgage loan. The down payment, the interest rate, and the length of the loan all make a difference in the monthly payment.

Complete the table. Round the amount of the monthly payment to the nearest cent.

	Purchase price	Down payment	Amount of down payment	Amount of loan	Interest rate	Time (years)	Monthly payment
	$48,000	20%	$9600	$38,400	12.5%	25	$418.56
1.	$50,000	20%	$10,000	$40,000	13.5%	30	$458.00
2.	$50,000	10%	$5000	$45,000	13.5%	20	$543.15
3.	$75,000	20%	$15,000	$60,000	12.5%	30	$640.20
4.	$75,000	30%	$22,500	$52,500	12.0%	25	$552.83
5.	$60,000	25%	$15,000	$45,000	13.0%	30	$497.70
6.	$82,000	30%	$24,600	$57,400	14.5%	30	$703.15
7.	$105,000	20%	$21,000	$84,000	11.5%	20	$895.44
8.	$94,000	25%	$23,500	$70,500	15.0%	25	$903.11

9. Find the difference in the amounts of the down payments for the two homes that cost $50,000. (Use the table above.)
$5000

10. Find the difference in the amounts of the down payments for the two homes that cost $75,000. (Use the table above.)
$7500

11. Find the difference in the monthly payments for these loans.

$32,500 at 14% interest for 20 years
$32,500 at 14% interest for 25 years
$13

12. Find the difference in the monthly payments for these loans.

$48,000 at 12% interest for 25 years
$48,000 at 12.5% interest for 25 years
$17.76

The purchase price of a certain home is $72,000.

13. Find the amount of the loan with a 25% down payment.
$54,000

14. Find the amount of the loan with a 20% down payment.
$57,600

15. Find the difference in the monthly payments for the loans in problems 13 and 14 at 14.5% interest for 30 years.
$44.10

Objective: Compute the amount of interest on a mortgage loan.

Warm-up: 243.70 × 300 [73,110]
268.50 × 360 [96,660]
274.83 × 240 [65,959.20]
154,640 − 58,000 [96,640]

Interest on a Mortgage Loan

On many home loans, people actually pay back three or four times the amount they borrow.

Problem

How much interest will be paid on a loan of $40,000 for 30 years if the annual interest rate is 13.5%?

Solution

Strategy

- Use the strategy on page 218 to find the monthly payment. $458
- Multiply the number of years by 12 to find the total number of payments. 12 × 30 = 360
- Multiply to find the total amount repaid. 360 × $458 = $164,880
- Subtract the amount borrowed to find the amount of interest. $164,880 − $40,000 = $124,880

Conclusion

$124,880 interest will be paid.

Related Problems

For problems 5–7, students need to use the strategy from the previous lesson to find the monthly payment.

Complete this table. Use the amortization table on page 218 for problems 5–7.

	Amount borrowed	Interest rate	Time (years)	Monthly payment	Total payments	Amount repaid	Amount of interest
	$40,000	13.5%	30	$458.00	360	$164,880	$124,880
1.	$40,000	13.5%	25	$466.40	300	$139,920	$99,920
2.	$40,000	14%	30	$474.00	360	$170,640	$130,640
3.	$40,000	14%	25	$481.60	300	$144,480	$104,480
4.	$40,000	14%	20	$497.60	240	$119,424	$79,424
5.	$35,500	13%	20	$416.06	240	$99,854.40	$64,354.40
6.	$55,500	10%	30	$487.29	360	$175,424.40	$119,924.40
7.	$55,500	18%	30	$836.94	360	$301,298.40	$245,798.40

Use the answers you found for the table to help you with the following problems.

8. Find the difference in the amounts of interest paid on these loans.

$40,000 at 14% interest for 30 years
$40,000 at 14% interest for 25 years
$26,160

9. Find the difference in the amounts of interest paid on these loans.

$40,000 at 14% interest for 30 years
$40,000 at 14% interest for 20 years
$51,216

10. Find the difference in the amounts of interest paid on these loans.

$40,000 at 13.5% interest for 25 years
$40,000 at 14% interest for 25 years
$4560

11. Find the difference in the amounts of interest paid on these loans.

$55,500 at 10% interest for 30 years
$55,500 at 18% interest for 30 years
(Notice that these are the lowest and highest interest rates on page 218.)
$125,874

12. In problem 1, the amount repaid is about how many times as great as the amount borrowed? (Round your answer to the nearest tenth.)
3.5

13. In problem 2, the amount repaid is about how many times as great as the amount borrowed? (Round your answer to the nearest tenth.)
4.3

Objective: Find the amount of interest paid and the amount paid on the principal in consecutive monthly mortgage payments.

Principal and Interest in a Monthly Payment

Warm-up: Write as a fraction.

$11\% = \blacksquare$ $[\frac{11}{100}]$

$9.5\% = \blacksquare$ $[\frac{95}{1000}]$

Round to the nearest hundredth.

$25{,}000 \times \frac{11}{100} \times \frac{1}{12}$ [229.17]

$38{,}000 \times \frac{14}{100} \times \frac{1}{12}$ [443.33]

Part of each monthly payment on a mortgage loan is the interest for that month. The rest of the payment is used to reduce the principal.

Problem

The Hermans are borrowing $54,000 at 14% annual interest to be repaid over 30 years. Their monthly payment will be $639.90. How much of their first monthly payment will go toward the principal and how much will be interest? What is the "new" principal (the amount still owed after the first month)?

Solution

Strategy

- Use the simple interest formula to find the interest for the first month. (1 month is $\frac{1}{12}$ of a year.)

$I = P \times R \times T$

$I = \$54{,}000 \times 14\% \times \frac{1}{12}$

$I = \$54{,}000 \times \frac{14}{100} \times \frac{1}{12}$

$I = \$630$

- Subtract to find the amount paid on the principal the first month.

$\$639.90 - \$630 = \$9.90$

- Subtract to find the new principal.

$\$54{,}000 - \$9.90 = \$53{,}990.10$

Conclusion

Of the Hermans' first monthly payment, $9.90 will go toward the principal and $630 will be interest. The new principal is $53,990.10.

Related Problems

Use the given information about the Hermans' loan to solve these problems. Round interest amounts to the nearest cent.

1. Find the amount of interest for the second month. Use the new principal, $53,990.10.
$629.88
2. Find the amount paid on the principal the second month.
$10.02
3. Find the new principal at the end of the second month.
$53,980.08
4. Find the amount of interest for the third month. Use the new principal from problem 3.
$629.77
5. Find the amount paid on the principal the third month.
$10.13
6. Find the new principal at the end of the third month.
$53,969.95
7. Find the amount of interest for the fourth month.
$629.65
8. Find the amount paid on the principal the fourth month.
$10.25
9. Find the new principal at the end of the fourth month.
$53,959.70

You might discuss the following information. For a 25-year mortgage loan with a 20% down payment:
After the down payment the buyer "owns" 20% of the home.
After 5 years, 29%.
After 10 years, 37%.
After 15 years, 51%.
After 20 years, 72%.
After 25 years, 100%.

See pages 254–255 for a computer application related to this lesson.

CALCULATOR APPLICATIONS

Amortization Tables

Point out that amortization tables are figured and printed by computers.

Many lending agencies provide their customers with an amortization table that shows how each monthly payment is divided between interest and principal. Scott Lynch is borrowing $40,000 at 13.5% annual interest for 25 years. His monthly payment will be $466.40. Use your calculator and the strategy on page 222 to complete these sections of Scott's amortization table.

Remind students that multiplying by $\frac{1}{12}$ is the same as dividing by 12.

	Payment number	Principal	Amount of interest	Amount paid on principal	New principal
	1	$40,000.00	$450.00	$16.40	$39,983.60
1.	2	$39,983.60	$449.82	$16.58	$39,967.02
2.	3	$39,967.02	$449.63	$16.77	$39,950.25
3.	4	$39,950.25	$449.44	$16.96	$39,933.29
4.	5	$39,933.29	$449.25	$17.15	$39,916.14
5.	6	$39,916.14	$449.06	$17.34	$39,898.80
6.	7	$39,898.80	$448.86	$17.54	$39,881.26
7.	8	$39,881.26	$448.66	$17.74	$39,863.52
8.	9	$39,863.52	$448.46	$17.94	$39,845.58
9.	10	$39,845.58	$448.26	$18.14	$39,827.44
10.	11	$39,827.44	$448.06	$18.34	$39,809.10
11.	12	$39,809.10	$447.85	$18.55	$39,790.55
	236	$21,253.33	$239.10	$227.30	$21,026.03
12.	237	$21,026.03	$236.54	$229.86	$20,796.17
13.	238	$20,796.17	$233.96	$232.44	$20,563.73
14.	239	$20,563.73	$231.34	$235.06	$20,328.67
15.	240 (20 yr.)	$20,328.67	$228.70	$237.70	$20,090.97

After students have solved problems 16 and 17, discuss the following:

On this 25-year mortgage, it will be almost 20 years before the principal portion of a payment is greater than the interest.

Approximately half of the principal will be paid back during the last 5 years of the mortgage term.

16. Beginning with which payment will the amount paid on the principal be greater than the amount of interest? **Payment 239**

17. After 20 years, what percent of the principal will be yet unpaid? Round to the nearest percent. **50%**

Objective: Compute an insurance premium for valuables in a home.

Homeowner's Insurance

The amount of homeowner's insurance required is usually the amount of the loan.

Carl Meil has a mortgage loan to pay for his house. The lender requires Carl to have homeowner's insurance.

The insurance company charges a basic annual premium to insure the house and its contents. The amount of this premium is based on many things including the type of materials used to build the house, the location of the house, and the amount for which the house is insured.

In addition to the basic insurance to cover the house and its contents, Carl wants coverage on several valuable articles. His insurance agent gave him the following table to determine the cost of insuring these items.

Personal property	One-year rate per $100 of value*
Jewelry	$1.40
Furs and garments trimmed with fur	$0.41
Fine art	$0.28
Cameras, projectors, etc.	$1.65
Musical instruments—amateur	$0.69
Musical instruments—professional and organs	$2.85
Silverware, silver-plated items, etc.	$0.50
Stamp collections	$0.90
Coin collections	$1.95

*Available only in multiples of $100.

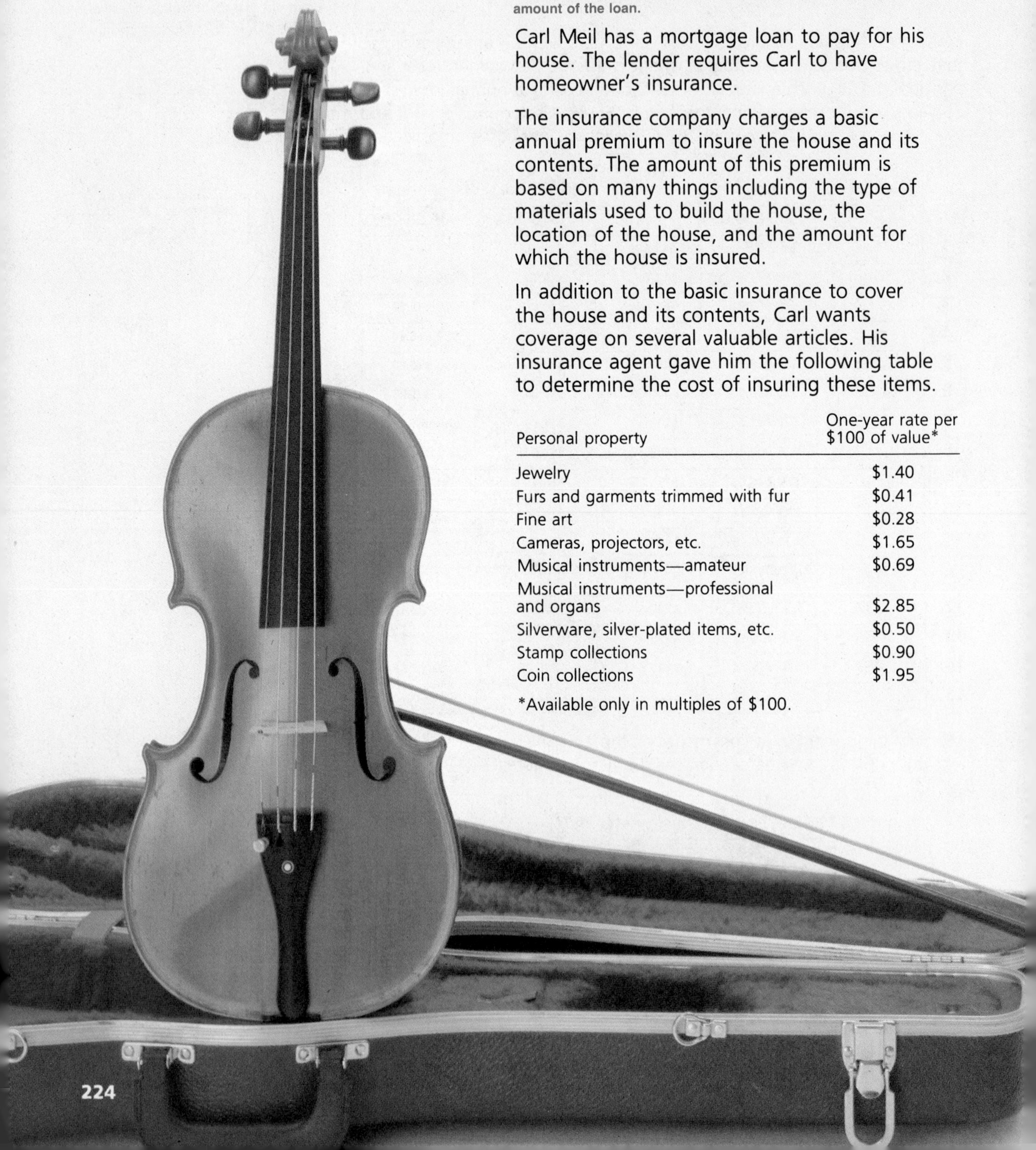

Warm-up: Round 345 up to the next hundred. [400]
Round 675 up to the next hundred. [700]
8 × 1.73 [13.84]
120 + 5.43 + 8.25 [133.68]

See pages 7 and 45 of *Consumer Forms and Problems.*

Problem

Carl's basic premium for his homeowner's insurance is $165. He has a gold ring worth $700 and a camera worth $225 that he wants to insure separately. What is the total premium for his insurance?

Solution

Strategy

- Read the table to find the rate for each item.

  Jewelry: $1.40 Camera: $1.65

- Multiply the rate by the number of hundreds of dollars each item is worth. (Round all values up to the next $100.)

  Ring: 7 × $1.40 = $9.80

  Camera: 3 × $1.65 = $4.95

- Add to find the total premium.

  $165 + $9.80 + $4.95 = $179.75

Conclusion

Carl's total insurance premium is $179.75.

Related Problems

Find the annual premium for each item. Then find each total premium.

Teresa Granados' basic premium is $175.

1. $600 ring
$8.40
2. $350 gold chain
$5.60
3. $300 flute (amateur)
$2.07
4. $450 painting
$1.40
5. Teresa's total premium
$192.47

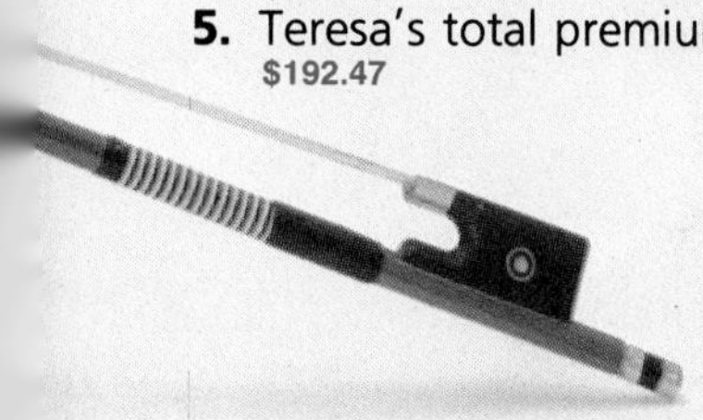

Lawrence Hetter's basic premium is $165.

6. $1250 organ
$37.05
7. $325 violin (amateur)
$2.76
8. $250 watch
$4.20
9. $800 coin collection
$15.60
10. Lawrence's total premium
$224.61

Sam and Polly Pfaff's basic premium is $140.

11. $325 camera
$6.60
12. $2500 in silverware
$12.50
13. $2300 stamp collection
$20.70
14. $425 coat with fur collar
$2.05
15. The Pfaffs' total premium
$181.85

Steve Davids is in a rock band that plays professionally. He insures his equipment as part of his homeowner's policy. Steve's basic premium is $130.

16. $325 drums
$11.40
17. $150 bass guitar
$5.70
18. $240 amplifier
$8.55
19. $435 ring
$7
20. Steve's total premium
$162.65

Many lending agencies require borrowers to pay $\frac{1}{12}$ of their annual homeowner's insurance premium every month. Find the amount each person listed below would pay for insurance each month. (Round each answer up to the next cent.)

21. Teresa Granados
$16.04
22. Lawrence Hetter
$18.72
23. Steve Davids
$13.56

The discussion for this lesson could include such things as the need for an appraisal of valuable items for insurance coverage. Also discuss the fact that many people forget to update their insurance as they accumulate valuables.

Objective: Compute the assessed valuation of property and the real estate taxes.

Real Estate Taxes

The method of tax computation presented here is basic. In various localities, other factors may be involved.

In most areas, the local government's chief source of income is the **real estate tax.** This is an annual tax based on the value of each taxpayer's property.

The local government taxes the property at a certain percentage of the current **market value.** This percentage is known as the **rate of assessment.** The market value multiplied by this rate gives the **assessed valuation** of the property.

A **tax rate** is used to determine the amount of the real estate tax. This rate is often expressed in terms of an amount per $100 of the assessed valuation of the property.

Problem

Show that a tax rate of $3.87 per $100 is just another way of saying 3.87%.

The market value of Peggy and Ed Wilson's condominium is $58,000. The rate of assessment in their area is 60% of the market value. The tax rate is $3.87 per $100 of assessed valuation. What is the amount of real estate tax on the Wilsons' condominium?

Discussion for this lesson could include how real estate taxes are used. This will be more meaningful if you use local tax rates. You could also point out that real estate taxes are tax deductible.

Solution

Strategy

- Multiply by 60% to find the assessed valuation.
  $0.60 \times \$58{,}000 = \$34{,}800$
- Multiply by the tax rate per hundred to find the amount of real estate tax. Think of 34,800 as 348 hundreds.
  $\$3.87 \times 348 = \$1346.76$

Conclusion

The real estate tax on the Wilsons' condominium is $1346.76.

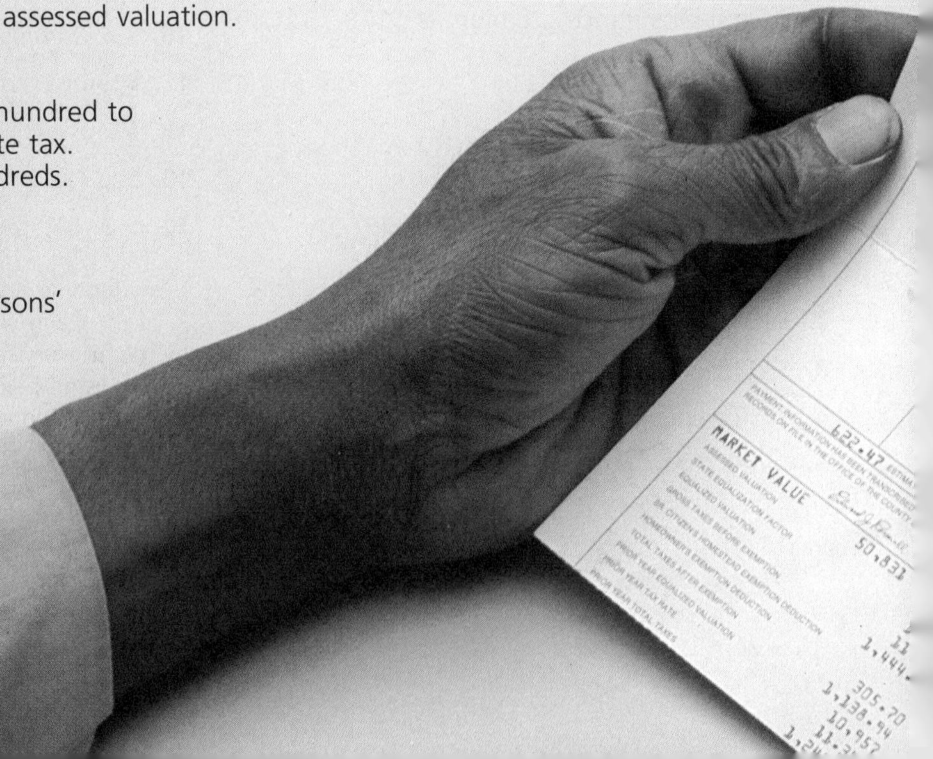

Warm-up: 60% of 45,000 [27,000]
How many hundreds in 25,600? [256]
How many hundreds in 34,570? [345.7]
2.30 × 342.5 [787.75]

See page 46 of *Consumer Forms and Problems*.

Related Problems

Complete the table. Round each answer to the nearest cent.

	Market value	Rate of assessment	Assessed valuation	Tax rate per \$100	Real estate tax
	\$58,000	60%	\$34,800	\$3.87	\$1346.76
1.	\$52,000	50%	\$26,000	\$2.75	\$715.00
2.	\$49,000	60%	\$29,400	\$3.50	\$1029.00
3.	\$68,000	50%	\$34,000	\$2.95	\$1003.00
4.	\$78,000	60%	\$46,800	\$3.12	\$1460.16
5.	\$60,000	60%	\$36,000	\$4.14	\$1490.40
6.	\$83,500	50%	\$41,750	\$3.70	\$1544.75
7.	\$105,000	30%	\$31,500	\$5.21	\$1641.15
8.	\$92,000	25%	\$23,000	\$7.05	\$1621.50
9.	\$64,500	30%	\$19,350	\$7.576	\$1465.96
10.	\$73,750	35%	\$25,812.50	\$5.321	\$1373.48

When discussing problem 11, point out that many banks include real estate taxes in the monthly payment. The bank places the money in an *escrow* account, to be used when the tax bill is due.

11. The Wilsons pay $\frac{1}{12}$ of their annual real estate tax every month to the bank which holds their mortgage loan. This is to assure the payment of these taxes each year. How much do the Wilsons pay for real estate tax each month?
\$112.23

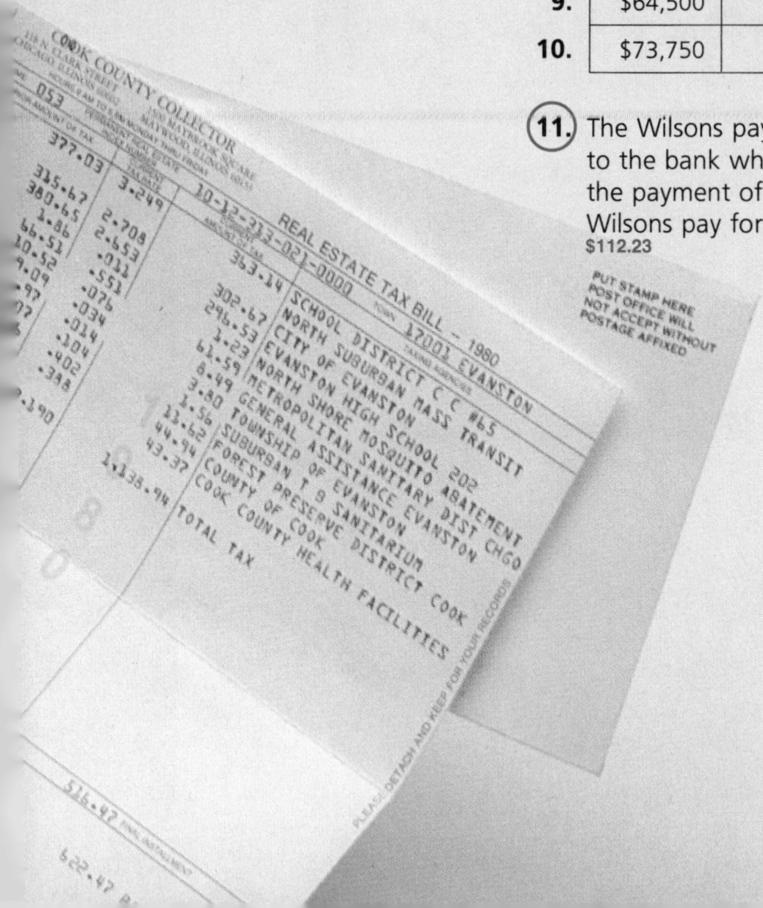

Objective: Find the closing costs involved in buying a home.

Closing Costs

At the time of signing the necessary papers for the purchase of a home, the buyer must pay a number of fees known as **closing costs.** The actual fees vary in different areas. Sometimes the fees involving the title are split with the seller, or fully paid by the seller. William and Angela Head were given the following information to help them determine their closing costs.

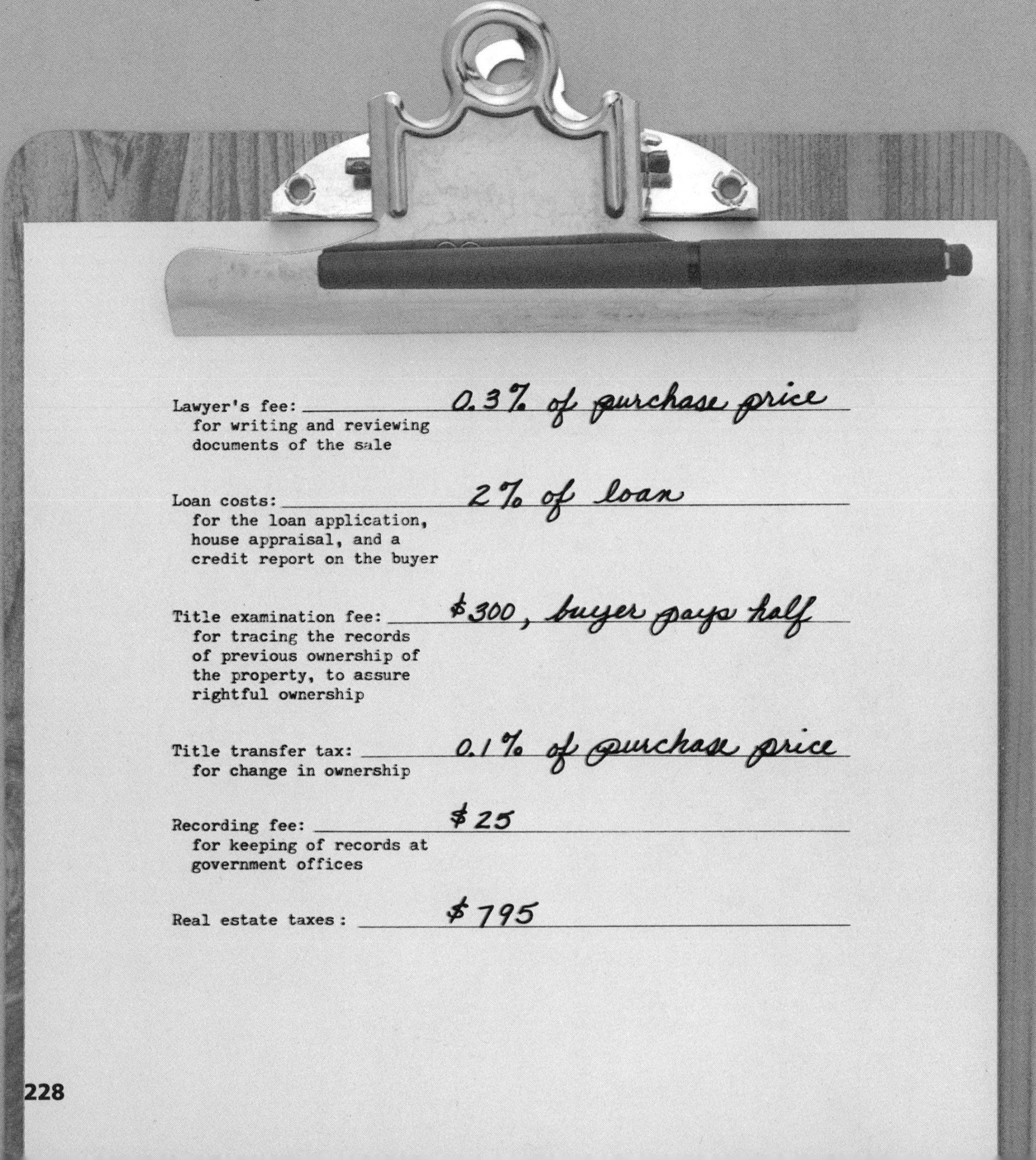

Lawyer's fee: 0.3% of purchase price
for writing and reviewing documents of the sale

Loan costs: 2% of loan
for the loan application, house appraisal, and a credit report on the buyer

Title examination fee: $300, buyer pays half
for tracing the records of previous ownership of the property, to assure rightful ownership

Title transfer tax: 0.1% of purchase price
for change in ownership

Recording fee: $25
for keeping of records at government offices

Real estate taxes: $795

Warm-up: 1.25% of 24,000 [300]
0.05% of 32,500 [16.25]
0.6% of 38,000 [228]
2.3% of 32,500 [747.5]

Problem

The purchase price of the Heads' home is $63,700. The amount of their loan is $50,000. What is the total of their closing costs?

Solution

Strategy

- Multiply the purchase price by 0.3% to find the lawyer's fee.

  $0.003 \times \$63{,}700 = \$191.10$

- Multiply the amount of the loan by 2% to find the loan costs.

  $0.02 \times \$50{,}000 = \$1000$

- Multiply the title examination fee by $\frac{1}{2}$ to find the Heads' share.

  $\frac{1}{2} \times \$300 = \$150$

- Multiply the purchase price by 0.1% to find the title transfer tax.

  $0.001 \times \$63{,}700 = \$63.70$

- Add to find total closing costs including recording fee and real estate taxes.

$$\begin{array}{r} \$\ 191.10 \\ 1000.00 \\ 150.00 \\ 63.70 \\ 25.00 \\ +\ 795.00 \\ \hline \$2224.80 \end{array}$$

Conclusion

The total of the Heads' closing costs is $2224.80.

Related Problems

For each buyer, find the amount of each fee listed. Then find total closing costs.

The Zobels: $58,000 purchase price
$45,000 loan

1. Lawyer: 0.2% of purchase price
   $116
2. Loan costs: 1.5% of loan
   $675
3. Title examination: $180, pay half
   $90
4. Title transfer: 0.1% of purchase price
   $58
5. The Zobels' total closing costs, including $575 for real estate taxes and $20 for recording fee
   $1534

June Kowalski: $52,000 purchase price
$40,000 loan

6. Loan costs: 2% of loan
   $800
7. Title transfer: 2% of purchase price, pay half
   $520
8. Recording: 0.05% of purchase price
   $26
9. June's total closing costs including $663.50 for real estate taxes and $200 for lawyer's fee
   $2209.50

The Corrins: $75,000 purchase price
$60,500 loan

10. Lawyer: 0.5% of purchase price
    $375
11. Loan costs: 1% of loan
    $605
12. Title examination: $235, pay half
    $117.50
13. Title transfer: 0.5% of purchase price, pay half
    $187.50
14. Recording: 0.1% of purchase price
    $75
15. The Corrins' total closing costs, including $425 for real estate taxes
    $1785

Objectives: Determine the list price for a house; use a table to determine the costs involved in buying a home in various geographical areas.

Real Estate Agent

Career Cluster: Business Contact Sarah Currier is a real estate agent. Her job involves bringing together people who want to sell property with those who want to buy property.

Problem

The agency Sarah works for charges a commission of 7% for selling a house. James and Lucille Whitewolf want to receive at least \$62,000 on the sale of their home. For what price should Sarah list the Whitewolfs' home?

Solution

Strategy

- Show the commission as 7% of the list price. Let L represent the list price.

$$\text{Commission} = 0.07 \times L$$

- Write an equation relating the list price, commission, and amount desired by the seller.

List price		Commission		Amount desired
L	$-$	$0.07L$	$=$	\$62,000

- Solve the equation. Remember, $L = 1L$. Round the answer up to the next hundred dollars.

$$1L - 0.07L = \$62{,}000$$
$$0.93L = \$62{,}000$$
$$\frac{0.93L}{0.93} = \frac{\$62{,}000}{0.93}$$
$$L \approx \$66{,}700$$

Conclusion

Sarah should list the Whitewolfs' home for \$66,700.

Warm-up: $T - 0.05T = \blacksquare T$ [0.95]

Solve for T to the nearest hundredth.

$0.95T = 38{,}000$ [40,000]

$T - 0.07T = 84{,}000$ [90,322.58]

$T - 0.06T = 105{,}000$ [111,702.13]

Related Problems

For what price should each house be listed? Use the commision rate given. Round each answer up to the next hundred dollars.

	Amount desired by seller	Commission	
1.	$65,000	6%	$69,200
2.	$83,500	7%	$89,800
3.	$73,800	8%	$80,300
4.	$58,800	7%	$63,300
5.	$97,900	8%	$106,500
6.	$105,300	7%	$113,300

7. Suppose Sarah's agency changes the commission rate to 8%. For what amount should Sarah then list the Whitewolfs' house?
$67,400

8. For the Whitewolfs' house, find the difference between the list prices with a 7% commission and an 8% commission.
$700

9. Suppose Sarah earns 3% on any house she sells. What would her earnings be on a $37,500 sale?
$1125

10. Sarah sold the Guytons' house for $51,000, the Wheatleys' house for $81,500, and the Garcias' house for $64,200 during a three-month period. At a 3.5% commission, how much did Sarah earn for that period?
$6884.50

11. The Walker Real Estate Agency sold Myoshi Tamura's house for $88,500. After the 7% commission was deducted, how much did Myoshi receive from the sale of her house?
$82,305

Some of Sarah's clients need information about home loans in various parts of the United States. To help them, Sarah uses a table prepared by the Federal Home Loan Bank Board.

Problem

Dave Peters is being transferred to Dallas. What can he expect to pay as a down payment on a $94,000 house?

Solution

Strategy

- Read the table to find the average down payment percent in Dallas.

  22.5%

- Multiply the cost of the house by 22.5% to find the amount of the down payment.

  $0.225 \times \$94{,}000 = \$21{,}150$

Conclusion

Dave can expect to pay $21,150 as a down payment.

Home Loans March, 1981

Metropolitan area	Average interest rate	Average purchase price	Average down payment
Atlanta	14.09%	$92,100	24.2%
Baltimore	13.67%	$89,100	26.6%
Boston	14.94%	$76,100	28.6%
Chicago-Northwestern Indiana	13.58%	$93,300	27.7%
Cleveland	13.57%	$70,600	26.6%
Dallas	13.45%	$93,700	22.5%
Denver	13.21%	$84,400	26.0%
Detroit	14.41%	$69,900	26.5%
Houston	13.79%	$92,200	19.7%
Los Angeles-Long Beach	14.46%	$110,100	24.4%
Miami	15.01%	$87,600	27.8%
Minneapolis-St. Paul	14.18%	$80,200	39.8%
New York-Northeastern New Jersey	14.91%	$88,900	34.5%
Philadelphia	14.10%	$65,100	29.5%
St. Louis	14.00%	$52,000	22.6%
San Francisco-Oakland	14.00%	$126,200	24.4%
Seattle-Tacoma	13.58%	$87,300	20.5%
Washington, D.C., Maryland, Virginia	14.21%	$101,200	23.6%

See page 47 of *Consumer Forms and Problems.*

Related Problems

12. Eleanor Hesen is moving to Boston. She expects to buy a home for $75,000. What can Eleanor expect to pay for her down payment?
$21,450

13. Grace and Oliver Matthews are moving to Seattle. They plan to spend $85,000 on a house. What can they expect to pay for a down payment?
$17,425

Of the metropolitan areas listed in the table on page 232, which area has

14. the lowest average purchase price?
St. Louis

15. the highest average purchase price?
San Francisco-Oakland

16. the lowest average interest rate?
Denver

17. the highest average interest rate?
Miami

Rosalee and Grayson Woodbury want to move to a warm climate. They are considering Atlanta, Houston, Los Angeles, and Miami.

18. How much greater is the average purchase price of a house in Los Angeles than in Miami?
$22,500

19. How much less could the Woodburys expect to pay as a down payment on a $90,000 house in Houston than in Miami?
$7290

20. Of the four areas the Woodburys are considering, which has the lowest average interest rate?
Houston

The answers to problems 14–20 could prompt a discussion of advantages and disadvantages of living in various parts of the country.

Break Time

Suppose you were given 1 billion dollars and were told to spend the money at the rate of 1 dollar per second. How long would it take you to spend the 1 billion dollars? Give your answer in years, days, hours, minutes, and seconds. (Use 365 days for 1 year.)
31 years, 259 days, 1 hour 46 minutes 40 seconds

Skills Tune-Up

Multiplying whole numbers, pages 8–9

1. 40 × 80 3200
2. 60 × 90 5400
3. 100 × 30 3000
4. 200 × 500 100,000
5. 700 × 400 280,000
6. 7000 × 30 210,000
7. 90 × 5000 450,000
8. 600 × 8000 4,800,000
9. 32 × 553 17,696
10. 784 × 292 228,928
11. 60 × 53 3180
12. 76 × 2384 181,184
13. 800 × 4300 3,440,000
14. 66 × 3 198
15. 51 × 16 816
16. 350 × 500 175,000
17. 679 × 3 2037
18. 603 × 4 2412
19. 7000 × 1200 8,400,000
20. 564 × 37 20,868
21. 536 × 404 216,544
22. 800 × 460 368,000
23. 5268 × 70 368,760
24. 2400 × 300 720,000
25. 943 × 1363 1,285,309
26. 5932 × 889 5,273,548
27. 209 × 3467 724,603
28. 7406 × 503 3,725,218

Renaming fractions and mixed numbers, pages 14–15

Rename in lowest terms.

1. $\frac{2}{8}$ $\frac{1}{4}$
2. $\frac{9}{15}$ $\frac{3}{5}$
3. $\frac{3}{6}$ $\frac{1}{2}$
4. $\frac{3}{9}$ $\frac{1}{3}$
5. $\frac{9}{12}$ $\frac{3}{4}$
6. $\frac{6}{9}$ $\frac{2}{3}$
7. $\frac{11}{22}$ $\frac{1}{2}$
8. $\frac{6}{18}$ $\frac{1}{3}$
9. $\frac{28}{32}$ $\frac{7}{8}$
10. $\frac{4}{16}$ $\frac{1}{4}$
11. $\frac{20}{24}$ $\frac{5}{6}$
12. $\frac{8}{32}$ $\frac{1}{4}$
13. $\frac{35}{50}$ $\frac{7}{10}$
14. $\frac{35}{56}$ $\frac{5}{8}$
15. $\frac{42}{56}$ $\frac{3}{4}$
16. $\frac{20}{25}$ $\frac{4}{5}$
17. $\frac{4}{42}$ $\frac{2}{21}$
18. $\frac{36}{48}$ $\frac{3}{4}$
19. $\frac{11}{33}$ $\frac{1}{3}$
20. $\frac{76}{100}$ $\frac{19}{25}$

Rename as a fraction.

21. $2\frac{2}{5}$ $\frac{12}{5}$
22. $10\frac{1}{8}$ $\frac{81}{8}$
23. $2\frac{3}{10}$ $\frac{23}{10}$
24. $5\frac{1}{4}$ $\frac{21}{4}$
25. $1\frac{4}{5}$ $\frac{9}{5}$
26. $2\frac{1}{3}$ $\frac{7}{3}$
27. $3\frac{1}{5}$ $\frac{16}{5}$
28. $4\frac{2}{3}$ $\frac{14}{3}$
29. $6\frac{5}{8}$ $\frac{53}{8}$
30. $8\frac{9}{10}$ $\frac{89}{10}$
31. $3\frac{3}{4}$ $\frac{15}{4}$
32. $12\frac{1}{2}$ $\frac{25}{2}$
33. $4\frac{3}{8}$ $\frac{35}{8}$
34. $5\frac{5}{6}$ $\frac{35}{6}$
35. $1\frac{1}{10}$ $\frac{11}{10}$
36. $3\frac{7}{8}$ $\frac{31}{8}$
37. $2\frac{5}{12}$ $\frac{29}{12}$
38. $6\frac{7}{10}$ $\frac{67}{10}$

Dividing fractions and mixed numbers, pages 16–17

1. $\frac{3}{8} \div \frac{1}{4}$ $1\frac{1}{2}$
2. $\frac{1}{4} \div \frac{2}{3}$ $\frac{3}{8}$
3. $\frac{3}{8} \div \frac{1}{3}$ $1\frac{1}{8}$
4. $\frac{9}{20} \div \frac{3}{8}$ $1\frac{1}{5}$
5. $\frac{3}{7} \div \frac{5}{8}$ $\frac{24}{35}$
6. $\frac{7}{15} \div \frac{4}{9}$ $1\frac{1}{20}$
7. $3 \div \frac{2}{5}$ $7\frac{1}{2}$
8. $\frac{1}{3} \div 2$ $\frac{1}{6}$
9. $10 \div \frac{5}{8}$ 16
10. $\frac{2}{5} \div 6$ $\frac{1}{15}$
11. $4\frac{1}{6} \div \frac{2}{3}$ $6\frac{1}{4}$
12. $\frac{2}{3} \div 1\frac{1}{2}$ $\frac{4}{9}$
13. $5\frac{1}{3} \div 3$ $1\frac{7}{9}$
14. $9 \div 1\frac{1}{2}$ 6
15. $5\frac{3}{4} \div 3\frac{3}{4}$ $1\frac{8}{15}$
16. $7\frac{2}{5} \div 2\frac{1}{5}$ $3\frac{4}{11}$
17. $3\frac{1}{8} \div 4\frac{1}{4}$ $\frac{25}{34}$
18. $6\frac{3}{5} \div 1\frac{4}{7}$ $4\frac{1}{5}$
19. $4\frac{3}{4} \div 6\frac{1}{3}$ $\frac{3}{4}$
20. $6\frac{2}{9} \div 2\frac{2}{3}$ $2\frac{1}{3}$
21. $3\frac{3}{8} \div 1\frac{4}{5}$ $1\frac{7}{8}$

Chapter 11 Review

Amount to borrow for a home, pages 216–217

1. Dawn Kenoi earns $7.45 per hour working 40 hours per week. What is the greatest amount she should borrow for a home? (Use the general guideline of 2 times annual income.)
   $30,992

Down payment and monthly payment, pages 218–219

2. Cecilia Diaz is buying a condominium for $58,500. She must make a 20% down payment. What is the amount of the loan after the down payment?
   $46,800
3. What is the monthly payment on a loan of $46,500 for 25 years if the annual interest rate is 12.5%? (Use the table on page 218.)
   $506.85

Interest on a mortgage loan, pages 220–221

4. What is the total amount of interest that will be paid on a loan of $45,000 for 30 years if the monthly payment is $463.05?
   $121,698

Principal and interest in a monthly payment, page 222

5. Bill Dunkle borrowed $37,000 at 13.5% annual interest. What is the amount of interest he will pay the first month?
   $416.25

Homeowner's insurance, pages 224–225

6. Walter's basic premium for his homeowner's insurance is $130. He has a stamp collection worth $2100 that he wants to insure separately. What is the total premium for his insurance? (Use the table on page 224.)
   $148.90

Real estate taxes, pages 226–227

7. The Lees' property has a market value of $78,500. The rate of assessment in the area is 60%. The tax rate is $3.23 per $100 of assessed valuation. What is the Lees' real estate tax?
   $1521.33

Closing costs, pages 228–229

8. The Condiffs paid a lawyer's fee of 0.5% of the purchase price of their home. What was the fee if the house cost $82,500?
   $412.50

Real estate agent, pages 230–231

9. Hal Parsons is a real estate agent. For what amount should he list a house so that the seller will receive at least $72,000? The commission is 7%. (Round the answer up to the next hundred dollars.)
   $77,500
10. The Days are moving to Denver. What can they expect to pay as a down payment on a $90,000 house? (Use the table on page 232.)
    $23,400

Chapter 11 Test

Number of test items - 10

Number missed	1	2	3	4	5
Percent correct	90	80	70	60	50

1. Paul Labe earns $10.50 per hour working 40 hours per week. What is the greatest amount he should borrow for a home? (Use the general guideline of 2 times annual income.)
$43,680

2. Elizabeth Markley is buying a home that costs $53,000. She made a 20% down payment. What is the amount of the loan after the down payment?
$42,400

3. What is the monthly payment on a loan of $37,000 for 30 years if the annual interest rate is 12.5%? (Use this table.)
$394.79

Monthly Payments for $1000 Loan

Interest rate	20-year loan	25-year loan	30-year loan
10.0%	$9.66	$9.09	$8.78
10.5%	$9.99	$9.45	$9.15
11.0%	$10.33	$9.81	$9.53
11.5%	$10.66	$10.16	$9.90
12.0%	$11.01	$10.53	$10.29
12.5%	$11.36	$10.90	$10.67
13.0%	$11.72	$11.28	$11.06

4. What is the total amount of interest that will be paid on a loan of $42,500 for 25 years if the monthly payment is $495.55?
$106,165

5. Machiko Ohira borrowed $38,000 at 15% annual interest. What is the amount of interest she will pay the first month?
$475

6. Joyce's basic premium for her homeowner's insurance is $125. She wants to insure a watch worth $200 separately. What is the total premium for her insurance? (Use this table.) **$127.80**

Personal property	One-year rate per $100 of value
Jewelry	$1.40
Furs and garments trimmed with fur	$0.41

7. The Waltons' property has a market value of $62,800. The rate of assessment in the area is 50%. The tax rate is $3.71 per $100 of assessed valuation. What is the Waltons' real estate tax?
$1164.94

8. In one area the recording fee is 0.1% of the purchase price of the home. What is the fee if a house costs $56,200?
$56.20

9. Tracy Johnson sells real estate. For what amount should she list a home if the sellers hope to get at least $84,000? The real estate commission is 7%. (Round the answer up to the next hundred dollars.)
$90,400

10. Dan Meza is moving to Baltimore. What can he expect to pay as a down payment on a $95,000 house? (Use this table.)
$25,270

Home Loans March, 1981

Metropolitan area	Average interest rate	Average purchase price	Average down payment
Atlanta	14.09%	$92,100	24.2%
Baltimore	13.67%	$89,100	26.6%

 See pages 27–28 of the *Test Masters* for an alternate form of the Chapter 11 Test.

Chapter 12 Building a Home

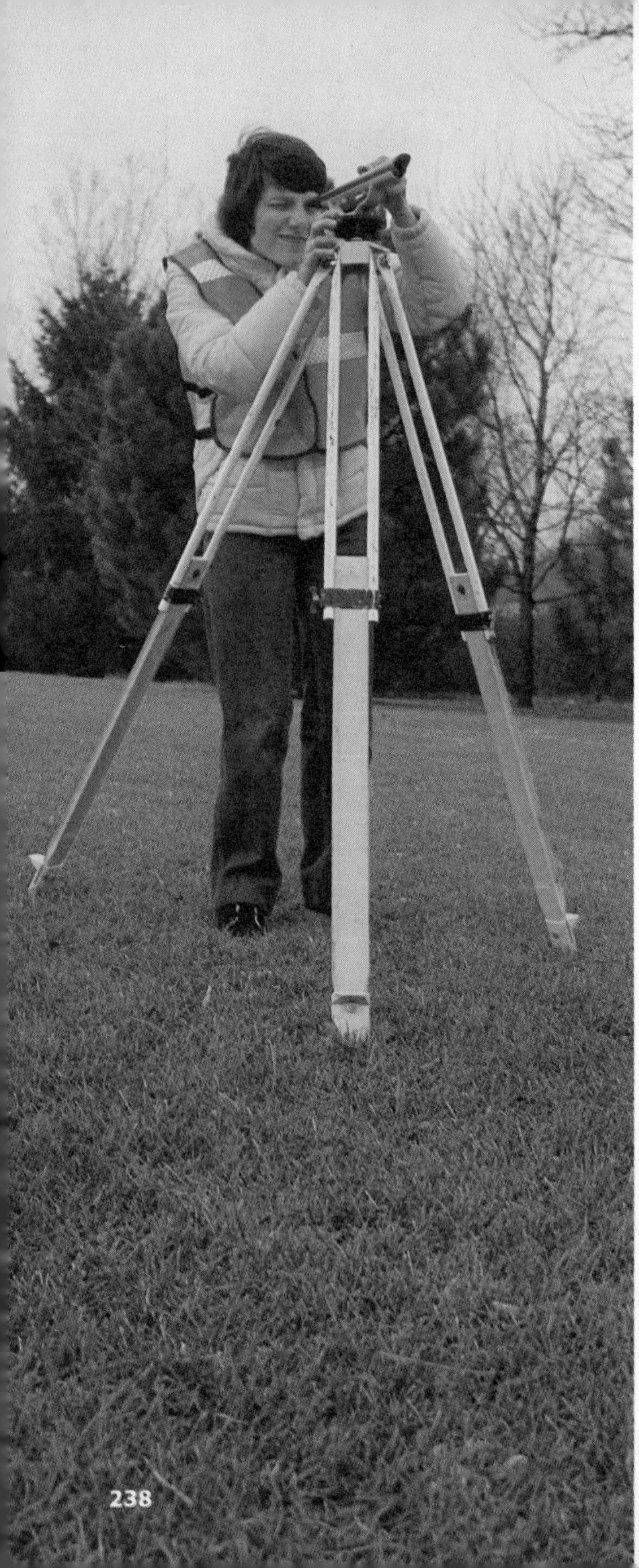

Objective: Make a scale drawing of a piece of property using a ruler and a protractor.

Surveyor

See page T37 for additional notes and activities for Chapter 12.

See the Careers Chart beginning on page 410 for more information about the careers in this cluster.

Career Cluster: Technology Rita Lawsen is a surveyor. She is often hired to make a land survey and a scale drawing of a piece of property.

To make a land survey, Rita determines the **bearings**, or direction, of each side of the property. She uses this information to make a scale drawing. In the diagram below, side XY has bearings N 81° E (81° east of north).

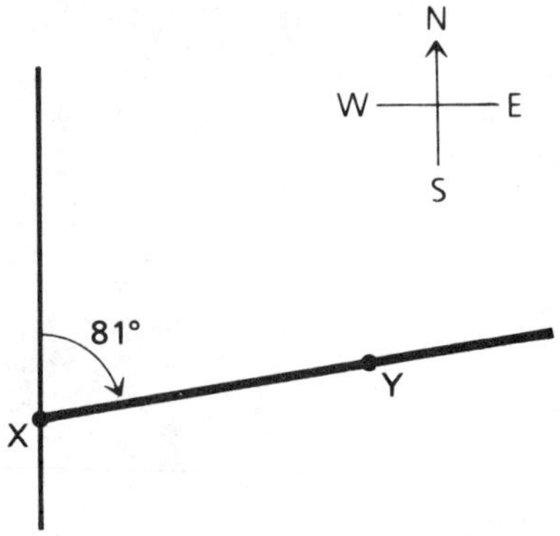

Problem

Materials: Protractor, ruler marked in millimeters

Make a scale drawing using this information from Rita's land survey. Use the scale of 1 cm → 10 m.

Side AB: N 11° W, 39 m
Side BC: S 85° E, 41 m
Side CD: S 8° W, 40 m
Side DA: N 80° W, 29 m

The numbers used in this lesson are rounded to the nearest unit of measure to simplify the work.

Warm-up: $\frac{1}{10} = \frac{x}{32}$ [3.2] $\frac{1}{10} = \frac{x}{98}$ [9.8]

$\frac{1}{10} = \frac{x}{46}$ [4.6] $\frac{1}{10} = \frac{x}{65}$ [6.5]

See page 48 of *Consumer Forms and Problems*.

Solution

You could suggest that students use a colored pencil to draw the north-south lines.

Strategy

- Select a starting point A. Draw a north-south line through A.
- Draw a line through A with bearings N 11° W. Use a protractor to draw the 11° angle.

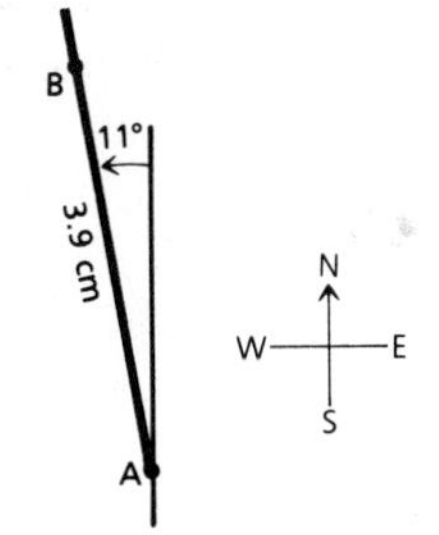

- Use a proportion to find the scale length of side AB.

$$\frac{1}{10} = \frac{x}{39} \begin{array}{l} \longleftarrow \text{Scale length (cm)} \\ \longleftarrow \text{Actual length (m)} \end{array}$$

$$x = 3.9$$

- Measure 3.9 cm from point A and label point B.
- Draw a north-south line through point B. Then draw a line through B with bearings S 85° E (85° east of south).

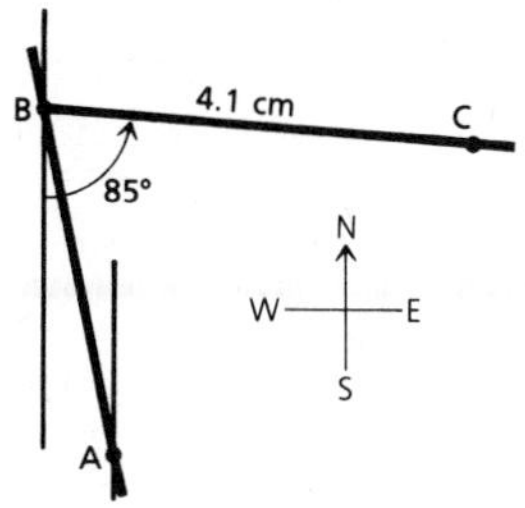

- Use a proportion to find that the scale length of side BC is 4.1 cm. Measure 4.1 cm from point B and label point C.
- Draw a north-south line through point C. Repeat the process and draw side CD.
- Draw side DA. If the drawing is correct, side DA is 2.9 cm long with bearings N 80° W (80° west of a north-south line through point D). Label each side with the bearings and the actual length.

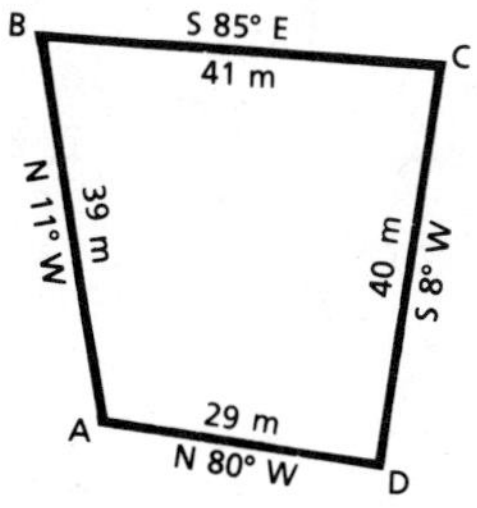

Conclusion

This is the scale drawing of the lot.

The last side drawn will provide a good self-check.

See Additional Answers beginning on page T44.

Related Problems

For each problem, draw the side of a lot with the given bearings and length. Use the scale of 1 cm ⟶ 10 m.

1. N 15° W, 20 m
2. N 87° W, 40 m
3. N 76° E, 38 m
4. N 32° E, 22 m
5. S 18° E, 54 m
6. S 65° E, 42 m
7. S 21° W, 35 m
8. S 9° W, 28 m

For problems 9-12, make a drawing of each lot using the given bearings and lengths. Use the scale of 1 cm ⟶ 10 m.

9. Side AB: N 10° W, 45 m
   Side BC: S 80° E, 40 m
   Side CD: S 5° W, 44 m
   Side DA: N 77° W, 27 m
10. Side KL: N 20° W, 50 m
    Side LM: N 75° E, 53 m
    Side MN: S 6° W, 64 m
    Side NK: N 84° W, 27 m
11. Side WX: N 12° E, 42 m
    Side XY: N 72° E, 38 m
    Side YZ: S 16° E, 65 m
    Side ZW: N 81° W, 64 m
12. Side QR: N 7° E, 54 m
    Side RS: S 73° E, 43 m
    Side ST: S 17° W, 36 m
    Side TQ: S 81° W, 38 m

Objective: Find the cost of building a house and garage by computing the area and using costs per square foot.

Cost of Building a House

Diana and Miguel Vasquez want to build a house. The cost will depend on the size and style of the house, the location, and the kind of building materials used.

Problem

Remind students that "′" means feet and "″" means inches.

Miguel and Diana have decided to build a one-story house with a brick exterior. The contractor told them that the house will cost \$43 per square foot to build. The garage will cost \$13.50 per square foot. What will be the total cost of building the house and garage?

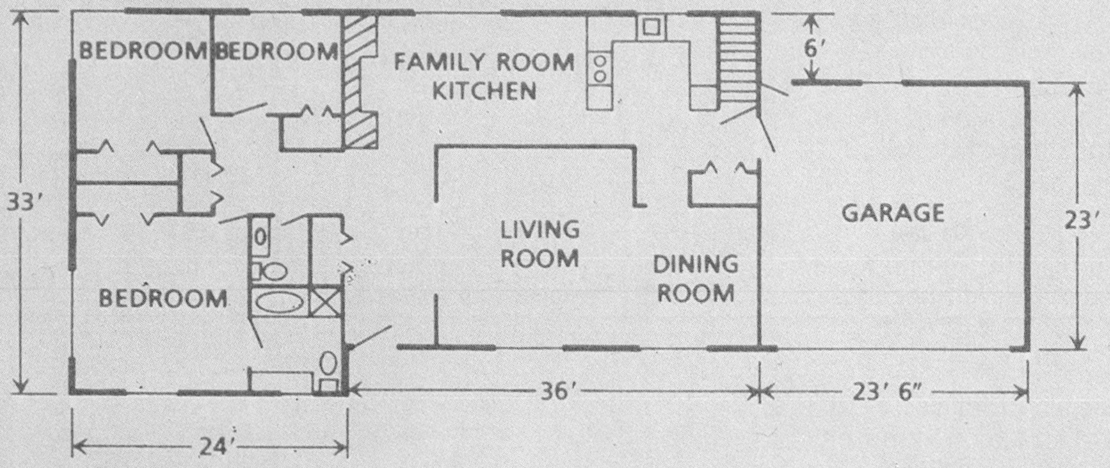

Solution

Strategy

- Multiply to find the area in square feet of each rectangular section of the house (excluding the garage). Then add to find the total area.
  Area of left side: $24 \times 33 = 792$
  Area of right side: $36 \times 29 = 1044$
  Total area: $792 + 1044 = 1836$
- Multiply to find the cost of building the house.
  $1836 \times \$43 = \$78{,}948$
- Multiply to find the area of the garage. Round up to the next square foot. Remember, $23'6'' = 23\frac{1}{2}'$.
  $23\frac{1}{2} \times 23 \approx 541$
- Multiply to find the cost of building the garage.
  $541 \times \$13.50 = \$7303.50$
- Add to find the total cost.
  $\$78{,}948 + \$7303.50 = \$86{,}251.50$

Conclusion

The total cost of building the house and garage will be \$86,251.50.

Warm-up: $23\frac{1}{2} \times 27$ [$634\frac{1}{2}$]

$26 \times 32\frac{1}{2}$ [845]

10.25×463 [4745.75]

39.50×1652 [65,254]

Related Problems

You might recommend that students check their answers by using estimation.

The two-story house below will cost about $38 per square foot to build, and the garage will cost about $13 per square foot.

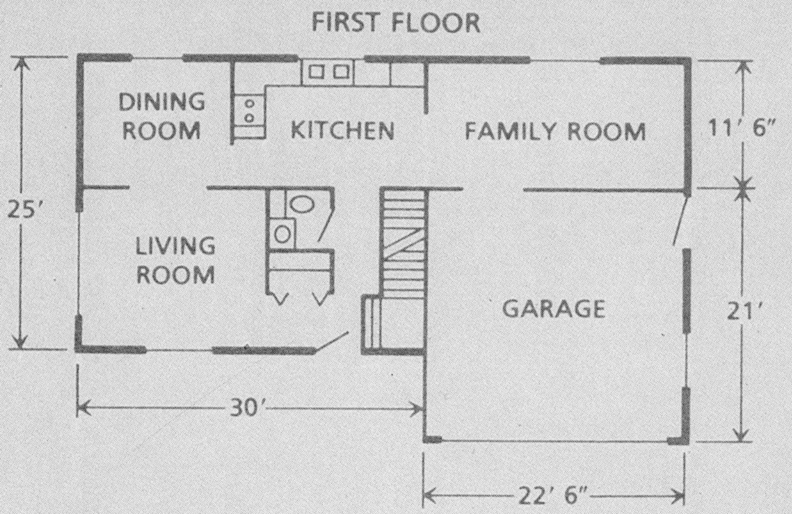

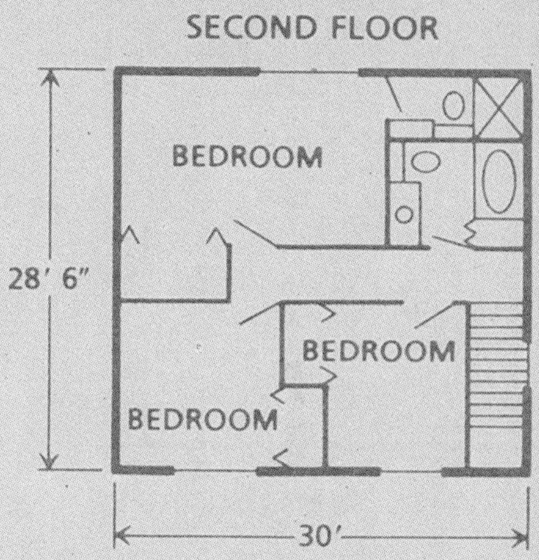

1. Find the area of the left side of the first floor.
   750 square feet
2. Find the area of the right side of the first floor (excluding the garage). $258\frac{3}{4}$ square feet
3. Find the area of the second floor.
   855 square feet
4. Find the total area of the house. Round up to the next square foot.
   1864 square feet
5. Find the cost of building the house.
   $70,832
6. Find the area of the garage. Round up to the next square foot.
   473 square feet
7. Find the cost of building the garage.
   $6149
8. Find the total cost of building the house and garage.
   $76,981

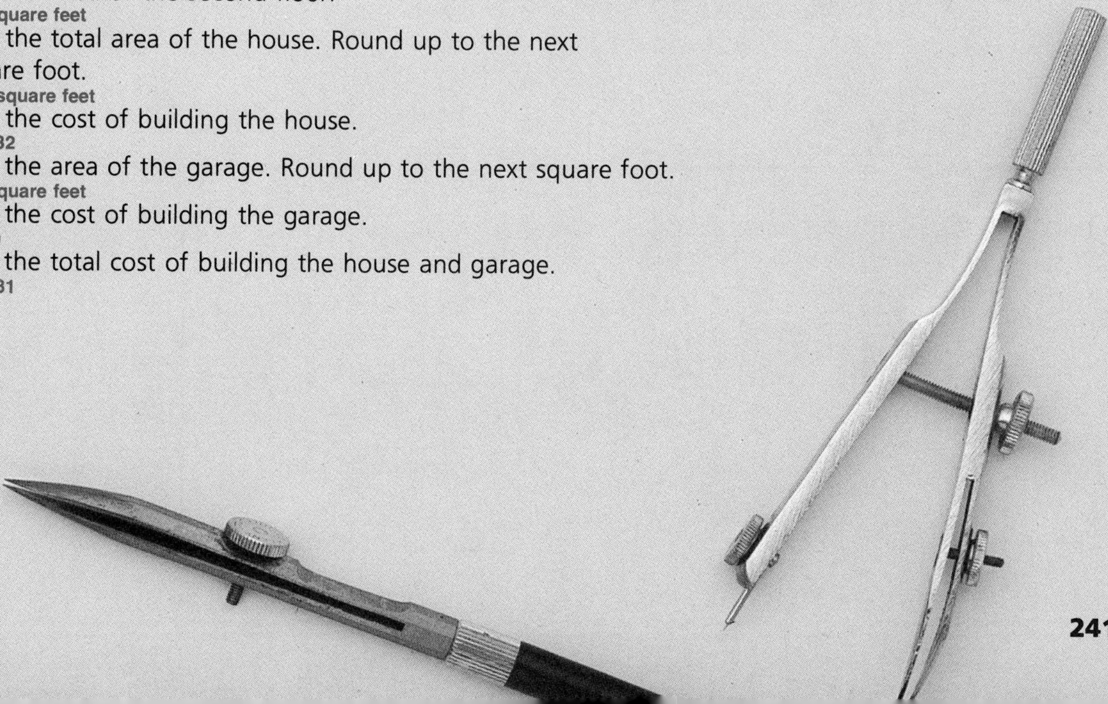

The split-level house below costs $40 per square foot to build. The garage costs $11.50 per square foot.

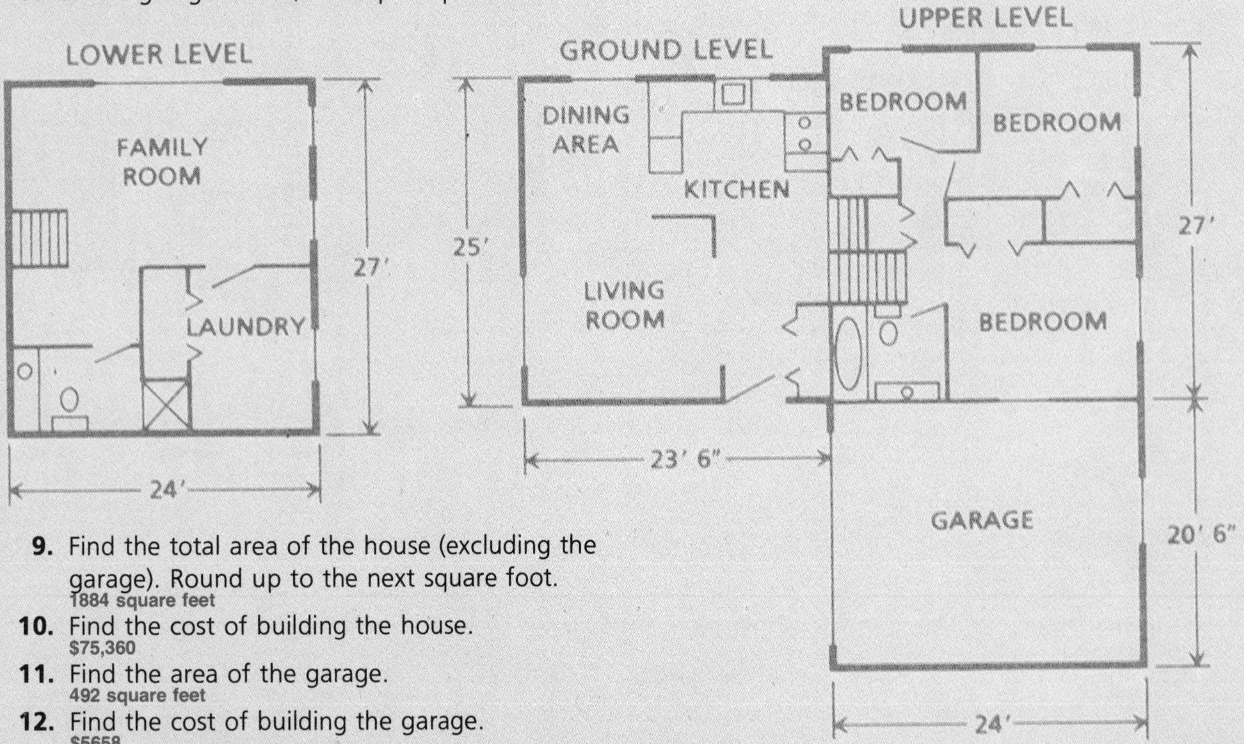

9. Find the total area of the house (excluding the garage). Round up to the next square foot.
1884 square feet

10. Find the cost of building the house.
$75,360

11. Find the area of the garage.
492 square feet

12. Find the cost of building the garage.
$5658

13. What is the total cost of building the house and garage?
$81,018

Break Time

Separate this lot into four smaller lots, each with the same shape as the larger lot. Each of the smaller lots should have the same area.

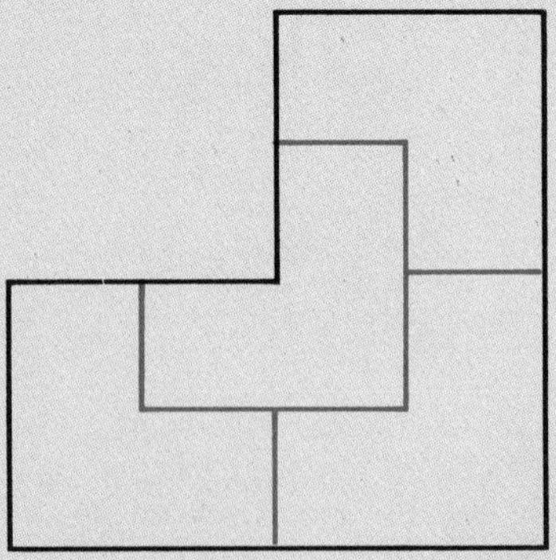

CALCULATOR APPLICATIONS

Building Costs

A builder is quoting the following prices for new homes. Complete the table and determine each total estimate.

Encourage students to use the calculator's memory with these applications.

	Style	Cost per square foot		Area (sq. ft.)				Cost		
		House	Garage	First level	Second level	Third level	Garage	House	Garage	Total
	Homes built with aluminum-siding exterior									
1.	One-story	$36.50	$12.00	1750	—	—	625	**$63,875.00**	**$7500.00**	**$71,375.00**
2.	Two-story	$32.50	$12.00	1000	950	—	450	**$63,375.00**	**$5400.00**	**$68,775.00**
3.	Split-level	$34.00	$11.50	570	580	725	425	**$63,750.00**	**$4887.50**	**$68,637.50**
	Homes built with brick exterior									
4.	One-story	$41.50	$13.50	1685	—	—	340	**$69,927.50**	**$4590.00**	**$74,517.50**
5.	Two-story	$37.00	$13.00	950	1065	—	615	**$74,555.00**	**$7995.00**	**$82,550.00**
6.	Split-level	$39.50	$13.00	615	700	775	625	**$82,555.00**	**$8125.00**	**$90,680.00**
	Homes built with stone exterior									
7.	One-story	$45.00	$15.00	1925	—	—	585	**$86,625.00**	**$8775.00**	**$95,400.00**
8.	Two-story	$40.50	$14.50	875	925	—	585	**$72,900.00**	**$8482.50**	**$81,382.50**
9.	Split-level	$42.50	$14.50	430	490	675	585	**$67,787.50**	**$8482.50**	**$76,270.00**
	Homes built with wood exterior									
10.	One-story	$35.00	$11.50	1875	—	—	500	**$65,625.00**	**$5750.00**	**$71,375.00**
11.	Two-story	$31.50	$11.50	1050	1100	—	585	**$67,725.00**	**$6727.50**	**$74,452.50**
12.	Split-level	$33.00	$11.00	650	670	580	550	**$62,700.00**	**$6050.00**	**$68,750.00**

Possible key sequence: Total area of house [×] Cost [=] [M+] Area of garage [×] Cost [=] [M+] [MR]

Objective: Find the cost of installing a driveway
by computing the area and using the cost per square foot.

Cost of Installing a Driveway

Peter Dubois is going to have a driveway installed. This will involve excavating the area, spreading and rolling gravel, and finally applying asphalt.

Problem

Peter drew this diagram of the driveway he wants installed. The contractor told him that the driveway will cost $1.35 per square foot. What will be the cost of installing the driveway?

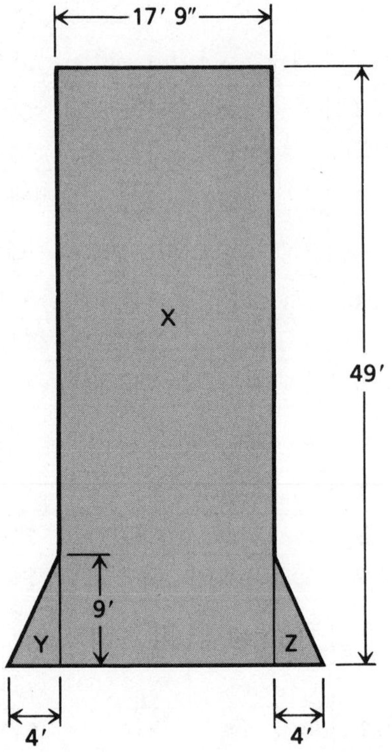

Solution

Strategy

- Multiply the length times the width to find the area in square feet of rectangular section X.
  Remember, 17′9″ = $17\frac{3}{4}'$.
  $49 \times 17\frac{3}{4} = 869\frac{3}{4}$
- For triangular sections Y and Z, multiply $\frac{1}{2}$ times the base times the height to find the area in square feet.
  Area of Y: $\frac{1}{2} \times 4 \times 9 = 18$
  Area of Z: $\frac{1}{2} \times 4 \times 9 = 18$
- Add to find the total area of the driveway. Round up to the next square foot.
  $869\frac{3}{4} + 18 + 18 \approx 906$
- Multiply by $1.35 to find the cost of installing the driveway.
  $1.35 × 906 = $1223.10

Conclusion

The cost of installing the driveway will be $1223.10.

Warm-up: $\frac{1}{2} \times 6 \times 9\frac{1}{4}$ [$27\frac{3}{4}$] $18 \times 10\frac{3}{4}$ [$193\frac{1}{2}$]

$\frac{1}{2} \times 7\frac{1}{2} \times 4$ [15] $526 + 49\frac{3}{4} + 16\frac{1}{2}$ [$592\frac{1}{4}$]

See page 49 of *Consumer Forms and Problems.*

Related Problems

You might recommend that students check their answers by using estimation.

Use the sketch of the driveway shown below for problems 1-10.

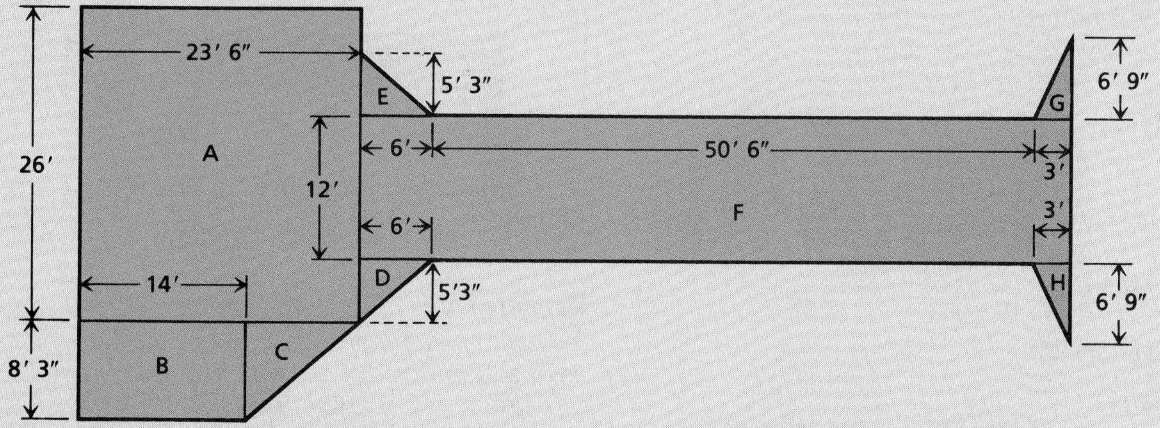

Find the area of each of the following sections of the driveway.

1. Section A **See right.**

2. Section B

3. Section C

4. Section D

5. Section E **$15\frac{3}{4}$ sq. ft.**

6. Section F **714 sq. ft.**

7. Section G **$10\frac{1}{8}$ sq. ft.**

8. Section H **$10\frac{1}{8}$ sq. ft.**

9. Find the total area of the driveway. Round up to the next square foot. **1532 sq. ft.**

10. Find the cost of installing the driveway at $1.35 per square foot. **$2068.20**

1. 611 sq. ft. **3. $39\frac{3}{16}$ sq. ft.**

2. $115\frac{1}{2}$ sq. ft. **4. $15\frac{3}{4}$ sq. ft.**

Objectives: Given a house or garage, find the number of square feet of surface to be covered with bricks; find the amount of materials needed.

Bricklayer

Career Cluster: Trades Bill Sewell is a bricklayer. He determines the number of bricks and the amount of mortar he needs for a job by first finding the number of square feet to be covered.

Problem

Bill is going to brick the front of the garage shown at the right. The door is 18 ft. by 6 ft. 6 in., and the window is 3 ft. by 4 ft. Find the number of square feet to be covered with bricks.

Solution

Strategy

- Multiply to find the area in square feet of the front of the garage.

  $24\frac{1}{2} \times 10 = 245$

- Multiply to find the area of each opening.

  Door: $18 \times 6\frac{1}{2} = 117$

  Window: $3 \times 4 = 12$

- Add to find the total area of the openings.

  $117 + 12 = 129$

- Subtract to find the number of square feet to be covered with bricks.

  $245 - 129 = 116$

Conclusion

116 sq. ft. will be covered with bricks.

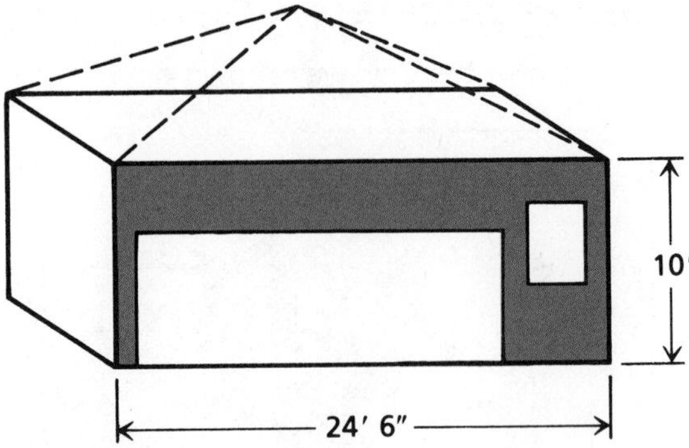

Problem

Bill estimates it will take 7 bricks to cover each square foot of surface. He uses 3 bags of cement and 9 cubic feet of sand to make enough mortar to cover 100 sq. ft. How many bricks, how much cement, and how much sand does he need for the front of the garage (116 sq. ft. of surface)?

Solution

Strategy

- Multiply the area to be covered by 7 to find the number of bricks needed.

  $7 \times 116 = 812$

- Use proportions to find the amount of cement and sand needed. Round up to the next whole number.

  $\frac{3}{100} = \frac{n}{116}$ ← Number of bags of cement (n); Square feet of surface to be covered (116)

  $n \approx 4$

  $\frac{9}{100} = \frac{n}{116}$ ← Cubic feet of sand (n); Square feet of surface to be covered (116)

  $n \approx 11$

Conclusion

Bill needs 812 bricks, 4 bags of cement, and 11 cu. ft. of sand.

Warm-up: $14\frac{3}{4} \times 18$ $[265\frac{1}{2}]$ $\frac{3}{100} = \frac{n}{156}$ [4.68]

$21 \times 13\frac{1}{2}$ $[283\frac{1}{2}]$ $\frac{9}{100} = \frac{n}{145}$ [13.05]

See page 50 of *Consumer Forms and Problems.*

Related Problems

All four sides of the house shown at the right will be covered with bricks.

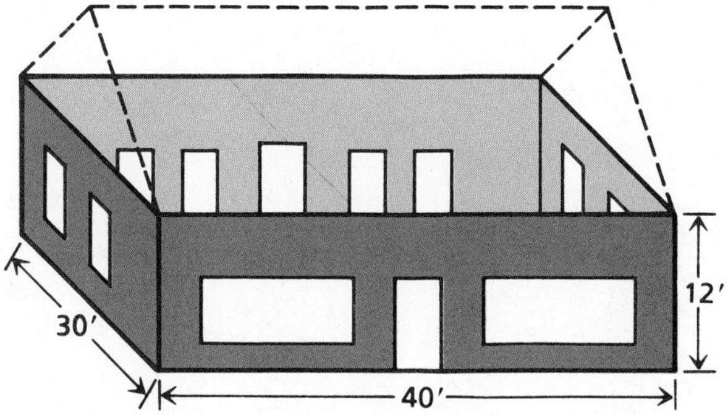

1. Find the area of the front of the house.
   480 square feet
2. Find the area of the left side of the house.
   360 square feet
3. Find the total area of all four sides. The back is the same size as the front, and the right side is the same size as the left side.
   1680 square feet
4. Each front window is 12 ft. by 5 ft. Find the total area of these two openings.
   120 square feet
5. There are eight windows, each 2 ft. 6 in. by 5 ft. Find the total area of these eight openings.
   100 square feet
6. There are two doors, each 3 ft. 6 in. by 7 ft. Find the total area of these two openings.
   49 square feet
7. Find the total area of the twelve openings.
   269 square feet
8. Find the number of square feet that will be covered with bricks.
   1411 square feet
9. Find the number of bricks needed for the house.
   9877 bricks
10. Find the number of bags of cement needed to make mortar for the house. Round up to the next whole number.
    43 bags
11. Find the number of cubic feet of sand needed to make the mortar. Round up to the next whole number.
    127 cubic feet

Skills Tune-Up

Multiplying fractions and mixed numbers, pages 16-17

1. $\frac{5}{8} \times \frac{7}{10}$ $\frac{7}{16}$
2. $\frac{5}{8} \times \frac{6}{7}$ $\frac{15}{28}$
3. $\frac{4}{9} \times \frac{9}{10}$ $\frac{2}{5}$
4. $\frac{7}{8} \times \frac{4}{7}$ $\frac{1}{2}$
5. $\frac{13}{28} \times \frac{21}{26}$ $\frac{3}{8}$
6. $9 \times \frac{1}{12}$ $\frac{3}{4}$
7. $\frac{2}{9} \times 36$ 8
8. $\frac{1}{3} \times 14$ $4\frac{2}{3}$
9. $2\frac{1}{2} \times \frac{1}{4}$ $\frac{5}{8}$
10. $6\frac{1}{4} \times \frac{5}{8}$ $3\frac{29}{32}$
11. $1\frac{3}{5} \times 1\frac{1}{2}$ $2\frac{2}{5}$
12. $3\frac{4}{7} \times 3\frac{1}{2}$ $12\frac{1}{2}$
13. $4\frac{3}{5} \times 8\frac{1}{3}$ $38\frac{1}{3}$
14. $2\frac{1}{12} \times 3\frac{9}{10}$ $8\frac{1}{8}$
15. $3\frac{3}{7} \times 5\frac{1}{2}$ $18\frac{6}{7}$
16. $8 \times 6\frac{5}{8}$ 53
17. $7\frac{5}{12} \times 3$ $22\frac{1}{4}$
18. $\frac{1}{7} \times \frac{7}{8} \times \frac{3}{5}$ $\frac{3}{40}$
19. $\frac{1}{4} \times 8\frac{2}{3} \times \frac{9}{13}$ $1\frac{1}{2}$
20. $2\frac{1}{10} \times 1\frac{2}{3} \times \frac{2}{3}$ $2\frac{1}{3}$

Adding fractions and mixed numbers, pages 18-19

1. $\frac{1}{3} + \frac{5}{12}$ $\frac{3}{4}$
2. $\frac{2}{15} + \frac{2}{5}$ $\frac{8}{15}$
3. $\frac{11}{12} + \frac{1}{2}$ $1\frac{5}{12}$
4. $\frac{5}{12} + \frac{1}{4}$ $\frac{2}{3}$
5. $\frac{1}{6} + \frac{7}{9}$ $\frac{17}{18}$
6. $\frac{11}{12} + \frac{2}{3}$ $1\frac{7}{12}$
7. $\frac{7}{10} + \frac{1}{2}$ $1\frac{1}{5}$
8. $\frac{3}{8} + \frac{9}{16}$ $\frac{15}{16}$
9. $\frac{1}{4} + 2\frac{1}{3}$ $2\frac{7}{12}$
10. $4\frac{1}{6} + \frac{1}{8}$ $4\frac{7}{24}$
11. $2\frac{1}{5} + 1\frac{3}{10}$ $3\frac{1}{2}$
12. $3\frac{3}{5} + 5\frac{3}{20}$ $8\frac{3}{4}$
13. $6\frac{3}{8} + 2\frac{5}{6}$ $9\frac{5}{24}$
14. $1\frac{3}{4} + 2\frac{7}{12}$ $4\frac{1}{3}$
15. $8\frac{7}{15} + 5\frac{2}{5}$ $13\frac{13}{15}$
16. $1\frac{1}{8} + 6\frac{2}{3}$ $7\frac{19}{24}$
17. $2\frac{7}{30} + 7\frac{9}{10}$ $10\frac{2}{15}$
18. $5\frac{7}{24} + 4\frac{5}{8}$ $9\frac{11}{12}$
19. $1\frac{1}{3} + 2\frac{1}{4} + 3\frac{5}{12}$ 7
20. $12\frac{4}{5} + 5\frac{11}{15} + 9\frac{2}{3}$ $28\frac{1}{5}$

Subtracting fractions and mixed numbers, pages 18-19

1. $\frac{11}{18} - \frac{1}{9}$ $\frac{1}{2}$
2. $\frac{13}{14} - \frac{3}{7}$ $\frac{1}{2}$
3. $\frac{3}{5} - \frac{1}{2}$ $\frac{1}{10}$
4. $\frac{17}{24} - \frac{1}{4}$ $\frac{11}{24}$
5. $\frac{7}{9} - \frac{11}{18}$ $\frac{1}{6}$
6. $\frac{17}{20} - \frac{1}{10}$ $\frac{3}{4}$
7. $\frac{13}{16} - \frac{5}{8}$ $\frac{3}{16}$
8. $\frac{3}{5} - \frac{13}{30}$ $\frac{1}{6}$
9. $10\frac{1}{3} - 1\frac{2}{3}$ $8\frac{2}{3}$
10. $20\frac{1}{7} - 2\frac{5}{7}$ $17\frac{3}{7}$
11. $3 - \frac{1}{3}$ $2\frac{2}{3}$
12. $9 - \frac{1}{5}$ $8\frac{4}{5}$
13. $6\frac{3}{8} - 4\frac{1}{4}$ $2\frac{1}{8}$
14. $17\frac{3}{5} - 2\frac{9}{10}$ $14\frac{7}{10}$
15. $6\frac{5}{6} - 3\frac{2}{9}$ $3\frac{11}{18}$
16. $13\frac{3}{7} - 4\frac{13}{14}$ $8\frac{1}{2}$
17. $5\frac{7}{9} - 2\frac{5}{6}$ $2\frac{17}{18}$
18. $13\frac{1}{3} - 6\frac{4}{5}$ $6\frac{8}{15}$
19. $7\frac{1}{4} - 5\frac{5}{12}$ $1\frac{5}{6}$
20. $15\frac{2}{3} - 4\frac{7}{9}$ $10\frac{8}{9}$

Chapter 12 Review

Materials: Protractor, ruler marked in millimeters

Surveyor, pages 238-239

1. Draw the side of a lot with bearings and length S 76° W, 42 m. Use the scale of 1 cm ⟶ 10 m.
See below.

Cost of building a house, pages 240-242

2. Find the total area of the house shown below. Round up to the next square foot.
1321 square feet

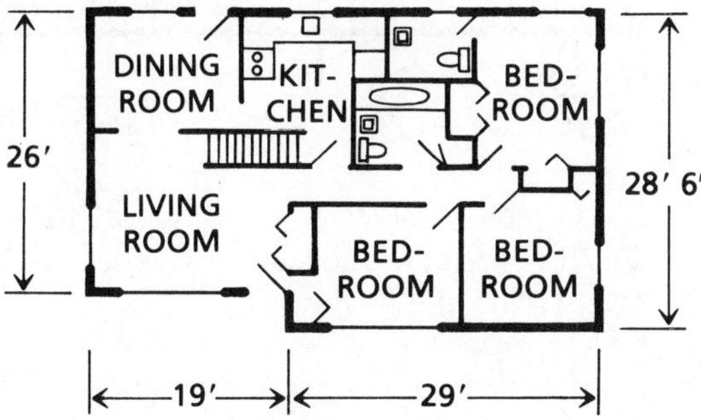

3. A builder will build this house for $39 per square foot. Find the cost of building this house.
$51,519
4. Find the cost of building the garage shown below at $12.50 per square foot.
$6037.50

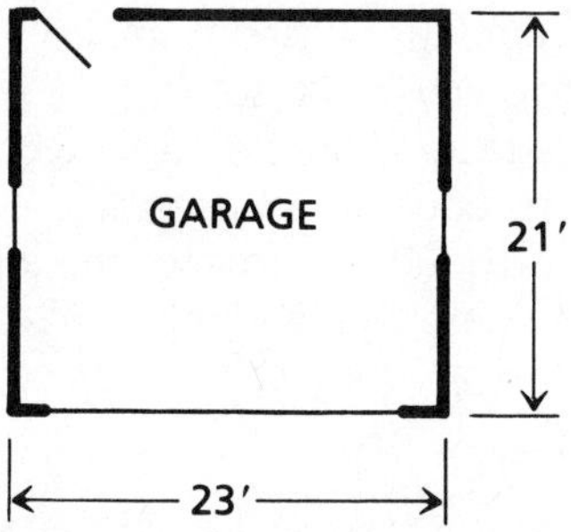

5. What will be the total cost of building the house and garage?
$57,556.50

Cost of installing a driveway, pages 244-245

6. Find the total area of the driveway shown below. Round up to the next square foot.
230 square feet

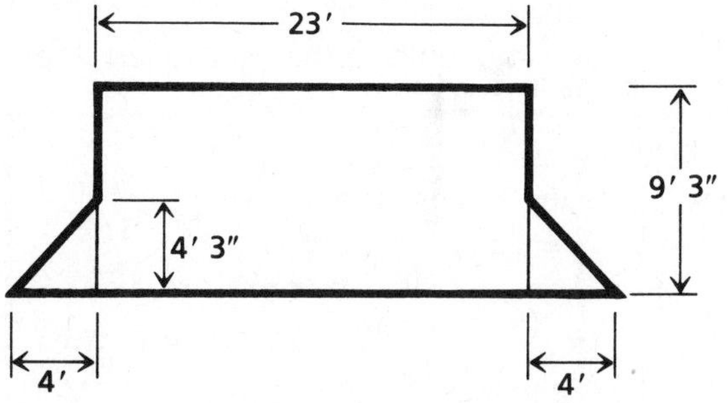

7. A contractor will install the driveway for $1.15 per square foot. What will be the cost of installing the driveway?
$264.50

Bricklayer, pages 246-247

8. The front of a garage 24 ft. 6 in. long and 10 ft. high is going to be covered with bricks. There is a garage door 17 ft. 6 in. by 8 ft. and a window 2 ft. by 3 ft. Find the number of square feet to be covered with bricks.
99 square feet
9. Seven bricks will cover one square foot of surface. How many bricks will be needed for 195 sq. ft. of surface?
1365 bricks
10. Nine cubic feet of sand are used to make enough mortar to cover 100 sq. ft. of surface. If 275 sq. ft. of surface is to be covered with bricks, how much sand is needed to make enough mortar for the job? Round up to the next whole number.
25 cubic feet

1.

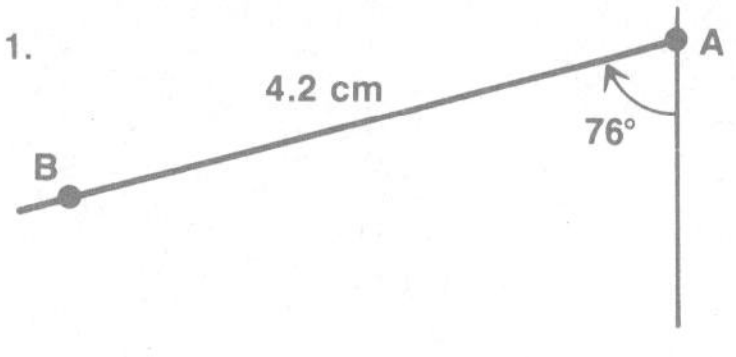

Chapter 12 Test

Materials: Protractor, ruler marked in millimeters

Number of test items - 10

Number missed	1	2	3	4	5
Percent correct	90	80	70	60	50

1. Draw the side of a lot with bearings and length N 84° E, 47 m. Use the scale of 1 cm → 10 m.
See below.

2. Find the total area of the house shown below. Round up to the next square foot.
1047 square feet

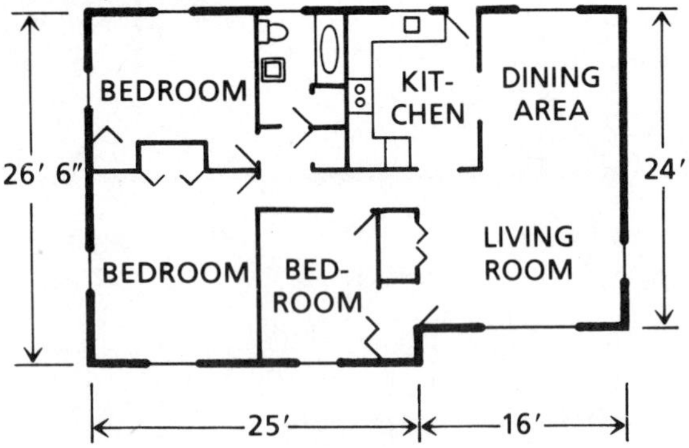

3. A builder will build this house for $41 per square foot. Find the cost of building this house.
$42,927

4. Find the cost of building the garage shown below at $14.50 per square foot.
$10,527

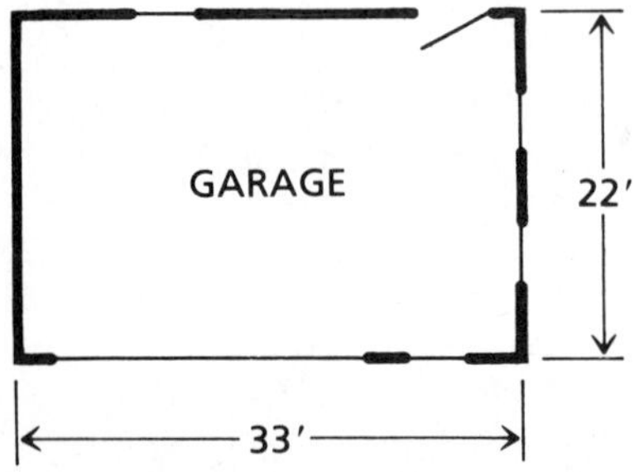

5. What will be the total cost of building the house and garage?
$53,454

6. Find the total area of the driveway shown below. Round up to the next square foot.
304 square feet

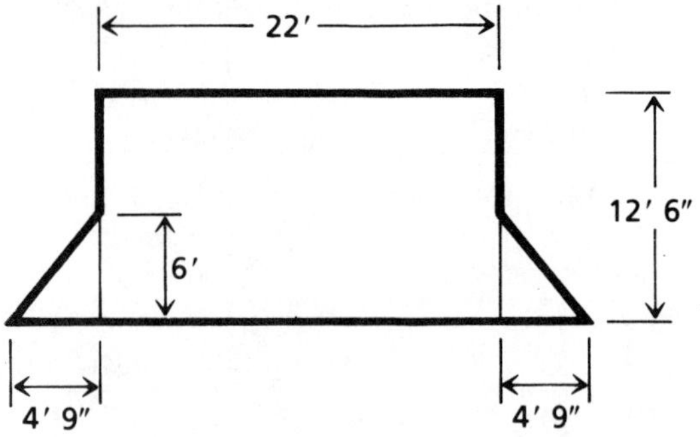

7. A contractor will install the driveway for $1.25 per square foot. What will be the cost of installing the driveway?
$380

8. The front of a store 30 ft. long and 9 ft. 6 in. high is going to be covered with bricks. There is a window 15 ft. by 6 ft. and a door 4 ft. by 7 ft. 6 in. Find the number of square feet to be covered with bricks.
165 square feet

9. Seven bricks will cover one square foot of surface. How many bricks will be needed for 286 sq. ft. of surface?
2002 bricks

10. Three bags of cement are used to make enough mortar to cover 100 sq. ft. If 325 sq. ft. of surface is to be covered with bricks, how many bags of cement are needed to make enough mortar for the job? Round up to the next whole number.
10 bags

1.

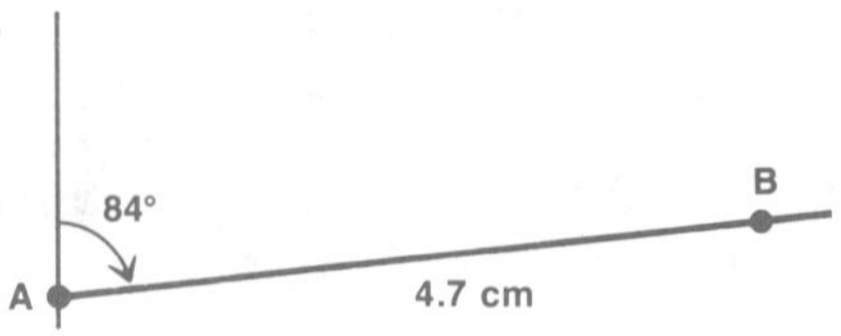

 See pages 29-30 of the *Test Masters* for an alternate form of the Chapter 12 Test.

Unit 4 Test

Number of test items - 20

Number missed	1	2	3	4	5	6	7	8	9	10
Percent correct	95	90	85	80	75	70	65	60	55	50

Choose the best answer.

Pages 194–195

1. Mario earns $7.50 per hour in a 40-hour work week. What is the most he should spend for rent each month? (Use the guideline of not spending more than one week's gross pay for shelter each month.)

A $47.50 **C** $1200

B $300 **D** $290

Pages 196–197

2. Shelley Big Eagle rented an apartment for $255 per month plus utilities. Electricity costs will average $25 per month and heating costs will average $35 per month. How much will Shelley pay for rent and utilities each month?

A $315 **C** $195

B $290 **D** $340

Pages 198–199

3. Give the reading for this electric meter.

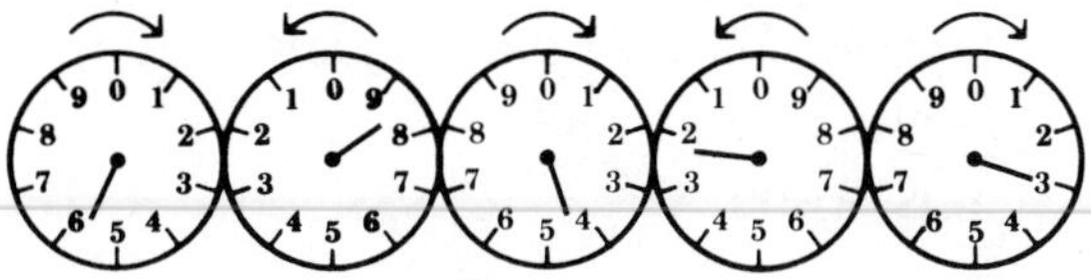

A 58521 **C** 58423

B 59521 **D** 12485

Pages 202–203

4. To the nearest tenth, what is the scale length of a table that is 1.5 m long? Use the scale of 1 cm ⟶ 0.2 m.

A 3.0 cm **C** 0.75 cm

B 0.3 cm **D** 7.5 cm

Pages 204–205

5. How many tiles will be needed to cover a floor 4.5 m by 3.0 m? Each tile is a square 30 cm by 30 cm.

A 900 tiles **C** 14 tiles

B 25 tiles **D** 150 tiles

Pages 206–207

6. A gallon of paint covers 400 sq. ft. About how much paint will be needed to paint the walls of a basement 35 ft. by 22 ft.? The walls are 7 ft. high.

A 1 gallon **C** 3 gallons

B 2 gallons **D** 13.5 gallons

Pages 208–209

7. A roll of wallpaper covers 30 sq. ft. How many rolls are needed for a room 15 ft. by 12 ft. with walls 8 ft. high? Subtract $\frac{1}{2}$ roll for each of the 2 windows and 2 doors.

A 13 rolls **C** 15 rolls

B 11 rolls **D** 46 rolls

Pages 210–211

8. Koyi has a $100-deductible insurance policy. His 5-year-old TV was stolen and will cost $800 to replace. If the annual rate of depreciation is 12%, how much will the insurance company pay?

A $96 **C** $220

B $320 **D** $380

Pages 216–217

9. Ruth earns $18,500 per year. What is the greatest amount she should borrow to buy a home? (Use the general guideline of 2 times annual income.)

A $37,000 **C** $9250

B $36,000 **D** $55,500

Pages 218–219

10. An amortization table shows that the monthly payment for a $1000 loan for 30 years at 12% interest is $10.29. Find the monthly payment on a 30-year home loan of $50,000 at 12% per year.

A $5145 **C** $514.50

B $308.70 **D** $600

Pages 220–221

11. How much interest will Lucita pay on a loan of $30,000 for 25 years if the monthly payments are $361.20?

A $20,970 **C** $277.87

(**B**) $78,360 **D** $108,360

Page 222

12. Maude borrowed $48,000 at an annual interest rate of 14%. How much interest will she pay the first month?

A $6720 **C** $286

B $5600 (**D**) $560

Pages 224–225

13. Drew's basic premium for homeowner's insurance is $195. He has a $600 camera and a $300 guitar he wants to insure separately. Use the table below and find the total premium for his insurance.

Personal property	One-year rate per $100 of value
Cameras, projectors, etc.	$1.65
Musical instruments—amateur	$0.69

(**A**) $206.97 **C** $183.03

B $1392 **D** $11.97

Pages 226–227

14. Find the assessed valuation of a home with a market value of $74,000. The rate of assessment is 60% of market value.

A $118,400 (**C**) $44,400

B $29,600 **D** $103,600

Pages 228–229

15. The recording fee is 0.1% of the purchase price of a home. What is the recording fee on a $94,000 home?

A $846 **C** $9400

(**B**) $94 **D** $940

Pages 230–233

16. A real estate salesperson's commission is 7% of the selling price of a home. For what amount should a house be listed if the seller wants at least $75,000? Round up to the next hundred dollars.

A $80,300 **C** $5300

(**B**) $80,700 **D** $525,000

Pages 238–239

17. Give the bearings of side XY.

A S 25° E **C** N 25° S

B N 25° E (**D**) S 25° W

Pages 240–242

18. A builder charges $42 per square foot to build a one-story house. Find the cost of building a house 35 feet wide and 50 feet long.

(**A**) $73,500 **C** $35,700

B $72,500 **D** $71,400

Pages 244–245

19. A contractor will install a driveway for $1.15 per square foot. What is the cost of a driveway 16 ft. 6 in. wide and 20 ft. long?

A $330 **C** $83.95

B $381.80 (**D**) $379.50

Pages 246–247

20. A store front is 30 ft. long and 10 ft. high. It contains one opening 8 ft. by 7 ft. If a bricklayer uses 7 bricks per square foot of surface covered, about how many bricks will be needed for the store front?

A 350 bricks (**C**) 1708 bricks

B 2100 bricks **D** 35 bricks

Break Time

Many items sold in stores have prices close to a multiple-of-10 amount or an even-dollar amount. For example, 89¢ is close to 90¢, and $7.98 is close to $8. Multiplying mentally to find total costs is easy with numbers like 90 and 8.

Blank cassette tapes cost 89¢ each. How much would 5 tapes cost?

THINK

89 cents is 1 cent less than 90 cents.
5 × 90 cents = 450 cents
5 × 1 cent = 5 cents
450 cents − 5 cents = 445 cents, or $4.45

The 5 tapes would cost $4.45.

Stereo tapes cost $7.98 each. How much would 4 stereo tapes cost?

THINK

$7.98 is 2 cents less than 8 dollars.
4 × 8 dollars = 32 dollars
4 × 2 cents = 8 cents
32 dollars − 8 cents = $31.92

The 4 stereo tapes would cost $31.92.

Find these products mentally. Write only the answer.

1. 4 × 79¢ $3.16
2. 6 × 99¢ $5.94
3. 8 × 59¢ $4.72
4. 2 × 88¢ $1.76
5. 7 × 48¢ $3.36
6. 5 × 35¢ $1.75
7. 9 × 39¢ $3.51
8. 15 × 19¢ $2.85
9. 4 × $1.99 $7.96
10. 3 × $3.98 $11.94
11. 6 × $1.97 $11.82
12. 2 × $4.99 $9.98
13. 5 × $2.95 $14.75
14. 8 × $2.99 $23.92
15. 4 × $5.98 $23.92
16. 12 × $1.99 $23.88

Now try these. A hint is given for exercise 17.

17. 3 × $2.09 $6.27

THINK

$2.09 is 9 cents more than 2 dollars.
3 × 2 dollars = 6 dollars
3 × 9 cents = 27 cents
6 dollars + 27 cents = ▦

18. 6 × $1.05 $6.30
19. 4 × $6.08 $24.32
20. 7 × $2.10 $14.70
21. 5 × $4.03 $20.15
22. 5 × 81¢ $4.05
23. 8 × 32¢ $2.56
24. 9 × 12¢ $1.08
25. 6 × 73¢ $4.38

Amortization Tables

The problems on pages 222–223 can be done using the program shown.

Betty Johnson is a loan officer at a savings and loan association. She uses the program shown to print amortization tables for mortgage loans.

Lines 40, 60, and 80 These values must be entered.

Data required	*Name*
Amount financed	P
Annual interest rate (%)	Y
Number of years to repay	N

Line 20 Each calculation in this program must be rounded, or error will compound. The DEF function can be used when rounding must be done many times. To define a function to round to the nearest cent, first use DEF, then a name of three letters beginning with FN, and then another name of one letter in parentheses.

Line 90 The number of years is multiplied by 12 to change it to the number of monthly payments.

Line 110 The monthly payment (A) is calculated.

Line 120 The monthly payment is rounded up to the next higher cent.

Lines 130 and 140 PRINT statements are used to print headings for the table.

Lines 160 and 240 A FOR–NEXT loop is used to calculate and print each payment of the amortization table. The calculations and PRINT statements go between lines 160 and 240. M counts the number of months.

Line 170 The interest (I) is calculated and rounded.

Line 180 The interest is subtracted from the payment to find the amount (P1) that is applied to the principal.

Line 190 As long as the amount applied to the principal doesn't exceed the principal, line 200 is skipped.

Line 200 On the last payment, the amount paid to the principal often exceeds the amount of principal left to be paid. In this case, P1 is changed so that only P is paid.

Line 210 The amount applied to the principal in line 180 is subtracted from the principal to find the new principal (P2).

Line 220 Each payment of the table is printed.

Line 230 The rounded new principal becomes the principal for the next time the loop is executed.

If your computer does not have a disc drive system, delete the statement on line 20. For every line that contains FNR as part of the statement, delete FNR and add a rounding statement as explained on page 128, line 120.

These problems should be done using a computer. Modifications can be paper-and-pencil activities.

```
10 REM  MORTGAGE AMORTIZATION TABLE
20 DEF FNR(Z)=INT(Z*100+.5)/100
30 PRINT "AMOUNT FINANCED";
40 INPUT P
50 PRINT "INTEREST RATE";
60 INPUT Y
70 PRINT "NUMBER OF YEARS";
80 INPUT N
90 LET N=N*12
100 LET R=Y/100/12
110 LET A=P*((R*(1+R)^N)/((1+R)^N-1))
120 LET A=INT(A*100+.999)/100
130 PRINT "PAYMENT";TAB(23);"AMOUNT OF";
TAB(35);"AMOUNT PAID";TAB(50);"'NEW'"
140 PRINT "NUMBER";TAB(11);"PRINCIPAL";
TAB(23);"INTEREST";TAB(35);"ON
PRINCIPAL";TAB(50);"PRINCIPAL"
150 PRINT
160 FOR M=1 TO N
170 LET I=FNR(P*R)
180 LET P1=FNR(A-I)
190 IF P1<=P THEN 210
200 LET P1=FNR(P)
210 LET P2=FNR(P-P1)
220 PRINT TAB(2);M;TAB(11);P;TAB(24);I;
TAB(38);P1;TAB(50);P2
230 LET P=FNR(P2)
240 NEXT M
250 END
```

Answers for computer applications are often in an abbreviated form. In all program modifications shown, the changes and/or additions incorporate previous modifications and will vary. Samples are given.

Give the output for the program above when

See Additional Answers beginning on page T51.

1. P is 2000, Y is 16, and N is 3.
2. P is 6500, Y is 14.5, and N is 2.5.
3. P is 4475, Y is 15.25, and N is 2.75.
4. P is 8000, Y is 17, and N is 2.25.
5. the principal is \$5000, the annual interest rate is 15%, and the number of years is 2.
6. the principal is \$7865, the annual interest rate is 16.5%, and the number of years is 2.75.
7. the principal is \$3600, the annual interest rate is 14.75%, and the number of years is 2.5.
8. the principal is \$2200, the annual interest rate is 17.5%, and the number of years is 1.5.
9. \$4000 is financed at 16.75% annually for 2.25 years.
10. \$1600 is financed at 18% annually for 0.75 years.
11. \$9500 is financed at 14% annually for 3 years.
12. \$6195 is financed at 16.5% annually for 2.5 years.
13. Modify the program so that a title, the principal, the annual rate of interest, the number of months, and the monthly payment are printed before the table. Only PRINT statements need to be added.
See below.
14. Give the output when the principal is \$3000, the annual interest rate is 14.75%, and the number of years is 2.
See Additional Answers on page T52.
15. Modify the program so that the total paid to interest and the total paid to principal are printed after the table. Use LET statements before the FOR–NEXT loop to make T1 and T2 equal to zero. Then use T1 and T2 inside the loop to keep running totals.
See below.
16. Give the output when the principal is \$3785, the annual interest rate is 15.5%, and the number of years is 2.5.
See Additional Answers on page T53 for problems 16 and 17.
17. Give the output when the principal is \$2755, the annual interest rate is 17.5%, and the number of years is 0.5.

13.
```
121 PRINT TAB(18);"MORTGAGE AMORTIZATION TABLE"
122 PRINT "PRINCIPAL AMOUNT";TAB(28);"$";P
123 PRINT "ANNUAL INTEREST RATE";TAB(29);Y;"%"
124 PRINT "TERM";TAB(29);N;"MONTHS"
125 PRINT "MONTHLY PAYMENT";TAB(28);"$";A
126 PRINT
```

15.
```
25 LET T1=0
26 LET T2=0
225 LET T1=T1+I
226 LET T2=T2+P1
241 PRINT
242 PRINT "TOTAL PAID TO INTEREST     $";FNR(T1)
243 PRINT "TOTAL PAID TO PRINCIPAL    $";FNR(T2)
244 PRINT TAB(28);"---------"
245 PRINT TAB(26);"$";FNR(T1+T2)
```

Unit 5 Taxes, Insurance, and Investments

Chapter 13 Income Tax

Objective: Determine who must file a federal income tax return.

Who Must File a Tax Return

See page T38 for additional notes and activities for Chapter 13.

1 Control number	22222
2 Employer's name, address, and ZIP code	Valley Supermarket 2307 Lake Street Spring Valley, MI 49100
3 Employer's identification number	
4 Employer's State number	
5 Stat. employee / Deceased / Pension plan / Legal rep. / 942 emp. / Subtotal / Correction / Void	☐ ☐ ☐ ☐ ☐ ☐ ☐ ☐
6	
7 Advance EIC payment	
8 Employee's social security number	999-32-5110
9 Federal income tax withheld	$105.77
10 Wages, tips, other compensation	$1,511.72
11 FICA tax withheld	$100.53
12 Employee's name, address, and ZIP code	Bert Steiger 562 Chestnut Street Spring Valley, MI 49100
13 FICA wages	$1,511.72
14 FICA tips	
16 Employer's use	
17 State income tax	$68.43
18 State wages, tips, etc.	$1,511.72
19 Name of State	MI
20 Local income tax	
21 Local wages, tips, etc.	
22 Name of locality	

Form **W-2 Wage and Tax Statement 1980** Copy B To be filed with employee's FEDERAL tax return. This information is being furnished to the Internal Revenue Service. Department of the Treasury Internal Revenue Service

At the end of each year, employers provide a **wage and tax statement**, Form W-2, to each person they have employed during the year. This form indicates the income earned and taxes withheld during the year. A copy of the W-2 form must accompany the person's **income tax return** when it is filed with the Internal Revenue Service (IRS).

The W-2 form shown above indicates that Bert Steiger earned $1511.72 at Valley Supermarket. It also shows that $105.77 was withheld for federal income tax, $100.53 was withheld for FICA (social security), and $68.43 was withheld for state income tax.

Two factors, **gross income** and **filing status**, are used to determine who must file a tax return. Gross income is total annual income that is taxed, such as income from wages, tips, interest, dividends, and self-employment. Filing status depends on marital status.

A person may not be required by law to file a tax return; but if he or she is entitled to a tax refund, a tax return must be filed in order to receive the refund.

General Instructions

Who Must File

Your income and your filing status generally determine whether or not you must file a tax return.

You must file a return for 1980, even if you owe no tax:	And your income was at least:
If you were single (this also means legally separated, divorced, or married with a dependent child and living apart from your spouse for all of 1980) and:	
Under 65	$3,300
65 or over	4,300
If you were married filing a joint return and were living with your spouse at the end of 1980 (or on the date your spouse died), and:	
Both were under 65	5,400
One was 65 or over	6,400
Both were 65 or over	7,400
If you were married filing a	

Warm-up: 1421.96 + 3347.82 [4769.78]
239.17 + 3301.55 [3540.72]
2890.43 + 3105.68 [5996.11]
184.62 + 1275.98 + 2315.50 [3776.10]

Problem

Bert Steiger is a single 18-year-old student. Last year he worked for both the Valley Supermarket, where he earned $1511.72, and the Ace Construction Company, where he earned $1396.26. What was his gross income for the year? Is he required to file a tax return?

Solution

Strategy

- Add to find the gross income.
  $1511.72 + $1396.26 = $2907.98
- Find the minimum income for a single person under 65 for which a tax return must be filed.
  $3300
- Compare Bert's income with the minimum income.
  $2907.98 < $3300

Conclusion

Bert's gross income was $2907.98. Bert is not required to file a tax return.

Even though Bert is not required to file a tax return, he must do so in order to obtain a refund if he is entitled to it.

Related Problems

For problems 1-8, find the gross income. Then write *yes* if a tax return is required or *no* if it is not required.

1. Louette Romas
Single (age 18)
Income: $2235.80 and $1310.75
$3546.55; yes

2. Patti and Greg Talman
Married filing joint return (ages 64 and 67)
Income: $4420.88 and $2132.18
$6553.06; yes

3. Martin and Sandra Weiler
Married filing joint return (both age 72)
Income: $3395.27, $2537.18, and $988.25
$6920.70; no

4. Norman Demato
Single (age 80)
Income: $3211.75, $1067.95, and $210.50
$4490.20; yes

5. Kevin and Bea Orzel
Married filing joint return (ages 68 and 70)
Income: $5100, $1273.14, $557.20, and $214.25
$7144.59; no

6. Clarence and Anne Friedman
Married filing joint return (both age 60)
Income: $2967.20, $1582.13, $456.63, and $272.95
$5278.91; no

7. Ruth Lampert
Single (age 66)
Income: $2116.25, $1349.31, and $714.30
$4179.86; no

8. Luke Kaywaykla
Single (age 21)
Income: $2182.50, $586.17, $436.15, and $118.23
$3323.05; yes

9. Samuel Taylor is single and 67 years old. He has earned $2875 so far this year. How much more can he earn and still remain under the minimum income for filing a tax return?
$1424.99

10. Marie and Tom Hannah are both 69 years old and will file a joint return. They have earned $5580 so far this year. How much more can they earn and still remain under the minimum income for filing a tax return?
$1819.99

Objective: Compute the adjusted gross income and tax credit as required on income tax Form 1040A.

Adjusted Gross Income and Tax Credit

By April 15 of each year, taxpayers should file an income tax return with the IRS. Most taxpayers complete either the **short form**, Form 1040A, or the **long form**, Form 1040.

The IRS allows taxpayers to round amounts to the nearest dollar on tax returns. The amounts shown on this tax return have been rounded to the nearest dollar.

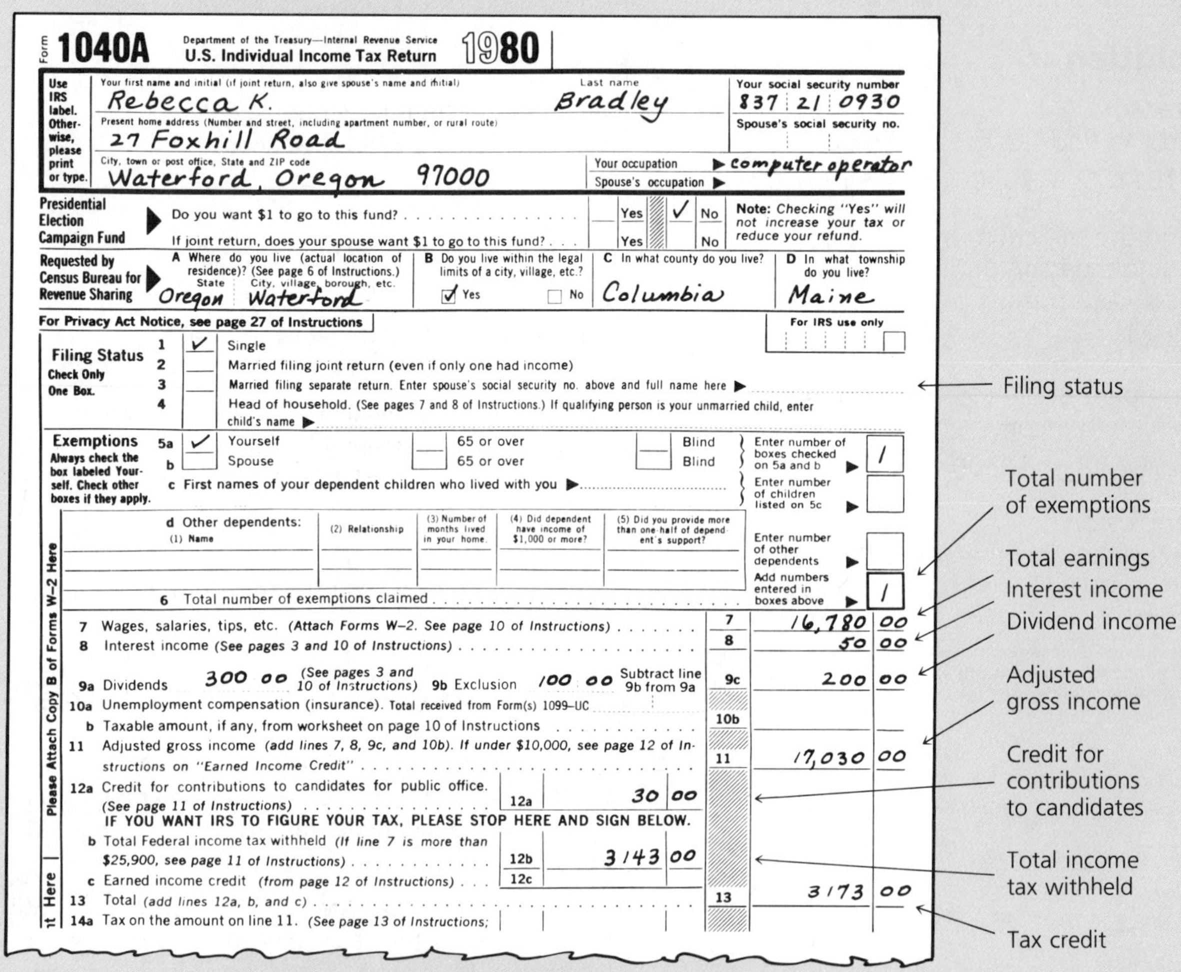

Form **1040A** Department of the Treasury—Internal Revenue Service **U.S. Individual Income Tax Return** **1980**

Use IRS label. Otherwise, please print or type.

Your first name and initial (if joint return, also give spouse's name and initial)	Last name	Your social security number
Rebecca K.	Bradley	837 21 0930
Present home address (Number and street, including apartment number, or rural route)		Spouse's social security no.
27 Foxhill Road		
City, town or post office, State and ZIP code	Your occupation ▶ computer operator	
Waterford, Oregon 97000	Spouse's occupation ▶	

Presidential Election Campaign Fund ▶ Do you want $1 to go to this fund? Yes ☐ No ✓ — If joint return, does your spouse want $1 to go to this fund? Yes ☐ No ☐ — **Note:** *Checking "Yes" will not increase your tax or reduce your refund.*

Requested by Census Bureau for Revenue Sharing ▶

A Where do you live (actual location of residence)? (See page 6 of Instructions.)	B Do you live within the legal limits of a city, village, etc.?	C In what county do you live?	D In what township do you live?
State: Oregon; City, village, borough, etc.: Waterford	✓ Yes ☐ No	Columbia	Maine

For Privacy Act Notice, see page 27 of Instructions — For IRS use only

Filing Status Check Only One Box.

1	✓	Single
2	☐	Married filing joint return (even if only one had income)
3	☐	Married filing separate return. Enter spouse's social security no. above and full name here ▶
4	☐	Head of household. (See pages 7 and 8 of Instructions.) If qualifying person is your unmarried child, enter child's name ▶

Exemptions Always check the box labeled Yourself. Check other boxes if they apply.

5a	✓ Yourself	☐ 65 or over	☐ Blind	Enter number of boxes checked on 5a and b ▶	1
b	☐ Spouse	☐ 65 or over	☐ Blind		
c	First names of your dependent children who lived with you ▶			Enter number of children listed on 5c ▶	

d Other dependents:

(1) Name	(2) Relationship	(3) Number of months lived in your home	(4) Did dependent have income of $1,000 or more?	(5) Did you provide more than one-half of dependent's support?

Enter number of other dependents ▶ ☐

Add numbers entered in boxes above ▶ 1

6 Total number of exemptions claimed

Please Attach Copy B of Forms W-2 Here

7	Wages, salaries, tips, etc. *(Attach Forms W-2. See page 10 of Instructions)*	7	16,780 00
8	Interest income *(See pages 3 and 10 of Instructions)*	8	50 00
9a	Dividends 300 00 *(See pages 3 and 10 of Instructions)* 9b Exclusion 100 00 Subtract line 9b from 9a	9c	200 00
10a	Unemployment compensation (insurance). Total received from Form(s) 1099–UC		
b	Taxable amount, if any, from worksheet on page 10 of Instructions	10b	
11	Adjusted gross income *(add lines 7, 8, 9c, and 10b). If under $10,000, see page 12 of Instructions on "Earned Income Credit"*	11	17,030 00
12a	Credit for contributions to candidates for public office. *(See page 11 of Instructions)* 12a 30 00		
	IF YOU WANT IRS TO FIGURE YOUR TAX, PLEASE STOP HERE AND SIGN BELOW.		
b	Total Federal income tax withheld *(If line 7 is more than $25,900, see page 11 of Instructions)* 12b 3143 00		
c	Earned income credit *(from page 12 of Instructions)* 12c		
13	Total *(add lines 12a, b, and c)*	13	3173 00
14a	Tax on the amount on line 11. *(See page 13 of Instructions;*		

Filing status

Total number of exemptions

Total earnings

Interest income

Dividend income

Adjusted gross income

Credit for contributions to candidates

Total income tax withheld

Tax credit

In this lesson and the following lessons, the amounts used are already rounded to the nearest dollar.

Warm-up: 15,287 + 40 + 35 [15,362]
21,837 + 160 + 45 [22,042]
Find $\frac{1}{2}$ of 80. [40]
Find $\frac{1}{2}$ of 120. [60]

The following is the information needed for filling out lines 7-13 of Form 1040A.

Line 7 is the total of all earnings for the year shown on W-2 forms.

Line 8 is all interest income for the year.

Line 9a is all dividend income. The exclusion on line 9b is determined as follows:

Single or Married Filing Separate Return: $100 exclusion

Married Filing Joint Return: $200 exclusion for stock owned jointly

Line 9c is the taxable dividend income.

Line 11 is the **adjusted gross income**.

Line 12a is credit for contributions to candidates running for public office. The credit is determined as follows:

Single or Married Filing Separate Return: One half of the contribution up to $50 maximum credit

Married Filing Joint Return: One half of the contribution up to $100 maximum credit

Line 12b is the total federal income tax withheld for the year as shown on W-2 forms.

Line 13 is the **tax credit**. This is the total amount of credits and taxes withheld.

Problem

Rebecca Bradley's tax return is shown on page 260. She contributed $60 to a candidate running for public office. What are her adjusted gross income and tax credit?

Solution

Strategy

- Fill in total earnings (line 7), interest income (line 8), and dividend income (line 9a).
- Determine exclusion (line 9b) for dividend income.
- Subtract the dividend exclusion (line 9b) from the dividends (line 9a) to find the dividend income that is taxed (line 9c).
- Determine if one half of the contribution to a candidate running for public office is less than the maximum allowed. Fill in the credit for contributions to candidates (line 12a).

$\frac{1}{2} \times \$60 = \$30$ — $30 is less than $50 maximum for a single person filing a separate return.

- Fill in income tax withheld (line 12b), and add to find the tax credit (line 13).

Conclusion

Rebecca's adjusted gross income is $17,030 (line 11). Her tax credit is $3173 (line 13).

The next two lessons will complete the tax return for Rebecca Bradley.

See pages 8–9 of
Consumer Forms and Problems.

Related Problems

Find the adjusted gross income and the tax credit.

1. Doug Erickson, Single
   Salary: $12,436
   Interest income: $47
   Dividend income: $378
   Contribution to candidates: $30
   Federal tax withheld: $1947
   $12,761; $1962
2. Viola Jackson, Single
   Salary: $14,682
   Interest income: $250
   Dividend income: $45
   Federal tax withheld: $2534
   $14,932; $2534
3. Margo Vitero
   Married filing separate return
   Salary: $18,200
   Interest income: $90
   Dividend income: $175
   Contribution to candidates: $100
   Federal tax withheld: $2554
   $18,365; $2604
4. Lisa and Joseph Rojas
   Married filing joint return
   Salary: $27,120
   Interest income: $175
   Contribution to candidates: $40
   Federal tax withheld: $4673
   $27,295; $4693
5. Gene and Kim Quan
   Married filing joint return
   Salaries: $15,800 and $10,300
   Interest income: $325
   Dividend income: $316
   Federal tax withheld: $1485 and $1060
   $26,541; $2545
6. Al and Kay McCarthy
   Married filing joint return
   Salaries: $10,995 and $4765
   Interest income: $95
   Dividend income: $160
   Contribution to candidates: $150
   Federal tax withheld: $1371 and $214
   $15,855; $1660

Break Time

The spoon weighs 22 grams. What is the total weight of a fork, knife, spoon, and plate?

154 grams
(Fork 22 grams; knife 44 grams; plate 66 grams)

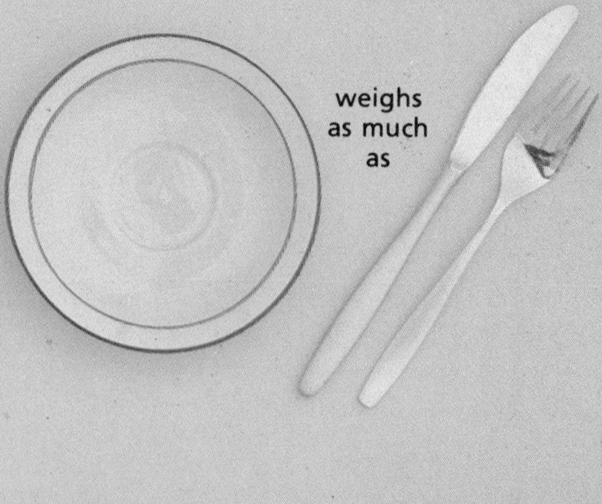

Objective: Use a tax table to find tax liability as required on Form 1040A.

Warm-up: Replace ● with < or >.
2436 ● 2582 [<]
387 ● 378 [>]
1642 ● 1289 [>]
2764 ● 2839 [<]

Tax Liability

Have students familiarize themselves with the tables before proceeding with the lesson.

The federal income tax is based on a graduated system in which the tax rate increases as income increases. Most people can use a tax table to find their **tax liability**. The table the taxpayer uses depends on his or her filing status. Parts of three of these tables are shown on pages 406-408.

Table A/Single
Table B/Married Filing Joint Return
Table C/Married Filing Separate Return
Table D/Head of Household has not been given.

The following section is from Table A.

1980 Tax Table A/Single

If line 11, Form 1040A, or line 34, Form 1040, is—		And the total number of exemptions claimed on line 6 is—		
Over	But not over	1	2	3
		Your tax is—		
16,900	16,950	2,883	2,586	2,326
16,950	17,000	2,898	2,599	2,339
17,000	17,050	2,913	2,613	2,352
17,050	17,100	2,928	2,628	2,365

Problem

Rebecca Bradley's tax return is shown on page 260.

Rebecca Bradley is single claiming 1 exemption. She has an adjusted gross income of $17,030. What is her tax liability?

Solution

Strategy

- Find the line in Tax Table A/Single for an adjusted gross income (line 11, Form 1040A) over $17,000 but not over $17,050.
- Read the tax liability for 1 exemption.
  $2913

Conclusion

Rebecca's tax liability is $2913.

Related Problems

Find the tax liability. Use the tax tables on pages 406-408.

1. Fred Livingston
   Single, 1 exemption
   Adjusted gross income: $11,543
   $1497
2. Harold and Yvonne Rader
   Married filing joint return, 3 exemptions
   Adjusted gross income: $19,775
   $2451
3. Nancy Madden
   Married filing separate return, 1 exemption
   Adjusted gross income: $14,029
   $2485
4. Robert and Karen Kato
   Married filing joint return, 4 exemptions
   Adjusted gross income: $25,725
   $3700
5. Shannon McGill
   Single, 2 exemptions
   Adjusted gross income: $19,820
   $3453
6. Charles Krueger
   Single, 1 exemption
   Adjusted gross income: $16,239
   $2673
7. Isabel and Jose Gomez
   Married filing joint return, 5 exemptions
   Adjusted gross income: $28,525
   $4204
8. Mary and Donald Hughes
   Married filing joint return, 7 exemptions
   Adjusted gross income: $19,160
   $1462
9. Gerald Ledder
   Married filing separate return, 3 exemptions
   Adjusted gross income: $18,725
   $3387

Find the tax liability on an adjusted gross income of $18,560 for a person with 2 exemptions whose filing status is

10. single.
    $3078
11. married filing joint return.
    $2403
12. married filing separate return.
    $3702

Discuss the situation in which an adjusted gross income (line 11, Form 1040A), such as $16,950, is at the upper limit for a line in the table. $16,950 is read in the line labeled "over $16,900 but not over $16,950." An adjusted gross income such as $16,951 is read in the line labeled "over $16,950 but not over $17,000."

Objective: Compute the tax refund or balance due the Internal Revenue Service as required on Form 1040A.

Tax Refund or Balance Due

The final step in completing an income tax return is comparing the tax liability with the tax credit.

If the tax credit is greater, find the **refund** due the taxpayer:

Tax credit − Tax liability = Refund

If the tax liability is greater, find the **balance due** the IRS:

Tax liability − Tax credit = Balance due

Problem

This lesson shows the completion of Rebecca Bradley's tax return.

Rebecca Bradley wrote her tax liability on lines 14a and 15 of her tax return. What is her refund or balance due?

Solution

Strategy

- Compare the tax credit (line 13) and the tax liability (line 15). The tax credit is greater.
- Subtract to find the refund (line 16).

Conclusion

Rebecca will receive a refund of $260.

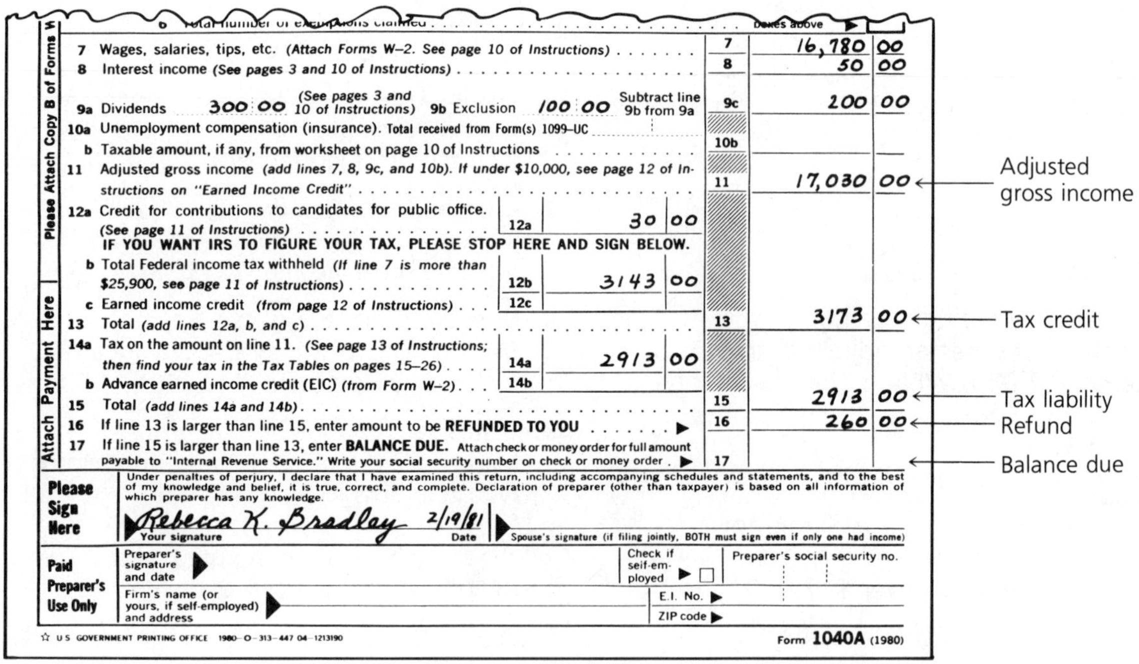

7	Wages, salaries, tips, etc. (Attach Forms W–2. See page 10 of Instructions)		7	16,780 00
8	Interest income (See pages 3 and 10 of Instructions)		8	50 00
9a	Dividends 300 00 (See pages 3 and 10 of Instructions) 9b Exclusion 100 00 Subtract line 9b from 9a		9c	200 00
10a	Unemployment compensation (insurance). Total received from Form(s) 1099–UC			
b	Taxable amount, if any, from worksheet on page 10 of Instructions		10b	
11	Adjusted gross income (add lines 7, 8, 9c, and 10b). If under $10,000, see page 12 of Instructions on "Earned Income Credit"		11	17,030 00
12a	Credit for contributions to candidates for public office. (See page 11 of Instructions)	12a 30 00		
	IF YOU WANT IRS TO FIGURE YOUR TAX, PLEASE STOP HERE AND SIGN BELOW.			
b	Total Federal income tax withheld (If line 7 is more than $25,900, see page 11 of Instructions)	12b 3143 00		
c	Earned income credit (from page 12 of Instructions)	12c		
13	Total (add lines 12a, b, and c)		13	3173 00
14a	Tax on the amount on line 11. (See page 13 of Instructions; then find your tax in the Tax Tables on pages 15–26)	14a 2913 00		
b	Advance earned income credit (EIC) (from Form W–2)	14b		
15	Total (add lines 14a and 14b)		15	2913 00
16	If line 13 is larger than line 15, enter amount to be REFUNDED TO YOU		16	260 00
17	If line 15 is larger than line 13, enter BALANCE DUE. Attach check or money order for full amount payable to "Internal Revenue Service." Write your social security number on check or money order		17	

Please Attach Copy B of Forms W

Attach Payment Here

Please Sign Here: Under penalties of perjury, I declare that I have examined this return, including accompanying schedules and statements, and to the best of my knowledge and belief, it is true, correct, and complete. Declaration of preparer (other than taxpayer) is based on all information of which preparer has any knowledge.

Rebecca K. Bradley 2/19/81
Your signature Date Spouse's signature (if filing jointly, BOTH must sign even if only one had income)

Paid Preparer's Use Only: Preparer's signature and date | Check if self-employed ☐ | Preparer's social security no.
Firm's name (or yours, if self-employed) and address | E.I. No. | ZIP code

☆ U.S. GOVERNMENT PRINTING OFFICE 1980—O—313—447 04—1213190 Form 1040A (1980)

Warm-up: 3144 − 2905 [239]
5923 − 5681 [242]
2200 − 1892 [308]
3118 − 2901 [217]

Related Problems

Find the refund or balance due. Then write *refund* or *balance due*.

1. Brad and Joyce Levy
   Tax liability: $2467
   Tax credit: $2568
   Refund: $101
2. Hank and Beth McGovern
   Tax liability: $1765
   Tax credit: $1692
   Balance due: $73
3. Emmett Lentz
   Tax liability: $1026
   Tax credit: $1155
   Refund: $129
4. Grace and Wilson Hardy
   Tax liability $1944
   Tax credit: $2027
   Refund: $83
5. Joe and Rita Blackfoot
   Tax liability: $2582
   Tax credit: $2533
   Balance due: $49
6. Olivia and Kurt Alvarez
   Tax liability: $2959
   Tax credit: $3197
   Refund: $238
7. Flora Westerfield
   Tax liability: $4539
   Tax credit: $4297
   Balance due: $242
8. Vernon Gracy
   Tax liability: $3619
   Tax credit: $3837
   Refund: $218
9. Juan and Ana Cabellon
   Tax liability: $1132
   Tax credit: $1007
   Balance due: $125
10. Sue and Tim Kennedy
    Tax liability: $1987
    Tax credit: $1818
    Balance due: $169
11. Hazel Widenaur
    Tax liability: $3180
    Tax credit: $3297
    Refund: $117
12. Dave and Kris Stewart
    Tax liability: $8300
    Tax credit: $7362
    Balance due: $938

Objective: Complete income tax Form 1040A.

Completing Form 1040A

Review the rules for determining dividend exclusion and credits for contributions to candidates.

Form **1040A** Department of the Treasury—Internal Revenue Service **U.S. Individual Income Tax Return** **1980**

Use IRS label. Otherwise, please print or type.

Your first name and initial (if joint return, also give spouse's name and initial): Albert R. and Ethel M. — Last name: Riley — Your social security number: 800 22 4116

Present home address (Number and street, including apartment number, or rural route): 3871 Ninth Street — Spouse's social security no.: 800 28 0917

City, town or post office, State and ZIP code: Middlefield, Texas 77200 — Your occupation ▶ Carpenter — Spouse's occupation ▶

Presidential Election Campaign Fund ▶ Do you want $1 to go to this fund? ✓ Yes ☐ No
If joint return, does your spouse want $1 to go to this fund? ✓ Yes ☐ No
Note: *Checking "Yes" will not increase your tax or reduce your refund.*

Requested by Census Bureau for Revenue Sharing ▶
A Where do you live (actual location of residence)? (See page 6 of Instructions.) State: TX — City, village, borough, etc.: Middlefield
B Do you live within the legal limits of a city, village, etc.? ✓ Yes ☐ No
C In what county do you live? Richmond
D In what township do you live? Clay

For Privacy Act Notice, see page 27 of Instructions — For IRS use only

Filing Status Check Only One Box.
1 ☐ Single
2 ✓ Married filing joint return (even if only one had income)
3 ☐ Married filing separate return. Enter spouse's social security no. above and full name here ▶
4 ☐ Head of household. (See pages 7 and 8 of Instructions.) If qualifying person is your unmarried child, enter child's name ▶

Exemptions Always check the box labeled Yourself. Check other boxes if they apply.
5a ✓ Yourself ☐ 65 or over ☐ Blind
b ✓ Spouse ☐ 65 or over ☐ Blind — Enter number of boxes checked on 5a and b ▶ 2
c First names of your dependent children who lived with you ▶ Susan, Jeffrey — Enter number of children listed on 5c ▶ 2

d Other dependents:

(1) Name	(2) Relationship	(3) Number of months lived in your home.	(4) Did dependent have income of $1,000 or more?	(5) Did you provide more than one-half of dependent's support?

Enter number of other dependents ▶
Add numbers entered in boxes above ▶ 4

6 Total number of exemptions claimed

Please Attach Copy B of Forms W-2 Here

Line	Description		Amount
7	Wages, salaries, tips, etc. (*Attach Forms W-2. See page 10 of Instructions*)		25,482 00
8	Interest income (*See pages 3 and 10 of Instructions*)		80 00
9a	Dividends 390 00 (*See pages 3 and 10 of Instructions*) 9b Exclusion 200 00 — Subtract line 9b from 9a	9c	190 00
10a	Unemployment compensation (insurance). Total received from Form(s) 1099–UC		
b	Taxable amount, if any, from worksheet on page 10 of Instructions	10b	
11	Adjusted gross income (*add lines 7, 8, 9c, and 10b*). *If under $10,000, see page 12 of Instructions on "Earned Income Credit"*	11	25,752 00
12a	Credit for contributions to candidates for public office. (*See page 11 of Instructions*) — 12a: 100 00		
	IF YOU WANT IRS TO FIGURE YOUR TAX, PLEASE STOP HERE AND SIGN BELOW.		
b	Total Federal income tax withheld (*If line 7 is more than $25,900, see page 11 of Instructions*) — 12b: 3515 00		
c	Earned income credit (*from page 12 of Instructions*) — 12c		
13	Total (*add lines 12a, b, and c*)	13	3615 00
14a	Tax on the amount on line 11. (*See page 13 of Instructions; then find your tax in the Tax Tables on pages 15–26*) — 14a: 3714 00		
b	Advance earned income credit (EIC) (*from Form W–2*) — 14b		
15	Total (*add lines 14a and 14b*)	15	3714 00
16	If line 13 is larger than line 15, enter amount to be **REFUNDED TO YOU** ▶	16	
17	If line 15 is larger than line 13, enter **BALANCE DUE.** Attach check or money order for full amount payable to "Internal Revenue Service." Write your social security number on check or money order ▶	17	99 00

Attach Payment Here

Please Sign Here Under penalties of perjury, I declare that I have examined this return, including accompanying schedules and statements, and to the best of my knowledge and belief, it is true, correct, and complete. Declaration of preparer (other than taxpayer) is based on all information of which preparer has any knowledge.
▶ Albert R. Riley — Your signature — 2/15/81 Date ▶ Ethel M. Riley — Spouse's signature (if filing jointly, BOTH must sign even if only one had income)

Paid Preparer's Use Only Preparer's signature and date ▶ — Check if self-employed ▶ ☐ — Preparer's social security no.
Firm's name (or yours, if self-employed) and address ▶ — E.I. No. ▶ — ZIP code ▶

☆ U.S. GOVERNMENT PRINTING OFFICE 1980—O—313-447 04-1213190 — Form **1040A** (1980)

Warm-up:
33,895 + 91 + 186 [34,172]
14,862 + 147 + 53 [15,062]
4102 − 3988 [114]
2517 − 2486 [31]

	Adjusted gross income	Tax credit	Tax liability	Refund/ Balance due
1.	$15,015	$2500	$2092	$408 refund
2.	$18,618	$1695	$1976	$281 balance due
3.	$17,836	$3250	$3153	$97 refund
4.	$17,662	$3552	$3369	$183 refund
5.	$26,425	$3548	$3616	$68 balance due

See pages 8-9 and 51 of *Consumer Forms and Problems.*

Problem

Albert and Ethel Riley are married, file a joint return, and claim 4 exemptions. Their completed Form 1040A is shown on page 266. Last year they earned $25,482 in wages, $80 in interest, and $390 from dividends. They contributed $250 to a political candidate, and they had $3515 withheld for federal tax. What are their adjusted gross income, tax credit, tax liability, and refund or balance due?

Solution

Strategy

- Compute the adjusted gross income (line 11).
- Compute the tax credit (line 13).
- Use Table B on page 407 to find the tax liability (lines 14a and 15).
- Compute the refund (line 16) or balance due (line 17).

Conclusion

The Rileys' adjusted gross income is $25,752, their tax credit is $3615, their tax liability is $3714, and their balance due is $99.

Related Problems

Students might arrange their answers in a table as shown above.

For each problem, find the adjusted gross income, tax credit, and tax liability. Then find the refund or balance due and write *refund* or *balance due*. Use the tax tables on pages 406-408.

See above.

1. Francis Turner
Single, 2 exemptions
Salary: $14,780
Interest income: $235
Federal tax withheld: $2500

2. Donald and Theresa Moore
Married, joint return, 4 exemptions
Salary: $18,568
Dividend income: $250
Federal tax withheld: $1695

3. Patsy Dotterweich
Single, 1 exemption
Salary: $17,763
Dividend income: $173
Contribution to candidates: $50
Federal tax withheld: $3225

4. Kate Watkins
Married, separate return, 2 exemptions
Salary: $17,565
Interest income: $21
Dividend income: $176
Contribution to candidates: $10
Federal tax withheld: $3547

5. Gary and Rose Masani
Married, joint return, 5 exemptions
Salary: $26,175
Interest income: $140
Dividend income: $310
Contribution to candidates: $350
Federal tax withheld: $3448

Objectives: Determine tax liability and refund or balance due when itemizing deductions; determine tax liability when income exceeds that given on the tax tables.

Tax Consultant

Career Cluster: Social Service Meyer Wolman is a tax consultant. Since income tax laws are complicated and always changing, taxpayers often come to him for advice. He finds that some of his clients cannot use Form 1040A because they have income that cannot be reported on the form, or because they claim more exemptions than are shown on the tax tables. These taxpayers must use Form 1040. Mr. Wolman also has clients who could use Form 1040A, but would pay less tax if they used Form 1040.

The government allows taxpayers a minimum deduction, or **zero bracket amount**. This amount is built into the tax tables.

Filing Status	Zero Bracket Amount
Single	$2300
Married Filing Joint Return	$3400
Married Filing Separate Return	$1700

A taxpayer's deductions may be greater than the zero bracket amount because of such things as medical and dental bills, interest expenses on mortgages and loans, state and local taxes, contributions to charities, casualty or theft losses, and other miscellaneous expenses. Such taxpayers should itemize deductions and use Form 1040.

Problem

Mr. Wolman has advised Anita and Jerry Prado to itemize deductions. Anita and Jerry file a joint return and claim 3 exemptions. They have an adjusted gross income of $21,175 and a tax credit of $2262. Their allowable itemized deductions are as follows:

Medical and dental expenses: $165
State and local taxes: $2255
Interest expenses: $2565
Contributions to charity: $947
Casualty loss: $120

What is the Prados' tax liability? What is their refund or balance due?

Discuss reasons for excess deductions. Point out that medical and dental expenses (excluding insurance) can be deducted only if they exceed 3% of the adjusted gross income. Also, there are limits on the amount of contributions that can be deducted.

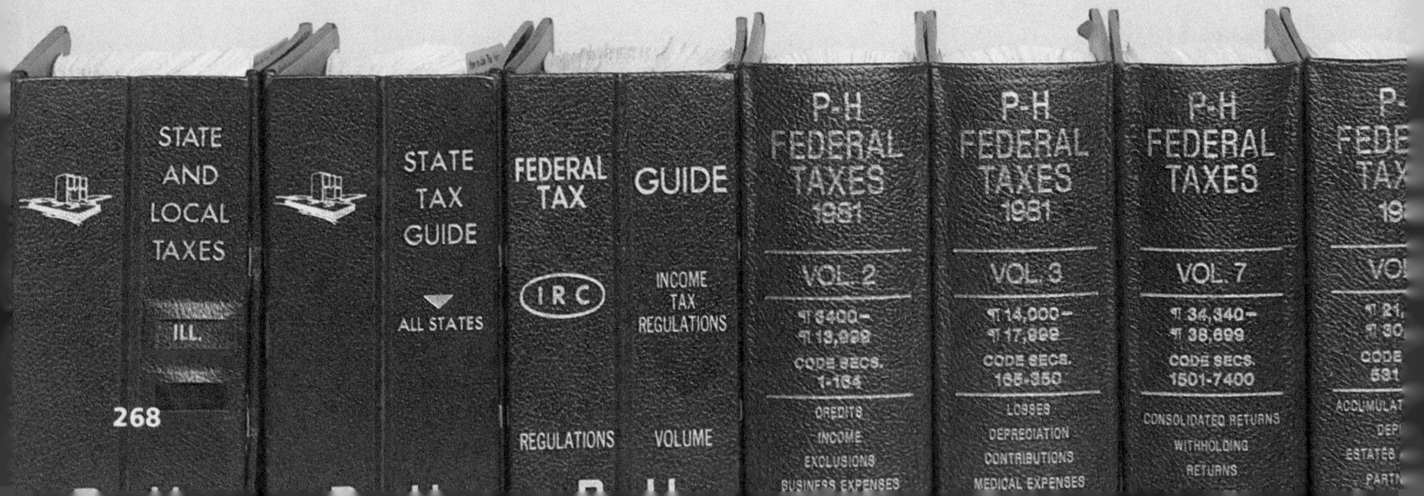

Warm-up: 3127 + 753 + 281 + 1037 [5198]
1903 + 672 + 56 + 158 [2789]
38,516 − 7983 [30,533]
5689 − 4973 [716]

Solution

Strategy

- Add to find the total itemized deductions.
  $165 + $2255 + $2565 + $947 + $120 = $6052
- Compare this total with the zero bracket amount for married filing joint return.
  $6052 > $3400
- Subtract to find the excess over the zero bracket amount.
  $6052 − $3400 = $2652
- Subtract from the adjusted gross income to find the amount to look for in the tax table (line 34, Form 1040).
  $21,175 − $2652 = $18,523
- Use Table B on page 407 to find the tax liability for $18,523.
  $2165
- Compare the tax liability with the tax credit.
  $2165 < $2262
- Subtract to find the amount of the refund.
  $2262 − $2165 = $97

Conclusion

The Prados' tax liability is $2165. They will receive a refund of $97.

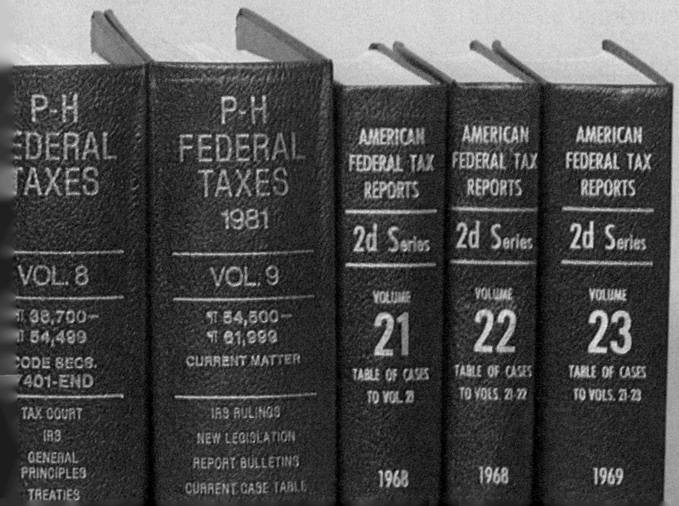

Related Problems

For each problem, find the tax liability. Then find the refund or balance due and write *refund* or *balance due*. Itemize deductions and use the zero bracket amounts on page 268. Use the tax tables on pages 406-408.

1. Jake and Mildred Bartlett
Married, joint return, 3 exemptions
Adjusted gross income: $29,895
Tax credit: $3886
Allowable itemized deductions
Medical and dental expenses: $250
State and local taxes: $2135
Interest expenses: $3200
Contributions to charity: $790
Miscellaneous: $240
$4246; balance due: $360

2. Willard Jones
Married, separate return, 3 exemptions
Adjusted gross income: $18,950
Tax credit: $3325
Allowable itemized deductions
State and local taxes: $2377
Interest expenses: $1750
Contributions to charity: $800
Theft losses: $395
Miscellaneous: $240
$2190; refund: $1135

3. Paula Swanson
Single, 1 exemption
Adjusted gross income: $18,380
Tax credit: $3150
Allowable itemized deductions
State and local taxes: $1745
Interest expenses: $495
Contributions to charity: $650
Miscellaneous: $350
$3033; refund: $117

4. Suppose Paula used Form 1040A and did not itemize deductions. Find her tax liability on $18,380. How much does she save by itemizing deductions?
$3318; $285

Schedule Z is for those who checked Filing Status Box 4, Head of Household. Since that category is not used here, Schedule Z is not included on page 409.

See page 52 of *Consumer Forms and Problems.*

Some of Mr. Wolman's clients cannot use the tax tables because the amount on line 34, Form 1040, exceeds the maximum listed on the tables. In these cases, they use Schedule TC and compute their tax using Schedule X, Y, or Z. Schedules X and Y are shown on page 409. The tax is based on **taxable income** (Schedule TC, Part 1, line 3), which is the income after all allowable deductions are made.

Part of Schedule Y for married couples filing a joint return is shown here.

If the amount on Schedule TC, Part I, line 3, is:		Enter on Schedule TC, Part I, line 4:	
Not over $3,400		—0—	
Over—	But not over—		of the amount over—
$3,400	$5,500	14%	$3,400
$5,500	$7,600	$294 + 16%	$5,500
$35,200	$45,800	$8,162 + 43%	$35,200
$45,800	$60,000	$12,720 + 49%	$45,800
$60,000	$85,600	$19,678 + 54%	$60,000

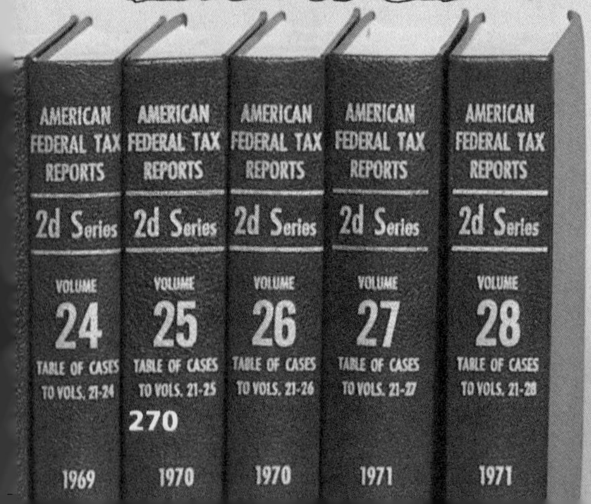

Problem

Mr. Wolman has determined that Alice and Ronald Winkner must use Schedule TC and Schedule Y. Alice and Ronald have a taxable income of $54,869, and they are filing a joint return. What is their tax liability?

Solution

Strategy

- Use Schedule Y. Read the tax information on the line for taxable income over $45,800 but not over $60,000.

  $12,720 + 49% of the amount over $45,800

- Subtract to find the taxable income over $45,800.

  $54,869 − $45,800 = $9069

- Find 49% of $9069. Round to the nearest dollar.

  0.49 × $9069 ≈ $4444

- Add to find the tax liability.

  $12,720 + $4444 = $17,164

Conclusion

The Winkners' tax liability is $17,164.

Related Problems

Compute the tax liability. Use Schedule X or Y on page 409. Round to the nearest dollar.

5. Gina Simpson
Single
Taxable income: $50,000
$18,067

6. Harry and May Thomas
Married, joint return
Taxable income: $116,500
$52,088

7. Brian Anderson
Married, separate return
Taxable income: $53,460
$23,040

8. William Fresco
Single
Taxable income: $79,600
$36,291

9. Amanda and Peter Stein
Married, joint return
Taxable income: $172,750
$88,502

10. Ed and Ida Ross
Married, joint return
Taxable income: $250,000
$141,724

CALCULATOR APPLICATIONS

Tax Penalty Charges

Self-employed people must estimate their income tax and pay it in four partial payments on or before these dates: April 15, June 15, September 15, and January 15. These payments must total at least 80% of the tax liability for the year. If they do not, there is a penalty charge on each underpayment based on an annual rate of 12%. For each underpayment the approximate rate of the penalty charge is shown below.

1st underpayment (1 year delinquent): 12% of underpayment
2nd underpayment ($\frac{5}{6}$ year delinquent): 10% of underpayment
3rd underpayment ($\frac{7}{12}$ year delinquent): 7% of underpayment
4th underpayment ($\frac{1}{4}$ year delinquent): 3% of underpayment

The actual rate of penalty charge is computed using this formula:

$$\frac{\text{Number of days from due date to April 15}}{365} \times 12\%$$

Last year, Gail Shaffer estimated her income tax at $3000. She paid this amount in four equal payments on the dates required. When she filed her tax return she had a tax liability of $5000. What is her penalty charge?

a. Estimated tax — $3000
b. Tax liability — $5000
c. 80% of tax liability — 0.80 × $5000 = $4000
d. Required partial payment (line c divided by 4) — $4000 ÷ 4 = $1000
e. Actual partial payment (line a divided by 4) — $3000 ÷ 4 = $750
f. Each underpayment (line d minus line e) — $1000 − $750 = $250
g. 1st penalty charge (12% of line f) — 0.12 × $250 = **$30.00**
h. 2nd penalty charge (10% of line f) — 0.10 × $250 = **$25.00**
i. 3rd penalty charge (7% of line f) — 0.07 × $250 = **$17.50**
j. 4th penalty charge (3% of line f) — 0.03 × $250 = **$7.50**
k. Total penalty charge (sum of lines g–h) — **$80.00**

Possible key sequence: 0.8 [×] 5000 [÷] 4 [=] [M+] 3000 [÷] 4 [=] [M−] [MR] [MC] [×] 0.12 [=] [M+] 0.10 [=] [M+] 0.07 [=] [M+] 0.03 [=] [M+] [MR]

For each problem, use steps a–k to find the total penalty charge to the nearest cent. Assume that the estimated tax was paid in four equal payments on the dates required.

The above key sequence assumes that the first factor can be used as an automatic constant.

	Estimated tax	Tax liability	
1.	$6000	$9000	$96.00
2.	$7500	$10,000	$40.00
3.	$1650	$4389	$148.90
4.	$16,500	$25,225	$294.40
5.	$25,000	$33,728	$158.59
6.	$0	$3890	$248.96

Objective: Compute state income tax using tax information from various states.

State Income Tax

Many states and some cities have income taxes that are similar to federal income tax. Different states include different items as income and allow varying amounts for deductions. Methods for determining the amount of tax in various states are shown below.

California

If taxable income is— OVER	BUT NOT OVER	YOUR TAX IS—
12,950	13,050	245
13,050	13,150	248
13,150	13,250	251
13,250	13,350	255
13,350	13,450	259
27,450	27,550	1,015
27,550	27,650	1,022
27,650	27,750	1,029
27,750	27,850	1,036
27,850	27,950	1,043
59,450	59,550	4,236
59,550	59,650	4,247
59,650	59,750	4,258
59,750	59,850	4,269
59,850	59,950	4,280
59,950	60,000	4,288
over 60,000		4,291 plus 11% of the amount over $60,000

Maryland

Maryland Income Tax		
Taxable income over	but not over	Amount of tax
$ 0	$1000	2% of taxable income
1000	2000	$20 plus 3% of amount over $1000
2000	3000	$50 plus 4% of amount over $2000
3000	—	$90 plus 5% of amount over $3000

Illinois

Amount of tax is 2.5% of the taxable income.

Michigan

Amount of tax is 4.6% of the taxable income.

Mississippi

Amount of tax is 3% of the first $5000 of taxable income plus 4% of the taxable income over $5000.

Warm-up: 16,850 − 3000 [13,850]
3% of 1575 [47.25]
4.6% of 25,725 [1183.35]
180 + 498.63 [678.63]

Problem

Ted Marten lives in Maryland. What is his state income tax on taxable income of $14,800?

Solution

Strategy

- Use the tax information for Maryland. $14,800 is greater than $3000. Subtract to find the amount over $3000.

  $14,800 − $3000 = $11,800

- Find 5% of the amount over $3000.

  0.05 × $11,800 = $590

- Add to $90 to find the total tax.

  $90 + $590 = $680

Conclusion

Ted's state income tax is $680.

Problem

Margaret Deitz lives in Mississippi. What is her state income tax on taxable income of $14,563?

Solution

Strategy

- Use the tax information for Mississippi. Find 3% of the first $5000.

  0.03 × $5000 = $150

- Subtract to find the taxable income over $5000.

  $14,563 − $5000 = $9563

- Find 4% of the amount over $5000.

  0.04 × $9563 = $382.52

- Add to find the total tax.

  $150 + $382.52 = $532.52

Conclusion

Margaret's state income tax is $532.52.

Related Problems

Find the state income tax to the nearest cent. Use the information on page 272.

	State	Taxable income		State	Taxable income
1.	Maryland $134.75	$3,895	**9.**	Michigan $1895.20	$41,200
2.	Maryland $511.45	$11,429	**10.**	Mississippi $221.68	$6,792
3.	Maryland $1344.55	$28,091	**11.**	Mississippi $793.36	$21,084
4.	Illinois $216.38	$8,655	**12.**	Mississippi $1510	$39,000
5.	Illinois $468.75	$18,750	**13.**	California $248	$13,075
6.	Illinois $890.50	$35,620	**14.**	California $1036	$27,825
7.	Michigan $204.84	$4,453	**15.**	California $4258	$59,750
8.	Michigan $813.28	$17,680	**16.**	California $5768.30	$73,430

Discuss the fact that some states allow fewer deductions than others. For this reason, a lower tax rate does not necessarily mean lower taxes.

Skills Tune-Up

Rounding whole numbers and decimals, pages 4-5

Round each number to the nearest thousand, nearest hundred, and nearest ten.

1. 832
   1000; 800; 830
2. 2484
   2000; 2500; 2480
3. 555
   1000; 600; 560
4. 8143
   8000; 8100; 8140
5. 9602
   10,000; 9600; 9600
6. 5478
   5000; 5500; 5480
7. 1071
   1000; 1100; 1070
8. 29,929
   30,000; 29,900; 29,930
9. 60,375
   60,000; 60,400; 60,380
10. 72,188
   72,000; 72,200; 72,190
11. 84,659
   85,000; 84,700; 84,660

Round each number to the nearest whole number, nearest tenth, and nearest hundredth.

12. 7.367
   7; 7.4; 7.37
13. 18.181
   18; 18.2; 18.18
14. 36.912
   37; 36.9; 36.91
15. 79.457
   79; 79.5; 79.46
16. 783.143
   783; 783.1; 783.14
17. 257.768
   258; 257.8; 257.77
18. 546.801
   547; 546.8; 546.80
19. 40.992
   41; 41.0; 40.99
20. 59.607
   60; 59.6; 59.61
21. 602.015
   602; 602.0; 602.02
22. 85.974
   86; 86.0; 85.97

Subtracting whole numbers and decimals, pages 6-7

1. 78 − 26
   52
2. 52 − 17
   35
3. 56 − 8
   48
4. 98 − 9
   89
5. 42 − 37
   5
6. 96 − 95
   1
7. 93.7 − 45.1
   48.6
8. 54.2 − 36.7
   17.5
9. 68.59 − 2.39
   66.2
10. 46.75 − 4.86
   41.89
11. 85.62 − 16.2
   69.42
12. 45.32 − 9.4
   35.92
13. 15.098 − 7.46
   7.638
14. 40.095 − 37.18
   2.915
15. 32.317 − 21.228
   11.089
16. 96.013 − 4.172
   91.841
17. 8.64 − 5.325
   3.315
18. 72.19 − 3.337
   68.853
19. 27.2 − 26.4
   0.8
20. 48.6 − 47.9
   0.7
21. 4.612 − 2
   2.612
22. 86.059 − 39
   47.059
23. 37 − 34.5
   2.5
24. 4 − 0.3
   3.7
25. 26 − 0.42
   25.58
26. 83 − 27.08
   55.92
27. 84.039 − 36.721
   47.318
28. 74.85 − 38.927
   35.923

Writing percents, decimals, and fractions, pages 32-33

Write as a fraction in lowest terms.

1. 12% $\frac{3}{25}$
2. 80% $\frac{4}{5}$
3. 55% $\frac{11}{20}$
4. 10% $\frac{1}{10}$
5. 47% $\frac{47}{100}$
6. 25% $\frac{1}{4}$
7. 62% $\frac{31}{50}$
8. 30% $\frac{3}{10}$
9. 16% $\frac{4}{25}$
10. 97% $\frac{97}{100}$
11. 70% $\frac{7}{10}$
12. 31% $\frac{31}{100}$
13. 27% $\frac{27}{100}$
14. 40% $\frac{2}{5}$
15. 65% $\frac{13}{20}$
16. 28% $\frac{7}{25}$
17. 225% $2\frac{1}{4}$
18. 132% $1\frac{8}{25}$
19. 103% $1\frac{3}{100}$
20. 450% $4\frac{1}{2}$

Write as a percent.

21. $\frac{1}{2}$ 50%
22. $\frac{1}{5}$ 20%
23. $\frac{1}{10}$ 10%
24. $\frac{3}{4}$ 75%
25. $\frac{3}{5}$ 60%
26. $\frac{1}{4}$ 25%
27. $\frac{7}{10}$ 70%
28. $\frac{9}{20}$ 45%
29. $\frac{19}{50}$ 38%
30. $\frac{4}{25}$ 16%
31. $\frac{9}{25}$ 36%
32. $\frac{11}{20}$ 55%
33. $\frac{3}{8}$ 37.5%
34. $\frac{15}{20}$ 75%
35. $\frac{9}{16}$ 56.25%
36. $\frac{7}{8}$ 87.5%
37. $\frac{9}{40}$ 22.5%
38. $\frac{13}{16}$ 81.25%
39. $\frac{17}{4}$ 425%
40. $\frac{11}{2}$ 550%
41. $\frac{38}{5}$ 760%
42. $\frac{13}{8}$ 162.5%

Chapter 13 Review

Who must file a tax return, pages 258-259

1. Ann and Tom White Eagle are 62 and 66 years old. They file a joint tax return. This year their incomes were $3822.50 and $2692.75. Are they required to file a tax return? (Use the information on page 258.)
Yes

Adjusted gross income and tax credit, pages 260-262

2. Mitzi Smith is single. Her salary was $14,950. She received $248 in interest and $180 in dividends. What is her adjusted gross income? (Use the information on page 261 for exclusion for dividend income.)
$15,278
3. Mitzi contributed $80 to a candidate running for public office and had $2157 withheld for federal income tax. What is her tax credit? (Use the information on page 261 for credit for contributions to candidates.)
$2197

Tax liability, page 263

4. A single person is filing a tax return claiming 2 exemptions. What is the tax liability on an adjusted gross income (line 11, Form 1040A) of $16,725? (Use the tax tables on pages 406-408.)
$2534

Tax refund or balance due, pages 264-265

5. Myung Lee has a tax liability of $1987 and a tax credit of $1822. What is his refund or balance due? Give the amount, and write *refund* or *balance due*.
Balance due: $165

Completing Form 1040A, pages 266-267

6. The Menards file a joint tax return and claim 5 exemptions. Their salary income was $26,816 and they received $518 in interest. They have a tax credit of $3950. What is their refund or balance due? Give the amount, and write *refund* or *balance due*. (Use the tax tables on pages 406-408.)
Refund: $82

Tax consultant, pages 268-270

7. Elaine Webster is single, claims 2 exemptions, and has an adjusted gross income of $17,500 and a tax credit of $2697. She itemizes these deductions:

   Medical and dental expenses: $685
   State and local taxes: $1598
   Interest expenses: $560
   Contributions to charity: $165

   What is Elaine's refund or balance due? Give the amount, and write *refund* or *balance due*. (Use the information on page 268 for zero bracket amounts. Use the tax tables on pages 406-408.)
Refund: $150
8. What is the tax liability for a single person with taxable income of $45,200? (Use Schedule X or Y on page 409.)
$15,427

State income tax, pages 272-273

9. The state income tax in Michigan is 4.6% of the taxable income. What is the state income tax on taxable income of $16,500?
$759
10. Maryland's state income tax for taxable income over $3000 is $90 plus 5% of the amount over $3000. What is the state income tax on taxable income of $10,900?
$485

Chapter 13 Test

Number of test items - 10

Number missed	1	2	3	4	5
Percent correct	90	80	70	60	50

1. A single person must file a federal income tax return if he or she is under 65 and has an income of at least $3300, or if he or she is 65 or over and has an income of at least $4300. Sara McDonald, age 70, is single and had incomes of $2387, $1543, and $175. Is she required to file a tax return?
No

2. A married couple filing a joint return can take a $200 exclusion for dividend income. The Yonans are filing a joint return. Their salary was $19,500. They received $83 in interest and $250 in dividends. What is their adjusted gross income?
$19,633

3. A married couple filing a joint return can claim one half of all contributions to candidates running for office up to a $100 maximum credit. The Yonans contributed $130 to a candidate and had $2155 withheld for federal income tax. What is their tax credit?
$2220

4. A married couple is filing a joint return claiming 3 exemptions. What is the tax liability on an adjusted gross income (line 11, Form 1040A) of $25,725? (Use the tax tables on pages 406-408.)
$3980

5. Louise Brown has a tax liability of $2188 and a tax credit of $2397. What is her refund or balance due? Give the amount, and write *refund* or *balance due*.
Refund: $209

6. Kay Murray is single and claims 1 exemption. Her salary was $17,100 and she received $125 in interest. She has a tax credit of $2714. What is her refund or balance due? Give the amount, and write *refund* or *balance due*. (Use the tax tables on pages 406-408.)
Balance due: $259

7. The zero bracket amount for a married couple filing a joint return is $3400. The Garzas file a joint return and claim 4 exemptions. They have an adjusted gross income of $26,700 and a tax credit of $3782. They itemized these deductions:

Medical and dental expenses: $975
State and local taxes: $2180
Interest expenses: $1250

What is their refund or balance due? Give the amount, and write *refund* or *balance due*. (Use the tax tables on pages 406-408.)
Refund: $96

8. What is the tax liability for a single person with a taxable income of $60,000? (Use Schedule X or Y on page 409.)
$23,943

9. The state income tax in Illinois is 2.5% of the taxable income. What is the tax on taxable income of $14,500?
$362.50

10. Mississippi's state income tax is 3% of the first $5000 of taxable income and 4% of the taxable income over $5000. What is the state income tax on taxable income of $18,900?
$706

 See pages 33–34 of the *Test Masters* for an alternate form of the Chapter 13 Test.

Chapter 14 Health, Life, and Retirement Insurance

Objective: Find the amount of medical expenses paid by an insurance company and the amount paid by the insured.

Health Insurance

See page T39 for additional notes and activities for Chapter 14.

Most people have some type of **health insurance** that pays for part or all of their medical expenses for doctors, hospitals, and medicine. The person covered by the insurance policy is called the **insured**.

Many health insurance policies have a deductible clause. The insurance company usually pays a certain portion of the total expenses after the deductible amount is subtracted. The insured pays the deductible amount and the remaining expenses.

The deductible usually applies to the medical expenses incurred during a calendar year.

Problem

Robert Pottinger works for a company that carries medical insurance on its employees. The insurance is a \$50-deductible policy. The insurance company pays 80% of the amount over the deductible.

Robert had surgery on his foot and was in the hospital for two days. His medical expenses amounted to \$1615. How much did the insurance company pay? How much did Robert pay?

Solution

Strategy

- Subtract to find the amount over the deductible.

  $\$1615 - \$50 = \$1565$

- Multiply by 80% to find the amount the insurance company paid.

  $0.80 \times \$1565 = \$1252$

- Subtract to find the amount Robert paid.

  $\$1615 - \$1252 = \$363$

Conclusion

The insurance company paid \$1252. Robert paid \$363.

The deductible amount is included in the \$363 paid by Robert.

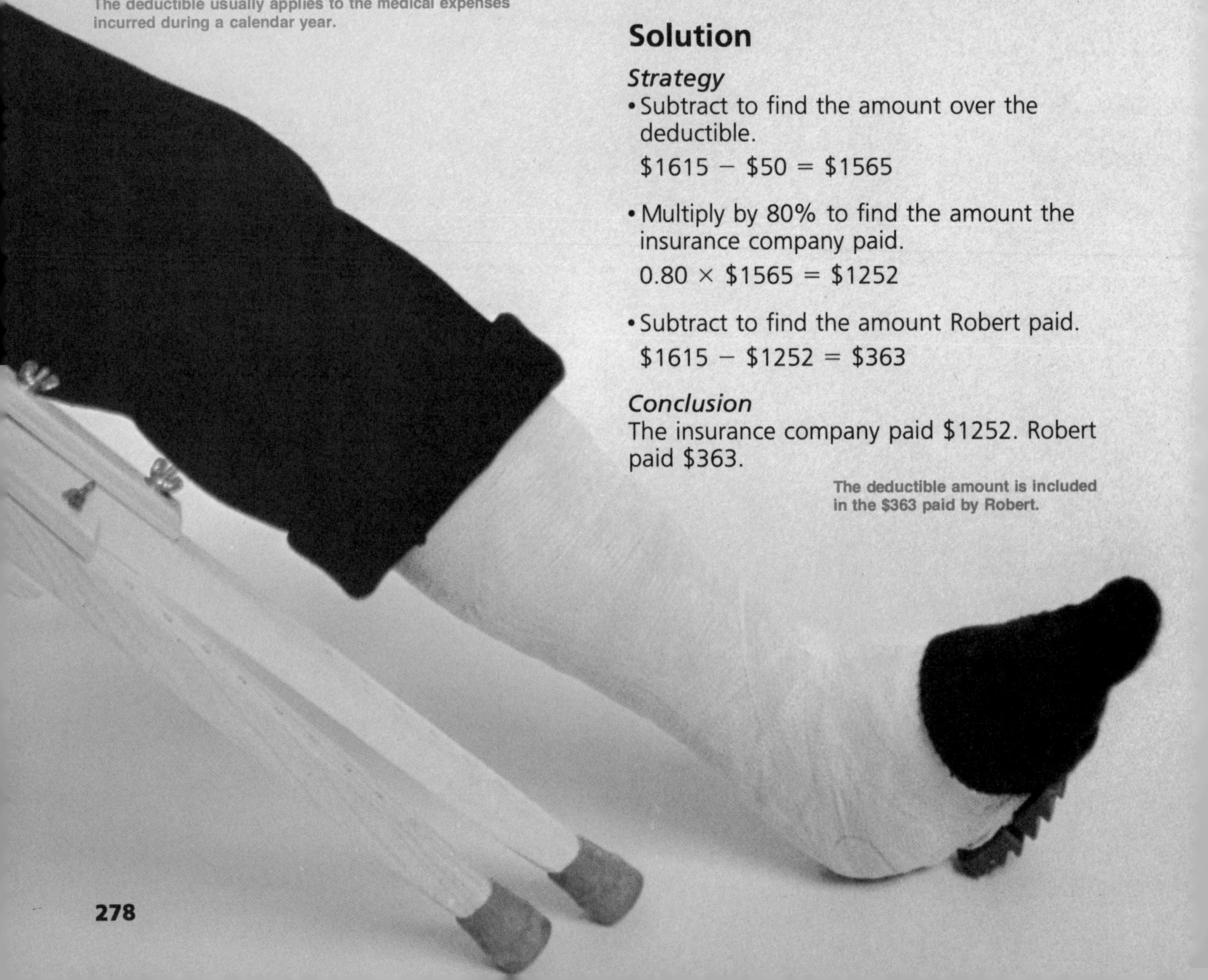

Warm-up: 80% of 3200 [2560]
85% of 2708 [2301.80]
(3200 − 50) × 0.8 [2520]
8413 − 6690.40 [1722.60]

See pages 53-54 of *Consumer Forms and Problems.*

Related Problems

For problems 1–10, find the amount paid by insurance and the amount paid by the insured.

	Insured	Deductible amount	Percent paid by insurance over deductible	Medical expenses	Paid by insurance	Paid by insured
	Robert Pottinger	$50	80%	$1615.00	$1252.00	$363.00
1.	Leonard Kaplan	$50	80%	$840.00	$632.00	$208.00
2.	Elsie Garden	$0	80%	$3165.00	$2532.00	$633.00
3.	Prudence Cook	$200	90%	$5100.00	$4410.00	$690.00
4.	Jaime Fisher	$100	90%	$3555.00	$3109.50	$445.50
5.	Elliott Cartier	$150	85%	$2750.00	$2210.00	$540.00
6.	Lydia Mayfair	$100	85%	$7600.00	$6375.00	$1225.00
7.	Jake Momaday	$0	75%	$4276.00	$3207.00	$1069.00
8.	Maxine Rice	$125	87%	$5714.00	$4862.43	$851.57
9.	Arturo Ruiz	$60	92%	$1980.00	$1766.40	$213.60
10.	Joan Fine	$40	84%	$6216.50	$5188.26	$1028.24

11. Chong Sun Lee has a $90-deductible health insurance policy. After $90, the insurance company pays 75% of all medical expenses including prescription medicines. Last year, Chong had $485 in doctor bills and spent $43 on prescription medicines. How much did the insurance company pay?
$328.50

12. Melissa Greenwald has a $60-deductible health insurance policy. After $60, the insurance company pays 80% of all medical expenses. Melissa's expenses totaled $5405. How much did Melissa pay?
$1129

13. Frances Zilliox has a $70-deductible health insurance policy. She has medical expenses that total $2482.60. Her insurance will pay whichever is less of these two amounts:

a. 85% of the amount over the deductible
b. $2000

How much will Frances pay?
$482.60

14. Mike Delgado has a $50-deductible health insurance policy. The insurance company pays 80% of all covered medical expenses from $50 through $3000. Above $3000, the insurance company pays 100%. Mike was in the hospital for major surgery. His medical expenses amounted to $8470. How much did the insurance company pay?
$7830

Objective: Compute annual premiums for term life insurance and the total premiums for a specified period of time for term life insurance.

Warm-up:
20 × 2.95 [59]
45 × 3.77 [169.65]
76 × 5.85 [444.60]
25 × 6.77 [169.25]

Term Life Insurance

Term life insurance is low-cost protection that is often bought to cover a "critical" period for a family such as when children are young or are in college or for the duration of a loan.

The main purpose of life insurance is to provide money for dependents of the insured person in case of his or her death. The persons named in the policy to receive the insurance money are called the **beneficiaries**. The amount of money that the beneficiaries would receive is the **face value** of the policy.

The least expensive type of life insurance is **term life insurance**. It is issued for a certain period of time, such as 5 or 10 years. If the insured does not die during that time, no money is paid by the insurance company and the policy is canceled.

This table shows annual premiums for a certain 5-year term insurance policy.

5-Year Term Insurance Annual Premiums per $1000					
	Premium			Premium	
Age	Male	Female	Age	Male	Female
18	$2.69	$2.05	32	$3.51	$2.94
19	2.71	2.13	33	3.66	3.05
20	2.72	2.21	34	3.71	3.16
21	2.74	2.27	35	3.98	3.29
22	2.76	2.31	36	4.19	3.44
23	2.78	2.36	37	4.43	3.60
24	2.79	2.41	38	4.69	3.77
25	2.80	2.47	39	4.98	3.95
26	2.87	2.53	40	5.27	4.14
27	2.95	2.58	41	5.56	4.35
28	3.05	2.63	42	5.85	4.56
29	3.16	2.68	43	6.15	4.78
30	3.27	2.74	44	6.46	5.01
31	3.38	2.83	45	6.77	5.26

Problem

Sally Geraci is 26 years old. She and her husband have two young children. Sally is buying a 5-year term life insurance policy with a face value of $70,000 to provide money to help her husband raise their children in case she dies. What is Sally's annual premium? How much will she pay for term insurance protection for 5 years?

Solution

Strategy

- Read the table to find the rate per $1000 for a 26-year-old female.

  $2.53

- Multiply by 70 to find the annual premium for $70,000.

  70 × $2.53 = $177.10

- Multiply by 5 to find the total amount of premiums for 5 years.

  5 × $177.10 = $885.50

Conclusion

Sally's annual premium is $177.10. She will pay $885.50 for 5 years of term insurance protection.

Related Problems

For problems 1-5, find the annual premium for each 5-year term policy.

	Age	Sex	Face value	
1.	25	Male	$60,000	$168
2.	39	Female	$80,000	$316
3.	40	Male	$75,000	$395.25
4.	38	Male	$250,000	$1172.50
5.	27	Female	$80,000	$206.40

6. Betty Neal is 30 years old. She is buying 5-year term insurance. How much will her annual premium be for a $55,000 policy?
$150.70

7. Jack Gomez is buying a 5-year term insurance policy with a face value of $25,000. He is 20 years old. How much will Jack pay for term insurance protection for 5 years?
$340

8. Theresa Banak is buying a 5-year term insurance policy with a face value of $90,000. She is 34 years old. If Theresa dies after three years, how much will her beneficiary receive? How much will Theresa pay for term insurance protection for 3 years?
$90,000; $853.20

9. Dan Ohira is 27 years old. He is buying a 5-year term insurance policy with a face value of $45,000. If Dan dies after four years, how much will his beneficiary receive? How much will Dan pay for term insurance protection for 4 years?
$45,000; $531

10. Ken Sawyer is 29 years old. How much 5-year term insurance (sold only in multiples of $1000) can he buy if he can spend no more than $125 a year?
$39,000

11. Alice Reinhardt is 33 years old. How much 5-year term insurance (sold only in multiples of $1000) can she buy if she can spend no more than $100 a year?
$32,000

For problems 10 and 11, point out that since the insurance is sold only in multiples of $1000, students must always round down after dividing (instead of rounding to the nearest whole number) in order to not spend more than the limit allowed for insurance.

Objectives: Find annual premiums for straight life, limited payment life, and endowment insurance; find cash values of insurance policies.

Straight Life, Limited Payment Life, and Endowment Insurance

One rule of thumb is that a family needs enough life insurance to cover 4 or 5 times its annual income.

Besides providing financial protection in case of death, some life insurance policies are a form of savings. After premiums have been paid for a certain length of time, the policy has a **cash value**. This amount of money increases as the policy gets older. The policy can be **surrendered**, or traded in, for its cash value. The insured can also borrow against the cash value at a very low rate of interest. Because these policies have a cash value, they are more expensive than term insurance.

One of the most common types of life insurance that has a cash value is **straight life insurance**. The insured pays premiums for life or until a certain age, usually 65 or 70. The insurance remains in force until the insured dies.

Another type of life insurance that has a cash value is **limited payment life insurance**. This type of policy is similar to straight life, but the premiums are paid for a specific length of time, usually 20 or 30 years. For this reason, the premiums are higher than for straight life. A limited payment policy that is paid for in 20 years is called a **20-payment life insurance** policy. The insurance remains in force until the insured dies.

The most expensive type of insurance is **endowment insurance**. Again, the premiums are paid for a specific length of time, usually 20 or 30 years. At the end of that time, the face value of the policy is paid to the insured and the insurance is no longer in force.

This table shows premium rates for certain life insurance policies. Rates given are for men. This table may also be used to figure premiums for a woman. Subtract 3 years from the woman's age and use the premiums for the resulting age.

Annual Insurance Premiums per $1000
(Rates shown are for a male. For a female, subtract 3 years from her age.)

Age	Straight life	20-payment life	20-year endowment
15	$11.05	$17.42	$41.80
16	11.35	17.84	41.86
17	11.66	18.27	41.92
18	11.99	18.72	41.98
19	12.31	19.15	42.04
20	12.67	19.63	42.08
21	13.02	20.08	42.12
22	13.39	20.54	42.16
23	13.79	21.04	42.20
24	14.21	21.54	42.24
25	14.64	22.07	42.27
26	15.06	22.55	42.30
27	15.51	23.07	42.33
28	15.97	23.60	42.36
29	16.46	24.14	42.39
30	16.98	24.69	42.44
31	17.52	25.27	42.51
32	18.07	25.87	42.60
33	18.67	26.49	42.70
34	19.29	27.14	42.82

You may want to compare these rates with the rates for term insurance in the previous lesson.

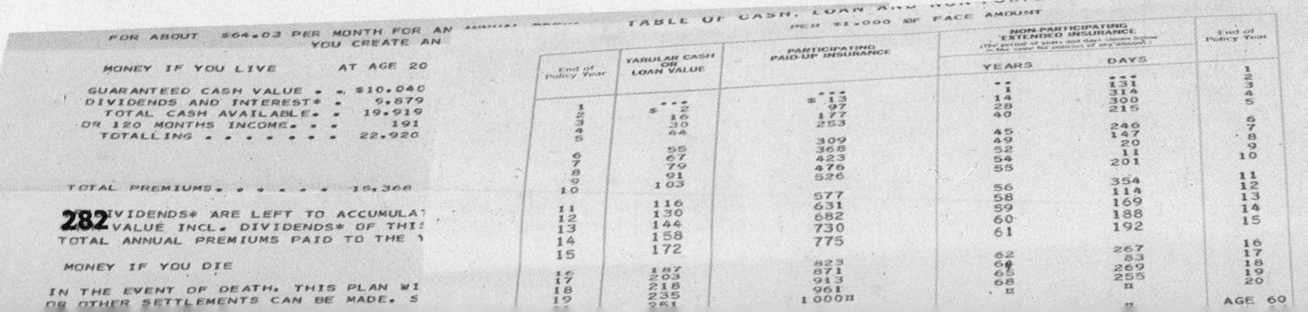
FOR ABOUT $64.03 PER MONTH FOR AN …
YOU CREATE AN
MONEY IF YOU LIVE AT AGE 20
GUARANTEED CASH VALUE . . $10,040
DIVIDENDS AND INTEREST* . 9,879
TOTAL CASH AVAILABLE. . 19,919
OR 120 MONTHS INCOME. . 191
TOTALLING 22,920
TOTAL PREMIUMS. 15,368
…IVIDENDS* ARE LEFT TO ACCUMULA…
…VALUE INCL. DIVIDENDS* OF THI…
TOTAL ANNUAL PREMIUMS PAID TO THE …
MONEY IF YOU DIE
IN THE EVENT OF DEATH, THIS PLAN WI…
OR OTHER SETTLEMENTS CAN BE MADE. S…

TABLE OF CASH, LOAN AND … PER $1,000 OF FACE AMOUNT

End of Policy Year	Tabular Cash or Loan Value	Participating Paid-Up Insurance	Non-Participating Extended Insurance Years	Days	End of Policy Year
1	---	---	--	---	1
2	$ 2	$ 13	1	131	2
3	16	97	14	314	3
4	30	177	28	300	4
5	44	253	40	215	5
6	55	309	45	246	6
7	67	368	49	147	7
8	79	423	52	20	8
9	91	476	54	11	9
10	103	526	55	201	10
11	116	577	56	354	11
12	130	631	58	114	12
13	144	682	59	169	13
14	158	730	60	188	14
15	172	775	61	192	15
16	187	823	62	267	16
17	203	871	64	83	17
18	218	913	65	269	18
19	235	961	68	255	19
	251	1000			20

AGE 60

Warm-up: 9 × 20.54 [184.86]
25 × 13.02 [325.50]
15 × 164.32 [2464.80]
18 × 235.72 [4242.96]

1. $413.70 2. $380.10 3. $1917 4. $1164.15 5. $221 6. $836 7. $1099.53 8. $1055 9. $772.48 10. $612.80 11. $303.16 12. $1254 13. $1004 14. $1153.50 15. $1684.80

Problem

Lisa Snowbird is 25 years old. She bought $20,000 worth of straight life insurance. What is her annual premium?

Solution

Strategy

- Subtract 3 years from Lisa's age.
  25 − 3 = 22
- Read the table on page 282 to find the annual premium for each $1000 of straight life insurance at age 22.
  $13.39
- Multiply by 20 to find the annual premium for $20,000.
  20 × $13.39 = $267.80

Conclusion

Lisa's annual premium is $267.80.

Related Problems

Find the annual premium for each policy.
See above.

	Policy	Age	Sex	Face value
1.	Straight life	23	Male	$30,000
2.	Straight life	23	Female	$30,000
3.	20-year endowment	32	Male	$45,000
4.	20-payment life	32	Male	$45,000
5.	Straight life	18	Female	$20,000
6.	20-year endowment	18	Female	$20,000
7.	Straight life	34	Male	$57,000
8.	20-year endowment	26	Female	$25,000
9.	20-payment life	29	Male	$32,000
10.	20-payment life	19	Male	$32,000
11.	Straight life	20	Female	$26,000
12.	20-year endowment	15	Male	$30,000
13.	20-payment life	24	Female	$50,000
14.	20-payment life	30	Female	$50,000
15.	20-year endowment	21	Male	$40,000

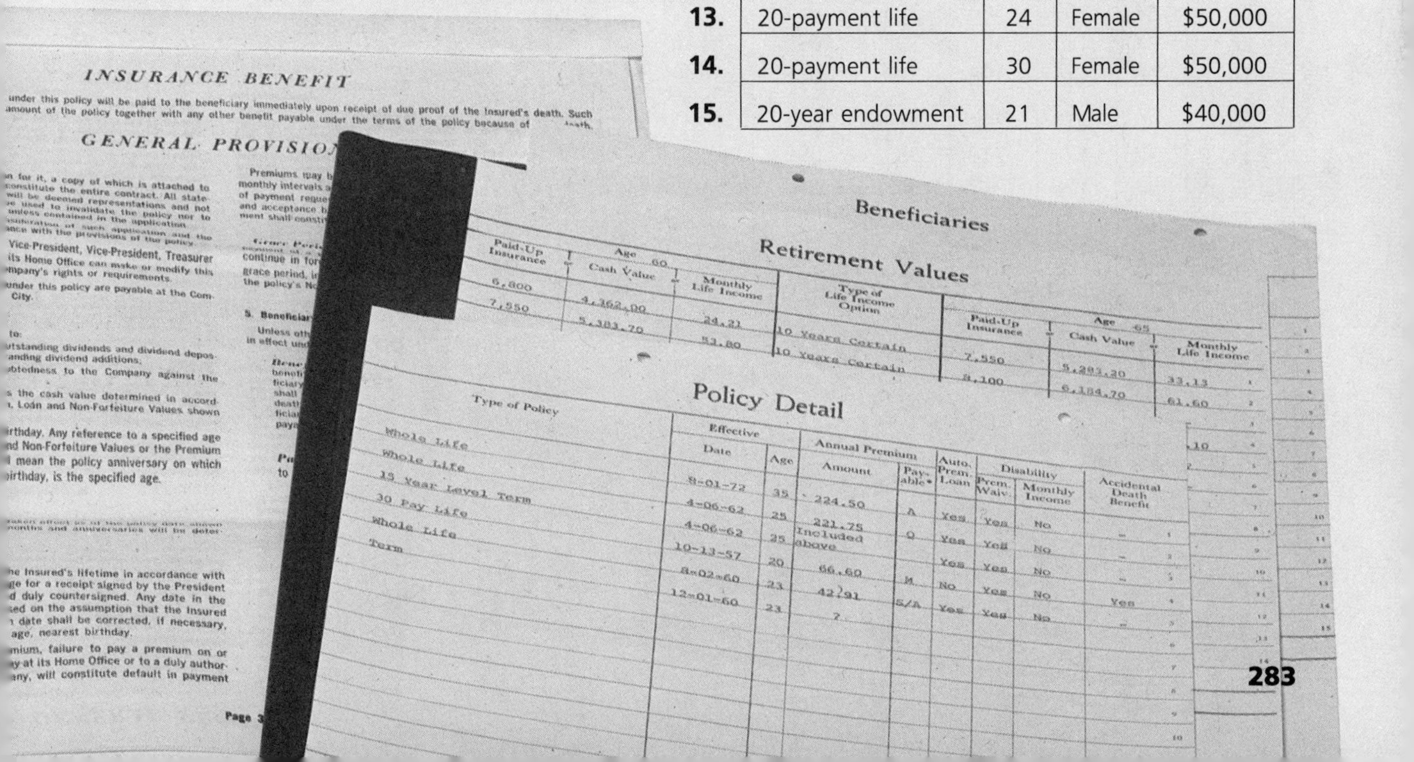

The cash value of a policy is the cash amount available to the insured if he or she were to surrender the policy or to borrow against the policy. This table shows the cash values for the straight life insurance policy included in the table on page 282.

Straight Life—Cash Value per $1000					
Age at time of issue	Cash value at end of year				Cash value at age 65
	5	10	15	20	
15	$21	$ 77	$133	$210	$729
16	22	79	136	216	726
17	23	82	140	222	723
18	24	84	144	228	719
19	25	86	148	234	714
20	26	89	152	241	710
21	27	91	156	247	703
22	28	94	161	254	696
23	29	97	165	262	690
24	30	99	171	270	682
25	31	102	176	278	673
26	32	105	181	286	663
27	33	109	186	295	651
28	34	112	192	303	639
29	35	115	198	313	625
30	36	119	204	323	611
31	37	123	210	333	596
32	38	126	217	343	578
33	39	131	224	355	560
34	40	135	231	367	540

Problem

Jason Williams is 20 years old. He wants to buy $25,000 worth of straight life insurance. What is the total amount he will pay in premiums in 15 years? What will be the cash value of his policy at the end of 15 years?

Solution

Strategy

- Read the table on page 282 to find the annual premium for each $1000 of straight life insurance at age 20.

  $12.67

- Multiply by 25 to find the annual premium for $25,000.

  $25 \times \$12.67 = \$316.75$

- Multiply by 15 to find the total amount of premiums for 15 years.

  $15 \times \$316.75 = \$4751.25$

- Read the table at the left to find the cash value at the end of 15 years for each $1000 of a policy issued at age 20.

  $152

- Multiply by 25 to find the cash value for $25,000 worth of insurance.

  $25 \times \$152 = \$3800$

Conclusion

Jason will pay $4751.25 in premiums in 15 years. The cash value of his policy at the end of 15 years will be $3800.

In problem 22, you might point out that this cash value is now greater than the amount paid in.

Related Problems

Use the tables on pages 282 and 284.

16. Alan Stansfield is 28 years old. He plans to buy $18,000 worth of straight life insurance. What is the total amount he will pay in premiums in 20 years?
$5749.20

17. What will be the cash value of Alan's insurance at the end of 20 years?
$5454

18. Jim Kuang is 19 years old. He plans to buy $15,000 worth of straight life insurance. What is the total amount he will pay in premiums in 10 years?
$1846.50

19. What will be the cash value of Jim's insurance at the end of 10 years?
$1290

20. David Kidd is 30 years old. He plans to buy $75,000 worth of straight life insurance. What will be his annual premium?
$1273.50

21. If David lives to be 65, how much will he have paid in premiums?
$44,572.50

22. When David is 65, what will be the cash value of his insurance?
$45,825

23. Carl Russell is 23 years old. He plans to buy $40,000 worth of straight life insurance. What will be the cash value of this insurance at the end of 5 years?
$1160

24. Quentin Jonas is 33 years old. He plans to buy $85,000 worth of straight life insurance. What will be the cash value of this insurance when Quentin is 65 years old?
$47,600

25. Dennis Tunney is 22 years old. He plans to buy $50,000 worth of straight life insurance. What will be the cash value of this insurance when Dennis is 37 years old?
$8050

Objective: Compare premium payment plans.

Insurance Agent

Career Cluster: Business Contact Roger Iverson is an insurance agent. Some of his customers prefer to pay their insurance premiums semiannually, quarterly, or monthly, instead of annually. These types of payments usually cost more per year than an annual payment. Roger uses a table like the one below to compute the amount of the premium.

Type of payment	Factor
Semiannually	0.51
Quarterly	0.26
Monthly	0.0875

You may wish to discuss why more frequent payments cost more. You might ask students what the factors would be if there were no cost differences for more frequent payments.

Warm-up: Round to the nearest hundredth.

0.51 × 238.50	[121.64]
0.26 × 307.80	[80.03]
4 × 80.03	[320.12]
320.12− 307.80	[12.32]

Problem

Joan Nakamura, one of Roger's customers, wants to pay her insurance premiums monthly. Her insurance policy has an annual premium of $237.28. What is the amount of her monthly premium? How much more per year will she pay than if she pays annually?

Solution

Strategy

- Read the table to find the factor for monthly premiums.

  0.0875

- Multiply times the annual premium to find the monthly premium. Round to the nearest cent.

  $0.0875 \times \$237.28 \approx \$20.76$

- Multiply by 12 to find the total of her monthly premiums for the year.

  $12 \times \$20.76 = \$249.12$

- Subtract the annual premium from the total of the monthly premiums to find the additional cost per year.

  $\$249.12 - \$237.28 = \$11.84$

Conclusion

Joan's monthly premium will be $20.76. She will pay $11.84 more per year if she makes monthly payments.

More frequent payments result in these differences from making one annual payment.
Monthly: 12 × 0.0875 = 1.05; pay 5% more.
Quarterly: 4 × 0.26 = 1.04; pay 4% more.
Semiannually: 2 × 0.51 = 1.02; pay 2% more.

Related Problems

1. The annual premium for Lisa Montel's straight life insurance policy is $342.50. What will be her monthly premium?
   $29.97
2. How much more per year will Lisa pay if she pays monthly?
   $17.14
3. Tony Falco's annual premium for his 5-year term life insurance is $149.30. If he pays quarterly, how much will his quarterly premium be?
   $38.82
4. How much more per year will Tony pay if he pays quarterly?
   $5.98
5. The annual premium for Jane Jansen's endowment policy is $462.80. What will be her semiannual premium?
   $236.03
6. How much more per year will Jane pay if she pays semiannually?
   $9.26
7. Jennifer Plain's annual premium for her 20-payment life insurance policy is $364.90. Her monthly premiums would be $31.93. What is the difference per year between paying annually and paying monthly?
   $18.26
8. Beth Duarte's endowment policy has an annual premium of $316.75. Her quarterly premium would be $82.36. What is the difference per year between paying annually and paying quarterly?
   $12.69
9. Justin Brown is 25 years old. He bought a $40,000, 20-year endowment policy. What is Justin's annual premium? (Use the table on page 282.)
   $1690.80
10. If Justin pays monthly, what will be his monthly premium?
    $147.95
11. At the end of 20 years, how much will Justin have saved if he pays his premiums annually rather than monthly?
    $1692

CALCULATOR APPLICATIONS

Insurance Premiums

For each problem, students will have to round the first answer to the nearest cent before continuing.

These tables show the annual premiums for various insurance policies. In the table headings, *A* means annual premium, *M* means monthly premium, *Q* means quarterly premium, and *S* means semiannual premium. Use your calculator and the factors given on page 286 to complete the tables.

For problems 1–7, the last column is the yearly difference between paying premiums monthly and annually.

	A	*M*	12*M*	12*M* − *A*
	$138.12	$12.09	$145.08	$6.96
1.	$172.49	**$15.09**	**$181.08**	**$8.59**
2.	$254.68	**$22.28**	**$267.36**	**$12.68**
3.	$127.46	**$11.15**	**$133.80**	**$6.34**
4.	$229.23	**$20.06**	**$240.72**	**$11.49**
5.	$148.77	**$13.02**	**$156.24**	**$7.47**
6.	$89.41	**$7.82**	**$93.84**	**$4.43**
7.	$124.55	**$10.90**	**$130.80**	**$6.25**

Remind students that 12M means 12 times the monthly premium.

For problems 8–14, the last column is the yearly difference between paying premiums quarterly and annually.

	A	*Q*	4*Q*	4*Q* − *A*
	$127.19	$33.07	$132.28	$5.09
8.	$218.73	**$56.87**	**$227.48**	**$8.75**
9.	$157.42	**$40.93**	**$163.72**	**$6.30**
10.	$309.50	**$80.47**	**$321.88**	**$12.38**
11.	$148.71	**$38.66**	**$154.64**	**$5.93**
12.	$272.18	**$70.77**	**$283.08**	**$10.90**
13.	$197.45	**$51.34**	**$205.36**	**$7.91**
14.	$314.89	**$81.87**	**$327.48**	**$12.59**

For problems 15–20, the last column is the yearly difference between paying premiums semiannually and annually.

	A	*S*	2*S*	2*S* − *A*
	$237.80	$121.28	$242.56	$4.76
15.	$193.42	**$98.64**	**$197.28**	**$3.86**
16.	$246.55	**$125.74**	**$251.48**	**$4.93**
17.	$311.71	**$158.97**	**$317.94**	**$6.23**
18.	$275.84	**$140.68**	**$281.36**	**$5.52**
19.	$329.09	**$167.84**	**$335.68**	**$6.59**
20.	$254.81	**$129.95**	**$259.90**	**$5.09**

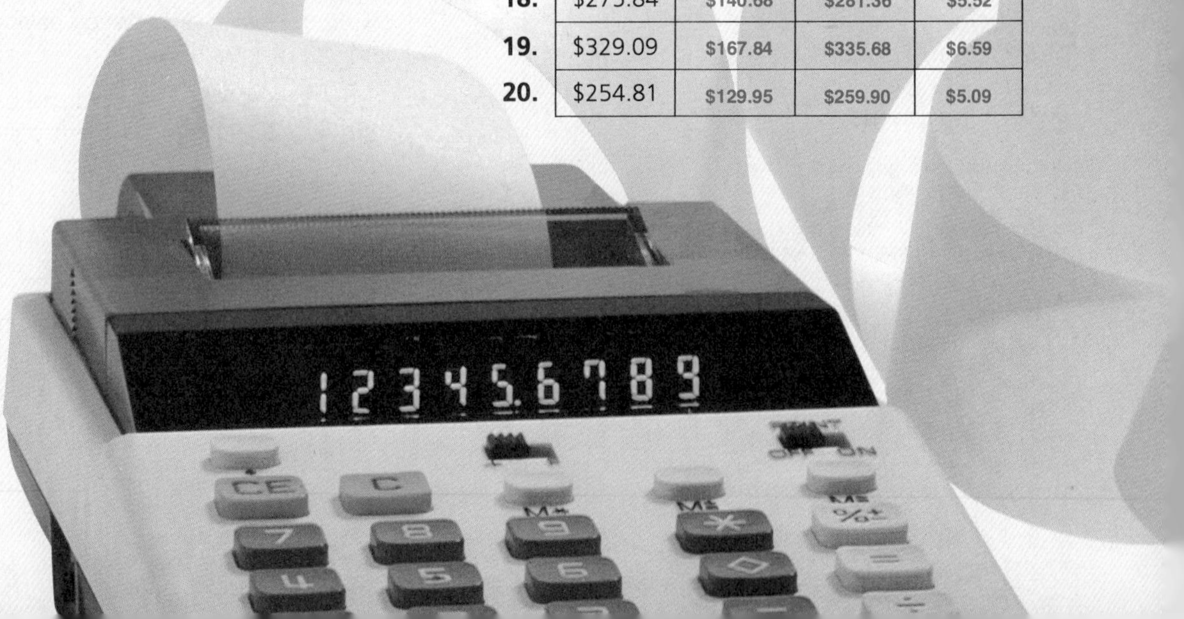

Break Time

On Monday, Mrs. Lee put two pitchers of juice into the refrigerator.

On Tuesday, Willy Lee poured from the black pitcher into the tan pitcher the amount of juice the tan pitcher contained on Monday.

On Wednesday, Tilly Lee poured from the tan pitcher into the black pitcher the amount of juice the black pitcher contained on Tuesday.

On Thursday, Milly Lee poured from the black pitcher into the tan pitcher the amount of juice the tan pitcher contained on Wednesday.

On Friday, Lilly Lee poured from the tan pitcher into the black pitcher the amount of juice the black pitcher contained on Thursday.

On Saturday, Mr. Lee measured the amount of juice in the pitchers. He found that each one contained 960 milliliters of juice.

How much juice had each pitcher contained on Monday?

Black pitcher: 1260 milliliters
Tan pitcher: 660 milliliters

Objective: Find the amount of insurance that can be purchased and the amount of savings that can be accumulated for a budgeted amount.

Choosing Insurance and Savings Plans

Many people combine their program of insurance protection with a long-term savings plan.

Problem

Fred Post is 25. An efficient way for him to provide insurance protection and save money is to buy straight life insurance, paying premiums monthly. How much straight life insurance (sold only in multiples of $1000) can he buy for a maximum of $60 a month? What will be the cash value of the insurance at the end of 20 years?

Solution

Students will have to refer to the strategies used in previous lessons.

Strategy

- Read the table on page 282 to find the annual premium for each $1000 of straight life insurance at age 25.

  $14.64

- Read the table on page 286 to find the factor for monthly premiums. Multiply this factor times the annual premium for each $1000 to find the monthly premium for each $1000. Round to the nearest cent.

  $0.0875 \times \$14.64 \approx \$1.28$

- Divide $60 by $1.28. Then find the number of $1000 units that can be purchased for a maximum of $60 a month. Remember, this insurance is sold only in multiples of $1000.

  $\$60 \div \$1.28 = 46.875 \longrightarrow 46$

  See note below.

- Multiply times $1000 to find the amount of insurance Fred can buy.

  $46 \times \$1000 = \$46{,}000$

Students must always round down after dividing in order to not spend more than the limit allowed for insurance.

- Read the table on page 284 to find the cash value at the end of 20 years for each $1000 of a straight life insurance policy issued at age 25. Multiply by 46 to find the cash value for $46,000 worth of insurance.

  $46 \times \$278 = \$12{,}788$

Conclusion

For a maximum of $60 a month, Fred can buy $46,000 worth of straight life insurance. The cash value of Fred's policy at the end of 20 years will be $12,788.

In 20 years, Fred Post will be 45. Discuss how he might change his insurance program.

Related Problems

For each problem, find the amount of straight life insurance that can be purchased for no more than the given amount. Then give the cash value of each policy at the end of 20 years. Use the tables on pages 282, 284, and 286. Assume that each person is a male.

	Age	Amount to spend each month	Amount that can be purchased	Cash value
1.	20	$75	$67,000	$16,147
2.	17	$40	$39,000	$8658
3.	18	$85	$80,000	$18,240
4.	33	$85	$52,000	$18,460
5.	23	$45	$37,000	$9694
6.	28	$65	$46,000	$13,938
7.	30	$60	$40,000	$12,920
8.	19	$70	$64,000	$14,976
9.	26	$90	$68,000	$19,448
10.	34	$80	$47,000	$17,249

Warm-up: Round to the nearest hundredth.

0.0875 × 12.67	[1.11]
65 ÷ 1.12	[58.04]
75 ÷ 1.56	[48.08]
28.5 × 290.82	[8288.37]

This table shows the results of depositing $1 each month in a savings account for a certain amount of time. Interest has been compounded monthly.

Long-Term Savings Balance (For $1 deposited each month with interest compounded monthly)		
Years	6%	7%
5	$ 69.77	$ 71.59
10	163.88	173.08
15	290.82	316.96
20	462.04	520.93
25	692.99	810.07
30	1004.52	1219.97

Problem

Linda Miley is buying a $45,000 term life insurance policy that she plans to keep for 20 years. The annual premium is $155. She is setting aside $60 each month for insurance and savings. The amount that is not spent for her insurance premium each month will be put in a savings account that earns 6% interest. How much can Linda save each month? If Linda keeps all of the interest in the savings account, how much will she have in the account at the end of 20 years?

Solution

Strategy

- Multiply the annual insurance premium by 0.0875 to find the monthly insurance premium. Round to the nearest cent.

  0.0875 × $155 ≈ $13.56

- Subtract to find the amount to be put in savings each month.

  $60 − $13.56 = $46.44

As Linda's savings accumulate, she probably will transfer the money to an account that pays a higher rate of interest.

- Read the table at the left to find the result at the end of 20 years of depositing $1 each month in a savings account at 6% interest.

  $462.04

- Multiply by 46.44 to find the result at the end of 20 years of depositing $46.44 each month in a savings account at 6% interest. Round to the nearest cent.

  46.44 × $462.04 ≈ $21,457.14

Conclusion

Linda can save $46.44 each month. At the end of 20 years, she will have $21,457.14 in her savings account.

Compare the insurance protection and savings for Fred Post and Linda Miley at the end of 20 years.

Related Problems

11. Jeannie Pope is 33 years old. Her annual premium for $70,000 worth of term life insurance is $195. How much does she pay per month for this insurance? The factor for monthly premiums is 0.0875.
$17.06

12. Jeannie spends a total of $60 per month for insurance and savings. What amount does she put in her savings account each month?
$42.94

13. Jeannie's savings account pays 7% interest compounded monthly. If she continues to deposit the same amount each month, how much will be in the savings account at the end of 20 years?
$22,368.73

14. Paul Jaeger spends a total of $75 a month for insurance and savings. His monthly insurance premium is $35.41. The amount that is not spent on his insurance premium is deposited each month in a savings account that earns 7% interest compounded monthly. How much will he have in the account at the end of 15 years?
$12,548.45

Objectives: Compute annual social security retirement benefits; compare retirement benefits at different ages.

Social Security Retirement Benefits

Most people in the United States are covered by social security. A portion of each person's paycheck is withheld for social security. When a person aged 62 or older **retires**, or stops working full-time, the government provides the person retirement benefits from the social security fund.

Problem

David Dawson wants to determine his average annual income subject to social security. The work sheet at the right gives the maximum annual income on which a person pays social security for 1955 through 1981. In the third column, David recorded his annual earnings that were covered by social security. He has been contributing to social security for 23 years. What is his average annual income subject to social security?

Work Sheet			
Year	Maximum annual income on which social security is paid	Actual annual earnings	Earnings subject to social security
1955	$4,200		
1956	4,200		
1957	4,200		
1958	4,200		
1959	4,800	$3,380	$3,380
1960	4,800	3,580	3,580
1961	4,800	3,790	3,790
1962	4,800	4,020	4,020
1963	4,800	4,260	4,260
1964	4,800	4,700	4,700
1965	4,800	4,800	4,800
1966	6,600	5,450	5,450
1967	6,600	5,860	5,860
1968	7,800	6,300	6,300
1969	7,800	7,400	7,400
1970	7,800	8,500	7,800
1971	7,800	9,650	7,800
1972	9,000	10,300	9,000
1973	10,800	11,100	10,800
1974	13,200	12,800	12,800
1975	14,100	14,200	14,100
1976	15,300	15,300	15,300
1977	16,500	15,900	15,900
1978	17,700	16,050	16,050
1979	22,900	17,000	17,000
1980	25,900	17,670	17,670
1981	29,700	18,010	18,010
		Total	$215,770

Solution

Strategy

- Use the information in the work sheet to list David's earnings that are subject to social security. If the earnings for any year are more than the maximum, list only the maximum. The last column of the work sheet shows these earnings.
- Add the earnings that are subject to social security. Then divide by the number of years to find the average annual income subject to social security. Round to the nearest dollar.

  $\$215{,}770 \div 23 \approx \$9381$

Conclusion

David's average annual income subject to social security is $9381.

Warm-up: 196,489 ÷ 23 [8543]
12 × 451.10 [5413.20]
12 × 291.20 [3494.40]
12 × 394.40 [4732.80]

Problem

David is planning to retire at age 65. He has one dependent. His average annual income subject to social security is $9381. What is the annual retirement benefit that David's family should receive?

Solution

Strategy

- In the table at the right, find the entry for average annual income subject to social security that is closest to $9381.

  $9400

- Read the table for $9400 to find David's monthly benefit at age 65 and his dependent's monthly benefit.

  For David: $520.40
  For his dependent: $260.20

- Add to find the total monthly benefit. If the total of the monthly benefits exceeds the maximum shown in the table, then the maximum family benefit is received.

  $520.40 + $260.20 = $780.60

- Multiply by 12 to find the family's annual retirement benefit.

  12 × $780.60 = $9367.20

Conclusion

The annual retirement benefit for David's family is $9367.20.

Monthly Social Security Retirement Benefits

Average annual income subject to social security	Benefit for worker, retirement at age 65	64	63	62	Benefit per dependent	Maximum family benefit
$923 or less	$121.80	$113.70	$105.60	$ 97.50	$ 60.90	$182.70
1,200	156.70	146.30	135.90	125.40	78.40	235.10
2,600	230.10	214.80	199.50	184.10	115.10	345.20
3,000	251.80	235.10	218.30	201.50	125.90	384.90
3,400	270.00	252.00	234.00	216.00	135.00	434.90
4,000	296.20	276.50	256.80	237.00	148.10	506.20
4,400	317.30	296.20	275.00	253.90	158.70	562.50
4,800	336.00	313.60	291.20	268.80	168.00	612.70
5,200	353.20	329.70	306.20	282.60	176.60	662.70
5,600	370.60	345.90	321.20	296.50	185.30	687.10
6,000	388.20	362.40	336.50	310.60	194.10	712.10
6,400	405.60	378.60	351.60	324.50	202.80	737.10
6,800	424.10	395.90	367.60	339.30	212.10	762.30
7,200	446.00	416.30	386.60	356.80	223.00	788.90
7,600	465.60	434.60	403.60	372.50	232.80	814.70
8,000	482.60	450.50	418.30	386.10	241.30	844.50
8,400	492.90	460.10	427.20	394.40	246.50	862.60
8,800	505.10	471.50	437.80	404.10	252.60	883.80
9,200	516.00	481.60	447.20	412.80	258.00	903.00
9,400	520.40	485.80	451.10	416.40	260.20	910.40
9,600	524.60	489.70	454.70	419.70	262.30	918.00
9,800	530.40	495.10	459.70	424.40	265.20	928.00
10,000	534.70	499.10	463.50	427.80	267.40	935.70

This table gives only a rough estimate of what retirement benefits will be. Actual social security tables give benefit amounts for dependents at various ages. This table has been simplified to show only one column of benefits for a dependent.

Related Problems

1. This table gives Clara Denby's annual earnings covered by social security. Use the information in the work sheet on page 292 to find Clara's average annual income subject to social security. $7043 See Additional Answers beginning on page T44 for completed worksheet.

Year	Actual earnings	Year	Actual earnings	Year	Actual earnings
1958	$3,290	1966	$5,800	1974	$ 8,750
1959	3,760	1967	6,430	1975	9,060
1960	3,800	1968	6,890	1976	9,300
1961	4,270	1969	7,430	1977	9,470
1962	4,500	1970	7,900	1978	9,650
1963	4,960	1971	8,100	1979	9,970
1964	4,990	1972	7,460	1980	10,350
1965	5,300	1973	8,000	1981	10,850

2. The total of Jim Wald's annual earnings subject to social security is $171,160. He has been contributing to social security for 26 years. What is his average annual income subject to social security?
$6583
3. Anna Caliendo's annual earnings subject to social security total $228,740. She has been contributing to social security for 23 years. What is her average annual income subject to social security?
$9945

For problems 4-9, read the table on page 293 to find the annual retirement benefit.

	Average annual income	Retirement at age	Number of dependents	
4.	$5815	64	0	$4348.80
5.	$7300	65	0	$5352.00
6.	$6142	65	1	$6987.60
7.	$7420	63	1	$7636.80
8.	$4616	62	2	$7257.60
9.	$9115	65	2	$10,836.00

For problem 9, the total of the monthly benefits is more than the maximum family benefit.

10. Albert Bach is planning to retire at age 62. He has no dependents. He has contributed to social security for 25 years. The total of his annual earnings subject to social security is $198,264. What is his annual retirement benefit?
$4633.20

Problems are based on using the same table for benefits at different ages of retirement, even though the table changes each year.

Problem

Anita Romero is planning for her retirement. If she retires in 1981 at age 62, her monthly retirement benefit will be $339.30. Anita estimated that if she waits until 1984 when she is 65, she will receive $482.60 each month. What will be Anita's annual retirement benefit if she retires at age 62? at age 65? In what year will the total benefits for retirement at 65 be more than the total benefits for retirement at 62?

Solution

Strategy

- Multiply by 12 to find the annual retirement benefit at age 62.

  12 × $339.30 = $4071.60

- Multiply by 12 to find the annual retirement benefit at age 65.

  12 × $482.60 = $5791.20

- Construct a table to show the total benefits to be received by Anita if she retires at age 62 and if she retires at age 65.

Year	Retirement at 62	Retirement at 65
1981	$ 4,071.60	
1982	8,143.20	
1983	12,214.80	
1984	16,286.40	$ 5,791.20
1985	20,358.00	11,582.40
1986	24,429.60	17,373.60
1987	28,501.20	23,164.80
1988	32,572.80	28,956.00
1989	36,644.40	34,747.20
1990	40,716.00	40,538.40
1991	44,787.60	46,329.60

Conclusion

If Anita retires at age 62, her annual retirement benefit will be $4071.60. If she waits until she is 65 to retire, she will receive $5791.20 annually. In 1991, the total benefits received by Anita if she retires at age 65 will be more than the total received if she retires at age 62.

Related Problems

11. Judith Hank can retire in 1981 when she is 63 years old and receive $403.60 per month from social security. What will be her annual benefit?
$4843.20

12. If Judith retires at age 63, how much will she receive in retirement benefits in 5 years?
$24,216

13. If Judith retires in 1983 when she is 65, she will receive $492.90 per month. What will be her annual benefit if she retires at age 65?
$5914.80

14. Construct a table to show the total benefits to be received by Judy if she retires at age 65 and if she retires at age 63. In what year will the total benefits for retirement at 65 be more than the total benefits for retirement at 63? 1992
For table, see Additional Answers beginning on page T44.

15. Rudy Aldinger receives $405.60 per month from social security. If social security benefits were increased by 14.2%, how much would Rudy receive each month? (Round to the nearest ten cents.)
$463.20

Skills Tune-Up

Adding whole numbers and decimals, pages 6-7

1. 17 + 24 + 14
   55
2. 6 + 29 + 18
   53
3. 75 + 36 + 59
   170
4. 39 + 28 + 97
   164
5. 62 + 19 + 27
   108
6. 91 + 25 + 46
   162
7. 13 + 38 + 55 + 14
   120
8. 7 + 89 + 68 + 32
   196
9. 61 + 27 + 91 + 52
   231
10. 98 + 25 + 13 + 43
    179
11. 414 + 296 + 172
    882
12. 867 + 329 + 541
    1737
13. 540 + 177 + 354
    1071
14. 805 + 643 + 784
    2232
15. 937 + 659 + 135
    1731
16. 5.7 + 4.27
    9.97
17. 12.74 + 9.2
    21.94
18. 11.35 + 43.43
    54.78
19. 67.59 + 48.07
    115.66
20. 0.2 + 0.4 + 0.3
    0.9
21. 3.1 + 7.3 + 5.65
    16.05
22. 1.97 + 0.14 + 0.68
    2.79
23. 9.82 + 3.25 + 4.74
    17.81
24. 3.4 + 6.68 + 2.52
    12.6
25. 0.59 + 0.18 + 0.67
    1.44
26. 2.82 + 9.95 + 4.59
    17.36
27. 0.37 + 8.18 + 2.719
    11.269
28. 7.1 + 2.58 + 5.1 + 8.9
    23.68

Multiplying whole numbers, pages 8-9

1. 80 × 30
   2400
2. 40 × 500
   20,000
3. 200 × 300
   60,000
4. 9000 × 500
   4,500,000
5. 3000 × 4000
   12,000,000
6. 100 × 680
   68,000
7. 35 × 40
   1400
8. 600 × 350
   210,000
9. 50 × 6400
   320,000
10. 2000 × 170
    340,000
11. 150 × 2800
    420,000
12. 170 × 1800
    306,000
13. 450 × 1800
    810,000
14. 5 × 17
    85
15. 78 × 24
    1872
16. 70 × 36
    2520
17. 367 × 8
    2936
18. 2721 × 3
    8163
19. 388 × 76
    29,488
20. 19 × 2193
    41,667
21. 490 × 672
    329,280
22. 2366 × 132
    312,312
23. 506 × 397
    200,882
24. 50 × 2409
    120,450
25. 217 × 2965
    643,405
26. 901 × 6867
    6,187,167
27. 12,274 × 12
    147,288
28. 7260 × 706
    5,125,560

Percent problems, pages 34-37

1. 5% of 188 is ____.
   9.4
2. $19\frac{1}{2}\%$ of 180 is ____.
   35.1
3. $1\frac{1}{4}\%$ of 1600 is ____.
   20
4. Find 80% of 30.
   24
5. Find 89% of 2.
   1.78
6. What number is 8.5% of 62?
   5.27
7. What number is 12% of 750?
   90
8. ____% of 76 is 19.
   25%
9. ____% of 84 is 79.8.
   95%
10. ____% of 60 is 7.5.
    12.5%
11. ____% of 40 is 34.
    85%
12. What percent of 900 is 288?
    32%
13. 2.38 is what percent of 68?
    3.5%
14. 559 is what percent of 860?
    65%
15. $3\frac{3}{4}\%$ of ____ is 30.
    800
16. 25% of ____ is 2.05.
    8.2
17. 72% of ____ is 28.8.
    40
18. $42\frac{1}{2}\%$ of ____ is 3.06.
    7.2
19. 32% of ____ is 64.
    200
20. 8.3% of what number is 29.05?
    350
21. 18.75 is 15% of what number?
    125
22. 340.3 is 83% of what number?
    410

Chapter 14 Review

Health insurance, pages 278-279

1. Pam Tanaka has a $50-deductible health insurance policy. The insurance company pays 75% of all covered medical expenses over the deductible amount. Her medical expenses amounted to $2735. How much did Pam pay?
$721.25

Term life insurance, pages 280-281

2. Beth Bauer is 25 years old. She bought a 5-year term life insurance policy with a face value of $75,000. What is her annual premium? **$185.25**

5-Year Term Insurance Annual Premiums per $1000		
	Premium	
Age	Male	Female
24	$2.79	$2.41
25	2.80	2.47
26	2.87	2.53

Straight life, limited payment life, and endowment insurance, pages 282-285

3. Ted Larson bought $60,000 worth of straight life insurance at age 27. What is his annual premium? **$930.60**

Annual Insurance Premiums per $1000			
Age	Straight life	20-payment life	20-year endowment
26	$15.06	$22.55	$42.30
27	15.51	23.07	42.33
28	15.97	23.60	42.36

4. What will be the cash value of Ted's insurance at the end of 20 years? **$17,700**

Straight Life—Cash Value per $1000				
Age at time of issue	Cash value at end of year			
	5	10	15	20
26	$32	$105	$181	$286
27	33	109	186	295
28	34	112	192	303

Insurance agent, pages 286-287

5. The annual premium for Angela Manuel's insurance is $384.72. The factor for monthly premiums is 0.0875. How much more per year will Angela pay if she pays monthly rather than annually?
$19.20

Choosing insurance and savings plans, pages 290-291

6. Andy Willoya, age 28, will pay monthly premiums for straight life insurance. The factor for monthly premiums is 0.0875. How much insurance (sold only in multiples of $1000) can he buy for a maximum of $65 a month? Use the table in problem 3.
$46,000

7. Janet Martin deposits $40 each month in a savings account that pays 6% interest compounded monthly. How much will be in the account at the end of 20 years? **$18,481.60**

Savings Balance (For $1 deposited each month with interest compounded monthly)		
Years	6%	7%
20	$462.04	$520.93

Social security retirement benefits, pages 292-295

8. The total of Lou Gacek's annual earnings subject to social security is $171,175. He has been contributing to social security for 25 years. What is his average annual income subject to social security?
$6847

9. Meg Sowa plans to retire at age 64. She has no dependents. Her average annual income subject to social security is $7465. What will be Meg's annual retirement benefit? **$5215.20**

Average annual income	Monthly benefit, retirement at age 64
$7200	$416.30
7600	434.60

10. Phil Damico is retired and receives $388.20 per month from social security. How much will he receive in 5 years?
$23,292

Chapter 14 Test

Number of test items - 10

Number missed	1	2	3	4	5
Percent correct	90	80	70	60	50

1. Wilma Racine has a $60-deductible health insurance policy. The insurance company pays 80% of all medical expenses over the deductible amount. Her medical expenses amounted to $957. How much did Wilma pay?
$239.40

2. Alma Torres is 30 years old. She bought a 5-year term insurance policy with a face value of $60,000. What is her annual premium?
$164.40

5-Year Term Insurance Annual Premiums per $1000		
	Premium	
Age	Male	Female
29	$3.16	$2.68
30	3.27	2.74
31	3.38	2.83

3. Russell Elliot bought $50,000 worth of straight life insurance at age 32. How much is his annual premium? $903.50

Annual Insurance Premiums per $1000			
Age	Straight life	20-payment life	20-year endowment
31	$17.52	$25.27	$42.51
32	18.07	25.87	42.60
33	18.67	26.49	42.70

4. What will be the cash value of Russell's insurance at the end of 20 years? $17,150

Straight Life—Cash Value per $1000				
Age at time of issue	Cash value at end of year			
	5	10	15	20
31	$37	$123	$210	$333
32	38	126	217	343
33	39	131	224	355

5. The annual premium for Liz Diehl's insurance is $583.50. The factor for quarterly premiums is 0.26. How much more will Liz pay each year if she pays quarterly rather than annually?
$23.34

6. Juan Carrido, age 33, is buying straight life insurance and will pay monthly premiums. The factor for monthly premiums is 0.0875. How much straight life insurance (sold only in multiples of $1000) can he buy for a maximum of $50 a month? Use the table in problem 3.
$30,000

7. Marie Kwon deposits $30 each month in a savings account that pays 7% interest compounded monthly. How much will be in the account at the end of 20 years? $15,627.90

Savings Balance (For $1 deposited each month with interest compounded monthly)		
Years	6%	7%
20	$462.04	$520.93

8. The total of Ray Wuttunee's annual earnings subject to social security is $168,100. He has been contributing to social security for 25 years. What is his average annual income subject to social security?
$6724

9. Ginny Tufo is planning to retire at age 63. She has no dependents. Her average annual income subject to social security is $7364. What will be Ginny's annual retirement benefit? $4639.20

Average annual income	Monthly benefit, retirement at age 63
$7200	$386.60
7600	403.60

10. Glen Conway is retired and receives $378.60 per month from social security. How much will he receive in 5 years?
$22,716

 See pages 35-36 of the *Test Masters* for an alternate form of the Ch[illegible]er 14 Test.

Chapter 15 Investments

Objective: Compute the cost and the redemption value of Series EE Savings Bonds.

United States Savings Bonds

See page T40 for additional notes and activities for Chapter 15.

Many people purchase **Series EE Savings Bonds** as an investment.

Series EE Bonds can be purchased with **face values** of \$50, \$75, \$100, \$200, \$500, \$1000, \$5000, and \$10,000. The cost of these bonds is $\frac{1}{2}$ of the face value.

A bond can be **redeemed**, or cashed in, any time after six months from the date of purchase. The **redemption value** of the bond is the cost of the bond plus interest for the time the bond was held. If held to **maturity**, which is 8 years, the interest is 9% compounded semiannually on the cost of the bond. The redemption value of any Series EE bond is based on the redemption value of a \$50 bond.

\$50 Savings Bond Series EE (Cost: \$25)	
After	Redemption value is
6 months	\$25.56
1 year	\$26.52
1.5 years	\$27.31
2 years	\$28.13
2.5 years	\$28.98
3 years	\$29.85
3.5 years	\$30.74
4 years	\$31.66
4.5 years	\$32.61
5 years	\$37.90
5.5 years	\$39.51
6 years	\$41.19
6.5 years	\$42.94
7 years	\$44.77
7.5 years	\$46.67
8 years	\$50.55
8.5 years	\$52.83
9 years	\$55.21
9.5 years	\$57.69
10 years	\$60.29
15 years	\$93.63
20 years	\$145.40

Maturity: 8 years

Warm-up: 7×250 [1750]
5×37.50 [187.50]
$\frac{42.94}{50} = \frac{r}{500}$ [$r = 429.40$]
$\frac{26.52}{50} = \frac{r}{250}$ [$r = 132.60$]

Problem

Bill Murphy wants to purchase a $200 Series EE Savings Bond. How much will the bond cost? If he redeems the bond in 8 years, how much will Bill receive?

Solution

Strategy

- Multiply $200 by $\frac{1}{2}$ to find the cost of the bond.
  $\frac{1}{2} \times \$200 = \$100$
- Read the table on page 300 to find the redemption value after 8 years for a $50 bond.
  $50.55
- Use a proportion to find the redemption value after 8 years for a $200 bond.

$$\frac{50.55}{50} = \frac{r}{200} \quad \begin{matrix} \longleftarrow \text{Redemption value} \\ \longleftarrow \text{Face value} \end{matrix}$$

$50r = 10{,}110$ Find the cross-products.

$r = 202.2$ Divide each side by 50.

Conclusion

The bond will cost $100. If Bill redeems the bond after 8 years, he will receive $202.20.

Related Problems

Complete the table.

	Number of bonds	Face value of each bond	Cost of 1 bond	Total cost
1.	1	$50	$25.00	——
2.	1	$75	$37.50	——
3.	3	$100	$50.00	$150
4.	3	$500	$250.00	$750
5.	6	$200	$100.00	$600
6.	4	$75	$37.50	$150
7.	12	$5,000	$2500.00	$30,000
8.	2	$10,000	$5000.00	$10,000
9.	20	$1,000	$500.00	$10,000

Find the redemption value of each bond to the nearest cent.

	Years held	Face value	
10.	3	$50	$29.85
11.	7	$50	$44.77
12.	5	$75	$56.85
13.	8	$500	$505.50
14.	2.5	$100	$57.96
15.	9.5	$75	$86.54
16.	15	$200	$374.52
17.	3.5	$1,000	$614.80
18.	6.5	$10,000	$8588.00
19.	20	$5,000	$14,540.00

20. Karl bought these Series EE Savings Bonds: three $50 bonds, one $75 bond, and three $100 bonds. To the nearest cent, what will be the total redemption value of these bonds after 10 years?
$633.05

Objective: Compute the interest and the annual yield for a certificate of deposit.

Certificates of Deposit

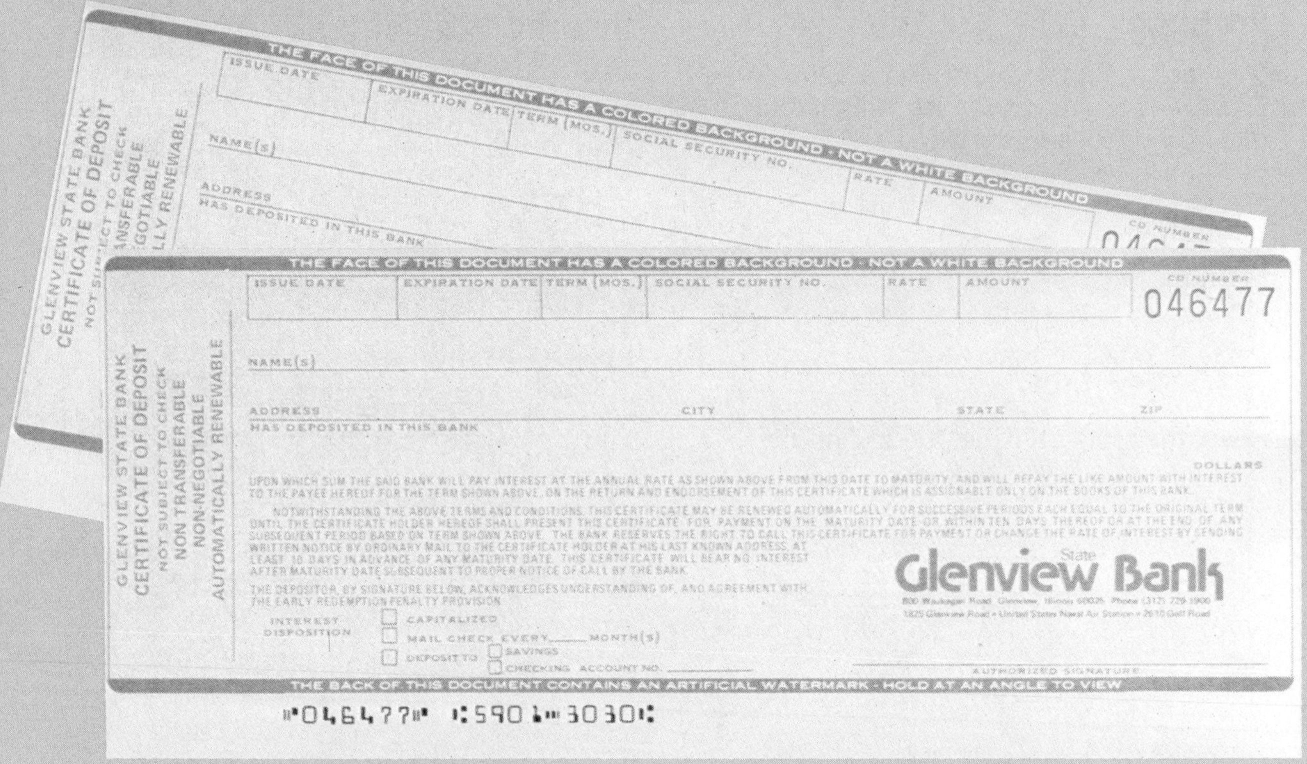

Most banks and savings institutions offer their customers **certificates of deposit.** A certificate of deposit (CD) earns a higher interest rate than a regular savings account.

Some types of certificates require a minimum deposit, usually $1000. Money invested in a CD must be left on deposit a certain length of time to earn the higher interest rate. If the money is withdrawn early, part of the interest is lost. This penalty for early withdrawal is required by federal law.

Generally, the interest on a CD is compounded daily. A table for interest compounded daily is shown at the right.

Interest Factors per $1 Invested

Annual rate	Interest period			
	3 mo.	6 mo.	9 mo.	1 yr.
5.25%	0.01303	0.02623	0.03960	0.05390
5.5%	0.01365	0.02749	0.04152	0.05654
5.75%	0.01428	0.02876	0.04345	0.05918
6%	0.01490	0.03003	0.04538	0.06183
6.25%	0.01553	0.03130	0.04731	0.06449
6.5%	0.01616	0.03257	0.04925	0.06715
6.75%	0.01678	0.03384	0.05119	0.06982
7%	0.01741	0.03512	0.05314	0.07250
7.25%	0.01804	0.03640	0.05509	0.07519
7.5%	0.01866	0.03767	0.05704	0.07788
7.75%	0.01929	0.03895	0.05900	0.08057
8%	0.01992	0.04024	0.06096	0.08328

Warm-up: 0.01428 × 1000 [14.28]
0.05119 × 5000 [255.95]
Round to the nearest hundredth.
0.01345 = ■% [1.35]
225.50 ÷ 2000 = ■% [11.28]

Problem

Millie Dunn decided to invest $2000 in a 4-year CD that earns 7.25% interest compounded daily. She agreed to leave her money on deposit for the full 4 years. The bank will send her a check for the interest each year. How much interest will Millie receive at the end of each year?

Solution

Strategy

- Read the table on page 302 to find the interest factor for 7.25% compounded daily for 1 year. 0.07519
- Multiply $2000 by the factor to find the annual interest. 0.07519 × $2000 = $150.38

Conclusion

Millie will receive $150.38 at the end of each year.

Related Problems

You may wish to allow students to use calculators for these problems.

Complete the table.

	Amount invested	Annual rate	Interest period	Interest factor	Interest
1.	$1,000	7.5%	1 year	0.07788	$77.88
2.	$5,000	7.75%	1 year	0.08057	$402.85
3.	$10,000	8%	9 months	0.06096	$609.60
4.	$3,000	6.25%	6 months	0.03130	$93.90
5.	$4,000	6.5%	6 months	0.03257	$130.28
6.	$2,000	6%	3 months	0.01490	$29.80
7.	$2,500	5.75%	3 months	0.01428	$35.70

8. Gail bought a $2000, 1-year CD that earns 7.5% interest compounded daily. She withdrew her money after 6 months. She received 6 months' interest at the regular savings-account rate of 5.25% compounded daily. How much interest did she receive?
$52.46

9. How much interest did Gail lose by withdrawing her money early?
$103.30

Problems 8 and 9 show how some banks compute the penalty for early withdrawal.

See page 55 of
Consumer Forms and Problems.

One method used to compare certificates of deposit is to find the **annual yield** of each CD. The CD with the highest annual yield will earn the most interest.

$$\text{Annual yield} = \frac{\text{Amount earned in 1 year}}{\text{Amount invested}}$$

Annual yield is usually expressed as a percent.

Problem

Millie's \$2000 CD earned \$150.38 interest each year. What was the annual yield to the nearest hundredth of a percent on this investment?

Solution

Strategy

- Use the formula to find the annual yield. Round to the nearest hundredth of a percent.

$$\text{Annual yield} = \frac{\$150.38}{\$2000} \approx 7.52\%$$

Conclusion

The annual yield was about 7.52%.

Related Problems

You may wish to discuss the effect of the interest period on the annual yield with respect to the annual interest rate.

Complete the table. Round the annual yield to the nearest hundredth of a percent.

	Amount invested	Annual rate	Interest period	Interest paid every period	Amount earned in 1 year	Annual yield
10.	\$1000	7.5%	1 year	\$77.88	\$77.88	7.79%
11.	\$3000	7.5%	6 months	\$113.01	\$226.02 (2 × \$113.01)	7.53%
12.	\$2000	5.75%	1 year	\$118.36	\$118.36	5.92%
13.	\$5000	6.25%	1 year	\$322.45	\$322.45	6.45%
14.	\$5000	6.5%	6 months	\$162.85	\$325.70	6.51%
15.	\$2000	5.75%	3 months	\$28.56	\$114.24	5.71%
16.	\$1000	7.5%	3 months	\$18.66	\$74.64	7.46%

17. Which has the higher annual yield: a \$1000 CD at 6% that earns \$61.83 each year, or a \$2000 CD at 6% that earns \$60.06 every 6 months?
\$1000 CD paying \$61.83 each year

18. Which has the higher annual yield: a \$1000 CD at 7.5% that earns \$77.88 each year, or a \$5000 CD at 7% that earns \$362.50 each year?
\$1000 CD paying \$77.88 each year

CALCULATOR APPLICATIONS

Compound Interest

The Acoyas bought a $2500 CD that earns 7.75% interest compounded daily. They plan to leave the $2500 and the interest it earns in the account for 10 years.

After the first year, the interest earned is 0.08057 × $2500, or $201.43. The compound amount, or the amount invested plus the interest earned, is $2500 + $201.43, or $2701.43. Notice that the amount invested each year is the same as the compound amount for the previous year.

Complete the table to find the value of the CD after 10 years. Round each answer to the nearest cent.

Encourage students to investigate the use of memory to facilitate completing the table.

	Year	Amount invested	Interest factor	Interest	Compound amount
	1	$2500	0.08057	$201.43	$2701.43
1.	2	$2701.43	0.08057	$217.65	$2919.08
2.	3	$2919.08	0.08057	$235.19	$3154.27
3.	4	$3154.27	0.08057	$254.14	$3408.41
4.	5	$3408.41	0.08057	$274.62	$3683.03
5.	6	$3683.03	0.08057	$296.74	$3979.77
6.	7	$3979.77	0.08057	$320.65	$4300.42
7.	8	$4300.42	0.08057	$346.48	$4646.90
8.	9	$4646.90	0.08057	$374.40	$5021.30
9.	10	$5021.30	0.08057	$404.57	$5425.87

10. Subtract the original $2500 invested from the compound amount after 10 years to find the amount of interest this CD will earn in 10 years.
$2925.87

11. This CD earned $201.43 in interest the first year. If the interest had been withdrawn each year, the total interest earned in 10 years would have been $201.43 × 10. Find this amount.
$2014.30

12. If the amount invested and the interest are compounded daily for the full 10 years, how much more interest will be earned than if the interest is withdrawn each year?
$911.57

13. Study the compound amounts for the 10 years. How many years does it take for the $2500 to double in value?
9 years

Objectives: Find the total cost of an investment in common stock; find the profit or loss and the annual yield of a stock investment.

Common Stock

Many people invest their money in **common stock**. The holder of **shares** of common stock is a partial owner of the company that issues the stock. If the company makes a profit during the year, it may pay **dividends**, or part of the profits, to its stockholders.

To purchase stocks, a buyer usually contacts a **broker**. The broker buys and sells stocks for the buyer, and can give advice about which stocks may be good investments. The buyer pays the broker a commission, or a fee for services, each time stocks are bought and sold.

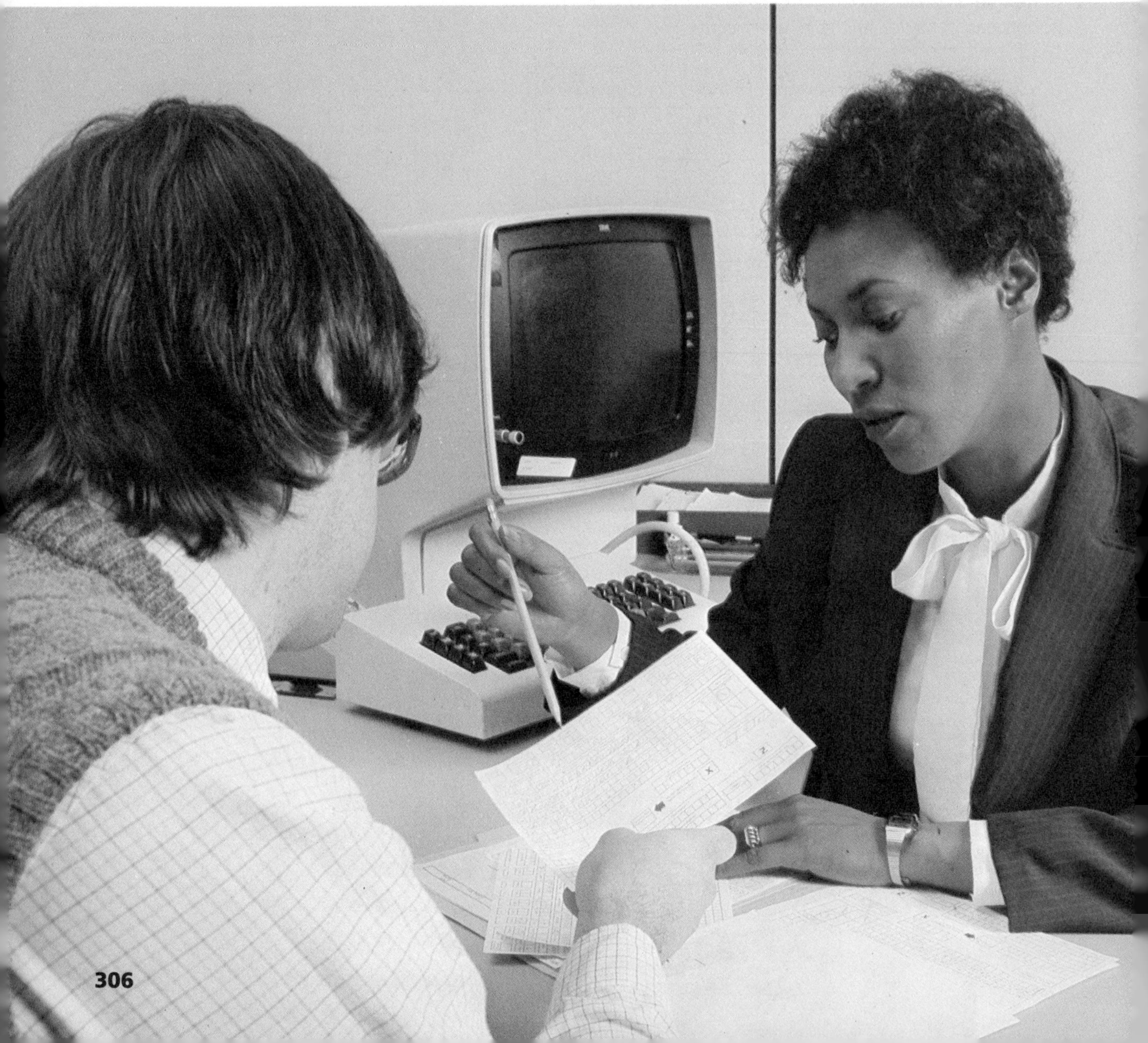

Warm-up: 120 × 6.125 [735]
200 × 55.875 [11,175]
Round to the nearest hundredth.
25 ÷ 450 = ■% [5.56]
215.5 ÷ 5000 = ■% [4.31]

The current prices of many stocks are listed in the financial sections of most newspapers. Part of a listing for a given day is shown below. An explanation of the columns is also given.

1	2 Div	3 P.E.	4 Sales (hds.)	5 High	6 Low	7 Close	8 Net Chg.
AAR	.44	8	28	11¾	11½	11½ −	⅛
ACF	2.76	10	89	48	47⅝	47⅞ −	⅛
AMF	1.24	13	136	24⅞	24⅝	24⅞ −	⅛
AM Intl		...	673	14¾	13½	13½ −	¾
APL		...	19	6⅛	6⅛	6⅛ −	⅛
ARA	1.94	7	138	33⅞	33	33⅜ +	⅛
ASA	5.00a	...	273	49¼	48⅝	49 −	¼
AVX	.32	24	223	35½	34¼	35 +	¼
AbtLb s		17	852	30½	29⅞	30½ +	⅞
AcmeC	1.40	8	6	27⅞	27⅞	27⅞	......
AdmDg	.04	8	27	6	5¾	5⅞ −	⅛
AdaEx	1.88e	...	75	14⅝	14⅜	14½	......
AdmMI	.20e	6	17	6¼	6⅛	6⅛	......
AMD s		17	328	26¾	26	26¾ +	⅞
AetnL f	2.32	6	2767 u	42¾	41⅜	42¾ +	1⅝

1 An abbreviation for the name of the stock.

2 *Div* Dividends paid in the last year. For example, .44 means $0.44 per share was paid in dividends in the last year.

3 *P.E.* Price-earnings ratio. The ratio of the market price per share to the earnings per share.

4 *Sales* (*hds.*) Hundreds of shares sold. 28 means 2800 shares were sold.

5 *High* The highest price paid for a share. $11\frac{3}{4}$ means $11\frac{3}{4}$ dollars, or $11.75.

6 *Low* The lowest price paid.

7 *Close* The last price paid.

8 *Net Chg*. Net change. The amount by which the closing price is different from the previous day's closing price. For example, $-\frac{1}{8}$ means that the closing price was $\frac{1}{8}$ of a dollar, or $0.125, per share lower than the previous day's closing price.

To give students experience in reading quotations, ask for example, "What was the closing price for Aetna Life?"

Problem

Craig Jarvis bought 25 shares of stock at $35\frac{3}{8}$, or $35.375, per share. He paid a commission of $21.50. To the nearest cent, what was the total amount that Craig invested?

Solution

Strategy

- Multiply to find the cost of the shares. Round to the nearest cent.
  $25 \times \$35.375 \approx \$884.38$
- Add the commission Craig paid to find the total amount invested.
  $\$884.38 + \$21.50 = \$905.88$

Conclusion

The total amount that Craig invested was $905.88.

Related Problems

For each problem, find the total amount invested to the nearest cent.

	Number of shares	Cost per share	Commission paid	
1.	45	$4.00	$13.88	$193.88
2.	90	$15.125	$39.25	$1400.50
3.	55	$10.125	$28.75	$585.63
4.	20	$35.125	$21.00	$723.50
5.	75	$28.75	$45.88	$2202.13
6.	100	$63.50	$91.75	$6441.75
7.	200	$58.75	$165.00	$11,915.00
8.	150	$26.125	$76.25	$3995.00
9.	60	$103.25	$83.50	$6278.50
10.	120	$100.375	$163.61	$12,208.61

Commissions may vary. Commission charges from several brokers should be compared before stocks are bought or sold.

Problem

Craig sold his 25 shares of stock several months after he bought them. The sale price was $36.75 per share. He paid a commission of $22. What was the profit or loss on the $905.88 that Craig invested?

Solution

Strategy

- Multiply the price per share by 25 to find the total sale price of the stock. $25 \times \$36.75 = \$918.75$
- Subtract the amount of commission to find the amount received from the sale of the stock. $\$918.75 - \$22 = \$896.75$
- Since the amount received was less than the amount invested, there was a loss. Subtract to find the loss. $\$905.88 - \$896.75 = \$9.13$

Conclusion

Craig had a loss of $9.13 on his investment.

Related Problems

Complete the table.

		Sale of stock				
	Amount invested	Number of shares	Sale price per share	Commission paid	Amount received	Profit or loss
	$905.88	25	$36.75	$22.00	$896.75	$9.13 loss
11.	$116.25	16	$5.625	$6.75	$83.25	$33.00 loss
12.	$2320.00	40	$63.50	$43.00	$2497.00	$177.00 profit
13.	$740.75	50	$15.75	$20.00	$767.50	$26.75 profit
14.	$1150.30	100	$13.375	$29.50	$1308.00	$157.70 profit
15.	$5950.15	100	$57.625	$74.00	$5688.50	$261.65 loss
16.	$1484.00	65	$27.25	$31.25	$1740.00	$256.00 profit
17.	$320.00	10	$32.125	$11.00	$310.25	$9.75 loss
18.	$6880.49	200	$41.00	$107.75	$8092.25	$1211.76 profit

See page 56 of
Consumer Forms and Problems.

Problem

Sandy MacKay invested $550 in 30 shares of stock. During the following year, the company paid dividends of $1.20 per share. To the nearest hundredth of a percent, what was the annual yield on Sandy's investment?

Solution

Strategy

- Multiply the dividend per share by 30 to find the total amount received.

  $30 \times \$1.20 = \$36$

- Use the formula on page 304 to find the annual yield. Round to the nearest hundredth of a percent.

  $\text{Annual yield} = \frac{\$36}{\$550} \approx 6.55\%$

Conclusion

The annual yield on Sandy's investment was about 6.55%.

Related Problems

Complete the table. Round the annual yield to the nearest hundredth of a percent.

	Amount invested	Number of shares	Dividends per share	Amount of dividends	Annual yield
19.	$2100	40	$3.00	**$120.00**	**5.71%**
20.	$6400	100	$4.20	**$420.00**	**6.56%**
21.	$4000	150	$1.06	**$159.00**	**3.98%**
22.	$3100	100	$2.15	**$215.00**	**6.94%**
23.	$7000	210	$1.72	**$361.20**	**5.16%**
24.	$2225	125	$5.76	**$720.00**	**32.36%**
25.	$5750	250	$3.10	**$775.00**	**13.48%**

Break Time

Copy each figure. Then trace each figure without lifting your pencil from the paper. Do not trace any line more than once.
Answers may vary.

Start

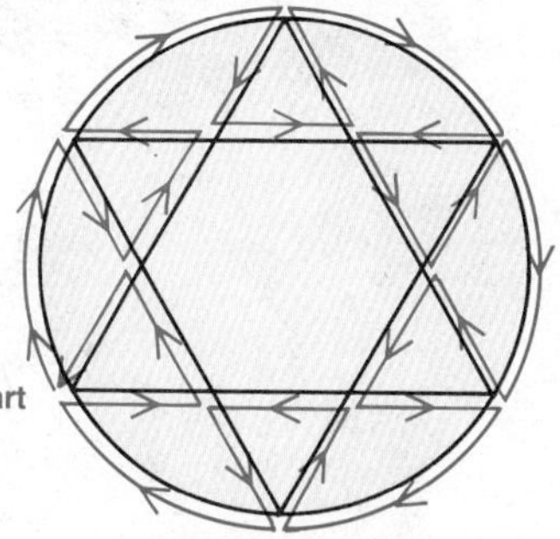

Start

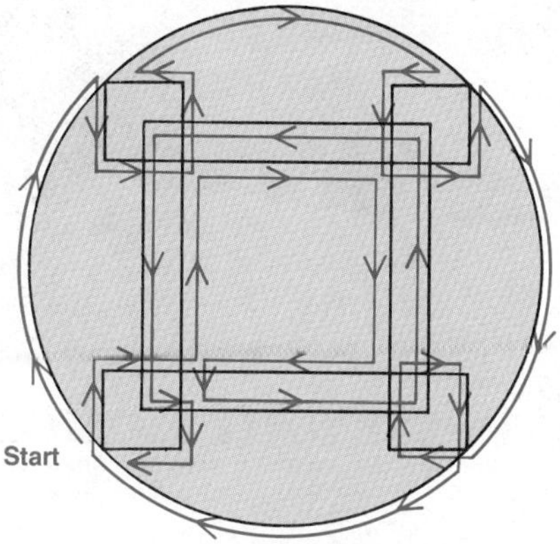

Start

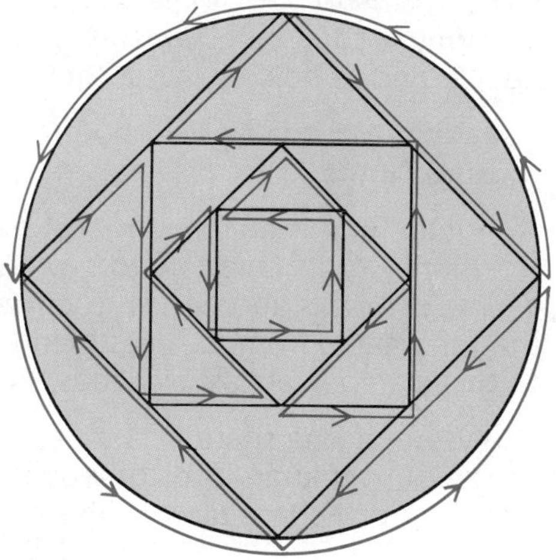

Investment Counselor

Objective: Find the cost of shares of mutual funds.

Career Cluster: Social Service As an investment counselor, Carla Reyes helps people decide how to invest their money.

Carla told Melinda Collier about **mutual funds.**

A mutual fund is a company that combines the money of its investors to buy a large variety of stocks and bonds. The money that the fund earns from its investments is paid to the shareholders as dividends.

The value of one share of a mutual fund is the amount that an investor would receive by selling one share back to the fund.

The amount that a new investor would have to pay to buy a share of a mutual fund sometimes includes a sales charge, or **load**. Thus, the price (buy price) is the value of a share (sell price) plus the load.

Mutual funds that do not have a sales charge are called **no-load** (NL) mutual funds. For these funds, the buy price is the same as the sell price.

The current prices of many funds are listed in the financial sections of most daily newspapers.

Warm-up: 25 × 14.75 [368.75]
80 × 6.66 [532.80]
31 × 17.59 [545.29]
47 × 15.06 [707.82]

Problem

Melinda was considering two mutual funds, the AB Mut. F. and the DX Mut. F. How much would Melinda pay for 50 shares of each fund?

MUTUAL FUNDS		
Name	Sell	Buy
AB Mut. F.	10.86	NL
AE Fund	13.05	14.26
BG Inv.	11.01	12.00
DX Mut. F.	9.97	10.90
GV Fund	7.63	8.34
Fin. Pln.	4.50	NL
HTH Grp.	12.12	13.25
Jay Fund	19.91	NL
MBT Grp.	5.79	NL
New Inv.	19.53	21.23
Park Fd.	24.97	NL
Va. Fund	4.01	NL

Solution

Strategy

- Read the table to find the buy price per share for each fund.

$10.86 AB Mut. F. (no-load)
$10.90 DX Mut. F. (includes load)

- Multiply each buy price by 50 to find the total price.

50 × $10.86 = $543 50 shares of AB Mut. F.
50 × $10.90 = $545 50 shares of DX Mut. F.

Conclusion

Melinda would pay $543 for 50 shares of the AB Mut. F. and $545 for 50 shares of the DX Mut. F.

Related Problems

Complete the table.

	Number of shares	Mutual fund	Buy price	Total cost
1.	5	Jay Fund	$19.91	$99.55
2.	20	New Inv.	$21.23	$424.60
3.	15	AE Fund	$14.26	$213.90
4.	50	Va. Fund	$4.01	$200.50
5.	75	Fin. Pln.	$4.50	$337.50
6.	40	BG Inv.	$12.00	$480.00
7.	12	GV Fund	$8.34	$100.08
8.	21	MBT Grp.	$5.79	$121.59
9.	16	Park Fd.	$24.97	$399.52

10. How much would Melinda receive if she sold 50 shares of the GV Fund back to the fund?
$381.50

11. How much would Melinda receive if she sold 40 shares of the Jay Fund back to the fund?
$796.40

12. What is the sales charge on each share of the DX Mut. F.?
$0.93

13. What is the sales charge on each share of the HTH Grp. fund?
$1.13

14. How many shares of the Fin. Pln. fund can be bought for $500? Round to the nearest ten-thousandth.
111.1111 shares

15. How many shares of the BG Inv. fund can be bought for $500? Round to the nearest ten-thousandth.
41.6667 shares

In many cases, investors need not buy a whole number of mutual-fund shares. Problems 14-15 are based on the common practice of computing each investment to the nearest ten-thousandth of a share.

Skills Tune-Up

Rounding whole numbers and decimals, pages 4-5

Round each number to the nearest thousand, nearest hundred, and nearest ten.

1. 719
   1000; 700; 720
2. 653
   1000; 700; 650
3. 3491
   3000; 3500; 3490
4. 6137
   6000; 6100; 6140
5. 9359
   9000; 9400; 9360
6. 4773
   5000; 4800; 4770
7. 56,202
   56,000; 56,200; 56,200
8. 2815
   3000; 2800; 2820
9. 999
   1000; 1000; 1000
10. 50,744
    51,000; 50,700; 50,740

Round each number to the nearest whole number, nearest tenth, and nearest hundredth.

11. 5.628
    6; 5.6; 5.63
12. 12.195
    12; 12.2; 12.20
13. 47.459
    47; 47.5; 47.46
14. 81.604
    82; 81.6; 81.60
15. 376.287
    376; 376.3; 376.29
16. 140.436
    140; 140.4; 140.44
17. 764.972
    765; 765.0; 764.97
18. 99.181
    99; 99.2; 99.18
19. 68.018
    68; 68.0; 68.02
20. 417.905
    418; 417.9; 417.91
21. 346.997
    347; 347.0; 347.00

Dividing decimals, pages 12-13

Find the quotient to the nearest hundredth.

1. $27.3 \div 9$
   3.03
2. $60.6 \div 7$
   8.66
3. $33.22 \div 37$
   0.90
4. $19.41 \div 43$
   0.45
5. $7.036 \div 78$
   0.09
6. $3.277 \div 63$
   0.05
7. $0.0027 \div 0.11$
   0.02
8. $0.0089 \div 0.58$
   0.02
9. $0.8 \div 3.6$
   0.22
10. $5.3 \div 8.3$
    0.64
11. $16.89 \div 6.1$
    2.77
12. $11.47 \div 9.5$
    1.21
13. $0.291 \div 0.08$
    3.64
14. $0.289 \div 0.03$
    9.63
15. $56 \div 0.7$
    80.00
16. $96 \div 0.4$
    240.00
17. $5.2 \div 1.11$
    4.68
18. $4.71 \div 9.43$
    0.50
19. $1.07 \div 28$
    0.04
20. $2.81 \div 9.06$
    0.31
21. $0.4877 \div 27$
    0.02
22. $0.725 \div 0.648$
    1.12
23. $0.932 \div 0.423$
    2.20
24. $0.6525 \div 0.042$
    15.54
25. $9.524 \div 0.039$
    244.21
26. $9.41 \div 1.04$
    9.05

Ratio and proportion, pages 30-31

Find the cross-products. Tell whether the ratios are equal.

1. $\frac{3}{5}$ $\frac{2}{3}$ **$9 \neq 10$**
2. $\frac{4}{6}$ $\frac{30}{45}$ **$180 = 180$**
3. $\frac{3}{7}$ $\frac{2}{12}$ **$36 \neq 14$**
4. $\frac{9}{2.7}$ $\frac{2}{0.6}$ **$5.4 = 5.4$**
5. $\frac{20.4}{100}$ $\frac{1.8}{9}$ **$183.6 \neq 180$**
6. $\frac{6}{9.95}$ $\frac{2}{2.99}$ **$17.94 \neq 19.9$**

Solve and check.

7. $\frac{5}{8} = \frac{15}{a}$ **$a = 24$**
8. $\frac{5}{4} = \frac{c}{28}$ **$c = 35$**
9. $\frac{49}{n} = \frac{14}{18}$ **$n = 63$**
10. $\frac{d}{8} = \frac{3.6}{6}$ **$d = 4.8$**
11. $\frac{0.75}{1} = \frac{18}{x}$ **$x = 24$**
12. $\frac{4.5}{a} = \frac{0.09}{0.2}$ **$a = 10$**
13. $\frac{0.48}{0.06} = \frac{y}{2}$ **$y = 16$**
14. $\frac{n}{6.3} = \frac{1.2}{2.7}$ **$n = 2.8$**

Chapter 15 Review

United States Savings Bonds, pages 300-301

1. The cost of any Series EE Savings Bond is $\frac{1}{2}$ of the face value. Find the cost of a $75 Series EE Savings Bond.
   $37.50
2. The redemption value of a $50 bond is $41.19 after 6 years. What is the redemption value of a $100 bond after 6 years?
   $82.38

Certificates of deposit, pages 302-304

3. Marie Wong bought a $4000 CD that earns 5.75% interest compounded daily. She receives an interest check every 3 months. How much interest does she receive every 3 months? A table for interest compounded daily is given below.
   $57.12

Interest Factors per $1 Invested

Annual rate	Interest period			
	3 mo.	6 mo.	9 mo.	1 yr.
5.25%	0.01303	0.02623	0.03960	0.05390
5.5%	0.01365	0.02749	0.04152	0.05654
5.75%	0.01428	0.02876	0.04345	0.05918
6%	0.01490	0.03003	0.04538	0.06183

4. Stan Larsen has a $3000 CD that earns $46.59 interest every 3 months. What is the annual yield on Stan's investment? Round to the nearest hundredth of a percent.
   6.21%

Common stock, pages 306-309

5. Ellen Drake bought 70 shares of stock for $43.375 per share. She paid a commission of $54. What was the total amount Ellen invested?
   $3090.25
6. Ronald May sold 50 shares of stock for $63.625 per share. He paid a commission of $49. How much did Ronald receive from the sale?
   $3132.25
7. Ronald's original investment was $3000. What was the profit or loss on his investment?
   $132.25 profit
8. Kirk invested $800 in 30 shares of stock. During the following year, he was paid dividends of $1.25 per share. What was the annual yield on his investment? Round to the nearest hundredth of a percent.
   4.69%

Investment counselor, pages 310-311

Use the table below for problems 9 and 10.

MUTUAL FUNDS		
Name	Sell	Buy
RV Fund	14.85	NL
Est. Grp.	12.20	14.00

9. Find the total price of 20 shares of the RV Fund.
   $297
10. Find the sales charge on each share of the Est. Grp. fund.
   $1.80

Chapter 15 Test

Number of test items - 10

Number missed	1	2	3	4	5
Percent correct	90	80	70	60	50

1. The cost of any Series EE Savings Bond is $\frac{1}{2}$ of the face value. Find the cost of a $500 Series EE Savings Bond.
$250

2. The redemption value of a $50 bond is $37.90 after 5 years. What is the redemption value of a $500 bond after 5 years?
$379

3. David Tooley bought a $3000 CD that earns 6% interest compounded daily. He receives an interest check every 6 months. How much interest does he receive every 6 months? A table for interest compounded daily is given below.
$90.09

Interest Factors per $1 Invested

Annual rate	Interest period			
	3 mo.	6 mo.	9 mo.	1 yr.
5.25%	0.01303	0.02623	0.03960	0.05390
5.5%	0.01365	0.02749	0.04152	0.05654
5.75%	0.01428	0.02876	0.04345	0.05918
6%	0.01490	0.03003	0.04538	0.06183

4. Barbara Vernon has a $5000 CD that earns $150.15 interest every 6 months. What is the annual yield on Barbara's investment? Round to the nearest hundredth of a percent.
6.01%

5. Eva Ventura bought 30 shares of stock for $42.875 per share. She paid a commission of $32. What was the total amount Eva invested?
$1318.25

6. Donald Ross sold 40 shares of stock for $52.625 per share. He paid a commission of $43. How much did Donald receive from the sale?
$2062

7. Donald's original investment was $2625. What was the profit or loss on his investment?
$563 loss

8. Renee invested $575 in 25 shares of stock. During the following year, she was paid dividends of $2.50 per share. What was the annual yield on her investment? Round to the nearest hundredth of a percent.
10.87%

Use the table below for problems 9 and 10.

MUTUAL FUNDS		
Name	Sell	Buy
Ntl. Inv.	27.10	NL
QA Fund	7.50	8.14

9. Find the total price of 30 shares of the Ntl. Inv. fund.
$813

10. Find the sales charge on each share of the QA Fund.
$0.64

 See pages 37-38 of the *Test Masters* for an alternate form of the Chapter 15 Test.

Unit 5 Test

Number of test items - 17

Number missed	1	2	3	4	5	6	7	8
Percent correct	94	88	82	76	71	65	59	53

Choose the best answer.

Pages 258–259

1. Last year, Elena earned $1545.25, $698, $1128.50, and $58.25. Find her gross income.

A $2740.50 **(C)** $3430

B $3421 **D** $15,478.75

Pages 260–262

2. Last year, Terry received $11,250 in salary, $140 in interest, and $250 in dividends. Find her adjusted gross income. Terry can claim a $100 exclusion for dividend income.

(A) $11,540 **C** $11,640

B $11,470 **D** $11,740

Page 263

3. Al and Sue Mendoza file a joint tax return and claim 2 exemptions. Their adjusted gross income (line 11, Form 1040A) is $19,475. Use the tax table below to find their tax liability.

1980 Tax Table B/Married Filing Joint Return

If line 11, Form 1040A, or line 34, Form 1040, is—		And the total number of exemptions claimed on line 6 is—					
Over	But not over	2	3	4	5	6	7
		Your tax is—					
19,400	19,450	2,607	2,367	2,144	1,934	1,724	1,514
19,450	19,500	2,619	2,379	2,155	1,945	1,735	1,525
19,500	19,550	2,631	2,391	2,165	1,955	1,745	1,535
19,550	19,600	2,643	2,403	2,176	1,966	1,756	1,546
19,600	19,650	2,655	2,415	2,186	1,976	1,766	1,556

A $2379 **(C)** $2619

B $2155 **D** $2607

Pages 264–265

4. Kate has a tax liability of $2975 and a tax credit of $2892. Find her refund or balance due.

A $5867 refund **C** $83 refund

(B) $83 balance due **D** $5867 balance due

Pages 266–267

5. The Red Clouds file a joint tax return and claim 5 exemptions. Their adjusted gross income is $19,565 and their tax credit is $2173. Find their refund or balance due. (Use the tax table in problem 3.)

A $207 balance due **C** $218 refund

(B) $207 refund **D** $218 balance due

Pages 268–270

6. Use the information below and the tax table in problem 3 to find the Edmonds' tax liability on a joint return.

Number of exemptions: 3
Adjusted gross income: $19,700
Zero bracket amount: $3400
Itemized deductions
State and local taxes: $1575
Interest expenses: $2100

A $2391 **C** $2379

B $2415 **(D)** $2367

Pages 272–273

7. Michigan's state income tax is 4.6% of taxable income. Find the tax on $12,500.

(A) $575 **C** $57.50

B $5750 **D** $83,950

Pages 278–279

8. A health insurance company pays 80% of all medical expenses over the $50-deductible amount. What will the company pay on medical expenses of $1495?

A $1196 **C** $289

B $1236 **(D)** $1156

Pages 280–281

9. The annual premium for a 5-year term life insurance policy for an 18-year-old male is $2.69 per $1000. Find the annual premium on a $50,000 policy.

A $672.50 **(C)** $134.50

B $1345 **D** $2690

Pages 282–285

10. Quan bought $75,000 worth of straight life insurance at age 21. Find the total cash value at age 65.

Straight Life—Cash Value per $1000			
Age at time of issue	Cash value at end of year		Cash value at age 65
	10	20	
20	$89	$241	$710
21	91	247	703
22	94	254	696

(A) $52,725 C $53,250

B $527,250 D $52,200

Pages 286–287

11. Beth's annual insurance premium is $508.50. How much more will she pay per year if she pays quarterly rather than annually? The factor for quarterly payments is 0.26.

A $132.21 C $376.29

B $528.84 (D) $20.34

Pages 290–291

12. Larry is buying straight life insurance at age 24. He wants to pay monthly premiums. How much of this insurance can he buy for a maximum of $60 a month? The factor for monthly premiums is 0.0875.

Annual Premiums per $1000 for Males			
Age	Straight life	20-payment life	20-year endowment
23	$13.79	$21.04	$42.20
24	14.21	21.54	42.24
25	14.64	22.07	42.27

A $40,000 C $49,000

(B) $48,000 D $45,000

Pages 292–295

13. The Cords can receive monthly social security retirement benefits of $419.70 plus $262.30 for one dependent. Find their annual retirement benefit.

A $682 C $3147.60

B $5036.40 (D) $8184

Pages 300–301

14. The cost of any Series EE Savings Bond is $\frac{1}{2}$ of the face value. Find the cost of a $100 bond.

A $100. C $75

(B) $50 D $200

Pages 302–304

15. Chad bought a $3000 CD that earns 7% interest compounded daily. He receives an interest check at the end of each year. How much interest does he receive at the end of each year?

Interest Factors per $1 Invested

Annual rate	Interest period		
	6 mo.	9 mo.	1 yr.
6.75%	0.03384	0.05119	0.06982
7%	0.03512	0.05314	0.07250
7.25%	0.03640	0.05509	0.07519

(A) $217.50 C $3217.50

B $225.60 D $225.57

Pages 306–309

16. Mrs. Leonard sold 80 shares of stock at $24.75 per share. She paid a commission of $36. How much did she receive?

(A) $1944 C $2016

B $1980 D $2880

Pages 310–311

17. DJR Mutual Fund is a no-load fund. The current selling price is $14.07 per share. Find the cost of 60 shares.

A $882.60 C $8826.40

(B) $844.20 D $8442.50

 For an alternate form of the Unit 5 Test, see pages T65–T66 of this book and pages 39–40 of the *Test Masters.*

Often it is easy to find percentages mentally. Study these examples for some helpful hints. The answers are rounded to the nearest cent.

When more than one computation is needed, round after the first computation.

Problem	**Hint**	THINK	**Answer**
10% of \$18	10% $= \frac{1}{10}$, so divide by 10.	\$18 ÷ 10 = \$1.80	\$1.80
10% of 18¢	Divide by 10.	18¢ ÷ 10 = 1.8¢ ≈ 2¢	2¢
5% of 79¢	5% $= \frac{1}{2}$ of 10%, so divide by 10 and then divide by 2.	79¢ ÷ 10 = 7.9¢ ≈ 8¢ 8¢ ÷ 2 = 4¢	4¢
20% of \$25	20% = 2 × 10%, so divide by 10 and then multiply by 2.	\$25 ÷ 10 = \$2.50 2 × \$2.50 = \$5	\$5
40% of \$1.50	40% = 4 × 10%, so divide by 10 and then multiply by 4.	\$1.50 ÷ 10 = \$0.15 = 15¢ 4 × 15¢ = 60¢	60¢
50% of 75¢	50% $= \frac{1}{2}$, so divide by 2.	75¢ ÷ 2 = 37.5¢ ≈ 38¢	38¢
25% of \$12	25% $= \frac{1}{4}$, so divide by 4.	\$12 ÷ 4 = \$3	\$3
$33\frac{1}{3}$% of \$3.60	$33\frac{1}{3}$% $= \frac{1}{3}$, so divide by 3.	\$3.60 ÷ 3 = \$1.20	\$1.20

Note, 20% also may be thought of as $\frac{1}{5}$. One would then divide by 5 when finding 20%.

Find the answers mentally. Round each answer to the nearest cent. Write only the answer.

1. 10% of \$45 **\$4.50**
2. 10% of 45¢ **5¢**
3. 5% of \$98 **\$4.90**
4. 5% of 98¢ **5¢**
5. 20% of \$30 **\$6**
6. 20% of 30¢ **6¢**
7. 40% of \$27 **\$10.80**
8. 40% of 27¢ **12¢**
9. 50% of \$15 **\$7.50**
10. 50% of 15¢ **8¢**
11. 25% of \$48 **\$12**
12. 25% of 48¢ **12¢**
13. $33\frac{1}{3}$% of \$63 **\$21**
14. $33\frac{1}{3}$% of 63¢ **21¢**
15. 10% of \$3.79 **38¢**
16. 10% of \$14.25 **\$1.43**
17. 20% of \$2.95 **60¢**
18. $33\frac{1}{3}$% of \$6.39 **\$2.13**
19. 50% of \$5.50 **\$2.75**
20. 5% of \$8.79 **44¢**
21. 25% of \$12.50 **\$3.13**
22. 40% of \$2.50 **\$1**
23. 30% of \$12 **\$3.60**
24. 80% of \$20 **\$16**

Payroll Deductions

The problems on page 79 can be done using the program shown.

John Weber works in the payroll department of a small company. The computational methods for finding the amount of federal income tax withheld were entered into the computer using the program shown.

Lines 50, 70, 90, and 110 These values need to be entered.

Data required	*Name*
Number of pay periods per year	P
Gross pay for this period	G
Number of exemptions	E
Filing status (Use 0 for single and 1 for married.)	S

Line 20 Rounding, to be used throughout the program, is defined.

Lines 30–38 These are DATA statements. Each line of data indicates a tax bracket. The first three numbers of each line are for single taxpayers, while the last three numbers of each line are for married taxpayers.

Line 120 The gross pay for the year (I) is estimated.

Line 130 Each exemption is a $1000 deduction which is subtracted from the yearly gross pay to compute the adjusted gross income (A).

Line 140 The RESTORE statement is placed before the READ statements so that the DATA lines can be reused.

Line 150 An IF . . . THEN statement is used to separate the calculations for a single filing status and a married filing status.

Lines 160, 170, 240, and 250 X eliminates data items in these statements. The entire DATA statement is read but numbers for X are not used.

Lines 160–230 and 240–310 These lines are used to find the line of data to use for the computations. The DATA lines are read until the adjusted gross income is less than B1, the first number used from the DATA statement that was read last. Then the computer is sent to line 320.

Line 320 D is the amount by which the adjusted gross income exceeds the bottom of the tax bracket from B to B1.

Line 330 Y, the federal tax for the year, is made up of two parts: a flat tax (F) for the bracket and a tax on the excess (D).

Line 340 The amount of federal withholding tax for the year is divided by the number of pay periods per year to find W, the amount to be withheld for one pay period.

If your computer does not have a disc drive system, delete the statement on line 20. For every line that contains FNR as part of the statement, delete FNR and add a rounding statement as explained on page 128, line 120.

These problems can be used either with a computer or as paper-and-pencil activities.

```
10 REM  FEDERAL INCOME TAX
20 DEF FNR(Z)=INT(Z*100+.5)/100
30 DATA 0,0,0,0,0,0
31 DATA 1420,0,.15,2400,0,.15
32 DATA 3300,282,.18,6600,630,.18
33 DATA 6800,912,.21,10900,1404,.21
34 DATA 10200,1626,.26,15000,2265,.24
35 DATA 14200,2666,.30,19200,3273,.28
36 DATA 17200,3566,.34,23600,4505,.32
37 DATA 22500,5368,.39,28900,6201,.37
38 DATA 0,0,0,0,0,0
40 PRINT "NUMBER OF PAY PERIODS";
50 INPUT P
60 PRINT "GROSS PAY";
70 INPUT G
80 PRINT "NUMBER OF EXEMPTIONS";
90 INPUT E
100 PRINT "FILING STATUS";
110 INPUT S
120 LET I=FNR(P*G)
130 LET A=FNR(I-E*1000)
140 RESTORE
150 IF S=1 THEN 240
160 READ B,F,T,X,X,X
170 READ B1,F1,T1,X,X,X
180 IF B1=0 THEN 320
190 IF A<B1 THEN 320
200 LET B=B1
210 LET F=F1
220 LET T=T1
230 GO TO 170
240 READ X,X,X,B,F,T
250 READ X,X,X,B1,F1,T1
260 IF B1=0 THEN 320
270 IF A<B1 THEN 320
280 LET B=B1
290 LET F=F1
300 LET T=T1
310 GO TO 250
320 LET D=FNR(A-B)
330 LET Y=FNR(T*D+F)
340 LET W=FNR(Y/P)
350 PRINT "FEDERAL WITHHOLDING TAX";W
360 END
```

Answers for computer applications are often in an abbreviated form. In all program modifications shown, the changes and/or additions incorporate previous modifications and will vary. Samples are given.

Give the output for the program above when

1. P is 52, G is 155, E is 2, and S is 0.
   FEDERAL WITHHOLDING TAX 14.98
2. P is 26, G is 264.44, E is 4, and S is 1.
   FEDERAL WITHHOLDING TAX 2.74
3. P is 26, G is 572.87, E is 3, and S is 1.
   FEDERAL WITHHOLDING TAX 62.03
4. P is 52, G is 302.18, E is 1, and S is 0.
   FEDERAL WITHHOLDING TAX 54.23
5. P is 26, G is 488.76, E is 2, and S is 1.
   FEDERAL WITHHOLDING TAX 52.67
6. a married person has 3 exemptions, there are 52 pay periods, and the pay for this pay period is $432.07.
   FEDERAL WITHHOLDING TAX 64.38
7. a single person has 1 exemption, there are 52 pay periods, and the pay for this pay period is $432.07.
   FEDERAL WITHHOLDING TAX 96.48
8. a single person has 3 exemptions, there are 26 pay periods, and the pay for this pay period is $678.45.
   FEDERAL WITHHOLDING TAX 107.61
9. a married person has 5 exemptions, there are 26 pay periods, and the pay for this pay period is $872.11.
   FEDERAL WITHHOLDING TAX 111.81
10. Modify the program so that the number of pay periods per year, the gross pay for this period, the number of exemptions, and the filing status are included in the printout.
    See below.
11. Give the output when there are 26 pay periods, the gross pay for this period is $478.93, there is 1 exemption, and the filing status is married.
    See below.
12. Modify the program to calculate a state withholding tax. For this tax, use 2.5% of the adjusted gross pay. (Adjusted gross pay is the amount after subtracting the deductions for exemptions.)
    See below.
13. Give the output when there are 52 pay periods, the gross pay for this period is $392.61, there is 1 exemption, and the filing status is single.
    FEDERAL WITHHOLDING TAX 83.06
    STATE WITHHOLDING TAX 9.33

10.
```
345 PRINT "NUMBER OF PAY PERIODS PER YEAR";P
346 PRINT "GROSS PAY FOR THIS PERIOD";G
347 PRINT "NUMBER OF EXEMPTIONS";E
348 PRINT "FILING STATUS";S
```

11.
```
NUMBER OF PAY PERIODS PER YEAR 26
GROSS PAY FOR THIS PERIOD 478.93
NUMBER OF EXEMPTIONS 1
FILING STATUS 1
FEDERAL WITHHOLDING TAX 58.46
```

12.
```
341 LET M=FNR(.025*A/P)
351 PRINT "STATE WITHHOLDING TAX";M
```

Unit 6 Purchasing and Budgeting

Chapter 16 Buying Food

Objective: Find the total number of calories in a meal, using a calorie chart.

Nutritionist

See page T41 for additional notes and activities for Chapter 16.

See the Careers Chart beginning on page 410 for more information about the careers in this cluster.

Career Cluster: Health Henry Robinson is a nutritionist at a hospital. His job is to plan nutritious, well-balanced meals.

When Henry plans meals for people, he takes into consideration these four main food groups.

— Meat, poultry, eggs, and fish
— Milk and dairy products
— Fruits and vegetables
— Breads and cereals

He also uses a calorie chart. A portion of one is shown below. A **calorie** is a heat unit that is used to express the fuel value of foods.

CALORIE CHART	Portion	Calories
Meat, poultry		
Bacon	1 slice	45
Chicken, broiled	1 piece	185
Meat loaf	1 slice	200
Dairy products and eggs		
Butter	1 pat	50
Cheddar cheese	55 g	225
Cottage cheese	55 g	50
Egg, poached	1	80
Milk	240 mL	160
Fruits		
Apple	1	70
Grapefruit	$\frac{1}{2}$	55
Orange juice	120 mL	55
Peaches, canned	1 serving	100
Vegetables		
Lettuce	2 leaves	10
Peas	1 serving	60
Potato, baked	1	90
Tomato	1	30
Breads and cereals		
Oatmeal	240 mL	150
Whole-wheat bread	1 slice	55
Sandwiches		
Chicken salad	1	280
Tuna salad	1	280
Miscellaneous		
French dressing	15 mL	60
Vegetable soup	240 mL	80

Problem

Henry is planning a low-calorie diet for Rose Benson. Find the number of calories in the breakfast that Henry has planned for Rose.

Monday breakfast
$\frac{1}{2}$ grapefruit
240 mL oatmeal
120 mL milk
2 slices bacon

Solution

Strategy

- Use the calorie chart to compute the number of calories in each item.

  Grapefruit: 55 cal.
  Oatmeal: 150 cal.
  Milk: 80 cal. (160 ÷ 2)
  Bacon: 90 cal. (45 × 2)

- Add to find the total number of calories.

  55 + 150 + 80 + 90 = 375

Conclusion

The breakfast contains 375 calories.

Warm-up: 2 × 45 [90]
2 × 185 [370]
150 ÷ 2 [75]
45 + 200 + 30 + 60 [335]

Related Problems

Find the number of calories in each meal.

1. Monday lunch
   535 calories
   240 mL vegetable soup
   $\frac{1}{2}$ tomato
   240 mL milk
   1 tuna salad sandwich

2. Monday dinner
   740 calories
   2 pieces broiled chicken
   55 g cottage cheese
   1 serving peas
   240 mL milk
   1 serving canned peaches

3. Tuesday breakfast
   480 calories
   120 mL orange juice
   2 poached eggs
   1 slice whole-wheat toast
   1 pat butter
   240 mL milk

4. Tuesday lunch
   595 calories
   $\frac{1}{2}$ chicken salad sandwich
   55 g cheddar cheese
   240 mL milk
   1 apple

5. Tuesday dinner
   530 calories
   1 slice meat loaf
   1 baked potato
   4 leaves of lettuce
   15 mL French dressing
   240 mL milk

6. Find the total number of calories planned for Monday. Include breakfast.
   1650 calories
7. Find the total number of calories planned for Tuesday.
   1605 calories

Objective: Find the number of calories used in various activities.

Calorie Usage

Jed Horton's doctor gave him information about the number of calories used in certain activities. Jed kept track of how long he participated in each activity one day. Then he completed the table below.

Activity	Calories used per kilogram of body weight in one hour	Number of hours spent one day
Sleeping	0.9	$7\frac{3}{4}$
Sitting quietly reading, writing, talking on the telephone, watching TV, attending classes	1.8	$9\frac{1}{2}$
Light exercise walking slowly, playing the piano, typing, driving a car	2.4	$4\frac{1}{2}$
Moderate exercise bicycling 8 km per hour, walking briskly, bowling, playing catch	3.9	$\frac{1}{2}$
Active exercise dancing, doing calisthenics, raking leaves, playing table tennis	5.7	$\frac{1}{4}$
Very active exercise jogging 8 km per hour, swimming, playing tennis	6.4	$1\frac{1}{2}$
	Total hours	24

Problem

Jed weighs 69 kg. How many calories did he use while sleeping?

Solution

Strategy

- Read the table to find the factor for sleeping.

  0.9

- Multiply times Jed's weight to find the number of calories used in one hour of sleeping.

  $0.9 \times 69 = 62.1$

- Read the table to find the number of hours Jed slept. Rename as a decimal.

  $7\frac{3}{4} = 7.75$

- Multiply times the number of calories used in one hour of sleeping. Round to the nearest whole number.

  $7.75 \times 62.1 \approx 481$

Conclusion

Jed used about 481 calories while sleeping.

Warm-up: 2.4×62 [148.8]
5.7×68 [387.6]
68.3×7.25 [495.175]
402.5×0.5 [201.25]

Related Problems

For problems 1–5, find the number of calories used during each activity listed in the chart. Round each answer to the nearest whole number.

1. Sitting quietly
   1180 calories
2. Light exercise
   745 calories
3. Moderate exercise
   135 calories
4. Active exercise
   98 calories
5. Very active exercise
   662 calories
6. Find the total number of calories Jed used on that day. Include the calories used for sleeping.
   3301 calories

Find the number of calories used by Betty Granville during each activity listed. The number of hours Betty spent on each activity on Monday is given. She weighs 58 kg.

7. Sleeping, 8 hours
   418 calories
8. Sitting quietly, $10\frac{1}{2}$ hours
   1096 calories
9. Light exercise, $2\frac{3}{4}$ hours
   383 calories
10. Moderate exercise, $1\frac{1}{4}$ hours
    283 calories
11. Active exercise, 1 hour
    331 calories
12. Very active exercise, $\frac{1}{2}$ hour
    186 calories
13. Find the total number of calories used by Betty on Monday.
    2697 calories
14. Betty is trying to use more calories than are in the food she eats. On Monday her meals contained 1375 calories. How many more calories did Betty use than were in the food she ate?
    1322 calories

Objectives: Compute the cost of a grocery item; compare the costs of two different brands or sizes of an item after computing the unit prices.

Grocery Shopping

Jaime and Alicia Lorenzo plan their weekly menus before they shop. From these menus the Lorenzos make a shopping list. This helps them buy only the items they need. They use ads in the newspaper to find the cost of the items they want to buy.

Problem

Bananas cost $0.87 per kilogram. Find the cost of 1.3 kg of bananas.

Solution

Point out that the answers are rounded up, and explain why.

Strategy

- Multiply the weight of the bananas times the cost per kilogram. Round up to the next whole cent.

  $1.3 \times \$0.87 \approx \$1.14$

Conclusion

1.3 kg of bananas cost $1.14.

Problem

Beef gravy mix is marked 3/$1.00. This means 3 packages cost $1.00. How much would 2 packages of gravy mix cost?

Solution

Strategy

- Divide by 3 to find the cost of one package. Round up to the next whole cent.

  $\$1.00 \div 3 \approx \$0.34$

- Multiply by 2 to find the cost of 2 packages.

  $2 \times \$0.34 = \$0.68$

Conclusion

2 packages of gravy mix cost $0.68.

Warm-up: 1.7 × 0.38 [0.646]
1.19 ÷ 4 [0.2975]
0.47 × 2 [0.94]
179 ÷ 500 [0.358]

In problem 9, the first two cans should cost $0.95. To find the cost of three cans, add the cost of a single can to $0.95.

Related Problems

Find the cost of each item listed.

1. 1.2 kg of apples at $1.54 per kilogram
   $1.85
2. 3 cans of pears at $0.69 each
   $2.07
3. 0.5 kg of steak at $6.05 per kilogram
   $3.03
4. 2 cans of peas at 4 for $1.00
   $0.50
5. 2 bottles of salad dressing at 3 for $2.00
   $1.34
6. 3 packages of pudding mix at 5 for $1.29
   $0.78
7. 2 cans of fruit drink at $0.62 each
   $1.24
8. 3.6 kg of onions at $0.65 per kilogram
   $2.34
9. 3 cans of pork and beans at 2 for $0.95
   $1.43
10. 8 cans of soup at 3 for $0.98
    $2.62
    In problem 10, the cost of the first six cans should be 2 × $0.98. To find the cost of eight cans, add the cost of two single cans to $1.96.

When Jaime and Alicia shop, they often compare prices to determine the best buys. To do this, they find the **unit price** of each item. This is the price per unit of measure.
Some stores post unit prices for quick comparisons.

Problem

Find the unit price of a 300-gram jar of peanut butter priced at $1.28.

Solution

Strategy

- Write the price in cents.

  $\$1.28 = 128¢$

- Divide by the number of grams. Round to the nearest hundredth of a cent.

  $128¢ \div 300 \approx 0.43¢$

Conclusion

The unit price is about 0.43¢ per gram.

Related Problems

Find the unit price for each item to the nearest hundredth of a cent.

11. 340-gram bottle of chili sauce for $0.63
0.19¢ per gram

12. 312-gram box of raisins for $1.40
0.45¢ per gram

13. 675-gram jar of applesauce for $0.81
0.12¢ per gram

14. 3.5-liter bottle of bleach for $0.77
22¢ per liter

15. 950-milliliter bottle of apple juice for $0.89
0.09¢ per milliliter

16. 908-gram can of peaches for $0.99
0.11¢ per gram

17. 535-milliliter can of tomato juice for $0.45
0.08¢ per milliliter

18. 0.5-kilogram bag of noodles for $0.65
$1.30 per kilogram

19. 300-gram jar of mustard for $0.48
0.16¢ per gram

20. 1.5-liter bottle of vinegar for $0.74
49.33¢ per liter

See pages 57–58 of
Consumer Forms and Problems.

Problem

Which is the better buy for vegetable oil?

1.2-liter bottle for \$1.99 1.6-liter bottle for \$2.89

Solution

Strategy

- Find the unit price for each item to the nearest whole cent. $\$1.99 \div 1.2 \approx \$1.66$ 1.2-liter bottle; $\$2.89 \div 1.6 \approx \$1.81$ 1.6-liter bottle
- Compare the unit prices. $\$1.66 < \$1.81$

Conclusion

The 1.2-liter bottle is the better buy.

Related Problems

This table shows some of the items on the Lorenzos' grocery list. For each brand, find the unit price to the nearest whole cent. Then find the cost of the item if the Lorenzos choose the better buy. Round each cost up to the next whole cent.

	Item	Name brand	Unit price	Store brand	Unit price	Cost
	Vegetable oil, 1 bottle	1.2-L bottle: \$1.99	\$1.66/L	1.6-L bottle: \$2.89	\$1.81/L	\$1.99
21.	Milk, 4 L	2-L carton: \$0.99	\$0.50/L	4-L carton: \$1.89	\$0.47/L	\$1.89
22.	Flour, 5 kg	2.5-kg sack: \$1.39	\$0.56/kg	5-kg sack: \$2.69	\$0.54/kg	\$2.69
23.	Detergent, 10 kg	5-kg box: \$7.29	\$1.46/kg	2-kg box: \$2.55	\$1.28/kg	\$12.75
24.	Swiss cheese, 1 kg	0.5-kg chunk: \$3.19	\$6.38/kg	1-kg chunk: \$6.45	\$6.45/kg	\$6.38
25.	Potatoes, 5 kg	2.5-kg sack: \$1.47	\$0.59/kg	\$0.53/kg	\$0.53/kg	\$2.65
26.	Butter, 1 kg	1-kg package: \$4.39	\$4.39/kg	0.5-kg package: \$2.35	\$4.70/kg	\$4.39
27.	Bread, 1 loaf	0.5-kg loaf: \$0.89	\$1.78/kg	0.6-kg loaf: \$0.95	\$1.58/kg	\$0.95
28.	Orange juice, 2 L	1-L bottle: \$0.89	\$0.89/L	2-L bottle: \$1.69	\$0.85/L	\$1.69

29. Find the total cost.
\$35.38

30. If a \$1-off coupon can be applied to either size, which is the better buy: 5 kg of charcoal for \$2.89, or 10 kg of charcoal for \$5.09?
5 kg for \$2.89

CALCULATOR APPLICATIONS

Food Costs

Sometimes a proportion can be used to find the price of an item.

Find the price of 1.4 kg of pears priced at 2 kg for $1.99.

Write a proportion.

$$\frac{1.99}{2} = \frac{n}{1.4} \begin{array}{l} \longleftarrow \text{Price (dollars)} \\ \longleftarrow \text{Weight (kilograms)} \end{array}$$

Solve the proportion, rounding up to the next whole cent.

$1.99 \times 1.4 = 2 \times n$

Key sequence:

1.99 [×] 1.4 [÷] 2 [=]

$$\frac{2.786}{2} = \frac{2n}{2}$$

$1.40 \approx n$

1.4 kg of pears cost $1.40.

Costs calculated by using proportions may differ from costs calculated by the methods shown on page 326.

Find the cost of each item listed. Round each answer up to the next whole cent.

1. 3.1 kg of oranges at 2 kg for $2.39
   $3.71
2. 0.7 kg of steak at $6.05 per kilogram
   $4.24
3. 7 cans of tomato sauce at 5 for $0.99
   $1.39
4. 2 packages of gelatin at 3 for $1.00
   $0.67
5. 2.6 kg of onions at 4 kg for $2.77
   $1.81
6. 1.2 kg of ham at 0.5 kg for $3.69
   $8.86
7. 1 jar of jelly at 3 for $1.66
   $0.56
8. 25 cans of juice at 2 for $0.79
   $9.88
9. 0.4 kg of nuts at $7.12 per kilogram
   $2.85
10. 5 cantaloupes at 3 for $1.39
    $2.32
11. 12 lemons at 5 for $0.79
    $1.90
12. 5 bars of soap at 2 for $0.49
    $1.23
13. 3 loaves of bread at 2 for $1.39
    $2.09
14. 0.8 kg of cheese at 0.5 kg for $2.99
    $4.79
15. 4 cans of soup at 3 for $0.98
    $1.31
16. 10 cans of dog food at 4 for $0.59
    $1.48

Objectives: Compute the percent of loss and the cost of a side of beef after butchering; compare the cost of a side of beef with the cost of buying the separate cuts at a grocery store.

Comparing Meat Prices

Ned Kuri belongs to a food-buying cooperative. He and his friends save money by sharing in the purchase of large quantities of food. The cooperative is interested in buying a side of beef. A side of beef is half of all the meat obtained from the animal. During butchering, there is a 20% to 30% loss due to trimming away fat, discarding bone, and normal shrinkage.

Problem

Before butchering, a side of beef weighed 135 kg. After butchering, the usable meat weighed 97.2 kg. What was the percent of loss?

Solution

Strategy

- Subtract to find the amount of loss.

  $135 - 97.2 = 37.8$

- Divide by the total weight of the side of beef to find the percent of loss.

  $\frac{37.8}{135} = 28\%$

Conclusion

The percent of loss was 28%.

Problem

The price of the 135-kilogram side of beef before butchering was $3.29 per kilogram. Find the cost per kilogram of usable meat (97.2 kg).

Solution

Strategy

- Multiply to find the total cost of the side of beef before butchering.

  $135 \times \$3.29 = \$444.15$

- Divide to find the cost per kilogram of usable meat. Round to the nearest whole cent.

  $\$444.15 \div 97.2 \approx \$4.57$

Conclusion

The usable meat cost $4.57 per kilogram.

Related Problems

Complete the table. Round each cost to the nearest whole cent.

	Weight of beef before butchering	Amount of usable meat	Percent of loss	Cost per kilogram before butchering	Cost per kilogram of usable meat
	135 kg	97.2 kg	28%	$3.29	$4.57
1.	130 kg	91.0 kg	30%	$3.29	$4.70
2.	145 kg	107.3 kg	26%	$3.19	$4.31
3.	125 kg	95.0 kg	24%	$3.33	$4.38
4.	155 kg	116.6 kg	25%	$3.19	$4.24
5.	165 kg	123.75 kg	25%	$3.19	$4.25

Warm-up: $\frac{37.4}{170} = ■\%$ [22%]

$\frac{40.3}{155} = ■\%$ [26%]

375.16 ÷ 90.4 [4.15]

17.5 × 3.29 [57.575]

Problem

A 140-kilogram side of beef yields 15.5 kg of ground beef. The current price for ground beef in a grocery store is \$3.99 per kilogram. Using this price, find the value of the ground beef obtained from the side of beef.

Solution

Strategy

- Multiply to find the store value of the ground beef. Round up to the next whole cent. $15.5 \times \$3.99 \approx \$61.85$

Conclusion

The ground beef would cost about \$61.85 in a grocery store.

Related Problems

The 140-kilogram side of beef yields the amounts listed in the table. Find the value for each cut of meat. Round up to the next whole cent.

	Cut of meat	Amount obtained	Current cost per kilogram	Value at the current price
	Ground beef	15.5 kg	\$3.99	\$61.85
6.	Round steak	15.4 kg	\$4.89	\$75.31
7.	Stew meat	14.4 kg	\$5.99	\$86.26
8.	Chuck blade roast	12.5 kg	\$4.09	\$51.13
9.	Sirloin steak	11.6 kg	\$5.39	\$62.53
10.	Rib roast	8.5 kg	\$5.89	\$50.07
11.	Chuck arm roast (boneless)	8.1 kg	\$5.09	\$41.23
12.	Porterhouse, T-bone, club steaks	7.1 kg	\$8.99	\$63.83
13.	Rump roast (boneless)	4.7 kg	\$4.59	\$21.58
14.	Brisket (boneless)	2.9 kg	\$5.29	\$15.35
15.	Flank steak	0.7 kg	\$8.09	\$5.67
16.	Kidney	0.4 kg	\$1.99	\$0.80

17. What is the total store value of the meat?
\$535.61
18. The price of the 140-kilogram side of beef is \$3.29 per kilogram before butchering. What is the difference between the total cost of the side of beef and the total value of the meat at current store prices?
\$75.01

Objectives: Compute the amount of tip for a restaurant meal; compare the cost of preparing a meal at home with the costs of various alternatives.

Comparing Meal Costs

Warm-up: 10% of 12 [1.2] 10% of 8 [0.8] $\frac{1}{2}$ of 0.60 [0.30] $\frac{1}{2}$ of 1.80 [0.90]

There are alternatives to preparing and eating meals at home. Many people choose to eat in restaurants or to purchase prepared foods and carry-out meals.

When eating at a restaurant, most people give the waiter or waitress a tip for serving the food. This amount is usually about 15% of the bill.

Problem

Irene and Stan Ochita want to compare the cost of eating in a restaurant with the cost of having the same dinner at home. They recently had fish dinners at a restaurant. The bill was $12.35 plus $0.62 tax. They left a 15% tip. Preparing the same meal at home costs $8.25. How much more does the restaurant meal cost?

Solution

Stress the mental calculation of the 15% tip. Since the bill is first rounded, the tip only approximates 15% of the bill.

Strategy

- Round the food bill to the nearest dollar.

  $12.35 ≈ $12.00

- Mentally calculate the amount of a 15% tip.

$1.20	10% of bill (10% of $12.00 = $1.20)
+ 0.60	5% of bill (5% = $\frac{1}{2}$ of 10%; $\frac{1}{2}$ of $1.20 = $0.60)
$1.80	Tip (15% = 10% + 5%)

- Find the total restaurant cost.

$12.35	Food bill
0.62	Tax
1.80	Tip
$14.77	Total cost

- Subtract the cost of preparing the same meal at home.

  $14.77 − $8.25 = $6.52

Conclusion

The restaurant meal costs $6.52 more.

See page 59 of *Consumer Forms and Problems*.

Remind students that the tip is calculated before the sales tax is added in problems 3 and 7.

Related Problems

Sales tax is included in problems 1, 2, 5, and 6.

Find the total cost for two people for each meal listed.

1. *Chicken carry-out* **$6.12**

Bucket of 8 pieces	$4.88
Cole slaw	$0.84
Beverage at home	$0.20 per person

2. *Chicken prepared at home* **$3.02**

Whole chicken	$2.10
Cole slaw ingredients	$0.52
Beverage	$0.20 per person

3. *Chicken at a restaurant* **$11.90**

Chicken and cole slaw dinner for two	$8.80
Beverage	$0.55 per person
Sales tax	$0.50
Include 15% tip.	

4. Find the difference in the total costs of the most expensive and the least expensive chicken dinners.
$8.88

5. *Beef stew dinner served at home* **$4.54**

Frozen beef stew	$3.59
Salad ingredients	$0.55
Beverage	$0.20 per person

6. *Beef stew prepared at home* **$3.07**

Beef	$1.70
Potatoes	$0.35
Carrots	$0.07
Salad ingredients	$0.55
Beverage	$0.20 per person

7. *Beef stew dinner at a restaurant* **$11.52**

Stew and salad for two	$8.40
Beverage	$0.60 per person
Sales tax	$0.42
Include 15% tip.	

8. Find the difference in the total costs of the most expensive and the least expensive beef stew dinners.
$8.45

Break Time

Fill in the squares in the diagram with all the numbers from 1 to 8. No two consecutive numbers can be next to each other vertically, horizontally, or diagonally.
Answers may vary.

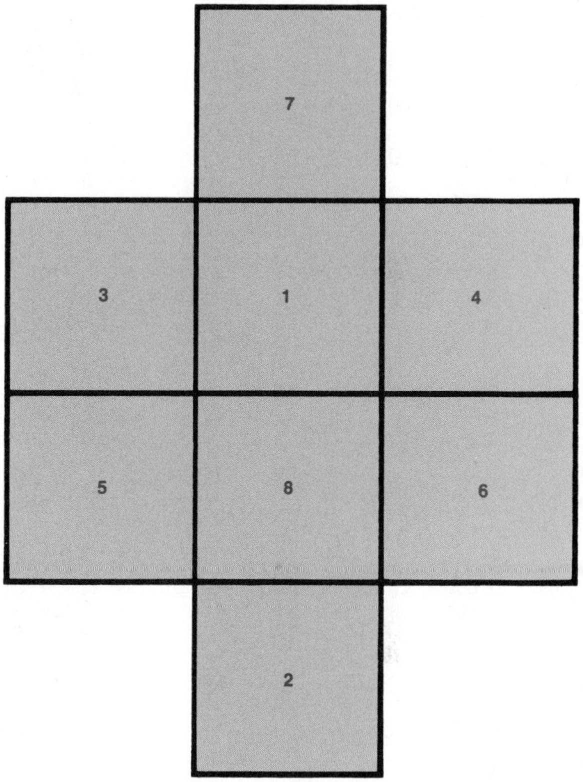

Skills Tune-Up

Multiplying decimals, pages 10-11

1. 0.6×0.5 0.3
2. 0.1×0.7 0.07
3. 0.03×0.3 0.009
4. 0.04×0.4 0.016
5. 0.07×0.05 0.0035
6. 0.06×0.07 0.0042
7. 0.004×0.01 0.00004
8. 0.09×0.011 0.00099
9. 300×0.4 120
10. 800×0.8 640
11. 900×0.02 18
12. 0.04×150 6
13. 0.004×300 1.2
14. 500×0.011 5.5
15. 0.005×0.008 0.00004
16. 0.007×0.004 0.000028
17. 6000×0.0011 6.6
18. 0.0013×8000 10.4
19. 4.3×9.7 41.71
20. 1.56×7.1 11.076
21. 6.7×3.02 20.234
22. 14.1×0.035 0.4935
23. 3.276×5.15 16.8714
24. 6.776×12.9 87.4104
25. 273.6×558 152,668.8
26. 0.55×0.0023 0.001265
27. 0.446×0.0068 0.0030328

Dividing fractions and mixed numbers, pages 16-17

1. $\frac{1}{2} \div \frac{5}{8}$ $\frac{4}{5}$
2. $\frac{2}{3} \div \frac{3}{4}$ $\frac{8}{9}$
3. $\frac{5}{8} \div \frac{15}{16}$ $\frac{2}{3}$
4. $\frac{2}{5} \div \frac{1}{10}$ 4
5. $\frac{5}{8} \div \frac{2}{7}$ $2\frac{3}{16}$
6. $\frac{2}{5} \div \frac{4}{7}$ $\frac{7}{10}$
7. $6 \div \frac{3}{4}$ 8
8. $\frac{1}{4} \div 4$ $\frac{1}{16}$
9. $\frac{4}{5} \div 3$ $\frac{4}{15}$
10. $6 \div \frac{3}{8}$ 16
11. $1\frac{3}{4} \div \frac{7}{10}$ $2\frac{1}{2}$
12. $\frac{2}{3} \div 1\frac{1}{5}$ $\frac{5}{9}$
13. $11\frac{3}{4} \div 4$ $2\frac{15}{16}$
14. $12 \div 2\frac{2}{7}$ $5\frac{1}{4}$
15. $9 \div 7\frac{1}{2}$ $1\frac{1}{5}$
16. $1\frac{4}{5} \div 2\frac{1}{10}$ $\frac{6}{7}$
17. $2\frac{4}{5} \div 1\frac{3}{4}$ $1\frac{3}{5}$
18. $1\frac{13}{14} \div 1\frac{1}{7}$ $1\frac{11}{16}$
19. $9\frac{2}{7} \div 1\frac{6}{7}$ 5
20. $4\frac{5}{6} \div 1\frac{2}{3}$ $2\frac{9}{10}$
21. $7\frac{7}{8} \div 8\frac{1}{6}$ $\frac{27}{28}$

Percent problems, pages 34-37

1. $12\frac{1}{2}$% of 10 is ____. 1.25
2. 30% of 20 is ____. 6
3. 5% of 300 is ____. 15
4. 5.5% of 85 is ____. 4.675
5. Find 12% of 5. 0.6
6. Find $2\frac{1}{2}$% of 700. 17.5
7. What number is 24% of 35? 8.4
8. What number is 6.6% of 50? 3.3
9. ____% of 32 is 24. 75%
10. ____% of 50 is 47.5. 95%
11. ____% of 70 is 17.5. 25%
12. ____% of 5.78 is 2.89. 50%
13. What percent of 64 is 48? 75%
14. What percent of 60 is 15? 25%
15. 81 is what percent of 120? 67.5%
16. 35% of ____ is 2.52. 7.2
17. 7.25% of ____ is 4.06. 56
18. 3% of ____ is 0.84. 28
19. $12\frac{1}{2}$% of ____ is 2.5. 200
20. 6% of what number is 2.22? 37
21. 60% of what number is 90? 150
22. 5.4 is $4\frac{1}{2}$% of what number? 120

Chapter 16 Review

Nutritionist, pages 322-323

1. Use the chart to find the number of calories in this meal.
490 calories
Lunch

55 g cottage cheese
2 slices whole-wheat bread
2 pats butter
1 apple
240 mL milk

CALORIE CHART	Portion	Calories
Meat		
Meat loaf	1 slice	200
Pot roast	1 slice	220
Dairy products		
Butter	1 pat	50
Cottage cheese	55 g	50
Milk	240 mL	160
Fruits and vegetables		
Apple	1	70
Cantaloupe	$\frac{1}{2}$	40
Cole slaw	1 serving	35
Green beans	1 serving	15
Breads		
Whole-wheat bread	1 slice	55
Roll	1	100

Calorie usage, pages 324-325

2. Angela weighs 60 kg. She went bicycling for $2\frac{1}{2}$ hours. Bicycling requires 3.9 calories per kilogram of body weight each hour. How many calories did she use? Round the answer to the nearest whole number.
585 calories

Grocery shopping, pages 326-328

3. Apples cost $1.39 per kilogram. Find the cost of 1.6 kg of apples.
$2.23
4. Find the cost of 2 cans of beans at 3 for $0.98.
$0.66
5. Find the unit price of a 520-gram box of macaroni for $0.69. Round the answer to the nearest hundredth of a cent.
0.13¢ per gram
6. Which is the better buy for onions?
3.5 kilograms for $2.19
3.5-kilogram bag for $2.19
5-kilogram bag for $3.65

Comparing meat prices, pages 330-331

7. Before butchering, a side of beef weighed 145 kg. After butchering, the usable meat weighed 107.3 kg. What was the percent of loss?
26%
8. The price of a 145-kilogram side of beef before butchering was $3.19 per kilogram. The usable meat weighed 107.3 kg. Find the cost per kilogram of usable meat. Round the answer to the nearest whole cent.
$4.31
9. The current price for sirloin steak in a grocery store is $5.39 per kilogram. Using this price, find the value of 11.9 kg of sirloin steak. Round the answer up to the next whole cent.
$64.15

Comparing meal costs, pages 332-333

10. Lana and Jay had fish dinners at a restaurant. The bill was $9.00 plus $0.45 tax. They left a 15% tip. Making the same meal at home costs $5.25. How much more does the restaurant meal cost?
$5.55

Chapter 16 Test

Number of test items - 10

Number missed	1	2	3	4	5
Percent correct	90	80	70	60	50

1. Use the chart to find the number of calories in this meal.
775 calories
Dinner

2 slices pot roast
1 serving cole slaw
$\frac{1}{2}$ cantaloupe
1 roll
240 mL milk

CALORIE CHART	Portion	Calories
Meat		
Meat loaf	1 slice	200
Pot roast	1 slice	220
Dairy products		
Butter	1 pat	50
Cottage cheese	55 g	50
Milk	240 mL	160
Fruits and vegetables		
Apple	1	70
Cantaloupe	$\frac{1}{2}$	40
Cole slaw	1 serving	35
Green beans	1 serving	15
Breads		
Whole-wheat bread	1 slice	55
Roll	1	100

2. Stu weighs 78 kg. He played table tennis for $1\frac{1}{2}$ hours. Playing table tennis requires 5.7 calories per kilogram of body weight each hour. How many calories did he use? Round the answer to the nearest whole number.
667 calories

3. Find the cost of 0.7 kg of pork chops at $3.99 per kilogram.
$2.80

4. Find the cost of 3 cans of tomatoes at 4 for $1.19.
$0.90

5. Find the unit price of a 350-milliliter can of soup for $0.33. Round the answer to the nearest hundredth of a cent.
0.09¢ per milliliter

6. Which is the better buy for fabric softener?
2 liters for $1.79
2-liter bottle for $1.79
3.5-liter bottle for $3.23

7. Before butchering, a side of beef weighed 140 kg. After butchering, the usable meat weighed 99.4 kg. What was the percent of loss?
29%

8. The price of a 140-kilogram side of beef before butchering was $3.29 per kilogram. The usable meat weighed 99.4 kg. Find the cost per kilogram of usable meat. Round the answer to the nearest whole cent.
$4.63

9. The current price for rump roast in a grocery store is $4.59 per kilogram. Using this price, find the value of 4.9 kg of rump roast. Round the answer up to the next whole cent.
$22.50

10. Michelle and Doug had spaghetti dinners at a restaurant. The bill was $11.00 plus $0.44 tax. They left a 15% tip. Making the same meal at home costs $5.80. How much more does the restaurant meal cost?
$7.29

 See pages 41–42 of the *Test Masters* for an alternate form of the Chapter 16 Test.

Chapter 17 Buying, Making, and Renting Goods

Objective: Compute the total cost of a catalog order by finding the cost of the merchandise, the amount of sales tax, and the charges for shipping and handling as given in a table.

Catalog Buying

Warm-up:
4% of 15.25 [0.61]
5% of 24.80 [1.24]
20 oz. = ■ lb. ■ oz. [1 lb. 4 oz.]
1 lb. 22 oz. = ■ lb. ■ oz. [2 lb. 6 oz.]

See page T42 for additional notes and activities for Chapter 17.

Dave and Diane Tomlinson order many items from catalogs. Together they can look through the catalogs at home and choose the items they want to buy.

When people buy merchandise shown in a catalog, they usually pay shipping and handling charges. These charges are shown in the table.

Shipping and Handling Charges				
Shipping weight	Local zone	Zones 1 & 2	Zone 3	Zone 4
1 oz. to 8 oz.	$1.27	$1.34	$1.36	$1.40
9 oz. to 15 oz.	$1.49	$1.60	$1.64	$1.68
1 lb. to 2 lb.	$1.97	$2.11	$2.14	$2.26
2 lb. 1 oz. to 3 lb.	$2.07	$2.39	$2.43	$2.53
3 lb. 1 oz. to 5 lb.	$2.20	$2.57	$2.63	$2.68
5 lb. 1 oz. to 10 lb.	$2.43	$2.84	$2.91	$3.04
10 lb. 1 oz. to 15 lb.	$2.73	$2.99	$3.21	$3.60
15 lb. 1 oz. to 25 lb.	$3.89	$4.14	$4.48	$5.02
25 lb. 1 oz. to 45 lb.	$4.77	$5.03	$5.59	$6.56

Point out that in many catalogs the cost of shipping and handling is determined by the total cost of the merchandise.

Problem

Diane wants to buy the woman's warm-up suit shown on page 339. She wants the jacket and pants in tan, both in size 10. The sales tax rate in her state is 4%. She lives in zone 3. Fill in the order form for Diane's warm-up suit. What is the total amount she must enclose with the order?

Solution

Strategy

- Fill in the merchandise information in the order form below.
- Add to find the total cost of the items.
- Multiply to find the tax. Round to the nearest cent.
- Add to find the total weight of the items. Remember, 1 pound = 16 ounces.
- Read the table for shipping and handling charges.
- Add to find the total cost of the order.

Conclusion

Diane must enclose $30.69 with the order.

Item	Catalog number	How many	Size	Color	Price for one	Total price	Shipping weight lb.	Shipping weight oz.
Jacket	G 38-0672	1	10	tan	$14.99	$14.99	1	8
Pants	G 38-0677	1	10	tan	11.99	11.99	1	10

	Merchandise total	26.98	Total weight	
4% of $26.98 →	Tax	1.08	lb.	oz.
Charges for 3 lb. 2 oz. in zone 3 →	Shipping and handling	2.63	3	2
Total cost →	AMOUNT ENCLOSED	$30.69		

A WARM-UP JACKET—Acrylic knit with fleece lining. Full zip front. Colors: Blue, red, tan. Sizes: Misses 6, 8, 10, 12, 14, 16. Wt. 1 lb. 8 oz. $14.99
G38-0672

B WARM-UP PANTS—Acrylic knit with fleece lining. Elasticized waist. Colors: Blue, red, tan. Sizes: Misses 6, 8, 10, 12, 14, 16. Wt. 1 lb. 10 oz. $11.99
G38-0677

C RUNNING SHOES—Nylon and leather uppers. Colors: Tan, blue, brown. D-width sizes: $7\frac{1}{2}$, 8, $8\frac{1}{2}$, 9, $9\frac{1}{2}$, 10, $10\frac{1}{2}$, 11, $11\frac{1}{2}$, 12. Wt. 1 lb. 14 oz. $26.50
W33-7881

D RUNNING SOCKS—65% cotton, 35% nylon. White with striped trim. Colors: Gold, brown, blue, burgundy. Sizes: M, L. Wt. 4 oz. $1.79
T59-5218

E RUNNING SUIT—100% polyester tricot. Elasticized waist. Colors: Green, blue, brown, gray. Sizes: S, M, L, XL. Wt. 1 lb. 10 oz. $17.99
N45-8603

11

Related Problems

Dave wants to buy the running suit, running shoes, and socks shown here. He wants all of them in blue. His suit size is Large. He wears a $10\frac{1}{2}$D shoe. And his sock size is Large.

1. What is the total cost of the items?
   $46.28
2. What is the amount of tax if the sales tax rate is 4%? Round to the nearest cent.
   $1.85
3. What is the total weight of the items?
   3 lb. 12 oz.
4. What are the shipping and handling costs for zone 3?
   $2.63
5. What is the total amount Dave must enclose with his order?
   $50.76

A SHOULDER PADS—Durable construction. 100% nylon covering. Sizes: S(26-28), M(28-30), L(30-32)
Wt. 2 lb. 2 oz.
P 232-9851 .... $15.99

B FOOTBALL—Genuine cowhide-leather football. Official size. Tee included. Wt. 1 lb. 7 oz.
M 430-4562 .... $12.99

C FIELDER'S GLOVE—Large pocket with tough lacing across the top. For right-handed throwers.
Wt. 13 oz.
V 516-4392 .... $17.99

D BASEBALL—Little League approved. Wt. 7 oz.
W 916-7342 .... $4.99

E BASEBALL CAP—Colors: navy, red, gold, green. Sizes: S, M, L. Wt. 5 oz.
Y 327-8420 .... $5.69

F SPORT SHOES—Black leather uppers, white stripes, padded ankle collar. 13 molded cleats. Medium width. Sizes: 4-10.
Wt. 1 lb. 15 oz.
T 829-3901 .... $18.79

G HELMET—Fully padded for maximum protection, white only. Sizes: S($6\frac{1}{4}$-$6\frac{1}{2}$), M($6\frac{5}{8}$-7), L($7\frac{1}{8}$-$7\frac{3}{8}$).
Wt. 2 lb. 1 oz.
R 342-6917 .... $19.99

34

Clarence wants to buy a football, a helmet (size M), and shoulder pads (size M).

6. What is the total cost of these items?
$48.97
7. Find the amount of tax if the sales tax rate is 5%. Round to the nearest cent.
$2.45
8. Find the total weight of the merchandise.
5 lb. 10 oz.
9. Use the table on page 338 to find the shipping and handling charges. Clarence lives in the local zone.
$2.43
10. What is the total amount Clarence must enclose with his order?
$53.85

Nancy wants to buy a baseball, a fielder's glove, a cap (red, size M), and a pair of sport shoes (size 8).

11. What is the total cost of these items?
$47.46
12. Find the amount of tax if the sales tax rate is 6%. Round to the nearest cent.
$2.85
13. Find the total weight of the merchandise.
3 lb. 8 oz.
14. Use the table on page 338 to find the shipping and handling charges. Nancy lives in zone 4.
$2.68
15. What is the total amount Nancy must enclose with her order?
$52.99

CALCULATOR APPLICATIONS

Completing Order Forms

Sally D'Avito is ordering office supplies for her stationery store. She needs 200 portfolios at \$0.96 each. The cost of the portfolios is 200 × \$0.96, or \$192.00.

The portfolios are packed 10 to a box. The number of boxes needed is 200 ÷ 10, or 20, boxes.

Each box weighs 1 lb. 6 oz. The total weight of the 20 boxes is 20 × 1 lb. 6 oz., or 20 lb. 120 oz. Since 1 pound = 16 ounces, the total weight is 27 lb. 8 oz.

Complete this order form.

For problems 7 and 8, remind students that a dozen is a group of 12.

	Name of item	Quantity	Catalog number	Unit price	Total price	Number per box	Number of boxes	Weight each box LB.	Weight each box OZ.	Total weight LB.	Total weight OZ.
	Portfolios	200	3-47A	\$0.96	\$192.00	10	20	1	6	27	8
1.	Legal ruled pads	180	5-62X	\$0.35	\$63.00	12	15	1	4	18	12
2.	Payroll record pads	50	9-51C	\$0.45	\$22.50	10	5	2	7	12	3
3.	Requisition pads	72	7-13R	\$0.40	\$28.80	12	6	1	12	10	8
4.	Letter openers	24	1-34T	\$1.59	\$38.16	12	2	2	12	5	8
5.	Legal-size envelopes	7 boxes	8-21B	\$9.32	\$65.24	——	7	3	13	26	11
6.	Staplers	25	2-63F	\$5.65	\$141.25	5	5	4	6	21	14
7.	Pencils	288	6-40D	\$1.35/doz.	\$32.40	12	24		7	10	8
8.	Pens	96	6-37Y	\$3.17/doz.	\$25.36	12	8		15	7	8
9.	Total for goods				\$608.71			Total		141	0
10.	Tax (5%)				\$30.44						
11.	Shipping charges (\$0.11/lb.)				\$15.51						
12.	TOTAL				\$654.66						

The tax is rounded to the nearest cent.

Objective: Compute the amount and cost of materials needed for a sewing project.

Sewing Costs

The cast of the Aberdeen High School Variety Show need costumes for some of the dance numbers. They want skirts for the girls and matching vests for the boys. The school is willing to pay for the material if some of the cast members will make the skirts and the vests.

There are 32 girls and 21 boys in the cast. Seven of the girls wear size 8. Ten wear size 10. Eleven wear size 12. And four wear size 14. Six of the boys need a small (S) vest. Ten need a medium (M). And five need a large (L).

Skirt

Size	8	10	12	14
Fabric width	Yards required			
35/36 in.	3¼	3¼	3⅜	3½
44/45 in.	1⅞	2	2	2⅛
54 in.	1⅞	1⅞	1⅞	1⅞

Vest (to be lined)

Size	S	M	L
Fabric width	Yards required		
35/36 in.	1⅜	1⅜	1½
44/45 in.	1⅛	1⅛	1¼
54 in.	¾	¾	¾

Vest lining - Purchase same amount of fabric as shown for vest.

Warm-up: $5 \times 1\frac{1}{4}$ $[6\frac{1}{4}]$

$32\frac{1}{2} + 12\frac{1}{4} + 9\frac{5}{8}$ $[54\frac{3}{8}]$

4.25×2.79 [11.8575]

15% of 18.30 [2.745]

See page 60 of *Consumer Forms and Problems.*

Problem

The fabric selected for the skirts is 45 inches wide. How many yards are needed for the seven skirts in size 8?

Solution

Strategy

- Read the chart. Find the row for 45-inch fabric and the column for size 8.

$1\frac{7}{8}$

- Multiply by 7 to find the amount needed for 7 skirts.

$7 \times 1\frac{7}{8} = 7 \times \frac{15}{8} = \frac{105}{8} = 13\frac{1}{8}$

Conclusion

The amount of fabric needed for the 7 skirts is $13\frac{1}{8}$ yards.

Related Problems

Discuss why the answers for problems 13 and 16 are rounded up.

1. How many yards of 45-inch fabric are needed for 10 skirts, size 10?
20 yards
2. How many yards of 45-inch fabric are needed for 11 skirts, size 12?
22 yards
3. How many yards of 45-inch fabric are needed for 4 skirts, size 14? $8\frac{1}{2}$ yards
4. How many yards of 45-inch fabric are needed for 6 vests, size S? $6\frac{3}{4}$ yards
5. How many yards of 45-inch fabric are needed for 10 vests, size M? $11\frac{1}{4}$ yards
6. How many yards of 45-inch fabric are needed for 5 vests, size L? $6\frac{1}{4}$ yards
7. What is the total number of yards needed for the 32 skirts and 21 vests? Include the fabric for the size 8 skirts. $87\frac{7}{8}$ yards
8. At $4.80 per yard, what is the cost of fabric for the skirts and vests?
$421.80

Suggest to the students that they change the yardage to a decimal before multiplying by the price in problems 8 and 9.

The answer for problem 9 is based on $24\frac{1}{4}$ yards of lining.

9. The 45-inch lining is $1.60 per yard. What is the cost of the lining for the vests?
$38.80
10. Each skirt pattern costs $1.75. The cast decides to buy two patterns for each size. Find the cost of the skirt patterns.
$14
11. Each vest pattern costs $1.50. The cast decides to buy one pattern for each size. Find the cost of the vest patterns.
$4.50
12. Each skirt has a zipper and a fastener. At $0.55 each, what is the total cost of the zippers?
$17.60
13. There are 3 fasteners in a package. How many packages of fasteners are needed?
11 packages
14. At $0.79 per package, what is the total cost of the fasteners?
$8.69
15. Five buttons are required for each vest. How many buttons are needed for all the vests?
105 buttons
16. There are 6 buttons in a package. How many packages of buttons are needed?
18 packages
17. At $1.35 per package, what is the total cost of the buttons?
$24.30
18. Thread costs $0.60 per spool. The cast estimates that they will need 12 spools. What is the cost of the thread?
$7.20
19. What is the total cost of all the materials (fabric, lining, patterns, zippers, fasteners, buttons, and thread)?
$536.89
20. If the fabric store gives a 15% discount to the school, what is the cost of the materials? (Round the discount to the nearest cent.)
$456.36

The discounted cost could also be found by multiplying the total cost by 85%.

Objectives: Determine the best month for buying certain items, using a chart; compute the amount of discount and the sale price of an item.

Seasonal Sales

When Barbara and Jim King plan some of their purchases, they use a chart like the one shown here. It gives the best times of the year for buying certain items.

Problem

Jim needs a new coat. The regular price of the coat that Jim wants is \$75.99. He expects to save at least 15% by shopping during the best months. What are the best months for buying men's coats? What can Jim expect to pay for the coat?

Solution

The sale price can also be found by subtracting the discount from 100% and then multiplying by the regular price.

Strategy

- Read the chart to find the best months for buying men's coats. — January and August
- Multiply the cost of the coat by 15% to find the discount. Round to the nearest cent. — $0.15 \times \$75.99 \approx \$11.40$
- Subtract to find the sale price. — $\$75.99 - \$11.40 = \$64.59$

Conclusion

The best months for buying men's coats are January and August. Jim can expect to pay about \$64.59 for the coat.

January	February	March	April
Men's coats Dresses Shoes Books Linens Toys	Men's shirts Furniture Curtains Rugs Small appliances	Winter clothes Ski equipment Hosiery Housewares Gardening supplies	Dresses Infants' wear Men's suits Shoes Paint
May	**June**	**July**	**August**
Handbags Linens Wallpaper Jewelry Luggage	Sleepwear Dresses Building materials TV sets	Fabric Bathing suits Men's shirts Shoes	Women's coats Men's coats School clothes School supplies New cars Linens
September	**October**	**November**	**December**
Dishes Bicycles Carpeting	Hosiery School clothes Women's coats Lamps	Blankets Used cars Major appliances Water heaters	Women's coats Shoes Party goods Men's and children's wear

Warm-up: Round to the nearest hundredth.

16.312	[16.31]
18.295	[18.30]
76.057	[76.06]
25% of 43.25	[10.81]

Related Problems

For each problem, list the best month or months to buy each item. Then find the amount of the expected discount, rounded to the nearest cent, and the expected sale price of the item.

	Item	Best months to buy	Regular price	Expected discount	Amount of discount	Sale price
	Man's coat	January, August	$75.99	15%	$11.40	$64.59
1.	Shoes	Jan., April, July, Dec.	$37.00	15%	$5.55	$31.45
2.	Paint	April	$13.69	20%	$2.74	$10.95
3.	Clothes dryer	November	$359.95	25%	$89.99	$269.96
4.	TV set	June	$689.95	15%	$103.49	$586.46
5.	Bedroom set	February	$895.99	20%	$179.20	$716.79
6.	Sheets	Jan., May, Aug.	$9.99	30%	$3.00	$6.99
7.	Handbag	May	$17.50	15%	$2.63	$14.87
8.	Curtains	February	$37.47	25%	$9.37	$28.10
9.	Bathing suit	July	$26.30	35%	$9.21	$17.09
10.	Dress	Jan., April, June	$48.00	40%	$19.20	$28.80

Break Time

There are 16 small squares in this large square. ABEF forms a square. ABCEFGIJK forms another square. How many new squares can you form?

14 new squares
(A total of 30 squares)

A	B	C	D
E	F	G	H
I	J	K	L
M	N	O	P

The small squares can also form rectangles. AB forms a rectangle. ABCEFG and BCDFGH form two more rectangles. How many new rectangles can you form?

67 new rectangles
(A total of 70 rectangles)

The order in which the letters are listed is irrelevant. For example, ABEF is the same square as AEFB.

Objective: Compute the total cost of materials for a craft project.

Buying Craft Supplies

Many people enjoy making items for their homes or themselves, or as gifts. This stained-glass window was made from various colors of glass, solder, copper foil, and edging. The solder is sold in 1-pound reels for $7.75 a pound. The foil comes in rolls for $3.00 a roll. The edging is sold in 8-foot strips for $3.75 each. Glass is sold only in 1- or $\frac{1}{2}$ - square foot sections. The prices are listed below.

Color	Price (sq. ft.)	Color	Price (sq. ft.)
Black	$5.00	Orange	$7.00
Blue	$3.00	Red	$9.00
Brown	$4.00	Salmon	$4.00
Camel	$4.00	White	$4.00
Gray	$4.50	Yellow	$5.00
Green	$5.00		

Problem

Find the total cost of materials for the scuba-diver window. The amounts of glass needed are listed below. The window takes 2 pounds of solder, 1 roll of foil, $7\frac{1}{2}$ feet of edging, and 17 glass bubbles at $0.15 each.

Black—1 square foot
Blue—$1\frac{1}{2}$ square feet
Brown—$1\frac{1}{3}$ square feet
Camel—$\frac{1}{3}$ square foot
Gray—3 square feet
Green—$3\frac{1}{2}$ square feet
White—$\frac{1}{3}$ square foot
Yellow—2 square feet

Solution

Be sure students understand that for $\frac{1}{4}$ or $\frac{1}{3}$ square foot of glass they must figure the cost for $\frac{1}{2}$ square foot.

Strategy

- Multiply to find the cost for each color of glass. Remember, glass is sold only in 1- or $\frac{1}{2}$ - square foot sections. Add to find the total cost for the glass.

1 × $5.00 =	$5.00	Black
$1\frac{1}{2}$ × $3.00 =	$4.50	Blue
$1\frac{1}{2}$ × $4.00 =	$6.00	Brown
$\frac{1}{2}$ × $4.00 =	$2.00	Camel
3 × $4.50 =	$13.50	Gray
$3\frac{1}{2}$ × $5.00 =	$17.50	Green
$\frac{1}{2}$ × $4.00 =	$2.00	White
2 × $5.00 =	$10.00	Yellow
	$60.50	Total

- Multiply to find the costs for the solder and bubbles.
  2 × $7.75 = $15.50 Solder
  17 × $0.15 = $2.55 Bubbles
- Add to find the total cost including foil and edging.
  $60.50 + $15.50 + $2.55 + $3.00 + $3.75 = $85.30

Conclusion

The total cost of materials for the window is $85.30.

Warm-up: $3\frac{1}{2} \times 6.00$ [21.00]

$2\frac{1}{2} \times 5.00$ [12.50]

3×2.79 [8.37]

12×0.18 [2.16]

See page 61 of *Consumer Forms and Problems.*

Point out that the solder, foil, and edging can be purchased only in the units mentioned in the example. The ribbon in problem 4, however, may be purchased by the $\frac{1}{4}$ yard. For problems 3 and 4, students may add the strands of yarn needed *before* multiplying by the price per strand.

Related Problems

Find the total cost for each stained-glass project. Use the prices on page 346.

1. **Glass** (sq. ft.)
   Brown—$\frac{1}{4}$
   Green—$1\frac{1}{2}$
   Orange—$\frac{1}{4}$
   Salmon—$1\frac{1}{2}$
   White—$\frac{2}{3}$
   Solder—1 pound
   Foil—$\frac{1}{2}$ roll
   Edging—4 feet
   $37.50

2. **Glass** (sq. ft.)
   Blue—$\frac{1}{2}$
   Brown—1
   Gray—4
   Red—2
   Orange—$\frac{1}{2}$
   White—$\frac{1}{4}$
   Solder $1\frac{1}{2}$ pounds
   Foil—$\frac{2}{3}$ roll
   Edging—7 feet
   $69.25

Find the cost for each needlepoint project. Yarn is $0.04 per strand.

3. **Yarn** (strands)
   Blue—38
   Gold—2
   Green—10
   Red—1
   Yellow—2
   Painted canvas mesh—$17.50
   $19.62

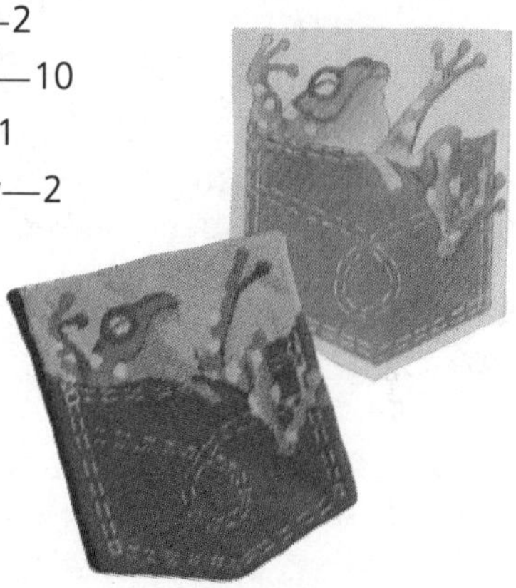

4. **Yarn** (strands)
   Black—8
   Blue—2
   Gold—5
   Gray—36
   Red—48
   White—1

   Stuffing—2 pounds at $1.59 a pound

   Buttons—4 at $0.10 each

   Felt—1 square at $0.29

   Ribbon—$\frac{1}{4}$ yard at $0.60 a yard

   Painted canvas mesh—$12.50

   $20.52

See pages 376–377 for a computer application related to this lesson.

Objective: Compute the cost of lumber and other materials for a building project.

Buying Building Materials

Virginia and Walter Harbold are buying various materials to build this frame storage shed.

Nails are referred to by their size. A 2-penny nail (2d), for example, is 1 in. long. A 20d nail is 4 in. long. Nails are often sold by the pound.

Lumber is also specified by size. The actual thickness and width of a board are smaller than the given measurements because the wood has been sawed and smoothed. The length, however, is about the same as given. For example, a 2 in. by 4 in. by 10 ft. board actually measures about $1\frac{1}{2}$ in. by $3\frac{1}{2}$ in. by 10 ft.

Lumber can be purchased in several ways. One way is by the linear foot. The cost of the lumber depends on just the length of the board. Another way is by the board foot. A board foot is the amount of lumber in a board 1 in. thick, 1 ft. wide, and 1 ft. long.

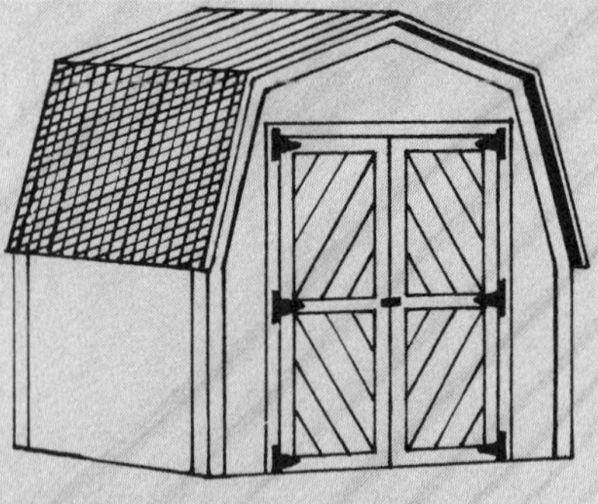

Problem

Two boards, each 2 in. by 6 in. by 14 ft., are needed for the ridge beam of the shed. At $0.33 per board foot, find the cost of the two boards.

Solution

Strategy

- Multiply the measurements to find the number of board feet in one board. Remember, 6 inches = $\frac{1}{2}$ foot.

Thickness in inches		Width in feet		Length in feet		Board feet
2	×	$\frac{1}{2}$	×	14	=	14

- Multiply to find the total cost.

Number of boards		Board feet per board		Cost per board foot		Total cost
2	×	14	×	$0.33	=	$9.24

Conclusion

The cost of the two boards is $9.24.

Problem

Battens are strips of wood that fasten the main structure. The shed requires 40 battens, each 1 in. by 3 in. by 8 ft. At $0.09 per linear foot, what is the cost of the 40 battens?

Solution

Strategy

- Multiply to find the total cost.

Number of battens		Length in feet		Cost per linear foot		Total cost
40	×	8	×	$0.09	=	$28.80

Conclusion

The cost of the 40 battens is $28.80.

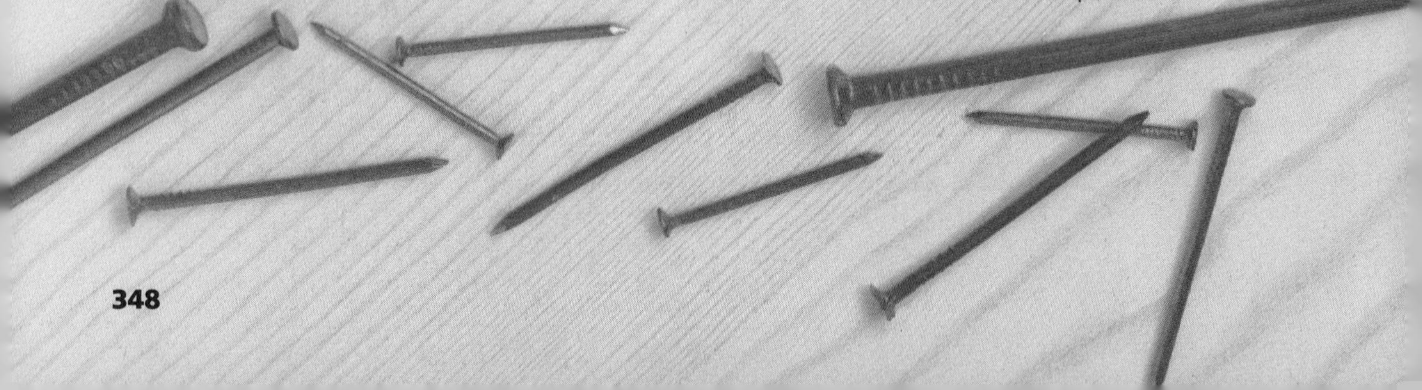

Warm-up: $2 \times \frac{1}{2} \times 16$ [16] $2 \times \frac{1}{3} \times 8$ [$5\frac{1}{3}$]

$2 \times \frac{2}{3} \times 18$ [24] $2\frac{1}{3} \times 0.33$ [0.77]

See page 62 of *Consumer Forms and Problems.*

Related Problems

Point out that problems 9 and 10 could be solved by using a proportion. Remind students that 1 ton = 2000 pounds.

Find the cost of each item for the storage shed. Round costs up to the next cent.

	Description	Size	Amount	Unit price	Cost
	Ridge beam	2 in. by 6 in. by 14 ft.	2	\$0.33/board foot	\$9.24
1.	Battens	1 in. by 3 in. by 8 ft.	40	\$0.09/ linear foot	\$28.80
		1 in. by 3 in. by 10 ft.	2	\$0.09/linear foot	\$1.80
2.	Framing and forms for concrete	2 in. by 2 in. by 6 ft.	6	\$0.33/board foot	\$3.96
		2 in. by 8 in. by 12 ft.	4	\$0.33/board foot	\$21.12
		2 in. by 4 in. by 4 ft.	1	\$0.33/board foot	\$0.88
		2 in. by 4 in. by 8 ft.	8	\$0.33/board foot	\$14.08
		2 in. by 4 in. by 10 ft.	11	\$0.33/board foot	\$24.20
		2 in. by 4 in. by 12 ft.	5	\$0.33/board foot	\$13.20
		2 in. by 4 in. by 14 ft.	24	\$0.33/board foot	\$73.92
3.	Galvanized nails	3d	$\frac{1}{2}$ lb.	\$1.09/lb.	\$0.55
		6d	5 lb.	\$1.09/lb.	\$5.45
4.	Common nails	10d	$3\frac{1}{2}$ lb.	\$0.89/lb.	\$3.12
		16d	7 lb.	\$0.89/lb.	\$6.23
		20d	3 lb.	\$0.89/lb.	\$2.67
5.	T-hinges	Heavy steel	2 pairs	\$3.95/pair	\$7.90
6.	Anchor bolts	$\frac{1}{2}$ in. by $5\frac{1}{2}$ in.	8	\$0.65 each	\$5.20
7.	Plywood	$\frac{1}{2}$ in. by 4 ft. by 8 ft.	28 sheets	\$16.95/sheet	\$474.60
8.	Concrete for pad		1.6 cu. yd.	\$50/cu. yd.	\$80.00
9.	Gravel for pad		3100 lb.	\$8/ton	\$12.40
10.	Roofing shingles	240 lb./100 sq. ft.	180 sq. ft.	\$27.95/100 sq. ft.	\$50.31
11.	Door trim and doorway	1 in. by 4 in. by 10 ft.	2	\$0.17/linear foot	\$3.40
		1 in. by 4 in. by 8 ft.	4	\$0.17/linear foot	\$5.44
		1 in. by 4 in. by 7 ft.	7	\$0.17/linear foot	\$8.33
12.	Door stop	1 in. by 2 in. by 4 ft.	1	\$0.07/linear foot	\$0.28
		1 in. by 2 in. by 7 ft.	2	\$0.07/linear foot	\$0.98

13. Find the total cost of all the materials for the storage shed.
\$858.06

Objective: Compute the cost of renting an item.

Rental Clerk

Career Cluster: Business Contact Leslie Deutsch works at Park Rental. This company rents various types of equipment to its customers. Leslie's job is to explain to the customers how to use the items they rent.

Leslie also fills out rental receipts. Customers pay a deposit when they pick up the equipment. If the rental charge is different when the equipment is returned, they either get a refund or pay the extra amount.

When Leslie computes the rental charge, she refers to the schedule of charges given in the table. First, she uses the hourly rate. Then she compares this charge to the minimum charge and the daily rate. The customer must pay at least the minimum charge. The daily rate is the maximum charge the customer will have to pay for each 24-hour period.

Item	Minimum charge	Hourly rate	Daily rate
Circular saw	$4.50	$1.50	$9.00
Drill	$3.00	$1.00	$6.00
Disc sander	$4.50	$1.50	$8.50
Hand-belt sander	$6.00	$2.00	$12.00
Metal detector	$10.50	$3.50	$15.00
Car polisher	$5.25	$1.75	$10.50
Chain saw	$20.00	$5.00	$28.00
Rug shampooer	$6.00	$2.00	$12.00
Rug steamer	$9.00	$3.00	$17.00
Wet vacuum	$9.00	$3.00	$13.00
Floor sander	$12.00	$4.00	$20.00
Extension ladder	$4.50	$1.50	$9.00
Tiller	$12.00	$6.00	$32.00
Lawn aerator	$8.00	$2.50	$12.00

Warm-up: 2.25×5 [11.25]
3.50×4 [14]
$58 \div 14.50$ [4]
$105 \div 2.50$ [42]

Problem

Elliott Dakota rented a disc sander one day. He used it for $6\frac{1}{4}$ hours. What did Leslie charge Elliott for the rental?

Solution

Strategy

- Round the number of hours up to the next full hour.

  $6\frac{1}{4} \rightarrow 7$

- Multiply the hourly rate by 7 to find the rental cost for 7 hours.

  $7 \times \$1.50 = \$10.50$

- Compare the rental cost for 7 hours to the minimum charge.

  $\$10.50 > \$4.50$

- Compare the rental cost for 7 hours to the daily rate.

  $\$10.50 > \$8.50$

Conclusion

Leslie charged Elliott $8.50.

Related Problems

Find the cost of renting each item for the number of hours given. Remember, the cost must be at least as much as the minimum charge, but not more than the daily rate.

	Item	Time	
1.	Chain saw	4 hours	$20
2.	Wet vacuum	$5\frac{1}{2}$ hours	$13
3.	Extension ladder	$3\frac{1}{2}$ hours	$6
4.	Drill	2 hours	$3
5.	Rug steamer	9 hours	$17
6.	Lawn aerator	$8\frac{1}{4}$ hours	$12
7.	Floor sander	$7\frac{1}{4}$ hours	$20
8.	Metal detector	1 hour	$10.50
9.	Circular saw	4 hours	$6
10.	Hand-belt sander	3 hours	$6

11. Fred uses a tiller for 2 full days a year. A tiller costs about $525. After how many years will the total rental costs exceed the price of the tiller?
9 years

12. The price of a rug shampooer is $75. Kazuko shampoos her rugs twice a year. It takes a full day each time. After how many years will the total rental costs exceed the price of a rug shampooer?
4 years

13. The owner of Park Rental bought a new car polisher for $45 and a new wet vacuum for $85. Based on the hourly rate, which one "pays for itself" sooner?
Car polisher

14. One of the circular saws at Park Rental needs replacement after about 330 hours of rental. The owner had paid $55 for it. Based on the hourly rate, find the number of times the saw had "paid for itself."
9 times

Skills Tune-Up

Dividing whole numbers, pages 12-13

1. 6564 ÷ 3
2188
2. 2846 ÷ 8
355 R6
3. 7993 ÷ 9
888 R1
4. 8214 ÷ 3
2738
5. 1358 ÷ 7
194
6. 8108 ÷ 7
1158 R2
7. 2203 ÷ 52
42 R19
8. 4295 ÷ 89
48 R23
9. 9786 ÷ 14
699
10. 4803 ÷ 83
57 R72
11. 5373 ÷ 47
114 R15
12. 9180 ÷ 64
143 R28
13. 5333 ÷ 77
69 R20
14. 7938 ÷ 27
294
15. 2770 ÷ 97
28 R54
16. 5840 ÷ 73
80
17. 3047 ÷ 41
74 R13
18. 23,397 ÷ 43
544 R5
19. 86,210 ÷ 27
3192 R26
20. 93,016 ÷ 44
2114
21. 285,797 ÷ 24
11,908 R5
22. 484,569 ÷ 88
5506 R41
23. 957,671 ÷ 78
12,277 R65
24. 828,129 ÷ 206
4020 R9
25. 156,648 ÷ 696
225 R48
26. 638,668 ÷ 530
1205 R18
27. 880,528 ÷ 964
913 R396

Adding fractions and mixed numbers, pages 18-19

1. $\frac{8}{15} + \frac{2}{5}$ $\frac{14}{15}$
2. $\frac{4}{5} + \frac{7}{10}$ $1\frac{1}{2}$
3. $\frac{5}{8} + \frac{1}{12}$ $\frac{17}{24}$
4. $\frac{3}{14} + \frac{5}{7}$ $\frac{13}{14}$
5. $\frac{1}{2} + \frac{1}{3}$ $\frac{5}{6}$
6. $\frac{1}{3} + \frac{5}{8}$ $\frac{23}{24}$
7. $\frac{7}{20} + \frac{9}{10}$ $1\frac{1}{4}$
8. $\frac{1}{9} + \frac{7}{45}$ $\frac{4}{15}$
9. $\frac{5}{6} + \frac{2}{9}$ $1\frac{1}{18}$
10. $\frac{1}{3} + 5\frac{1}{12}$ $5\frac{5}{12}$
11. $7\frac{3}{10} + \frac{1}{2}$ $7\frac{4}{5}$
12. $2\frac{7}{10} + 2\frac{13}{30}$ $5\frac{2}{15}$
13. $5\frac{5}{6} + 2\frac{1}{3}$ $8\frac{1}{6}$
14. $5\frac{2}{7} + 12\frac{5}{7}$ 18
15. $15\frac{5}{9} + 5\frac{5}{18}$ $20\frac{5}{6}$
16. $10\frac{2}{5} + 6\frac{1}{3}$ $16\frac{11}{15}$
17. $4\frac{11}{24} + 2\frac{1}{4}$ $6\frac{17}{24}$
18. $3\frac{1}{15} + 7\frac{4}{5}$ $10\frac{13}{15}$
19. $9\frac{11}{20} + \frac{1}{5} + 8\frac{3}{5}$ $18\frac{7}{20}$
20. $5\frac{1}{2} + 4\frac{4}{9} + 8\frac{1}{18}$ 18

Subtracting fractions and mixed numbers, pages 18-19

1. $\frac{5}{6} - \frac{1}{2}$ $\frac{1}{3}$
2. $\frac{3}{5} - \frac{7}{15}$ $\frac{2}{15}$
3. $\frac{5}{6} - \frac{1}{8}$ $\frac{17}{24}$
4. $\frac{25}{36} - \frac{2}{9}$ $\frac{17}{36}$
5. $\frac{1}{6} - \frac{1}{8}$ $\frac{1}{24}$
6. $\frac{3}{5} - \frac{8}{15}$ $\frac{1}{15}$
7. $\frac{5}{7} - \frac{13}{21}$ $\frac{2}{21}$
8. $\frac{11}{24} - \frac{1}{8}$ $\frac{1}{3}$
9. $18 - 3\frac{6}{7}$ $14\frac{1}{7}$
10. $8 - 2\frac{1}{4}$ $5\frac{3}{4}$
11. $4 - \frac{1}{2}$ $3\frac{1}{2}$
12. $12\frac{49}{64} - 8\frac{57}{64}$ $3\frac{7}{8}$
13. $10 - \frac{3}{5}$ $9\frac{2}{5}$
14. $4 - \frac{2}{3}$ $3\frac{1}{3}$
15. $7\frac{1}{3} - 7\frac{1}{8}$ $\frac{5}{24}$
16. $17\frac{1}{2} - 9\frac{3}{10}$ $8\frac{1}{5}$
17. $37\frac{3}{8} - 29\frac{23}{24}$ $7\frac{5}{12}$
18. $22\frac{23}{30} - 18\frac{5}{6}$ $3\frac{14}{15}$
19. $26\frac{5}{8} - 9\frac{19}{24}$ $16\frac{5}{6}$
20. $11\frac{2}{15} - 9\frac{5}{6}$ $1\frac{3}{10}$

Chapter 17 Review

Catalog buying, pages 338-340

Kaye Kwail wants to buy 2 AM-FM radios from the catalog.

AM-FM RADIO—100% solid state chassis with 3-inch speaker. Built-in AM, telescoping FM antennas. Operates on AC cord or 4 optional "C" batteries. Black plastic case with handle. Wt. 2 lb. 10 oz.
S 5-398 ....$38.95

1. What is the total cost of the merchandise?
$77.90

2. What is the amount of sales tax if the tax rate is 5%? Round to the nearest cent.
$3.90

3. Kaye lives in zone 2. Use this table to find the shipping and handling charges.
$2.84

Shipping and Handling Charges			
Shipping weight	Local zone	Zones 1 & 2	Zone 3
1 oz. to 8 oz.	$1.27	$1.34	$1.36
9 oz. to 15 oz.	$1.49	$1.60	$1.64
1 lb. to 2 lb.	$1.97	$2.11	$2.14
2 lb. 1 oz. to 3 lb.	$2.07	$2.39	$2.43
3 lb. 1 oz. to 5 lb.	$2.20	$2.57	$2.63
5 lb. 1 oz. to 10 lb.	$2.43	$2.84	$2.91

4. What is the total amount Kaye must enclose with her order?
$84.64

Sewing costs, pages 342-343

5. If $1\frac{1}{4}$ yd. of fabric is needed to make one vest, how much fabric is needed to make 9 vests? **$11\frac{1}{4}$ yards**

Seasonal sales, pages 344-345

6. TV sets are often on sale in June. The regular price of a certain model is $375. With a 15% discount, what is the sale price of the TV set?
$318.75

Craft supplies, pages 346-347

7. A stained-glass window takes the amounts of glass listed. Find the total cost. Remember, glass is sold only in 1- or $\frac{1}{2}$- square foot sections.

Blue—$2\frac{1}{2}$ sq. ft. at $3 a square foot
Green—1 sq. ft. at $5 a square foot
Red—$2\frac{3}{4}$ sq. ft. at $9 a square foot
Yellow—3 sq. ft. at $5 a square foot
$54.50

8. The stained-glass window in problem 7 takes $1\frac{1}{2}$ pounds of solder at $7.75 a pound, $\frac{2}{3}$ of a roll of foil at $3 a roll, and 8 feet of edging at $3.75 for 8 feet. Find the total cost of materials, including glass.
$76.75

Buying building materials, pages 348-349

9. Find the cost of three boards, each 1 in. by 4 in. by 6 ft. at $0.18 per linear foot. Remember, when lumber is priced by the linear foot, the cost of each board depends only on its length.
$3.24

Rental clerk, pages 350-351

10. Find the cost of renting a car polisher for 4 hours at $1.75 per hour.
$7

Chapter 17 Test

Number of test items – 10					
Number missed	1	2	3	4	5
Percent correct	90	80	70	60	50

George Wright wants to buy 2 sweaters from the catalog.

SWEATER—100% wool. Pull-over style with ribbed neckline, wrist, and bottom edge. Long sleeve, raglan shoulder. Machine wash warm, tumble dry low. Colors: navy, brown, light blue, yellow, red. Sizes: S, M, L, XL. Wt. 15 oz.
Q 5-391 .... $24.98

1. What is the total cost of the merchandise?
$49.96

2. What is the amount of sales tax if the tax rate is 4%? Round to the nearest cent.
$2.00

3. George lives in zone 1. Use this table to find the shipping and handling charges.
$2.11

Shipping and Handling Charges			
Shipping weight	Local zone	Zones 1 & 2	Zone 3
1 oz. to 8 oz.	$1.27	$1.34	$1.36
9 oz. to 15 oz.	$1.49	$1.60	$1.64
1 lb. to 2 lb.	$1.97	$2.11	$2.14
2 lb. 1 oz. to 3 lb.	$2.07	$2.39	$2.43
3 lb. 1 oz. to 5 lb.	$2.20	$2.57	$2.63
5 lb. 1 oz. to 10 lb.	$2.43	$2.84	$2.91

4. What is the total amount George must enclose with his order?
$54.07

5. If $3\frac{1}{4}$ yd. of fabric is needed to make one skirt, how much fabric is needed to make 7 skirts? **$22\frac{3}{4}$ yards**

6. Men's suits are often on sale in April. The regular price of one suit is $145. With a 20% discount, what is the sale price of the suit?
$116

7. A stained-glass planter takes the amounts of glass listed. Find the total cost. Remember, glass is sold only in 1- or $\frac{1}{2}$ - square foot sections.

Gold—$1\frac{1}{3}$ sq. ft. at $4 a square foot
Clear—$1\frac{1}{2}$ sq. ft. at $3 a square foot
Yellow—2 sq. ft. at $5 a square foot
$20.50

8. The stained-glass planter in problem 7 takes 2 pounds of solder at $7.75 a pound and 1 roll of foil at $3 a roll. Find the total cost of materials, including glass.
$39.00

9. Find the cost of five boards, each 2 in. by 8 in. by 12 ft., at $0.36 per linear foot. Remember, when lumber is priced by the linear foot, the cost of each board depends only on its length.
$21.60

10. Find the cost of renting a lawn aerator for 3 hours at $2.50 per hour.
$7.50

 See pages 43-44 of the *Test Masters* for an alternate form of the Chapter 17 Test.

Chapter 18 Budgeting

Objective: Analyze spending by keeping organized records of variable monthly expenses.

Analyzing Spending Habits

See page T43 for additional notes and activities for Chapter 18.

A **budget** is an organized plan for spending money. The first step in making a budget is to find out how money is currently being spent.

The expenses that usually change from one month to the next are **variable monthly expenses**. Julie Brown, a high-school senior with a part-time job, started recording her variable expenses in February.

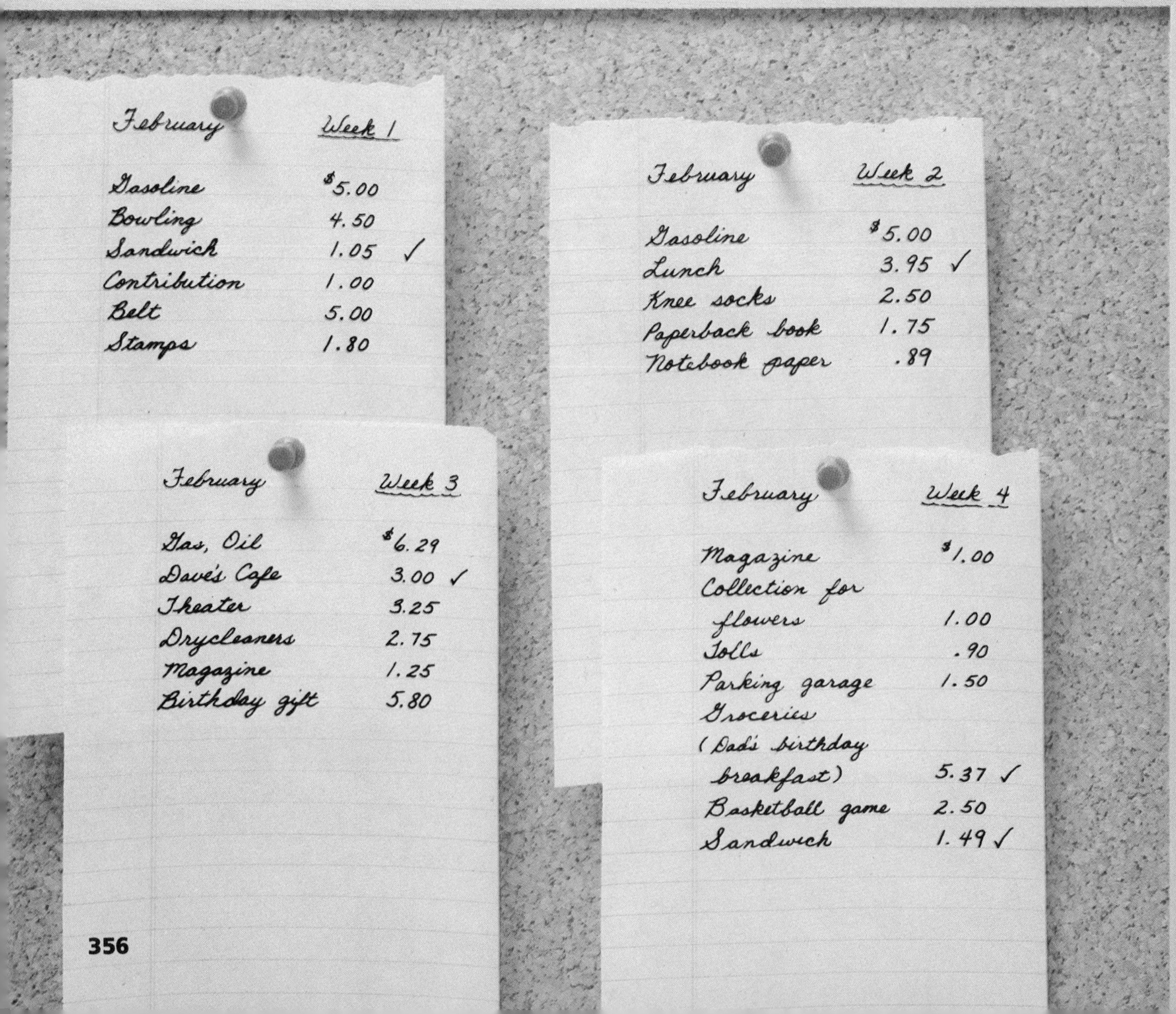

February Week 1
Gasoline $5.00
Bowling 4.50
Sandwich 1.05 ✓
Contribution 1.00
Belt 5.00
Stamps 1.80
February Week 2
Gasoline $5.00
Lunch 3.95 ✓
Knee socks 2.50
Paperback book 1.75
Notebook paper .89
February Week 3
Gas, Oil $6.29
Dave's Cafe 3.00 ✓
Theater 3.25
Drycleaners 2.75
Magazine 1.25
Birthday gift 5.80
February Week 4
Magazine $1.00
Collection for flowers 1.00
Tolls .90
Parking garage 1.50
Groceries (Dad's birthday breakfast) 5.37 ✓
Basketball game 2.50
Sandwich 1.49 ✓

Warm-up: Round each sum to the nearest whole number.

10 + 7.50 + 3.82	[21]
1.50 + 1.75 + 4.29	[8]
0.79 + 0.75 + 0.25 + 1	[3]
16 + 8.80 + 10 + 11.25	[46]

Problem

Julie realized that her expenses fall into categories, such as food and entertainment. How much did Julie spend for food during February?

Solution

Strategy

- Read Julie's spending records. List all of her food expenses and add to find the total amount spent for food. Round the answer to the nearest dollar.

$\$1.05 + \$3.95 + \$3.00 + \$5.37 + \$1.49 \approx \$15.00$

Conclusion

Julie spent about $15 for food during February.

Related Problems

Throughout this chapter, problems appear in groups. The entire group of related problems should be assigned.

Julie chose six categories of spending, including a category for miscellaneous purchases. Find the monthly total for each category and the total of all variable expenses for the month. Round each total to the nearest dollar.

	Variable Expenses for February					
	Category	Week 1	Week 2	Week 3	Week 4	Category total
	Food	$1.05	$3.95	$3.00	$5.37 + $1.49	$15
1.	Car	$5.00	$5.00	$6.29	$0.90 + $1.50	$19
2.	Entertainment	$4.50	—	$3.25	$2.50	$10
3.	Clothes and clothing care	$5.00	$2.50	$2.75	—	$10
4.	Gifts, contributions	$1.00	—	$5.80	$1.00	$8
5.	Miscellaneous (All other spending)	$1.80	$1.75 + $0.89	$1.25	$1.00	$7
6.	TOTAL					$69

Since Robert Wright's bus transportation is the same amount each month, it is not included here. It appears in the Wrights' budget sheet on page 364.

The Wright family's variable expenses for February are given below. Helen Wright drives to and from work. Her husband Robert takes the bus. Their children, Andy and Tina, are in junior high school.

Unlike Julie Brown, the Wrights consider eating in a restaurant as part of their entertainment. Other eating costs are included under "Food." Personal expenses like magazines and haircuts are not listed here because they are covered by a fixed monthly allowance that each family member receives.

February – Variable Expenses

FIRST WEEK			
Groceries	45.50	Contributions	10.00
Robert's lunches	15.50	Dry cleaner	22.00
Helen's lunches	10.20	Groceries	20.17
Gas bill	65.32	Movie	12.00
Electric bill	41.71	2 pr. jeans	32.90
Gasoline	15.00	Miscellaneous	9.85
SECOND WEEK			
Groceries	57.25	Basketball game	7.25
Robert's lunches	12.50	Restaurant	9.25
Helen's lunches	9.00	Tina's boots (on sale)	21.95
Gasoline	17.50	Miscellaneous	8.50
Helen's shoes	24.00		
THIRD WEEK			
Groceries	58.88	Chelsea's Restaurant	37.82
Robert's lunches	12.57	Contributions	13.00
Helen's lunches	8.47	Miscellaneous	1.42
Telephone	25.40	Miscellaneous	6.00
Gasoline	18.00		
FOURTH WEEK			
Groceries	60.04	Museum	6.00
Robert's lunches	13.75	Robert's jacket	75.00
Helen's lunches	14.00	Parking	1.25
Gasoline	17.25	Miscellaneous	13.00

Break Time: Compare the weight of three diamonds with the weight of any other three. If they balance, weigh two of the remaining diamonds. If one goes down, it is the counterfeit. If they balance, the remaining stone is the counterfeit. If they do not balance, weigh two of the diamonds from the heavier tray. If one goes down, it is the counterfeit. If they balance, the third diamond is the counterfeit.

Related Problems

Use the Wrights' record of variable expenses to complete the following table. Round each total to the nearest dollar.

	Variable Expenses for *February*					
	Category	Week 1	Week 2	Week 3	Week 4	Category total
7.	Food	\$45.50; \$15.50; \$10.20; \$20.17	\$57.25; \$12.50; \$9.00	\$58.88; \$12.57; \$8.47	\$60.04; \$13.75; \$14.00	\$338
8.	Utilities (gas, phone, electric)	\$65.32 \$41.71	——	\$25.40	——	\$132
9.	Car	\$15.00	\$17.50	\$18.00	\$17.25; \$1.25	\$69
10.	Entertainment	\$12.00	\$7.25; \$9.25	\$37.82	\$6.00	\$72
11.	Contributions	\$10.00	——	\$13.00	——	\$23
12.	Clothing and maintenance	\$22.00 \$32.90	\$24.00 \$21.95	——	\$75.00	\$176
13.	Miscellaneous	\$9.85	\$8.50	\$1.42; \$6.00	\$13.00	\$39
14.	TOTAL					\$849

Break Time

Except for one counterfeit stone, all of these diamonds have the same weight. The counterfeit is slightly heavier than each of the other stones.

Describe how to use no more than two weighings of the diamonds on a balance scale to decide which stone is counterfeit.
See above.

Objective: Budget variable expenses by using average expenses from records of several months' spending.

Budgeting Variable Expenses

Julie Brown has been recording her variable expenses for three months. If she averages the amounts she has spent in each category, she can predict expenses for the next month. Each average becomes the **amount budgeted**.

Problem

Julie's records show that in the last three months she has spent \$15, \$19, and \$18 for food. How much should she allow in her budget for food for next month?

Solution

Strategy

- Add to find the total amount spent for food.

  $\$15 + \$19 + \$18 = \$52$

- Divide by 3 to find the average amount. Round the answer to the nearest dollar.

  $\$52 \div 3 \approx \$17$

Conclusion

Julie should allow about \$17 for food next month.

Warm-up: Find the average. Round to the nearest whole number.

25, 30, 18	[24]
16, 20, 20	[19]
300, 360, 342	[334]
81, 105, 97	[94]

Related Problems

Complete each chart to find the amounts that should be budgeted for the next month. Round each answer to the nearest dollar.

Julie Brown

	Variable monthly expenses	February	March	April	Amount budgeted
	Food	$ 15	$ 19	$ 18	$ 17
1.	Car	$ 19	$ 23	$ 20	$ 21
2.	Entertainment	$ 10	$ 11	$ 15	$ 12
3.	Clothes and clothing care	$ 10	$ 7	$ 10	$ 9
4.	Gifts, contributions ...	$ 8	$ 5	$ 9	$ 7
5.	Miscellaneous	$ 7	$ 5	$ 5	$ 6
6.	Total amount to be budgeted for next month				$ 72

The Wright family

	Variable monthly expenses	February	March	April	Amount budgeted
7.	Food	$ 338	$ 347	$ 370	$ 352
8.	Utilities	$ 132	$ 165	$ 113	$ 137
9.	Car	$ 69	$ 81	$ 75	$ 75
10.	Entertainment	$ 72	$ 60	$ 64	$ 65
11.	Contributions	$ 23	$ 20	$ 30	$ 24
12.	Clothing and maintenance	$ 176	$ 125	$ 130	$ 144
13.	Miscellaneous	$ 39	$ 65	$ 46	$ 50
14.	Total amount to be budgeted for next month				$ 847

Another way to determine the amount to be budgeted involves using the largest amount spent during any one month. On tight budgets, however, this practice is rarely feasible.

Objective: Make a budget by using total variable monthly expenses, total fixed monthly expenses, and the monthly reserve determined from total annual expenses.

Making a Budget

Give students enough time to become familiar with the first three parts of the budget sheet so that they can understand how those parts relate to the fourth part, the monthly spending plan.

After graduation, Julie Brown will be working full time. Her monthly take-home pay will be about $540. To plan her spending, she filled out a budget sheet.

Under variable monthly expenses, Julie increased the amounts she budgets for clothes and clothing care and for miscellaneous spending.

Fixed monthly expenses, such as a car payment and rent, do not vary from month to month. Some people also consider amounts that they save or invest each month as fixed expenses. Julie intends to open a savings account.

Budget sheet for *Julie Brown*

Monthly take-home pay $ *540*

Variable monthly expenses

Food *($17 budgeted now)*	$ *17*
Car *($21 now)*	$ *21*
Entertainment *($12 now)*	$ *12*
Clothes and clothing care *($9 now)*	$ *40*
Gifts, contributions *($7 now)*	$ *7*
Miscellaneous *($6 now)*	$ *15*
TOTAL	$ *112*

Fixed monthly expenses

Car payment	$ *125*
Rent *(Room and board)*	$ *100*
Savings account	$ *35*
TOTAL	$ *260*

Annual expenses

Car insurance	$ *500*
Car repairs	$ *300*
License plates	$ *18*
Medical, dental bills	$ *100*
Vacation	$ *300*
Miscellaneous *(Computer course)*	$ *80*
TOTAL	$
Monthly reserve (TOTAL ÷ 12)	$

MONTHLY SPENDING PLAN

Total variable expenses	$
Total fixed expenses	$
Monthly reserve for annual expenses	$
SUBTOTAL	$
Plus 5% of subtotal for unexpected expenses	$
SPENDING TOTAL	$

Some people maintain a separate bank account into which they deposit the monthly reserve. Annual expenses are paid for out of this account.

Warm-up: 15 + 42 + 7 + 10 + 15 [89]
369 + 20 + 150 + 200 + 500 [1239]
864 ÷ 12 [72]
4740 ÷ 12 [395]

See page 10 of *Consumer Forms and Problems.*

Everyone is faced with expenses that occur only occasionally, such as bills for insurance or car repair. These expenses are listed as **annual expenses**.

Problem

What is the total of Julie's annual expenses? How much money should she set aside each month (monthly reserve) for these expenses?

Solution

Strategy

- Use Julie's budget sheet to list her annual expenses. Then add to find the total.

$500	Car insurance
300	Car repairs
18	License plates
100	Medical, dental bills
300	Vacation
+ 80	Computer course
$1298	Total

- Divide by 12 to find the monthly reserve. Round to the nearest dollar. $\$1298 \div 12 \approx \$108$

Conclusion

Julie's annual expenses will be about $1298. She should set aside $108 each month for these expenses.

Related Problems

Discuss how the use of a 5% "cushion" can help prevent a person from budgeting the last dollar of take-home pay.

To complete Julie's monthly spending plan, find the sum of monthly variable expenses, monthly fixed expenses, and the monthly reserve. Then add on 5% of this sum to find the spending total.

MONTHLY SPENDING PLAN

1.	Total variable expenses	$ 112
2.	Total fixed expenses	$ 260
	Monthly reserve for annual expenses	$108
3.	SUBTOTAL	$ 480
4.	Plus 5% of subtotal for unexpected expenses	$ 24
5.	SPENDING TOTAL	$ 504

6. If the spending total is greater than the monthly take-home pay, the budget must be revised. Does Julie need to revise her budget?
No

Emphasize that all budgets are based on take-home pay, not gross pay.

See page 63 of *Consumer Forms and Problems.*

Establish that while the four parts of this budget sheet are the same as those of Julie Brown's budget sheet, some of the categories of spending are different.

This budget sheet for the Wright family includes budgeted amounts for variable monthly expenses as determined on page 361. Complete the budget sheet. In problem 9, round the answer to the nearest dollar.

Budget sheet for The Wrights

Monthly take-home pay $ 2166

Variable monthly expenses	
Food	$352
Utilities	$137
Car	$ 75
Entertainment	$ 65
Contributions	$ 24
Clothing and maintenance	$144
Miscellaneous	$ 50
TOTAL	$847

	Fixed monthly expenses	
	Mortgage (including real estate tax payment)	$ 335
	Installment payments	
	a. Car	$170
	b. Furniture	$ 68
	Savings	$100
	Miscellaneous	
	Robert's bus fare	$ 22
	School lunches	$ 40
	Robert's allowance	$ 35
	Helen's allowance	$ 35
	Andy's allowance	$ 15
	Tina's allowance	$ 15
7.	TOTAL	$ 835

	Annual expenses	
	Homeowner's insurance	$250
	Home repairs	$1500
	Water, garbage bills (4 x $45)	$180
	Car insurance	$435
	Car repairs	$200
	License plates	$ 22
	City registration	$ 12
	Life insurance	$375
	Medical, dental bills	$500
	Clubs, professional organizations	$ 25
	Vacation	$600
	Gifts	$120
	Newspaper, magazine subscriptions	$ 75
8.	TOTAL	$ 4294
9.	Monthly reserve (TOTAL ÷ 12)	$ 358

	MONTHLY SPENDING PLAN	
10.	Total variable expenses	$ 847
11.	Total fixed expenses	$ 835
12.	Monthly reserve for annual expenses	$ 358
13.	SUBTOTAL	$ 2040
14.	Plus 5% of subtotal for unexpected expenses	$ 102
15.	SPENDING TOTAL	$ 2142

16. Which is greater, the spending total or the take-home pay for one month?
The take-home pay

17. Do the Wrights need to revise their budget?
No

CALCULATOR APPLICATIONS

Percent of Increase

A year ago, George Vanda moved from a small city to a large city. He wants to find the **percent of increase** in some of his spending categories.

George spent \$500 in contributions during the last year and \$467 the previous year. To find the percent of increase, first find the difference between the two amounts.

$\$500 - \$467 = \$33$

Divide the difference by the previous year's expense. Write the answer as a decimal rounded to the nearest hundredth.

$\$33 \div \$467 \approx 0.07$

Possible key sequence:
500 [−] 467 [÷] 467 [=]

Write the decimal as a percent.

$0.07 = 7\%$

George's expenses for contributions increased by 7%.

Find the percent of increase in each of these categories of George's spending.

	Category	Last year's expense	Previous year's expense	Difference	Difference ÷ previous year's expense	Percent of increase
	Contributions	\$500	\$467	\$33	0.07	7%
1.	Food	\$1322	\$1172	\$150	0.13	13%
2.	Rent	\$3660	\$2400	\$1260	0.53	53%
3.	Car insurance	\$523	\$278	\$245	0.88	88%
4.	Other car expenses	\$887	\$650	\$237	0.36	36%
5.	Clothing	\$616	\$565	\$51	0.09	9%

Objectives: Adjust a budget to reflect changes in expenses or income; make a decision about future spending.

Adjusting a Budget

The changes described in this lesson are to be made on the budget given on pages 362–363.

Two of Julie Brown's girlfriends want her to move in with them when their roommate leaves in six months. This change would create new expenses for Julie. She cannot increase her income right now, but she may be able to adjust her budget by reducing some current expenses.

Problem

The three girls would allow about $150 per month for groceries. Julie would also allow $15 for lunches and $20 per month for eating in a restaurant. What amount should Julie budget for food?

Solution

Strategy

- Divide by 3 to find Julie's share of the grocery expense.
  $150 ÷ 3 = $50
- Add to find the total amount she should budget for food.

$50	Groceries
15	Lunches
+ 20	Eating in a restaurant
$85	

Conclusion

Julie should budget $85 for food.

Related Problems

Besides sharing the cost of groceries, the three girls would also equally share the costs for telephone, electricity, and rent. Make the changes described in problems 1-10.

Variable monthly expenses

1. The girls budget $30 each month for the telephone bill. How much would Julie pay?
   $10
2. The girls budget $20 each month for electricity. How much would Julie pay?
   $7
3. If Julie cuts her budgeted amount of $40 for clothing in half, what would be the new amount?
   $20
4. Julie would budget $85 for food. Her other variable monthly expenses should stay the same, as listed below.

   Car $21
   Entertainment $12
   Gifts and contributions $7
   Miscellaneous $15

   Use these amounts, along with your answers to problems 1-3, to find the new total of Julie's variable monthly expenses.
   $177

Fixed monthly expenses

5. The $100 for room and board would be replaced by Julie's share of $330 for rent. How much would Julie pay for rent?
   $110
6. Add Julie's share of the rent to her car payment of $125 and her savings deposit of $35. What would be the new total for fixed monthly expenses?
   $270

Warm-up: 48 ÷ 3 [16]
68 + 20 + 25 + 19 [132]
1092 ÷ 12 [91]
5% of 520 [26]

See page 10 of
Consumer Forms and Problems.

Annual expenses

7. Julie would need renter's insurance to protect her stereo and some furniture. Premiums of $35 each are payable two times a year. What would be Julie's annual expense for this insurance?
$70

8. If she reduces the $300 budgeted for a vacation by $100, what would be the new amount budgeted?
$200

9. In six months, Julie would no longer have to budget $80 for her computer course, which would be completed. Her other annual expenses would stay about the same.

Car insurance $500
Car repairs $300
License plates $18
Medical, dental bills $100

Use these amounts, along with your answers to problems 7 and 8, to find the new total of Julie's annual expenses.
$1188

10. How much would Julie have to reserve each month to pay for annual expenses?
$99

Use the answers to problems 4, 6, and 10 to help you complete Julie's new monthly spending plan. Round your answers to the nearest dollar.

	MONTHLY SPENDING PLAN	
11.	Total variable expenses	$ 177
12.	Total fixed expenses	$ 270
13.	Monthly reserve for annual expenses	$ 99
14.	SUBTOTAL	$ 546
15.	Plus 5% of subtotal for unexpected expenses	$ 27
16.	SPENDING TOTAL	$ 573

17. Julie's take-home pay from the full-time job will be $540. Can she afford to move into the apartment in six months?
No

18. In nine months, Julie will have a chance to get a promotion. Her take-home pay would be increased by 10%. What would be her new monthly take-home pay?
$594

19. Could Julie afford to move if she gets the promotion?
Yes

20. If Julie does not get the promotion but cuts out the vacation allowance entirely, could she afford to move?
No

Objective: Compute annual spending of gross income for a family of four by using information from a graph.

Economist

See the Careers Chart beginning on page 410 for more information about the careers in this cluster.

Career Cluster: Science Tony Bartlett is an economist and a university instructor. He is involved in a research project that will explain how people spend their money, depending on their level of income and the part of the country in which they live. The country is divided into six regions, and eight different levels of income are included.

Tony made the bar graph on page 369. It shows how families of four in a certain region of the country spend their gross income. Three levels of income are used in the graph.

Have students check local sources for similar data on the cost of living in your area.

Problem

At income level B, how much money does the typical family spend for food?

Solution

Strategy

- Read the graph to determine what percent of income a family at level B spends for food.

  29%

- Read the list of income levels to find the family's gross income.

  $12,000

- Multiply $12,000 by 29% to find the amount spent for food.

  $0.29 \times \$12{,}000 = \$3480$

Conclusion

The typical family at income level B spends $3480 for food during the year.

Warm-up: 23% of 14,000 [3220]
15% of 22,000 [3300]
8% of 22,000 [1760]
17% of 45,000 [7650]

See page 64 of *Consumer Forms and Problems.*

Region I
Annual spending for typical families of four

Income levels B $12,000 D $21,000 F $35,000

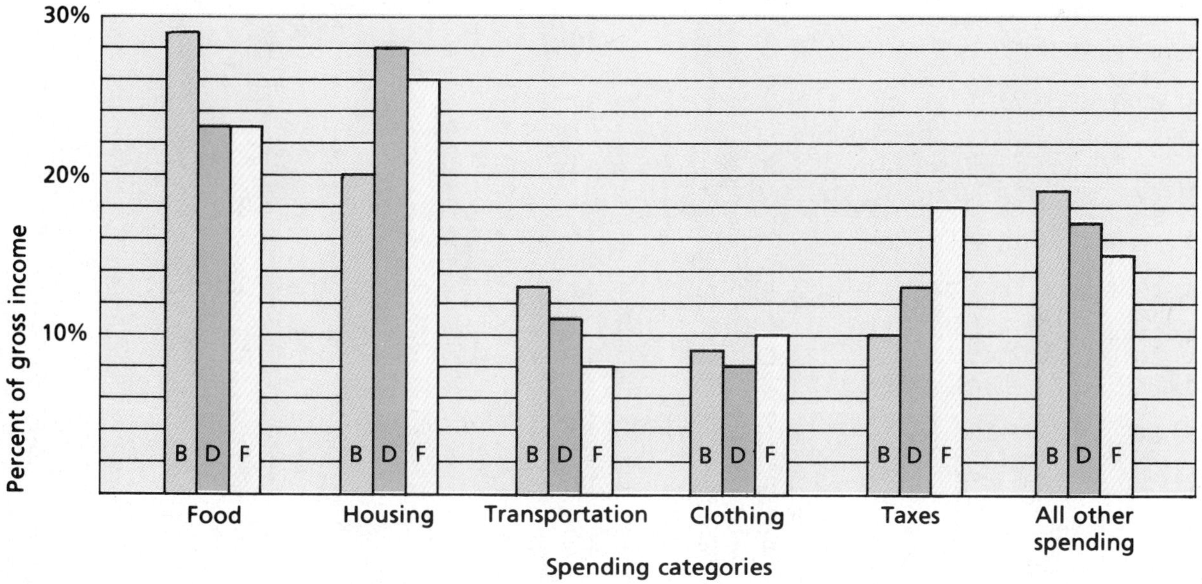

Related Problems

Find the amount spent for each category.

	Category	Income level B	Income level D	Income level F
1.	Food	$3480	$4830	$8050
2.	Housing	$2400	$5880	$9100
3.	Transportation	$1560	$2310	$2800
4.	Clothing	$1080	$1680	$3500
5.	Taxes	$1200	$2730	$6300
6.	All other spending	$2280	$3570	$5250

Refer to your answers to problems 1-6.

What is the most expensive category for a family

7. at income level B?
Food

8. at income level D?
Housing

9. at income level F?
Housing

10. How much more does a family at level B pay for food than for housing?
$1080

11. How much more does a family at level D pay in taxes than it spends for clothing?
$1050

12. How much more does a family at level F pay for housing than it spends for transportation?
$6300

Skills Tune-Up

Adding whole numbers and decimals, pages 6-7

1. 14 + 37 + 21
   72
2. 28 + 15 + 7
   50
3. 43 + 97 + 21
   161
4. 81 + 49 + 23
   153
5. 97 + 55 + 47
   199
6. 67 + 80 + 79
   226
7. 26 + 43 + 78 + 55
   202
8. 17 + 83 + 48 + 24
   172
9. 97 + 39 + 27 + 70
   233
10. 668 + 202 + 341
    1211
11. 548 + 913 + 188
    1649
12. 300 + 784 + 456
    1540
13. 224 + 384 + 170
    778
14. 3.5 + 4.24
    7.74
15. 13.42 + 4.65
    18.07
16. 33.17 + 19.05
    52.22
17. 15.85 + 82.76
    98.61
18. 0.29 + 0.32 + 0.13
    0.74
19. 5.8 + 8.3 + 3.75
    17.85
20. 0.75 + 3.07 + 0.08
    3.9
21. 9.43 + 7.55 + 3.09
    20.07
22. 3.45 + 2.41 + 9.7
    15.56
23. 0.78 + 0.46 + 0.01
    1.25
24. 4.04 + 1.16 + 7.82
    13.02
25. 0.06 + 3.179 + 7.26
    10.499
26. 7.8 + 2.99 + 3.4 + 5.6
    19.79
27. 3.7 + 1.33 + 8.8 + 7.4
    21.23

Comparing and renaming fractions and mixed numbers, pages 14-15

Compare these fractions.
Replace ● with <, >, or =.

1. $\frac{3}{5}$ ● $\frac{2}{7}$ >
2. $\frac{3}{4}$ ● $\frac{8}{9}$ <
3. $\frac{2}{3}$ ● $\frac{7}{8}$ <
4. $\frac{5}{9}$ ● $\frac{1}{3}$ >
5. $\frac{1}{2}$ ● $\frac{4}{7}$ <
6. $\frac{11}{12}$ ● $\frac{5}{8}$ >
7. $\frac{5}{9}$ ● $\frac{6}{7}$ <
8. $\frac{3}{7}$ ● $\frac{1}{2}$ <
9. $\frac{6}{7}$ ● $\frac{12}{14}$ =
10. $\frac{5}{8}$ ● $\frac{11}{16}$ <
11. $\frac{1}{2}$ ● $\frac{4}{9}$ >
12. $\frac{7}{8}$ ● $\frac{8}{9}$ <
13. $\frac{2}{3}$ ● $\frac{5}{12}$ >
14. $\frac{5}{7}$ ● $\frac{10}{14}$ =
15. $\frac{4}{7}$ ● $\frac{3}{4}$ <
16. $\frac{9}{14}$ ● $\frac{1}{2}$ >
17. $\frac{1}{3}$ ● $\frac{3}{8}$ <
18. $\frac{8}{11}$ ● $\frac{4}{5}$ <

Rename as a mixed number.

19. $\frac{9}{2}$ $4\frac{1}{2}$
20. $\frac{15}{4}$ $3\frac{3}{4}$
21. $\frac{21}{6}$ $3\frac{1}{2}$
22. $\frac{19}{5}$ $3\frac{4}{5}$
23. $\frac{18}{12}$ $1\frac{1}{2}$
24. $\frac{21}{8}$ $2\frac{5}{8}$
25. $\frac{13}{2}$ $6\frac{1}{2}$
26. $\frac{26}{3}$ $8\frac{2}{3}$
27. $\frac{25}{10}$ $2\frac{1}{2}$
28. $\frac{37}{5}$ $7\frac{2}{5}$
29. $\frac{31}{8}$ $3\frac{7}{8}$
30. $\frac{45}{36}$ $1\frac{1}{4}$
31. $\frac{48}{11}$ $4\frac{4}{11}$
32. $\frac{29}{7}$ $4\frac{1}{7}$
33. $\frac{44}{33}$ $1\frac{1}{3}$
34. $\frac{57}{8}$ $7\frac{1}{8}$
35. $\frac{65}{10}$ $6\frac{1}{2}$
36. $\frac{25}{15}$ $1\frac{2}{3}$

Dividing fractions and mixed numbers, pages 16-17

1. $\frac{1}{4} \div \frac{1}{3}$ $\frac{3}{4}$
2. $\frac{8}{9} \div \frac{4}{7}$ $1\frac{5}{9}$
3. $\frac{2}{5} \div \frac{2}{3}$ $\frac{3}{5}$
4. $\frac{3}{7} \div \frac{3}{8}$ $1\frac{1}{7}$
5. $\frac{1}{10} \div \frac{2}{3}$ $\frac{3}{20}$
6. $\frac{21}{25} \div \frac{7}{15}$ $1\frac{4}{5}$
7. $7 \div \frac{7}{8}$ 8
8. $\frac{8}{15} \div 16$ $\frac{1}{30}$
9. $4 \div \frac{3}{7}$ $9\frac{1}{3}$
10. $\frac{15}{16} \div 3$ $\frac{5}{16}$
11. $5\frac{5}{6} \div \frac{5}{6}$ 7
12. $\frac{3}{7} \div 2\frac{2}{3}$ $\frac{9}{56}$
13. $1\frac{1}{5} \div 10$ $\frac{3}{25}$
14. $20 \div 6\frac{1}{4}$ $3\frac{1}{5}$
15. $1\frac{2}{5} \div 2\frac{1}{3}$ $\frac{3}{5}$
16. $9\frac{1}{6} \div 1\frac{4}{7}$ $5\frac{5}{6}$
17. $1\frac{1}{7} \div 1\frac{1}{3}$ $\frac{6}{7}$
18. $4\frac{3}{8} \div 1\frac{1}{6}$ $3\frac{3}{4}$
19. $2\frac{6}{7} \div 8\frac{3}{4}$ $\frac{16}{49}$
20. $2\frac{5}{14} \div 3\frac{1}{7}$ $\frac{3}{4}$

Chapter 18 Review

Analyzing spending habits, pages 356-359

Use the spending record below. Round each answer to the nearest dollar.

Sweater \$20.00	Food \$3.30
Food \$7.80	Shirt \$13.50
Movie \$4.50	Bus tokens \$4.50
Books \$7.15	Dance \$10.00
Miscellaneous \$2.45	Food \$8.50
Mittens \$7.20	Art exhibit \$3.50
Ball game \$3.50	

1. Find the total expense for clothing.
\$41
2. Find the total expense for entertainment.
\$22

Budgeting variable expenses, pages 360-361

3. Use this 3-month spending record. Find the amount that should be budgeted for this variable expense. Round to the nearest dollar.

	May	June	July	Amount budgeted
Food	\$40	\$55	\$60	\$52

4. The budgeted amounts for Rae's variable monthly expenses are: food, \$15; car, \$20; entertainment, \$20; clothes, \$15; gifts, \$7; and miscellaneous, \$10. What is the total of her variable monthly expenses?
\$87

Making a budget, pages 362-364

5. Rae's fixed expenses are \$25 for savings and \$18 to repay a loan from her parents. What is the total of her fixed monthly expenses?
\$43

6. The total of Rae's annual expenses is \$920. To the nearest dollar, how much should she set aside each month to pay her annual expenses?
\$77
7. Complete this monthly spending plan for the Etheridge family.

MONTHLY SPENDING PLAN	
Total variable expenses	\$650
Total fixed expenses	\$492
Monthly reserve for annual expenses	\$298
SUBTOTAL	\$ 1440
Plus 5% of subtotal for unexpected expenses	\$ 72
SPENDING TOTAL	\$ 1512

8. Take-home pay for the Etheridges is \$1550 per month. Does their budget need to be revised?
No

Adjusting a budget, pages 366-367

9. The Springer family budgets \$78 per month for car expenses. If Mr. Springer joins a car pool, he can cut this expense in half. What would be the new amount budgeted?
\$39

Economist, pages 368-369

10. In one part of the country, a typical family spends 27% of its gross income for housing. If the family's income is \$19,000 per year, what is the amount spent for housing?
\$5130

Chapter 18 Test

Number of test items - 10					
Number missed	1	2	3	4	5
Percent correct	90	80	70	60	50

Use the spending record below. Round each answer to the nearest dollar.

Gas $8.20	Gift $8.75
Food $3.55	Charity $4.00
Album $6.15	Gas & oil $7.90
Miscellaneous $3.27	Food $7.00
Tennis $7.50	Haircut $4.75
Food $2.30	Books $6.30
Gas $4.25	

1. Find the total expense for food.
$13
2. Find the total expense for gas and oil.
$20

3. Use this 3-month spending record. Find the amount that should be budgeted for this variable expense.

	May	June	July	Amount budgeted
Utilities	$92	$100	$117	$103

4. The budgeted amounts for Brian's variable expenses are: food, $25; car, $60; entertainment, $35; and miscellaneous, $20. What is the total of Brian's variable monthly expenses?
$140

5. Brian's fixed expenses are $210 per month for his car payment and $45 per month for savings. What is the total of Brian's fixed monthly expenses?
$255

6. The total of Brian's annual expenses is $850. To the nearest dollar, how much should he set aside each month to pay his annual expenses?
$71
7. Complete this monthly spending plan for the Hahn family.

MONTHLY SPENDING PLAN	
Total variable expenses	$617
Total fixed expenses	$500
Monthly reserve for annual expenses	$423
SUBTOTAL	$ 1540
Plus 5% of subtotal for unexpected expenses	$ 77
SPENDING TOTAL	$ 1617

8. Take-home pay for the Hahns is $1682 per month. Does their budget need to be revised?
No

9. The James family budgets $1825 annually for clothes. Mr. and Mrs. James hope to save $350 annually by making some of their clothes. What should be the new amount budgeted for clothes?
$1475

10. One survey showed that a typical family spends 22% of its income for food. If the family's income is $30,000 per year, what amount is spent for food?
$6600

 See pages 45–46 of the *Test Masters* for an alternate form of the Chapter 18 Test.

Unit 6 Test

Number of test items - 16								
Number missed	1	2	3	4	5	6	7	8
Percent correct	94	88	81	75	69	63	56	50

Choose the best answer.

Pages 322–323

1. Find the number of calories in 3 slices of bacon if 1 slice contains 45 calories.

   A 48 calories **(C)** 135 calories

   B 125 calories **D** 15 calories

Pages 324–325

2. Lori weighs 66 kilograms. She went bowling for 1.5 hours. At 3.9 calories per kilogram per hour, how many calories did she use? Round to the nearest whole number.

   (A) 386 calories **C** 184 calories

   B 257 calories **D** 92 calories

Pages 326–328

3. Find the cost of 1.5 kilograms of grapes at $1.79 per kilogram. Round to the nearest cent.

   A $1.19 **C** $3.29

   (B) $2.69 **D** $0.29

Pages 330–331

4. Before butchering, a side of beef weighed 150 kilograms. After butchering, the usable meat weighed 114 kilograms. What was the percent of loss?

   A 32% **(C)** 24%

   B 76% **D** 132%

Pages 332–333

5. Find the total cost of this meal for two people. The prices given are per person. Include a 15% tip.

Shrimp	$9.25
Beverage	$0.50
Salad	$1.25

   A $11 **C** $12.65

   B $22 **(D)** $25.30

Pages 338–340

6. Use the table below. Find the shipping and handling charges for an order weighing 3 lb. 7 oz. and going to zone 2.

Shipping and Handling Charges			
Shipping weight	Local zone	Zones 1 & 2	Zone 3
1 oz. to 8 oz.	$1.27	$1.34	$1.36
9 oz. to 15 oz.	$1.49	$1.60	$1.64
1 lb. to 2 lb.	$1.97	$2.11	$2.14
2 lb. 1 oz. to 3 lb.	$2.07	$2.39	$2.43
3 lb. 1 oz. to 5 lb.	$2.20	$2.57	$2.63
5 lb. 1 oz. to 10 lb.	$2.43	$2.84	$2.91

   A $2.07 **C** $7.71

   B $2.39 **(D)** $2.57

Pages 342–343

7. If $2\frac{1}{4}$ yards of fabric is needed to make one blouse, how much fabric is needed to make two blouses?

   A $4\frac{1}{16}$ yd. **C** $4\frac{1}{4}$ yd.

   (B) $4\frac{1}{2}$ yd. **D** $4\frac{1}{8}$ yd.

Pages 344–345

8. Laundry appliances are often on sale in March. The regular price of a clothes washer is $400. What is the sale price of the washer if the discount is 15%?

   A $385 **(C)** $340

   B $60 **D** $460

Pages 346–347

9. A stained-glass planter takes 5 sq. ft. of gold glass at $4 a square foot. It also takes 2 pounds of solder at $7.75 a pound and 1 roll of foil at $3 a roll. Find the total cost of the materials for the planter.

A $14.75 **C** $30.75

B $38.50 **D** $22.50

Pages 348–349

10. Find the total cost of 4 boards, each 2 in. by 4 in. by 8 ft. at $0.18 per linear foot. Remember, when lumber is priced by the linear foot, the cost of each board depends only on its length.

A $5.76 **C** $11.52

B $1.44 **D** $2.56

Pages 350–351

11. A rug shampooer rents for $2.50 per hour. Find the cost of renting the shampooer for 6 hours.

A $12 **C** $15

B $8.50 **D** $10

Pages 356–359

12. Find the total expense for entertainment for January. Round to the nearest dollar.

Entertainment expenses—January

Concert	$6.00
Hockey game	$8.75
Bowling	$4.35

A $19 **C** $18

B $20 **D** $17

Pages 360–361

13. A 3-month spending record for gasoline, oil, and tolls is given below. Find the amount that should be budgeted per month for this variable expense.

June: $28
July: $31
August: $28

A $87 **C** $30

B $28 **D** $29

Pages 362–364

14. Don Kim's annual expenses total $585. To the nearest dollar, how much should he reserve each month to pay annual expenses?

A $600 **C** $49

B $59 **D** $40

Pages 366–367

15. The Stowe family usually budgets $1500 for a summer vacation. This year they hope to save $425 by driving instead of flying to their destination. How much should they budget this year for the vacation?

A $1925 **C** $1075

B $425 **D** $125

Pages 368–369

16. One survey indicates that an average family spends 28% of its income on housing. If the family income is $17,200 per year, what is the amount spent for housing?

A $12,384 **C** $401

B $4816 **D** $1433

For an alternate form of the Unit 6 Test, see pages T67–T68 of this book and pages 47–48 of the *Test Masters.*
For an end-of-book test, see pages T69–T72 of this book and pages 49–52 of the *Test Masters.*

Winter carnival tickets cost 25¢ each. How much would a book of 18 tickets cost?

Here is a short way to find 18 × 25.

$$\begin{array}{r} 25 \\ \times\ 18 \\ \hline 450 \end{array}$$

THINK

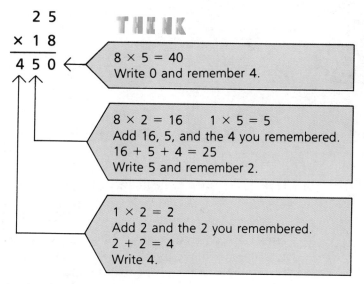

- 8 × 5 = 40
  Write 0 and remember 4.
- 8 × 2 = 16 1 × 5 = 5
  Add 16, 5, and the 4 you remembered.
  16 + 5 + 4 = 25
  Write 5 and remember 2.
- 1 × 2 = 2
  Add 2 and the 2 you remembered.
  2 + 2 = 4
  Write 4.

The book of tickets would cost $4.50.

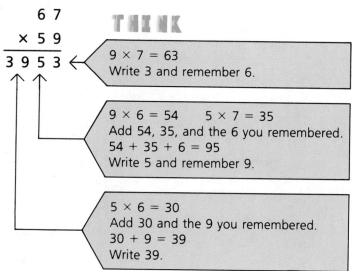

Find 59 × 67.

$$\begin{array}{r} 67 \\ \times\ 59 \\ \hline 3953 \end{array}$$

THINK

- 9 × 7 = 63
  Write 3 and remember 6.
- 9 × 6 = 54 5 × 7 = 35
  Add 54, 35, and the 6 you remembered.
  54 + 35 + 6 = 95
  Write 5 and remember 9.
- 5 × 6 = 30
  Add 30 and the 9 you remembered.
  30 + 9 = 39
  Write 39.

Use the method described at the left to multiply mentally. Write only the answer.

1. 25 × 32 (800)
2. 24 × 31 (744)
3. 13 × 21 (273)
4. 23 × 42 (966)
5. 36 × 18 (648)
6. 21 × 43 (903)
7. 35 × 26 (910)
8. 43 × 15 (645)
9. 62 × 35 (2170)
10. 46 × 28 (1288)
11. 52 × 36 (1872)
12. 19 × 28 (532)
13. 42 × 16 (672)
14. 63 × 24 (1512)
15. 16 × 35 (560)
16. 45 × 36 (1620)
17. 82 × 14 (1148)
18. 46 × 33 (1518)
19. 73 × 48 (3504)
20. 56 × 37 (2072)
21. 91 × 85 (7735)

Cash Registers

The problems on page 347 can be extended using the program for problem 19 if an amount given is added to the problems.

Cash registers at many stores are computerized. They provide an accounting for money received and keep track of inventory. Some read labels on merchandise, ''ring up'' a sale without having their keys pressed by a clerk, and make change. The program shown causes a computer to figure change as a cash register does.

Lines 40 and 60 These values are entered.

Data required	*Name*
Amount of total bill	T
Amount given	A

Lines 30 and 50 A PRINT statement before each INPUT statement shows what data to enter.

Lines 20 and 25 DATA statements indicate the value and name of each bill and coin used to make change.

Line 80 The amount of the total bill is subtracted from the amount given to find the amount of change (S).

Line 90 The DATA statement is read. The bill with the highest value is read first.

Line 110 When the amount of change is less than the value of the bill or coin, the computer is sent to line 160.

Line 120 When the amount of change is equal to or greater than the value of the bill or coin, the value (V) of the bill or coin is subtracted.

Lines 100 and 130 N is used to keep track of the number of times a bill or coin is used.

Lines 70 and 140 C is used to keep a running total of the change received.

Line 150 The computer is sent back to line 110 and lines 110–140 are repeated to check if a bill or coin is used more than once.

Line 160 When a bill or coin is not used, the computer is sent to line 180.

Line 170 When a bill or coin is used, the name and the number of times it is used is printed.

Line 180 When the amount of change does not equal zero, the computer is sent back to read the next bill or coin.

Line 190 The total amount of change is printed.

1.
TENS	1
FIVES	1
ONES	1
NICKELS	1
CHANGE	$ 16.05

2.
ONES	3
DIMES	1
PENNIES	2
CHANGE	$ 3.12

3.
ONES	2
QUARTERS	3
PENNIES	2
CHANGE	$ 2.77

4.
FIVES	1
ONES	2
QUARTERS	3
NICKELS	1
PENNIES	3
CHANGE	$ 7.83

The comma in line 170 will send the computer to the next zone to print the values for N.

These problems can be used either with a computer or as paper-and-pencil activities.

```
10 REM  CASH REGISTER
20 DATA 20,"TWENTIES",10,"TENS",5,
"FIVES",1,"ONES"
25 DATA .25,"QUARTERS",.10,"DIMES",
.05,"NICKELS",.01,"PENNIES"
30 PRINT "TOTAL BILL";
40 INPUT T
50 PRINT "AMOUNT GIVEN";
60 INPUT A
70 LET C=0
80 LET S=A-T
90 READ V,D$
100 LET N=0
110 IF S<V THEN 160
120 LET S=S-V
130 LET N=N+1
140 LET C=C+V
150 GO TO 110
160 IF N=0 THEN 180
170 PRINT D$,N
180 IF S>=.01 THEN 90
190 PRINT "CHANGE   $";C
200 END
```

Answers for computer applications are often in an abbreviated form. In all program modifications shown, the changes and/or additions incorporate previous modifications and will vary. Samples are given.

Give the output for the program above when
See below.

1. T is 23.95 and A is 40.

2. T is 16.88 and A is 20.

3. T is 37.23 and A is 40.

4. T is 2.17 and A is 10.

5. T is 11.62 and A is 15.

6. the amount of the total bill is $3.46 and the amount given is $5.00.

7. the amount of the total bill is $43.78 and the amount given is $50.00.

8. the amount of the total bill is $22.45 and the amount given is $30.00.

9. the amount of the total bill is $2.56 and the amount given is $20.00.

10. the amount of the total bill is $10.50 and the amount given is $15.00.
See above.

11. purchases totaling $15.97 are paid for with $20.
See above.

12. purchases totaling $21.94 are paid for with $40.
See Additional Answers beginning on page T53.

13. purchases totaling $21.94 are paid for with $30.

14. purchases totaling $21.94 are paid for with $22.

15. Modify the program so that a statement is printed for the situation where the amount given is less than the total bill. Have the computer go back to line 50 so that another amount can be entered.

16. Give the output when the total cost is $22.78 and the first amount given is $20 and the next amount given is $25.

17. Modify the program so that instead of the amount of the total bill, the total cost of the merchandise is entered. Add a 5% sales tax to the total cost.

18. Give the output when the total cost is $37.26 and the amount given is $40.

19. Modify the program so that instead of the total cost, the number of items and the price per item are entered. Then have the total cost calculated in the program.

20. Give the output for 3 items for $0.78 each, 2 items for $1.99 each, 5 items for $0.87 each, 2 items for $1.44 each, and 1 item for $5.79. The amount given is $30.

10.

ONES	4
QUARTERS	2
CHANGE	$ 4.5

11.

ONES	4
PENNIES	3
CHANGE	$ 4.03

5.

ONES	3
QUARTERS	1
DIMES	1
PENNIES	3
CHANGE	$ 3.38

6.

ONES	1
QUARTERS	2
PENNIES	4
CHANGE	$ 1.54

7.

FIVES	1
ONES	1
DIMES	2
PENNIES	2
CHANGE	$ 6.22

8.

FIVES	1
ONES	2
QUARTERS	2
NICKELS	1
CHANGE	$ 7.55

9.

TENS	1
FIVES	1
ONES	2
QUARTERS	1
DIMES	1
NICKELS	1
PENNIES	4
CHANGE	$ 17.44

Skills File

Computer Literacy

Tables

Skills File

Rounding whole numbers and decimals, pages 4–5

Round each number to the nearest thousand and nearest ten.

1. 709 1000; 710
2. 518 1000; 520
3. 676 1000; 680
4. 983 1000; 980
5. 845 1000; 850
6. 597 1000; 600
7. 1386 1000; 1390
8. 4427 4000; 4430
9. 8391 8000; 8390
10. 6852 7000; 6850
11. 2416 2000; 2420
12. 9637 10,000; 9640
13. 5234 5000; 5230
14. 8891 9000; 8890
15. 7084 7000; 7080
16. 2498 2000; 2500
17. 9536 10,000; 9540
18. 5167 5000; 5170
19. 8698 9000; 8700
20. 3094 3000; 3090
21. 4972 5000; 4970
22. 7889 8000; 7890
23. 6503 7000; 6500
24. 1484 1000; 1480
25. 6728 7000; 6730
26. 4102 4000; 4100
27. 2776 3000; 2780
28. 9383 9000; 9380
29. 8671 9000; 8670
30. 1867 2000; 1870
31. 7561 8000; 7560
32. 5555 6000; 5560
33. 9674 10,000; 9670
34. 2021 2000; 2020
35. 4999 5000; 5000
36. 7903 8000; 7900
37. 96,932 97,000; 96,930
38. 20,248 20,000; 20,250
39. 84,853 85,000; 84,850
40. 50,626 51,000; 50,630
41. 61,472 61,000; 61,470
42. 22,319 22,000; 22,320
43. 11,707 12,000; 11,710
44. 30,858 31,000; 30,860
45. 43,674 44,000; 43,670
46. 94,153 94,000; 94,150
47. 74,906 75,000; 74,910
48. 56,521 57,000; 56,520
49. 35,032 35,000; 35,030
50. 10,791 11,000; 10,790
51. 46,957 47,000; 46,960
52. 52,385 52,000; 52,390
53. 97,503 98,000; 97,500
54. 71,807 72,000; 71,810
55. 25,013 25,000; 25,010
56. 47,203 47,000; 47,200
57. 58,689 59,000; 58,690
58. 62,474 62,000; 62,470
59. 79,619 80,000; 79,620
60. 89,795 90,000; 89,800

Round each number to the nearest whole number and nearest hundredth.

61. 4.167 4; 4.17
62. 1.408 1; 1.41
63. 7.856 8; 7.86
64. 5.714 6; 5.71
65. 6.293 6; 6.29
66. 8.641 9; 8.64
67. 2.9381 3; 2.94
68. 3.0857 3; 3.09
69. 9.7292 10; 9.73
70. 2.3904 2; 2.39
71. 3.4729 3; 3.47
72. 6.5175 7; 6.52
73. 37.109 37; 37.11
74. 94.014 94; 94.01
75. 49.658 50; 49.66
76. 88.761 89; 88.76
77. 68.256 68; 68.26
78. 40.322 40; 40.32
79. 31.493 31; 31.49
80. 22.945 23; 22.95
81. 71.547 72; 71.55
82. 55.008 55; 55.01
83. 90.232 90; 90.23
84. 16.874 17; 16.87
85. 79.5301 80; 79.53
86. 41.2674 41; 41.27
87. 26.3788 26; 26.38
88. 59.6684 60; 59.67
89. 86.0473 86; 86.05
90. 25.7857 26; 25.79
91. 11.9353 12; 11.94
92. 72.4822 72; 72.48
93. 99.8294 100; 99.83
94. 33.5738 34; 33.57
95. 65.0687 65; 65.07
96. 84.7111 85; 84.71
97. 268.866 269; 268.87
98. 689.742 690; 689.74
99. 912.049 912; 912.05
100. 567.605 568; 567.61
101. 403.188 403; 403.19
102. 741.222 741; 741.22
103. 100.885 101; 100.89
104. 808.351 808; 808.35
105. 352.879 353; 352.88
106. 973.624 974; 973.62
107. 735.038 735; 735.04
108. 270.181 270; 270.18
109. 646.7184 647; 646.72
110. 439.8209 440; 439.82
111. 574.1852 574; 574.19
112. 671.4135 671; 671.41
113. 821.6397 822; 821.64
114. 757.2531 757; 757.25
115. 248.3418 248; 248.34
116. 189.7416 190; 189.74
117. 545.5665 546; 545.57
118. 337.2746 337; 337.27
119. 499.8283 500; 499.83
120. 986.9772 987; 986.98

Skills File

Adding whole numbers and decimals, pages 6–7

1. 65 + 18 — 83

2. 27 + 43 — 70

3. 89 + 57 — 146

4. 65 + 96 — 161

5. 18, 7 + 75 — 100

6. 21, 36 + 3 — 60

7. 54, 78 + 39 — 171

8. 17, 42 + 73 — 132

9. 81, 40 + 25 — 146

10. 50, 65 + 94 — 209

11. 64, 37 + 18 — 119

12. 45, 3, 22 + 14 — 84

13. 41, 35, 14 + 7 — 97

14. 56, 80, 21 + 15 — 172

15. 92, 77, 23 + 40 — 232

16. 11, 42, 30 + 12 — 95

17. 56, 48, 70 + 62 — 236

18. 19, 54, 68 + 72 — 213

19. 96, 85, 22 + 58 — 261

20. 371 + 265 — 636

21. 203 + 978 — 1181

22. 189 + 726 — 915

23. 426 + 609 — 1035

24. 404, 82 + 360 — 846

25. 343, 261 + 35 — 639

26. 472, 148 + 606 — 1226

27. 229, 705 + 991 — 1925

28. 316, 283 + 257 — 856

29. 589, 884 + 625 — 2098

30. 873, 559 + 167 — 1599

31. 7.38 + 2.9 — 10.28

32. 8.4 + 3.56 — 11.96

33. 1.17 + 4.39 — 5.56

34. 5.04 + 6.79 — 11.83

35. 21.53 + 65.08 — 86.61

36. 84.77 + 40.62 — 125.39

37. 0.2, 0.7 + 0.8 — 1.7

38. 2.4, 0.6 + 3.2 — 6.2

39. 7.5, 3.23 + 6.1 — 16.83

40. 8.49, 2.3 + 1.52 — 12.31

41. 7.9, 9.04 + 2.83 — 19.77

42. 5.46, 8.02 + 0.63 — 14.11

43. 8.52, 0.04 + 3.07 — 11.63

44. 4.67, 1.82 + 9.05 — 15.54

45. 4.06, 5.72 + 3.108 — 12.888

46. 4.452, 2.19 + 9.68 — 16.322

47. 8.1, 2.8, 7.5 + 5.4 — 23.8

48. 7.3, 0.7, 6.8 + 4.39 — 19.19

49. 8.2, 3.04, 1.5 + 9.7 — 22.44

50. 4.03, 0.14, 0.8 + 1.9 — 6.87

51. 6.7, 2.05, 7.36 + 0.4 — 16.51

52. 3.8, 5.27, 1.13 + 5.05 — 15.25

53. 7.64, 4.38, 0.95 + 8.5 — 21.47

54. 0.28, 9.51, 0.04 + 2.97 — 12.8

55. 8.65, 0.23, 3.14 + 6.37 — 18.39

56. 8.13, 0.285, 9.47 + 0.39 — 18.275

57. 0.17, 9.59, 4.509 + 1.26 — 15.529

58. 9.19, 5.26, 0.48 + 2.606 — 17.536

59. 8.776, 4.81, 3.03 + 6.45 — 23.066

Skills File

Subtracting whole numbers and decimals, pages 6–7

1.	78 − 35	43
2.	94 − 83	11
3.	34 − 9	25
4.	21 − 8	13
5.	52 − 3	49
6.	60 − 4	56
7.	94 − 69	25
8.	76 − 47	29
9.	63 − 17	46
10.	44 − 25	19
11.	80 − 37	43
12.	50 − 19	31
13.	32 − 29	3
14.	87 − 79	8
15.	283 − 191	92
16.	763 − 488	275
17.	970 − 343	627
18.	708 − 314	394
19.	413 − 86	327
20.	865 − 81	784
21.	607 − 38	569
22.	7946 − 2871	5075
23.	5126 − 3718	1408
24.	7103 − 1214	5889
25.	5001 − 3745	1256
26.	1782 − 649	1133
27.	8124 − 315	7809
28.	4334 − 702	3632
29.	88.4 − 53.7	34.7
30.	74.8 − 2.5	72.3
31.	17.5 − 6.9	10.6
32.	90.1 − 65.3	24.8
33.	76.47 − 21.35	55.12
34.	41.96 − 38.59	3.37
35.	53.07 − 21.64	31.43
36.	17.42 − 8.17	9.25
37.	47.79 − 0.38	47.41
38.	28.537 − 14.216	14.321
39.	32.045 − 18.637	13.408
40.	71.894 − 4.968	66.926
41.	27.158 − 6.253	20.905
42.	50.297 − 8.759	41.538
43.	87.26 − 59.8	27.46
44.	23.74 − 18.4	5.34
45.	97.16 − 3.2	93.96
46.	54.07 − 6.1	47.97
47.	73.85 − 31.4	42.45
48.	91.32 − 38.4	52.92
49.	58.241 − 3.19	55.051
50.	45.939 − 21.87	24.069
51.	70.427 − 27.99	42.437
52.	40.176 − 26.5	13.676
53.	56.714 − 23.4	33.314
54.	15.673 − 8.8	6.873
55.	85.061 − 9.4	75.661
56.	59.347 − 18.9	40.447
57.	61.4 − 48	13.4
58.	80.7 − 49	31.7
59.	93.2 − 57	36.2
60.	26.6 − 8	18.6
61.	73.7 − 48	25.7
62.	42.61 − 35	7.61
63.	28.53 − 19	9.53
64.	71.29 − 55	16.29
65.	90.14 − 67	23.14
66.	87 − 4.1	82.9
67.	27 − 6.3	20.7
68.	84 − 59.5	24.5
69.	52 − 18.3	33.7
70.	30 − 29.6	0.4
71.	28 − 14.81	13.19
72.	63 − 21.84	41.16
73.	55 − 7.39	47.61
74.	70 − 43.06	26.94
75.	18.75 − 6.672	12.078
76.	95.03 − 32.671	62.359
77.	20.05 − 18.164	1.886
78.	43.09 − 21.426	21.664
79.	82.91 − 7.525	75.385
80.	57.6 − 3.244	54.356
81.	83.7 − 5.625	78.075
82.	92.1 − 17.066	75.034
83.	50.3 − 36.218	14.082
84.	41.2 − 29.489	11.711

Skills File

Multiplying whole numbers, pages 8–9

1.	700	× 3	2100
2.	100	× 6	600
3.	200	× 8	1600
4.	900	× 5	4500
5.	400	× 7	2800
6.	200	× 5	1000
7.	1000	× 8	8000
8.	3000	× 4	12,000
9.	6000	× 9	54,000
10.	9000	× 2	18,000
11.	5000	× 4	20,000
12.	7000	× 6	42,000
13.	10	× 30	300
14.	20	× 80	1600
15.	40	× 70	2800
16.	60	× 10	600
17.	50	× 30	1500
18.	80	× 50	4000
19.	100	× 90	9000
20.	300	× 80	24,000
21.	900	× 40	36,000
22.	200	× 90	18,000
23.	500	× 60	30,000
24.	700	× 10	7000
25.	400	× 30	12,000
26.	800	× 50	40,000
27.	600	× 20	12,000
28.	200	× 70	14,000
29.	300	× 90	27,000
30.	400	× 80	32,000
31.	7000	× 60	420,000
32.	3000	× 80	240,000
33.	9000	× 50	450,000
34.	800	× 900	720,000
35.	500	× 700	350,000
36.	100	× 600	60,000
37.	4000	× 100	400,000
38.	2000	× 800	1,600,000
39.	7000	× 400	2,800,000
40.	6000	× 2000	12,000,000
41.	1000	× 3000	3,000,000
42.	5000	× 4000	20,000,000
43.	67	× 26	1742
44.	41	× 53	2173
45.	34	× 22	748
46.	40	× 67	2680
47.	82	× 80	6560
48.	28	× 74	2072
49.	55	× 73	4015
50.	84	× 59	4956
51.	388	× 45	17,460
52.	679	× 18	12,222
53.	612	× 33	20,196
54.	507	× 86	43,602
55.	801	× 45	36,045
56.	428	× 67	28,676
57.	325	× 89	28,925
58.	567	× 14	7938
59.	208	× 95	19,760
60.	223	× 149	33,227
61.	257	× 306	78,642
62.	803	× 142	114,026
63.	643	× 718	461,674
64.	978	× 535	523,230
65.	161	× 824	132,664
66.	432	× 218	94,176
67.	686	× 504	345,744
68.	6530	× 49	319,970
69.	7238	× 72	521,136
70.	1472	× 40	58,880
71.	9053	× 80	724,240
72.	5416	× 26	140,816
73.	6923	× 35	242,305
74.	7672	× 54	414,288
75.	6958	× 63	438,354
76.	3042	× 51	155,142
77.	8821	× 68	599,828
78.	9455	× 26	245,830
79.	7158	× 247	1,768,026
80.	5904	× 832	4,912,128
81.	9268	× 107	991,676
82.	5296	× 308	1,631,168
83.	2087	× 645	1,346,115
84.	7009	× 836	5,859,524

Skills File

Multiplying decimals, pages 10–11

No.	Number	Multiplier	Answer
1.	0.6	× 0.4	0.24
2.	0.5	× 0.9	0.45
3.	0.7	× 0.8	0.56
4.	0.01	× 0.6	0.006
5.	0.02	× 0.7	0.014
6.	0.08	× 0.3	0.024
7.	0.04	× 0.5	0.02
8.	0.03	× 0.01	0.0003
9.	0.07	× 0.04	0.0028
10.	0.02	× 0.09	0.0018
11.	0.06	× 0.08	0.0048
12.	0.003	× 0.6	0.0018
13.	0.001	× 0.7	0.0007
14.	0.008	× 0.2	0.0016
15.	0.004	× 0.5	0.002
16.	0.02	× 8	0.16
17.	0.08	× 1	0.08
18.	0.05	× 7	0.35
19.	0.03	× 2	0.06
20.	0.001	× 3	0.003
21.	0.004	× 9	0.036
22.	0.007	× 6	0.042
23.	0.008	× 2	0.016
24.	0.005	× 50	0.25
25.	0.003	× 70	0.21
26.	0.006	× 80	0.48
27.	2000	× 0.9	1800
28.	4000	× 0.1	400
29.	9000	× 0.6	5400
30.	5000	× 0.3	1500
31.	0.004	× 0.06	0.00024
32.	0.003	× 0.08	0.00024
33.	0.007	× 0.02	0.00014
34.	0.002	× 0.04	0.00008
35.	300	× 0.06	18
36.	100	× 0.09	9
37.	700	× 0.04	28
38.	200	× 0.06	12
39.	4000	× 0.03	120
40.	9000	× 0.05	450
41.	6000	× 0.01	60
42.	5000	× 0.08	400
43.	770	× 0.68	523.6
44.	580	× 0.34	197.2
45.	409	× 0.23	94.07
46.	604	× 0.19	114.76
47.	0.24	× 89	21.36
48.	0.36	× 37	13.32
49.	0.68	× 16	10.88
50.	0.7501	× 22	16.5022
51.	0.2034	× 58	11.7972
52.	0.5083	× 27	13.7241
53.	3652	× 0.15	547.8
54.	7378	× 0.21	1549.38
55.	5447	× 0.87	4738.89
56.	0.452	× 8.1	3.6612
57.	0.723	× 1.4	1.0122
58.	0.639	× 9.2	5.8788
59.	0.741	× 3.6	2.6676
60.	0.873	× 0.72	0.62856
61.	0.206	× 0.63	0.12978
62.	0.592	× 0.78	0.46176
63.	0.749	× 3.16	2.36684
64.	0.412	× 7.23	2.97876
65.	40.2	× 5.07	203.814
66.	81.3	× 6.38	518.694
67.	57.8	× 5.81	335.818
68.	62.9	× 7.3	459.17
69.	84.1	× 1.9	159.79
70.	47.8	× 2.7	129.06
71.	30.5	× 8.5	259.25
72.	0.124	× 0.362	0.044888
73.	0.819	× 0.703	0.575757
74.	0.376	× 0.105	0.03948
75.	8.051	× 36.8	296.2768
76.	4.695	× 73.2	343.674
77.	2.597	× 98.6	256.0642
78.	7.002	× 65.9	461.4318
79.	0.076	× 29.08	2.21008
80.	0.802	× 90.46	72.54892
81.	0.538	× 74.13	39.88194
82.	0.6087	× 23.41	14.249667
83.	0.3043	× 91.82	27.940826
84.	0.5309	× 84.52	44.871668

Skills File

Dividing whole numbers, pages 12–13

1. 2)463 — 231 R1
2. 7)821 — 117 R2
3. 9)846 — 94
4. 8)702 — 87 R6
5. 7)4136 — 590 R6
6. 6)8256 — 1376
7. 4)1273 — 318 R1
8. 3)6728 — 2242 R2
9. 6)7108 — 1184 R4
10. 9)3618 — 402
11. 7)5920 — 845 R5
12. 2)9523 — 4761 R1
13. 4)3007 — 751 R3
14. 5)1234 — 246 R4
15. 8)8867 — 1108 R3
16. 3)2050 — 683 R1
17. 4)8756 — 2189
18. 6)81429 — 13,571 R3
19. 7)50633 — 7233 R2
20. 5)31954 — 6390 R4
21. 9)92648 — 10,294 R2
22. 61)725 — 11 R54
23. 14)359 — 25 R9
24. 36)288 — 8
25. 42)176 — 4 R8
26. 79)870 — 11 R1
27. 82)563 — 6 R71
28. 27)937 — 34 R19
29. 51)428 — 8 R20
30. 66)255 — 3 R57
31. 93)986 — 10 R56
32. 56)805 — 14 R21
33. 31)172 — 5 R17
34. 17)643 — 37 R14
35. 64)781 — 12 R13
36. 85)999 — 11 R64
37. 77)200 — 2 R46
38. 43)136 — 3 R7
39. 50)487 — 9 R37
40. 94)950 — 10 R10
41. 22)215 — 9R17
42. 68)404 — 5 R64
43. 42)5862 — 139 R24
44. 76)4972 — 65 R32
45. 91)2634 — 28 R86
46. 23)1288 — 56
47. 39)8114 — 208 R2
48. 75)3435 — 45 R60
49. 57)3592 — 63 R1
50. 63)1286 — 20 R26
51. 27)8346 — 309 R3
52. 32)3159 — 98 R23
53. 70)9403 — 134 R23
54. 81)7342 — 90 R52
55. 65)7878 — 121 R13
56. 51)9161 — 179 R32
57. 31)8835 — 285
58. 47)1048 — 22 R14
59. 66)3308 — 50 R8
60. 25)2463 — 98 R13
61. 88)9006 — 102 R30
62. 94)5526 — 58 R74
63. 46)4407 — 95 R37
64. 22)39378 — 1789 R20
65. 52)39728 — 764
66. 60)48901 — 815 R1
67. 72)65989 — 916 R37
68. 17)83424 — 4907 R5
69. 91)85736 — 942 R14
70. 87)90480 — 1040
71. 37)30555 — 825 R30
72. 49)86047 — 1756 R3
73. 28)94613 — 3379 R1
74. 56)823914 — 14,712 R42
75. 20)149298 — 7464 R18
76. 64)173696 — 2714
77. 16)181457 — 11,341 R1
78. 97)482582 — 4975 R7
79. 33)347096 — 10,518 R2
80. 71)375534 — 5289 R15
81. 46)920414 — 20,009
82. 68)234405 — 3447 R9
83. 86)261379 — 3039 R25
84. 32)974021 — 30,438 R5
85. 441)89027 — 201 R386
86. 703)24368 — 34 R466
87. 282)76446 — 271 R24
88. 927)42175 — 45 R460
89. 870)10653 — 12 R213
90. 376)68808 — 183
91. 135)87146 — 645 R71
92. 564)55364 — 98 R92
93. 656)23209 — 35 R249
94. 488)70216 — 143 R432
95. 834)625549 — 750 R49
96. 263)248745 — 945 R210
97. 454)476246 — 1049
98. 622)818288 — 1315 R358
99. 185)140535 — 759 R120
100. 506)345092 — 682
101. 313)920369 — 2940 R149
102. 911)702636 — 771 R255
103. 586)900413 — 1536 R317
104. 204)863446 — 4232 R118
105. 781)532931 — 682 R289

Skills File

Dividing decimals, pages 12-13

Find each quotient to the nearest hundredth.

3.84 **1.** 2)7.67	1.04 **21.** 95)98.9	2.41 **41.** 3.2)7.7	4.32 **61.** 0.19)0.82	6.67 **81.** 4.05)27
5.09 **2.** 7)35.63	1.15 **22.** 64)73.8	0.18 **42.** 7.4)1.3	0.58 **62.** 0.25)0.145	5.04 **82.** 8.33)42
232.18 **3.** 4)928.7	2.06 **23.** 39)80.4	1.64 **43.** 2.8)4.6	0.48 **63.** 0.64)0.309	7.59 **83.** 6.19)47
213.63 **4.** 3)640.9	1.25 **24.** 41)51.2	1.51 **44.** 6.1)9.2	2.42 **64.** 0.38)0.918	20.35 **84.** 1.72)35
53.77 **5.** 6)322.6	1.23 **25.** 53)65.23	0.43 **45.** 9.5)4.1	1.64 **65.** 0.51)0.836	18.05 **85.** 29.8)538
94.46 **6.** 5)472.3	0.38 **26.** 81)31.06	0.87 **46.** 8.3)7.2	0.52 **66.** 0.98)0.505	10.63 **86.** 70.2)746
1112.63 **7.** 8)8901	0.85 **27.** 98)83.54	0.47 **47.** 5.9)2.8	0.88 **67.** 0.73)0.641	21.55 **87.** 40.1)864
792.44 **8.** 9)7132	30.84 **28.** 23)709.41	23.95 **48.** 4.1)98.2	0.17 **68.** 0.62)0.103	6.45 **88.** 93.2)601
925.57 **9.** 7)6479	6.12 **29.** 77)471.29	4.14 **49.** 7.4)30.6	12.88 **69.** 3.24)41.72	5.85 **89.** 69.7)408
1597.17 **10.** 6)9583	5.21 **30.** 46)239.75	11.87 **50.** 5.2)61.7	6.11 **70.** 9.38)57.35	12.87 **90.** 32.4)417
0.36 **11.** 12)4.37	12.59 **31.** 324)4078	5.67 **51.** 4.8)27.2	10.68 **71.** 2.98)31.82	5.98 **91.** 95.8)573
0.07 **12.** 55)3.72	6.11 **32.** 938)5735	7.38 **52.** 6.3)46.5	3.92 **72.** 6.07)23.79	10.74 **92.** 29.6)318
0.07 **13.** 86)5.64	10.68 **33.** 298)3182	18.56 **53.** 2.7)50.1	31.39 **73.** 1.69)53.05	19.36 **93.** 0.47)9.1
0.12 **14.** 31)3.78	3.92 **34.** 607)2379	8.15 **54.** 9.6)78.2	8.33 **74.** 8.43)70.24	23.23 **94.** 0.31)7.2
0.78 **15.** 67)52.4	31.39 **35.** 169)5305	0.22 **55.** 0.65)0.14	12.91 **75.** 7.36)95.01	3.78 **95.** 2.51)9.5
0.24 **16.** 74)17.6	0.08 **36.** 843)70.24	1.63 **56.** 0.24)0.39	4.65 **76.** 4.26)19.82	1.03 **96.** 8.46)8.7
2.65 **17.** 28)74.2	0.12 **37.** 736)90.51	5.59 **57.** 0.17)0.95	18.21 **77.** 3.13)57	0.47 **97.** 5.09)2.4
0.55 **18.** 93)50.8	0.31 **38.** 142)43.57	0.68 **58.** 0.41)0.28	30.52 **78.** 2.49)76	2.28 **98.** 3.77)8.6
1.58 **19.** 40)63.1	0.23 **39.** 305)68.72	0.56 **59.** 0.93)0.52	48.19 **79.** 1.93)93	0.86 **99.** 9.21)7.9
1.61 **20.** 17)27.4	0.08 **40.** 718)58.34	0.37 **60.** 0.57)0.21	9.83 **80.** 7.02)69	0.41 **100.** 7.62)3.1

Skills File

Comparing and renaming fractions and mixed numbers, pages 14–15

Compare. Replace ● with <, >, or =.

1. $\frac{7}{8}$ ● $\frac{5}{8}$ $>$	10. $\frac{5}{6}$ ● $\frac{3}{4}$ $>$
2. $\frac{2}{3}$ ● $\frac{9}{12}$ $<$	11. $\frac{5}{8}$ ● $\frac{7}{12}$ $>$
3. $\frac{6}{16}$ ● $\frac{3}{8}$ $=$	12. $\frac{3}{10}$ ● $\frac{4}{15}$ $>$
4. $\frac{11}{15}$ ● $\frac{3}{5}$ $>$	13. $3\frac{4}{5}$ ● $4\frac{1}{8}$ $<$
5. $\frac{3}{7}$ ● $\frac{1}{3}$ $>$	14. $7\frac{2}{3}$ ● $8\frac{7}{8}$ $<$
6. $\frac{1}{2}$ ● $\frac{2}{5}$ $>$	15. $2\frac{3}{5}$ ● $2\frac{3}{7}$ $>$
7. $\frac{3}{4}$ ● $\frac{6}{7}$ $<$	16. $1\frac{7}{8}$ ● $1\frac{7}{9}$ $>$
8. $\frac{2}{5}$ ● $\frac{4}{9}$ $<$	17. $5\frac{1}{4}$ ● $5\frac{1}{3}$ $<$
9. $\frac{1}{9}$ ● $\frac{1}{6}$ $<$	18. $6\frac{9}{10}$ ● $6\frac{27}{30}$ $=$

Rename as a fraction.

46. $6\frac{3}{7}$ $\frac{45}{7}$	55. $8\frac{3}{5}$ $\frac{43}{5}$	64. $10\frac{3}{4}$ $\frac{43}{4}$
47. $1\frac{1}{4}$ $\frac{5}{4}$	56. $2\frac{9}{10}$ $\frac{29}{10}$	65. $8\frac{5}{8}$ $\frac{69}{8}$
48. $4\frac{1}{6}$ $\frac{25}{6}$	57. $4\frac{7}{8}$ $\frac{39}{8}$	66. 12 $\frac{12}{1}$
49. 7 $\frac{7}{1}$	58. $1\frac{4}{7}$ $\frac{11}{7}$	67. $7\frac{3}{11}$ $\frac{80}{11}$
50. $5\frac{1}{5}$ $\frac{26}{5}$	59. $6\frac{5}{6}$ $\frac{41}{6}$	68. $4\frac{7}{16}$ $\frac{71}{16}$
51. $2\frac{5}{8}$ $\frac{21}{8}$	60. 4 $\frac{4}{1}$	69. $6\frac{2}{15}$ $\frac{92}{15}$
52. $9\frac{2}{3}$ $\frac{29}{3}$	61. $3\frac{2}{9}$ $\frac{29}{9}$	70. $3\frac{5}{18}$ $\frac{59}{18}$
53. $8\frac{1}{10}$ $\frac{81}{10}$	62. $9\frac{7}{11}$ $\frac{106}{11}$	71. $11\frac{10}{11}$ $\frac{131}{11}$
54. $3\frac{1}{2}$ $\frac{7}{2}$	63. $5\frac{1}{12}$ $\frac{61}{12}$	72. $12\frac{13}{16}$ $\frac{205}{16}$

Rename in lowest terms.

19. $\frac{6}{10}$ $\frac{3}{5}$	28. $\frac{11}{88}$ $\frac{1}{8}$	37. $\frac{14}{63}$ $\frac{2}{9}$
20. $\frac{3}{15}$ $\frac{1}{5}$	29. $\frac{7}{14}$ $\frac{1}{2}$	38. $\frac{21}{48}$ $\frac{7}{16}$
21. $\frac{6}{18}$ $\frac{1}{3}$	30. $\frac{3}{24}$ $\frac{1}{8}$	39. $\frac{16}{80}$ $\frac{1}{5}$
22. $\frac{4}{14}$ $\frac{2}{7}$	31. $\frac{60}{100}$ $\frac{3}{5}$	40. $\frac{72}{81}$ $\frac{8}{9}$
23. $\frac{5}{35}$ $\frac{1}{7}$	32. $\frac{48}{54}$ $\frac{8}{9}$	41. $\frac{20}{90}$ $\frac{2}{9}$
24. $\frac{10}{12}$ $\frac{5}{6}$	33. $\frac{12}{72}$ $\frac{1}{6}$	42. $\frac{84}{100}$ $\frac{21}{25}$
25. $\frac{16}{24}$ $\frac{2}{3}$	34. $\frac{21}{27}$ $\frac{7}{9}$	43. $\frac{18}{81}$ $\frac{2}{9}$
26. $\frac{25}{100}$ $\frac{1}{4}$	35. $\frac{24}{30}$ $\frac{4}{5}$	44. $\frac{28}{42}$ $\frac{2}{3}$
27. $\frac{39}{42}$ $\frac{13}{14}$	36. $\frac{18}{63}$ $\frac{2}{7}$	45. $\frac{49}{56}$ $\frac{7}{8}$

Rename as a mixed number.

73. $\frac{5}{2}$ $2\frac{1}{2}$	82. $\frac{38}{7}$ $5\frac{3}{7}$	91. $\frac{50}{30}$ $1\frac{2}{3}$
74. $\frac{9}{4}$ $2\frac{1}{4}$	83. $\frac{33}{6}$ $5\frac{1}{2}$	92. $\frac{78}{12}$ $6\frac{1}{2}$
75. $\frac{7}{5}$ $1\frac{2}{5}$	84. $\frac{45}{9}$ 5	93. $\frac{56}{24}$ $2\frac{1}{3}$
76. $\frac{25}{6}$ $4\frac{1}{6}$	85. $\frac{29}{8}$ $3\frac{5}{8}$	94. $\frac{63}{15}$ $4\frac{1}{5}$
77. $\frac{19}{3}$ $6\frac{1}{3}$	86. $\frac{18}{4}$ $4\frac{1}{2}$	95. $\frac{45}{27}$ $1\frac{2}{3}$
78. $\frac{27}{8}$ $3\frac{3}{8}$	87. $\frac{25}{2}$ $12\frac{1}{2}$	96. $\frac{64}{8}$ 8
79. $\frac{42}{7}$ 6	88. $\frac{53}{5}$ $10\frac{3}{5}$	97. $\frac{121}{10}$ $12\frac{1}{10}$
80. $\frac{13}{8}$ $1\frac{5}{8}$	89. $\frac{51}{7}$ $7\frac{2}{7}$	98. $\frac{84}{11}$ $7\frac{7}{11}$
81. $\frac{73}{9}$ $8\frac{1}{9}$	90. $\frac{40}{16}$ $2\frac{1}{2}$	99. $\frac{143}{12}$ $11\frac{11}{12}$

Skills File

Multiplying fractions and mixed numbers, pages 16–17

1. $\frac{1}{3} \times \frac{4}{5}$ $\frac{4}{15}$
2. $\frac{3}{5} \times \frac{1}{4}$ $\frac{3}{20}$
3. $\frac{1}{2} \times \frac{5}{6}$ $\frac{5}{12}$
4. $\frac{2}{7} \times \frac{2}{3}$ $\frac{4}{21}$
5. $\frac{1}{2} \times \frac{5}{8}$ $\frac{5}{16}$
6. $\frac{3}{7} \times \frac{1}{3}$ $\frac{1}{7}$
7. $\frac{4}{5} \times \frac{3}{4}$ $\frac{3}{5}$
8. $\frac{2}{3} \times \frac{7}{8}$ $\frac{7}{12}$
9. $\frac{6}{11} \times \frac{1}{3}$ $\frac{2}{11}$
10. $\frac{2}{9} \times \frac{9}{10}$ $\frac{1}{5}$
11. $\frac{5}{9} \times \frac{3}{5}$ $\frac{1}{3}$
12. $\frac{3}{8} \times \frac{4}{15}$ $\frac{1}{10}$
13. $\frac{5}{6} \times \frac{4}{5}$ $\frac{2}{3}$
14. $\frac{2}{9} \times \frac{8}{9}$ $\frac{16}{81}$
15. $\frac{3}{4} \times \frac{8}{9}$ $\frac{2}{3}$
16. $\frac{5}{6} \times \frac{7}{10}$ $\frac{7}{12}$
17. $\frac{5}{12} \times \frac{7}{12}$ $\frac{35}{144}$
18. $\frac{5}{8} \times \frac{16}{25}$ $\frac{2}{5}$
19. $\frac{3}{14} \times \frac{7}{18}$ $\frac{1}{12}$
20. $\frac{22}{25} \times \frac{10}{11}$ $\frac{4}{5}$
21. $\frac{8}{9} \times \frac{15}{28}$ $\frac{10}{21}$
22. $\frac{1}{2} \times 5$ $2\frac{1}{2}$
23. $\frac{2}{3} \times 7$ $4\frac{2}{3}$
24. $\frac{3}{4} \times 8$ 6
25. $\frac{1}{4} \times 12$ 3
26. $4 \times \frac{1}{3}$ $1\frac{1}{3}$
27. $24 \times \frac{1}{12}$ 2
28. $20 \times \frac{3}{10}$ 6
29. $6 \times \frac{2}{5}$ $2\frac{2}{5}$
30. $\frac{3}{8} \times 16$ 6
31. $42 \times \frac{2}{9}$ $9\frac{1}{3}$
32. $56 \times \frac{6}{7}$ 48
33. $\frac{1}{10} \times 36$ $3\frac{3}{5}$
34. $\frac{2}{3} \times 51$ 34
35. $\frac{4}{5} \times 35$ 28
36. $72 \times \frac{1}{8}$ 9
37. $100 \times \frac{7}{10}$ 70
38. $\frac{5}{12} \times 28$ $11\frac{2}{3}$
39. $14 \times \frac{2}{11}$ $2\frac{6}{11}$
40. $22 \times \frac{3}{7}$ $9\frac{3}{7}$
41. $\frac{8}{9} \times 30$ $26\frac{2}{3}$
42. $\frac{7}{10} \times 64$ $44\frac{4}{5}$
43. $\frac{4}{7} \times 1\frac{2}{5}$ $\frac{4}{5}$
44. $\frac{1}{2} \times 1\frac{1}{5}$ $\frac{3}{5}$
45. $4\frac{3}{8} \times \frac{2}{5}$ $1\frac{3}{4}$
46. $3\frac{1}{2} \times \frac{6}{7}$ 3
47. $\frac{2}{3} \times 1\frac{5}{16}$ $\frac{7}{8}$
48. $2\frac{5}{8} \times \frac{4}{7}$ $1\frac{1}{2}$
49. $1\frac{3}{8} \times \frac{8}{11}$ 1
50. $\frac{9}{10} \times 1\frac{1}{4}$ $1\frac{1}{8}$
51. $\frac{5}{6} \times 2\frac{1}{3}$ $1\frac{17}{18}$
52. $3\frac{1}{9} \times \frac{1}{2}$ $1\frac{5}{9}$
53. $\frac{3}{5} \times 6\frac{2}{3}$ 4
54. $5\frac{1}{4} \times \frac{1}{6}$ $\frac{7}{8}$
55. $4\frac{2}{7} \times \frac{3}{5}$ $2\frac{4}{7}$
56. $\frac{5}{9} \times 15\frac{3}{4}$ $8\frac{3}{4}$
57. $1\frac{1}{4} \times 8$ 10
58. $3 \times 1\frac{1}{2}$ $4\frac{1}{2}$
59. $12 \times 1\frac{1}{8}$ $13\frac{1}{2}$
60. $9 \times 3\frac{2}{3}$ 33
61. $1\frac{7}{8} \times 6$ $11\frac{1}{4}$
62. $2\frac{1}{3} \times 7$ $16\frac{1}{3}$
63. $4 \times 5\frac{1}{6}$ $20\frac{2}{3}$
64. $5 \times 3\frac{3}{10}$ $16\frac{1}{2}$
65. $4 \times 4\frac{1}{2}$ 18
66. $1\frac{1}{6} \times 9$ $10\frac{1}{2}$
67. $24 \times 4\frac{1}{3}$ 104
68. $1\frac{1}{12} \times 8$ $8\frac{2}{3}$
69. $4 \times 7\frac{2}{3}$ $30\frac{2}{3}$
70. $5\frac{5}{12} \times 6$ $32\frac{1}{2}$
71. $2\frac{1}{2} \times 3\frac{1}{3}$ $8\frac{1}{3}$
72. $3\frac{3}{4} \times 1\frac{1}{3}$ 5
73. $1\frac{1}{2} \times 2\frac{1}{6}$ $3\frac{1}{4}$
74. $5\frac{1}{3} \times 1\frac{1}{8}$ 6
75. $3\frac{1}{2} \times 2\frac{1}{3}$ $8\frac{1}{6}$
76. $2\frac{2}{3} \times 1\frac{3}{4}$ $4\frac{2}{3}$
77. $3\frac{8}{9} \times 2\frac{2}{5}$ $9\frac{1}{3}$
78. $2\frac{1}{3} \times 1\frac{2}{7}$ 3
79. $5\frac{1}{4} \times 1\frac{2}{3}$ $8\frac{3}{4}$
80. $3\frac{3}{5} \times 4\frac{4}{9}$ 16
81. $1\frac{3}{7} \times 8\frac{3}{4}$ $12\frac{1}{2}$
82. $2\frac{2}{15} \times 2\frac{1}{12}$ $4\frac{4}{9}$
83. $6\frac{3}{5} \times 2\frac{7}{9}$ $18\frac{1}{3}$
84. $4\frac{4}{15} \times 5\frac{5}{16}$ $22\frac{2}{3}$
85. $\frac{1}{2} \times \frac{2}{5} \times \frac{1}{3}$ $\frac{1}{15}$
86. $\frac{2}{3} \times \frac{1}{2} \times \frac{5}{8}$ $\frac{5}{24}$
87. $\frac{1}{4} \times \frac{4}{5} \times \frac{3}{8}$ $\frac{3}{40}$
88. $\frac{1}{2} \times \frac{5}{6} \times 3\frac{3}{5}$ $1\frac{1}{2}$
89. $\frac{1}{6} \times 3 \times \frac{5}{8}$ $\frac{5}{16}$
90. $2 \times \frac{5}{8} \times \frac{6}{7}$ $1\frac{1}{14}$
91. $1\frac{2}{3} \times \frac{4}{5} \times 9$ 12
92. $\frac{1}{2} \times 4\frac{1}{2} \times 3\frac{1}{2}$ $7\frac{7}{8}$
93. $\frac{2}{3} \times \frac{3}{8} \times 7$ $1\frac{3}{4}$
94. $\frac{5}{6} \times 3 \times \frac{4}{15}$ $\frac{2}{3}$
95. $2\frac{1}{4} \times 5\frac{1}{3} \times \frac{7}{8}$ $10\frac{1}{2}$
96. $3\frac{1}{5} \times \frac{1}{2} \times 1\frac{3}{4}$ $2\frac{4}{5}$
97. $4\frac{1}{8} \times 1\frac{3}{5} \times \frac{2}{3}$ $4\frac{2}{5}$
98. $2\frac{1}{2} \times 3\frac{1}{3} \times 2\frac{1}{4}$ $18\frac{3}{4}$
99. $1\frac{5}{16} \times \frac{2}{3} \times 2\frac{2}{3}$ $2\frac{1}{3}$
100. $10 \times \frac{4}{5} \times 3\frac{1}{12}$ $24\frac{2}{3}$
101. $2\frac{1}{4} \times \frac{3}{5} \times 8$ $10\frac{4}{5}$
102. $2\frac{2}{3} \times 1\frac{3}{4} \times 5$ $23\frac{1}{3}$
103. $4 \times 2\frac{1}{5} \times 3\frac{1}{8}$ $27\frac{1}{2}$
104. $6\frac{1}{4} \times 5\frac{1}{2} \times 8$ 275
105. $3\frac{3}{4} \times 4\frac{4}{5} \times 5\frac{5}{6}$ 105

Skills File

Dividing fractions and mixed numbers, pages 16–17

1. $\frac{3}{4} \div \frac{1}{2}$ $1\frac{1}{2}$
2. $\frac{1}{4} \div \frac{2}{3}$ $\frac{3}{8}$
3. $\frac{3}{5} \div \frac{7}{8}$ $\frac{24}{35}$
4. $\frac{1}{2} \div \frac{5}{8}$ $\frac{4}{5}$
5. $\frac{2}{3} \div \frac{1}{6}$ 4
6. $\frac{7}{8} \div \frac{2}{5}$ $2\frac{3}{16}$
7. $\frac{4}{9} \div \frac{2}{7}$ $1\frac{5}{9}$
8. $\frac{1}{10} \div \frac{2}{3}$ $\frac{3}{20}$
9. $\frac{12}{25} \div \frac{4}{15}$ $1\frac{4}{5}$
10. $\frac{1}{2} \div 3$ $\frac{1}{6}$
11. $\frac{3}{5} \div 9$ $\frac{1}{15}$
12. $\frac{1}{8} \div 2$ $\frac{1}{16}$
13. $\frac{4}{5} \div 3$ $\frac{4}{15}$
14. $\frac{4}{15} \div 8$ $\frac{1}{30}$
15. $\frac{15}{16} \div 3$ $\frac{5}{16}$
16. $\frac{4}{5} \div 10$ $\frac{2}{25}$
17. $\frac{8}{9} \div 12$ $\frac{2}{27}$
18. $\frac{7}{12} \div 4$ $\frac{7}{48}$
19. $5 \div \frac{2}{3}$ $7\frac{1}{2}$
20. $6 \div \frac{3}{8}$ 16
21. $6 \div \frac{3}{4}$ 8
22. $10 \div \frac{5}{8}$ 16
23. $7 \div \frac{3}{4}$ $9\frac{1}{3}$
24. $5 \div \frac{2}{3}$ $7\frac{1}{2}$
25. $1 \div \frac{3}{4}$ $1\frac{1}{3}$
26. $2 \div \frac{4}{5}$ $2\frac{1}{2}$
27. $9 \div \frac{6}{7}$ $10\frac{1}{2}$
28. $\frac{2}{3} \div 1\frac{1}{2}$ $\frac{4}{9}$
29. $\frac{3}{10} \div 1\frac{1}{5}$ $\frac{1}{4}$
30. $\frac{3}{8} \div 2\frac{1}{3}$ $\frac{9}{56}$
31. $\frac{1}{3} \div 1\frac{1}{9}$ $\frac{3}{10}$
32. $\frac{1}{2} \div 1\frac{1}{4}$ $\frac{2}{5}$
33. $\frac{3}{4} \div 7\frac{1}{2}$ $\frac{1}{10}$
34. $\frac{2}{5} \div 2\frac{3}{5}$ $\frac{2}{13}$
35. $\frac{3}{8} \div 3\frac{1}{2}$ $\frac{3}{28}$
36. $\frac{7}{10} \div 2\frac{4}{5}$ $\frac{1}{4}$
37. $3\frac{3}{4} \div \frac{3}{5}$ $6\frac{1}{4}$
38. $2\frac{1}{4} \div \frac{9}{10}$ $2\frac{1}{2}$
39. $5\frac{3}{5} \div \frac{4}{5}$ 7
40. $7\frac{1}{2} \div \frac{1}{2}$ 15
41. $1\frac{1}{8} \div \frac{5}{6}$ $1\frac{7}{20}$
42. $3\frac{3}{4} \div \frac{3}{8}$ 10
43. $8\frac{1}{3} \div \frac{1}{6}$ 50
44. $6\frac{2}{3} \div \frac{15}{16}$ $7\frac{1}{9}$
45. $5\frac{1}{4} \div \frac{7}{10}$ $7\frac{1}{2}$
46. $5\frac{1}{3} \div 3$ $1\frac{7}{9}$
47. $5\frac{7}{8} \div 2$ $2\frac{15}{16}$
48. $1\frac{4}{5} \div 15$ $\frac{3}{25}$
49. $8\frac{1}{4} \div 3$ $2\frac{3}{4}$
50. $2\frac{2}{3} \div 3$ $\frac{8}{9}$
51. $5\frac{1}{4} \div 7$ $\frac{3}{4}$
52. $3\frac{1}{5} \div 8$ $\frac{2}{5}$
53. $9\frac{1}{3} \div 7$ $1\frac{1}{3}$
54. $8\frac{3}{4} \div 14$ $\frac{5}{8}$
55. $8 \div 1\frac{1}{3}$ 6
56. $9 \div 1\frac{5}{7}$ $5\frac{1}{4}$
57. $12 \div 3\frac{3}{4}$ $3\frac{1}{5}$
58. $4 \div 1\frac{2}{3}$ $2\frac{2}{5}$
59. $6 \div 1\frac{1}{8}$ $5\frac{1}{3}$
60. $10 \div 4\frac{3}{8}$ $2\frac{2}{7}$
61. $25 \div 3\frac{1}{3}$ $7\frac{1}{2}$
62. $7 \div 2\frac{1}{2}$ $2\frac{4}{5}$
63. $40 \div 1\frac{3}{5}$ 25
64. $2\frac{7}{8} \div 1\frac{7}{8}$ $1\frac{8}{15}$
65. $9\frac{1}{4} \div 2\frac{3}{4}$ $3\frac{4}{11}$
66. $4\frac{1}{6} \div 5\frac{2}{3}$ $\frac{25}{34}$
67. $2\frac{3}{4} \div 3\frac{2}{3}$ $\frac{3}{4}$
68. $7\frac{4}{5} \div 1\frac{6}{7}$ $4\frac{1}{5}$
69. $8\frac{5}{9} \div 3\frac{2}{3}$ $2\frac{1}{3}$
70. $1\frac{1}{8} \div 1\frac{5}{16}$ $\frac{6}{7}$
71. $3\frac{3}{5} \div 2\frac{1}{4}$ $1\frac{3}{5}$
72. $2\frac{7}{10} \div 1\frac{3}{5}$ $1\frac{11}{16}$
73. $9\frac{3}{8} \div 1\frac{7}{8}$ 5
74. $7\frac{1}{4} \div 2\frac{1}{2}$ $2\frac{9}{10}$
75. $5\frac{5}{8} \div 5\frac{5}{6}$ $\frac{27}{28}$
76. $1\frac{3}{5} \div 2\frac{2}{3}$ $\frac{3}{5}$
77. $1\frac{7}{8} \div 3\frac{1}{3}$ $\frac{9}{16}$
78. $7\frac{1}{2} \div 1\frac{1}{2}$ 5
79. $3\frac{7}{8} \div 1\frac{1}{4}$ $3\frac{1}{10}$
80. $8\frac{1}{6} \div 1\frac{2}{5}$ $5\frac{5}{6}$
81. $4\frac{1}{2} \div 2\frac{2}{5}$ $1\frac{7}{8}$
82. $6\frac{1}{4} \div 2\frac{1}{2}$ $2\frac{1}{2}$
83. $6\frac{2}{3} \div 7\frac{1}{2}$ $\frac{8}{9}$
84. $3\frac{3}{5} \div 4\frac{1}{5}$ $\frac{6}{7}$
85. $3\frac{3}{5} \div 2\frac{1}{4}$ $1\frac{3}{5}$
86. $8\frac{2}{3} \div 2\frac{1}{6}$ 4
87. $3\frac{1}{3} \div 2\frac{1}{12}$ $1\frac{3}{5}$
88. $2\frac{7}{10} \div 1\frac{5}{8}$ $1\frac{43}{65}$
89. $6\frac{7}{8} \div 1\frac{5}{6}$ $3\frac{3}{4}$
90. $4\frac{1}{6} \div 3\frac{3}{4}$ $1\frac{1}{9}$
91. $10\frac{1}{2} \div 1\frac{3}{4}$ 6
92. $2\frac{3}{5} \div 3\frac{9}{10}$ $\frac{2}{3}$
93. $2\frac{2}{7} \div 5\frac{1}{3}$ $\frac{3}{7}$
94. $2\frac{4}{5} \div 1\frac{3}{4}$ $1\frac{3}{5}$
95. $1\frac{1}{4} \div 7\frac{1}{2}$ $\frac{1}{6}$
96. $1\frac{5}{7} \div 5\frac{1}{4}$ $\frac{16}{49}$
97. $4\frac{2}{3} \div 1\frac{1}{6}$ 4
98. $4\frac{1}{2} \div 2\frac{1}{4}$ 2
99. $8\frac{2}{3} \div 2\frac{3}{5}$ $3\frac{1}{3}$
100. $2\frac{3}{8} \div 1\frac{1}{2}$ $1\frac{7}{12}$
101. $3\frac{3}{10} \div 4\frac{2}{5}$ $\frac{3}{4}$
102. $10\frac{1}{2} \div 2\frac{1}{3}$ $4\frac{1}{2}$
103. $5\frac{5}{6} \div 1\frac{5}{9}$ $3\frac{3}{4}$
104. $13\frac{3}{4} \div 1\frac{2}{3}$ $8\frac{1}{4}$
105. $16\frac{2}{3} \div 2\frac{3}{11}$ $7\frac{1}{3}$

Skills File

Adding fractions and mixed numbers, pages 18–19

1. $\frac{1}{3} + \frac{3}{4}$ $1\frac{1}{12}$
2. $\frac{1}{10} + \frac{3}{5}$ $\frac{7}{10}$
3. $\frac{5}{6} + \frac{1}{2}$ $1\frac{1}{3}$
4. $\frac{3}{5} + \frac{2}{15}$ $\frac{11}{15}$
5. $\frac{1}{2} + \frac{5}{7}$ $1\frac{3}{14}$
6. $\frac{7}{10} + \frac{1}{2}$ $1\frac{1}{5}$
7. $\frac{7}{9} + \frac{7}{12}$ $1\frac{13}{36}$
8. $\frac{3}{4} + \frac{2}{3}$ $1\frac{5}{12}$
9. $\frac{1}{6} + \frac{8}{9}$ $1\frac{1}{18}$
10. $\frac{3}{4} + \frac{5}{6}$ $1\frac{7}{12}$
11. $\frac{9}{10} + \frac{1}{2}$ $1\frac{2}{5}$
12. $\frac{5}{16} + \frac{1}{4}$ $\frac{9}{16}$
13. $\frac{4}{5} + \frac{7}{10}$ $1\frac{1}{2}$
14. $\frac{7}{8} + \frac{1}{3}$ $1\frac{5}{24}$
15. $\frac{7}{8} + \frac{1}{6}$ $1\frac{1}{24}$
16. $\frac{7}{12} + \frac{2}{3}$ $1\frac{1}{4}$
17. $\frac{1}{10} + \frac{1}{6}$ $\frac{4}{15}$
18. $\frac{5}{6} + \frac{2}{9}$ $1\frac{1}{18}$
19. $\frac{2}{5} + \frac{7}{8}$ $1\frac{11}{40}$
20. $\frac{9}{16} + \frac{3}{4}$ $1\frac{5}{16}$
21. $\frac{5}{8} + \frac{2}{3}$ $1\frac{7}{24}$
22. $\frac{8}{15} + \frac{4}{5}$ $1\frac{1}{3}$
23. $\frac{11}{18} + \frac{5}{6}$ $1\frac{4}{9}$
24. $\frac{4}{9} + \frac{7}{12}$ $1\frac{1}{36}$
25. $5\frac{1}{6} + \frac{7}{8}$ $6\frac{1}{24}$
26. $3\frac{5}{6} + \frac{7}{10}$ $4\frac{8}{15}$
27. $4\frac{7}{9} + \frac{1}{4}$ $5\frac{1}{36}$
28. $2\frac{3}{8} + \frac{5}{24}$ $2\frac{7}{12}$
29. $3\frac{5}{8} + \frac{2}{3}$ $4\frac{7}{24}$
30. $1\frac{9}{10} + \frac{1}{5}$ $2\frac{1}{10}$
31. $5\frac{3}{8} + \frac{1}{24}$ $5\frac{5}{12}$
32. $7\frac{1}{2} + \frac{3}{10}$ $7\frac{4}{5}$
33. $3\frac{2}{5} + \frac{2}{3}$ $4\frac{1}{15}$
34. $3\frac{15}{16} + \frac{7}{8}$ $4\frac{13}{16}$
35. $12\frac{1}{10} + \frac{4}{5}$ $12\frac{9}{10}$
36. $16\frac{4}{5} + \frac{1}{6}$ $16\frac{29}{30}$
37. $3\frac{8}{15} + 4\frac{4}{5}$ $8\frac{1}{3}$
38. $6\frac{2}{3} + 4\frac{7}{12}$ $11\frac{1}{4}$
39. $2\frac{2}{9} + 3\frac{7}{18}$ $5\frac{11}{18}$
40. $3\frac{1}{2} + 1\frac{5}{8}$ $5\frac{1}{8}$
41. $2\frac{3}{5} + 6\frac{5}{8}$ $9\frac{9}{40}$
42. $5\frac{1}{2} + 3\frac{1}{4}$ $8\frac{3}{4}$
43. $7\frac{5}{8} + 1\frac{1}{6}$ $8\frac{19}{24}$
44. $2\frac{3}{4} + 1\frac{7}{12}$ $4\frac{1}{3}$
45. $4\frac{2}{3} + 8\frac{1}{5}$ $12\frac{13}{15}$
46. $3\frac{1}{8} + 7\frac{2}{3}$ $10\frac{19}{24}$
47. $1\frac{4}{5} + 5\frac{1}{3}$ $7\frac{2}{15}$
48. $8\frac{3}{5} + 9\frac{2}{5}$ 18
49. $12\frac{1}{4} + 8\frac{7}{12}$ $20\frac{5}{6}$
50. $2\frac{7}{8} + 3\frac{5}{6}$ $6\frac{17}{24}$
51. $2\frac{2}{5} + 7\frac{7}{15}$ $9\frac{13}{15}$
52. $6\frac{1}{4} + 2\frac{4}{5}$ $9\frac{1}{20}$
53. $5\frac{1}{6} + 9\frac{3}{10}$ $14\frac{7}{15}$
54. $8\frac{5}{12} + 7\frac{3}{4}$ $16\frac{1}{6}$
55. $8\frac{7}{10} + 5\frac{2}{3}$ $14\frac{11}{30}$
56. $4\frac{11}{12} + 3\frac{1}{4}$ $8\frac{1}{6}$
57. $7\frac{1}{2} + 2\frac{2}{3}$ $10\frac{1}{6}$
58. $5\frac{1}{7} + 3\frac{2}{3}$ $8\frac{17}{21}$
59. $16\frac{1}{3} + 2\frac{1}{6}$ $18\frac{1}{2}$
60. $15\frac{3}{8} + 9\frac{3}{16}$ $24\frac{9}{16}$
61. $\frac{1}{2} + \frac{2}{3} + \frac{1}{4}$ $1\frac{5}{12}$
62. $\frac{1}{3} + \frac{5}{8} + \frac{5}{6}$ $1\frac{19}{24}$
63. $1\frac{1}{2} + \frac{4}{5} + 2\frac{1}{3}$ $4\frac{19}{30}$
64. $3\frac{3}{8} + 4\frac{1}{2} + \frac{1}{6}$ $8\frac{1}{24}$
65. $2\frac{5}{12} + 2\frac{2}{3} + 1\frac{1}{4}$ $6\frac{1}{3}$
66. $4\frac{1}{6} + 1\frac{2}{5} + 3\frac{2}{3}$ $9\frac{7}{30}$
67. $1\frac{3}{8} + 1\frac{1}{3} + 1\frac{5}{6}$ $4\frac{13}{24}$
68. $3\frac{3}{4} + 4\frac{2}{5} + 3\frac{1}{2}$ $11\frac{13}{20}$

Skills File

Subtracting fractions and mixed numbers, pages 18–19

1. $\frac{5}{6} - \frac{1}{3}$ $\frac{1}{2}$
2. $\frac{3}{4} - \frac{1}{2}$ $\frac{1}{4}$
3. $\frac{7}{8} - \frac{1}{4}$ $\frac{5}{8}$
4. $\frac{4}{5} - \frac{1}{3}$ $\frac{7}{15}$
5. $\frac{7}{8} - \frac{1}{6}$ $\frac{17}{24}$
6. $\frac{5}{6} - \frac{2}{3}$ $\frac{1}{6}$
7. $\frac{1}{2} - \frac{2}{7}$ $\frac{3}{14}$
8. $\frac{3}{4} - \frac{3}{10}$ $\frac{9}{20}$
9. $\frac{4}{5} - \frac{3}{10}$ $\frac{1}{2}$
10. $\frac{5}{8} - \frac{1}{6}$ $\frac{11}{24}$
11. $\frac{17}{18} - \frac{7}{9}$ $\frac{1}{6}$
12. $\frac{4}{15} - \frac{1}{10}$ $\frac{1}{6}$
13. $\frac{4}{5} - \frac{2}{3}$ $\frac{2}{15}$
14. $\frac{5}{6} - \frac{1}{8}$ $\frac{17}{24}$
15. $\frac{9}{10} - \frac{5}{6}$ $\frac{1}{15}$
16. $\frac{2}{3} - \frac{4}{7}$ $\frac{2}{21}$
17. $\frac{8}{15} - \frac{2}{5}$ $\frac{2}{15}$
18. $\frac{13}{16} - \frac{3}{4}$ $\frac{1}{16}$
19. $\frac{5}{7} - \frac{1}{2}$ $\frac{3}{14}$
20. $\frac{5}{8} - \frac{1}{6}$ $\frac{11}{24}$
21. $\frac{7}{10} - \frac{2}{15}$ $\frac{17}{30}$
22. $\frac{11}{15} - \frac{5}{9}$ $\frac{8}{45}$
23. $\frac{5}{6} - \frac{7}{10}$ $\frac{2}{15}$
24. $\frac{11}{12} - \frac{1}{8}$ $\frac{19}{24}$
25. $2 - \frac{5}{8}$ $1\frac{3}{8}$
26. $8 - \frac{2}{5}$ $7\frac{3}{5}$
27. $9 - \frac{1}{3}$ $8\frac{2}{3}$
28. $13 - \frac{4}{7}$ $12\frac{3}{7}$
29. $3 - \frac{7}{8}$ $2\frac{1}{8}$
30. $15 - \frac{3}{10}$ $14\frac{7}{10}$
31. $10 - \frac{6}{7}$ $9\frac{1}{7}$
32. $6 - \frac{1}{4}$ $5\frac{3}{4}$
33. $10 - 4\frac{2}{3}$ $5\frac{1}{3}$
34. $7 - 6\frac{7}{10}$ $\frac{3}{10}$
35. $18 - 8\frac{3}{5}$ $9\frac{2}{5}$
36. $9 - 5\frac{2}{3}$ $3\frac{1}{3}$
37. $3 - 1\frac{5}{7}$ $1\frac{2}{7}$
38. $12 - 6\frac{5}{6}$ $5\frac{1}{6}$
39. $16 - 9\frac{3}{8}$ $6\frac{5}{8}$
40. $6 - 5\frac{1}{16}$ $\frac{15}{16}$
41. $3\frac{1}{2} - \frac{2}{5}$ $3\frac{1}{10}$
42. $4\frac{7}{8} - \frac{3}{16}$ $4\frac{11}{16}$
43. $5\frac{1}{10} - \frac{3}{5}$ $4\frac{1}{2}$
44. $4\frac{4}{9} - \frac{5}{6}$ $3\frac{11}{18}$
45. $9\frac{1}{3} - 6$ $3\frac{1}{3}$
46. $15\frac{4}{9} - 7$ $8\frac{4}{9}$
47. $21\frac{7}{8} - 17$ $4\frac{7}{8}$
48. $12\frac{3}{10} - 11$ $1\frac{3}{10}$
49. $14\frac{5}{6} - 8\frac{1}{2}$ $6\frac{1}{3}$
50. $10\frac{4}{5} - 8\frac{3}{4}$ $2\frac{1}{20}$
51. $7\frac{3}{4} - 2\frac{3}{16}$ $5\frac{9}{16}$
52. $2\frac{7}{12} - 2\frac{3}{8}$ $\frac{5}{24}$
53. $5\frac{7}{8} - 5\frac{5}{12}$ $\frac{11}{24}$
54. $8\frac{3}{4} - 2\frac{1}{3}$ $6\frac{5}{12}$
55. $9\frac{3}{10} - 5\frac{1}{5}$ $4\frac{1}{10}$
56. $8\frac{5}{8} - 4\frac{3}{16}$ $4\frac{7}{16}$
57. $3\frac{4}{5} - 1\frac{3}{20}$ $2\frac{13}{20}$
58. $9\frac{5}{6} - 2\frac{1}{3}$ $7\frac{1}{2}$
59. $10\frac{7}{8} - 5\frac{5}{12}$ $5\frac{11}{24}$
60. $12\frac{13}{15} - 9\frac{5}{6}$ $3\frac{1}{30}$
61. $5\frac{1}{4} - 2\frac{3}{4}$ $2\frac{1}{2}$
62. $8\frac{3}{8} - 4\frac{5}{8}$ $3\frac{3}{4}$
63. $9\frac{1}{6} - 4\frac{5}{9}$ $4\frac{11}{18}$
64. $7\frac{5}{6} - 4\frac{8}{9}$ $2\frac{17}{18}$
65. $10\frac{1}{3} - 3\frac{4}{5}$ $6\frac{8}{15}$
66. $5\frac{1}{4} - 2\frac{7}{10}$ $2\frac{11}{20}$
67. $6\frac{3}{4} - 4\frac{4}{5}$ $1\frac{19}{20}$
68. $11\frac{3}{8} - 9\frac{2}{3}$ $1\frac{17}{24}$
69. $18\frac{5}{6} - 13\frac{11}{12}$ $4\frac{11}{12}$
70. $14\frac{4}{9} - 7\frac{3}{4}$ $6\frac{25}{36}$
71. $13\frac{7}{12} - 9\frac{5}{8}$ $3\frac{23}{24}$
72. $16\frac{1}{10} - 15\frac{7}{15}$ $\frac{19}{30}$

Skills File

Ratio and proportion, pages 30–31

Find the cross-products. Tell whether the ratios are equal.

1. $\frac{6}{30}$ $\frac{4}{20}$
   $120 = 120$
2. $\frac{3}{13}$ $\frac{5}{15}$
   $45 \neq 65$
3. $\frac{10}{12}$ $\frac{12}{14}$
   $140 \neq 144$
4. $\frac{7}{6}$ $\frac{21}{18}$
   $126 = 126$
5. $\frac{40}{8}$ $\frac{160}{30}$
   $1200 \neq 1280$
6. $\frac{5}{12}$ $\frac{15}{36}$
   $180 = 180$
7. $\frac{5}{9}$ $\frac{11}{18}$
   $90 \neq 99$
8. $\frac{2}{15}$ $\frac{6}{45}$
   $90 = 90$
9. $\frac{15}{24}$ $\frac{5}{8}$
   $120 = 120$
10. $\frac{7}{12}$ $\frac{28}{48}$
    $336 = 336$
11. $\frac{4}{5}$ $\frac{12}{16}$
    $64 \neq 60$
12. $\frac{6}{14}$ $\frac{15}{35}$
    $210 = 210$
13. $\frac{5}{13}$ $\frac{4}{12}$
    $60 \neq 52$
14. $\frac{8}{5}$ $\frac{28}{15}$
    $120 \neq 140$
15. $\frac{14}{38}$ $\frac{21}{57}$
    $798 = 798$
16. $\frac{42}{28}$ $\frac{63}{42}$
    $1764 = 1764$
17. $\frac{12}{15}$ $\frac{26}{30}$
    $360 \neq 390$
18. $\frac{17}{35}$ $\frac{27}{54}$
    $918 \neq 945$
19. $\frac{2.1}{0.7}$ $\frac{6}{2}$
    $4.2 = 4.2$
20. $\frac{18}{4.5}$ $\frac{100}{25}$
    $450 = 450$
21. $\frac{8.4}{12}$ $\frac{12}{14}$
    $117.6 \neq 144$
22. $\frac{6}{1.8}$ $\frac{3}{0.9}$
    $5.4 = 5.4$
23. $\frac{30.6}{100}$ $\frac{1.8}{6}$
    $183.6 \neq 180$
24. $\frac{0.16}{0.06}$ $\frac{0.55}{0.4}$
    $0.064 \neq 0.033$
25. $\frac{3}{3.98}$ $\frac{5}{5.98}$
    $17.94 \neq 19.9$
26. $\frac{11}{15}$ $\frac{0.99}{1.35}$
    $14.85 = 14.85$
27. $\frac{8}{12}$ $\frac{2.4}{3.2}$
    $25.6 \neq 28.8$
28. $\frac{1.8}{2.7}$ $\frac{42}{63}$
    $113.4 = 113.4$
29. $\frac{2}{0.3}$ $\frac{42}{6.3}$
    $12.6 = 12.6$
30. $\frac{0.8}{3}$ $\frac{2.7}{10}$
    $8 \neq 8.1$
31. $\frac{7.9}{4}$ $\frac{16.1}{8.6}$
    $67.94 \neq 64.4$
32. $\frac{2.8}{4.5}$ $\frac{2.1}{3.5}$
    $9.8 \neq 9.45$
33. $\frac{25.5}{15.3}$ $\frac{0.5}{0.3}$
    $7.65 = 7.65$
34. $\frac{1.8}{16.5}$ $\frac{0.6}{5.5}$
    $9.9 = 9.9$
35. $\frac{0.9}{2.1}$ $\frac{0.25}{0.5}$
    $0.45 \neq 0.525$

Solve and check.

36. $\frac{4}{3} = \frac{s}{27}$
    $s = 36$
37. $\frac{25}{n} = \frac{5}{20}$
    $n = 100$
38. $\frac{24}{8} = \frac{9}{x}$
    $x = 3$
39. $\frac{a}{42} = \frac{5}{14}$
    $a = 15$
40. $\frac{x}{45} = \frac{7}{9}$
    $x = 35$
41. $\frac{5}{7} = \frac{b}{42}$
    $b = 30$
42. $\frac{36}{w} = \frac{12}{21}$
    $w = 63$
43. $\frac{65}{10} = \frac{13}{d}$
    $d = 2$
44. $\frac{34}{72} = \frac{17}{m}$
    $m = 36$
45. $\frac{c}{21} = \frac{19}{57}$
    $c = 7$
46. $\frac{4}{30} = \frac{t}{36}$
    $t = 4.8$
47. $\frac{3}{y} = \frac{10}{15}$
    $y = 4.5$
48. $\frac{4}{f} = \frac{24}{9}$
    $f = 1.5$
49. $\frac{18}{15} = \frac{s}{18}$
    $s = 21.6$
50. $\frac{r}{6} = \frac{4}{5}$
    $r = 4.8$
51. $\frac{16}{3} = \frac{8}{h}$
    $h = 1.5$
52. $\frac{9}{5} = \frac{v}{8}$
    $v = 14.4$
53. $\frac{5}{k} = \frac{4}{3}$
    $k = 3.75$
54. $\frac{0.07}{0.56} = \frac{2}{w}$
    $w = 16$
55. $\frac{d}{1.6} = \frac{2.4}{3.2}$
    $d = 1.2$
56. $\frac{18}{y} = \frac{2.4}{2.8}$
    $y = 21$
57. $\frac{0.07}{0.02} = \frac{3.5}{b}$
    $b = 1$
58. $\frac{g}{8} = \frac{23.7}{3}$
    $g = 63.2$
59. $\frac{1.5}{0.6} = \frac{d}{0.36}$
    $d = 0.9$
60. $\frac{0.4}{0.14} = \frac{18}{y}$
    $y = 6.3$
61. $\frac{n}{1.26} = \frac{4}{0.72}$
    $n = 7$
62. $\frac{10.6}{5} = \frac{a}{2.5}$
    $a = 5.3$
63. $\frac{0.9}{g} = \frac{0.4}{4.8}$
    $g = 10.8$
64. $\frac{0.08}{0.6} = \frac{c}{3.3}$
    $c = 0.44$
65. $\frac{0.03}{0.27} = \frac{9}{v}$
    $v = 81$
66. $\frac{0.8}{n} = \frac{4.8}{9}$
    $n = 1.5$
67. $\frac{a}{21} = \frac{7.8}{63}$
    $a = 2.6$
68. $\frac{0.18}{0.29} = \frac{2.88}{t}$
    $t = 4.64$
69. $\frac{9.6}{4.7} = \frac{m}{2.35}$
    $m = 4.8$
70. $\frac{4.9}{h} = \frac{2.1}{1.2}$
    $h = 2.8$

Skills File

Writing percents, decimals, and fractions, pages 32–33

Write as a percent.

1. 0.39	39%	**13.** 0.2946	29.46%
2. 0.62	62%	**14.** 0.4372	43.72%
3. 0.04	4%	**15.** 0.7708	77.08%
4. 0.08	8%	**16.** 0.9021	90.21%
5. 0.7	70%	**17.** 0.1008	10.08%
6. 0.5	50%	**18.** 0.0566	5.66%
7. 0.727	72.7%	**19.** 3.62	362%
8. 0.345	34.5%	**20.** 4.78	478%
9. 0.802	80.2%	**21.** 9.01	901%
10. 0.109	10.9%	**22.** 2.149	214.9%
11. 0.061	6.1%	**23.** 7.681	768.1%
12. 0.557	55.7%	**24.** 5.023	502.3%

Write as a decimal.

52. 17%	0.17	**64.** 3.08%	0.0308
53. 82%	0.82	**65.** 5.91%	0.0591
54. 30%	0.3	**66.** $8\frac{3}{4}\%$	0.0875
55. 90%	0.9	**67.** $4\frac{1}{2}\%$	0.045
56. 75%	0.75	**68.** $1\frac{1}{4}\%$	0.0125
57. 46%	0.46	**69.** $23\frac{1}{4}\%$	0.2325
58. 5%	0.05	**70.** $50\frac{1}{2}\%$	0.505
59. 8%	0.08	**71.** $47\frac{3}{8}\%$	0.47375
60. 51.3%	0.513	**72.** 172%	1.72
61. 20.7%	0.207	**73.** 206%	2.06
62. 19.6%	0.196	**74.** 270%	2.7
63. 7.42%	0.0742	**75.** 159%	1.59

Write as a percent.

25. $\frac{1}{2}$	50%	**34.** $\frac{9}{10}$	90%	**43.** $\frac{5}{32}$	15.625%
26. $\frac{3}{4}$	75%	**35.** $\frac{1}{20}$	5%	**44.** $\frac{29}{32}$	90.625%
27. $\frac{2}{5}$	40%	**36.** $\frac{37}{50}$	74%	**45.** $\frac{3}{8}$	37.5%
28. $\frac{1}{4}$	25%	**37.** $\frac{18}{25}$	72%	**46.** $\frac{9}{16}$	56.25%
29. $\frac{2}{25}$	8%	**38.** $\frac{1}{8}$	12.5%	**47.** $\frac{7}{8}$	87.5%
30. $\frac{6}{20}$	30%	**39.** $\frac{15}{32}$	46.875%	**48.** $\frac{3}{2}$	150%
31. $\frac{21}{50}$	42%	**40.** $\frac{3}{16}$	18.75%	**49.** $\frac{13}{4}$	325%
32. $\frac{8}{25}$	32%	**41.** $\frac{15}{16}$	93.75%	**50.** $\frac{19}{5}$	380%
33. $\frac{7}{10}$	70%	**42.** $\frac{5}{8}$	62.5%	**51.** $\frac{27}{20}$	135%

Write as a fraction in lowest terms.

76. 10%	$\frac{1}{10}$	**88.** 41%	$\frac{41}{100}$
77. 80%	$\frac{4}{5}$	**89.** 24%	$\frac{6}{25}$
78. 30%	$\frac{3}{10}$	**90.** 68%	$\frac{17}{25}$
79. 90%	$\frac{9}{10}$	**91.** 79%	$\frac{79}{100}$
80. 25%	$\frac{1}{4}$	**92.** 86%	$\frac{43}{50}$
81. 75%	$\frac{3}{4}$	**93.** 13%	$\frac{13}{100}$
82. 45%	$\frac{9}{20}$	**94.** 51%	$\frac{51}{100}$
83. 95%	$\frac{19}{20}$	**95.** 34%	$\frac{17}{50}$
84. 5%	$\frac{1}{20}$	**96.** 160%	$1\frac{3}{5}$
85. 8%	$\frac{2}{25}$	**97.** 172%	$1\frac{18}{25}$
86. 3%	$\frac{3}{100}$	**98.** 103%	$1\frac{3}{100}$
87. 1%	$\frac{1}{100}$	**99.** 250%	$2\frac{1}{2}$

Skills File

Using percent, pages 34–37

1. 25% of 60 is ____.
15
2. 90% of 50 is ____.
45
3. 7% of 82 is ____.
5.74
4. 14.8% of 45 is ____.
6.66
5. 5.3% of 94 is ____.
4.982
6. 32.6% of 72 is ____.
23.472
7. $4\frac{1}{2}$% of 25 is ____.
1.125
8. $18\frac{3}{4}$% of 30 is ____.
5.625
9. Find 41% of 17.
6.97
10. Find 89% of 52.
46.28
11. Find 1.9% of 200.
3.8
12. Find 8.5% of 350.
29.75
13. Find $5\frac{1}{2}$% of 63.
3.465
14. Find $6\frac{5}{8}$% of 100.
6.625
15. Find 108% of 80.
86.4
16. Find 150% of 35.
52.5
17. 7% of 81 is what number?
5.67
18. 23% of 57 is what number?
13.11
19. 52% of 90 is what number?
46.8
20. 7.2% of 18 is what number?
1.296
21. What number is 9.6% of 54?
5.184
22. What number is $3\frac{1}{2}$% of 100?
3.5
23. What number is $9\frac{3}{4}$% of 270?
26.325
24. ____% of 25 is 17.
68%
25. ____% of 50 is 4.
8%
26. ____% of 35 is 7.
20%
27. ____% of 64 is 16.
25%
28. ____% of 60 is 45.
75%
29. ____% of 40 is 1.2.
3%
30. ____% of 66 is 36.3.
55%
31. ____% of 82 is 11.48.
14%
32. ____% of 75 is 45.75.
61%
33. ____% of 44 is 15.4.
35%
34. ____% of 27 is 10.8.
40%
35. ____% of 50 is 44.5.
89%
36. What percent of 90 is 18?
20%
37. What percent of 40 is 6?
15%
38. What percent of 48 is 18?
37.5%
39. What percent of 56 is 35?
62.5%
40. What percent of 50 is 47?
94%
41. 42 is what percent of 48?
87.5%
42. 70 is what percent of 80?
87.5%
43. 18.4 is what percent of 23?
80%
44. 12 is what percent of 32?
37.5%
45. 40% of ____ is 30.
75
46. 5% of ____ is 2.
40
47. 14% of ____ is 21.
150
48. 25% of ____ is 1.8.
7.2
49. 2% of ____ is 0.56.
28
50. 5% of ____ is 0.41.
8.2
51. 75% of ____ is 5.4
7.2
52. $82\frac{1}{2}$% of ____ is 33.
40
53. $6\frac{1}{4}$% of ____ is 12.5.
200
54. $3\frac{3}{4}$% of ____ is 7.5.
200
55. 12.5% of ____ is 6.
48
56. 7.3% of ____ is 0.73.
10
57. 60% of what number is 18?
30
58. 8% of what number is 10?
125
59. 17% of what number is 14.45?
85
60. $37\frac{1}{2}$% of what number is 26.25?
70
61. 54.8% of what number is 8.22?
15
62. 6.3 is 20% of what number?
31.5
63. 1.12 is 32% of what number?
3.5
64. 8.4 is 70% of what number?
12
65. 27.2 is 85% of what number?
32

COMPUTER LITERACY

The PRINT and END Statements

The programs and exercises in this section have been written so that they can be used either with a computer or as a paper-and-pencil activity.

A computer is a very fast and accurate machine. A computer does not think. It needs instructions from a human. A computer **program** is a set of instructions. BASIC is a common programming language. In BASIC, numbers are written as decimals or decimal approximations. The data that is put into the program is called **input**. The computer executes the program, and what it prints out is called the **output**.

The computer recognizes these symbols of operation:

* (multiply)	+ (add)
/ (divide)	− (subtract)

The instructions to a computer are called statements. The PRINT statement causes the computer to print what is between quotation marks or answers to calculations.

The END statement stops the program. It should be the last statement in a program.

Program A

Input	Output
10 PRINT "HELLO"	HELLO
20 PRINT "MY NAME"	MY NAME
30 PRINT "IS"	IS
40 PRINT "HAL."	HAL.
50 END	

Every statement of a program is given a line number. Although the statements do not have to be typed in order, the computer always executes them in numerical order. Many people number the statements by tens so that statements can be added to the program if necessary.

Statement numbers can be any integer from 1 to 99,999. Some computers have an automatic numbering feature.

Program B

Input	Output
10 PRINT 6+2	8
20 PRINT 6-2	4
30 PRINT 6*2	12
40 PRINT 6/2	3
50 END	

A semicolon separates items in a PRINT statement.

A semicolon used at the end of a PRINT statement causes the computer to print the next PRINT statement on the same line.

Program C

Input	Output
10 PRINT "9/3=";9/3	9/3= 3
20 PRINT "10/4=";10/4	10/4= 2.5
30 PRINT "8/3=";8/3	8/3= 2.666666667
40 END	

Give the output for each program.

1.
```
10 PRINT "THIS IS"
20 PRINT "A BASIC"
30 PRINT "PROGRAM."
40 END
```
THIS IS
A BASIC
PROGRAM.

2.
```
10 PRINT 3+4
20 PRINT 7-2
30 PRINT 5*8
40 PRINT 24/4
50 END
```
2. 7
5
40
6

3.
```
10 PRINT "2+4=";2+4
20 PRINT "9-7=";9-7
30 PRINT 8*4;"=8*4"
40 PRINT 9/5;"=9/5"
50 END
```
See page T54.

4. Give the output for Program A if the following statement is added after line 50.

```
35 PRINT "NOT"
```
See Additional Answers on page T54.

5. Write a program to print your name, your age, and the name of your school.

6. Write a program to compute 12 + 5, 9 − 4, 6 × 18, and 15 ÷ 3.

COMPUTER LITERACY

The LET and INPUT Statements

A computer has thousands of memory locations. Each location can hold exactly one value at a time. When a memory location is used, it is given a name. A name can be either a single letter or a single letter followed by a single digit. C and B3 are examples of names that can be used.

In BASIC, the LET statement is used to put a value in a memory location. In Program A, lines 10 and 20 assign values into memory locations. In line 30, the values for R and S are retrieved from the memory, the computation is performed, and the resulting value is stored in another memory location (T).

Program A

The LET statement is a command to perform calculations, not a statement of algebraic equality.

Input	Output
10 LET R=6	54
20 LET S=R+3	
30 LET T=R*S	
40 PRINT T	
50 END	

The general form of the LET statement is:
LET (variable) = (expression)

The INPUT statement is another way to put a value into a memory location. When the computer gets to an INPUT statement in a program, it prints a question mark and waits for a number to be typed in. In Program B, the user typed 5 for X and 8 for Y.

Program B

Input	Output
10 INPUT X	? 5
20 INPUT Y	? 8
30 PRINT 2*(X+Y)-3	23
40 END	

The INPUT statement allows you, the user, to run the same program more than once, using a different value each time. Use commas between names in INPUT statements.

A letter followed by $ can be used to put letters and/or numbers into a memory location. This is called a string variable and is often used for names and addresses. In a LET statement, quotation marks must be used to show where the string begins and ends.

Program C

Input	Output
10 INPUT N$	? B.HUFFMAN
20 LET T$="TEST AVERAGE="	? 97,95,96
30 INPUT S1,S2,S3	B.HUFFMAN
40 LET A=(S1+S2+S3)/3	TEST AVERAGE= 96
50 PRINT N$	
60 PRINT T$;A	
70 END	

1. ? 7
? 15
41

2. ? 20
? 35
107

Give the output for Program B when

1. X is 7; Y is 15. See above.

2. X is 20; Y is 35. See above.

3. Give the output for Program C when N$ is your name, S1 is 88, S2 is 95, and S3 is 90.
Answers will vary. See below.

Give the output for each program. Use 7 for B and 8 for H.

4. DISTANCE
240

4.
```
10 PRINT "DISTANCE"
20 LET R=80
30 LET T=3
40 PRINT R*T
50 END
```

5.
```
10 INPUT B        ? 7
20 INPUT H        ? 8
30 LET A=B*H      56
40 PRINT A
50 END
```

6. Use INPUT statements to write a program to find the area of a triangle. Programs may vary.
```
10 INPUT B
20 INPUT H
30 LET A=B*H/2
40 PRINT A
50 END
```

3. ? DON WEE
? 88,95,90
DON WEE
TEST AVERAGE= 91

COMPUTER LITERACY

The GO TO and IF . . . THEN Statements

A computer executes a program in the order of the line numbers unless the program tells the computer to go to a specific statement. The GO TO statement tells the computer to skip ahead or to go back to a specified line. It is often used to repeat a set of statements.

Program A

Input	Output
10 INPUT X 20 PRINT 3*X 30 GO TO 10 40 END	? 4 12 ? 9 27 ?

Consult your manual to learn how to stop this program.

In Program A, line 30 sends the computer to line 10 where another value for X is to be entered. The user first typed 4 for X, then 9. The computer will keep asking for values for X until the program is stopped by the user.

The IF . . . THEN statement compares two values. If the comparison is true, the statement sends the computer to a specified line. If the statement is false, the computer will go to the next higher statement number.

BASIC recognizes these comparisons:

= (equal)	<> (not equal)
< (less than)	<= (less than or equal)
> (greater than)	>= (greater than or equal)

In Program B, when the user types YES for line 30, line 40 sends the computer back to line 10. If the user types anything other than YES for line 30, the computer will go to line 50.

Program B

Input	Output
10 INPUT A,B 20 PRINT "A+B=";A+B 30 INPUT Q$ 40 IF Q$="YES" THEN 10 50 PRINT "DONE" 60 END	? 6,8 A+B= 14 ? YES ? 15,23 A+B= 38 ? NO DONE

The statement on line 20 of the program in exercise 4 will cause the computer to stop asking for input if 999 is entered for A. A similar statement is on line 30 of the program in exercise 5.

Give the output for Program A when

1. X is 20, 34, 56, and 128.

1. ? 20
60
? 34
102
? 56
168
? 128
384
?

Give the output for Program B when

2. A is 34; B is 57; Q$ is YES.
See below.

3. A is 66; B is 75; Q$ is NO.
See below.

4. Give the output. Enter 7, 2, 3, 12, 17, 9, 999, and 0.

```
10 INPUT A,B
20 IF A=999 THEN 50
30 PRINT A;"*";B;"=";A*B
40 GO TO 10
50 PRINT "NO MORE DATA"
60 END
```

? 7,2
7 * 2 = 14
? 3,12
3 * 12 = 36
? 17,9
17 * 9 = 153
? 999,0
NO MORE DATA

5. Give the output. Enter your name for N$ and 7, 25, and 130 for A.
Answers will vary.

```
10 INPUT N$
20 INPUT A
30 IF A>99 THEN 60
40 PRINT 3*A+14
50 GO TO 20
60 PRINT "THAT'S ALL ";N$
70 END
```

? J.KELLY
? 7
35
? 25
89
? 130
THAT'S ALL J.KELLY

6. Rewrite Program A so that it will end if you put in a number greater than 244.
Programs may vary.

10 INPUT X
20 IF X>244 THEN 50
30 PRINT 3*X
40 GO TO 10
50 END

2. ? 34,57
A+B= 91
? YES
?

3. ? 66,75
A+B= 141
? NO
DONE

COMPUTER LITERACY

The READ, DATA, and REM Statements

The LET and INPUT statements are used to put values into a program. Another way to tell the computer the values of A and B is to use the READ and DATA statements. As the computer executes the READ statement, it looks for a DATA statement in the program. The word DATA is followed by the values, each value separated from the next by a comma.

In Program A, the first time the computer reads L and W, it uses 4 for L and 2.5 for W. The second time, it uses 18 for L and 11 for W. The computer keeps track of where it is in the data line. On the third pass through Program A, the computer will type a message that it is out of data and stop.

Program A

In Programs A and B and exercises 2 and 5, lines of type were broken to save space.

Input

```
10 READ L,W
20 LET P=2*L+2*W
30 PRINT "PERIMETER -";P
40 GO TO 10
50 DATA 4,2.5,18,11
60 END
```

Output

```
PERIMETER = 13
PERIMETER = 58
OUT OF DATA AT
LINE 10
```

Some computers will print an error message when the computer is out of data. Check your computer before assigning these exercises so that you can tell your students what to expect when the computer runs out of data.

The REM statement is ignored by the computer. REM stands for remark. This statement is used to supply information to someone looking at the program.

Program B

Input

```
10 REM  FINDING INTEREST
20 READ P,R,T
30 PRINT "INTEREST =";P*R*T
40 GO TO 20
50 DATA 1000,.08,2,1800,
.065,1.75
60 END
```

Output

```
INTEREST = 160
INTEREST = 204.75
OUT OF DATA AT
LINE 20
```

1. PERIMETER = 13
PERIMETER = 58
PERIMETER = 34
PERIMETER = 18
PERIMETER = 5
PERIMETER = 74
OUT OF DATA AT LINE 10

2. INTEREST = 160
INTEREST = 204.75
INTEREST = 269.5
INTEREST = 669.5
OUT OF DATA AT LINE 20

1. Give the output for Program A when this statement is added to the program. **See below.**

```
55 DATA 12,5,7,2,1.4,1.1,23,14
```

2. Give the output for Program B when this statement is added to the program. **See below.**

```
52 DATA 2200,.07,1.75,2575,
.065,4
```

Give the output for each program.
See Additional Answers on page T55.

3.
```
10 READ R
20 REM  CIRCUMFERENCE
30 LET C=3.14*2*R
40 PRINT "R =";R;" C =";C
50 GO TO 10
60 DATA 5,10,17
70 END
```

4.
```
10 READ P
20 REM  20% DISCOUNT
30 LET S=.8*P
40 PRINT "REGULAR PRICE IS";P
50 PRINT "SALE PRICE IS    ";S
60 GO TO 10
70 DATA 15,22,27.50,30,42.75
80 END
```

5.
```
10 REM  GROSS PAY
20 READ N$,R,H
30 IF H>40 THEN 70
40 LET P=R*H
50 PRINT N$;"  PAY =";P
60 GO TO 20
70 LET P=40*R+(H-40)*1.5*R
80 GO TO 50
90 DATA ANDERSON,10.50,35,
JENSEN,11.75,42
100 DATA RIEDELL,12,45,
BRETZLAUF,10.75,38
110 END
```

6. Given the regular price and the sale price for several items, write a program to find the amount of discount and the rate of discount.

COMPUTER LITERACY

The FOR and NEXT Statements

A loop is a set of statements that are executed over and over again. When the number of times a loop is to be executed is known, the FOR and NEXT statements can be used. The FOR statement specifies the first and last values to use. The NEXT statement decides whether the loop is to be executed again. The statements that are repeated are placed between the FOR and NEXT statements.

In Program A, line 10 tells the computer to go through the loop using 1 as the first value for X. Line 30 sends the computer back to line 10 and the computer goes through the loop using 2 as the value for X. Each time the loop is executed, the value for X increases by 1. The loop is completed after the last value of X (4) that is indicated in the FOR statement is used, and the computer goes to the line following the NEXT statement.

Program A

Input	Output
10 FOR X=1 TO 4	1
20 PRINT X	2
30 NEXT X	3
40 END	4

In Program B, STEP 3 tells the computer to increase the value of Y by 3 each time the loop is executed. If no step is given, the value increases by 1.

Program B

Input	Output
10 FOR Y=6 TO 15 STEP 3	6
20 PRINT Y	9
30 NEXT Y	12
40 END	15

Program C adds the even numbers from 2 to 10, printing each sum as it goes. Notice that in line 30, a different value is assigned to S each time the loop is executed.

Program C

LET S=S+N can be a difficult concept for students. Work through Program C with your students before assigning exercise 4.

Input	Output
10 LET S=0	2
20 FOR N=2 TO 10 STEP 2	6
30 LET S=S+N	12
40 PRINT S	20
50 NEXT N	30
60 END	

Give the output for each program.

1.
```
10 FOR N=3 TO 8
20 PRINT N
30 NEXT N
40 END
```
3
4
5
6
7
8

2.
```
10 FOR M=12 TO 20 STEP 4
20 PRINT M
30 NEXT M
40 END
```
12
16
20

See Additional Answers on page T55.

3.
```
10 REM  COST OF 6 ITEMS
20 FOR N=1 TO 6
30 LET C=19.95*N
40 PRINT "NUMBER:";N;"COST:";C
50 NEXT N
60 END
```

4.
```
10 REM  ANNUAL COMPOUND INTEREST
20 REM  $100 AT 8%
30 LET P=100
40 FOR T=1 TO 5
50 LET P=P+I
60 LET I=P*.08
70 PRINT "YEAR:";T;"INTEREST: $";I
80 NEXT T
90 END
```
You may wish to add line 25, LET I = 0, if your computer does not initialize variables at zero.

5. Write a program to find the amount earned by working from 1 to 8 hours at a rate of $4.50 an hour.

COMPUTER LITERACY

The INT and TAB Functions

INT(X) is the greatest integer function. The computer will determine the greatest integer that is less than or equal to the number specified in parentheses following INT. Some examples are:

INT(8) = 8 INT(0.07) = 0
INT(3.87) = 3 INT(9/2) = 4

An important use for INT is to determine whether one number is divisible by another number. If so, the quotient will be the same as the INT of the quotient. Program A uses the INT function to determine the even integers between 1 and 10.

Program A

Input	Output
10 FOR N=1 TO 10	2
20 IF INT(N/2)=N/2 THEN 50	4
30 NEXT N	6
40 GO TO 70	8
50 PRINT N	10
60 GO TO 30	
70 END	

The TAB function is used only in PRINT statements. It moves the computer across to a specified position. It is used to place output below headings.

Program B

The statement on line 30 of Program B will cause the computer to stop if 99 is entered for R.

Input	Output
10 PRINT "RADIUS AREA"	RADIUS AREA
20 INPUT R	? 5
30 IF R=99 THEN 60	5 78.5
40 PRINT R;TAB(8);3.14*R*R	? 8
50 GO TO 20	8 200.96
60 END	? 99

In Program B, TAB(8) sends the computer across to the eighth column. Then, since a number is being printed, the computer moves one more space to the right in case there is a negative sign. The other programs shown follow this style.

Give the output for each program.

1. 5 10 15 20 25 30 35 40 45 50 55 60

1.
```
10 FOR X=1 TO 60
20 IF INT(X/5)=X/5 THEN 50
30 NEXT X
40 GO TO 70
50 PRINT X
60 GO TO 30
70 END
```

2.
```
10 READ N
20 PRINT "DIVISORS OF";N;"ARE:"
30 FOR D=1 TO N
40 IF INT(N/D)<>N/D THEN 60
50 PRINT D
60 NEXT D
70 GO TO 10
80 DATA 24,36,56,59
90 END
```

See Additional Answers on page T55.

3.
```
10 PRINT "PRICE  5% TAX  TOTAL"
20 READ P
30 PRINT P;TAB(8);.05*P;TAB(16);
P+.05*P
40 GO TO 20
50 DATA 1.20,6.80,12.60
60 END
```

4.
```
10 REM  CCM BANK SERVICE CHARGE
20 PRINT "ACCOUNT  SERVICE CHARGE"
30 READ A,B,N
40 REM  N IS NUMBER OF CHECKS
50 IF B>300 THEN 90
60 LET S=.1*N
70 PRINT "#";A;TAB(10);"$";S
80 GO TO 30
90 PRINT "#";A;TAB(10);"NO CHARGE"
100 GO TO 30
110 DATA 1519,85.72,16,1520,
234.87,15
120 DATA 1521,328.41,23,1522,
261.35,19
130 END
```

5. Write a program that will test if a number is divisible by 3. **Programs may vary.**

```
10 INPUT N
20 IF N=0 THEN 80
30 IF INT(N/3)=N/3 THEN 60
40 PRINT N;"IS NOT DIVISIBLE BY 3"
50 GO TO 10
60 PRINT N;"IS DIVISIBLE BY 3"
70 GO TO 10
80 END
```

Tables

Metric System

Length

10 millimeters (mm)	= 1 centimeter (cm)
10 centimeters 100 millimeters	= 1 decimeter (dm)
10 decimeters 100 centimeters	= 1 meter (m)
1000 meters	= 1 kilometer (km)

Area

100 square millimeters (mm^2)	= 1 square centimeter (cm^2)
10,000 square centimeters	= 1 square meter (m^2)
100 square meters	= 1 are (a)
10,000 square meters	= 1 hectare (ha)

Volume

1000 cubic millimeters (mm^3)	= 1 cubic centimeter (cm^3)
1000 cubic centimeters	= 1 cubic decimeter (dm^3)
1,000,000 cubic centimeters	= 1 cubic meter (m^3)

Mass

1000 milligrams (mg)	= 1 gram (g)
1000 grams	= 1 kilogram (kg)
1000 kilograms	= 1 metric ton (t)

Capacity

1000 milliliters (mL)	= 1 liter (L)
1000 liters	= 1 kiloliter (kL)

United States Customary System

Length

12 inches (in.)	= 1 foot (ft.)
3 feet 36 inches	= 1 yard (yd.)
1760 yards 5280 feet	= 1 mile (mi.)
6076 feet	= 1 nautical mile

Area

144 square inches (sq. in.)	= 1 square foot (sq. ft.)
9 square feet	= 1 square yard (sq. yd.)
4840 square yards	= 1 acre (A.)

Volume

1728 cubic inches (cu. in.)	= 1 cubic foot (cu. ft.)
27 cubic feet	= 1 cubic yard (cu. yd.)

Weight

16 ounces (oz.)	= 1 pound (lb.)
2000 pounds	= 1 ton (T.)

Capacity

8 fluid ounces (fl. oz.)	= 1 cup (c.)
2 cups	= 1 pint (pt.)
2 pints	= 1 quart (qt.)
4 quarts	= 1 gallon (gal.)

Symbols

$\approx$	approximately equal to
$\overline{AB}$	segment AB
$\angle G$	angle G
$45°$	45 degrees
∟	right angle
$\sqrt{25}$	square root of 25

Geometric Formulas

Perimeter

rectangle $P = 2l + 2w$

Circumference

circle $C = \pi d$ or $C = 2\pi r$

Area

rectangle $A = lw$

square $A = s^2$

parallelogram $A = bh$

triangle $A = \frac{1}{2}bh$

trapezoid $A = \frac{1}{2}h(a + b)$

circle $A = \pi r^2$

Surface area

rectangular prism $A = 2lw + 2lh + 2wh$

cube $A = 6s^2$

cylinder $A = 2\pi rh + 2\pi r^2$

Volume

rectangular prism $V = lwh$

cube $V = s^3$

cylinder $V = \pi r^2 h$

rectangular pyramid $V = \frac{1}{3}lwh$

cone $V = \frac{1}{3}\pi r^2 h$

sphere $V = \frac{4}{3}\pi r^3$

Monthly Payment per $1 Borrowed						
	Number of equal monthly payments					
Annual rate	6	12	18	24	30	36
12%	0.17255	0.08885	0.06098	0.04707	0.03875	0.03321
13%	0.17304	0.08932	0.06145	0.04754	0.03922	0.03369
14%	0.17354	0.08979	0.06192	0.04801	0.03970	0.03418
15%	0.17403	0.09026	0.06238	0.04849	0.04019	0.03467
15.5%	0.17428	0.09049	0.06262	0.04872	0.04042	0.03491
16%	0.17453	0.09073	0.06286	0.04896	0.04066	0.03516
16.5%	0.17478	0.09097	0.06309	0.04920	0.04091	0.03540
17%	0.17503	0.09120	0.06333	0.04944	0.04115	0.03565
17.5%	0.17528	0.09144	0.06357	0.04968	0.04139	0.03590
18%	0.17553	0.09168	0.06381	0.04992	0.04164	0.03615
18.5%	0.17577	0.09192	0.06404	0.05017	0.04189	0.03640
19%	0.17602	0.09216	0.06428	0.05041	0.04213	0.03666
19.5%	0.17627	0.09240	0.06452	0.05065	0.04238	0.03691
20%	0.17652	0.09263	0.06476	0.05090	0.04263	0.03716
20.5%	0.17677	0.09287	0.06500	0.05114	0.04288	0.03742
21%	0.17702	0.09311	0.06524	0.05139	0.04313	0.03768
21.5%	0.17727	0.09335	0.06549	0.05163	0.04338	0.03793
22%	0.17752	0.09359	0.06573	0.05188	0.04363	0.03819
22.5%	0.17777	0.09384	0.06597	0.05213	0.04389	0.03845
23%	0.17802	0.09408	0.06621	0.05237	0.04414	0.03871
23.5%	0.17827	0.09432	0.06646	0.05262	0.04439	0.03897
24%	0.17853	0.09456	0.06670	0.05287	0.04465	0.03923

SINGLE Persons—WEEKLY Payroll Period

And the wages are—		Exemptions claimed										
At least	But less than	0	1	2	3	4	5	6	7	8	9	10 or more
		The amount of income tax to be withheld shall be—										
$0	$28	$0	$0	$0	$0	$0	$0	$0	$0	$0	$0	$0
28	29	.20	0	0	0	0	0	0	0	0	0	0
29	30	.30	0	0	0	0	0	0	0	0	0	0
30	31	.50	0	0	0	0	0	0	0	0	0	0
31	32	.60	0	0	0	0	0	0	0	0	0	0
32	33	.80	0	0	0	0	0	0	0	0	0	0
33	34	.90	0	0	0	0	0	0	0	0	0	0
34	35	1.10	0	0	0	0	0	0	0	0	0	0
35	36	1.20	0	0	0	0	0	0	0	0	0	0
36	37	1.40	0	0	0	0	0	0	0	0	0	0
37	38	1.50	0	0	0	0	0	0	0	0	0	0
38	39	1.70	0	0	0	0	0	0	0	0	0	0
39	40	1.80	0	0	0	0	0	0	0	0	0	0
40	41	2.00	0	0	0	0	0	0	0	0	0	0
41	42	2.10	0	0	0	0	0	0	0	0	0	0
42	43	2.30	0	0	0	0	0	0	0	0	0	0
43	44	2.40	0	0	0	0	0	0	0	0	0	0
44	45	2.60	0	0	0	0	0	0	0	0	0	0
45	46	2.70	0	0	0	0	0	0	0	0	0	0
46	47	2.90	0	0	0	0	0	0	0	0	0	0
47	48	3.00	.10	0	0	0	0	0	0	0	0	0
48	49	3.20	.30	0	0	0	0	0	0	0	0	0
49	50	3.30	.40	0	0	0	0	0	0	0	0	0
50	51	3.50	.60	0	0	0	0	0	0	0	0	0
51	52	3.60	.70	0	0	0	0	0	0	0	0	0
52	53	3.80	.90	0	0	0	0	0	0	0	0	0
53	54	3.90	1.00	0	0	0	0	0	0	0	0	0
54	55	4.10	1.20	0	0	0	0	0	0	0	0	0
55	56	4.20	1.30	0	0	0	0	0	0	0	0	0
56	57	4.40	1.50	0	0	0	0	0	0	0	0	0
57	58	4.50	1.60	0	0	0	0	0	0	0	0	0
58	59	4.70	1.80	0	0	0	0	0	0	0	0	0
59	60	4.80	1.90	0	0	0	0	0	0	0	0	0
60	62	5.10	2.20	0	0	0	0	0	0	0	0	0
62	64	5.40	2.50	0	0	0	0	0	0	0	0	0
64	66	5.70	2.80	0	0	0	0	0	0	0	0	0
66	68	6.10	3.10	.20	0	0	0	0	0	0	0	0
68	70	6.40	3.40	.50	0	0	0	0	0	0	0	0
70	72	6.80	3.70	.80	0	0	0	0	0	0	0	0
72	74	7.10	4.00	1.10	0	0	0	0	0	0	0	0
74	76	7.50	4.30	1.40	0	0	0	0	0	0	0	0
76	78	7.90	4.60	1.70	0	0	0	0	0	0	0	0
78	80	8.20	4.90	2.00	0	0	0	0	0	0	0	0
80	82	8.60	5.20	2.30	0	0	0	0	0	0	0	0
82	84	8.90	5.50	2.60	0	0	0	0	0	0	0	0
84	86	9.30	5.80	2.90	0	0	0	0	0	0	0	0
86	88	9.70	6.20	3.20	.30	0	0	0	0	0	0	0
88	90	10.00	6.60	3.50	.60	0	0	0	0	0	0	0
90	92	10.40	6.90	3.80	.90	0	0	0	0	0	0	0
92	94	10.70	7.30	4.10	1.20	0	0	0	0	0	0	0
94	96	11.10	7.60	4.40	1.50	0	0	0	0	0	0	0
96	98	11.50	8.00	4.70	1.80	0	0	0	0	0	0	0
98	100	11.80	8.40	5.00	2.10	0	0	0	0	0	0	0
100	105	12.50	9.00	5.50	2.60	0	0	0	0	0	0	0
105	110	13.40	9.90	6.40	3.40	.50	0	0	0	0	0	0
110	115	14.30	10.80	7.30	4.10	1.20	0	0	0	0	0	0
115	120	15.20	11.70	8.20	4.90	2.00	0	0	0	0	0	0
120	125	16.10	12.60	9.10	5.70	2.70	0	0	0	0	0	0
125	130	17.00	13.50	10.00	6.60	3.50	.60	0	0	0	0	0
130	135	17.90	14.40	10.90	7.50	4.20	1.40	0	0	0	0	0

And the wages are—		Exemptions claimed										
At least	But less than	0	1	2	3	4	5	6	7	8	9	10 or more
		The amount of income tax to be withheld shall be—										
$135	$140	$19.00	$15.30	$11.80	$8.40	$5.00	$2.10	$0	$0	$0	$0	$0
140	145	20.00	16.20	12.70	9.30	5.80	2.90	0	0	0	0	0
145	150	21.10	17.10	13.60	10.20	6.70	3.60	.70	0	0	0	0
150	160	22.60	18.60	15.00	11.50	8.10	4.70	1.80	0	0	0	0
160	170	24.70	20.70	16.80	13.30	9.90	6.40	3.30	.50	0	0	0
170	180	26.80	22.80	18.80	15.10	11.70	8.20	4.80	2.00	0	0	0
180	190	28.90	24.90	20.90	16.90	13.50	10.00	6.50	3.50	.60	0	0
190	200	31.00	27.00	23.00	18.90	15.30	11.80	8.30	5.00	2.10	0	0
200	210	33.60	29.10	25.10	21.00	17.10	13.60	10.10	6.70	3.60	.70	0
210	220	36.20	31.20	27.20	23.10	19.10	15.40	11.90	8.50	5.10	2.20	0
220	230	38.80	33.80	29.30	25.20	21.20	17.20	13.70	10.30	6.80	3.70	.80
230	240	41.40	36.40	31.40	27.30	23.30	19.20	15.50	12.10	8.60	5.20	2.30
240	250	44.00	39.00	34.00	29.40	25.40	21.30	17.30	13.90	10.40	6.90	3.80
250	260	46.60	41.60	36.60	31.60	27.50	23.40	19.40	15.70	12.20	8.70	5.30
260	270	49.20	44.20	39.20	34.20	29.60	25.50	21.50	17.50	14.00	10.50	7.10
270	280	51.80	46.80	41.80	36.80	31.80	27.60	23.60	19.60	15.80	12.30	8.90
280	290	54.80	49.40	44.40	39.40	34.40	29.70	25.70	21.70	17.60	14.10	10.70
290	300	57.80	52.10	47.00	42.00	37.00	32.00	27.80	23.80	19.70	15.90	12.50
300	310	60.80	55.10	49.60	44.60	39.60	34.60	29.90	25.90	21.80	17.80	14.30
310	320	63.80	58.10	52.30	47.20	42.20	37.20	32.20	28.00	23.90	19.90	16.10
320	330	66.80	61.10	55.30	49.80	44.80	39.80	34.80	30.10	26.00	22.00	17.90
330	340	70.00	64.10	58.30	52.50	47.40	42.40	37.40	32.40	28.10	24.10	20.00
340	350	73.40	67.10	61.30	55.50	50.00	45.00	40.00	35.00	30.20	26.20	22.10
350	360	76.80	70.30	64.30	58.50	52.80	47.60	42.60	37.60	32.60	28.30	24.20
360	370	80.20	73.70	67.30	61.50	55.80	50.20	45.20	40.20	35.20	30.40	26.30
370	380	83.60	77.10	70.50	64.50	58.80	53.00	47.80	42.80	37.80	32.80	28.40
380	390	87.00	80.50	73.90	67.50	61.80	56.00	50.40	45.40	40.40	35.40	30.50
390	400	90.40	83.90	77.30	70.80	64.80	59.00	53.20	48.00	43.00	38.00	33.00
400	410	93.80	87.30	80.70	74.20	67.80	62.00	56.20	50.60	45.60	40.60	35.60
410	420	97.20	90.70	84.10	77.60	71.10	65.00	59.20	53.50	48.20	43.20	38.20
420	430	100.60	94.10	87.50	81.00	74.50	68.00	62.20	56.50	50.80	45.80	40.80
430	440	104.10	97.50	90.90	84.40	77.90	71.30	65.20	59.50	53.70	48.40	43.40
440	450	108.00	100.90	94.30	87.80	81.30	74.70	68.20	62.50	56.70	51.00	46.00
450	460	111.90	104.40	97.70	91.20	84.70	78.10	71.60	65.50	59.70	53.90	48.60
460	470	115.80	108.30	101.10	94.60	88.10	81.50	75.00	68.50	62.70	56.90	51.20
470	480	119.70	112.20	104.70	98.00	91.50	84.90	78.40	71.80	65.70	59.90	54.20
480	490	123.60	116.10	108.60	101.40	94.90	88.30	81.80	75.20	68.70	62.90	57.20
490	500	127.50	120.00	112.50	105.00	98.30	91.70	85.20	78.60	72.10	65.90	60.20
500	510	131.40	123.90	116.40	108.90	101.70	95.10	88.60	82.00	75.50	69.00	63.20
510	520	135.30	127.80	120.30	112.80	105.30	98.50	92.00	85.40	78.90	72.40	66.20
520	530	139.20	131.70	124.20	116.70	109.20	101.90	95.40	88.80	82.30	75.80	69.20
530	540	143.10	135.60	128.10	120.60	113.10	105.60	98.80	92.20	85.70	79.20	72.60
540	550	147.00	139.50	132.00	124.50	117.00	109.50	102.20	95.60	89.10	82.60	76.00
550	560	150.90	143.40	135.90	128.40	120.90	113.40	105.90	99.00	92.50	86.00	79.40
560	570	154.80	147.30	139.80	132.30	124.80	117.30	109.80	102.40	95.90	89.40	82.80
570	580	158.70	151.20	143.70	136.20	128.70	121.20	113.70	106.20	99.30	92.80	86.20
580	590	162.60	155.10	147.60	140.10	132.60	125.10	117.60	110.10	102.70	96.20	89.60
590	600	166.50	159.00	151.50	144.00	136.50	129.00	121.50	114.00	106.50	99.60	93.00
600	610	170.40	162.90	155.40	147.90	140.40	132.90	125.40	117.90	110.40	103.00	96.40
610	620	174.30	166.80	159.30	151.80	144.30	136.80	129.30	121.80	114.30	106.80	99.80
620	630	178.20	170.70	163.20	155.70	148.20	140.70	133.20	125.70	118.20	110.70	103.20
630	640	182.10	174.60	167.10	159.60	152.10	144.60	137.10	129.60	122.10	114.60	107.10
640	650	186.00	178.50	171.00	163.50	156.00	148.50	141.00	133.50	126.00	118.50	111.00
650	660	189.90	182.40	174.90	167.40	159.90	152.40	144.90	137.40	129.90	122.40	114.90
660	670	193.80	186.30	178.80	171.30	163.80	156.30	148.80	141.30	133.80	126.30	118.80
		39 percent of the excess over $670 plus—										
$670 and over		195.80	188.30	180.80	173.30	165.80	158.30	150.80	143.30	135.80	128.30	120.80

MARRIED Persons—WEEKLY Payroll Period

And the wages are—		Exemptions claimed										
At least	But less than	0	1	2	3	4	5	6	7	8	9	10 or more
		The amount of income tax to be withheld shall be—										
$0	$46	$0	$0	$0	$0	$0	$0	$0	$0	$0	$0	$0
46	47	.10	0	0	0	0	0	0	0	0	0	0
47	48	.20	0	0	0	0	0	0	0	0	0	0
48	49	.40	0	0	0	0	0	0	0	0	0	0
49	50	.50	0	0	0	0	0	0	0	0	0	0
50	51	.70	0	0	0	0	0	0	0	0	0	0
51	52	.80	0	0	0	0	0	0	0	0	0	0
52	53	1.00	0	0	0	0	0	0	0	0	0	0
53	54	1.10	0	0	0	0	0	0	0	0	0	0
54	55	1.30	0	0	0	0	0	0	0	0	0	0
55	56	1.40	0	0	0	0	0	0	0	0	0	0
56	57	1.60	0	0	0	0	0	0	0	0	0	0
57	58	1.70	0	0	0	0	0	0	0	0	0	0
58	59	1.90	0	0	0	0	0	0	0	0	0	0
59	60	2.00	0	0	0	0	0	0	0	0	0	0
60	62	2.20	0	0	0	0	0	0	0	0	0	0
62	64	2.50	0	0	0	0	0	0	0	0	0	0
64	66	2.80	0	0	0	0	0	0	0	0	0	0
66	68	3.10	.20	0	0	0	0	0	0	0	0	0
68	70	3.40	.50	0	0	0	0	0	0	0	0	0
70	72	3.70	.80	0	0	0	0	0	0	0	0	0
72	74	4.00	1.10	0	0	0	0	0	0	0	0	0
74	76	4.30	1.40	0	0	0	0	0	0	0	0	0
76	78	4.60	1.70	0	0	0	0	0	0	0	0	0
78	80	4.90	2.00	0	0	0	0	0	0	0	0	0
80	82	5.20	2.30	0	0	0	0	0	0	0	0	0
82	84	5.50	2.60	0	0	0	0	0	0	0	0	0
84	86	5.80	2.90	.10	0	0	0	0	0	0	0	0
86	88	6.10	3.20	.40	0	0	0	0	0	0	0	0
88	90	6.40	3.50	.70	0	0	0	0	0	0	0	0
90	92	6.70	3.80	1.00	0	0	0	0	0	0	0	0
92	94	7.00	4.10	1.30	0	0	0	0	0	0	0	0
94	96	7.30	4.40	1.60	0	0	0	0	0	0	0	0
96	98	7.60	4.70	1.90	0	0	0	0	0	0	0	0
98	100	7.90	5.00	2.20	0	0	0	0	0	0	0	0
100	105	8.50	5.60	2.70	0	0	0	0	0	0	0	0
105	110	9.20	6.30	3.40	.50	0	0	0	0	0	0	0
110	115	10.00	7.10	4.20	1.30	0	0	0	0	0	0	0
115	120	10.70	7.80	4.90	2.00	0	0	0	0	0	0	0
120	125	11.50	8.60	5.70	2.80	0	0	0	0	0	0	0
125	130	12.20	9.30	6.40	3.50	.70	0	0	0	0	0	0
130	135	13.10	10.10	7.20	4.30	1.40	0	0	0	0	0	0
135	140	14.00	10.80	7.90	5.00	2.20	0	0	0	0	0	0
140	145	14.90	11.60	8.70	5.80	2.90	0	0	0	0	0	0
145	150	15.80	12.40	9.40	6.50	3.70	.80	0	0	0	0	0
150	160	17.20	13.70	10.60	7.70	4.80	1.90	0	0	0	0	0
160	170	19.00	15.50	12.10	9.20	6.30	3.40	.50	0	0	0	0
170	180	20.80	17.30	13.80	10.70	7.80	4.90	2.00	0	0	0	0
180	190	22.60	19.10	15.60	12.20	9.30	6.40	3.50	.60	0	0	0
190	200	24.40	20.90	17.40	14.00	10.80	7.90	5.00	2.10	0	0	0
200	210	26.20	22.70	19.20	15.80	12.30	9.40	6.50	3.60	.80	0	0
210	220	28.10	24.50	21.00	17.60	14.10	10.90	8.00	5.10	2.30	0	0
220	230	30.20	26.30	22.80	19.40	15.90	12.50	9.50	6.60	3.80	.90	0
230	240	32.30	28.30	24.60	21.20	17.70	14.30	11.00	8.10	5.30	2.40	0
240	250	34.40	30.40	26.40	23.00	19.50	16.10	12.60	9.60	6.80	3.90	1.00
250	260	36.50	32.50	28.50	24.80	21.30	17.90	14.40	11.10	8.30	5.40	2.50
260	270	38.60	34.60	30.60	26.60	23.10	19.70	16.20	12.70	9.80	6.90	4.00
270	280	40.70	36.70	32.70	28.60	24.90	21.50	18.00	14.50	11.30	8.40	5.50
280	290	42.80	38.80	34.80	30.70	26.70	23.30	19.80	16.30	12.90	9.90	7.00
290	300	45.10	40.90	36.90	32.80	28.80	25.10	21.60	18.10	14.70	11.40	8.50

MARRIED Persons—**WEEKLY** Payroll Period

And the wages are—		Exemptions claimed										
At least	But less than	0	1	2	3	4	5	6	7	8	9	10 or more
		The amount of income tax to be withheld shall be—										
$300	$310	$47.50	$43.00	$39.00	$34.90	$30.90	$26.90	$23.40	$19.90	$16.50	$13.00	$10.00
310	320	49.90	45.30	41.10	37.00	33.00	28.90	25.20	21.70	18.30	14.80	11.50
320	330	52.30	47.70	43.20	39.10	35.10	31.00	27.00	23.50	20.10	16.60	13.20
330	340	54.70	50.10	45.50	41.20	37.20	33.10	29.10	25.30	21.90	18.40	15.00
340	350	57.10	52.50	47.90	43.30	39.30	35.20	31.20	27.20	23.70	20.20	16.80
350	360	59.50	54.90	50.30	45.70	41.40	37.30	33.30	29.30	25.50	22.00	18.60
360	370	61.90	57.30	52.70	48.10	43.50	39.40	35.40	31.40	27.30	23.80	20.40
370	380	64.60	59.70	55.10	50.50	45.90	41.50	37.50	33.50	29.40	25.60	22.20
380	390	67.40	62.10	57.50	52.90	48.30	43.70	39.60	35.60	31.50	27.50	24.00
390	400	70.20	64.80	59.90	55.30	50.70	46.10	41.70	37.70	33.60	29.60	25.80
400	410	73.00	67.60	62.30	57.70	53.10	48.50	43.80	39.80	35.70	31.70	27.60
410	420	75.80	70.40	65.00	60.10	55.50	50.90	46.20	41.90	37.80	33.80	29.70
420	430	78.60	73.20	67.80	62.50	57.90	53.30	48.60	44.00	39.90	35.90	31.80
430	440	81.40	76.00	70.60	65.20	60.30	55.70	51.00	46.40	42.00	38.00	33.90
440	450	84.20	78.80	73.40	68.00	62.70	58.10	53.40	48.80	44.20	40.10	36.00
450	460	87.00	81.60	76.20	70.80	65.40	60.50	55.80	51.20	46.60	42.20	38.10
460	470	90.20	84.40	79.00	73.60	68.20	62.90	58.20	53.60	49.00	44.40	40.20
470	480	93.40	87.30	81.80	76.40	71.00	65.60	60.60	56.00	51.40	46.80	42.30
480	490	96.60	90.50	84.60	79.20	73.80	68.40	63.10	58.40	53.80	49.20	44.60
490	500	99.80	93.70	87.50	82.00	76.60	71.20	65.90	60.80	56.20	51.60	47.00
500	510	103.00	96.90	90.70	84.80	79.40	74.00	68.70	63.30	58.60	54.00	49.40
510	520	106.20	100.10	93.90	87.70	82.20	76.80	71.50	66.10	61.00	56.40	51.80
520	530	109.40	103.30	97.10	90.90	85.00	79.60	74.30	68.90	63.50	58.80	54.20
530	540	112.60	106.50	100.30	94.10	88.00	82.40	77.10	71.70	66.30	61.20	56.60
540	550	115.80	109.70	103.50	97.30	91.20	85.20	79.90	74.50	69.10	63.70	59.00
550	560	119.00	112.90	106.70	100.50	94.40	88.20	82.70	77.30	71.90	66.50	61.40
560	570	122.70	116.10	109.90	103.70	97.60	91.40	85.50	80.10	74.70	69.30	63.90
570	580	126.40	119.30	113.10	106.90	100.80	94.60	88.50	82.90	77.50	72.10	66.70
580	590	130.10	123.00	116.30	110.10	104.00	97.80	91.70	85.70	80.30	74.90	69.50
590	600	133.80	126.70	119.50	113.30	107.20	101.00	94.90	88.70	83.10	77.70	72.30
600	610	137.50	130.40	123.20	116.50	110.40	104.20	98.10	91.90	85.90	80.50	75.10
610	620	141.20	134.10	126.90	119.80	113.60	107.40	101.30	95.10	89.00	83.30	77.90
620	630	144.90	137.80	130.60	123.50	116.80	110.60	104.50	98.30	92.20	86.10	80.70
630	640	148.60	141.50	134.30	127.20	120.10	113.80	107.70	101.50	95.40	89.20	83.50
640	650	152.30	145.20	138.00	130.90	123.80	117.00	110.90	104.70	98.60	92.40	86.30
650	660	156.00	148.90	141.70	134.60	127.50	120.40	114.10	107.90	101.80	95.60	89.50
660	670	159.70	152.60	145.40	138.30	131.20	124.10	117.30	111.10	105.00	98.80	92.70
670	680	163.40	156.30	149.10	142.00	134.90	127.80	120.70	114.30	108.20	102.00	95.90
680	690	167.10	160.00	152.80	145.70	138.60	131.50	124.40	117.50	111.40	105.20	99.10
690	700	170.80	163.70	156.50	149.40	142.30	135.20	128.10	121.00	114.60	108.40	102.30
700	710	174.50	167.40	160.20	153.10	146.00	138.90	131.80	124.70	117.80	111.60	105.50
710	720	178.20	171.10	163.90	156.80	149.70	142.60	135.50	128.40	121.20	114.80	108.70
720	730	181.90	174.80	167.60	160.50	153.40	146.30	139.20	132.10	124.90	118.00	111.90
730	740	185.60	178.50	171.30	164.20	157.10	150.00	142.90	135.80	128.60	121.50	115.10
740	750	189.30	182.20	175.00	167.90	160.80	153.70	146.60	139.50	132.30	125.20	118.30
750	760	193.00	185.90	178.70	171.60	164.50	157.40	150.30	143.20	136.00	128.90	121.80
760	770	196.70	189.60	182.40	175.30	168.20	161.10	154.00	146.90	139.70	132.60	125.50
770	780	200.40	193.30	186.10	179.00	171.90	164.80	157.70	150.60	143.40	136.30	129.20
780	790	204.10	197.00	189.80	182.70	175.60	168.50	161.40	154.30	147.10	140.00	132.90
790	800	207.80	200.70	193.50	186.40	179.30	172.20	165.10	158.00	150.80	143.70	136.60
800	810	211.50	204.40	197.20	190.10	183.00	175.90	168.80	161.70	154.50	147.40	140.30
810	820	215.20	208.10	200.90	193.80	186.70	179.60	172.50	165.40	158.20	151.10	144.00
820	830	218.90	211.80	204.60	197.50	190.40	183.30	176.20	169.10	161.90	154.80	147.70
830	840	222.60	215.50	208.30	201.20	194.10	187.00	179.90	172.80	165.60	158.50	151.40
840	850	226.30	219.20	212.00	204.90	197.80	190.70	183.60	176.50	169.30	162.20	155.10
		37 percent of the excess over $850 plus—										
$850 and over		228.10	221.00	213.90	206.80	199.70	192.50	185.40	178.30	171.20	164.10	157.00

1980 Tax Table A/Single (Filing Status Box 1)

If line 11, Form 1040A, or line 34, Form 1040, is—		And the total number of exemptions claimed on line 6 is—		
Over	But not over	1	2	3
		Your tax is—		
11,100	11,150	1,413	1,203	1,001
11,150	11,200	1,424	1,214	1,010
11,200	11,250	1,434	1,224	1,020
11,250	11,300	1,445	1,235	1,029
11,300	11,350	1,455	1,245	1,039
11,350	11,400	1,466	1,256	1,048
11,400	11,450	1,476	1,266	1,058
11,450	11,500	1,487	1,277	1,067
11,500	11,550	1,497	1,287	1,077
11,550	11,600	1,508	1,298	1,088
11,600	11,650	1,518	1,308	1,098
11,650	11,700	1,529	1,319	1,109
11,700	11,750	1,539	1,329	1,119
11,750	11,800	1,550	1,340	1,130
11,800	11,850	1,561	1,350	1,140
11,850	11,900	1,573	1,361	1,151
11,900	11,950	1,585	1,371	1,161
11,950	12,000	1,597	1,382	1,172
12,000	12,050	1,609	1,392	1,182
12,050	12,100	1,621	1,403	1,193
12,100	12,150	1,633	1,413	1,203
12,150	12,200	1,645	1,424	1,214
12,200	12,250	1,657	1,434	1,224
12,250	12,300	1,669	1,445	1,235
12,300	12,350	1,681	1,455	1,245
12,350	12,400	1,693	1,466	1,256
12,400	12,450	1,705	1,476	1,266
12,450	12,500	1,717	1,487	1,277
12,500	12,550	1,729	1,497	1,287
12,550	12,600	1,741	1,508	1,298
12,600	12,650	1,753	1,518	1,308
12,650	12,700	1,765	1,529	1,319
12,700	12,750	1,777	1,539	1,329
12,750	12,800	1,789	1,550	1,340
12,800	12,850	1,801	1,561	1,350
12,850	12,900	1,813	1,573	1,361
12,900	12,950	1,825	1,585	1,371
12,950	13,000	1,837	1,597	1,382
13,000	13,050	1,849	1,609	1,392
13,050	13,100	1,861	1,621	1,403
13,100	13,150	1,873	1,633	1,413
13,150	13,200	1,885	1,645	1,424
13,200	13,250	1,897	1,657	1,434
13,250	13,300	1,909	1,669	1,445
13,300	13,350	1,921	1,681	1,455
13,350	13,400	1,933	1,693	1,466
13,400	13,450	1,945	1,705	1,476
13,450	13,500	1,957	1,717	1,487
13,500	13,550	1,969	1,729	1,497
13,550	13,600	1,981	1,741	1,508
13,600	13,650	1,993	1,753	1,518
13,650	13,700	2,005	1,765	1,529
13,700	13,750	2,017	1,777	1,539
13,750	13,800	2,029	1,789	1,550
13,800	13,850	2,041	1,801	1,561
13,850	13,900	2,053	1,813	1,573
13,900	13,950	2,066	1,825	1,585
13,950	14,000	2,079	1,837	1,597
14,000	14,050	2,092	1,849	1,609
14,050	14,100	2,105	1,861	1,621

Continued next column

If line 11, Form 1040A, or line 34, Form 1040, is—		And the total number of exemptions claimed on line 6 is—		
Over	But not over	1	2	3
		Your tax is—		
14,100	14,150	2,118	1,873	1,633
14,150	14,200	2,131	1,885	1,645
14,200	14,250	2,144	1,897	1,657
14,250	14,300	2,157	1,909	1,669
14,300	14,350	2,170	1,921	1,681
14,350	14,400	2,183	1,933	1,693
14,400	14,450	2,196	1,945	1,705
14,450	14,500	2,209	1,957	1,717
14,500	14,550	2,222	1,969	1,729
14,550	14,600	2,235	1,981	1,741
14,600	14,650	2,248	1,993	1,753
14,650	14,700	2,261	2,005	1,765
14,700	14,750	2,274	2,017	1,777
14,750	14,800	2,287	2,029	1,789
14,800	14,850	2,300	2,041	1,801
14,850	14,900	2,313	2,053	1,813
14,900	14,950	2,326	2,066	1,825
14,950	15,000	2,339	2,079	1,837
15,000	15,050	2,352	2,092	1,849
15,050	15,100	2,365	2,105	1,861
15,100	15,150	2,378	2,118	1,873
15,150	15,200	2,391	2,131	1,885
15,200	15,250	2,404	2,144	1,897
15,250	15,300	2,417	2,157	1,909
15,300	15,350	2,430	2,170	1,921
15,350	15,400	2,443	2,183	1,933
15,400	15,450	2,456	2,196	1,945
15,450	15,500	2,469	2,209	1,957
15,500	15,550	2,482	2,222	1,969
15,550	15,600	2,495	2,235	1,981
15,600	15,650	2,508	2,248	1,993
15,650	15,700	2,521	2,261	2,005
15,700	15,750	2,534	2,274	2,017
15,750	15,800	2,547	2,287	2,029
15,800	15,850	2,560	2,300	2,041
15,850	15,900	2,573	2,313	2,053
15,900	15,950	2,586	2,326	2,066
15,950	16,000	2,599	2,339	2,079
16,000	16,050	2,613	2,352	2,092
16,050	16,100	2,628	2,365	2,105
16,100	16,150	2,643	2,378	2,118
16,150	16,200	2,658	2,391	2,131
16,200	16,250	2,673	2,404	2,144
16,250	16,300	2,688	2,417	2,157
16,300	16,350	2,703	2,430	2,170
16,350	16,400	2,718	2,443	2,183
16,400	16,450	2,733	2,456	2,196
16,450	16,500	2,748	2,469	2,209
16,500	16,550	2,763	2,482	2,222
16,550	16,600	2,778	2,495	2,235
16,600	16,650	2,793	2,508	2,248
16,650	16,700	2,808	2,521	2,261
16,700	16,750	2,823	2,534	2,274
16,750	16,800	2,838	2,547	2,287
16,800	16,850	2,853	2,560	2,300
16,850	16,900	2,868	2,573	2,313
16,900	16,950	2,883	2,586	2,326
16,950	17,000	2,898	2,599	2,339
17,000	17,050	2,913	2,613	2,352
17,050	17,100	2,928	2,628	2,365

Continued next column

If line 11, Form 1040A, or line 34, Form 1040, is—		And the total number of exemptions claimed on line 6 is—		
Over	But not over	1	2	3
		Your tax is—		
17,100	17,150	2,943	2,643	2,378
17,150	17,200	2,958	2,658	2,391
17,200	17,250	2,973	2,673	2,404
17,250	17,300	2,988	2,688	2,417
17,300	17,350	3,003	2,703	2,430
17,350	17,400	3,018	2,718	2,443
17,400	17,450	3,033	2,733	2,456
17,450	17,500	3,048	2,748	2,469
17,500	17,550	3,063	2,763	2,482
17,550	17,600	3,078	2,778	2,495
17,600	17,650	3,093	2,793	2,508
17,650	17,700	3,108	2,808	2,521
17,700	17,750	3,123	2,823	2,534
17,750	17,800	3,138	2,838	2,547
17,800	17,850	3,153	2,853	2,560
17,850	17,900	3,168	2,868	2,573
17,900	17,950	3,183	2,883	2,586
17,950	18,000	3,198	2,898	2,599
18,000	18,050	3,213	2,913	2,613
18,050	18,100	3,228	2,928	2,628
18,100	18,150	3,243	2,943	2,643
18,150	18,200	3,258	2,958	2,658
18,200	18,250	3,273	2,973	2,673
18,250	18,300	3,288	2,988	2,688
18,300	18,350	3,303	3,003	2,703
18,350	18,400	3,318	3,018	2,718
18,400	18,450	3,333	3,033	2,733
18,450	18,500	3,348	3,048	2,748
18,500	18,550	3,363	3,063	2,763
18,550	18,600	3,378	3,078	2,778
18,600	18,650	3,393	3,093	2,793
18,650	18,700	3,408	3,108	2,808
18,700	18,750	3,423	3,123	2,823
18,750	18,800	3,438	3,138	2,838
18,800	18,850	3,453	3,153	2,853
18,850	18,900	3,468	3,168	2,868
18,900	18,950	3,483	3,183	2,883
18,950	19,000	3,498	3,198	2,898
19,000	19,050	3,513	3,213	2,913
19,050	19,100	3,528	3,228	2,928
19,100	19,150	3,543	3,243	2,943
19,150	19,200	3,558	3,258	2,958
19,200	19,250	3,574	3,273	2,973
19,250	19,300	3,591	3,288	2,988
19,300	19,350	3,608	3,303	3,003
19,350	19,400	3,625	3,318	3,018
19,400	19,450	3,642	3,333	3,033
19,450	19,500	3,659	3,348	3,048
19,500	19,550	3,676	3,363	3,063
19,550	19,600	3,693	3,378	3,078
19,600	19,650	3,710	3,393	3,093
19,650	19,700	3,727	3,408	3,108
19,700	19,750	3,744	3,423	3,123
19,750	19,800	3,761	3,438	3,138
19,800	19,850	3,778	3,453	3,153
19,850	19,900	3,795	3,468	3,168
19,900	19,950	3,812	3,483	3,183
19,950	20,000	3,829	3,498	3,198

1980 Tax Table B/Married Filing Joint Return (Filing Status Box 2)

If line 11, Form 1040A, or line 34, Form 1040, is—		And the total number of exemptions claimed on line 6 is—							
Over	But not over	2	3	4	5	6	7	8	9
		Your tax is—							
18,400	18,450	2,367	2,144	1,934	1,724	1,514	1,319	1,139	959
18,450	18,500	2,379	2,155	1,945	1,735	1,525	1,328	1,148	968
18,500	18,550	2,391	2,165	1,955	1,745	1,535	1,337	1,157	977
18,550	18,600	2,403	2,176	1,966	1,756	1,546	1,346	1,166	986
18,600	18,650	2,415	2,186	1,976	1,766	1,556	1,355	1,175	995
18,650	18,700	2,427	2,197	1,987	1,777	1,567	1,364	1,184	1,004
18,700	18,750	2,439	2,207	1,997	1,787	1,577	1,373	1,193	1,013
18,750	18,800	2,451	2,218	2,008	1,798	1,588	1,382	1,202	1,022
18,800	18,850	2,463	2,228	2,018	1,808	1,598	1,391	1,211	1,031
18,850	18,900	2,475	2,239	2,029	1,819	1,609	1,400	1,220	1,040
18,900	18,950	2,487	2,249	2,039	1,829	1,619	1,409	1,229	1,049
18,950	19,000	2,499	2,260	2,050	1,840	1,630	1,420	1,238	1,058
19,000	19,050	2,511	2,271	2,060	1,850	1,640	1,430	1,247	1,067
19,050	19,100	2,523	2,283	2,071	1,861	1,651	1,441	1,256	1,076
19,100	19,150	2,535	2,295	2,081	1,871	1,661	1,451	1,265	1,085
19,150	19,200	2,547	2,307	2,092	1,882	1,672	1,462	1,274	1,094
19,200	19,250	2,559	2,319	2,102	1,892	1,682	1,472	1,283	1,103
19,250	19,300	2,571	2,331	2,113	1,903	1,693	1,483	1,292	1,112
19,300	19,350	2,583	2,343	2,123	1,913	1,703	1,493	1,301	1,121
19,350	19,400	2,595	2,355	2,134	1,924	1,714	1,504	1,310	1,130
19,400	19,450	2,607	2,367	2,144	1,934	1,724	1,514	1,319	1,139
19,450	19,500	2,619	2,379	2,155	1,945	1,735	1,525	1,328	1,148
19,500	19,550	2,631	2,391	2,165	1,955	1,745	1,535	1,337	1,157
19,550	19,600	2,643	2,403	2,176	1,966	1,756	1,546	1,346	1,166
19,600	19,650	2,655	2,415	2,186	1,976	1,766	1,556	1,355	1,175
19,650	19,700	2,667	2,427	2,197	1,987	1,777	1,567	1,364	1,184
19,700	19,750	2,679	2,439	2,207	1,997	1,787	1,577	1,373	1,193
19,750	19,800	2,691	2,451	2,218	2,008	1,798	1,588	1,382	1,202
19,800	19,850	2,703	2,463	2,228	2,018	1,808	1,598	1,391	1,211
19,850	19,900	2,715	2,475	2,239	2,029	1,819	1,609	1,400	1,220
19,900	19,950	2,727	2,487	2,249	2,039	1,829	1,619	1,409	1,229
19,950	20,000	2,739	2,499	2,260	2,050	1,840	1,630	1,420	1,238
20,000	20,050	2,751	2,511	2,271	2,060	1,850	1,640	1,430	1,247
20,050	20,100	2,763	2,523	2,283	2,071	1,861	1,651	1,441	1,256
20,100	20,150	2,775	2,535	2,295	2,081	1,871	1,661	1,451	1,265
20,150	20,200	2,787	2,547	2,307	2,092	1,882	1,672	1,462	1,274
20,200	20,250	2,799	2,559	2,319	2,102	1,892	1,682	1,472	1,283
20,250	20,300	2,811	2,571	2,331	2,113	1,903	1,693	1,483	1,292
20,300	20,350	2,823	2,583	2,343	2,123	1,913	1,703	1,493	1,301
20,350	20,400	2,835	2,595	2,355	2,134	1,924	1,714	1,504	1,310
20,400	20,450	2,847	2,607	2,367	2,144	1,934	1,724	1,514	1,319
20,450	20,500	2,859	2,619	2,379	2,155	1,945	1,735	1,525	1,328
20,500	20,550	2,871	2,631	2,391	2,165	1,955	1,745	1,535	1,337
20,550	20,600	2,883	2,643	2,403	2,176	1,966	1,756	1,546	1,346
20,600	20,650	2,895	2,655	2,415	2,186	1,976	1,766	1,556	1,355
20,650	20,700	2,907	2,667	2,427	2,197	1,987	1,777	1,567	1,364
20,700	20,750	2,919	2,679	2,439	2,207	1,997	1,787	1,577	1,373
20,750	20,800	2,931	2,691	2,451	2,218	2,008	1,798	1,588	1,382
20,800	20,850	2,943	2,703	2,463	2,228	2,018	1,808	1,598	1,391
20,850	20,900	2,955	2,715	2,475	2,239	2,029	1,819	1,609	1,400
20,900	20,950	2,967	2,727	2,487	2,249	2,039	1,829	1,619	1,409
20,950	21,000	2,979	2,739	2,499	2,260	2,050	1,840	1,630	1,420
21,000	21,050	2,991	2,751	2,511	2,271	2,060	1,850	1,640	1,430
21,050	21,100	3,003	2,763	2,523	2,283	2,071	1,861	1,651	1,441
21,100	21,150	3,015	2,775	2,535	2,295	2,081	1,871	1,661	1,451
21,150	21,200	3,027	2,787	2,547	2,307	2,092	1,882	1,672	1,462
21,200	21,250	3,039	2,799	2,559	2,319	2,102	1,892	1,682	1,472
21,250	21,300	3,051	2,811	2,571	2,331	2,113	1,903	1,693	1,483
21,300	21,350	3,063	2,823	2,583	2,343	2,123	1,913	1,703	1,493
21,350	21,400	3,075	2,835	2,595	2,355	2,134	1,924	1,714	1,504
21,400	21,450	3,087	2,847	2,607	2,367	2,144	1,934	1,724	1,514
21,450	21,500	3,099	2,859	2,619	2,379	2,155	1,945	1,735	1,525
21,500	21,550	3,111	2,871	2,631	2,391	2,165	1,955	1,745	1,535
21,550	21,600	3,123	2,883	2,643	2,403	2,176	1,966	1,756	1,546
21,600	21,650	3,135	2,895	2,655	2,415	2,186	1,976	1,766	1,556
21,650	21,700	3,147	2,907	2,667	2,427	2,197	1,987	1,777	1,567
21,700	21,750	3,159	2,919	2,679	2,439	2,207	1,997	1,787	1,577
21,750	21,800	3,171	2,931	2,691	2,451	2,218	2,008	1,798	1,588
21,800	21,850	3,183	2,943	2,703	2,463	2,228	2,018	1,808	1,598
21,850	21,900	3,195	2,955	2,715	2,475	2,239	2,029	1,819	1,609
21,900	21,950	3,207	2,967	2,727	2,487	2,249	2,039	1,829	1,619
21,950	22,000	3,219	2,979	2,739	2,499	2,260	2,050	1,840	1,630

1980 Tax Table B/Married Filing Joint Return (Filing Status Box 2)

If line 11, Form 1040A, or line 34, Form 1040, is—		And the total number of exemptions claimed on line 6 is—							
Over	But not over	2	3	4	5	6	7	8	9
		Your tax is—							
25,600	25,650	4,232	3,952	3,672	3,392	3,135	2,895	2,655	2,415
25,650	25,700	4,246	3,966	3,686	3,406	3,147	2,907	2,667	2,427
25,700	25,750	4,260	3,980	3,700	3,420	3,159	2,919	2,679	2,439
25,750	25,800	4,274	3,994	3,714	3,434	3,171	2,931	2,691	2,451
25,800	25,850	4,288	4,008	3,728	3,448	3,183	2,943	2,703	2,463
25,850	25,900	4,302	4,022	3,742	3,462	3,195	2,955	2,715	2,475
25,900	25,950	4,316	4,036	3,756	3,476	3,207	2,967	2,727	2,487
25,950	26,000	4,330	4,050	3,770	3,490	3,219	2,979	2,739	2,499
26,000	26,050	4,344	4,064	3,784	3,504	3,231	2,991	2,751	2,511
26,050	26,100	4,358	4,078	3,798	3,518	3,243	3,003	2,763	2,523
26,100	26,150	4,372	4,092	3,812	3,532	3,255	3,015	2,775	2,535
26,150	26,200	4,386	4,106	3,826	3,546	3,267	3,027	2,787	2,547
26,200	26,250	4,400	4,120	3,840	3,560	3,280	3,039	2,799	2,559
26,250	26,300	4,414	4,134	3,854	3,574	3,294	3,051	2,811	2,571
26,300	26,350	4,428	4,148	3,868	3,588	3,308	3,063	2,823	2,583
26,350	26,400	4,442	4,162	3,882	3,602	3,322	3,075	2,835	2,595
26,400	26,450	4,456	4,176	3,896	3,616	3,336	3,087	2,847	2,607
26,450	26,500	4,470	4,190	3,910	3,630	3,350	3,099	2,859	2,619
26,500	26,550	4,484	4,204	3,924	3,644	3,364	3,111	2,871	2,631
26,550	26,600	4,498	4,218	3,938	3,658	3,378	3,123	2,883	2,643
26,600	26,650	4,513	4,232	3,952	3,672	3,392	3,135	2,895	2,655
26,650	26,700	4,529	4,246	3,966	3,686	3,406	3,147	2,907	2,667
26,700	26,750	4,545	4,260	3,980	3,700	3,420	3,159	2,919	2,679
26,750	26,800	4,561	4,274	3,994	3,714	3,434	3,171	2,931	2,691
26,800	26,850	4,577	4,288	4,008	3,728	3,448	3,183	2,943	2,703
26,850	26,900	4,593	4,302	4,022	3,742	3,462	3,195	2,955	2,715
26,900	26,950	4,609	4,316	4,036	3,756	3,476	3,207	2,967	2,727
26,950	27,000	4,625	4,330	4,050	3,770	3,490	3,219	2,979	2,739
27,000	27,050	4,641	4,344	4,064	3,784	3,504	3,231	2,991	2,751
27,050	27,100	4,657	4,358	4,078	3,798	3,518	3,243	3,003	2,763
27,100	27,150	4,673	4,372	4,092	3,812	3,532	3,255	3,015	2,775
27,150	27,200	4,689	4,386	4,106	3,826	3,546	3,267	3,027	2,787
27,200	27,250	4,705	4,400	4,120	3,840	3,560	3,280	3,039	2,799
27,250	27,300	4,721	4,414	4,134	3,854	3,574	3,294	3,051	2,811
27,300	27,350	4,737	4,428	4,148	3,868	3,588	3,308	3,063	2,823
27,350	27,400	4,753	4,442	4,162	3,882	3,602	3,322	3,075	2,835
27,400	27,450	4,769	4,456	4,176	3,896	3,616	3,336	3,087	2,847
27,450	27,500	4,785	4,470	4,190	3,910	3,630	3,350	3,099	2,859
27,500	27,550	4,801	4,484	4,204	3,924	3,644	3,364	3,111	2,871
27,550	27,600	4,817	4,498	4,218	3,938	3,658	3,378	3,123	2,883
27,600	27,650	4,833	4,513	4,232	3,952	3,672	3,392	3,135	2,895
27,650	27,700	4,849	4,529	4,246	3,966	3,686	3,406	3,147	2,907
27,700	27,750	4,865	4,545	4,260	3,980	3,700	3,420	3,159	2,919
27,750	27,800	4,881	4,561	4,274	3,994	3,714	3,434	3,171	2,931
27,800	27,850	4,897	4,577	4,288	4,008	3,728	3,448	3,183	2,943
27,850	27,900	4,913	4,593	4,302	4,022	3,742	3,462	3,195	2,955
27,900	27,950	4,929	4,609	4,316	4,036	3,756	3,476	3,207	2,967
27,950	28,000	4,945	4,625	4,330	4,050	3,770	3,490	3,219	2,979
28,000	28,050	4,961	4,641	4,344	4,064	3,784	3,504	3,231	2,991
28,050	28,100	4,977	4,657	4,358	4,078	3,798	3,518	3,243	3,003
28,100	28,150	4,993	4,673	4,372	4,092	3,812	3,532	3,255	3,015
28,150	28,200	5,009	4,689	4,386	4,106	3,826	3,546	3,267	3,027
28,200	28,250	5,025	4,705	4,400	4,120	3,840	3,560	3,280	3,039
28,250	28,300	5,041	4,721	4,414	4,134	3,854	3,574	3,294	3,051
28,300	28,350	5,057	4,737	4,428	4,148	3,868	3,588	3,308	3,063
28,350	28,400	5,073	4,753	4,442	4,162	3,882	3,602	3,322	3,075
28,400	28,450	5,089	4,769	4,456	4,176	3,896	3,616	3,336	3,087
28,450	28,500	5,105	4,785	4,470	4,190	3,910	3,630	3,350	3,099
28,500	28,550	5,121	4,801	4,484	4,204	3,924	3,644	3,364	3,111
28,550	28,600	5,137	4,817	4,498	4,218	3,938	3,658	3,378	3,123
28,600	28,650	5,153	4,833	4,513	4,232	3,952	3,672	3,392	3,135
28,650	28,700	5,169	4,849	4,529	4,246	3,966	3,686	3,406	3,147
28,700	28,750	5,185	4,865	4,545	4,260	3,980	3,700	3,420	3,159
28,750	28,800	5,201	4,881	4,561	4,274	3,994	3,714	3,434	3,171
28,800	28,850	5,217	4,897	4,577	4,288	4,008	3,728	3,448	3,183
28,850	28,900	5,233	4,913	4,593	4,302	4,022	3,742	3,462	3,195
28,900	28,950	5,249	4,929	4,609	4,316	4,036	3,756	3,476	3,207
28,950	29,000	5,265	4,945	4,625	4,330	4,050	3,770	3,490	3,219
29,000	29,050	5,281	4,961	4,641	4,344	4,064	3,784	3,504	3,231
29,050	29,100	5,297	4,977	4,657	4,358	4,078	3,798	3,518	3,243
29,100	29,150	5,313	4,993	4,673	4,372	4,092	3,812	3,532	3,255
29,150	29,200	5,329	5,009	4,689	4,386	4,106	3,826	3,546	3,267

1980 Tax Table C/Married Filing Separate Return (Filing Status Box 3)

If line 11, Form 1040A, or line 34, Form 1040, is—		And the total number of exemptions claimed on line 6 is—		
Over	But not over	1	2	3
		Your tax is—		
10,800	10,850	1,571	1,331	1,096
10,850	10,900	1,583	1,343	1,106
10,900	10,950	1,595	1,355	1,117
10,950	11,000	1,607	1,367	1,127
11,000	11,050	1,619	1,379	1,139
11,050	11,100	1,631	1,391	1,151
11,100	11,150	1,644	1,403	1,163
11,150	11,200	1,658	1,415	1,175
11,200	11,250	1,672	1,427	1,187
11,250	11,300	1,686	1,439	1,199
11,300	11,350	1,700	1,451	1,211
11,350	11,400	1,714	1,463	1,223
11,400	11,450	1,728	1,475	1,235
11,450	11,500	1,742	1,487	1,247
11,500	11,550	1,756	1,499	1,259
11,550	11,600	1,770	1,511	1,271
11,600	11,650	1,784	1,523	1,283
11,650	11,700	1,798	1,535	1,295
11,700	11,750	1,812	1,547	1,307
11,750	11,800	1,826	1,559	1,319
11,800	11,850	1,840	1,571	1,331
11,850	11,900	1,854	1,583	1,343
11,900	11,950	1,868	1,595	1,355
11,950	12,000	1,882	1,607	1,367
12,000	12,050	1,896	1,619	1,379
12,050	12,100	1,910	1,631	1,391
12,100	12,150	1,924	1,644	1,403
12,150	12,200	1,938	1,658	1,415
12,200	12,250	1,952	1,672	1,427
12,250	12,300	1,966	1,686	1,439
12,300	12,350	1,980	1,700	1,451
12,350	12,400	1,994	1,714	1,463
12,400	12,450	2,008	1,728	1,475
12,450	12,500	2,022	1,742	1,487
12,500	12,550	2,036	1,756	1,499
12,550	12,600	2,050	1,770	1,511
12,600	12,650	2,064	1,784	1,523
12,650	12,700	2,078	1,798	1,535
12,700	12,750	2,092	1,812	1,547
12,750	12,800	2,106	1,826	1,559
12,800	12,850	2,120	1,840	1,571
12,850	12,900	2,134	1,854	1,583
12,900	12,950	2,148	1,868	1,595
12,950	13,000	2,162	1,882	1,607
13,000	13,050	2,176	1,896	1,619
13,050	13,100	2,190	1,910	1,631
13,100	13,150	2,204	1,924	1,644
13,150	13,200	2,218	1,938	1,658
13,200	13,250	2,232	1,952	1,672
13,250	13,300	2,246	1,966	1,686
13,300	13,350	2,261	1,980	1,700
13,350	13,400	2,277	1,994	1,714
13,400	13,450	2,293	2,008	1,728
13,450	13,500	2,309	2,022	1,742
13,500	13,550	2,325	2,036	1,756
13,550	13,600	2,341	2,050	1,770
13,600	13,650	2,357	2,064	1,784
13,650	13,700	2,373	2,078	1,798
13,700	13,750	2,389	2,092	1,812
13,750	13,800	2,405	2,106	1,826

Continued next column

If line 11, Form 1040A, or line 34, Form 1040, is—		And the total number of exemptions claimed on line 6 is—		
Over	But not over	1	2	3
		Your tax is—		
13,800	13,850	2,421	2,120	1,840
13,850	13,900	2,437	2,134	1,854
13,900	13,950	2,453	2,148	1,868
13,950	14,000	2,469	2,162	1,882
14,000	14,050	2,485	2,176	1,896
14,050	14,100	2,501	2,190	1,910
14,100	14,150	2,517	2,204	1,924
14,150	14,200	2,533	2,218	1,938
14,200	14,250	2,549	2,232	1,952
14,250	14,300	2,565	2,246	1,966
14,300	14,350	2,581	2,261	1,980
14,350	14,400	2,597	2,277	1,994
14,400	14,450	2,613	2,293	2,008
14,450	14,500	2,629	2,309	2,022
14,500	14,550	2,645	2,325	2,036
14,550	14,600	2,661	2,341	2,050
14,600	14,650	2,677	2,357	2,064
14,650	14,700	2,693	2,373	2,078
14,700	14,750	2,709	2,389	2,092
14,750	14,800	2,725	2,405	2,106
14,800	14,850	2,741	2,421	2,120
14,850	14,900	2,757	2,437	2,134
14,900	14,950	2,773	2,453	2,148
14,950	15,000	2,789	2,469	2,162
15,000	15,050	2,805	2,485	2,176
15,050	15,100	2,821	2,501	2,190
15,100	15,150	2,837	2,517	2,204
15,150	15,200	2,853	2,533	2,218
15,200	15,250	2,869	2,549	2,232
15,250	15,300	2,885	2,565	2,246
15,300	15,350	2,901	2,581	2,261
15,350	15,400	2,917	2,597	2,277
15,400	15,450	2,933	2,613	2,293
15,450	15,500	2,949	2,629	2,309
15,500	15,550	2,965	2,645	2,325
15,550	15,600	2,981	2,661	2,341
15,600	15,650	2,997	2,677	2,357
15,650	15,700	3,013	2,693	2,373
15,700	15,750	3,029	2,709	2,389
15,750	15,800	3,045	2,725	2,405
15,800	15,850	3,061	2,741	2,421
15,850	15,900	3,077	2,757	2,437
15,900	15,950	3,093	2,773	2,453
15,950	16,000	3,110	2,789	2,469
16,000	16,050	3,128	2,805	2,485
16,050	16,100	3,147	2,821	2,501
16,100	16,150	3,165	2,837	2,517
16,150	16,200	3,184	2,853	2,533
16,200	16,250	3,202	2,869	2,549
16,250	16,300	3,221	2,885	2,565
16,300	16,350	3,239	2,901	2,581
16,350	16,400	3,258	2,917	2,597
16,400	16,450	3,276	2,933	2,613
16,450	16,500	3,295	2,949	2,629
16,500	16,550	3,313	2,965	2,645
16,550	16,600	3,332	2,981	2,661
16,600	16,650	3,350	2,997	2,677
16,650	16,700	3,369	3,013	2,693
16,700	16,750	3,387	3,029	2,709
16,750	16,800	3,406	3,045	2,725

Continued next column

If line 11, Form 1040A, or line 34, Form 1040, is—		And the total number of exemptions claimed on line 6 is—		
Over	But not over	1	2	3
		Your tax is—		
16,800	16,850	3,424	3,061	2,741
16,850	16,900	3,443	3,077	2,757
16,900	16,950	3,461	3,093	2,773
16,950	17,000	3,480	3,110	2,789
17,000	17,050	3,498	3,128	2,805
17,050	17,100	3,517	3,147	2,821
17,100	17,150	3,535	3,165	2,837
17,150	17,200	3,554	3,184	2,853
17,200	17,250	3,572	3,202	2,869
17,250	17,300	3,591	3,221	2,885
17,300	17,350	3,609	3,239	2,901
17,350	17,400	3,628	3,258	2,917
17,400	17,450	3,646	3,276	2,933
17,450	17,500	3,665	3,295	2,949
17,500	17,550	3,683	3,313	2,965
17,550	17,600	3,702	3,332	2,981
17,600	17,650	3,720	3,350	2,997
17,650	17,700	3,739	3,369	3,013
17,700	17,750	3,757	3,387	3,029
17,750	17,800	3,776	3,406	3,045
17,800	17,850	3,794	3,424	3,061
17,850	17,900	3,813	3,443	3,077
17,900	17,950	3,831	3,461	3,093
17,950	18,000	3,850	3,480	3,110
18,000	18,050	3,868	3,498	3,128
18,050	18,100	3,887	3,517	3,147
18,100	18,150	3,905	3,535	3,165
18,150	18,200	3,924	3,554	3,184
18,200	18,250	3,942	3,572	3,202
18,250	18,300	3,961	3,591	3,221
18,300	18,350	3,979	3,609	3,239
18,350	18,400	3,998	3,628	3,258
18,400	18,450	4,016	3,646	3,276
18,450	18,500	4,035	3,665	3,295
18,500	18,550	4,053	3,683	3,313
18,550	18,600	4,072	3,702	3,332
18,600	18,650	4,092	3,720	3,350
18,650	18,700	4,113	3,739	3,369
18,700	18,750	4,135	3,757	3,387
18,750	18,800	4,156	3,776	3,406
18,800	18,850	4,178	3,794	3,424
18,850	18,900	4,199	3,813	3,443
18,900	18,950	4,221	3,831	3,461
18,950	19,000	4,242	3,850	3,480
19,000	19,050	4,264	3,868	3,498
19,050	19,100	4,285	3,887	3,517
19,100	19,150	4,307	3,905	3,535
19,150	19,200	4,328	3,924	3,554
19,200	19,250	4,350	3,942	3,572
19,250	19,300	4,371	3,961	3,591
19,300	19,350	4,393	3,979	3,609
19,350	19,400	4,414	3,998	3,628
19,400	19,450	4,436	4,016	3,646
19,450	19,500	4,457	4,035	3,665
19,500	19,550	4,479	4,053	3,683
19,550	19,600	4,500	4,072	3,702
19,600	19,650	4,522	4,092	3,720
19,650	19,700	4,543	4,113	3,739
19,700	19,750	4,565	4,135	3,757
19,750	19,800	4,586	4,156	3,776
19,800	19,850	4,608	4,178	3,794
19,850	19,900	4,629	4,199	3,813
19,900	19,950	4,651	4,221	3,831
19,950	20,000	4,672	4,242	3,850

1980 Tax Rate Schedules

If you cannot use one of the Tax Tables, figure your tax on the amount on Schedule TC, Part I, line 3, by using the appropriate Tax Rate Schedule on this page. Enter the tax on Schedule TC, Part I, line 4.
Note: *Your zero bracket amount has been built into these Tax Rate Schedules.*

SCHEDULE X—Single Taxpayers

Use this schedule if you checked **Filing Status Box 1** on Form 1040—

If the amount on Schedule TC, Part I, line 3, is: / Enter on Schedule TC, Part I, line 4:

Not over $2,300 . . . . . —0—

Over—	But not over—		of the amount over—
$2,300	$3,400	14%	$2,300
$3,400	$4,400	$154+16%	$3,400
$4,400	$6,500	$314+18%	$4,400
$6,500	$8,500	$692+19%	$6,500
$8,500	$10,800	$1,072+21%	$8,500
$10,800	$12,900	$1,555+24%	$10,800
$12,900	$15,000	$2,059+26%	$12,900
$15,000	$18,200	$2,605+30%	$15,000
$18,200	$23,500	$3,565+34%	$18,200
$23,500	$28,800	$5,367+39%	$23,500
$28,800	$34,100	$7,434+44%	$28,800
$34,100	$41,500	$9,766+49%	$34,100
$41,500	$55,300	$13,392+55%	$41,500
$55,300	$81,800	$20,982+63%	$55,300
$81,800	$108,300	$37,677+68%	$81,800
$108,300	....	$55,697+70%	$108,300

SCHEDULE Y—Married Taxpayers and Qualifying Widows and Widowers

Married Filing Joint Returns and Qualifying Widows and Widowers

Use this schedule if you checked **Filing Status Box 2 or 5** on Form 1040—

If the amount on Schedule TC, Part I, line 3, is: / Enter on Schedule TC, Part I, line 4:

Not over $3,400 . . . . . —0—

Over—	But not over—		of the amount over—
$3,400	$5,500	14%	$3,400
$5,500	$7,600	$294+16%	$5,500
$7,600	$11,900	$630+18%	$7,600
$11,900	$16,000	$1,404+21%	$11,900
$16,000	$20,200	$2,265+24%	$16,000
$20,200	$24,600	$3,273+28%	$20,200
$24,600	$29,900	$4,505+32%	$24,600
$29,900	$35,200	$6,201+37%	$29,900
$35,200	$45,800	$8,162+43%	$35,200
$45,800	$60,000	$12,720+49%	$45,800
$60,000	$85,600	$19,678+54%	$60,000
$85,600	$109,400	$33,502+59%	$85,600
$109,400	$162,400	$47,544+64%	$109,400
$162,400	$215,400	$81,464+68%	$162,400
$215,400	....	$117,504+70%	$215,400

Married Filing Separate Returns

Use this schedule if you checked **Filing Status Box 3** on Form 1040—

If the amount on Schedule TC, Part I, line 3, is: / Enter on Schedule TC, Part I, line 4:

Not over $1,700 . . . . . —0—

Over—	But not over—		of the amount over—
$1,700	$2,750	14%	$1,700
$2,750	$3,800	$147.00+16%	$2,750
$3,800	$5,950	$315.00+18%	$3,800
$5,950	$8,000	$702.00+21%	$5,950
$8,000	$10,100	$1,132.50+24%	$8,000
$10,100	$12,300	$1,636.50+28%	$10,100
$12,300	$14,950	$2,252.50+32%	$12,300
$14,950	$17,600	$3,100.50+37%	$14,950
$17,600	$22,900	$4,081.00+43%	$17,600
$22,900	$30,000	$6,360.00+49%	$22,900
$30,000	$42,800	$9,839.00+54%	$30,000
$42,800	$54,700	$16,751.00+59%	$42,800
$54,700	$81,200	$23,772.00+64%	$54,700
$81,200	$107,700	$40,732.00+68%	$81,200
$107,700	....	$58,752.00+70%	$107,700

Careers Chart

This four-page chart gives information about selected careers in eight career clusters: Trades, Technology, Science, Health, Arts, Social Service, Business Contact, and Business Detail.* Information given includes training qualifications of most workers, estimated employment in 1978, and projected average annual openings to 1990 due to growth and replacement needs.

The following code is used under the heading "Qualifications."

C 4 years or more of college required
S Special training required (technical or vocational school, junior college, or apprenticeship)
— No college or special training required

Trades	Qualifications	Estimated employment in 1978	Average annual openings to 1990
Air-conditioning, refrigeration, or heating mechanic	S	210,000	8200
Aircraft mechanic	S	132,000	3500
Appliance repairer	—	145,000	6900
Assembler	—	1,164,000	77,000
Automobile mechanic	—	860,000	37,000
Bricklayer	S	205,000	6200
Carpenter	S	1,253,000	58,000
Electrician (construction)	S	290,000	12,900
Industrial machinery repairer	S	655,000	58,000
Inspector (manufacturing)	—	771,000	35,000
Instrument maker (mechanical)	S	6000	300
Machine tool operator	—	542,000	19,600
Machinist	S	484,000	22,500
Maintenance electrician	S	300,000	15,500
Meatcutter	S	204,000	5200
Millwright	S	95,000	4700
Painter or paperhanger	—	504,000	27,000
Plumber or pipefitter	S	428,000	20,000
Power truck operator	—	363,000	14,000
Supervisor	S	1,671,000	69,000
Television or radio service technician	S	131,000	6100
Tool and die maker	S	170,000	8600
Truck and bus mechanic	—	165,000	6800
Welder	—	679,000	35,000

*Cluster titles are based on interest areas measured by the Vocational Interest Profile used in The American College Testing Career Planning Program. Reprinted by permission. Information about qualifications and employment is from *Occupational Projections and Training Data, 1980 Edition.*

The eight career clusters are first mentioned in career lessons on pages 74–75, 98–99, 112–113, 156–159, 202–203, 238–239, 322–323, 368–369. When a cluster is first mentioned, you might have the students turn to this chart and read the data for the careers in that cluster. Remind students that employment prospects depend on many factors, such as the number of people seeking employment in a particular career.

Technology

	Qualifications	Estimated employment in 1978	Average annual openings to 1990
Aerospace engineer	C	60,000	1900
Air traffic controller	C	21,000	700
Chemical engineer	C	53,000	1800
Civil engineer	C	155,000	7800
Drafter	S	296,000	11,000
Electrical engineer	C	300,000	10,500
Engineering and science technician	S	600,000	23,000
Forester	C	31,200	1400
Mechanical engineer	C	195,000	7500
Pilot or copilot	S	76,000	3800
Surveyor or surveying technician	S	62,000	2300

Science

Chemist	C	143,000	6100
Economist	C	130,000	7800
Geologist	C	31,000	1700
Life scientist	C	215,000	11,200
Mathematician	C	33,500	1000
Meteorologist	C	7300	300
Physicist	C	44,000	1000

Health

Dental assistant	—	150,000	11,000
Dental hygienist	S	35,000	6000
Dentist	C	120,000	5500
Dietitian	C	35,000	3300
Hospital attendant or nursing aide	—	1,037,000	94,000
Licensed practical nurse	S	518,000	60,000
Medical laboratory worker	S,C	210,000	14,800
Pharmacist	C	135,000	7800
Physician	C	405,000	19,000
Radiologic technologist	S	100,000	9000
Registered nurse	S,C	1,060,000	85,000
Surgical technician	S	35,000	2600
Veterinarian	C	33,500	1700

Arts	Qualifications	Estimated employment in 1978	Average annual openings to 1990
Actor or actress	S	13,400	850
Architect	C	54,000	4000
Dancer	S	8000	550
Display worker	—	44,000	3300
Interior designer	S	79,000	3600
Musician or music teacher	S,C	127,000	8900
Newspaper reporter	C	45,000	2400
Photographer	—	93,000	3800
Radio or television announcer	—	27,000	850
Singer or singing teacher	S,C	22,000	1600

Social Service

Barber	S	121,000	9700
Building custodian	—	2,251,000	176,000
College or university teacher	C	673,000	11,000
Cook or chef	—	1,186,000	86,000
Cosmetologist	S	542,000	29,000
Firefighter	—	220,000	7500
Flight attendant	S	48,000	4800
Gasoline service station attendant	—	340,000	5200
Guard	—	550,000	70,000
Kindergarten or elementary school teacher	C	1,322,000	86,000
Lawyer	C	487,000	37,000
Librarian	C	142,000	8000
Mail carrier	—	245,000	7000
Mortician	S	45,000	2200
Personnel or labor relations worker	C	405,000	17,000
Police officer (municipal)	—	450,000	16,500
Private household worker	—	1,162,000	45,000
School counselor	C	45,000	1700
Secondary school teacher	C	1,087,000	7200
Social service aide	—	134,000	7500
Social worker	C	385,000	22,000
State police officer	—	47,000	1800
Teacher aide	—	342,000	26,000
Telephone operator	—	311,000	9900
Waiter or waitress	—	1,383,000	70,000

Business Contact	Qualifications	Estimated employment in 1978	Average annual openings to 1990
Airline passenger agent	—	56,000	2200
Automobile parts clerk	—	97,000	4200
Automobile sales agent	—	158,000	10,400
Bank officer or manager	C	330,000	28,000
Bank teller	—	410,000	17,000
Conductor (railroad)	—	37,000	1700
Hotel manager or assistant	C	168,000	8900
Local truckdriver	—	1,720,000	64,000
Long-distance truckdriver	—	584,000	21,500
Manufacturers' sales representative	C	402,000	21,700
Postal clerk	—	260,000	2000
Public relations worker	C	185,000	7500
Purchasing agent	C	185,000	13,400
Real estate sales agent or broker	S	555,000	50,000
Retail sales worker	—	2,851,000	226,000
Securities sales worker	S	109,000	5500
Taxi driver	—	94,000	4300
Wholesale trade salesworker	—	840,000	40,000

Business Detail			
Accountant	C	985,000	61,000
Bank clerk	—	505,000	45,000
Bookkeeping worker	—	1,830,000	96,000
Cashier	—	1,400,000	119,000
Computer operator	—	666,000	12,500
File clerk	—	273,000	16,500
Front office clerk (hotel)	—	79,000	5400
Insurance actuary	C	9000	500
Office machine operator	—	160,000	9700
Programmer	S,C	247,000	9200
Receptionist	—	588,000	41,000
Shipping and receiving clerk	—	461,000	22,000
Stenographer or secretary	—	3,684,000	305,000
Stock clerk	—	507,000	23,000
Systems analyst	C	182,000	7900
Typist	—	1,044,000	59,000

Glossary

Brief descriptions of certain important terms are listed in this glossary. These descriptions need not be considered formal, complete definitions.

amortization table
Table showing amount of each payment of a loan and sometimes the breakdown of each payment into interest and principal.

annual
For one year, or 12 months.

annual yield
Percent of interest earned for 1 year; the rule is

$$\frac{\text{amount earned in 1 year}}{\text{amount invested}}.$$

The answer is expressed as a percent.

area
Measure of an amount of surface, given in square units, inside a closed, plane figure.

assessed valuation
Value of property, usually a percentage of actual market value, upon which the property tax is based.

average daily balance
Average of the daily unpaid amounts in an account; used to determine the finance charge.

bank statement
Record from a bank showing deposits, canceled checks, and other information concerning an account.

bearings
Position or direction of boundaries, used in making a scale drawing of a piece of property.

beneficiary
Person named in an insurance policy to receive benefits if the insured person dies.

bodily injury insurance
Type of liability insurance that protects a car owner financially if someone is injured by the car.

bond
Type of investment in which a person lends money to a company or a government agency that will repay the amount of the loan with interest.

broker
Person who buys and sells for others; stocks, bonds, and real estate are often handled by brokers.

budget
Organized spending plan.

calorie
Unit of heat used to express the fuel value of food.

canceled checks
Checks, written on an account, that have been paid by the bank, marked "paid," and returned to the depositor with the bank statement.

capacity
Greatest number of units a container can hold.

cash on delivery
Amount paid at the time of delivery of a purchase.

cash value
Amount of money that can be borrowed from a life insurance policy by the insured; the policy can be traded in for this amount.

CD
Certificate of deposit.

certificate of deposit
Savings account of a specified size (often a multiple of $1000) that earns interest at a rate higher than that of a regular savings account.

charge account
Allows a customer to buy goods or services and pay at a later date or on an installment plan.

check
Written order to a bank directing the bank to pay out money from a depositor's account.

checking account
Bank account into which money is deposited; the money is withdrawn by using forms called checks.

check register
Depositor's record that a check has been written; gives the same information as a check stub.

check stub
Depositor's record that a check has been written; gives the same information as a check register.

classified ads
Short advertisements placed in a special section of newspapers or magazines; the ads concern such things as jobs available, jobs wanted, and property for rent or for sale; also called wants ads.

closing costs
Various fees and taxes that must be paid to complete the purchase of real estate.

collision insurance
Type of insurance that pays for repair of damage to the insured person's car caused by an accident.

commission
Straight commission: a percentage of total sales that is paid to a salesperson as wages. Graduated commission: wages in which the rate of commission varies, depending on the total sales.

common stock
Share of a business bought as an investment.

compound interest
Interest computed on the principal and on the interest previously earned.

comprehensive insurance
Type of insurance that pays for repair or replacement of a car in case of fire, theft, vandalism, or acts of nature.

consumer
A person who buys or rents goods and services offered to the public.

cross-products
The cross-products for the ratios below are 3×8 and 4×6; two ratios are equal if their cross-products are equal.
$\frac{3}{4} = \frac{6}{8}$ because $3 \times 8 = 4 \times 6$.

data
Information such as scores, values, and measurement.

deductible amount
Amount subtracted from an insured loss and not replaced by the insurance; \$50 and \$100 are common deductible amounts.

deductions
Money withheld from a person's pay for taxes, insurance, social security, and so on; also, amounts a person may subtract from gross income when computing income tax.

deferred-payment price
Sum of the down payment and total paid in monthly installments.

denominator
In the fraction $\frac{5}{6}$, the denominator is 6.

deposit
Money given to a bank to open or to add to a checking or a savings account; also, an amount paid when a person orders an item.

depreciation
Decrease in value of a piece of property because of age and wear; for automobiles, the greatest depreciation usually occurs in the first two years.

discount
Amount deducted from list price to obtain sale price; a percent of the list price.

dividend
In $820 \div 20 = 41$, the dividend is 820.

dividends (stock)
Part of a company's profits that is paid periodically to stockholders.

divisor
In $820 \div 20 = 41$, the divisor is 20.

down payment
Amount paid at the time of an installment purchase to reduce the amount of loan needed.

equation
Mathematical sentence that uses the equal sign; examples are $5 + 6 = 11$ and $4n = 28$.

exemptions
Persons claimed by a taxpayer as legally dependent on the taxpayer for support.

face value
Value stated on a bond, note, insurance policy, etc.

factor
Number used in multiplication; in $18 \times 4 = 72$, the numbers 18 and 4 are factors.

Federal Insurance Contributions Act (FICA)
Commonly called social security; provides retirement income, medical payments, and survivors' benefits to those who qualify.

FICA deduction
Amount withheld from a person's pay for social security.

finance charge
Amount charged for buying an item on credit or on an installment plan.

financing
Purchasing goods or services through installment buying.

fixed monthly expenses
Costs that require the same amount to be paid every month, such as rent.

fuel economy rate
Quotient of the distance traveled divided by the amount of fuel consumed; usually expressed as kilometers per liter or as miles per gallon.

graph
Picture used to show data; the picture could be a bar, line, or circle graph, or a pictograph. A graph might also be points on a grid matched with given ordered pairs of numbers.

gross income
Income before any deductions are made.

gross pay
Wages or salary before any deductions are made.

hourly rate
Dollar amount paid for each hour worked or fraction thereof.

income tax return
Form that must be completed to determine one's tax liability; depending on circumstances, a taxpayer may use the short form (1040A) or the long form (1040).

installment
Part of a sum of money or debt to be paid at certain stated times.

insurance
Provides protection against financial loss; common types of insurance are health, life (term, straight, limited payment, endowment), automobile, homeowner's, and personal property.

insured
Person covered by an insurance policy.

interest
Amount paid for the use of money; usually a percent of the amount invested, loaned, or borrowed.

investment
Expenditure of money for something that is expected to produce a profit.

itemized deductions
Expenses a taxpayer may list on which no tax is paid; used only if the total exceeds the zero bracket amount.

landlord
Person who owns buildings or land that is rented to others.

lease
Right to use real estate or other property for a given length of time with a payment of rent.

level-payment loan
Loan that is repaid in equal monthly installments.

liability insurance
Automobile insurance that includes bodily injury insurance and property damage insurance.

list price
Original price or regular price before discounts, fees, or commissions are subtracted.

loan
Amount of money that is borrowed for a certain period of time and upon which interest is usually paid.

mean
Average; the sum of a set of numbers divided by the number of addends.

median
Middle number in a set of numbers arranged in order.

minimum payment
Least amount that can be paid on a monthly bill for credit card expenses.

mode
Number occurring most often in a set of numbers.

mortgage loan
Money borrowed to buy a home.

mutual fund
Investment company that sells shares and combines the investors' money in order to buy a large variety of stocks and bonds.

net deposit
Amount deposited in an account, less cash received.

net pay
Amount left after all deductions have been subtracted from gross pay; sometimes called take-home pay.

numerator
In the fraction $\frac{5}{6}$, the numerator is 5.

overtime
Time worked beyond the regular hours; an increase in the hourly rate is often given for this time.

percent
Word that indicates "hundredths" or "out of 100"; 4 percent (4%) means 0.04, or $\frac{4}{100}$.

perimeter
Measure of the distance around a closed figure.

policy (insurance)
Written agreement between the person being insured and the insurer.

premium
Cost of an insurance policy; premiums can be paid monthly, semiannually, or annually.

principal
Amount of money upon which interest is computed.

product
Answer in a multiplication problem; in $8 \times 12 = 96$, the product is 96.

promissory note
Written statement that is signed by a borrower and tells to whom, how much, and when payment will be made.

property damage insurance
Type of liability insurance that protects the car owner financially if the car damages the property of others.

proportion
Statement that two ratios are equal; an example is
$\frac{3}{8} = \frac{9}{24}$.

protractor
Instrument used to draw or measure angles.

quarterly
Every 3 months, or 4 times a year.

quotient
Answer in a division problem; in $48 \div 6 = 8$, the quotient is 8.

real estate tax
Tax based upon the value of real estate owned.

reconciling a bank statement
Procedure used to see that the checkbook balance and the bank statement agree; this verifies the balance left in the account.

remainder
When 15 is divided by 6, the remainder is 3.
$$6\overline{)15}\ \to\ 2\text{ R3}$$

salary
Fixed amount paid to an employee at regular intervals for regular hours of work; usually paid every week, every 2 weeks, or every month.

sales tax
Tax imposed by state or local government on the retail price of certain goods and services.

savings account
Account at a bank or other savings institution into which money is deposited to earn interest.

scale drawing
Drawing in which all distances are measured and are in a constant ratio to the actual distances.

semiannual
Every 6 months, or twice a year.

service charge
Amount charged by a bank for handling an account; the service charge is printed on the bank statement.

share of stock
One unit of ownership in a company or corporation.

simple interest formula
Basic method of computing interest; the interest (I) equals the principal (p) times the rate (r) times the time (t) expressed in years.
$$I = p \times r \times t$$

social security
See Federal Insurance Contributions Act.

statistics
Collection of data, usually numbers, relating to any topic.

sticker price
Quoted price of a car, including the suggested retail price and the price of optional equipment.

surveyor
Person who accurately determines boundaries, measures distances, and makes scale drawings of land.

time and a half
Overtime rate of pay; 1.5 times the regular hourly rate.

tip
Small amount of money in excess of regular charges paid by a customer for a service, such as a tip paid to a waiter or a waitress for serving a meal.

trade-in allowance
Amount of money allowed for a used article as part of the purchase price of a new item.

unit price
Price per unit of measure of an item.

utilities
Public-service items, such as gas electricity, water, or telephone service, that are usually paid for by the individual consumer.

variable monthly expenses
Costs that change from month to month; most of a person's expenses are variable to some extent.

volume
Measure of an amount of space, given in cubic units.

wage and tax statement
Form W-2; a form, issued by an employer to an employee, that states the income earned and taxes withheld for the employee during the calendar year.

want ads
See classified ads.

zero bracket amount
The minimum deduction allowed a taxpayer when a federal income tax return is filed.

Selected Answers

page 5

Set A **1.** 2000; 1500; 1540 **3.** 5000; 4900; 4870 **5.** 1000; 900; 930 **7.** 6000; 6000; 6010 **9.** 7000; 7000; 7000

Set B **11.** 13; 12.7; 12.68 **13.** 14; 13.9; 13.88 **15.** 48; 48.0; 47.97 **17.** 321; 320.7; 320.71 **19.** 100; 100.1; 100.08

Related Problems **21.** 4,000,000 **23.** $28.10; $28 **25.** $30.20; $30

page 7

Set A **1.** 110; 109 **3.** 100; 104 **5.** 430; 434 **7.** 140; 136 **9.** 1200; 1165

Set B **11.** 45; 44.95 **13.** 7; 7.19 **15.** 18; 18.46 **17.** 3; 2.73

Set C **19.** 40; 44 **21.** 80; 84 **23.** 200; 204

Set D **25.** 88; 87.69 **27.** 5; 4.733 **29.** 9; 9.31 **31.** 15; 14.55 **33.** 31; 30.614

Related Problems **35.** $12.08

page 9

Set A **1.** 4500 **3.** 14,000 **5.** 480,000 **7.** 5,400,000 **9.** 40,000 **11.** 1800 **13.** 81,000 **15.** 2400

Set B **17.** 1500; 1484 **19.** 1000; 1026 **21.** 14,000; 13,616 **23.** 18,000; 17,632 **25.** 100,000; 108,072 **27.** 60,000; 64,414 **29.** 50,000; 54,135 **31.** 720,000; 716,374 **33.** 1,600,000; 1,560,780 **35.** 2,000,000; 2,127,224

Mixed Practice **37.** 320,000 **39.** 353,792 **41.** 29,852 **43.** 246,000 **45.** 48,600,000 **47.** 6071 **49.** 3120 **51.** 34,486 **53.** 66,000 **55.** 3298 **57.** 16,000 **59.** 364,000

Related Problems **61.** 6000 bushels **63.** 4200 pounds

page 11

Set A **1.** 0.08 **3.** 0.064 **5.** 0.0036 **7.** 0.0056 **9.** 2.5 **11.** 0.081 **13.** 4000 **15.** 0.02 **17.** 150 **19.** 5.4

Set B **21.** 180; 179.2 **23.** 0.04; 0.04108 **25.** 24; 23.994 **27.** 0.1; 0.13412 **29.** 18; 18.4968 **31.** 500; 504.45 **33.** 0.18; 0.176902 **35.** 24; 23.9328 **37.** 360; 359.6899 **39.** 18; 17.98563

Mixed Practice **41.** 0.032 **43.** 14.11 **45.** 0.0024 **47.** 3.6 **49.** 2.2715 **51.** 1239.92 **53.** 48.5007 **55.** 0.7

Related Problems **57.** $82.81 **59.** $288.61

page 13

Set A **1.** 394 **3.** 36 R2 **5.** 49 R53 **7.** 471 R1 **9.** 175 R115

Set B **11.** 29.86 **13.** 2.19 **15.** 0.20 **17.** 2.12 **19.** 4.83

Set C **21.** 8 **23.** 4 **25.** 5 **27.** 3 **29.** 9

Related Problems **31.** 89.3 feet

page 15

Set A **1.** $>$ **3.** $<$ **5.** $>$ **7.** $>$ **9.** $>$

Set B **11.** $\frac{3}{4}$ **13.** $\frac{2}{5}$ **15.** $\frac{3}{4}$ **17.** $\frac{1}{3}$

Set C **19.** $\frac{29}{3}$ **21.** $\frac{53}{12}$ **23.** $\frac{55}{8}$ **25.** $\frac{71}{10}$

Set D **27.** $4\frac{2}{3}$ **29.** 9 **31.** $2\frac{2}{5}$ **33.** 3

Related Problems **35.** No

page 17

Set A **1.** $\frac{5}{12}$ **3.** $\frac{1}{2}$ **5.** $\frac{4}{5}$

Set B **7.** 4; $4\frac{1}{5}$ **9.** 16; $15\frac{3}{5}$ **11.** 36; $35\frac{1}{2}$

Set C **13.** $\frac{5}{6}$ **15.** $1\frac{4}{5}$ **17.** $3\frac{5}{7}$

Mixed Practice **19.** $2\frac{1}{7}$ **21.** $1\frac{1}{2}$ **23.** $2\frac{3}{16}$ **25.** 4 **27.** $\frac{5}{24}$

Related Problems **29.** 375 miles

page 19

Set A **1.** $\frac{11}{24}$ **3.** $\frac{13}{14}$ **5.** $1\frac{3}{16}$ **7.** $\frac{29}{36}$ **9.** $1\frac{23}{24}$ **11.** 7; $7\frac{1}{6}$ **13.** 3; $2\frac{17}{20}$
15. 11; $10\frac{11}{12}$ **17.** 13; $13\frac{1}{24}$ **19.** 11; $10\frac{15}{16}$ **21.** 8; $7\frac{19}{20}$

Set B **23.** $\frac{1}{8}$ **25.** $\frac{1}{4}$ **27.** $\frac{1}{24}$ **29.** $\frac{1}{24}$ **31.** $3\frac{2}{5}$ **33.** 3; $3\frac{1}{4}$
35. 12; $11\frac{5}{8}$ **37.** 5; $5\frac{2}{9}$ **39.** 14; $13\frac{13}{16}$ **41.** 8; $7\frac{17}{20}$ **43.** 5; $5\frac{11}{24}$

Related Problems **45.** $16\frac{3}{8}$

page 20 **1.** 0.833 **3.** 0.846 **5.** 0.625 **7.** 0.389 **9.** 0.288 **11.** 1.071
13. 2.622 **15.** 7.600 **17.** 2.800 **19.** 14.417 **21.** 31.067 **23.** 2.182
25. 17.273 **27.** 53.444 **29.** 15.333 **31.** 6.354

page 21 **1.** 7000; 7500; 7480 **2.** 24; 23.7; 23.72 **3.** 141 **4.** 8.28 **5.** 34
6. 41.46 **7.** 21,000 **8.** 24,192 **9.** 3.5 **10.** 35.041 **11.** 582

12. 6.23 **13.** 350 **14.** $>$ **15.** $\frac{2}{3}$ **16.** $\frac{39}{8}$ **17.** $9\frac{1}{3}$ **18.** $\frac{5}{21}$ **19.** $3\frac{1}{9}$

20. $4\frac{1}{2}$ **21.** $2\frac{4}{5}$ **22.** $\frac{19}{20}$ **23.** $6\frac{5}{24}$ **24.** $\frac{19}{40}$ **25.** $3\frac{5}{9}$

page 25

Set A **1.** $a = 15$ **3.** $f = 1.53$ **5.** $c = 6.3$ **7.** $y = 4.1$ **9.** $m = 21$
11. $t = 8.9$ **13.** $m = 6$

Set B **15.** $g = 23$ **17.** $h = 1.38$ **19.** $n = 24$ **21.** $k = 0.79$ **23.** $m = 147$
25. $t = 35.8$ **27.** $x = 8.02$

Mixed Practice **29.** $t = 27$ **31.** $m = 12$ **33.** $t = 0.93$ **35.** $s = 5.6$
37. $w = 51.19$ **39.** $y = 53$ **41.** $p = 91$ **43.** $b = 2.76$ **45.** $z = 9.05$
47. $g = 33.4$

Related Problems **49.** $r - 1.25 = 11.85$; \$13.10

page 27

Set A **1.** $a = 47$ **3.** $c = 17$ **5.** $x = 0.9$

Set B **7.** $f = 0.6$ **9.** $r = 15.2$

Set C **11.** $a = 3$ **13.** $t = 9$ **15.** $x = 12$

Mixed Practice **17.** $f = 0.096$ **19.** $y = 0$ **21.** $z = 90$ **23.** $s = 4$ **25.** $x = 0$
27. $x = 50$ **29.** $k = 0$

Related Problems **31.** $0.85g = 7.65$; 9 games **33.** $15t = 135$; 9 teams

page 29

Set A **1.** $a = 1$ **3.** $n = 9$ **5.** $b = 3.5$ **7.** $m = 5$ **9.** $n = 1$

Set B **11.** $m = 6$ **13.** $t = 7$ **15.** $n = 36$ **17.** $b = 144$ **19.** $x = 81$

Mixed Practice **21.** $z = 8$ **23.** $x = 18$ **25.** $m = 0.2$ **27.** $x = 2$ **29.** $b = 4$

Related Problems **31.** $3r - 450 = 315$; \$255

page 31

Set A **1.** $84 = 84$ **3.** $210 \neq 222$ **5.** $192 = 192$ **7.** $528 = 528$ **9.** $2.4 = 2.4$
11. $21.6 = 21.6$ **13.** $0.1 = 0.1$ **15.** $453.6 \neq 420$

Set B **17.** $a = 15$ **19.** $d = 9$ **21.** $x = 3.75$ **23.** $h = 4.2$ **25.** $x = 40$
27. $s = 200$ **29.** $t = 0.006$ **31.** $y = 0.5$

Related Problems **33.** 18 meters

pages 32–33

Set A **1.** 43% **3.** 9% **5.** 2.7% **7.** 22.5% **9.** 19.75% **11.** 7.45%
13. 125% **15.** 246.5%

Set B **17.** 50% **19.** 80% **21.** 68% **23.** 5% **25.** 62.5% **27.** 37.5%
29. 220%

Set C **31.** 0.23 **33.** 0.02 **35.** 0.135 **37.** 0.0875 **39.** 0.035
41. 0.3225 **43.** 1.35 **45.** 1.07

Set D **47.** $\frac{7}{10}$ **49.** $\frac{1}{2}$ **51.** $\frac{3}{4}$ **53.** $\frac{7}{20}$ **55.** $\frac{47}{100}$ **57.** $\frac{61}{100}$ **59.** $1\frac{9}{100}$

Related Problems **61.** 0.22 **63.** 75%

pages 35–37
Set A **1.** 14 **3.** 2.5 **5.** 32.34 **7.** 21.25 **9.** 42 **11.** 0.7125
Set B **13.** 60% **15.** 88% **17.** 75% **19.** 8% **21.** 15% **23.** 67.5%
Set C **25.** 40 **27.** 90 **29.** 450 **31.** 11 **33.** 30 **35.** 144
Mixed Practice **37.** 17 **39.** 160 **41.** 350 **43.** 75% **45.** 47% **47.** 14.5
Related Problems **49.** \$0.36 **51.** \$0.17 **53.** 21% **55.** \$2.90 **57.** \$140
59. \$6.38; \$14.88

page 38 **1.** \$709.59 **3.** \$636.23 **5.** \$471.49 **7.** \$1387.08 **9.** \$2415.19
11. \$1011.95; \$758.96; \$762.75

page 39 **1.** $d = 4.5$ **2.** $m = 8.5$ **3.** $f = 7.99$ **4.** $g = 7.95$ **5.** $x = 53$
6. $t = 7$ **7.** $b = 2.16$ **8.** $a = 4$ **9.** $c = 5$ **10.** $y = 8$ **11.** $a = 68$
12. $x = 6$ **13.** $250 \neq 260$ **14.** $28.8 = 28.8$ **15.** $c = 24$ **16.** $t = 88$
17. 6% **18.** 46.5% **19.** 76% **20.** 31.25% **21.** 0.57 **22.** 0.0575
23. $\frac{41}{100}$ **24.** $\frac{19}{50}$ **25.** 31.62 **26.** 24 **27.** 15% **28.** 87.5% **29.** 45
30. 150

page 43
Set A **1.** 3.87 km **3.** 14 mm **5.** 2130 km
Set B **7.** 60 m **9.** 4590 km
Related Problems **11–15.** Answers will vary.

page 45
Set A **1.** 392.0 mm^2 **3.** 9.4 km^2 **5.** 322.5 m^2
Set B **7.** 210.0 mm^2 **9.** 36.4 m^2
Set C **11.** 8177.0 mm^3 **13.** 104.5 cm^3 **15.** 1131.5 cm^3
Related Problems **17.** 0.8 m^3

page 47
Set A **1.** 250 mL **3.** 40 L **5.** 150 mL
Set B **7.** 85 g **9.** 165 g
Related Problems **11.** Liter **13.** Milliliter **15.** Gram

page 49
Set A **1.** 500 cm **3.** 93 mm **5.** 1275 cm **7.** 500 mL **9.** 2100 mg
Set B **11.** 0.935 km **13.** 0.429 m **15.** 6.7 cm **17.** 0.084 L **19.** 1.375 g
Mixed Practice **21.** 23,000 m **23.** 180 mm **25.** 0.06 m **27.** 0.25 L
29. 1.296 g
Related Problems **31.** 1000 grams **33.** 500 milliliters

page 51 **1.** 0°C **3.** 3°C **5.** 125°C **7.** 39.8°C **9.** 10°C
Related Problems **11.** ⁻28°C **13.** ⁻10°C **15.** 25 km/h

page 53
Set A **1.** 8 hours 35 minutes **3.** 8 hours 20 minutes
Set B **5.** 11:35 A.M. **7.** 6:25 A.M.
Set C **9.** 3 hours 10 minutes **11.** 6 hours 35 minutes
Related Problems **13.** 8 hours 5 minutes **15.** 4:15 P.M.

page 55
Set A **1.**

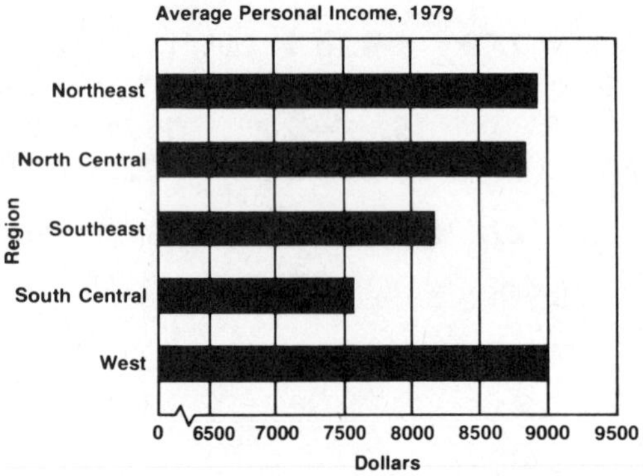

Set B **3.**

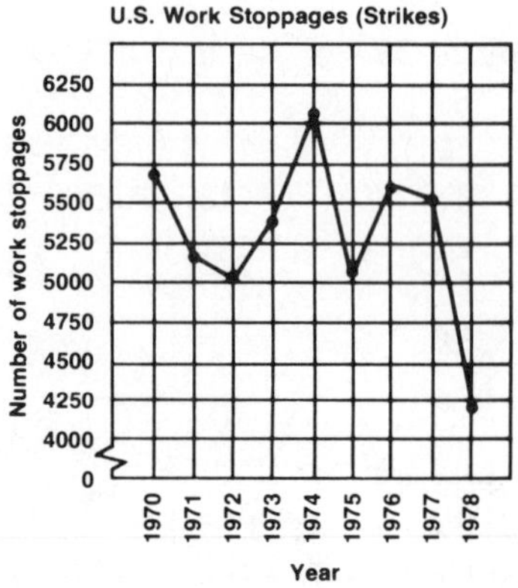

Related Problems **5.** $5 billion **7.** $15 billion; $28 billion

page 57
Set A **1.** 1,443,600,000 t **3.** 561,400,000 t **5.** 320,800,000 t **7.** $5250
9. $1400 **11.** $1750
Set B **13.**

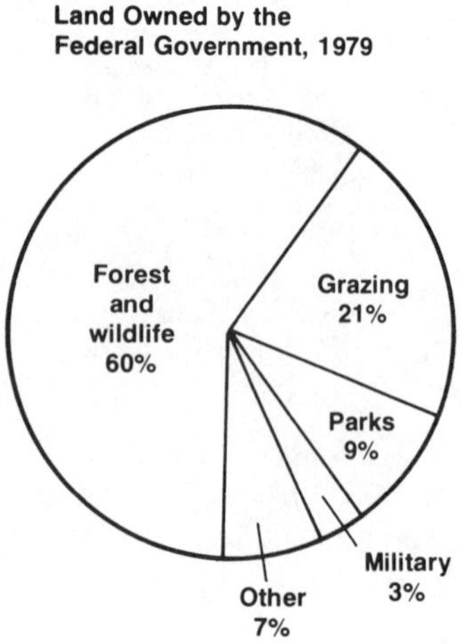

15.

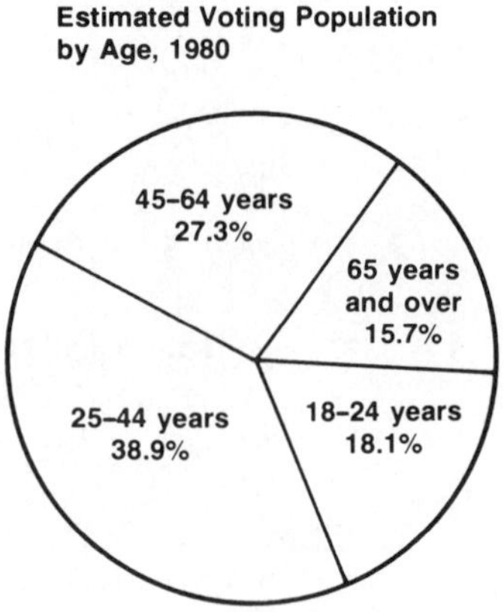

page 57 continued

Related Problems **17.** 3,104,000 managers **19.** 25.8%

page 59

Set A **1.** 6 **3.** 38 **5.** 26 **7.** 121 **9.** 10.3

Set B **11.** 7 **13.** 21 **15.** 25 **17.** 121 **19.** 10.3

Set C **21.** 7 **23.** 21 **25.** 29 **27.** 116 and 132 **29.** 10.3

Related Problems **31.** Bob 131, Matt 156; handicap: Bob 25

33. Bev 119, John 115; handicap: John 4

page 60 **1.** 600.5 **3.** 4567 **5.** 50,883.6 **7.** 68,802.1 **9.** 241.3

11. 1757 students **13.** 56,501 people

page 61 **1.** 3 cm **2.** 1 m **3.** 33.6 m^2 **4.** 51.7 cm^2 **5.** 576.6 cm^3

6. 13 L **7.** 600 g **8.** 7630 g **9.** 0.34 m **10.** 80°C

11. 10 hours 5 minutes **12.** 8:05 P.M. **13.** 3 hours 45 minutes

14.

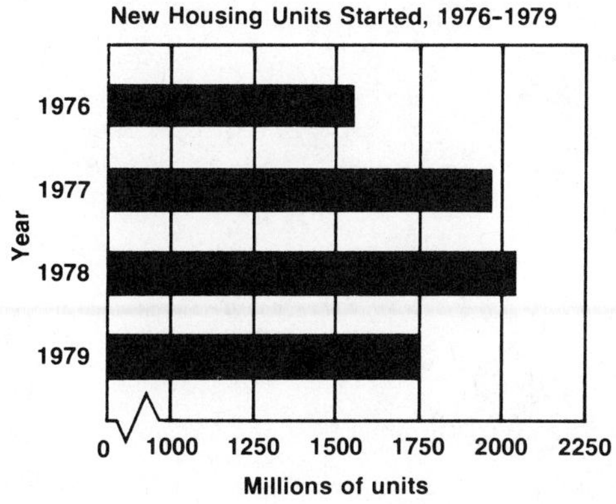

15.

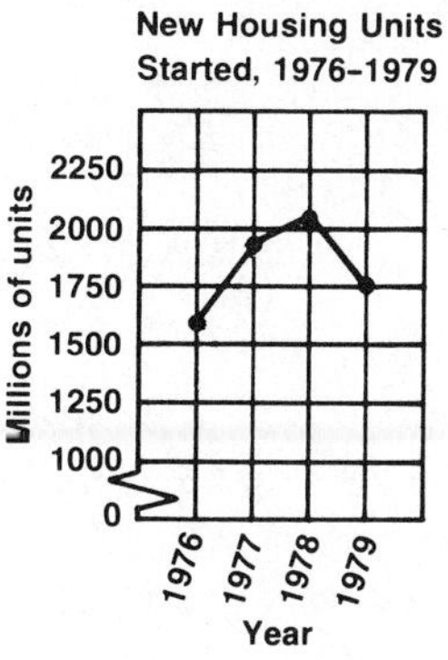

16. 8,840,000 households

17.

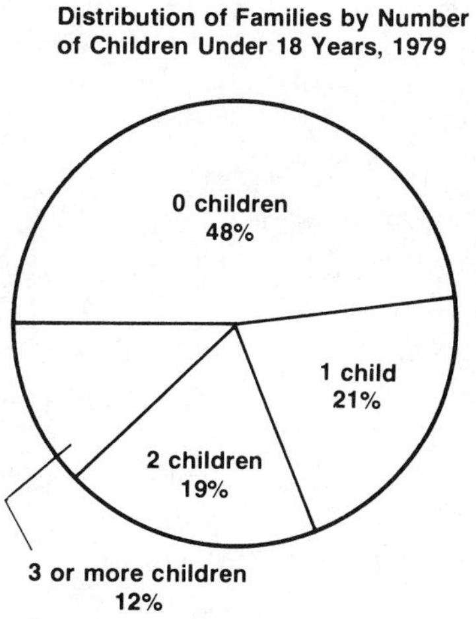

18. 18 **19.** 18 **20.** 21

page 65 **1.** 44 **3.** 55 **5.** 68 **7.** 69 **9.** 90

page 69 **1.** $404.00; $404.00 **3.** $260.00; $9.75; $48.75; $308.75
5. $248.00; $9.30; $74.40; $322.40 **7.** $320.80; $12.03; $27.07; $347.87
9. $341.20; $12.80; $44.80; $386.00 **11.** $321.20; $12.05; $63.26; $384.46

page 71 **1.** $410.00 **3.** $298.40 **5.** $428.20 **7.** $375.07 **9.** $550

page 73 **1.** $1.58 **3.** $1.29 **5.** $1.66 **7.** $0.82 **9.** $0.37
11. $11.98; $4.79 **13.** $2.29; $0.92 **15.** $4.50; $1.80 **17.** $11.96; $4.78

page 75 **1.** $242.50 **3.** $336.50 **5.** $265.57 **7.** $318.92 **9.** $269
11. $834

page 76 **1.** $1020.00 **3.** $1225.00 **5.** $1264.75

page 77 **1.** $9073.00; 14.0% **3.** $10,692.97; 14.3% **5.** $15,281.85; 11.5%
7. $16,254.34; 10.2% **9.** $16,680.94; 14.2% **11.** $19,976.87; 9.3%

pages 79–81 **1.** $13.50 **3.** $18.80 **5.** $84.40 **7.** $65.20 **9.** $46.20
11. $39.00 **13.** $10.70 **15.** $85.20 **17.** $6.29 **19.** $15.08 **21.** $12.07
23. $102.88 **25.** None **27.** $24.60; $15.69; $195.63
29. $58.10; $20.69; $223.16 **31.** $80.50; $25.90; $267.68

page 83 **1.** M; $2432 **3.** G; $200 **5.** $16,125 **7.** $185.52 **9.** $24,612.50

page 84
Rounding whole numbers and decimals **1.** 1000; 700; 670 **3.** 1000; 1200; 1250
5. 5000; 5000; 5040 **7.** 65,000; 65,200; 65,190 **9.** 88,000; 87,900; 87,900
11. 3; 3.3; 3.28 **13.** 75; 74.5; 74.52 **15.** 153; 152.8; 152.80
17. 391; 391.5; 391.48 **19.** 85; 84.7; 84.67 **21.** 479; 479.0; 478.98
Subtracting whole numbers and decimals **1.** 31 **3.** 66 **5.** 9 **7.** 12.5 **9.** 12.71
11. 15.81 **13.** 3.482 **15.** 17.345 **17.** 0.353 **19.** 0.6 **21.** 5.103
23. 71.4 **25.** 4.39 **27.** 12.516
Multiplying whole numbers **1.** 1500 **3.** 42,000 **5.** 540,000 **7.** 180,000
9. 301 **11.** 3,400,000 **13.** 7857 **15.** 2125 **17.** 3,570,000 **19.** 4032
21. 34,408 **23.** 217,994 **25.** 8,113,050 **27.** 2,169,288

page 85 **1.** \$194.40 **2.** \$288 **3.** \$155.82 **4.** \$234 **5.** \$240 **6.** \$522.50 **7.** \$30.70 **8.** \$24.30 **9.** \$208.00 **10.** B; \$420

page 89 **1.** \$514.65; \$454.65 **3.** \$70.31; \$70.31 **5.** \$419.18; \$344.18 **7.** \$182.07 **9.** \$469.52

pages 90–91 **1.** Twenty-seven and $\frac{81}{100}$ **3.** Sixty and $\frac{00}{100}$ **5.** Fifteen and $\frac{00}{100}$ **7.** Three hundred ninety-five and $\frac{13}{100}$ **9.** One thousand two and $\frac{30}{100}$ **11.** \$146.86; \$97.91 **13.** \$438.80

page 93 **1.** \$282.22 **3.** \$244.84 **5.** \$528.87 **7.** \$459.16 **9.** \$373.54 **11.** \$432.34 **13.** \$304.66 **15.** \$457.80

page 96 **1.** \$71.29 **3.** \$39.61 **5.** \$174.72

page 97 **1.** \$789.99 **3.** \$1403.81 **5.** \$745.99 **7.** \$13.02 **9.** \$221.88 **11.** \$647.68 **13.** \$534.50 **15.** \$340.05

page 99 **1.** \$1.25 **3.** \$34.13 **5.** \$23.93 **7.** \$34.31 **9.** \$72.52 **11.** \$58.59 **13.** \$918.13 **15.** \$167.40

pages 100–101 **1.** \$31.08 **3.** \$101.46 **5.** \$242.30 **7.** \$28.74 **9.** \$148.59 **11.** \$136.48 **13.** \$30.45

page 103 **1.** \$26.25 **3.** \$1629.15 **5.** \$136.04 **7.** \$787.69 **9.** \$971.80 **11.** \$872.10

page 104

Multiplying decimals **1.** 0.35 **3.** 0.016 **5.** 0.0018 **7.** 0.00008 **9.** 140 **11.** 32 **13.** 2.1 **15.** 0.00002 **17.** 4.4 **19.** 34.944 **21.** 0.243 **23.** 153.51063 **25.** 1.574944 **27.** 1.701

Ratio and proportion **1.** $120 = 120$ **3.** $140 \neq 144$ **5.** $0.064 \neq 0.033$ **7.** $n = 36$ **9.** $x = 15$ **11.** $d = 21$ **13.** $y = 81$

page 104 continued

Writing percents, decimals, and fractions **1.** 0.17 **3.** 0.01 **5.** 0.96 **7.** 0.99 **9.** 0.0775 **11.** 0.125 **13.** 0.0675 **15.** 0.328 **17.** 0.0575 **19.** 1.03 **21.** 8.56 **23.** 0.0025 **25.** $\frac{1}{2}$ **27.** $\frac{7}{20}$ **29.** $\frac{3}{5}$ **31.** $\frac{6}{25}$ **33.** $\frac{1}{5}$ **35.** $\frac{9}{100}$ **37.** $\frac{33}{100}$ **39.** $\frac{9}{20}$ **41.** $\frac{19}{20}$ **43.** $\frac{3}{8}$ **45.** $1\frac{1}{10}$ **47.** $3\frac{1}{2}$

page 105 **1.** \$81.18; \$56.18 **2.** Thirty-eight and $\frac{72}{100}$ **3.** \$206.62; \$131.42 **4.** \$419.44 **5.** \$384.74 **6.** \$109.11 **7.** \$58.50 **8.** \$98.88 **9.** \$82.43 **10.** \$137.56

page 109 **1.** \$38.25 **3.** \$17.64 **5.** \$1.11 **7.** \$115 **9.** \$106.25 **11.** \$108 interest; \$1908 total due **13.** \$840 interest; \$3240 total due

page 111 **1.** \$47.16; \$0.71; \$47.87 **3.** \$106.38; \$1.60; \$107.98 **5.** \$22.33; \$0.33; \$47.32 **7.** \$173.77; \$2.61; \$206.02 **9.** \$0; \$0; \$20.94 **11.** \$150.00; \$2.25; \$187.85

page 113 **1.** 10 days; \$1471.90 **3.** \$122.19; 19 days; \$2321.61 **5.** \$130.52 **7.** \$122.19 **9.** \$0.47; \$42.47 **11.** \$1.57; \$83.30

page 114 **1.** \$459.75 **3.** \$409.75; 4 days; \$1639.00 **5.** \$422.06; 8 days; \$3376.48 **7.** \$441.05; 4 days; \$1764.20 **9.** \$456.84; 2 days; \$913.68 **11.** \$13,369.05; \$431.26 **13.** Total of payments, \$50.00; Balance after payments, \$385.78; Total of purchases, \$71.06; Finance charge, \$7.76; New balance, \$464.60

page 115 **1.** \$42.16; \$54.70; \$10.00 **3.** \$107.36; \$194.47; \$20.00 **5.** \$190.93; \$193.79; \$20.00 **7.** \$9.68; \$9.83; \$9.83

page 117 **1.** \$87.89 **3.** \$122 **5.** \$13.09 **7.** \$46.51 **9.** \$159.53 **11.** \$3.36; \$255.00; \$202.64 **13.** \$152.98; \$2.04; \$155.02; \$102.66 **15.** \$51.67; \$0.69; \$52.36; \$0

page 119 **1.** \$277.32; \$27.82 **3.** \$729.95; \$891.60; \$161.65 **5.** \$174.20; \$222.90; \$48.70 **7.** \$553.71; \$740.88; \$187.17 **9.** \$202.77; \$271.08; \$68.31 **11.** \$45.84; \$550.08; \$50.08 **13.** \$18.08; \$650.88; \$150.88 **15.** \$25.70; \$616.80; \$116.80 **17.** \$25.82; \$619.68; \$119.68

page 121 **1.** \$90.21 **3.** Ace Appliance Store **5.** \$72 **7.** \$116.59
9. The 17% loan for 36 months in problem 8 **11.** \$23.52 **13.** \$16.44
15. The \$100 a month at 2% per month in problem 14

page 122
Dividing whole numbers **1.** 2604 **3.** 183 **5.** 1653 R2 **7.** 44 R57 **9.** 104 R43
11. 41 R10 **13.** 458 **15.** 209 R25 **17.** 45 R26 **19.** 679 **21.** 2274 R25
23. 3654 R13 **25.** 11,292 R57 **27.** 87 R96
Dividing decimals **1.** 1.84 **3.** 0.66 **5.** 0.09 **7.** 5.42 **9.** 0.11 **11.** 6.39
13. 4.57 **15.** 280 **17.** 5.65 **19.** 0.78 **21.** 0.05 **23.** 1.39 **25.** 7.23
Multiplying fractions and mixed numbers **1.** $\frac{2}{15}$ **3.** $\frac{1}{5}$ **5.** $\frac{1}{2}$ **7.** $6\frac{2}{3}$ **9.** $1\frac{4}{5}$
11. 5 **13.** $3\frac{1}{8}$ **15.** 6 **17.** $15\frac{3}{4}$ **19.** $\frac{5}{14}$ **21.** $16\frac{2}{3}$

page 123 **1.** \$1567.50 **2.** \$108.91 **3.** \$80 **4.** \$2.35 **5.** \$211.83
6. \$51.14 **7.** \$50.29 **8.** \$461.66 **9.** \$68 **10.** Plan B

page 127 **1.** 74 **3.** 82 **5.** 65 **7.** 89 **9.** 66 **11.** 161 **13.** 121
15. 104 **17.** 174 **19.** 482 **21.** 512 **23.** 58 **25.** 126 **27.** 139

page 129 Program modifications may vary. Samples are given.

1.

```
          MEYER'S DEPARTMENT STORE
          CHARGE-ACCOUNT STATEMENT

BEGINNING OF AUGUST
   BALANCE                          211.85
PAYMENTS DURING AUGUST              50
FINANCE CHARGE ON
   BALANCE OF $  161.85               2.43
CHARGES DURING AUGUST               37.82
NEW BALANCE                         202.1
```

3.

```
          MEYER'S DEPARTMENT STORE
          CHARGE-ACCOUNT STATEMENT

BEGINNING OF JANUARY
   BALANCE                          37.42
PAYMENTS DURING JANUARY             37.42
FINANCE CHARGE ON
   BALANCE OF $  0                   0
CHARGES DURING JANUARY              23.51
NEW BALANCE                         23.51
```

5.

```
          MEYER'S DEPARTMENT STORE
          CHARGE-ACCOUNT STATEMENT

BEGINNING OF JUNE
   BALANCE                          83.92
PAYMENTS DURING JUNE                40
FINANCE CHARGE ON
   BALANCE OF $  43.92                .66
CHARGES DURING JUNE                 27.35
NEW BALANCE                         71.93
```

7.

```
          MEYER'S DEPARTMENT STORE
          CHARGE-ACCOUNT STATEMENT

BEGINNING OF FEBRUARY
   BALANCE                          287.93
PAYMENTS DURING FEBRUARY            35
FINANCE CHARGE ON
   BALANCE OF $  252.93               3.79
CHARGES DURING FEBRUARY             29.68
NEW BALANCE                         286.4
```

9.

```
          MEYER'S DEPARTMENT STORE
          CHARGE-ACCOUNT STATEMENT

BEGINNING OF OCTOBER
   BALANCE                          87.21
PAYMENTS DURING OCTOBER             10
FINANCE CHARGE ON
   BALANCE OF $  77.21                1.16
CHARGES DURING OCTOBER              19.58
NEW BALANCE                         97.95
```

11.

```
182 IF P>0 THEN 190
183 IF B=0 THEN 190
184 PRINT "NO PAYMENT RECEIVED"
185 PRINT "IF PAYMENT IS IN MAIL, THANK YOU"
```

page 129 continued

13.
```
15 LET C=0
90 INPUT C1
91 IF C1=0 THEN 100
92 LET C=C+C1
93 GO TO 90
```
With this modification, zero must be entered for the last input for line 90 so the program can continue.

15.
```
75 PRINT "RETURNS";
76 INPUT R
101 IF R>U THEN 104
102 LET U=U-R
103 GO TO 110
104 LET A=0
105 LET A=R-U
106 LET F=0
107 GO TO 130
191 IF R=0 THEN 200
192 PRINT "$";R;"HAS BEEN CREDITED TO YOUR ACCOUNT"
225 IF A=0 THEN 230
226 PRINT "NEW BALANCE";TAB(30);"$";A;"CREDIT"
227 GO TO 240
```

17.
```
91 IF C1=0 THEN 97
97 PRINT "FINANCE CHARGE RATE";
98 INPUT Y
110 LET F=Y*U/100
```

page 133 **1.** \$8160.49 **3.** \$8771.49 **5.** \$7989.49; yes **7.** AM radio, \$51; Sport-style mirrors, driver's remote, \$53; Steel-belted, blackwall tires with 2.8-liter engine, \$67 **9.** AM-FM stereo radio with 40 channel CB, \$413; Sport-style mirrors, both remote, \$80; Steel-belted, wide oval, billboard-lettered tires with 2.8-liter engine, \$119

page 134 **1.** \$8300 **3.** \$8800 **5.** \$7100 **7.** \$8400 **9.** \$6700

page 137 **1.** \$41.25; \$1036.75 **3.** \$68.85; \$2393.35 **5.** \$129.15; \$1998.15 **7.** \$3738.95 **9.** \$152.24; \$3223.92 **11.** \$28.14 **13.** \$116.80 **15.** \$3113.90 **17.** \$9432.25 **19.** \$741.75

page 139 **1.** \$6125 **3.** \$6165 **5.** \$6805 **7.** \$6708 **9.** \$6698 **11.** \$7342 **13.** \$8539 **15.** \$8445 **17.** \$10,214 Subcompact model: Suburban, Ltd. Compact model: Colonial Motors Mid-sized model: Heritage, Ltd. Full-sized model: Cass St. Motors Luxury sedan: Prospect Sales Sports car: Congress Motors **19.** \$8073 **21.** \$8672.61

pages 141–142 **1.** \$6000; \$7258.80; \$1258.80; \$8998.80 **3.** \$6853; \$7870.68; \$1017.68; \$10,865.68 **5.** \$6180; \$6869.76; \$689.76; \$9344.76 **7.** \$6853; \$9662.88; \$2809.88; \$12,727.88 **9.** \$4889; \$5943.36; \$1054.36; \$9593.36

pages 141–142 continued

11. SALE SUMMARY

Suggested Retail Price		$6845.00
Optional equipment	$ 739.00	
Destination charge	$ 260.00	
Sticker Price		$7844.00
Price reduction	$ 500.00	
Selling Price		$7344.00
Sales tax (4%)	$ 293.76	
License-plate fee	$ 18.00	
Title fee	$ 5.00	
Other charges	$ ----	
Total Cost		$7660.76
Trade-in allowance	$ ----	
Cash deposit	$3060.76	
Amount Financed		$4600.00
Finance charge	$ 965.36	
ANNUAL PERCENTAGE RATE		
Number of payments	24	
Monthly payment	$ 231.89	
Total of payments	$5565.36	
Total Sale Price (deferred-payment price)		$8626.12

page 143 **1.** 18.57% **3.** 20.92% **5.** 18.83% **7.** 21.03%

page 145 **1.** $1813.50; $800; $2613.50 **3.** $1752.50; $800; $2552.50 **5.** $1984.00; $1400; $3384.00 **7.** $1350.00; $75; $1425.00 **9.** $1533.75; $350; $1883.75 **11.** $902.50; $0; $902.50 **13.** $400 **15.** $1443.75 **17.** $1793.75

page 146

Subtracting whole numbers and decimals **1.** 34 **3.** 24 **5.** 67 **7.** 21.1 **9.** 18.2 **11.** 20.97 **13.** 3.781 **15.** 21.272 **17.** 0.363 **19.** 0.9 **21.** 5.789 **23.** 26.6 **25.** 1.96 **27.** 47.504

Writing percents, decimals, and fractions **1.** 0.29 **3.** 0.09 **5.** 0.82 **7.** 0.73 **9.** 0.1842 **11.** 0.675 **13.** 0.0825 **15.** 0.184 **17.** 0.0825 **19.** 0.205 **21.** 4.05 **23.** 2.5 **25.** 56% **27.** 3% **29.** 50% **31.** 49% **33.** 5.3% **35.** 33.9% **37.** 90.6% **39.** 1.25% **41.** 32.25% **43.** 90.54% **45.** 506% **47.** 112.1%

Percent problems **1.** 4.9 **3.** 39 **5.** 207 **7.** 6.6 **9.** 12.5% **11.** 3% **13.** 32% **15.** 44% **17.** 25 **19.** 340 **21.** 3 **23.** 30

page 147 **1.** $9264 **2.** $6100 **3.** $98.75 **4.** $3096.65 **5.** $6675 **6.** $7488; $7598; $7522; Sayo Imports **7.** $1089.74 **8.** $11,013.28 **9.** $1083 **10.** $2205

page 151 **1.** 1104.7 kilometers **3.** 6.5 kilometers per liter **5.** 5.9¢ per kilometer **7.** 349.5 km; 6.1 km/L; 6.2¢ **9.** 242.0 km; 4.0 km/L; 9.5¢ **11.** 342.5 km; 4.5 km/L; 8.4¢

page 153 **1.** $4060; $3190; $2320; $2030; $1740; $4060
3. $4340; $3410; $2480; $2170; $1860; $4340
5. $4970; $3905; $2840; $2485; $2130; $4970
7. $5950; $4675; $3400; $2975; $2550; $5950
9. $6790; $5335; $3880; $3395; $2910; $6790

page 154 **1.** $3123 **3.** $1823 **5.** $3120 **7.** $3619 **9.** $4186 **11.** $2652 **13.** $2597 **15.** $5677 **17.** $2080 **19.** $3706 **21.** $2814 **23.** $5848

page 155 **1.** 8.586 km/L **3.** 7.55 km/L **5.** 7.736 km/L **7.** 7.06 km/L **9.** 10.45; 8.70; 1.75; 16.75% **11.** 7.31; 6.85; 0.46; 6.29%

pages 157–159 **1.** $65.50 **3.** $6.70 **5.** $26.20 **7.** $9.06 **9.** $113.96 **11.** $27.50 **13.** $236.48

page 161 **1.** $250,000 **3.** $100,000 **5.** $217.81 **7.** $223.04 **9.** $342.47 **11.** $429.76 **13.** $372.68

page 163 **1.** $692.04; $81.60; $773.64 **3.** $280.32; $81.60; $361.92 **5.** $652.54; $55.60; $708.14 **7.** $264.32; $55.60; $319.92 **9.** $726.80; $76.20; $803.00

page 165 **1.** $4073.81 **3.** $6196.20 **5.** Depreciation; gas **7.** $728.13 **9.** $2848.63 **11.** Radial tires

page 167 **1.** $71.60 **3.** $36 **5.** $42 **7.** $54 **9.** 2.7¢ per kilometer **11.** $3792 **13.** $2340 **15.** $3096 **17.** $4440 **19.** $5220

page 168
Adding whole numbers and decimals **1.** 52 **3.** 157 **5.** 189 **7.** 232 **9.** 320 **11.** 1732 **13.** 1566 **15.** 12.85 **17.** 59.51 **19.** 18.87 **21.** 21.6 **23.** 1.44 **25.** 7.904 **27.** 154.07

Multiplying decimals **1.** 0.18 **3.** 0.036 **5.** 0.003 **7.** 0.00024 **9.** 320 **11.** 3.6 **13.** 5.6 **15.** 0.00003 **17.** 8.4 **19.** 34.452 **21.** 0.3588 **23.** 35.1568 **25.** 6.26824 **27.** 5.4846

Renaming fractions and mixed numbers **1.** $\frac{11}{8}$ **3.** $\frac{17}{6}$ **5.** $\frac{26}{5}$ **7.** $\frac{19}{2}$ **9.** $\frac{32}{9}$ **11.** $\frac{63}{10}$ **13.** $\frac{12}{1}$ **15.** $\frac{35}{16}$ **17.** $\frac{59}{10}$ **19.** $\frac{52}{11}$ **21.** $2\frac{1}{4}$ **23.** $1\frac{1}{2}$ **25.** $2\frac{1}{6}$ **27.** $4\frac{2}{3}$ **29.** $4\frac{1}{3}$ **31.** $1\frac{5}{16}$ **33.** $2\frac{3}{8}$ **35.** $1\frac{4}{5}$ **37.** $7\frac{4}{9}$

page 169 **1.** 6.8 kilometers per liter **2.** $3360 **3.** $2418 **4.** $71.75 **5.** $19.20 **6.** $372.68 **7.** $448.56 **8.** 27.5¢ per kilometer **9.** $59.10 **10.** $2340

page 173 **1.** 3600 kilometers **3.** 2108 kilometers **5.** 4274 kilometers **7.** 4623 kilometers **9.** 5138 kilometers **11.** 142 kilometers **13.** 4434 kilometers

page 175 **1.** 167 kilometers; 2 hours **3.** 334 kilometers; 4 hours **5.** 167 kilometers; 2 hours **7.** 338 kilometers; 4 hours **9.** 301 kilometers; 4 hours **11.** 110 kilometers **13.** 80 kilometers **15.** 80 kilometers **17.** 132 km; 120 km **19.** 160 km; 150 km **21.** 6 hours

page 177 **1.** $45.20 **3.** $671.80 **5.** $53.20

page 179 **1.** $184 **3.** $577.50 **5.** $1143.25 **7.** $497 **9.** $1000

page 180 **1.** $150 **3.** $149.60 **5.** $261.81 **7.** $138.14 **9.** $211.84

page 181 **1.** 828 km; $124.20; $175; $299.20 **3.** 544 km; $87.04; $112; $199.04 **5.** 379 km; $75.80; $96; $171.80 **7.** $206 **9.** $186 **11.** $129 **13.** $349 **15.** Compact Getaway Special; $135

page 183 **1.** $135 **3.** $212 **5.** $347.50 **7.** $585 **9.** $2356

page 184

Dividing decimals **1.** 10.79 **3.** 0.08 **5.** 14.05 **7.** 0.81 **9.** 6.27 **11.** 11.94 **13.** 6 **15.** 6 **17.** 3 **19.** 8 **21.** 80 **23.** 32

Adding fractions and mixed numbers **1.** $1\frac{1}{12}$ **3.** $1\frac{1}{3}$ **5.** $1\frac{1}{14}$ **7.** $1\frac{11}{36}$ **9.** $4\frac{1}{15}$ **11.** $8\frac{1}{3}$ **13.** $7\frac{5}{6}$ **15.** $6\frac{14}{15}$ **17.** $8\frac{3}{16}$ **19.** 19 **21.** $18\frac{17}{24}$

Subtracting fractions and mixed numbers **1.** $\frac{1}{2}$ **3.** $\frac{3}{8}$ **5.** $\frac{17}{24}$ **7.** $\frac{1}{14}$ **9.** $2\frac{3}{8}$ **11.** $2\frac{1}{2}$ **13.** $4\frac{1}{3}$ **15.** $9\frac{9}{16}$ **17.** $6\frac{7}{15}$ **19.** $6\frac{1}{3}$ **21.** $7\frac{5}{12}$

page 185 **1.** 1214 kilometers **2.** 269 kilometers **3.** 100 kilometers **4.** $81.20 **5.** $73 **6.** $508.75 **7.** $1880 **8.** $200.95 **9.** $606 **10.** $969

page 189 **1.** 44 **3.** 58 **5.** 37 **7.** 44 **9.** 29 **11.** 13 **13.** 36 **15.** 37 **17.** 65 **19.** 58 **21.** 107 **23.** 235 **25.** 219 **27.** 128

page 191 Program modifications may vary. A sample is given.

1.
```
AMOUNT TO FINANCE       $ 2500
ANNUAL INTEREST RATE  17  %
NUMBER OF MONTHS 18
MONTHLY PAYMENT       $ 158.33
```

3.
```
AMOUNT TO FINANCE       $ 5250
ANNUAL INTEREST RATE  19  %
NUMBER OF MONTHS 24
MONTHLY PAYMENT       $ 264.65
```

5.
```
AMOUNT TO FINANCE       $ 7185
ANNUAL INTEREST RATE  17.75  %
NUMBER OF MONTHS 36
MONTHLY PAYMENT       $ 258.85
```

7.
```
AMOUNT TO FINANCE       $ 7210
ANNUAL INTEREST RATE  16.75  %
NUMBER OF MONTHS 36
MONTHLY PAYMENT       $ 256.16
```

9.
```
AMOUNT TO FINANCE       $ 6820
ANNUAL INTEREST RATE  17.5  %
NUMBER OF MONTHS 18
MONTHLY PAYMENT       $ 433.53
```

11.
```
AMOUNT TO FINANCE       $ 3000
ANNUAL INTEREST RATE  17.5  %
NUMBER OF MONTHS 24
MONTHLY PAYMENT       $ 149.05
```

```
AMOUNT TO FINANCE       $ 3500
ANNUAL INTEREST RATE  18  %
NUMBER OF MONTHS 30
MONTHLY PAYMENT       $ 145.74
```

$3500 at 18% annually for 30 months

13.
```
AMOUNT TO FINANCE       $ 4785
ANNUAL INTEREST RATE  18.5  %
NUMBER OF MONTHS 18
MONTHLY PAYMENT       $ 306.45
```

```
AMOUNT TO FINANCE       $ 5000
ANNUAL INTEREST RATE  17  %
NUMBER OF MONTHS 24
MONTHLY PAYMENT       $ 247.21
```

$5000 at 17% annually for 24 months

15.
```
20 PRINT "TOTAL COST";
30 INPUT T
32 PRINT "DOWN PAYMENT";
33 INPUT D
34 LET P=T-D
105 PRINT "TOTAL COST     $";T
106 PRINT "DOWN PAYMENT     $";D
```

17.
```
TOTAL COST       $ 8745
DOWN PAYMENT     $ 4000
AMOUNT TO FINANCE       $ 4745
ANNUAL INTEREST RATE  16.5  %
NUMBER OF MONTHS 28
MONTHLY PAYMENT       $ 205.32
```

```
TOTAL COST       $ 9282
DOWN PAYMENT     $ 5000
AMOUNT TO FINANCE       $ 4282
ANNUAL INTEREST RATE  16.8  %
NUMBER OF MONTHS 24
MONTHLY PAYMENT       $ 211.3
```

$8745 with a $4000 down payment at 16.5% annually for 28 months

page 191 continued

19. TOTAL COST $ 8378
DOWN PAYMENT $ 3500
AMOUNT TO FINANCE $ 4878
ANNUAL INTEREST RATE 18.5 %
NUMBER OF MONTHS 24
COST OF FINANCING $ 995.04
MONTHLY PAYMENT $ 244.71

21. TOTAL COST $ 10583
DOWN PAYMENT $ 4000
AMOUNT TO FINANCE $ 6583
ANNUAL INTEREST RATE 16.75 %
NUMBER OF MONTHS 30
COST OF FINANCING $ 1519.4
TOTAL SALE PRICE $ 12102.4
MONTHLY PAYMENT $ 270.08

pages 194–195 **1.** \$252 **3.** \$344 **5.** \$290 **7.** \$500 **9.** \$208 **11.** \$300 **13.** \$229 **15.** \$268 **17.** \$365 **19.** \$490 **21.** \$472

page 197 **1.** \$370 **3.** \$410 **5.** \$285 **7.** The Villas, \$265; Colony Point, \$285; 750 Nichols Road, \$295; Summit, \$370; Middletown Apartments, \$380; Cranbrook Square, \$410; Meadow Green, \$415 **9.** \$205

page 199 **1.** 58915 **3.** 60279 **5.** 62750 **7.** 64431 **9.** Feb.–April 677; April–June 643; June–Aug. 1828; Aug.–Oct. 1134; Oct.–Dec. 547

page 200 **1.** \$0.90 **3.** \$7.16 **5.** \$18.05 **7.** \$1.94 **9.** \$22.13 **11.** \$2.29 **13.** \$22.78 **15.** \$5.42 **17.** \$0.90; \$9.53; \$7.22; \$58.95; \$18.21; \$2.51; \$1.96; \$49.82; \$22.33; \$61.46; \$2.31; \$13.14; \$22.98; \$4.31; \$5.47; \$0.10

page 203 **1.** 17.0 cm **3.** 7.7 cm by 4.3 cm **5.** 7.5 cm by 2.9 cm **7.** 6.4 cm by 3.0 cm **9.** 7.8 cm by 5.4 cm **11.** 2.6 cm by 1.8 cm **13.** 6.7 cm by 1.9 cm **15.** Outline should be 14.4 cm by 13.8 cm

pages 204–205 For problems **1–5,** answers are given in this order: length, width, total.
1. 8; 5; 40 **3.** 15; 13; 195
5. 21; 17; 357 **7.** \$162.50

9.

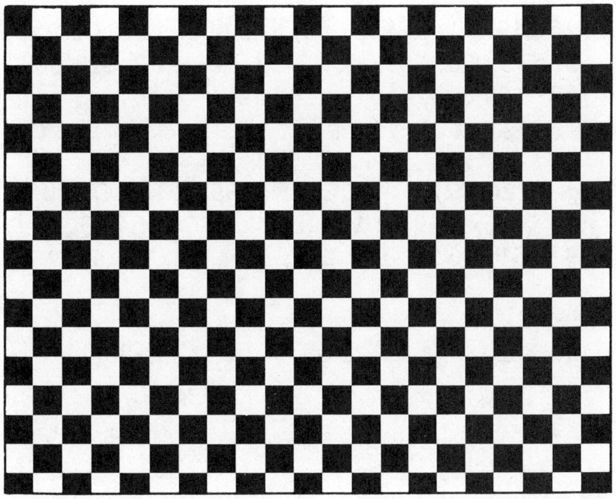

11. 178 tiles **13.** \$216

page 207 **1.** 400 sq. ft.; 154 sq. ft.; 554 sq. ft.; 2 gal. **3.** 176 sq. ft.; 30 sq. ft.; 206 sq. ft.; 1 gal. **5.** 480 sq. ft.; 125 sq. ft.; 605 sq. ft.; 2 gal.

page 209 **1.** 480 sq. ft **3.** 3 rolls **5.** $110.37 **7.** 22 rolls **9.** 19 rolls **11.** 3 rolls

page 211 **1.** $90.00 **3.** $57.20 **5.** $88.00 **7.** $131.25 **9.** $406.00 **11.** $129.50 **13.** $273.00 **15.** $51.00

page 212

Dividing whole numbers **1.** 511 **3.** 324 R4 **5.** 4742 **7.** 126 R28 **9.** 108 R21 **11.** 121 R47 **13.** 44 **15.** 207 **17.** 80 R32 **19.** 1203 R3 **21.** 7814 R16 **23.** 4285 R86 **25.** 204 **27.** 1646 R189

Multiplying fractions and mixed numbers **1.** $\frac{5}{24}$ **3.** $\frac{2}{7}$ **5.** $\frac{1}{12}$ **7.** $3\frac{1}{2}$ **9.** $1\frac{1}{5}$ **11.** $1\frac{1}{4}$ **13.** 27 **15.** 9 **17.** $24\frac{2}{5}$ **19.** $10\frac{1}{2}$

Ratio and proportion **1.** $24 \neq 28$ **3.** $1200 \neq 1280$ **5.** $117.6 \neq 144$ **7.** $a = 30$ **9.** $c = 3$ **11.** $n = 5.3$ **13.** $n = 400$

page 213 **1.** $314 **2.** $238 **3.** $370 **4.** 40593 **5.** 22 cm **6.** 285 tiles **7.** $65 **8.** 2 gallons **9.** 15 rolls **10.** $177.40

page 217 **1.** $36,000 **3.** $18,720 **5.** $29,120 **7.** $28,288 **9.** $22,880 **11.** No **13.** Yes

page 219 **1.** $10,000; $40,000; $458.00 **3.** $15,000; $60,000; $640.20 **5.** $15,000; $45,000; $497.70 **7.** $21,000; $84,000; $895.44 **9.** $5000 **11.** $13 **13.** $54,000 **15.** $44.10

pages 220–221 **1.** 300; $139,920; $99,920 **3.** 300; $144,480; $104,480 **5.** $416.06; 240; $99,854.40; $64,354.40 **7.** $836.94; 360; $301,298.40; $245,798.40 **9.** $51,216 **11.** $125,874 **13.** 4.3

page 222 **1.** $629.88 **3.** $53,980.08 **5.** $10.13 **7.** $629.65 **9.** $53,959.70

page 223 **1.** \$449.82; \$16.58; \$39,967.02 **3.** \$39,950.25; \$449.44; \$16.96; \$39,933.29 **5.** \$39,916.14; \$449.06; \$17.34; \$39,898.80 **7.** \$39,881.26; \$448.66; \$17.74; \$39,863.52 **9.** \$39,845.58; \$448.26; \$18.14; \$39,827.44 **11.** \$39,809.10; \$447.85; \$18.55; \$39,790.55 **13.** \$20,796.17; \$233.96; \$232.44; \$20,563.73 **15.** \$20,328.67; \$228.70; \$237.70; \$20,090.97 **17.** 50%

page 225 **1.** \$8.40 **3.** \$2.07 **5.** \$192.47 **7.** \$2.76 **9.** \$15.60 **11.** \$6.60 **13.** \$20.70 **15.** \$181.85 **17.** \$5.70 **19.** \$7 **21.** \$16.04 **23.** \$13.56

page 227 **1.** \$26,000; \$715.00 **3.** \$34,000; \$1003.00 **5.** \$36,000; \$1490.40 **7.** \$31,500; \$1641.15 **9.** \$19,350; \$1465.96 **11.** \$112.23

page 229 **1.** \$116 **3.** \$90 **5.** \$1534 **7.** \$520 **9.** \$2209.50 **11.** \$605 **13.** \$187.50 **15.** \$1785

pages 231–233 **1.** \$69,200 **3.** \$80,300 **5.** \$106,500 **7.** \$67,400 **9.** \$1125 **11.** \$82,305 **13.** \$17,425 **15.** San Francisco-Oakland **17.** Miami **19.** \$7290

page 234

Multiplying whole numbers **1.** 3200 **3.** 3000 **5.** 280,000 **7.** 450,000 **9.** 17,696 **11.** 3180 **13.** 3,440,000 **15.** 816 **17.** 2037 **19.** 8,400,000 **21.** 216,544 **23.** 368,760 **25.** 1,285,309 **27.** 724,603

Renaming fractions and mixed numbers **1.** $\frac{1}{4}$ **3.** $\frac{1}{2}$ **5.** $\frac{3}{4}$ **7.** $\frac{1}{2}$ **9.** $\frac{7}{8}$ **11.** $\frac{5}{6}$ **13.** $\frac{7}{10}$ **15.** $\frac{3}{4}$ **17.** $\frac{2}{21}$ **19.** $\frac{1}{3}$ **21.** $\frac{12}{5}$ **23.** $\frac{23}{10}$ **25.** $\frac{9}{5}$ **27.** $\frac{16}{5}$ **29.** $\frac{53}{8}$ **31.** $\frac{15}{4}$ **33.** $\frac{35}{8}$ **35.** $\frac{11}{10}$ **37.** $\frac{29}{12}$

Dividing fractions and mixed numbers **1.** $1\frac{1}{2}$ **3.** $1\frac{1}{8}$ **5.** $\frac{24}{35}$ **7.** $7\frac{1}{2}$ **9.** 16 **11.** $6\frac{1}{4}$ **13.** $1\frac{7}{9}$ **15.** $1\frac{8}{15}$ **17.** $\frac{25}{34}$ **19.** $\frac{3}{4}$ **21.** $1\frac{7}{8}$

page 235 **1.** \$30,992 **2.** \$46,800 **3.** \$506.85 **4.** \$121,698 **5.** \$416.25 **6.** \$148.90 **7.** \$1521.33 **8.** \$412.50 **9.** \$77,500 **10.** \$23,400

page 239

1.

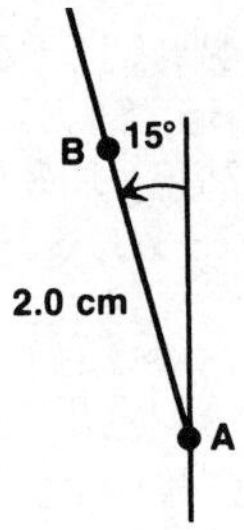

3.

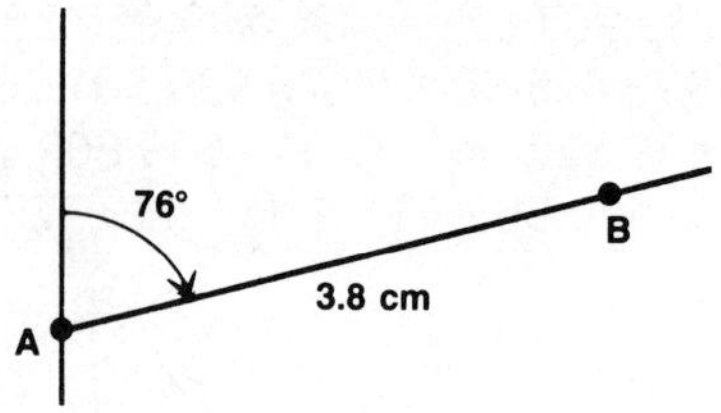

5.

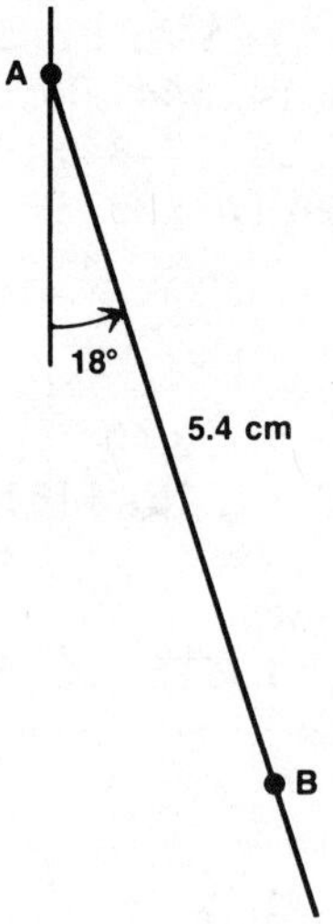

7.

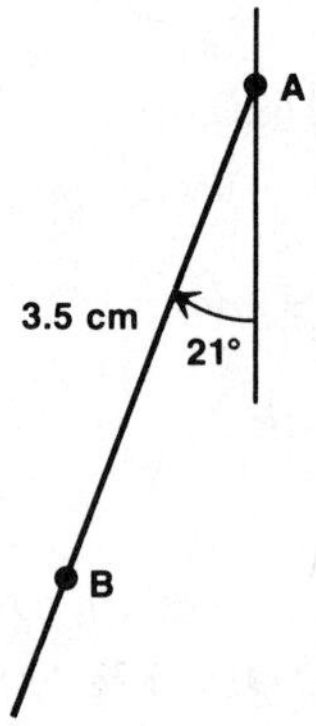

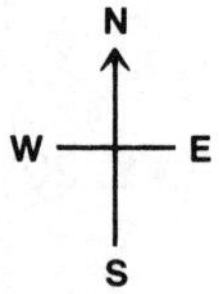

1 cm → 10 m

9.

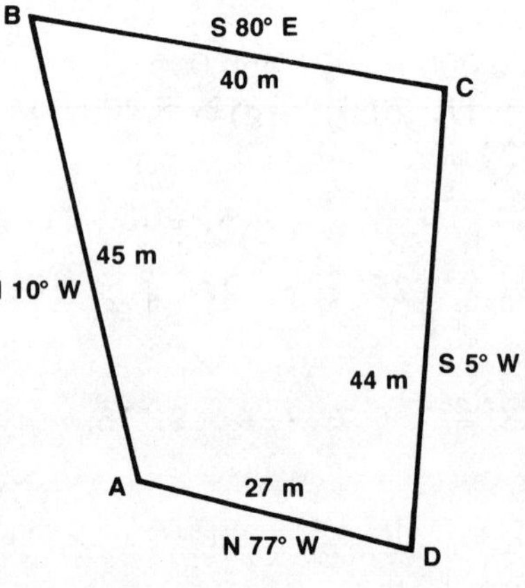

11.

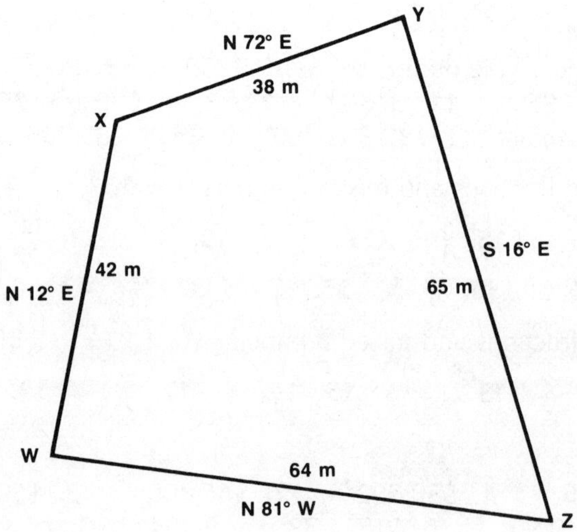

pages 241–242 **1.** 750 square feet **3.** 855 square feet **5.** \$70,832 **7.** \$6149 **9.** 1884 square feet **11.** 492 square feet **13.** \$81,018

page 243 **1.** \$63,875.00; \$7500.00; \$71,375.00 **3.** \$63,750.00; \$4887.50; \$68,637.50 **5.** \$74,555.00; \$7995.00; \$82,550.00 **7.** \$86,625.00; \$8775.00; \$95,400.00 **9.** \$67,787.50; \$8482.50; \$76,270.00 **11.** \$67,725.00; \$6727.50; \$74,452.50

page 245 **1.** 611 sq. ft. **3.** $39\frac{3}{16}$ sq. ft. **5.** $15\frac{3}{4}$ sq. ft. **7.** $10\frac{1}{8}$ sq. ft. **9.** 1532 sq. ft.

page 247 **1.** 480 square feet **3.** 1680 square feet **5.** 100 square feet **7.** 269 square feet **9.** 9877 bricks **11.** 127 cubic feet

page 248

Multiplying fractions and mixed numbers **1.** $\frac{7}{16}$ **3.** $\frac{2}{5}$ **5.** $\frac{3}{8}$ **7.** 8 **9.** $\frac{5}{8}$ **11.** $2\frac{2}{5}$ **13.** $38\frac{1}{3}$ **15.** $18\frac{6}{7}$ **17.** $22\frac{1}{4}$ **19.** $1\frac{1}{2}$

Adding fractions and mixed numbers **1.** $\frac{3}{4}$ **3.** $1\frac{5}{12}$ **5.** $\frac{17}{18}$ **7.** $1\frac{1}{5}$ **9.** $2\frac{7}{12}$ **11.** $3\frac{1}{2}$ **13.** $9\frac{5}{24}$ **15.** $13\frac{13}{15}$ **17.** $10\frac{2}{15}$ **19.** 7

Subtracting fractions and mixed numbers **1.** $\frac{1}{2}$ **3.** $\frac{1}{10}$ **5.** $\frac{1}{6}$ **7.** $\frac{3}{16}$ **9.** $8\frac{2}{3}$ **11.** $2\frac{2}{3}$ **13.** $2\frac{1}{8}$ **15.** $3\frac{11}{18}$ **17.** $2\frac{17}{18}$ **19.** $1\frac{5}{6}$

page 249 **1.**

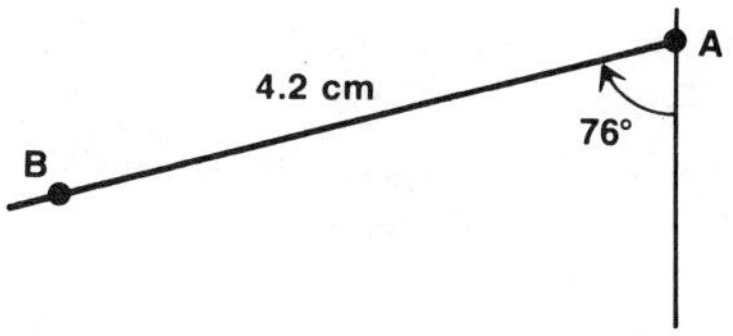

2. 1321 square feet **3.** \$51,519 **4.** \$6037.50 **5.** \$57,556.50 **6.** 230 square feet **7.** \$264.50 **8.** 99 square feet **9.** 1365 bricks **10.** 25 cubic feet

page 253 **1.** \$3.16 **3.** \$4.72 **5.** \$3.36 **7.** \$3.51 **9.** \$7.96 **11.** \$11.82 **13.** \$14.75 **15.** \$23.92 **17.** \$6.27 **19.** \$24.32 **21.** \$20.15 **23.** \$2.56 **25.** \$4.38

page 255 Program modifications may vary. Samples are given.

1.

PAYMENT NUMBER	PRINCIPAL	AMOUNT OF INTEREST	AMOUNT PAID ON PRINCIPAL	'NEW' PRINCIPAL
1	2000	26.67	43.65	1956.35
2	1956.35	26.08	44.24	1912.11
3	1912.11	25.49	44.83	1867.28
4	1867.28	24.9	45.42	1821.86
5	1821.86	24.29	46.03	1775.83
6	1775.83	23.68	46.64	1729.19
7	1729.19	23.06	47.26	1681.93
8	1681.93	22.43	47.89	1634.04
9	1634.04	21.79	48.53	1585.51
10	1585.51	21.14	49.18	1536.33
11	1536.33	20.48	49.84	1486.49
12	1486.49	19.82	50.5	1435.99
13	1435.99	19.15	51.17	1384.82
14	1384.82	18.46	51.86	1332.96
15	1332.96	17.77	52.55	1280.41
16	1280.41	17.07	53.25	1227.16
17	1227.16	16.36	53.96	1173.2
18	1173.2	15.64	54.68	1117.52
19	1118.52	14.91	55.41	1063.11
20	1063.11	14.17	56.15	1006.96
21	1006.96	13.43	56.89	950.07
22	950.07	12.67	57.65	892.42
23	892.42	11.9	58.42	834
24	834	11.12	59.2	774.8
25	774.8	10.33	59.99	714.81
26	714.81	9.53	60.79	654.02
27	654.02	8.72	61.6	592.42
28	592.42	7.9	62.42	530
29	530	7.07	63.25	466.75
30	466.75	6.22	64.1	402.65
31	402.65	5.37	64.95	337.7
32	337.7	4.5	65.82	271.88
33	271.88	3.63	66.69	205.19
34	205.19	2.74	67.58	137.61
35	137.61	1.83	68.49	69.12
36	69.12	.92	69.12	0

3.

PAYMENT NUMBER	PRINCIPAL	AMOUNT OF INTEREST	AMOUNT PAID ON PRINCIPAL	'NEW' PRINCIPAL
1	4475	56.87	110.01	4364.99
2	4364.99	55.47	111.41	4253.58
.	.	.	.	.
.	.	.	.	.
.	.	.	.	.
33	164.4	2.09	164.4	0

5.

PAYMENT NUMBER	PRINCIPAL	AMOUNT OF INTEREST	AMOUNT PAID ON PRINCIPAL	'NEW' PRINCIPAL
1	5000	62.5	179.94	4820.06
2	4820.06	60.25	182.19	4637.87
.	.	.	.	.
.	.	.	.	.
.	.	.	.	.
24	239.25	2.99	239.25	0

page 255 continued

7.

PAYMENT NUMBER	PRINCIPAL	AMOUNT OF INTEREST	AMOUNT PAID ON PRINCIPAL	'NEW' PRINCIPAL
1	3600	44.25	99.96	3500.04
2	3500.04	43.02	101.19	3398.85
.	.	.	.	.
.	.	.	.	.
.	.	.	.	.
30	142.43	1.75	142.43	0

9.

PAYMENT NUMBER	PRINCIPAL	AMOUNT OF INTEREST	AMOUNT PAID ON PRINCIPAL	'NEW' PRINCIPAL
1	4000	55.83	123.01	3876.99
2	3876.99	54.12	124.72	3752.27
.	.	.	.	.
.	.	.	.	.
.	.	.	.	.
27	176.18	2.46	176.18	0

11.

PAYMENT NUMBER	PRINCIPAL	AMOUNT OF INTEREST	AMOUNT PAID ON PRINCIPAL	'NEW' PRINCIPAL
1	9500	110.83	213.86	9286.14
2	9286.14	108.34	216.35	9069.79
.	.	.	.	.
.	.	.	.	.
.	.	.	.	.
36	320.83	3.74	320.83	0

13.

```
121 PRINT TAB(18);"MORTGAGE AMORTIZATION TABLE"
122 PRINT "PRINCIPAL AMOUNT";TAB(28);"$";P
123 PRINT "ANNUAL INTEREST RATE";TAB(29);Y;"%"
124 PRINT "TERM";TAB(29);N;"MONTHS"
125 PRINT "MONTHLY PAYMENT";TAB(28);"$";A
126 PRINT
```

15.

```
25 LET T1=0
26 LET T2=0
225 LET T1=T1+I
226 LET T2=T2+P1
241 PRINT
242 PRINT "TOTAL PAID TO INTEREST     $";FNR(T1)
243 PRINT "TOTAL PAID TO PRINCIPAL    $";FNR(T2)
244 PRINT TAB(28);"---------"
245 PRINT TAB(26);"$";FNR(T1+T2)
```

17.

```
                    MORTGAGE AMORTIZATION TABLE
PRINCIPAL AMOUNT                    $  2755
ANNUAL INTEREST RATE                   17.5  %
TERM                                   6 MONTHS
MONTHLY PAYMENT                     $  482.89
```

PAYMENT NUMBER	PRINCIPAL	AMOUNT OF INTEREST	AMOUNT PAID ON PRINCIPAL	'NEW' PRINCIPAL
1	2755	40.18	442.71	2312.29
2	2312.29	33.72	449.17	1863.12
3	1863.12	27.17	455.72	1407.4
4	1407.4	20.52	462.37	945.03
5	945.03	13.78	469.11	475.92
6	475.92	6.94	475.92	0

Program continued on next page.

page 255 continued

17. continued

```
TOTAL PAID TO INTEREST          $ 142.31
TOTAL PAID TO PRINCIPAL         $ 2755
                                ---------
                                $ 2897.31
```

page 259 **1.** $3546.55; yes **3.** $6920.70; no **5.** $7144.59; no **7.** $4179.86; no **9.** $1424.99

page 262 **1.** $12,761; $1962 **3.** $18,365; $2604 **5.** $26,541; $2545

page 263 **1.** $1497 **3.** $2485 **5.** $3453 **7.** $4204 **9.** $3387 **11.** $2403

page 265 **1.** Refund: $101 **3.** Refund: $129 **5.** Balance due: $49 **7.** Balance due: $242 **9.** Balance due: $125 **11.** Refund: $117

page 267 **1.** $15,015; $2500; $2092; $408 refund **3.** $17,836; $3250; $3153; $97 refund **5.** $26,425; $3548; $3616; $68 balance due

pages 269–270 **1.** $4246; balance due: $360 **3.** $3033; refund: $117 **5.** $18,067 **7.** $23,040 **9.** $88,502

page 271 **1.** $96.00 **3.** $148.90 **5.** $158.59

page 273 **1.** $134.75 **3.** $1344.55 **5.** $468.75 **7.** $204.84 **9.** $1895.20 **11.** $793.36 **13.** $248 **15.** $4258

page 274

Rounding whole numbers and decimals **1.** 1000; 800; 830 **3.** 1000; 600; 560 **5.** 10,000; 9600; 9600 **7.** 1000; 1100; 1070 **9.** 60,000; 60,400; 60,380 **11.** 85,000; 84,700; 84,660 **13.** 18; 18.2; 18.18 **15.** 79; 79.5; 79.46 **17.** 258; 257.8; 257.77 **19.** 41; 41.0; 40.99 **21.** 602; 602.0; 602.02

Subtracting whole numbers and decimals **1.** 52 **3.** 48 **5.** 5 **7.** 48.6 **9.** 66.2 **11.** 69.42 **13.** 7.638 **15.** 11.089 **17.** 3.315 **19.** 0.8 **21.** 2.612 **23.** 2.5 **25.** 25.58 **27.** 47.318

page 274 continued
Writing percents, decimals, and fractions **1.** $\frac{3}{25}$ **3.** $\frac{11}{20}$ **5.** $\frac{47}{100}$ **7.** $\frac{31}{50}$ **9.** $\frac{4}{25}$
11. $\frac{7}{10}$ **13.** $\frac{27}{100}$ **15.** $\frac{13}{20}$ **17.** $2\frac{1}{4}$ **19.** $1\frac{3}{100}$ **21.** 50% **23.** 10%
25. 60% **27.** 70% **29.** 38% **31.** 36% **33.** 37.5% **35.** 56.25%
37. 22.5% **39.** 425% **41.** 760%

page 275 **1.** Yes **2.** $15,278 **3.** $2197 **4.** $2534 **5.** Balance due: $165
6. Refund: $82 **7.** Refund: $150 **8.** $15,427 **9.** $759 **10.** $485

page 279 **1.** $632.00; $208.00 **3.** $4410.00; $690.00 **5.** $2210.00; $540.00
7. $3207.00; $1069.00 **9.** $1766.40; $213.60 **11.** $328.50 **13.** $482.60

page 281 **1.** $168 **3.** $395.25 **5.** $206.40 **7.** $340 **9.** $45,000; $531
11. $32,000

pages 283–285 **1.** $413.70 **3.** $1917 **5.** $221 **7.** $1099.53 **9.** $772.48
11. $303.16 **13.** $1004 **15.** $1684.80 **17.** $5454 **19.** $1290
21. $44,572.50 **23.** $1160 **25.** $8050

page 287 **1.** $29.97 **3.** $38.82 **5.** $236.03 **7.** $18.26 **9.** $1690.80
11. $1692

page 288 **1.** $15.09; $181.08; $8.59 **3.** $11.15; $133.80; $6.34
5. $13.02; $156.24; $7.47 **7.** $10.90; $130.80; $6.25 **9.** $40.93; $163.72; $6.30
11. $38.66; $154.64; $5.93 **13.** $51.34; $205.36; $7.91 **15.** $98.64; $197.28; $3.86
17. $158.97; $317.94; $6.23 **19.** $167.84; $335.68; $6.59

pages 290–291 **1.** $67,000; $16,147 **3.** $80,000; $18,240 **5.** $37,000; $9694
7. $40,000; $12,920 **9.** $68,000; $19,448 **11.** $17.06 **13.** $22,368.73

pages 294–295 **1.** $7043 **3.** $9945 **5.** $5352.00 **7.** $7636.80 **9.** $10,836.00
11. $4843.20 **13.** $5914.80 **15.** $463.20

page 296
Adding whole numbers and decimals **1.** 55 **3.** 170 **5.** 108 **7.** 120 **9.** 231
11. 882 **13.** 1071 **15.** 1731 **17.** 21.94 **19.** 115.66 **21.** 16.05
23. 17.81 **25.** 1.44 **27.** 11.269

page 296 continued

Multiplying whole numbers **1.** 2400 **3.** 60,000 **5.** 12,000,000 **7.** 1400 **9.** 320,000 **11.** 420,000 **13.** 810,000 **15.** 1872 **17.** 2936 **19.** 29,488 **21.** 329,280 **23.** 200,882 **25.** 643,405 **27.** 147,288

Percent problems **1.** 9.4 **3.** 20 **5.** 1.78 **7.** 90 **9.** 95% **11.** 85% **13.** 3.5% **15.** 800 **17.** 40 **19.** 200 **21.** 125

page 297 **1.** $721.25 **2.** $185.25 **3.** $930.60 **4.** $17,700 **5.** $19.20 **6.** $46,000 **7.** $18,481.60 **8.** $6847 **9.** $5215.20 **10.** $23,292

page 301 **1.** $25.00 **3.** $50.00; $150 **5.** $100.00; $600 **7.** $2500.00; $30,000 **9.** $500.00; $10,000 **11.** $44.77 **13.** $505.50 **15.** $86.54 **17.** $614.80 **19.** $14,540.00

pages 303–304 **1.** 0.07788; $77.88 **3.** 0.06096; $609.60 **5.** 0.03257; $130.28 **7.** 0.01428; $35.70 **9.** $103.30 **11.** $226.02; 7.53% **13.** $322.45; $322.45; 6.45% **15.** $28.56; $114.24; 5.71% **17.** $1000 CD paying $61.83 each year

page 305 **1.** $217.65; $2919.08 **3.** $3154.27; $254.14; $3408.41 **5.** $3683.03; $296.74; $3979.77 **7.** $4300.42; $346.48; $4646.90 **9.** $5021.30; $404.57; $5425.87 **11.** $2014.30 **13.** 9 years

pages 307–309 **1.** $193.88 **3.** $585.63 **5.** $2202.13 **7.** $11,915.00 **9.** $6278.50 **11.** $83.25; $33.00 loss **13.** $767.50; $26.75 profit **15.** $5688.50; $261.65 loss **17.** $310.25; $9.75 loss **19.** $120.00; 5.71% **21.** $159.00; 3.98% **23.** $361.20; 5.16% **25.** $775.00; 13.48%

page 311 **1.** $19.91; $99.55 **3.** $14.26; $213.90 **5.** $4.50; $337.50 **7.** $8.34; $100.08 **9.** $24.97; $399.52 **11.** $796.40 **13.** $1.13 **15.** 41.6667 shares

page 312

Rounding whole numbers and decimals **1.** 1000; 700; 720 **3.** 3000; 3500; 3490 **5.** 9000; 9400; 9360 **7.** 56,000; 56,200; 56,200 **9.** 1000; 1000; 1000 **11.** 6; 5.6; 5.63 **13.** 47; 47.5; 47.46 **15.** 376; 376.3; 376.29 **17.** 765; 765.0; 764.97 **19.** 68; 68.0; 68.02 **21.** 347; 347.0; 347.00

Dividing decimals **1.** 3.03 **3.** 0.90 **5.** 0.09 **7.** 0.02 **9.** 0.22 **11.** 2.77 **13.** 3.64 **15.** 80.00 **17.** 4.68 **19.** 0.04 **21.** 0.02 **23.** 2.20 **25.** 244.21

page 312 continued

Ratio and proportion **1.** $9 \neq 10$ **3.** $36 \neq 14$ **5.** $183.6 \neq 180$ **7.** $a = 24$ **9.** $n = 63$ **11.** $x = 24$ **13.** $y = 16$

page 313 **1.** $37.50 **2.** $82.38 **3.** $57.12 **4.** 6.21% **5.** $3090.25 **6.** $3132.25 **7.** $132.25 profit **8.** 4.69% **9.** $297 **10.** $1.80

page 317 **1.** $4.50 **3.** $4.90 **5.** $6 **7.** $10.80 **9.** $7.50 **11.** $12 **13.** $21 **15.** 38¢ **17.** 60¢ **19.** $2.75 **21.** $3.13 **23.** $3.60

page 319 **1.** FEDERAL WITHHOLDING TAX 14.98 **3.** FEDERAL WITHHOLDING TAX 62.03 **5.** FEDERAL WITHHOLDING TAX 52.67 **7.** FEDERAL WITHHOLDING TAX 96.48 **9.** FEDERAL WITHHOLDING TAX 111.81

11. NUMBER OF PAY PERIODS PER YEAR 26
GROSS PAY FOR THIS PERIOD 478.93
NUMBER OF EXEMPTIONS 1
FILING STATUS 1
FEDERAL WITHHOLDING TAX 58.46

13. NUMBER OF PAY PERIODS PER YEAR 52
GROSS PAY FOR THIS PERIOD 392.61
NUMBER OF EXEMPTIONS 1
FILING STATUS 0
FEDERAL WITHHOLDING TAX 83.06
STATE WITHHOLDING TAX 9.33

page 323 **1.** 535 calories **3.** 480 calories **5.** 530 calories **7.** 1605 calories

page 325 **1.** 1180 calories **3.** 135 calories **5.** 662 calories **7.** 418 calories **9.** 383 calories **11.** 331 calories **13.** 2697 calories

pages 326–328 **1.** $1.85 **3.** $3.03 **5.** $1.34 **7.** $1.24 **9.** $1.43 **11.** 0.19¢ per gram **13.** 0.12¢ per gram **15.** 0.09¢ per milliliter **17.** 0.08¢ per milliliter **19.** 0.16¢ per gram **21.** $0.50/L; $0.47/L; $1.89 **23.** $1.46/kg; $1.28/kg; $12.75 **25.** $0.59/kg; $0.53/kg; $2.65 **27.** $1.78/kg; $1.58/kg; $0.95 **29.** $35.38

page 329 **1.** $3.71 **3.** $1.39 **5.** $1.81 **7.** $0.56 **9.** $2.85 **11.** $1.90 **13.** $2.09 **15.** $1.31

pages 330–331 **1.** 30%; $4.70 **3.** 24%; $4.38 **5.** 25%; $4.25 **7.** $86.26 **9.** $62.53 **11.** $41.23 **13.** $21.58 **15.** $5.67 **17.** $535.61

page 333 **1.** $6.12 **3.** $11.90 **5.** $4.54 **7.** $11.52

page 334

Multiplying decimals **1.** 0.3 **3.** 0.009 **5.** 0.0035 **7.** 0.00004 **9.** 120 **11.** 18 **13.** 1.2 **15.** 0.00004 **17.** 6.6 **19.** 41.71 **21.** 20.234 **23.** 16.8714 **25.** 152,668.8 **27.** 0.0030328

Dividing fractions and mixed numbers **1.** $\frac{4}{5}$ **3.** $\frac{2}{3}$ **5.** $2\frac{3}{16}$ **7.** 8 **9.** $\frac{4}{15}$ **11.** $2\frac{1}{2}$ **13.** $2\frac{15}{16}$ **15.** $1\frac{1}{5}$ **17.** $1\frac{3}{5}$ **19.** 5 **21.** $\frac{27}{28}$

Percent problems **1.** 1.25 **3.** 15 **5.** 0.6 **7.** 8.4 **9.** 75% **11.** 25% **13.** 75% **15.** 67.5% **17.** 56 **19.** 200 **21.** 150

page 335 **1.** 490 calories **2.** 585 calories **3.** $2.23 **4.** $0.66 **5.** 0.13¢ per gram **6.** 3.5 kilograms for $2.19 **7.** 26% **8.** $4.31 **9.** $64.15 **10.** $5.55

pages 339–340 **1.** $46.28 **3.** 3 lb. 12 oz. **5.** $50.76 **7.** $2.45 **9.** $2.43 **11.** $47.46 **13.** 3 lb. 8 oz. **15.** $52.99

page 341 **1.** $63.00; 15 boxes; 18 lb. 12 oz. **3.** $28.80; 6 boxes; 10 lb. 8 oz. **5.** $65.24; 7 boxes; 26 lb. 11 oz. **7.** $32.40; 24 boxes; 10 lb. 8 oz. **9.** $608.71; 141 lb. 0 oz. **11.** $15.51

page 343 **1.** 20 yards **3.** $8\frac{1}{2}$ yards **5.** $11\frac{1}{4}$ yards **7.** $87\frac{7}{8}$ yards **9.** $38.80 **11.** $4.50 **13.** 11 packages **15.** 105 buttons **17.** $24.30 **19.** $536.89

page 345 **1.** Jan., April, July, Dec.; $5.55; $31.45 **3.** November; $89.99; $269.96 **5.** February; $179.20; $716.79 **7.** May; $2.63; $14.87 **9.** July; $9.21; $17.09

page 347 **1.** $37.50 **3.** $19.62

page 349 **1.** $1.80 **3.** $0.55; $5.45 **5.** $7.90 **7.** $474.60 **9.** $12.40 **11.** $3.40; $5.44; $8.33 **13.** $858.06

page 351 **1.** $20 **3.** $6 **5.** $17 **7.** $20 **9.** $6 **11.** 9 years **13.** Car polisher

page 352
Dividing whole numbers **1.** 2188 **3.** 888 R1 **5.** 194 **7.** 42 R19 **9.** 699 **11.** 114 R15 **13.** 69 R20 **15.** 28 R54 **17.** 74 R13 **19.** 3192 R26 **21.** 11,908 R5 **23.** 12,277 R65 **25.** 225 R48 **27.** 913 R396

Adding fractions and mixed numbers **1.** $\frac{14}{15}$ **3.** $\frac{17}{24}$ **5.** $\frac{5}{6}$ **7.** $1\frac{1}{4}$ **9.** $1\frac{1}{18}$ **11.** $7\frac{4}{5}$ **13.** $8\frac{1}{6}$ **15.** $20\frac{5}{6}$ **17.** $6\frac{17}{24}$ **19.** $18\frac{7}{20}$

Subtracting fractions and mixed numbers **1.** $\frac{1}{3}$ **3.** $\frac{17}{24}$ **5.** $\frac{1}{24}$ **7.** $\frac{2}{21}$ **9.** $14\frac{1}{7}$ **11.** $3\frac{1}{2}$ **13.** $9\frac{2}{5}$ **15.** $\frac{5}{24}$ **17.** $7\frac{5}{12}$ **19.** $16\frac{5}{6}$

page 353 **1.** $77.90 **2.** $3.90 **3.** $2.84 **4.** $84.64 **5.** $11\frac{1}{4}$ yards **6.** $318.75 **7.** $54.50 **8.** $76.75 **9.** $3.24 **10.** $7

pages 357–359 **1.** $5.00; $5.00; $6.29; $0.90 + $1.50; $19 **3.** $5.00; $2.50; $2.75; $10 **5.** $1.80; $1.75 + $0.89; $1.25; $1.00; $7
7. Week 1: $45.50, $15.50, $10.20, $20.17; Week 2: $57.25, $12.50, $9.00; Week 3: $58.88, $12.57, $8.47; Week 4: $60.04, $13.75, $14.00; Total: $338
9. Week 1: $15.00; Week 2: $17.50; Week 3: $18.00; Week 4: $17.25, $1.25; Total: $69
11. Week 1: $10.00; Week 3: $13.00; Total: $23 **13.** Week 1: $9.85; Week 2: $8.50; Week 3: $1.42, $6.00; Week 4: $13.00; Total: $39

page 361 **1.** $21 **3.** $9 **5.** $6 **7.** $352 **9.** $75 **11.** $24 **13.** $50

pages 363–364 **1.** $112 **3.** $480 **5.** $504 **7.** $835 **9.** $358 **11.** $835 **13.** $2040 **15.** $2142 **17.** No

page 365 **1.** $150; 0.13; 13% **3.** $245; 0.88; 88% **5.** $51; 0.09; 9%

pages 366–367 **1.** $10 **3.** $20 **5.** $110 **7.** $70 **9.** $1188 **11.** $177 **13.** $99 **15.** $27 **17.** No **19.** Yes

page 369 **1.** $4830; $8050 **3.** $1560; $2310; $2800 **5.** $1200; $2730; $6300 **7.** Food **9.** Housing **11.** $1050

page 370

Adding whole numbers and decimals **1.** 72 **3.** 161 **5.** 199 **7.** 202 **9.** 233 **11.** 1649 **13.** 778 **15.** 18.07 **17.** 98.61 **19.** 17.85 **21.** 20.07 **23.** 1.25 **25.** 10.499 **27.** 21.23

Comparing and renaming fractions and mixed numbers **1.** $>$ **3.** $<$ **5.** $<$ **7.** $<$ **9.** $=$ **11.** $>$ **13.** $>$ **15.** $<$ **17.** $<$ **19.** $4\frac{1}{2}$ **21.** $3\frac{1}{2}$ **23.** $1\frac{1}{2}$ **25.** $6\frac{1}{2}$ **27.** $2\frac{1}{2}$ **29.** $3\frac{7}{8}$ **31.** $4\frac{4}{11}$ **33.** $1\frac{1}{3}$ **35.** $6\frac{1}{2}$

Dividing fractions and mixed numbers **1.** $\frac{3}{4}$ **3.** $\frac{3}{5}$ **5.** $\frac{3}{20}$ **7.** 8 **9.** $9\frac{1}{3}$ **11.** 7 **13.** $\frac{3}{25}$ **15.** $\frac{3}{5}$ **17.** $\frac{6}{7}$ **19.** $\frac{16}{49}$

page 371 **1.** \$41 **2.** \$22 **3.** \$52 **4.** \$87 **5.** \$43 **6.** \$77 **7.** \$1440; \$72; \$1512 **8.** No **9.** \$39 **10.** \$5130

page 375 **1.** 800 **3.** 273 **5.** 648 **7.** 910 **9.** 2170 **11.** 1872 **13.** 672 **15.** 560 **17.** 1148 **19.** 3504 **21.** 7735

page 377 Program modifications may vary. Samples are given.

1.
```
TENS            1
FIVES           1
ONES            1
NICKELS         1
CHANGE     $ 16.05
```

3.
```
ONES            2
QUARTERS        3
PENNIES         2
CHANGE     $ 2.77
```

5.
```
ONES            3
QUARTERS        1
DIMES           1
PENNIES         3
CHANGE     $ 3.38
```

7.
```
FIVES           1
ONES            1
DIMES           2
PENNIES         2
CHANGE     $ 6.22
```

9.
```
TENS            1
FIVES           1
ONES            2
QUARTERS        1
DIMES           1
NICKELS         1
PENNIES         4
CHANGE     $ 17.44
```

11.
```
ONES            4
PENNIES         3
CHANGE     $ 4.03
```

13.
```
FIVES           1
ONES            3
NICKELS         1
PENNIES         1
CHANGE     $ 8.06
```

15.
```
85 IF S>=0 THEN 90
86 PRINT "NOT ENOUGH MONEY"
87 GO TO 50
```

17.
```
30 PRINT "AMOUNT OF MERCHANDISE";
40 INPUT M
45 LET X=M*.05
46 LET X=INT(X*100+.5)/100
47 LET T=M+X
182 PRINT
183 PRINT "COST OF MERCHANDISE     $";M
184 PRINT "SALES TAX";TAB(22);"$";X
185 PRINT "TOTAL";TAB (22); "$";T
186 PRINT "AMOUNT GIVEN";TAB(22);"$";A
190 PRINT "CHANGE";TAB(22);"$";C
```

page 377 continued

19.

```
27 LET M = 0
28 PRINT "NO. OF ITEMS    COST/ITEM    COST"
30 PRINT "NUMBER OF ITEMS";
31 INPUT Q
32 IF Q = 0 THEN 45
33 PRINT "COST PER ITEM";
34 INPUT P
35 LET E = Q*P
36 LET E = INT(E*100+.5)/100
37 PRINT TAB(6);Q;TAB(17);P;TAB(25);E
38 LET M = M + E
39 GO TO 30
65 PRINT
```

Line 40 was deleted.

page 379 **1.** 1000; 710 **3.** 1000; 680 **5.** 1000; 850 **7.** 1000; 1390 **9.** 8000; 8390 **11.** 2000; 2420 **13.** 5000; 5230 **15.** 7000; 7080 **17.** 10,000; 9540 **19.** 9000; 8700 **21.** 5000; 4970 **23.** 7000; 6500 **25.** 7000; 6730 **27.** 3000; 2780 **29.** 9000; 8670 **31.** 8000; 7560 **33.** 10,000; 9670 **35.** 5000; 5000 **37.** 97,000; 96,930 **39.** 85,000; 84,850 **41.** 61,000; 61,470 **43.** 12,000; 11,710 **45.** 44,000; 43,670 **47.** 75,000; 74,910 **49.** 35,000; 35,030 **51.** 47,000; 46,960 **53.** 98,000; 97,500 **55.** 25,000; 25,010 **57.** 59,000; 58,690 **59.** 80,000; 79,620 **61.** 4; 4.17 **63.** 8; 7.86 **65.** 6; 6.29 **67.** 3; 2.94 **69.** 10; 9.73 **71.** 3; 3.47 **73.** 37; 37.11 **75.** 50; 49.66 **77.** 68; 68.26 **79.** 31; 31.49 **81.** 72; 71.55 **83.** 90; 90.23 **85.** 80; 79.53 **87.** 26; 26.38 **89.** 86; 86.05 **91.** 12; 11.94 **93.** 100; 99.83 **95.** 65; 65.07 **97.** 269; 268.87 **99.** 912; 912.05 **101.** 403; 403.19 **103.** 101; 100.89 **105.** 353; 352.88 **107.** 735; 735.04 **109.** 647; 646.72 **111.** 574; 574.19 **113.** 822; 821.64 **115.** 248; 248.34 **117.** 546; 545.57 **119.** 500; 499.83

page 380 **1.** 83 **3.** 146 **5.** 100 **7.** 171 **9.** 146 **11.** 119 **13.** 97 **15.** 232 **17.** 236 **19.** 261 **21.** 1181 **23.** 1035 **25.** 639 **27.** 1925 **29.** 2098 **31.** 10.28 **33.** 5.56 **35.** 86.61 **37.** 1.7 **39.** 16.83 **41.** 19.77 **43.** 11.63 **45.** 12.888 **47.** 23.8 **49.** 22.44 **51.** 16.51 **53.** 21.47 **55.** 18.39 **57.** 15.529 **59.** 23.066

page 381 **1.** 43 **3.** 25 **5.** 49 **7.** 25 **9.** 46 **11.** 43 **13.** 3 **15.** 92 **17.** 627 **19.** 327 **21.** 569 **23.** 1408 **25.** 1256 **27.** 7809 **29.** 34.7 **31.** 10.6 **33.** 55.12 **35.** 31.43 **37.** 47.41 **39.** 13.408 **41.** 20.905 **43.** 27.46 **45.** 93.96 **47.** 42.45 **49.** 55.051 **51.** 42.437 **53.** 33.314 **55.** 75.661 **57.** 13.4 **59.** 36.2 **61.** 25.7 **63.** 9.53 **65.** 23.14 **67.** 20.7 **69.** 33.7 **71.** 13.19 **73.** 47.61 **75.** 12.078 **77.** 1.886 **79.** 75.385 **81.** 78.075 **83.** 14.082

page 382 **1.** 2100 **3.** 1600 **5.** 2800 **7.** 8000 **9.** 54,000 **11.** 20,000 **13.** 300 **15.** 2800 **17.** 1500 **19.** 9000 **21.** 36,000 **23.** 30,000 **25.** 12,000 **27.** 12,000 **29.** 27,000 **31.** 420,000 **33.** 450,000 **35.** 350,000 **37.** 400,000 **39.** 2,800,000 **41.** 3,000,000 **43.** 1742 **45.** 748 **47.** 6560 **49.** 4015 **51.** 17,460 **53.** 20,196 **55.** 36,045 **57.** 28,925 **59.** 19,760 **61.** 78,642 **63.** 461,674 **65.** 132,664 **67.** 345,744 **69.** 521,136 **71.** 724,240 **73.** 242,305 **75.** 438,354 **77.** 599,828 **79.** 1,768,026 **81.** 991,676 **83.** 1,346,115

page 383 **1.** 0.24 **3.** 0.56 **5.** 0.014 **7.** 0.02 **9.** 0.0028 **11.** 0.0048 **13.** 0.0007 **15.** 0.002 **17.** 0.08 **19.** 0.06 **21.** 0.036 **23.** 0.016 **25.** 0.21 **27.** 1800 **29.** 5400 **31.** 0.00024 **33.** 0.00014 **35.** 18 **37.** 28 **39.** 120 **41.** 60 **43.** 523.6 **45.** 94.07 **47.** 21.36 **49.** 10.88 **51.** 11.7972 **53.** 547.8 **55.** 4738.89 **57.** 1.0122 **59.** 2.6676 **61.** 0.12978 **63.** 2.36684 **65.** 203.814 **67.** 335.818 **69.** 159.79 **71.** 259.25 **73.** 0.575757 **75.** 296.2768 **77.** 256.0642 **79.** 2.21008 **81.** 39.88194 **83.** 27.940826

page 384 **1.** 231 R1 **3.** 94 **5.** 590 R6 **7.** 318 R1 **9.** 1184 R4 **11.** 845 R5 **13.** 751 R3 **15.** 1108 R3 **17.** 2189 **19.** 7233 R2 **21.** 10,294 R2 **23.** 25 R9 **25.** 4 R8 **27.** 6 R71 **29.** 8 R20 **31.** 10 R56 **33.** 5 R17 **35.** 12 R13 **37.** 2 R46 **39.** 9 R37 **41.** 9 R17 **43.** 139 R24 **45.** 28 R86 **47.** 208 R2 **49.** 63 R1 **51.** 309 R3 **53.** 134 R23 **55.** 121 R13 **57.** 285 **59.** 50 R8 **61.** 102 R30 **63.** 95 R37 **65.** 764 **67.** 916 R37 **69.** 942 R14 **71.** 825 R30 **73.** 3379 R1 **75.** 7464 R18 **77.** 11,341 R1 **79.** 10,518 R2 **81.** 20,009 **83.** 3039 R25 **85.** 201 R386 **87.** 271 R24 **89.** 12 R213 **91.** 645 R71 **93.** 35 R249 **95.** 750 R49 **97.** 1049 **99.** 759 R120 **101.** 2940 R149 **103.** 1536 R317 **105.** 682 R289

page 385 **1.** 3.84 **3.** 232.18 **5.** 53.77 **7.** 1112.63 **9.** 925.57 **11.** 0.36 **13.** 0.07 **15.** 0.78 **17.** 2.65 **19.** 1.58 **21.** 1.04 **23.** 2.06 **25.** 1.23 **27.** 0.85 **29.** 6.12 **31.** 12.59 **33.** 10.68 **35.** 31.39 **37.** 0.12 **39.** 0.23 **41.** 2.41 **43.** 1.64 **45.** 0.43 **47.** 0.47 **49.** 4.14 **51.** 5.67 **53.** 18.56 **55.** 0.22 **57.** 5.59 **59.** 0.56 **61.** 4.32 **63.** 0.48 **65.** 1.64 **67.** 0.88 **69.** 12.88 **71.** 10.68 **73.** 31.39 **75.** 12.91 **77.** 18.21 **79.** 48.19 **81.** 6.67 **83.** 7.59 **85.** 18.05 **87.** 21.55 **89.** 5.85 **91.** 5.98 **93.** 19.36 **95.** 3.78 **97.** 0.47 **99.** 0.86

page 386 **1.** $>$ **3.** $=$ **5.** $>$ **7.** $<$ **9.** $<$ **11.** $>$ **13.** $<$ **15.** $>$ **17.** $<$ **19.** $\frac{3}{5}$ **21.** $\frac{1}{3}$ **23.** $\frac{1}{7}$ **25.** $\frac{2}{3}$ **27.** $\frac{13}{14}$ **29.** $\frac{1}{2}$ **31.** $\frac{3}{5}$ **33.** $\frac{1}{6}$ **35.** $\frac{4}{5}$ **37.** $\frac{2}{9}$ **39.** $\frac{1}{5}$ **41.** $\frac{2}{9}$ **43.** $\frac{2}{9}$ **45.** $\frac{7}{8}$ **47.** $\frac{5}{4}$ **49.** $\frac{7}{1}$ **51.** $\frac{21}{8}$ **53.** $\frac{81}{10}$ **55.** $\frac{43}{5}$ **57.** $\frac{39}{8}$ **59.** $\frac{41}{6}$ **61.** $\frac{29}{9}$ **63.** $\frac{61}{12}$ **65.** $\frac{69}{8}$ **67.** $\frac{80}{11}$

page 386 continued

69. $\frac{92}{15}$ **71.** $\frac{131}{11}$ **73.** $2\frac{1}{2}$ **75.** $1\frac{2}{5}$ **77.** $6\frac{1}{3}$ **79.** 6 **81.** $8\frac{1}{9}$ **83.** $5\frac{1}{2}$
85. $3\frac{5}{8}$ **87.** $12\frac{1}{2}$ **89.** $7\frac{2}{7}$ **91.** $1\frac{2}{3}$ **93.** $2\frac{1}{3}$ **95.** $1\frac{2}{3}$ **97.** $12\frac{1}{10}$ **99.** $11\frac{11}{12}$

page 387 **1.** $\frac{4}{15}$ **3.** $\frac{5}{12}$ **5.** $\frac{5}{16}$ **7.** $\frac{3}{5}$ **9.** $\frac{2}{11}$ **11.** $\frac{1}{3}$ **13.** $\frac{2}{3}$ **15.** $\frac{2}{3}$
17. $\frac{35}{144}$ **19.** $\frac{1}{12}$ **21.** $\frac{10}{21}$ **23.** $4\frac{2}{3}$ **25.** 3 **27.** 2 **29.** $2\frac{2}{5}$ **31.** $9\frac{1}{3}$
33. $3\frac{3}{5}$ **35.** 28 **37.** 70 **39.** $2\frac{6}{11}$ **41.** $26\frac{2}{3}$ **43.** $\frac{4}{5}$ **45.** $1\frac{3}{4}$ **47.** $\frac{7}{8}$
49. 1 **51.** $1\frac{17}{18}$ **53.** 4 **55.** $2\frac{4}{7}$ **57.** 10 **59.** $13\frac{1}{2}$ **61.** $11\frac{1}{4}$ **63.** $20\frac{2}{3}$
65. 18 **67.** 104 **69.** $30\frac{2}{3}$ **71.** $8\frac{1}{3}$ **73.** $3\frac{1}{4}$ **75.** $8\frac{1}{6}$ **77.** $9\frac{1}{3}$ **79.** $8\frac{3}{4}$
81. $12\frac{1}{2}$ **83.** $18\frac{1}{3}$ **85.** $\frac{1}{15}$ **87.** $\frac{3}{40}$ **89.** $\frac{5}{16}$ **91.** 12 **93.** $1\frac{3}{4}$ **95.** $10\frac{1}{2}$
97. $4\frac{2}{5}$ **99.** $2\frac{1}{3}$ **101.** $10\frac{4}{5}$ **103.** $27\frac{1}{2}$ **105.** 105

page 388 **1.** $1\frac{1}{2}$ **3.** $\frac{24}{35}$ **5.** 4 **7.** $1\frac{5}{9}$ **9.** $1\frac{4}{5}$ **11.** $\frac{1}{15}$ **13.** $\frac{4}{15}$ **15.** $\frac{5}{16}$
17. $\frac{2}{27}$ **19.** $7\frac{1}{2}$ **21.** 8 **23.** $9\frac{1}{3}$ **25.** $1\frac{1}{3}$ **27.** $10\frac{1}{2}$ **29.** $\frac{1}{4}$ **31.** $\frac{3}{10}$
33. $\frac{1}{10}$ **35.** $\frac{3}{28}$ **37.** $6\frac{1}{4}$ **39.** 7 **41.** $1\frac{7}{20}$ **43.** 50 **45.** $7\frac{1}{2}$ **47.** $2\frac{15}{16}$
49. $2\frac{3}{4}$ **51.** $\frac{3}{4}$ **53.** $1\frac{1}{3}$ **55.** 6 **57.** $3\frac{1}{5}$ **59.** $5\frac{1}{3}$ **61.** $7\frac{1}{2}$ **63.** 25
65. $3\frac{4}{11}$ **67.** $\frac{3}{4}$ **69.** $2\frac{1}{3}$ **71.** $1\frac{3}{5}$ **73.** 5 **75.** $\frac{27}{28}$ **77.** $\frac{9}{16}$ **79.** $3\frac{1}{10}$
81. $1\frac{7}{8}$ **83.** $\frac{8}{9}$ **85.** $1\frac{3}{5}$ **87.** $1\frac{3}{5}$ **89.** $3\frac{3}{4}$ **91.** 6 **93.** $\frac{3}{7}$ **95.** $\frac{1}{6}$ **97.** 4
99. $3\frac{1}{3}$ **101.** $\frac{3}{4}$ **103.** $3\frac{3}{4}$ **105.** $7\frac{1}{3}$

page 389 **1.** $1\frac{1}{12}$ **3.** $1\frac{1}{3}$ **5.** $1\frac{3}{14}$ **7.** $1\frac{13}{36}$ **9.** $1\frac{1}{18}$ **11.** $1\frac{2}{5}$ **13.** $1\frac{1}{2}$
15. $1\frac{1}{24}$ **17.** $\frac{4}{15}$ **19.** $1\frac{11}{40}$ **21.** $1\frac{7}{24}$ **23.** $1\frac{4}{9}$ **25.** $6\frac{1}{24}$ **27.** $5\frac{1}{36}$ **29.** $4\frac{7}{24}$
31. $5\frac{5}{12}$ **33.** $4\frac{1}{15}$ **35.** $12\frac{9}{10}$ **37.** $8\frac{1}{3}$ **39.** $5\frac{11}{18}$ **41.** $9\frac{9}{40}$ **43.** $8\frac{19}{24}$
45. $12\frac{13}{15}$ **47.** $7\frac{2}{15}$ **49.** $20\frac{5}{6}$ **51.** $9\frac{13}{15}$ **53.** $14\frac{7}{15}$ **55.** $14\frac{11}{30}$ **57.** $10\frac{1}{6}$
59. $18\frac{1}{2}$ **61.** $1\frac{5}{12}$ **63.** $4\frac{19}{30}$ **65.** $6\frac{1}{3}$ **67.** $4\frac{13}{24}$

page 390 **1.** $\frac{1}{2}$ **3.** $\frac{5}{8}$ **5.** $\frac{17}{24}$ **7.** $\frac{3}{14}$ **9.** $\frac{1}{2}$ **11.** $\frac{1}{6}$ **13.** $\frac{2}{15}$ **15.** $\frac{1}{15}$
17. $\frac{2}{15}$ **19.** $\frac{3}{14}$ **21.** $\frac{17}{30}$ **23.** $\frac{2}{15}$ **25.** $1\frac{3}{8}$ **27.** $8\frac{2}{3}$ **29.** $2\frac{1}{8}$ **31.** $9\frac{1}{7}$
33. $5\frac{1}{3}$ **35.** $9\frac{2}{5}$ **37.** $1\frac{2}{7}$ **39.** $6\frac{5}{8}$ **41.** $3\frac{1}{10}$ **43.** $4\frac{1}{2}$ **45.** $3\frac{1}{3}$ **47.** $4\frac{7}{8}$
49. $6\frac{1}{3}$ **51.** $5\frac{9}{16}$ **53.** $\frac{11}{24}$ **55.** $4\frac{1}{10}$ **57.** $2\frac{13}{20}$ **59.** $5\frac{11}{24}$ **61.** $2\frac{1}{2}$ **63.** $4\frac{11}{18}$
65. $6\frac{8}{15}$ **67.** $1\frac{19}{20}$ **69.** $4\frac{11}{12}$ **71.** $3\frac{23}{24}$

page 391 **1.** 120 = 120 **3.** 140 ≠ 144 **5.** 1200 ≠ 1280 **7.** 90 ≠ 99 **9.** 120 = 120 **11.** 64 ≠ 60 **13.** 60 ≠ 52 **15.** 798 = 798 **17.** 360 ≠ 390 **19.** 4.2 = 4.2 **21.** 117.6 ≠ 144 **23.** 183.6 ≠ 180 **25.** 17.94 ≠ 19.9 **27.** 25.6 ≠ 28.8 **29.** 12.6 = 12.6 **31.** 67.94 ≠ 64.4 **33.** 7.65 = 7.65 **35.** 0.45 ≠ 0.525 **37.** $n = 100$ **39.** $a = 15$ **41.** $b = 30$ **43.** $d = 2$ **45.** $c = 7$ **47.** $y = 4.5$ **49.** $s = 21.6$ **51.** $h = 1.5$ **53.** $k = 3.75$ **55.** $d = 1.2$ **57.** $b = 1$ **59.** $d = 0.9$ **61.** $n = 7$ **63.** $g = 10.8$ **65.** $v = 81$ **67.** $a = 2.6$ **69.** $m = 4.8$

page 392 **1.** 39% **3.** 4% **5.** 70% **7.** 72.7% **9.** 80.2% **11.** 6.1% **13.** 29.46% **15.** 77.08% **17.** 10.08% **19.** 362% **21.** 901% **23.** 768.1% **25.** 50% **27.** 40% **29.** 8% **31.** 42% **33.** 70% **35.** 5% **37.** 72% **39.** 46.875% **41.** 93.75% **43.** 15.625% **45.** 37.5% **47.** 87.5% **49.** 325% **51.** 135% **53.** 0.82 **55.** 0.9 **57.** 0.46 **59.** 0.08 **61.** 0.207 **63.** 0.0742 **65.** 0.0591 **67.** 0.045 **69.** 0.2325 **71.** 0.47375 **73.** 2.06 **75.** 1.59 **77.** $\frac{4}{5}$ **79.** $\frac{9}{10}$ **81.** $\frac{3}{4}$ **83.** $\frac{19}{20}$ **85.** $\frac{2}{25}$ **87.** $\frac{1}{100}$ **89.** $\frac{6}{25}$ **91.** $\frac{79}{100}$ **93.** $\frac{13}{100}$ **95.** $\frac{17}{50}$ **97.** $1\frac{18}{25}$ **99.** $2\frac{1}{2}$

page 393 **1.** 15 **3.** 5.74 **5.** 4.982 **7.** 1.125 **9.** 6.97 **11.** 3.8 **13.** 3.465 **15.** 86.4 **17.** 5.67 **19.** 46.8 **21.** 5.184 **23.** 26.325 **25.** 8% **27.** 25% **29.** 3% **31.** 14% **33.** 35% **35.** 89% **37.** 15% **39.** 62.5% **41.** 87.5% **43.** 80% **45.** 75 **47.** 150 **49.** 28 **51.** 7.2 **53.** 200 **55.** 48 **57.** 30 **59.** 85 **61.** 15 **63.** 3.5 **65.** 32

page 394

1.
```
THIS IS
A BASIC
PROGRAM.
```

3.
```
2+4=  6
9-7=  2
 32  =8*4
 1.8  =9/5
```

5. Answers will vary. A sample is given.

```
10 PRINT "MARY FRASER"
20 PRINT "AGE 16 YEARS"
30 PRINT "AUBURNDALE HIGH SCHOOL"
40 END
```

page 395

1.
```
? 7
? 15
 41
```

3. Answers will vary. A sample is given.

```
? DON WEE
? 88,95,90
DON WEE
TEST AVERAGE=  91
```

5.
```
? 7
? 8
 56
```

page 396

1.
```
? 20
 60
?34
 102
? 56
 168
? 128
 384
?
```

3.
```
? 66,75
A+B=  141
? NO
DONE
```

5. Answers will vary. A sample is given.

```
? J. KELLY
? 7
 35
? 25
 89
? 130
THAT'S ALL J. KELLY
```

page 397

1.
```
PERIMETER = 13
PERIMETER = 58
PERIMETER = 34
PERIMETER = 18
PERIMETER = 5
PERIMETER = 74
OUT OF DATA AT LINE 10
```

3.
```
R = 5     C = 31.4
R = 10    C = 62.8
R = 17    C = 106.76
OUT OF DATA AT LINE 10
```

5.
```
ANDERSON      PAY = 367.5
JENSEN     PAY = 505.25
RIEDELL     PAY = 570
BRETZLAUF      PAY = 408.5
OUT OF DATA AT LINE 20
```

page 398

1.
```
3
4
5
6
7
8
```

3.
```
NUMBER:  1  COST:  19.95
NUMBER:  2  COST:  39.9
NUMBER:  3  COST:  59.85
NUMBER:  4  COST:  79.8
NUMBER:  5  COST:  99.75
NUMBER:  6  COST:  119.7
```

5. Answers may vary. A sample is given.

```
10 FOR H=1 TO 8
20 LET P=4.5*H
30 PRINT "HOURS:";H;"PAY: $";P
40 NEXT H
50 END
```

page 399

1.
```
5
10
15
20
25
30
35
40
45
50
55
60
```

3.
```
PRICE     5% TAX     TOTAL
  1.2       .06        1.26
  6.8       .34        7.14
  12.6      .63        13.23
OUT OF DATA AT LINE 20
```

5. Answers may vary. A sample is given.

```
10 INPUT N
20 IF N=0 THEN 80
30 IF INT(N/3)=N/3 THEN 60
40 PRINT N;"IS NOT DIVISIBLE BY 3"
50 GO TO 10
60 PRINT N;"IS DIVISIBLE BY 3"
70 GO TO 10
80 END
```

Index